Europe in the Late Middle Ages

EUROPE
in the
LATE MIDDLE AGES

edited by
J. R. HALE
J. R. L. HIGHFIELD
B. SMALLEY

FABER AND FABER
London

First published in 1965
by Faber and Faber Limited
24 Russell Square London WC1
First published in this edition 1970
Printed in Great Britain by
Latimer Trend & Co Ltd., Whitstable
All rights reserved

SBN (paper edition) 571 09413 9
SBN (cloth edition) 571 06377 2

© *1965 by Faber and Faber Limited*

CONTENTS

ILLUSTRATIONS

MAPS

PHOTOGRAPHS

9

ACKNOWLEDGMENTS

Thanks are due to the Editors of *Medium Aevum*, *Past and Present* and the *Bulletin of the Institute of Historical Research* for permission to quote from recent articles by Dr P. S. Lewis in their journals.

INTRODUCTORY NOTE

The lack of guidance available to those who are interested in the history of late medieval Europe is notorious. This collection of essays is an attempt to make good part of that deficiency. It does not pretend to be a comprehensive study of the subject. The principle of the selection of individual topics represents a compromise between subjects which the editors hoped to be able to cover and those which they found that scholars were actually working on. Economic studies have not been included, because it was thought that they are still at a technical and regional stage which makes it difficult to fit them into a volume of this kind. Specific themes also unrepresented are the Conciliar and religious movements (whether orthodox or heretical). It was not possible to include everything, and in these instances it was thought best to omit subjects on which much was already available in print.

Some essays, as will be at once apparent, are by way of being syntheses or surveys of work in progress. Others reflect the research in depth which is currently being undertaken. Above all it is hoped that the collection shows the nature of the interest which English scholars are taking in the history of late medieval Europe.

I

BERYL SMALLEY

CHURCH AND STATE 1300–1377: THEORY AND FACT

A modern student of Church-State relations in the fourteenth century runs into an obstacle to understanding at once. 'Regarde ce chaos depuis que les mots ont quitté les choses'[1] will be his most likely reaction. Theorists seem to credit words with the power of sticks and stones to break one's bones. Their faith in mere verbal claims contrasts too sharply with our way of thinking for us to judge them sympathetically. A political theorist, we now assume, seeks either to analyse and justify the *status quo* or to argue for some kind of change which he supposes to be feasible as well as desirable. Even Rousseau backs down when he comes to apply his Social Contract to actual conditions, warning us that it may not work. The fourteenth century knew few such scruples. Conflicts between popes on one side, secular princes on the other, produced theories which grew in grandeur and precision in proportion to their distance from the facts of political life.

'Publicists', to use a modern term for those who joined in the battle of words, evolved on the popes' behalf what has been claimed as 'a full theory of sovereignty'.[2] The gist can be summarized as follows. Christ, as Son of God, possessed lordship,

---

[1] Y. Berger, *Le Sud* (Paris, 1962), 50. The speaker in the novel is criticizing modern civilization.

[2] M. J. Wilks, *The Problem of Sovereignty in the Later Middle Ages* (Cambridge, 1963). My debt to Dr Wilks for his clear and comprehensive analysis of fourteenth-century thinking will be obvious throughout this chapter. He also gives a full bibliography on his subject, which I need not duplicate. I refer readers to his short biographies of the leading political theorists for their dates. For criticism see H. S. Offler, *History*, xlix (1964), 216–18.

both spiritual and temporal, over the whole world, though he did not choose to reign as an earthly king. He avoided being acclaimed as king by the Jewish people, so it was argued, in order to show that his power was divine rather than human in origin. The pope was Vicar of Christ in both capacities. An all-embracing dominion passed to him through the commission to St Peter. He therefore wielded full power over all men, whether clerk or lay, Christian or infidel. Supreme pastor and universal ordinary, he guided, judged and corrected for sin through the machinery of the courts Christian and of other instruments of power, centred on the *Curia romana*. Secular and ecclesiastical rulers must obey him. It was heretical or at best schismatical to do otherwise. The secular state with its coercive and administrative powers was conceived as a mere function of the Church. Lay rulers acted as papal agents, enjoying a delegated authority which the pope allowed them or tolerated because it did not suit him to assume such functions himself. He preferred to restrict himself to his ecclesiastical duties in the normal course; but he could intervene directly in secular affairs in virtue of his supreme power, when he thought fit, conveying, deposing or transferring. His direct and discretionary powers depended on his position as intermediary between God and man, as well as on the more specific inheritance from St Peter. His authority to bind and loose, determine, establish, judge and legislate flowed directly from heaven. The pope stood above human history, in that he could reverse his predecessors' decisions and make new canons. That he would, in doing so, keep within the boundaries of the Catholic faith was assumed. These bounds, imposed on him by tradition, were more elastic than might be supposed. The government of a changing society must be dynamic; new problems come up and crises multiply. The limits recede even further if we look at theological trends in the early fourteenth century. Theologians speculated on the distinction between God's ordained and absolute power. The more adventurous and sceptical used the concept of God's absolute power as a dissolvent; by its use God could abrogate all ordained norms of morality.[1] The canon lawyers knew of the distinction, and some publicists argued on similar lines about politics: the pope could have recourse to his absolute power in

[1] See G. Leff, *Bradwardine and the Pelagians* (Cambridge, 1957), 127–264: *Gregory of Rimini* (Manchester, 1961), 18–28.

an extraordinary situation, though his ordained power sufficed as a rule. His spiritual function as supreme judge of men 'by reason of sin' would have amounted to absolute monarchy if pushed to its logical conclusions in a Christian community. He had in addition that discretionary power to act in an emergency which is essential to sovereignty.

As Hobbs realized, sovereignty is incompatible with built-in privileges or traditional rights and customs. The centralization of the Church under the papacy complemented absolutism. The pope, as sole channel of divine authority, was not only the apex but the master of the ecclesiastical hierarchy in all its degrees. In concrete terms he did not need to consult the college of cardinals nor could they bind him. Innocent VI frustrated the cardinals' attempt to impose conditions on him at his election; they had wanted to have more say in political and financial business and to safeguard their own rights and revenues.[1] The papacy also withstood pressure from the episcopate to uphold what the secular clergy thought of as their traditional, permanent rights of ministry against usurpation by the new mendicant orders of friars. It was natural that the papal monarchy should find its most extreme defenders in the ranks of the mendicants.[2]

Admittedly, the popes in their official pronouncements used more cautious language than their publicists, so much so that historians still differ in their interpretation of papal theory. What degree of absolutism did the popes themselves claim? When, if ever, was fullness of power in spiritual things stretched to include temporal things? When did indirect power over secular rulers 'by reason of sin' come to be reinforced by a claim to direct power? A good case has been made for tracing the claim to direct power back to Innocent III.[3] An expert in the history of canon law sees Innocent IV rather than Boniface VIII as reaching the highwater-mark of papal claims.[4] At

---

[1] The document stating the cardinals' claims and the pope's refusal to be bound by his promise, made before his election, to accept them, is printed in full by P. Gasnault and M.-H. Laurent, *Innocent VI (1352–1362), Lettres secrètes et curiales,* i, fasc. ii (Paris, 1960), no. 435, 137–8.

[2] See Y. M.-J. Congar, 'Aspects ecclésiologiques de la querelle entre mendiants et séculiers dans la seconde moitié du XIIIᵉ siècle et le début du XIVᵉ', *Archives d'histoire doctrinale et littéraire du Moyen Age,* xxviii (1962), 35–151.

[3] See a recent discussion by B. Tierney, ' "Tria quippe distinguit iudicia . . ." A Note on Innocent III's Decretal *Per venerabilem*', *Speculum,* xxxvii (1962), 48–59.

[4] L. Buisson, *Potestas und Caritas. Die päpstliche Gewalt im Spätmittelalter,* Forschungen zur kirchlichen Rechtsgeschichte und zum Kirchenrecht, ii (1958), 117.

least two points are clear. It is difficult to read 'dualism', the recognition of the temporal power as supreme 'in its own sphere', in the bull *Unam sanctam* issued by Boniface VIII. The bull stated that the spiritual power had to *institute* and to judge the temporal; *Unam sanctam* was incorporated into canon law. Secondly, the fourteenth-century popes never explicitly repudiated the claims made for them by their publicists in the same way as John XXII denounced Marsilius of Padua's opinions as heretical or as Innocent VI denounced the cardinals' attack on his fullness of power. On the contrary, *Unam sanctam* seems to quote certain passages from a treatise by Giles of Rome, defending the right of the papacy to both temporal and spiritual lordship.[1]

A sermon preached by Clement VI (6th November, 1346) is revealing. True, a sermon differs from a bull, in that the pope as preacher is not concerned to define doctrine, but to persuade an audience. Nevertheless, it shows how his mind worked.[2] Clement's generous, peace-loving temperament makes it all the more striking. His object, moreover, was to praise the emperor elect, his friend Charles of Luxemburg, and to open a new era of friendship and co-operation between pope and emperor. After praising Charles to the point of flattery, Clement reminds him that the empire has been translated many times from one race to another 'by the Church'. There are 'greater and lesser lights' (ecclesiastical and secular powers). All derive from God, but the lesser come from God mediately through the pope's. Hence the pope has the right 'to approve, judge and regulate'. The imperial power, therefore, must seek approval, submit to examination, and rule on the principle of moderation and right order. Powers are ordained, one above the other, the greater commanding the lesser. The pope is God's vicar. The apostolic command is as God's. Catholic imperial power originates with the pope, is modelled on the pope's, is directed by the pope, and ends with the pope. Clement here uses the word 'ends' in its teleological sense: the end of a thing, according to Aristotle, is its perfection or fullest development. That, 'so it seems to me', is the reason why popes and bishops have to judge in temporal as well as in spiritual matters. As judges of the end, they must

---

[1] J. Rivière, *Le problème de l'Eglise et de l'Etat au temps de Philippe le Bel* (Louvain/Paris, 1926), 394–404.

[2] *Mon. Germ. Hist. Legum* iv, *Constit.* viii, pars prior (1910), no. 100, 158–59.

also judge the means, that is, the behaviour of emperors. Clement concludes that the spiritual power can judge all temporal things. Current arguments from 'reason' in the form of scholastic philosophy and from 'authority' in the form of Scripture and canon law reinforce his thesis. In this sermon, at least, Clement makes the publicists' claims his own.

There was one hole in this giant wall of theory. The importance of canon law has been stressed in recent studies of medieval political thought: 'The publicists built the mansions; the canonists made the bricks'.[1] The *Corpus iuris canonici* included the case of a heretical pope: what was to be done with him? The most extreme papalist, denying that anyone had the right to judge Christ's vicar for his personal sins or for unwise use of his power, still had to consider the possibility, as found in canon law, that a pope might deviate from the faith. But this mattered little in the absence of any agreement as to how or by whom a heretical pope could be judged and deposed. Once the crisis of Boniface VIII's reign was safely over, the problem remained hypothetical rather than actual until the Schism of 1378. The papalist theory amounts to formulation of sovereignty in spite of this seeming flaw in it. After all, the most absolute monarchy imaginable needs machinery for replacing a mad ruler: assassination makes sorry precedent. Some readers may object that a religious theory of sovereignty is nonsense anyway: it depends on premises which cannot be proved by reason and is valid only for believers. But such an objection would rule out almost any political theory that has ever been put forward. Theorists have to start from assumptions which are acceptable at the time, but which will be questioned later.

The true weakness in the papal theory of sovereignty is its failure to consider the executive. It is a strange theory of sovereignty which ignores the problem of physical force: one might as well discuss it today without mentioning nuclear weapons. Granted that the pope had supreme lordship over temporal things, how could he enforce it? His absolute, universal rule was not conceived as a theocracy, which would at least have been logical. It is better described as a 'hierocracy'. Taking 'theocracy' to mean government by priests, we can see that it obtained only in certain spheres and in certain places, not everywhere. The clergy shared government with secular

[1] B. Tierney, *Foundations of the Conciliar Movement* (Cambridge, 1955), 197.

rulers; it was a large share by modern standards, but no more than a share. The papal states in central Italy offer the closest approximation to theocracy, in that here the pope had direct temporal as well as spiritual power. When and in as much as his power was effective, he used clerics as his agents and they controlled or tried to control the unruly inhabitants. The most logical and consistent of all the papal publicists, the Austin friar, Augustine of Ancona, came from a town in the papal states, which may not be accidental. But no one in his wildest dreams thought of making the temporal power effective elsewhere.[1] Again, the pope had royal vassals, who owed him homage as their feudal lord. The kingdom of Naples was a fief of the papacy. Here a minority or grave crisis would lead the pope to intervene directly in government. Clement VI and his legates exercised a protectorate over the girl queen and her kingdom when Joanna came to the throne in 1343. 'I have lost a true father' she wrote to her brother on Clement's death. She had cause to be grateful, although the pope had an interest in watching his rights in his fief.[2] But a feudal relationship existed only in special cases and for historical reasons: it could not have been generalized. The popes had hardly any physical force behind them. The papal states provided a small army and a derisory revenue at the best of times. The dues and taxes to be drawn from the rest of Christendom depended on the goodwill of princes. The popes had to fight by means of allies. To gain allies they had to act as politicians. That meant loss of confidence, their most precious asset. Most people today dislike the idea of theocracy because they think they can imagine what it would be like. Still, it is thinkable as a form of government, however unpleasant. A papal hierocracy, absolute power without force to back it, is not imaginable.

The contrast between fact and theory comes out in the papal registers themselves. The prelates assembled at the council of Vienne, opened by Clement V in 1311, presented a list of

---

[1] P. de Lapparent finds the idea that the pope might govern the world directly as its temporal ruler in a work by the Franciscan friar, Francis de Meyronnes, 'L'oeuvre politique de François de Meyronnes', *Archives d'hist. doctr. et lit. du M. A.*, xv–xvii (1942), 37; but if so, the idea is vaguely expressed, and no concrete suggestions are made; moreover, Meyronnes praises the vassal kingdom of Naples (p. 41), which makes it look as though he were quite satisfied with the existing arrangements. See the criticism of de Lapparent by F. Baethgen, 'Dante und Franz von Mayronis', *Deutsches Archiv für Erforschungen des Mittelalters*, xv (1959), 103–36.

[2] E. Léonard, *La jeunesse de Jeanne I*, ii (Paris, 1932), 388.

grievances, enumerating the wrongs currently suffered by clergy at the hands of laymen.[1] The first item states that temporal lords are claiming superiority over lands belonging to churches. The complainants go on to lay usurpation of ecclesiastical jurisdiction, refusal to punish attacks on the persons and property of clergy, the violation of church liberties and immunities. The dossier gives a full account, illustrated by examples, of the means by which laymen encroach on church property and privilege. The council then proceeded to discuss remedies. The debate was inconclusive. Some thought that excommunication might be stepped up, others that canon law already supplied redress for certain cases. Yet the whole trouble arose out of disrespect for canon law. Two incidents, picked at random from the papal registers for 1338, show what went on in the decades after the council. Two knights and two 'rectors of churches' with 'a great crowd of country folk' have attacked the bishop of Constance and seriously wounded some of his train; they still hold him in prison.[2] Here we see clerics in the persons of the two rectors, aiding and abetting a lay foray against a bishop. The second incident is the more shocking because it happened in the kingdom of Naples under an ardently guelf king, who recognized the pope as his overlord. Enemies of the bishop of Bisaccia have withdrawn his vassals from obedience on the ground that churches have no business to hold fiefs. They have forbidden anyone to sell food to the bishop or his household. Moreover they beat him, swearing 'to break his head', stripped him naked, tied him up, and tormented him for two days and a night.[3] The Neapolitan government could not protect a papal official, let alone bishops. The people of Gaeta attacked a papal tax-collector on a ship flying the papal flag in 1347. They stripped, insulted and imprisoned him, and seized the ship with its treasure on board. Though a royal galley sailed to his rescue, the Gaetans needed much persuasion before they would disgorge their loot, and they seem to have gone unpunished.[4] The Church fared better in a strongly governed state such as England, where self-help on the

[1] F. Ehrle, 'Ein Bruchstück der Akten des Concils von Vienne, *Archiv für Literatur-und-Kirchengeschichte*, iv (1888), 361–470.

[2] *Benoît XII (1334–1342), Lettres communes*, ii (Paris, 1910), no. 6308, 104.

[3] Ibid., no. 6261, 97.

[4] E. Léonard, op. cit., i, 650. On King Robert's inability to keep order and protect his clergy from attacks by laymen, see R. Caggesi, *Roberto d'Angiò e i suoi tempi*, i (Florence, 1922), 248–52.

part of anticlericals was generally repressed. A strong king, on the other hand, was a tougher customer to deal with in bargaining over papal rights in his territories.

Papal history is full of irony, as hopes for a brighter future rise and fall. Our period opens with the Jubilee of 1300. Its splendour and popularity implied a moral triumph for Boniface VIII: pressure to celebrate it had come from below, from the ranks of the faithful. The pope's temperament was secondary, though he made the most of his opportunities. The Jubilee formed a glorious backcloth to the publication of *Unam sanctam* in 1302. Less than a year later came the humiliation of Anagni. The French king's agents subjected the pope's person to violence and his memory to smears: Philip IV had succeeded better than any emperor in getting his way with the papacy. Clement V failed to save the Knights Templar from his brutal treatment and could do little to exonerate Boniface. The election of a series of Frenchmen as popes and their settlement at Avignon seemed to mark a victory for France.

Our period ends with the return to Rome in January 1377. There was to be another fresh start. The new pope's choice of name proclaimed his loyalties and his programme. Gregory I, Gregory VII and Gregory IX had been Romans and defenders of Rome, as well as forceful characters; Gregory X had worked for reform, unity and peace. Gregory XI, although a Frenchman, meant to renew the Gregorian tradition. He persisted in leaving Avignon, undeterred by the sad experience of his predecessor, Urban V, who had given up his plan to stay in Rome for good. The city welcomed home the exile; the Babylonian captivity had ended. Gregory's chaplain, the bishop of Senigallia, describes the journey and the Roman greeting in a poem which mixes rhetoric with realism. The travellers, tired and seasick, arrive at Ostia to be escorted to Rome along muddy roads. It was all as cheerless and exhausting as a long fête in depressing weather can be. Elaborate pageantry laid on for the occasion featured 'young dancers clad in white' and 'bald old dodderers playing loudly on trumpets by torchlight'.[1] We know as we read that the Schism with all its scandal and bitterness will begin after Gregory's death in the following year. Hence the bathos of his welcome must appear as symbolic. The chorus of baldheads making music for the weary pope signify those

[1] Ed. Muratori, *Script. rer. Ital.*, iii, fasc. ii (1734), 704–6.

arguments for hierocracy which had served the papacy so long and so badly.

Laymen could see the silliness of papal claims. 'I had a good laugh', says the knight in a *Dispute between Clerk and Knight* written in defence of Philip IV, 'when I heard of Lord Boniface VIII's new statute, where he claims that he is and ought to be set above all principalities and kingdoms. He can easily get a right to anything; he just writes it down'. To want is to have: 'He has only to write "I will that this should be law", when he wants my castle, my house or my cash'.[1]

The historian has to measure the distance between fact and theory, but that is not all. If he finds a wide gap, he must ask why it opened and try to understand the theorists. Dreamy idealism has never figured among the many faults ascribed to the Avignon popes from their own time onward. They must, therefore, have had some reason for claiming full power over things temporal. How did their minds work?

The development of papal bureaucracy at Avignon was a solid fact underlying the hierocratic theory. If the popes often failed to protect their servants, they at least worked out the means to exploit the resources of Christendom. The system held good because lay rulers and churchmen alike needed the Curia. They used it for litigation and for diplomatic services, as a source of promotion for themselves and their relatives and officials. The shareholders might quarrel over dividends; it did not suit them to liquidate the company. Consent, mutual profit and a nice balance of interests kept the institution going, as long as they lasted. For the present Avignon with all its *agréments* provided a climate, physically as well as metaphorically, which partly compensated for sentimental objections to the desertion of Rome.[2] The French monarchy and a politically sheltered site offered security until the armed companies begotten by the Anglo-French wars made even Provence unsafe. The nomadic habits of thirteenth-century popes had hindered the tendency, shared by papal government with all others, to expand and to pile up records. In Italy the popes had lived mainly in their hill strongholds or in Viterbo, paying occasional visits to their capital. Clement V moved restlessly

---

[1] Ed. M. Goldast, *Monarchia Sancti Romani Imperii*, i (Hanover, 1612), 62–3.

[2] Y. Renouard, *La Papauté à Avignon* (Paris, 1954); G. Mollat, *Les papes d'Avignon 1305–1378*, 9th ed. (Paris, 1950).

about southern France. Residence at Avignon was something new. What was thought of at first as a temporary stay turned into permanent settlement. Here, in a light roomy palace, archives could be filed, stored and consulted. An imperial promise in sealed letters, 'which we have put away in the archives of the Roman Church and are having carefully guarded',[1] had every prospect of remaining there. Offices could proliferate.

Expansion characterized fourteenth-century government in general, but papal bureaucracy differed from secular in a way favourable to the popes.[2] In England and France sections of the original royal household would 'go out of court' to become departments of state, no longer amenable to close royal control and jealous of the parent body, the king's permanent household, which remained attached to him, and which he might use as a reserve of power and initiative. The papal bureaucracy, on the contrary, continued to be patriarchal, a true 'household', watched over and regulated by its chief. The popes attended carefully to its running and would draw up ordinances to regulate it. Secondly, the popes could draw on the talent of Europe for their personnel. They staffed their administration mainly with Frenchmen, but neither nepotism nor local patriotism stood in the way of efficiency. Clement V continued to employ Italians and his successors followed his example. The reasons were probably that they wished to keep in touch with Rome rather than break the tradition, and that Italian trained secretaries excelled in their mastery of technique; the Italian law schools were the best in Europe. The papal penitentiaries had to be recruited from different countries in order to cope with the penitents of diverse speech and customs who came to the Curia or corresponded with its officials.

A government's first need is for money. The pope and his cardinals, who worked hard for their rents and perquisites, had to finance a vast machine. They maintained large households of personal servants and dispensed charity and patronage. The papacy, as a temporal power, had to pay for wars in Italy. The papal states must be reconquered from usurpers and local 'tyrants'. Innocent VI had to buy off the captain of an armed

[1] *Mon. Germ. Hist.*, *Legum* iv, *Constit.* iv, pars post. fasc. i (1908), no. 1165, 210, 1313/1314.
[2] B. Guillemain, *La Cour pontificale d'Avignon (1309–1376). Etude d'une société* (Paris, 1962).

company who held Avignon to ransom. Papal revenues, unlike royal, were normally adequate to the demands made on them. They differed from royal in that they came in from all over Europe and were less variable in quantity, nor were there any 'estates' to bargain with. Further, the papacy led the way in financial experiments and organization. A glance at its sources of revenue may suggest that they were chancey and subject to compromise; a secular prince's were much more so.[1]

The papal states brought in a low income on account of the prevalent war and disorder. The small county of the Venaissin, centred on Avignon, produced more relatively to its size. There were rents from vassal states; Peter's pence was paid by certain kingdoms. Add payments from exempt abbeys (subject to the immediate jurisdiction of the Holy See), gifts and payments traditionally made to the Curia on various occasions, revenues connected with papal provisions, and taxes. Direct taxation, assessed on property, originated in the war effort called for by the crusades, and was a papal invention. Gradually the papal 'tenths', raised on ecclesiastical property throughout Christendom, came to be levied for any war or urgent need which the popes regarded as touching the welfare of the Roman Church. Friction resulted as secular rulers followed their example. Two questions arose: had a secular government the right to tax its clergy for national needs? Would it tolerate papal taxation of its clergy, which drew money out of the kingdom? Both questions had been settled by a compromise after the bull *Clericis laicos*, issued in 1298.[2] On the first question, papal permission was required in principle for taxation of the clergy, except in case of 'urgent need'. The discretion to decide when 'urgent need' arose marked a step in the direction of autonomous lay states. One can understand Boniface VIII's claim to world dominion in compensation and as an ultimate sanction. The papal answer to the second question was to leave the principle intact and to compromise in practice. The more powerful princes allowed papal tenths to be levied on their clergy in return for a rake-off. Papal taxation of the clergy became royal in effect. The popes contented themselves with as large or as

---

[1] On papal finance and banking see Y. Renouard, op. cit., 101–5; *Les relations des papes d'Avignon et des compagnies commerciales et bancaires de 1316 à 1378* (Paris, 1941); D. P. Waley, 'An Account-Book of the Patrimony of St. Peter in Tuscany, 1304–1305', *Journal of Ecclesiastical History*, vi (1955), 18–25.
[2] See T. S. R. Boase, *Boniface VIII* (London, 1933), 129–56.

small, often very small, a share as they could bargain for in given circumstances. Their tax collectors got the odium, secular governments much of the benefit.

Collecting, transporting, accounting for and spending such diverse and scattered revenues raised acute problems; moreover, some income was divided between the pope and the cardinals. John XXII found a financial genius in the person of Gasbert Laval, who had charge of the apostolic chamber (the treasury) 1319–47. He overhauled the system and got it into working order. Banking is perhaps the most 'modern' aspect of papal finance. Most medieval governments ran on credit. Revenues came in slowly, were hard to collect and fell into staggering arrears. The development of business techniques, especially in the prosperous mercantile centres of northern Italy and Tuscany, put international credit largely into the hands of Italian firms, which combined banking with commerce. Hence nothing could be more vital to any government than to deal with stable firms, capable of supplying large-scale credit, and to have good relations with them, based on mutual advantage. Papal history taught many lessons. Innocent IV had been dunned for his predecessor's debts by Roman creditors soon after his consecration:[1] the Romans were impatient because they had little capital. Even the great Florentine firms would go bankrupt; they were at the mercy of local politics and of princely debtors who could not pay. The Avignon popes chose a limited number of Florentine firms for their most important business, except for a few years after the great crashes of the 'forties; then an Asti firm replaced the Florentines. The guelf commune was politically reliable as a rule. Its bankers had a grip on the papacy's main ally in Italy, Angevin Naples. The Florentine firms used the Rhône valley as their main route to northern Europe, where they had a network of connexions. By selecting a few companies to deal with out of the many available the papacy ensured confidence and favour as a trusted client. Papal bankers served mainly to transport or transfer bullion. The Bardi, for instance, could receive papal revenues in England and turn the money to account on the spot in the purchase of English wool for sale in Flanders and

---

[1] See his *Life*, written by da Calvi, Muratori (op. cit.), iii, 592. On Boniface VIII's difficulties with his bankers see G. Digard, *Philippe le Bel et le Saint-Siège de 1285 à 1304*, ii (Paris, 1936), 7–8.

Tuscany. Their agents in Avignon would pay the equivalent into the apostolic chamber, or perhaps the Bardi would have instructions to pay directly to the pope's allies or servants in Italy. Such arrangements obviated the risk of carrying precious metal across Europe. The bankers also provided deposit and postal services, exchanged currency, and could act as news agencies: their international relations and their own need for 'hard' news for business purposes made them useful here. They sometimes made loans or advances on incoming revenues. In that case they might receive interest in a concealed form, so as not to infringe the canon law prohibition of usury. But papal favour mattered enough to make them accommodating. As papal bankers they handled vast sums and were put in the way of profitable deals with the pope's clients, credit-hungry debtors or allies. The popes on their side acted prudently. Their bankers in this period were instruments to be used, not counsellors or pressure groups.

Finance was sound for most of the fourteenth century, indeed sounder than before. Clement V built up the treasure and his work was continued. Neither John XXII nor Benedict XII borrowed except for one loan raised in 1320 and repaid in 1321. No serious strains appeared until the pontificate of Innocent VI; then they arose from circumstances outside his control. Secular rulers, heavily in debt, must have envied the papacy.

Collation to ecclesiastical benefices supplemented taxes and formed a source of power and influence worth more than money. To understand the system of papal provisions one must notice that church property represented a high proportion of the landed wealth of every country, and that a church was seen as a revenue-producing unit like any other estate. This calls for a mental effort: 'the conception of the ecclesiastical benefice as primarily a pecuniary asset, a piece of real property, susceptible of most of the transactions associated with other forms of property and legally recognized as having this quality, has now practically vanished from the world'.[1] How and by whom were ecclesiastical benefices allocated? Before the development of papal provisions the system had been roughly that a cathedral chapter would elect its bishop, freely or under pressure, sometimes also its dean and other prebendaries. The rest went by patronage, under diocesan supervision where cure of souls was

[1] D. Knowles, *The Religious Orders in England*, ii (Cambridge, 1955), 288.

affected. Rights to present or nominate, being a form of property, reflected status; a king, an archbishop or an abbey would possess them in quantities; they differed in value according to the wealth of the benefice, and were often widely scattered. The centralization of the Church naturally brought an increasing share to the papacy.[1] The thirteenth-century popes began to reserve to themselves provision to certain categories of benefices. Petition to the Curia became a recognized way of seeking preferment. Clerks without influential friends would snatch at the chance. The area of papal reservation widened until Urban V in 1363 reserved all vacant bishoprics and monasteries for his lifetime; Gregory XI did likewise. These measures marked the highest degree of centralization ever reached from an administrative point of view. The granting of 'expectancies', that is provision to benefices not yet vacant, gave a new dimension to patronage.

Provisions enriched the Curia. Papal provisees paid a proportion of the value of a benefice if it were over a certain amount, and 'annates' or the first year's income, if it were below. The papacy claimed the right of 'spoils', that is the personal property of ecclesiastical origin which belonged to a deceased prelate, less the bequests he made on his deathbed for the good of his soul, payment of his debts, and funeral expenses. The area where spoils were exacted was limited; they fell most heavily on southern France.[2] There were other payments incidental to provisions. Further, the right to provide enabled the popes to reward and finance their staff and to put their friends into high positions, just as kings would put royal servants into bishoprics. Indeed, the process came into motion all the more smoothly since elections had almost ceased to be free; they were being managed by interested parties outside the chapters. Stalls in cathedral and collegiate churches, where obligation to residence could be dispensed with or reduced, were normally given to scholars and civil servants or to nobles

[1] Special studies on papal provisions are too numerous to mention; see especially E. Moreau, *Histoire de l'Eglise en Belgique*, iii (Brussels, 1945), 205–309; G. Mollat, *La collation des bénéfices ecclésiastiques sous les papes d'Avignon* (Paris, 1921); B. Guillemain, *La politique bénéficiale du Pape Benoît XII (1334–1342)*, Bibl. de l'Ecole des Hautes Etudes, ccxcix (1952); W. A. Pantin, *The English Church in the Fourteenth Century* (Cambridge, 1955); C. Davies, 'The Statute of Provisors of 1351', *History*, N.S. xxxviii (1953), 116–33.
[2] G. Mollat, 'A propos du droit de dépouille', *Revue d'histoire ecclésiastique*, xxix (1933), 316–43.

and their kinsfolk. The fourteenth-century popes cashed in on a valuable source of patronage. Benefices with cure of souls were less affected; the popes did not often provide non-resident foreigners to them. Once the system was going, everyone jumped on the bandwagon. Many complained, especially those whose rights of patronage were impeded; all wanted to get provisions for themselves or their servants and relatives.

An extremely complicated set of struggles went on behind the façade. There was endless litigation, bringing more business to the Curia. There were threats, political pressures, counter-measures and compromises. The operation of the system varied from one pontificate to another. Benedict XII (1334–42), a severe, upright monk, followed the example of the Dominican Pope Benedict XI (1303–4); he revoked expectancies and reduced pluralism; nor would he provide an excessive number of foreigners to local churches. At other times the system tended to get out of hand. It varied from one country to another according to the degree of resistance it met. Patrons with traditional rights, infringed by the system, could work it from inside: the pope would provide a royal nominee; in the case of an obstinate German chapter he would quash an election *pro forma* and then provide the man elected. The English kings had their own brand of secret diplomacy and blackmail. The metropolitans of decentralized Germany fought a rearguard action, but ended by accepting papal provision in principle; it made little difference to German practice. The popes had more success in the area covered by modern Belgium, where a topsy-turvy situation developed. The secular princes kept their independence *vis-à-vis* the French monarchy, while the Avignon popes made the churches 'annexes of France'. Provisions in northern France, except in Brittany and Burgundy, whose dukes negotiated separately, reflected the mutual dependence of king and pope. The latter needed protection, the former, once the wars had started, backing against the English. The popes tried to be impartial. Clement VI could write sincerely to Edward III in 1345: 'The Almighty knows that since divine mercy raised us to the highest apostolate we have worked loyally for concord between you and the king (of France)'.[1] But peace would have favoured the French at this

---

[1] *Clément VI (1342–1352), Lettres closes, etc.*, ed. E. Déprez, J. Glénisson and G. Mollat, ii, fasc. iii (1958), no. 1844, 22–3.

stage of the war. Clement loaned 300,000 gold florins to the French Crown in the following year.[1] The popes also supported the pro-French ecclesiastics in Flanders against the pro-English burghers and peasantry. The result was an understanding by which the popes often, by no means always, accepted royal nomination under cover of provision. Innocent VI (1352–62) had to yield to French cathedral chapters, demanding their traditional rights, for the reason that the royal government could not always protect papal provisees against local resistance in these critical years. The areas of greatest penetration were Italy, Spain and Portugal: here the pope 'disposed almost as a sovereign of many bishoprics, abbeys and lesser benefices'.[2]

The total effect of all this face-saving compromise behind the façade of papal taxation and collation is clearer to the modern historian, who has a bird's-eye view, than it was to contemporaries. The papacy had devised a method by which wealth could be tapped and canalized through the Curia. If the profits had to be shared, at least their distribution was centralized. That bureaucracy had triumphed was plain as daylight to all interested parties. Modern attempts to decide whether 'worthy candidates' for promotion fared better or worse under the new system of distribution run into insuperable difficulties. Can one estimate 'merit' in fourteenth-century terms? University men did well out of papal provisions, a fact which rather endears the system to academic historians; our judgments cannot but be subjective.

The judicial machinery for dealing with cases of first instance and appeals to the Curia continued to develop. Litigation concerning provisions reached such proportions that a separate tribunal was established to deal with them and with some related business. It came to be called the Rota from the round bench in the room in the papal palace where the judges sat, to distinguish it from the Consistory. It had split off from the papal chapel, where clerks had previously had temporary commissions to hear cases, and became a permanent court, staffed by professional judges with its own procedural traditions and *esprit de corps*.[3]

The early fourteenth-century popes were also great legislators,

[1] G. Mollat, 'Le Saint-Siège et la France sous le pontificat de Clément VI', *Revue d'histoire ecclésiastique*, lv (1960), 7.
[2] G. Mollat, 'La collation', op. cit., 131–2.
[3] B. Guillemain, *La Cour*, op. cit., 345–6.

working in touch with the canon lawyers. They would promulgate a collection of decretals or a separate constitution by
sending it to the canon law faculties of the major universities.
The professors certainly taught a 'live subject': their curriculum
had to be constantly adjusted so as to include new material.[1]
A papal definition or condemnation of doctrine would become
known at once. Decretals were lectured on and discussed
eagerly. Papal legislation impinged on almost all aspects of
life. To give one example: Boniface VIII's constitution *Cum ex eo*
affected both schools and parishes. It facilitated the education
of parish clergy by allowing bishops to grant leave of absence to
rectors with cure of souls for the purpose of study at a recognized academic centre for specified periods; the absentee had
to provide a suitable substitute of course. Boniface's successors
sympathized with his aims and the fourteenth century saw a
wide application of *Cum ex eo*.[2] Each new constitution brought
inquiries from the diocesans who had to implement it and
directives from the Curia. Initiative in the reform of the religious
orders now came from above rather than from below, as it had
so often done in previous centuries. It was the popes who
imposed and supervised a reform programme.[3]

Administrative centralization had reached a point where it
could become burdensome. Innocent VI appointed Cardinal
Albornoz as legate to reconquer the papal states in 1353. His
duties called for wide powers both civil and military. Hence the
pope had to delegate his supreme authority in detail. 'Here is
an excellent example of the difficulties of papal diplomacy,
aggravated as they were by the developments in the theory
of papal power. Many of the powers which the pope had
specifically taken to himself had to be carefully devolved upon
the cardinal, in order to give the head of the mission room to
manœuvre'.[4] Innocent's wordy preface to his instruments to
Albornoz betrays his sense of the awkwardness of the proceeding.

[1] L. E. Boyle, 'The Curriculum of the Faculty of Canon Law at Oxford in the
First Half of the Fourteenth Century', in *Oxford Studies presented to Daniel Callus*,
Oxford Historical Society (1964), 150–1, 158–60.
[2] L. E. Boyle, 'The Constitution "Cum ex eo" of Boniface VIII', *Mediaeval
Studies*, xxiv (1962), 263–302.
[3] See for example C. Schmitt, *Un pape réformateur et un défenseur de l'unité de
l'Eglise. Benoît XII et l'Ordre des Frères Mineurs* (Quaracchi, 1959).
[4] J. R. L. Highfield reviewing P. Gasnault and M.-H. Laurent, op. cit.,
English Historical Review, lxxviii (1963), 160.

On a wider front, the pope did sometimes take action in purely secular matters. Clement VI intervened with the French *parlement* to negotiate an accord between warring nobles, on the ground that his mission as representative of the King of Peace on earth obliged him to do so. He would ask for remission of penalties incurred by nobles for offences against the royal government, and even objected to an administrative measure for political reasons.[1]

The papacy was not so weak as to present no threat to secular governments. These still smelt danger. There was no guarantee that they would get their way by dint of bluff or bargaining. One episode will illustrate what ecclesiastical jurisdiction might entail in terms not only of money from fines, but even of national security.[2] Philip of Alençon, a noble of royal blood, was provided to the archbishopric of Rouen in 1359, probably as a royal nominee. Nevertheless, he at once asserted his rights of ecclesiastical jurisdiction against royal officials. His kinship with the enemy of the Valois, Charles the Bad of Navarre, made it risky to offend him. By 1370, however, the French Crown had regained strength. Revival of royal power brought a new drive to circumscribe privilege of clergy. The archbishop's conduct became a test case. He was arraigned for his action against the royal bailiff in *parlement*, the supreme law court for civil suits; the bailiff set forth his grievances. The judgment, given in 1373, ordered the temporalities of the see to be confiscated and sold up to the amount of the fine imposed on the archbishop and his official. He was not to receive them back until he had raised all sentences of excommunication on the bailiff. The royal chancellor presided at the hearing. *Parlement* even fixed the wages of a small army which would be sent to take possession of the temporalities. The archbishop would not budge, although urged to moderate his zeal by the pope himself. Finally he took refuge at Avignon, and was compensated for the loss of Rouen by receiving the archbishopric of Auch and a titular patriarchate. Charles V felt nervous enough to ask Gregory XI to 'kick him upstairs' by giving him the red hat, which the pope refused. The king had reason to fear him. Two agents of Navarre, caught and questioned in

---

[1] G. Mollat, 'Le Saint-Siège', op. cit., 12, 21.
[2] L. Mirot and E. Déprez, 'Un conflit de jurisdiction', *Le Moyen Age*, x (1897), 129–74.

1378, disclosed that Philip of Alençon, while still archbishop of Rouen, had plotted a revolt against Charles V in concert with their master. He went over to the side of the Roman pope when the Schism began, and died as a cardinal in Rome. Charles had rid himself of 'this turbulent priest' without bloodshed, thanks to his good understanding with Gregory XI, but only after much delay and anxiety. Suppose the pope had been hostile instead of friendly? No wonder that Charles did all he could to keep Urban V and Gregory XI at Avignon. Papal claims to supremacy over kings had little substance, but that little might sometimes be tiresome.

Resident at Avignon or in one of their summer villas nearby, the popes formed the hub of a great legal, judicial, financial, administrative and diplomatic machine. They worked in a setting of international splendour. The city on the Rhône was more accessible to northern visitors to the Curia than Rome had been, while being easy to reach by sea or road from Mediterranean countries. It became a cultural centre for men of letters and artists, patronized by popes and cardinals. Modern scholars, studying early humanism, have discovered the importance of Avignon as a link between Latin scholarship in the north and the new trends in Italy. Contacts between scholars and transmission of texts came about at the right moment. Petrarch's abuse of France and Frenchmen has concealed his debt to them.[1] Similarly the popes engaged artists and architects from England, Spain and Italy as well as from France. As soon as a long stay at Avignon was envisaged, they aimed at making it worthy of their choice. Italian painters brought their new techniques from the peninsula; there were interesting experiments in perspective and naturalism. Northerners, accustomed to two-dimensional art, saw a painted wall which seemed to dissolve into green landscape, opening up behind marble colonnades. Avignon not only assembled various artistic traditions, but radiated them outwards. Rich visitors, impressed by the scene, would engage artists and craftsmen to take home on their return journey.[2] The popes built up a

[1] R. J. Dean, 'Cultural Relations in the Middle Ages: Nicholas Trevet and Nicholas of Prato', *Studies in Philology*, lxv (1948), 541–64; Gius. Billanovich, 'Dal Livio di Raterio al Livio del Petrarca', *Italia medioevale e umanistica*, ii (1959), 133–78. On the cardinals see G. Mollat, 'Le sacré collège', *Revue d'histoire ecclésiastique*, xlvi (1951), 22–112.
[2] See E. Castelnuovo, *Un pittore italiano alla corte di Avignone. Matteo Giovannetti e la pittura in Provenza nel secolo XIV* (Turin, 1962).

magnificent library. Theologians of repute lectured to an international audience of clerks at the school attached to the Curia.[1] Some of their lectures have survived: one teacher, at least, used to illustrate his points with the aid of charming Provençal allusions, proverbs and tales.[2] An English prelate, Richard de Bury, boasted that he could get reports, hot from Avignon, of any good sermon which had been preached there or of any new question which had been disputed.[3] The town also had a law school; Boniface VIII had already granted it the status of a university. It served more than local needs. Englishmen, for instance, inscribed themselves as students, probably regarding it as a stepping stone to papal provision.[4]

Potentates secular and clerical with their agents, and a throng of scholars, bankers, artists, friars, monks, poor clerks and laymen queued up for audience or were received in private at the palace. People waited anxiously in the papal ante-room and returned sadly to their lodgings when the bell rang to signal that audiences were over for the day.[5] The papal prisons, too, housed an international assortment of delinquents and 'enthusiasts'. A French friar, who had visions of a dangerously political kind, has described this prison underworld. The worst of the riff-raff was a renegade English monk from Winchcombe Abbey, a coarse ox of a man. Although mad, with homicidal impulses, he upheld his country's fame for orthodoxy by calling the prophet, in English, 'heretic-tic-tic!'.[6] It was well for the establishment that both types of men should be kept under lock and key. The Inquisition functioned as before to repress, if it could not extirpate, actual heresy. The popes, moreover, could still get the better of ideological rebels within the Church, as John XXII defeated the 'spirituals' in the Franciscan order. If any men had the appearance of power, and power at its most beneficent and civilized, it was the Avignon popes and their cardinals.

---

[1] R. Creytens, 'Le *studium Romanae Curiae* et le maître du sacré palais', *Archivum Fratrum Praedicatorum*, xii (1942), 1–83.

[2] B. Smalley, *English Friars and Antiquity in the Early Fourteenth Century* (Oxford, 1960), 251–7. For sermons preached at Avignon see Th. Käppeli, 'Predigten am päpstliche Hof von Avignon', *Archivum Fratrum Praedicatorum*, xix (1949), 388–93.

[3] *Philobiblon Ricardi de Bury. Text and Translation*, ed. M. Maclagan (Oxford, 1960), 90–1.

[4] B. Guillemain, *La Cour*, op. cit., 613.

[5] B. Smalley, 'Robert Holcot O.P.', *Archivum Fratrum Praedicatorum*, xxvi (1956), 62.

[6] J. Bignani-Odier, *Etudes sur Jean de Roquetaillard* (Paris, 1952), 20–3.

Why should they have claimed less than their predecessors? Another factor reinforcing the hierocratic theory was tradition. Fourteenth-century men had more awareness of history in the sense of precedent than their forebears. It seems a large claim to make for them, given the sway of tradition over the whole Middle Ages, but it can be substantiated. In Italy hostile factions would fall back on the old pattern of guelf versus ghibelline, papalist versus imperialist, even when the labels did not fit. Florence made ready to oppose the emperor elect, Henry VII, in the name of Christ and the Church, and denied his title at a moment when he still had the papal blessing.[1] The hierocrats inherited the traditions of Gregorian reform; they had only to develop its inner logic. They excelled at this. 'To follow the thread of thought to its extreme limit' characterized their way of thinking.[2] Traditionalism betrays its addicts, especially when taken to its logical conclusions. The Gregorian reformers had been practical in that they hoped to bring theory and fact together. Dismiss their dated arguments, and it becomes clear that they wanted the Church, under papal guidance, to take its rightful place in society. Ecclesiastical institutions had developed faster than secular; hence 'to rule the Church in the Middle Ages was tantamount to ruling the world'.[3] By the fourteenth century, however, this was ceasing to be true. Secular governments were catching up. A literate laity in the upper reaches of society and the growth of vernacular cultures undermined the status of 'clergy'. The century produced at least three scholar kings: Robert the Wise, the emperor Charles IV, and Charles V of France. The first two even dabbled in theology: Robert loved to preach and the Church indulged him; he was a king and safely orthodox, as we know from his sermons; Charles IV experimented in the essentially clerical genre of 'moralities' on biblical themes.[4] The increasing sophistication of royal counsellors hurt the papacy more than the learned tastes of their masters. They were not only ruthless

[1] W. Bowski, 'Florence and Henry of Luxemburg. The Rebirth of Guelfism', *Speculum*, xxxiii (1958), 177–203.

[2] D. Knowles, 'A Characteristic of the Mental Climate of the Fourteenth Century', *Mélanges offerts à Etienne Gilson*, Etudes de philosophie médiévale, hors série (Toronto/Paris, 1959), 315–25.

[3] G. le Bras, 'Le droit romain au service de la domination pontificale', *Revue historique de droit français et étranger*, xxvii (1949), 393.

[4] W. Goetz, *König Robert von Neapel* (1309–1343) (Tübingen, 1910), 34, 63–6. See the bibliography on Charles IV, B. Gebhardt, *Handbuch der deutschen Geschichte*, i (1954), 480.

and clever; they had a rival ideology, based on civil law and its exaltation of the lay power.[1] Although they professed a regard for the priesthood as such, they could meet the hierocrats on their own ground as political theorists. That fatherly 'talking down' which marked clerical addresses to laymen no longer met the case when laymen could answer back. And yet it was natural. Fathers often refuse to treat their children as adults; the head of an institution is still more prone to cling on to power. History offers few examples of giving way gracefully.

The papal attitude to the empire illustrates the extraordinary pull of tradition.[2] The fourteenth-century empire, as the textbooks say, 'was but a shadow of its former self'. The setting sun cast shadows larger than life. Two facts remained to justify imperial intervention in Italy: an invader could always collect a party of malcontents, who wanted material help and a legal pretext; there was real need for peace and order. Dante generalized these facts into an argument for one supreme ruler over secular affairs. Frederick III of Sicily defended his alliance with Henry VII on the score that the emperor had universal dominion. The emperor, he wrote, 'is lord of the world and head of peoples in temporal things; the kings and princes of the earth are legally subject to him'. It followed that his imperial ban sufficed to deprive Robert of Naples of his kingdom. Therefore, Frederick had a lawful *casus belli* against his enemy, King Robert. Frederick put forward these high-sounding considerations when begging his brother of Aragon to send help against an invasion which Robert was planning for the next spring (1314).[3] The failure of Henry VII and then of Lewis IV to restore the empire pricked these bubbles. Some theorists argued that it was just an anachronism, which did more harm than good. King Robert of Naples, who admittedly had as much to lose from an imperial revival as Frederick had to gain by it, attacked the whole idea after Henry's death in 1313.[4] The pope should weigh up the damages which the

[1] G. de Lagarde, *La naissance de l'esprit laïque au déclin du Moyen Age*, i (Paris, 1934); R. Cazelles, *La société politique et la crise de la royauté sous Philippe de Valois* (Paris, 1958), 297–301.
[2] M. J. Wilks, *The Problem*, op. cit., 282, 433–51.
[3] A. de Stefano, *Frederico III d'Aragona re di Sicilia* (1296–1337) (Palermo, 1937); *Mon. Germ. Hist. Legum* iv, *Constit.* iv, pars post., fasc. ii (1909), no. 1302–4, 1441–5.
[4] Ibid., fasc. i (1908), no 1253, 1369–73. For proposals to split the empire up into separate kingdoms, see H. S. Offler, 'Empire and Papacy: the Last Struggle', *Transactions of the Royal Historical Society*, 5th series, vi (1956), 21–2.

empire had inflicted on Italy and on the Roman Church. Robert drew up a long dossier of imperial crimes, stretching from Domitian to the last Hohenstaufen emperor. The Roman empire had originated in force and in seizure of alien lands. Force is unnatural. It runs counter to the law of nature and to the law of nations. Force is self-defeating in consequence. In the course of nature the empire has been cut up in its turn. All powers, from the Chaldean to the Roman, must suffer change in spite of their one-time greatness. Where is now the wisdom of the Greeks and the almost universal dominion of the Romans? Precedent, in Robert's argument, is used to demolish tradition, or rather to make change itself traditional. He had other and more practical reasons, calculated to appeal to the pope as a politician. An emperor, given his claim (which Robert would disallow) to be above all kings and peoples, and to be protector of the Roman Church, is sure to get proud; he will set himself over the pope; he will attack French possessions across the Sâone and the Angevin kingdom in Italy. The election, now customary, of Germans commits a dangerous power to fierce barbarians, 'who don't count theft as a sin'. It was a serious matter, as Robert knew, to invite the pope to liquidate the empire. The pope might object that he could hardly refuse to confirm an imperial election, made in due form. Robert fell back on an argument from canon law: the pope could and should use his authority to prevent scandal.[1] To suppress an ancient institution because it no longer fulfilled any useful purpose would have been a formidable exercise of the pope's discretionary power. He did not take the advice.

'The empire to the scrapheap!' might have appealed to the popes as a slogan. It would, after all, have been a logical step in their policy of recognizing the independence of Christian states outside the boundaries of Germany and northern Italy. Innocent III's bull *Per venerabilem* of 1202 stated that the king of France had no superior in temporal matters. *Pastoralis cura* (1313) denied to the emperor any superiority over Robert of Naples, a papal vassal. In any case, the princes to the west of Germany had never allowed the emperor more than precedence in rank, or at best moral leadership. Then came Lewis the Bavarian to realize the gloomiest forecast of crimes to be

---

[1] For canon law teaching on the pope's plenary power and scandal, see L. Buisson, op. cit., 125-65.

expected from a German emperor. Lewis employed Marsilius of Padua and William of Ockham. The Bavarian was the least forgivable of all emperors to judge by Clement VI's diatribe against him.[1]

Strange to say, no sooner had he been defeated than the pope began to praise the empire. The epic struggle between empire and papacy had this anticlimax. Clement VI set forth in glowing terms the benefits which would accrue to the Roman Church, the faithful and the whole commonwealth from the election of 'an active, devout and Catholic emperor'. Lewis was still living, it is true; Charles of Luxemburg must be offered 'the real thing' to make it worth his while to stand as a rival candidate. But Clement went out of his way to exalt the empire as universal. His sermon to Charles, already quoted, while it puts the empire below the papacy, sets it above all kingdoms. French independence, admitted by canon law, is passed over lightly. The legists (civil lawyers) claim for the empire unlimited power over the world. Today there are limits set by canon law. 'Yet this is certain: it stretches far wider than any temporal kingdom and is nobler than all the rest'.[2]

This ambivalent attitude towards the empire disgusted the French publicists and played into their hands. Its results appear in the *Somnium viridarii*, a vast compilation of material on relations between Church and State and on royal rights in general. Charles V seems to have ordered it to be made for use as a dossier, perhaps in view of his drive against clerical privileges and jurisdiction. The anonymous compiler or compilers finished the 'Orchard Dream' in May 1376. Its argument is that the king should be supreme in all temporal matters. The tone is anticlerical. The 'Dream' provides the framework for a dispute between a clerk and a knight, like the earlier *Dispute*, which it incorporates. The compiler contrives very cleverly to present the knight as a good Catholic, however anticlerical, and the clerk as a bad Frenchman. The latter, strong for the papacy, objects to the knight's opinion that the king has a right to tax his clergy, pleading that they have an imperial privilege granting them immunity. The king, so the clerk argues, cannot revoke it because the emperor is his superior: the emperor 'is

[1] H. S. Offler, 'A Political "Collatio" of Pope Clement VI, O.S.B.', *Revue bénédictine*, lxv (1955), 132–41; the date is April 10th, 1343.
[2] See p. 18, n.2, above, and ibid. no. 16, 31–3.

lord of the world in temporal affairs'. The knight duly examines and refutes all the clerk's reasons in favour of imperial supremacy over kings. The clerk begins to look like a fifth columnist, working against France on the emperor's behalf as well as on the pope's. Worse still, he was undermining the king's 'imperial' rights over his own subjects in his own kingdom.[1]

The popes had nothing to gain and much to lose by associating themselves with an outmoded concept of imperial power. Flattery of the emperor would not increase his real strength in politics and was bad for Franco-papal relations. But the empire had a function in the hierocratic theory, which they felt unable to sacrifice. The empire resembled a wife whose husband cannot live either with or without her. He quarrels with her in health and is pledged to her in sickness. The marriage, celebrated some six centuries earlier, would last until her death. The papacy depended too much on a historical tradition, regarded as divine, to break free of the past.

Lastly, we must realize that the hierocratic theory was so flexible as to leave ample room for manœuvre. The two kinds of supremacy claimed by the popes did not exclude each other; they provided defence in depth. Their upholders could occupy either the outer or the inner ring, withdrawing or advancing at will. There was an element of bargaining: ask for more than you expect to get; if you ask for everything you may get something. The pope has dominion over the whole world; therefore he can at least forbid lay taxation of church property. An English Carmelite friar, John Baconthorpe, lecturing about 1336, offers a good example of the technique. Arguing on behalf of the papacy, he puts forward the extreme claim to dominion over all things, temporal as well as spiritual; but if anyone should dispute it, he must at least admit the pope's right to intervene 'by reason of sin'.[2]

The classic case of manœuvre arose from the Flemings'

---

[1] Ed. Goldast, op. cit., 58–229. On the sources of the *Somnium Viridarii* see M. Lièvre, 'Note sur les sources du "Somnium Viridarii" ', *Romania*, lxxxi (1960), 483–91; B. Smalley, 'Jean de Hesdin a Source of the *Somnium Viridarii*', *Recherches de théologie ancienne et médiévale*, xxx (1963), 154–9. The passage referred to here, pp. 67–8, has not yet been identified as a quotation. See also A. Bossuat, 'La formule "Le roi est empereur en son royaume" ', *Revue historique de droit français et étranger*, 4th series, iii (1961), 371–81.

[2] B. Smalley, 'John Baconthorpe's Postill on St. Matthew', *Mediaeval and Renaissance Studies*, iv (1958), 91–145.

appeal to Boniface VIII to protect their country against the aggression of Philip IV, their overlord. They could not dispute the fact that their count was Philip's vassal. Feudal law gave no remedy against him that would have been practical in the circumstances. They therefore sought the pope's intervention by reason of his supremacy over kings even in temporal matters. This, they argued, gave him the right to act as judge. A Flemish embassy to the Curia in 1298 threw back, so to speak, at Boniface all the arguments for his claim to supreme lordship as St Peter's successor, Christ's vicar and God's viceroy on earth. No papal publicist could have improved on their statement; in fact, a Franciscan cardinal may have helped them to draw it up; he reinforced their case in a sermon preached at the Curia. The pope was not at all pleased, as a report from the embassy noted. It did not suit him at this time to act as judge of appeal in a secular dispute between the count and the king. He drew in his horns, snubbed the upholders of his highest claims, and left the Flemings out of his arbitration, undertaken privately (not as pope), between France and England, in which Flanders was very much concerned. He was not so foolish, he said elsewhere, as to confuse the spiritual with the temporal power; both had been ordained by God.[1] Again we find Innocent VI making no protest against the Golden Bull of 1356, though it passed over in silence the papal claim to approve the choice of the electors. Innocent's restraint is all the more striking in view of Clement VI's lecture to Charles IV less then ten years earlier on his dependence on the papacy, with its special stress on papal approval of an emperor elect. The Golden Bull did not even worsen relations between Innocent and Charles, who remained on friendly terms afterwards.[2] Gregory XI lectured the over-zealous archbishop of Rouen on his duty to respect and honour the king, his lord. He should protect ecclesiastical liberties 'with that moderation which becomes a prelate'. Thus will he gain a triple reward, 'from his God, his pope and his king'.[3] Here was a very wide application of the hierocrats' theory that the pope ruled through secular rulers in temporal matters in the normal course. In this case the king of France was allowed rather free rein in spiritual matters as well. The

[1] Migne, *Patrologia latina*, clxxxv, coll. 1897–1902; Digard, op. cit., i, 362–5.
[2] W. Scheffler, 'Karl IV und Innocenz VI', *Historische Studien*, ci (1912), 18–107.
[3] Mirot and Déprez, op. cit., 159.

popes had both a claim and an alibi ready for any emergency.

The lay powers on their side worked differently. They would entrench themselves in a moderate position as a rule, admitting papal supremacy in spiritual things. From this fortress they consolidated their hold over a border territory, rich in fines and taxes. Alliance with the papacy proved to be a good method of mastering and exploiting local churches. Only in times of acute crisis would lay publicists make long-distance raids across the border or lay rulers proceed to extreme measures. The more adventurous raiders got cut off from their base. Marsilius was probably better known through papal condemnation of his doctrine than through study of the original. The compiler of the *Somnium viridarii* quotes the *Defensor pacis*, but in a watered down version. John of Gaunt used Wyclif as a propagandist up to a point; but the government never acted on his call to disendow the clergy, much less to break with Rome. Even Ockham's modest plea for lay intervention, in case of necessity, to correct error in the Church had little appeal until the Schism put it on the map of practical politics. On the legal side, an English judge made a far-reaching claim for Edward III in an action brought by the Crown against the archbishop and chapter of York in 1343 concerning the advowson of the deanery. The king, it was claimed, was 'patron paramount of the whole bishopric'; 'in former times the king gave the bishoprics, and although he has since given licence to the chapter to elect, the patronage remains with him'; he could still claim it during a vacancy. Judgment was given for the Crown, on the grounds that the king 'from his fullness of power' could provide whenever it should be necessary according to his rights.[1] Although a judge spoke these brave words on his behalf, Edward often found the papal 'fullness of power' more useful than his own in promoting his servants.

The stream of abuse directed against the Curia from all quarters has often misled historians. Abuse served as a safety valve and hides a deep acquiescence. Listen to an English chronicler, whose *Life of Edward II* is notoriously anti-papal. He criticizes papal claims and papal provisions so fiercely that he has been seen as anticipating Henry VIII. There is a change of tune when he tells how two cardinals were attacked and

[1] *Year Book 17 Edward III, Trinity Term, no. 17*, ed. L. O. Pike (Rolls Series, 1901) 524-40.

robbed on their way through England to Scotland in 1317. The attack horrified him. The brutal punishment which royal justice meted out to the robbers struck him as right and proper:

'To whose person is reverence due if it is not given to legates specially sent by the pope? . . . The Roman Church is accustomed to bestow pardon on the humble petitioner; but if the sacrilegious hand attacks the Curia itself, with what assurance, I ask, can pardon be demanded?'[1]

A warning to us not to take grumbles at their face value! Secular princes had their work cut out to control their own subjects. When Philip VI complained to Edward III that he was not master at home,[2] many of his fellow rulers would have sympathized.

The historian with his hindsight can say which of the fourteenth-century theorists were prophetic and which were not. We know that the hierocratic theory will lose its value to the papacy; it has come to be regarded as a mistake. We know that it will be turned upside down: lay rulers will take over the concept of sovereignty and will supply its defect, the absence of executive power in the ruler's hands. We know that the various compromise solutions, allowing each of the two powers autonomy 'in its own sphere' will cease to be valid, as the State claims more of those civic functions which had fallen to the medieval Church. The idea of compromise will revive with neo-Thomism, but only after the Church has retreated into narrower limits. The 'prize for modernity', if we award it, goes to the most daring thinkers on the lay side. Anticlericalism will cease to be a mere threat or attitude and will influence practical politics. Marsilius' ghost could converse happily with Thomas Cromwell's or with that of Henry Parker, who served a greater Cromwell.[3] We can see 'the inexorable development towards a national church in the late Middle Ages';[4] but this was hardly visible to contemporaries. Marsilius' argument in his *Defensor pacis*, outside its Italian background, bore as little relation to fact as did Augustine of Ancona's hierocratic theories. Prophetic, too, were those who distinguished between *de facto*

[1] *Vita Edwardi Secundi*, ed. N. Denholm-Young, Nelson's Medieval Texts (1957), 83–4.
[2] Cazelles, op. cit., 71–2.
[3] W. K. Jordan, *Men of Substance. A Study of the Thought of Two English Revolutionaries, Henry Parker and Henry Robinson* (Chicago, 1942), 66–86.
[4] G. L. Harriss, 'Medieval Government and Statecraft', *Past and Present*, no. 25 (1963), 17.

and *de iure*. What was rightly claimed at law, they pointed out, for instance the emperor's universal power, did not correspond to the actual state of things. Circumstances alter cases; respect the law, but don't be hidebound.[1] This tendency to divorce moral principle from expediency and to erect the latter into a principle in its own right looks forward to Machiavelli. The divorce had been accepted in practice; the germs of the theory itself are medieval.[2] But fourteenth-century writers still make the distinction between law and fact, right and expediency in a timid, incidental way. They have no idea of shouting it from the housetops as a great discovery. It would have shocked their hearers and would have exposed them to censure.

What would a bourgeois onlooker, say the Ménagier of Paris, who wrote a book for the guidance of his young wife, have foreseen, had he turned his mind to such high matters? I should say at a guess that the moderates would have attracted him. Extremists seemed to cancel one another out. Providence, working through sensible men, would arrange a compromise whereby Church and State could respect each other's rights, as they had sometimes done in the past and might do again. Or perhaps our bourgeois onlooker is pessimistic, sharing the apocalyptic forebodings of many contemporaries. If so, the coming of Antichrist will leave no room either for the hierocrats or for *The Prince*.

---

[1] See C. N. Woolfe, *Bartolus of Sassoferrato* (Cambridge, 1913), 22–36, 78–99.
[2] A. H. Gilbert, *Machiavelli's Prince and its Forerunners* (Durham, N.C., 1938).

II

NICOLAI RUBINSTEIN

MARSILIUS OF PADUA AND ITALIAN POLITICAL THOUGHT OF HIS TIME

When Marsilius of Padua completed the *Defensor pacis*, on 24th June, 1324, it was three months since John XXII had excommunicated Louis the Bavarian, and a few weeks since Louis had replied by denouncing the pope as a heretic. As the conflict between Philip the Fair and Boniface VIII at the turn of the century had raised once more the problem of the relationship between the papacy and the secular states, so did that between Louis and John XXII. The resulting controversy, in which Marsilius played a prominent part, revived, in a different context, the polemics of the time of Philip the Fair. Marsilius, who had spent several years in Paris before writing there the *Defender of the Peace*, was doubtless well-acquainted with the arguments of the antipapal publicists of Philip.[1] Yet although his work was to help support the cause of the German king against the pope, its original purpose was not to formulate an imperialist doctrine in answer to the papalist claims of plenitude of power. It was not until much later, after years of service with Louis the Bavarian, that Marsilius used some of the conclusions he had reached in the *Defensor pacis* to substantiate a theory of universal empire.[2] In that work, he states that a discussion of

---

[1] R. Scholz, *Die Publizistik zur Zeit Philipps des Schönen und Bonifaz' VIII* (Stuttgart, 1903), 152–5, and G. de Lagarde, *La naissance de l'esprit laïque au déclin du Moyen Age*, ii (Saint-Paul-Trois-Châteaux, 1934), 105–17.

[2] In the *Defensor minor*, written probably in 1342 (ed. C. K. Brampton, Birmingham, 1922). The *De translatione imperii*, which Marsilius composed perhaps a few years after the *Defensor pacis*, is, to all intents and purposes, a copy of Landulfus Colonna's *De statu et mutatione Romani imperii*, with Landulfus' papalist arguments reversed (ed. M. Goldast, *Monarchia Sancti Romani Imperii* (Hanover, 1611–14),

the empire conceived as universal monarchy would fall outside the scope he had set himself,[1] which was to discover the causes of the loss of civic peace. Marsilius' attitude may be clarified by comparing the introductory chapter of the *Defensor pacis* with the opening chapters of Dante's *Monarchia*.[2] Both authors agree that since peace is essential for attaining the earthly purpose of life, the present troubles were caused by the disturbance of that peace. But while Dante speaks of peace in terms of universal tranquillity in a world-empire, Marsilius does so with reference to Italy. The disastrous effects of discord, he says, can be readily illustrated by the example of the *Italicum regnum*, whose inhabitants once lived peacefully together, and as a result 'brought the entire habitable world under their sway'. But now that kingdom is torn by strife, to the extent of being nearly destroyed by it.[3] For this state of things, he concludes at the end of the first discourse, the papal usurpation of secular power is to blame: 'over a long period [it had] been impeding the due action of the ruler in the *Italicum regnum*, and is now doing so even more'.[4] The *regnum Italicum* had been, since Otto I's coronation in 962, part of the German empire; originally identical with the Longobard kingdom, it comprised most of northern and central Italy. Having long lost its former political significance, it retained its place in Italian constitutional law.[5] Marsilius was exclusively concerned with the *regnum Italicum*, when he stated that Louis the Bavarian was, by some ancient birthright, impelled to extinguish strife and

---

ii. 147–53, and 88–95). I disagree with the view expressed by M. J. Wilks, *The Problem of Sovereignty in the Later Middle Ages* (Cambridge, 1963), 111, according to which 'in general . . . by the *pars principans* Marsilius has in mind the Roman emperor'.

[1] I.xvii.10, ed. R. Scholz (Hanover, 1932), 118: 'utrum autem universitati civiliter vivencium et in orbe totali unicum numero supremum omnium principatum habere conveniat . . . racionabilem habet perscrutacionem, aliam tamen ab intencione presenti'.

[2] *De monarchia*, i.4,5, ed. E. Moore and P. Toynbee, in *Le Opere di Dante Alighieri*, 4th ed. (Oxford, 1924), 343–5; *Defensor pacis*, I.i.1, pp. 1–3. Cf. A. Gewirth, *Marsilius of Padua* (New York, 1951–6), i. 97.

[3] I.i.2, pp. 3–4. In my quotations, in the text, from the *Defensor pacis*, I shall usually follow Gewirth's translation, op. cit., ii, but shall occasionally modify it. On the Italian aspects of Dante's concept of peace, see below, p. 68.

[4] I.xix.4, p. 127. Gewirth translates *Italicum regnum* as 'Italian state'. It is true that in I.ii.2, pp. 10–11, Marsilius says that he is going to use the term *regnum* as applicable to all temperate constitutions, and not to that of the kingdom only. But *regnum Italicum* was, as we shall presently see, a current geographical and political term, to which that definition evidently does not apply.

[5] See F. Ercole, *Dal comune al principato* (Florence, 1929), 200–2.

establish peace;[1] and it is chiefly with a view to contemporary Italy and its problems and needs, that he develops, in the first discourse of his work, a political doctrine to which he attributes universal validity. For he considers it necessary to examine the nature and right order of the state, and the 'usual' causes of discord in it, before proceeding to investigate the 'singular' cause of present strife, namely the claims and actions of the papacy.[2]

This examination is, in its turn, focused on the Italian city-states. Whatever the imperial claims to rule over Italy, which had been pressed only a few years earlier by Henry VII, an imperial 'state' had ceased to exist in Italy after the death, in 1250, of Frederick II.[3] In 1324, northern Italy had no effective political structure beside the states into which the *regnum Italicum* had long been divided. Of these, Padua was, at the beginning of the fourteenth century, one of the most powerful and prosperous. In addressing, from Paris, the German king, Marsilius proudly states his Paduan origins: 'and so I, a son of Antenor, . . . have written down the sentences which follow'.[4] Antenor was the legendary founder of Padua, whose 'tomb' had been 'discovered' there around the time of Marsilius' birth. This had caused much excitement, and the leading personality in Padua's pre-humanist circle, Lovato Lovati, had written an epitaph for the tomb,[5] in which he had praised Antenor as *patriae vox*, who, having striven for peace, had brought fugitives from Troy to their new home. Marsilius must have been acquainted with these lines, and may have considered his own work to be a fitting task for a descendant of Padua's founder.

That the Italian city-states in general, and Padua in particular, provide the institutional background for much of Marsilius' theory of the state, has been amply demonstrated.[6]

---

[1] I.i.6, p. 8.
[2] Gewirth, II. xxi.
[3] See E. Kantorowicz, *Kaiser Friedrich II* (Berlin, 1927), 442 sqq.; idem, *Ergänzungsband* (Berlin, 1931), 195 sqq.
[4] I.i.6, pp. 7, 8.
[5] See R. Weiss, 'Lovato Lovati (1241–1309)', *Italian Studies*, vi (1951), 7–8, 20–1. The inscription has been published several times, e.g. by P. H. Wicksteed and E. G. Gardner, *Dante and Giovanni di Virgilio* (Westminster, 1902), 323.
[6] See C. W. Previté-Orton, 'Marsiglio of Padua. Doctrines', *E.H.R.*, xxxviii (1923), 1–18, and his edition of the *Defensor pacis* (Cambridge, 1928), *passim*; and Gewirth, i. 23–31. The frequent references to Italian communal institutions form, incidentally, the most powerful, though by no means the sole argument against the thesis that discourse one was composed not by Marsilius, but by his friend Jean de Jandun; cf. Scholz, introduction to his edition of the *Defensor pacis*,

His faithful rendering of Aristotle's account of the genesis of the state, as culminating in the perfect *communitas vocata civitas*,[1] indicates the focal point of his political theory. Marsilius' basic concept of the *legislator humanus* as the source of all political authority in the state recalls the legislative assemblies and councils of the Italian communes; the limits he sets to the powers of the *pars principans* resemble the strict controls to which the city magistrates were subjected; the election of the *pars principans* corresponds to that of the *podestà* and *capitano*. Last, but not least, the integration of the Church in the political community, and its consequent subjection to the government, which forms one of the principal aspects of Marsilius' doctrine, was also a major objective of communal governments. Padua provides a striking example both of the attempts of the commune to exercise control over the local church and priesthood, and of the ensuing conflicts.[2] Between 1270 and 1290, communal legislation abolished benefit of clergy for crimes committed against laymen, and deprived clerics who did not pay taxes of legal protection and civic rights. As a result, Padua was placed, in 1283, under an interdict, and did not make peace with the church authorities until 1290, after being threatened with the closure of the university. Yet by the 'concordat' of 1290, ecclesiastical exemptions remained substantially restricted. Similarly, the history of Florence from the early thirteenth century onwards was marked by conflicts caused by successive communal attempts to deprive the clergy of its privileged position.[3] Thus, between 1250 and 1260, the popular régime abolished clerical exemptions from communal taxation and jurisdiction; and even after the guelf reaction in 1266, Charles of Anjou could still forbid, in 1270, the observance of statutes

---

li–liii; Gewirth, 'John of Jandun and the *Defensor pacis*', *Speculum*, xxiii (1948), 267–72. M. J. Wilks' important work on the problem of sovereignty (above, p. 44, n. 2) appears to me to give a less than fair appraisal of Marsilius' political doctrine by all but ignoring Marsilius' Italian background.

[1] I.iii.5, p. 16. Cf., by way of contrast, St Thomas, *De regimine principum*, i.1, ed. J. Mathis (Turin, 1948), p. 3: 'in civitate vero, quae est perfecta communitas, quantum ad omnia necessaria vitae; sed adhuc magis in provincia una propter necessitatem compugnationis et mutui auxilii contra hostes'; Giles of Rome, *De regimine principum* (Rome, 1556), III.i.2,5, fols. 239v, 243r–v.

[2] See L. A. Botteghi, 'Clero e comune in Padova nel secolo XIII', *Nuovo Archivio Veneto*, n.s., ix (1905), 238–68. Cf. M. A. Zorzi, 'L'Ordinamento Comunale Padovano nella seconda metà del secolo XIII', *Miscellanea di storia Veneta* (Deputazione di storia patria per le Venezie), v (1931), 98 sqq.

[3] R. Davidsohn, *Geschichte von Florenz*, IV.1 (Berlin, 1922), 146–51.

ordering taxation of the clergy.[1] Conflicts over clerical exemption from communal tribunals continued, however: in 1322,
the new Statutes of the Captain of the People reasserted the
subjection of the clergy to the communal courts, while five
years later, the bishop of Florence threatened the officials in
charge of compiling the city's statutes with excommunication,
if they encroached upon the liberty of the Church.[2]

In fact, the Italian background of Marsilius' theory of the
state is not confined to its institutional setting, but extends to the
contemporary political problems of the city-states. Foremost
among these was civic strife. The failure of most communes to
put an end to internal factions and social conflicts was one of the
chief causes of the rise of despotism in the thirteenth century.
Another was the protection a despot could provide in inter-
state struggles. By the time Marsilius was writing, most of the
northern Italian communes had come under the sway of
Signori; regularly elected by communal councils and assemblies,
these had succeeded in establishing their autocratic rule, and
in securing what amounted to hereditary succession.[3] The
Signoria offered an alternative to republican government at the
price of sacrificing long-established liberties. But, despite the
attractions and the success of the new régime, opposition to it
was widespread and articulate. It was particularly forceful in
Marsilius' Padua.

At the beginning of the fourteenth century, Padua was one of
the few great cities of northern Italy which had preserved their
republican constitution, and under the popular régime
established after the fall of the despotic rule of Ezzelino in 1256,
antidespotic feeling ran high.[4] Thus the statute creating, in
1293, a military union of the Paduan guilds[5] explains that this
reorganization was effected in order to preserve Padua in a
peaceful state, and free from 'the rule of any tyrant or any
single person'. But in 1318, Jacopo da Carrara, one of the
leading citizens, was elected *Signore* for life. Civil strife had
broken out during Henry VII's Italian expedition of 1310-13,
and this, as well as the military threat from the lord of Verona,

---

[1] Ibid., II (Berlin, 1908), i.454-5, ii.51.
[2] Ibid., IV.i.149-50.
[3] See E. Salzer, *Ueber die Anfaenge der Signorie in Oberitalien* (Berlin, 1900),
233. See also below, 63-4.
[4] Zorzi, op. cit., 183 sqq.
[5] Ed. ibid., 205-6.

Cangrande della Scala, resulted in the leader of one of the rival factions being elected *Signore*, in spite of the statutes designed to prevent such an occurrence.[1] That Jacopo a year later resigned his authority in favour of the count of Gorizia, who seemed to offer better protection against Cangrande, was hardly due to military reasons alone,[2] but doubtless also reflects the strength of Padua's republican tradition. Jacopo died in 1324; and under his nephew Marsilio da Carrara the family reasserted and consolidated their ascendancy in the city, until Marsilio in his turn was elected *Signore* in 1328—only to hand over Padua to Cangrande. During the intervening period, Marsilius of Padua's friend Albertino Mussato emerged as the passionate spokesman of Paduan republicanism against the despotic régime that was threatening to engulf his city.[3] Marsilius' strictures on absolute government are, on a theoretical plane, concerned with problems similar to those Mussato was facing in Padua on a political and historical plane.[4]

In this, as in other respects, it is difficult to evaluate Marsilius' political theory adequately without taking into consideration contemporary political thinking in his native country, and the political developments in the city in which he was born and educated, and in which he spent his formative years.[5] However much Paris may have influenced him, Padua was his original intellectual home. On his return from France in or soon after 1313, we find him there as friend of two of the leading Paduan thinkers of his time, Albertino Mussato and Peter of Abano. He was thus in contact with the pre-humanist circle which

[1] See Ercole, op. cit., 58–60; Zorzi, 193–4.

[2] As Ercole seems to imply (61).

[3] On Mussato, see A. Zardo, *Albertino Mussato* (Padua, 1884) and M. Minoia, *Della vita e delle opere di Albertino Mussato* (Rome, 1884); on his friendship with Marsilius, F. Novati, 'Nuovi aneddoti sul cenacolo letterario padovano del primissimo Trecento', in *Scritti storici in memoria di G. Monticolo* (Venice, 1922), p. 178; J. Haller, 'Zur Lebensgeschichte des Marsilius von Padua', *Zeitschrift für Kirchengeschichte*, xlviii (1929), 168 sqq., and Lagarde, op. cit., 21–7.

[4] That he had been, at one time, in the service of Cangrande della Scala of Verona and Matteo Visconti of Milan—he was sent by them to France in 1319, in order to negotiate on behalf of the ghibelline league (cf. Previté-Orton, 'Marsilius of Padua and the Visconti', *E.H.R.*, xliv (1929), 278–9; Gewirth, i, 20–1)—and that he had been upbraided by Mussato for serving the former (in a metric epistle addressed to Marsilius, best edition Haller, op. cit., 195–7), need not be relevant for the views he held, in 1324, on constitutional problems in general, and on those of his city in particular. On Marsilius' attitude to absolutism, below, 71 sqq.

[5] On the chronological problems of Marsilius' biography before 1324, see Haller, 166–82, Lagarde, ii.17–30, and Gewirth, 1.20–1.

flourished in that city, as well as with its most prominent philosopher.[1] It was significant of the role Padua played in Marsilius' intellectual development that through him John of Jandun became the first of the Parisian teachers of philosophy to acquire Peter of Abano's commentary on Aristotle's *Problemata*.[2] Marsilius' self-chosen title, *Antenorides*, clearly has more than one meaning.

A systematic survey of Italian political thought at the time of Marsilius has never been attempted, and its absence explains the scant references to Italian political ideas in works on Marsilius. Such references as there are are mainly confined to Dante's *Monarchy*, which deals with the universal empire, and Thomist works such as Giles of Rome's *De regimine principum*, which are concerned with the problems of European monarchies.[3] In contrast to this, I shall attempt to discuss some of the principal themes in Italian political thought of Marsilius' age by confining myself to views that have direct bearing on the political or social conditions of northern Italy. In doing so, literary and historical sources, as well as political tracts, will be considered as valid evidence. Thus, Dante's *Monarchy* will appear significant in so far as it refers to specifically Italian problems; Guido Vernani's refutation of it,[4] on the other hand, will not be considered relevant to our purpose, for its scholastic arguments could have been formulated in France or Germany, as well as in Italy.

The specifically Italian contribution to contemporary political thought can perhaps best be shown in the use made of Aristotle's theory of constitutions. While St Thomas and nearly all his followers tried to make it fit into the medieval pattern by giving Aristotle's views on the ideal constitution a decidedly monarchical slant, Italian thinkers were able to provide an alternative

---

[1] On Paduan pre-humanism, see R. Weiss, *The Dawn of Humanism in Italy* (London, 1947), 6–12; on Peter of Abano, B. Nardi, *Saggi sull'Aristotelismo padovano dal secolo xiv al xvi* (Florence, s.d. [1958]), 1–74; on Marsilius' relations with Peter of Abano, Lagarde, op. cit., 20–1, 27–9.

[2] See Renan, *Averroes et l'averroïsme*, 3rd ed. (Paris, 1882), qu. by Gewirth i. 40, n. 37.

[3] His *De regimine* was written about 1277–9 for the instruction of the future king Philip IV of France; cf. W. Berges, *Die Fürstenspiegel des hohen und späten Mittelalters* (Stuttgart, 1938), 320.

[4] *De reprobatione Monarchiae composita a Dante*, ed. T. Kaeppeli, 'Der Dantegegner Guido Vernani O. P. von Rimini', *Quellen und Forschungen aus italienischen Archiven und Bibliotheken*, xxviii (1937–8), 107–46, and N. Matteini, *Il più antico oppositore politico di Dante: Guido Vernani da Rimini* (Padua, 1958).

interpretation. About sixty years before the *Defensor pacis*, and almost contemporaneously with St Thomas' *De regimine principum*, Brunetto Latini insisted, in his *Trésors*, on the superiority of the republican régime of the polity over the monarchy.[1] When he was writing the *Trésors*, between 1260 and 1266, he did not yet know the *Politics*,[2] and derived Aristotle's classification of true constitutions from the *Nicomachean Ethics*. The Latin version of the *Ethics*, which Brunetto used, reads: 'there are three forms of constitution, kingship, aristocracy and that of communities (*communitatum*). And of these, kingship is the best'.[3] Brunetto was clearly unaware of the modifications and distinctions which Aristotle added to this basic scheme in the *Politics*, by virtue of which the polity gained the highest place among the practicable constitutions. None the less, Brunetto rephrased the passage from the *Ethics* in such a way as to reverse its order of preference: 'one is kingship, the second aristocracy, the third that of the communes, which is by far the best'. In translating *comunitatum* by *communes*, and in altering the wording of the *Ethics*, Brunetto proclaims the communal régime as the best of the true constitutions.[4]

About forty years later, Ptolemy of Lucca expounded, in his continuation of St Thomas' *De regimine principum*,[5] a similar interpretation of the Aristotelian scheme of constitutions. But he did so in a much fuller and far more sophisticated manner.

[1] *Li Livres dou Tresor*, ii.44, ed. F. J. Carmody (Berkeley and Los Angeles, 1948), 211.

[2] The *Politics* was translated by William of Moerbeke around 1260; see M. Grabmann, *Guglielmo di Moerbeke O.P. il traduttore delle opere di Aristotele* (Rome, 1946), 111–13. For the date of the *De reg. princ.* (1265–6) see Grabmann, *Die Werke des Hl. Thomas von Aquin* (Munster, 1949), 333.

[3] 'Principatus civiles tres sunt, principatus regum et principatus bonorum et principatus communitatum. Et omnium optimus est regum principatus' (*Compendium Alexandrinum*, ed. C. Marchesi, *L'Etica Nicomachea nella tradizione latina Medievale* (Messina 1904), lxxiii; cf. *Nic. Ethics*, VIII. i–ii). Brunetto used the *Ethics* in the abridged version of the *Compendium Alexandrinum*, or *Summa Alexandrinorum*, which had been translated from the Arabic, in *c.* 1243, by Hermannus Alemannus; see Grabmann, *Mittelalterliches Geistesleben* (Munich, 1926–56), iii.135, and Carmody, introduction, xxviii.

[4] 'L'une est des rois, la seconde est des bons, la tierce est des communes, laquele est la trés millour entre ces autres' (loc. cit.). By way of contrast, we might compare this with Giles of Rome's classification: 'bonum est igitur regimen populi sive multitudinis, si sit rectum; melius est tamen regimen paucorum . . .; optima est autem monarchia . . .' (*De reg. princ.*, III.ii.3, fol. 270v).

[5] On Ptolemy of Lucca (Bartolomeo Fiadoni), see Grabmann, op. cit., iv. 354–60. For the date of the composition of the *Trésors*, see Carmody, xvii–xviii, and Th. Sundby, *Della vita e delle opere di Brunetto Latini*, tr. R. Renier (Florence, 1884), 10; for that of the continuation of the *De regimine principum* (probably between 1300 and 1305), Grabmann, *Die Werke des Hl. Thomas*, 335–6.

The newly translated *Politics* had provided ample evidence to show that Aristotle was by no means as favourable to monarchy as might have been assumed from the *Ethics*; but St Thomas continued to refer to its classification of constitutions in support of his arguments in favour of monarchy.[1] Ptolemy of Lucca, in concentrating on the polity, came much closer to Aristotle than his teacher had done. But then St Thomas, who belonged to the family of the counts of Aquino in the kingdom of Sicily, and had spent much of his life in Paris, viewed politics from the angle of the European monarchies; Bartolomeo (Tolomeo) Fiadoni of Lucca, a native of one of the great Tuscan city-republics, wrote from the viewpoint of the Italian communes.

This becomes immediately clear when we read, in book four of the *De regimine*, that 'those who are of virile spirit and brave heart, and confident in their intelligence, cannot be governed by any other régime than the *principatus politicus*, including in this, aristocracy. But this régime exists particularly (*maxime*) in Italy'.[2] Conversely, monarchy is counted as a despotic régime, suited for countries which are of 'servile nature'.[3] There could be no more drastic departure from St Thomas' praise of monarchy in the first book of that treatise.

Ptolemy of Lucca, who in his *Hexaemeron* distinguished, in household government, between the *principatus despoticus* over slaves, and the paternal rule of the *principatus regalis*,[4] may have derived his classification of constitutions from William of Moerbeke's translation of *Politics*, III.xvii.1. While the passage reads, in English translation: 'There is one sort of society which is meant by its nature for rule of the despotic type,

---

[1] *Summa theologica*, ia iiae, qu. 105, art. 1.

[2] iv.8, p. 76: 'Qui autem virilis animi et in audacia cordis, et in confidentia suae intelligentiae sunt, tales regi non possunt nisi principatu politico, communi nomine extendendo ipsum ad aristocraticum. Tale autem dominium maxime in Italia viget'. Cf. Aristotle, *Politics*, VII.vii.2–3. Ptolemy applies Aristotle's judgment on the Greeks, as possessing, in contrast to the northern European peoples, 'both spirit and intelligence', to the inhabitants of northern Italy.

[3] 'Quaedam autem provinciae sunt servilis naturae: et tales gubernari debent principatu despotico, includendo in despotico etiam regale' (loc. cit.). See also below, p. 60. Gewirth does not render Ptolemy's attitude correctly by presenting him as considering monarchy to be in many ways preferable to the *regimen politicum* (op. cit., i.240). What Ptolemy says is that, while the *regimen politicum* is preferable to the *regimen regale*, 'in natura corrupta regimen regale est fructuosius', and that some regions are suited for servitude, others for freedom (ii.9, p. 29). It must be stressed that he does not conceive corruption in terms of original sin only. The ancient Romans, he says, were virtuous, and hence for them 'regimen politicum melius fuit'. By seeing corruption as part of an historical process, Ptolemy comes close to Machiavelli.

[4] Ed. P.-Th. Masetti (Siena, 1880), 112.

another for rule by a king, and another still for rule of a constitutional type',[1] William of Moerbeke's translation leaves out the second, monarchical, type.[2] Accordingly, there are only two main categories of natural governments; and Ptolemy could consequently classify aristocratic with 'constitutional', and royal with despotic, government. *Politicus*, in this passage, is William of Moerbeke's translation of πολιτικός in the sense of 'constitutional'; *principatus* stands for 'rule', not for 'principality'. Aristotle says of political rule that it is, in contrast to the *principatus despoticus*, 'rule of the sort which is exercised over persons who are similar in birth to the ruler, and are similarly free'.[3] Ptolemy accordingly defines *principatus politicus* as a régime by which a region or a town is ruled by one or several men according to its statutes.[4] Later on, however, he identifies it with the *dominium* (or *principatus*) *plurium*.[5] If such rule is exercised by the few, it is called aristocracy, if by the many, *politia*, from *polis* or *civitas*. 'For this régime', he adds, 'is suitable for cities, as we can see particularly in Italy',[6] and it once flourished in Athens. Its opposite is royal or despotic rule.[7] Government in it is elective, and, unlike that of monarchies,[8] limited by the laws, and subjected to controls. Thus Ptolemy draws in his *principatus politicus* an ideal picture of republican government, which is based on the institutions of the Italian communes: *maxime in Italia viget*. If his familiarity with those institutions and his republican sentiments made him accept Aristotle's constitutional doctrine far more radically than St Thomas had done, Aristotle's authority also served to confirm

[1] E. Barker, *The Politics of Aristotle* (Oxford, 1946), 149 50. The Greek text reads: ἔστι γάρ τι φύσει δεσποτικὸν καὶ ἄλλο βασιλευτὸν καὶ ἄλλο πολιτικόν.

[2] 'Est enim aliquid natura despoticum et aliud politicum', *Aristotelis Politicorum libri octo cum vetusta translatione Guilelmi de Moerbeka*, ed. F. Susemihl (Leipzig, 1872), 233. On the various translations of πολιτικόα and of πολιτεία in contemporary works, see L. Minio-Paluello, 'Tre note alla "Monarchia"', in *Medioevo e Rinascimento. Studi in onore di Bruno Nardi* (Florence, 1955), ii. 511–22.

[3] *Politics*, III.iv.13; Barker, 104–5.

[4] *De reg. princ.*, ii.8, p. 27: 'Politicus quidem, quando regio, sive provincia, sive civitas, sive castrum, per unum vel plures regitur secundum ipsorum statuta.' Ptolemy refers, in this passage, to Aristotle's distinction between *principatus politicus* and *despoticus* in *Pol.* III.iv.13; but Aristotle does not define the former as rule according to the laws.

[5] Ibid., iv.i, p. 66. *Dominium* and *principatus* are used as interchangeable terms: 'Dominium . . . sive principatus' (ibid.).

[6] Ibid., 'hoc regimen proprie ad civitates pertinet, ut in partibus Italiae maxime videmus'.

[7] '. . . quocumque modo dividitur contra regnum, sive monarchiam' (ibid.); 'includendo in despotico [principatu] etiam regale, (iv.8, p. 76).

[8] iv.i, p. 66; see below, p. 65.

his patriotic conviction of the political superiority of the Italians, as demonstrated in the city-republics of northern Italy.[1]

Ptolemy of Lucca's reappraisal of the *Politics* constitutes the most vigorous formulation Italian communal theory had yet received by the beginning of the fourteenth century. About the same time, another Tuscan Dominican, Remigio Girolami, gave the Aristotelian concept of the common good fresh significance.[2] While the Thomists generally affirmed, even more than St Thomas himself had done, that the good of the community can be served best by a monarch, who alone can reduce it to unity,[3] for the Florentine Remigio the term *commune* had civic overtones. Accordingly, *bonum commune* could appear identical with the *bonum communis*, the common good with the good of the commune,[4] magistrates and citizens being responsible for its preservation. 'Since you have been appointed to your office by the commune', he warns the Priors of Florence, 'you must work for the common good'.[5] While his approach to the common good is thus more concrete and less conceptualist than that of other Thomists, he carries the Thomist doctrine of the subordination of private to common interest to an extreme.[6] 'The commune must be loved more than oneself', he states in his *De bono communi*, 'because of its similarity with God'.[7] Remigio's

[1] On the contrast between the republican and the despotic régime, see also below, pp. 60–1.

[2] On Remigio Girolami, see Grabmann, op. cit., i. 361–9, and Ch. T. Davis, 'An early Florentine political theorist: Fra Remigio de' Girolami', *Proceedings of the American Philosophical Society*, civ (1960), 662–76. Extracts from his treatise *De bono communi* have been edited by R. Egenter, 'Gemeinnutz vor Eigennutz . . .', *Scholastik* ix (1934), 79–92, and by L. Minio-Paluello, 'Remigio Girolami's *De bono communi*', *Italian Studies*, xi (1956), 56–71; his *De bono pacis* by Ch. T. Davis, 'Remigio de' Girolami and Dante . . .', *Studi Danteschi*, xxxvi (1959), 105–36; and extracts from his sermons by G. Salvadori and U. Federici, 'I sermoni d'occasione, le sequenze e i ritmi di Remigio Girolami fiorentino', in *Scritti vari di filologia a Ernesto Monaci* (Rome, 1901), 455–508. See also Lagarde, op. cit., iii (1942), 148–52, and E. H. Kantorowicz, *The King's Two Bodies. A Study in Mediaeval Political Theology* (Princeton, N.J., 1957), 478–80.

[3] St Thomas, *De reg. princ.*, i.2, 3–4; Giles of Rome, *De reg. princ.*, III.ii.4, fol. 271r; John of Paris, *De potestate regia et papali*, i, ed. J. Leclercq, *Jean de Paris et l'ecclésiologie du xiiie siècle* (Paris, 1942), pp. 176–8. Cf. Lagarde, iii. 155–6.

[4] See N. Rubinstein, 'Political ideas in Sienese art: the frescoes by Ambrogio Lorenzetti and Taddeo di Bartolo in the Palazzo Pubblico', *Journal of the Warburg and Courtauld Institutes*, xxi (1958), 185.

[5] 'Sicut estis facti et positi in officio per comune, ita laboretis pro comuni bono' (Salvadori and Federici, op. cit., 482).

[6] Lagarde, iii, 150; Kantorowicz, loc. cit.; Davis, 'An early Florentine political theorist', 670–1.

[7] Egenter, op. cit., 84, n. 11: the commune 'directe amatur, praeamatur autem post Deum propter similitudinem, quam habet ad Deum'.

view reminds us of the corporationalist theories of the Italian lawyers, which later in the century found expression in Bartolo of Sassoferrato's notion of the *universitas* as different from the sum total of its component parts.[1] Remigio has concrete situations in mind when he exclaims that, if Florence were destroyed, those who had been Florentine citizens would no longer be entitled to that name; for 'man being by nature a political animal, he who is not a citizen is not a man'.[2] The destruction of Florence is seen in terms of civic strife, in which individual interest is placed above the common good.[3] Remigio, in amplifying a passage from Aristotle's *Ethics*, and St Thomas' comment on it, states that 'the common good means peace, which is the highest end of society, just as health is the greatest good of the body'.[4] Such sentiments were widely shared in contemporary Italy; but nowhere was the connection between peace and the common good stated more emphatically and persuasively than in the frescoes which Ambrogio Lorenzetti painted between 1337 and 1340 in the council chamber of the government of Siena.[5] The majestic figure of the çivic ruler personifies the common good; he holds the cord symbolizing concord, which runs from the figure of Justice to that of Concord, and thence through the hands of a group of citizens: by obeying justice and the common good, the Sienese citizens will achieve peace and unity.

If allegiance to the common good was productive of internal peace in cities, it could be argued that it had identical effects in larger political units, and that the larger their size, the greater was its value. This was implied in St Thomas' comment on the statement in Aristotle's *Ethics* that 'the good of the state is

---

[1] Cf. Kantorowicz, 309–10, 476–7.

[2] *De bono communi*, qu. by Egenter, 83, n. 10, and Minio-Paluello, 60: 'Destructa civitate remanet civis lapideus aut depictus . . . Qui erat civis florentinus per destructionem Florentie iam non est florentinus dicendus sed potius "flerentinus". Et si non est civis non est homo, quia homo est naturaliter animal civile secundum Philosophum . . .'.

[3] Ibid., qu. by Minio-Paluello, 59–60.

[4] Summum bonum multitudinis est pax' (*De bono pacis*, op. cit., 124): '. . . summum bonum multitudinis et finis eius est pax . . . sicut sanitas est summum bonum totius corporis'. Cf. 118. Remigio refers to Aristotle *in tertio Ethicorum*; but Aristotle only says (III.v.11) that both physicians and statesmen take the end of their professions for granted, which is, in the case of the latter, peace. St Thomas comments on this passage as follows: 'Nec etiam politicus, idest rector civitatis, consiliatur an debeat facere pacem quae se habet ad civitatem sicut sanitas ad corpus hominis' (*In decem libros Ethicorum Aristotelis ad Nicomachum Expositio*, III.viii.474, ed. R. M. Spiazzi (Turin, 1949), 133).

[5] Rubinstein, op. cit., 179–89.

manifestly a greater and more perfect good than that of the individual'.[1] The Latin translation renders πόλις with *civitas*; but St Thomas observes that the common good of an entire nation is *multo divinius* than that of a single city. Remigio enlarges on this comment: 'the more general the common good, the more desirable it is'; hence the good of the city is more desirable than that of one citizen, the good of a province more than that of one city, and the good of a kingdom more than that of one province.[2] In the same vein, the Bolognese notary Graziolo Bambaglioli says, around 1335, that 'the more general a good, the greater its value; and unity and peace are its results'.[3] St Thomas focuses his attention on the *regnum* as a superior form of political organization, and claims that a monarch will be best suited to serve the common good;[4] Dante's monarchy, while conceived on a universal plane, also contains the specific Italian message that only an effective imperial authority could provide the peace Italians were longing for.[5] Remigio Girolami and Graziolo Bambaglioli, while recognizing the wider implications of this concept, keep their eyes firmly fixed on the cities. For if St Thomas' statement that 'bonum commune est divinius quam bonum unius'[6] had become an article of faith with the Thomists in general,[7] it had its special bearings on the Italian communes. The common good, raised to a position of supremacy in the state, would have the same unifying effects as monarchy. As Lorenzetti's frescoes in the Palazzo Pubblico in Siena show, by the thirties of the century the Aristotelian doctrine of the common good could become official political theory of a great Italian city-republic.

---

[1] I.ii.8. In William of Moerbeke's translation, ed. Spiazzi, op. cit., 6; see St Thomas' comment, I.ii.30, ibid., 8.

[2] *De bono communi*, qu. by Minio-Paluello, op. cit., 62: 'quanto bonum est communius, tanto est magis amandum', etc.

[3] *Trattato delle volgari sentenze sopra le virtù morali* (composed about 1335), in *Rimatori bolognesi del Trecento*, ed. L. Frati (Bologna, 1915), 19: 'Quanto è perfecto il ben, tanto più vale,/Quant'egl'è più comune e generale;/Perchè ciascun contenta e satisface,/E nascene unione e dolce pace'.

[4] *De reg. princ.*, i.2,3; pp. 3, 4.

[5] See below, p. 68.

[6] *In libros Politicorum Aristotelis Expositio*, i.1, ed. R. M. Spiazzi (Turin, 1951), 6. Cf. *Nic. Eth.*, I.ii.8; see above, n. 1.

[7] See Lagarde, iii, 151, n. 11, who erroneously attributes it to the *Ethics*, evidently following St Thomas' reference to that work. The passage St Thomas must have had in mind (*Nic. Eth.* I.ii.8) reads in the Latin translation: 'Amabile quidem enim [bonum] et uni soli: melius vero et divinius genti et civitatibus'.

While the concept of the common good could thus serve as the basis of a communal political theory, and hence as a reply to the challenge of the *Signoria*, it could also help to explain some of the endemic problems of the city-states, and of Italy at large. 'The prophecy of St Paul,' says Remigio Girolami in his *De bono communi*, ' "that perilous times shall come and men shall be lovers of their own selves, covetous, boasters, proud," etc., can clearly be seen fulfilled in these times in modern men, and alas! particularly among our Italian compatriots. These have, in their excessive unlimited love of self, neglected the common good, for which they care little or nothing; and being incited by a diabolical spirit, they continuously disturb and destroy villages, cities, provinces, and the entire country by their uncontrolled strife.'[1] Remigio gives St Paul's eschatological prophecy a contemporary political slant by omitting the reference to the last days. His diatribe is directed against the factionalism of Florence, which had its parallel in many other Italian cities. His complaints about the neglect of the common good, and the resulting loss of peace and unity, are echoed by other Italian writers. 'There is no place left for the common good,' laments Graziolo Bambaglioli, 'for everyone cares only for his own affairs'.[2] Filippo Ceffi's manual of rhetoric advises the *Podestà* to address a hostile faction in these words: 'They do not mind destroying their beautiful city by placing their own interest before the good of the commune, so that they may increase their power'.[3] That lack of civic unity could lead to the decline and destruction of cities, was by then a traditional theme in northern Italy: 'A town torn by faction,' says Brunetto Latini in his *Tesoretto*, 'cannot escape

---

[1] *De bono communi*, qu. by Minio-Paluello, op. cit., 59: 'Prophetia beati apostoli Pauli qua dixit (*Tim.* 3) "instabunt tempora periculosa et erunt homines se ipsos amantes, cupidi, elati, superbi etc." hiis temporibus aperte videtur impleta in modernis hominibus et, heu! maxime in Ytalicis nostris; qui quidem propter nimium amorem atque inordinatum sui ipsorum bona communia negligentes, parum vel nichil de ipsis curando, spiritu diabolico agitati, castra civitates provincias totamque regionem hostilitatibus inordinatis confundunt et destruunt incessanter.' I read *bona communia* for *bona contraria* (MS. Florence, Bibl. Nazionale, Conventi soppressi, C.4.940, fol. 97r).

[2] Op. cit., 47: 'A far lo ben comun non c'è più loco,/Perchè ciascun al suo mulin attende'. See also S. Morpurgo, 'Bruto, "il buon giudice" . . .', in *Miscellanea di storia dell' arte in onore di I. B. Supino* (Florence, 1933), 155–62, and Rubinstein, op. cit., 184–9.

[3] Ed. G. Giannardi, 'Le "Dicerie" di Filippo Ceffi', *Studi di filogia italiana*, vi (1942), 57: 'non curano distruggere la bella cittade per poter innalzare loro, mettendo la loro propria utilitade avante al generale bene del comune'.

destruction.'[1] Around 1270, Bellino Bissolo said of Milan that 'in se divisa ... desolata iacet';[2] and, in 1288, another Milanese grammarian, Bonvesin della Riva, indicted the Milanese whose greed for power would cause the destruction of their city through civil strife.[3]

In these circumstances, it must have been tempting to contrast the present with what appeared, in retrospect, a golden age of civic peace and unity. Dante was not alone in praising the good old days when 'Florence within her ancient limit-mark ... Was chaste and sober, and abode in peace'.[4] 'At that time', writes the author of a Ferrarese chronicle, of the years before 1240, 'the Ferrarese republic was prospering, and its citizens were enjoying wealth and peace ...'[5] Similarly, the picture which Mussato draws of thirteenth-century Padua is that of a peaceful city, which subjects its neighbours through love.[6] The decline sets in with the growing desire for wealth, which eventually results in the suppression of justice and in the breakdown of the political structure.[7] What is evil is not wealth itself, but the inordinate desire for it (*avaritia*); like that for power (*superbia*) it is one of the roots of the contemporary predicament. Avarice has destroyed the world, says Graziolo Bambaglioli, and ambition to rule causes strife.[8] In either case, the result is a

---

[1] *Tesoretto*, in *Poemetti allegorico-didattici del secolo xiii*, ed. L. di Benedetto (Bari, 1941), 8. Cf. Franceso da Barberino, *Documenti d'amore*, ed. F. Egidi (Rome 1905–27), ii. 227: 'non solamente citta ma province/per division lolor nemico vince'. Cf. Guittone d'Arezzo's letter to the Florentines after their defeat at Montaperti in 1260: 'E cierto non ebbero cominciamento li Romani più di voi bello, nè in tanto di tenpo più non feciero, nè tanto quanto avavate fatto et eravate inviati a ffare, stando a ccomune. O mizeri, mirate ove siete ora, e ben considerate ove sareste, fustevi retti a una comunitate. Li Romani suggiugono tutto il mondo: divizione tornati ali a neiente quazi ...' (*Le Lettere*, ed. F. Meriano [Bologna, 1922], 179).

[2] Qu. from his *Speculum vite* by R. Weiss, 'Bellino Bissolo, poeta milanese del duecento', *Archivio Storico Lombardo*, n.s., x (1950), 46. On its date—between 1260 and 1277—ibid., 34.

[3] *De magnalibus urbis Mediolani*, ed. F. Novati, in *Bullettino dell'Istituto Storico Italiano*, xx (1898), 175. For the date (1288) ibid., p. 40.

[4] *Paradiso*, xv, 97, 99: 'Fiorenza dentro dalla cerchia antica/. . . Si stava in pace, sobria, e pudica'. I quote from H. F. Cary's translation.

[5] *Chronica parva Ferrariensis*, in Muratori, *Rerum Italicarum Scriptores*, viii (Milan, 1726), 483: 'Huius pacis tempore floruit respublica Ferrariensis, et cives bonorum copia fruebantur et pace. Nemo nisi facinorosus et scelestus exulabat a patria ...' Probably by Riccobaldo da Ferrara; see A. F. Massèra in *Archivio Muratoriano*, ii. 239–44.

[6] Virtutibus praeditos cives gignit: illibata pace fruitur, finitimis civitatibus praeest, quas amore et beneficiis ad se allicit', *De gestis Italicorum post Henricum VII*, ibid., x (Milan, 1727), 715–16.   [7] Ibid.

[8] 'O avaritia nimica di dio   Che per cupidità d'esser signore,
Tu ai sì strutto il mondo e fatto rio,   O d'acquistar honor, cittade o terra,
....   L'un strugge l'altro, onde nasce la guerra.'

disturbance of the right political and social order, of 'the good disposition of the city'.[1]

The frequent political crises and constitutional changes in the city-states, as well as their social and economic developments, had made Italians keenly aware of the instability of institutions and society. That cities were subject to corruption and decline would be confirmed to them by Roman authors, and above all by Sallust, whose historical works were widely read.[2] Mussato tells us that the problem of political decline was a favourite subject of discussion in his circle at Padua.[3] No one has expounded this theme more persuasively than Mussato himself.[4] In his *History of the Deeds of the Italians after Henry VII*, he imitates Sallust's *Bellum Catilinarium* in describing his city's decline from the conditions of power and prosperity that had, in the past, been created by the virtues of its citizens.[5] But this decline was for him not only, as for Sallust, a matter of moral corruption; he sees it also reflected in the constitutional development of Padua. Accordingly, Mussato tries to explain recent events in that city by resorting to Aristotle's discussion of constitutional changes.[6] Padua had passed from a mixed constitution to democracy and thence to oligarchy; will it end up with tyranny? In his *History*, Mussato narrates Padua's gradual transition from republic to *Signoria*—'quo pacto urbs haec de communitate ad singulare dominium transacta devenerit'[7]—ending with Marsilio da Carrara's election as the city's lord in 1328, and his subjection of the city to Cangrande.

(op. cit., 42). Cf. Stefano da Vicomercate, (d. *c.* 1297), *De gestis in civitate Mediolani*, Muratori, *Rer. Ital. Script.*, new ed., ix. 1, ed. G. Calligaris (Città di Castello, 1912), 10–11 (on the beginnings of internal strife in Milan between 1259 and 1277): 'Diripit ambitio immeritos temeraria fasces./Gurges avaritie nullo saciabilis haustu/Fundamenta quatit, titubant hinc menia, casum/Inclinata gravem quasi iam ruitura minantur . . .'). On avarice as a cause of decline, cf. also Seneca, *Epistolae morales*, xix.38.

[1] *Defensor pacis*, I.xix.2, 125.
[2] See N. Rubinstein, 'Some ideas on municipal progress and decline in the Italy of the Communes', in *Fritz Saxl. A Volume of Memorial Essays . . .*, ed. D. J. Gordon (Edinburgh, 1957), 165–83, esp. 169 sqq.
[3] Ibid., 171.
[4] Muratori, *Scriptores*, x, 716; cf. Sallust, *Bell. Cat.*, x.
[5] Rubinstein, op. cit., 169–70, 173–4.
[6] *Politics*, III.xv.11–12, V.xii.7–18.
[7] *Historia de gestis Italicorum post Henricum VII*, extracts in [L. Padrin], *Il principato di Giacomo da Carrara* (Padua, 1891), 79ff, 90, and 'De traditione Paduae ad Canem grandem', in Muratori, *Scriptores*, x, 715 sqq. Mussato's compatriot Giovanni da Nono prophesied the coming of a second Ezzelino as a punishment of Paduan usury and civil strife (G. Fabris, 'La cronaca di Giovanni da Nono', *Bollettino del Museo Civico di Padova*, n.s. x–xi (1934–9), 3–4, who dates the *Cronaca* between 1329 and 1337: ibid., n.s. viii (1932), 22).

In medieval political thought, tyranny was considered the perversion of monarchy. A king who oppressed his subjects and violated justice, was turned into a tyrant; according to Isidore of Seville's immensely popular formula, 'recte igitur faciendo regis nomen tenetur, peccando amittitur'.[1] But already St Thomas observed, probably having Italian developments in mind, that not only monarchy, but also democracy could be replaced by the rule of a tyrant. Indeed, he adds, this happens perhaps more often in a democracy than in a monarchy: 'for nearly every *regimen multorum* has ended in tyranny, as can be clearly seen in the Roman republic'.[2] St Thomas makes this observation by way of digression; since monarchy is for him the normal form of government, he remains faithful to the medieval antithesis *rex-tyrannus*. Ptolemy of Lucca breaks with this tradition, by contrasting the *regimen despoticum*, not with the *regimen regale*, but with the *regimen politicum*.[3]

Ptolemy derived the term *despoticus* from the Latin translation of the *Politics*. William of Moerbeke translates δεσποτικός with *despoticus*, and Ptolemy was fully aware that Aristotle made a distinction between despots and tyrants. *Principatus despoticus*, he says correctly,[4] stands for rule over serfs. According to Aristotle, it was one of the three forms of household government; and while by nature autocratic, it was not necessarily tyrannical.[5] But it was precisely autocratic rule which was the principal characteristic of the Italian *Signoria*. Republicans were used, by Ptolemy's time, to call the new lords *tiranni*, and it could be argued, on theoretical grounds, that autocratic rulers were, by violating the statutes and suppressing civic liberties, *eo ipso* tyrants. For Ptolemy, this implication was evident, as appears from his statement that, with the exception of Venice, it was impossible in northern Italy to have rule for life, unless it was done by using tyrannical methods, *per viam tyrannicam*.[6] But at

---

[1] *Etymologiarum sive originum libri xx*, IX.iii.4, ed. W. M. Lindsay (Oxford, 1911). On the origin of this formula, cf. J. Balogh, ' "Rex a recte regendo" ', *Speculum*, iii (1928), 580–2. Cf. e.g. John of Salisbury, *Policraticus*, iv.1, viii. 17, ed. C. Webb (Oxford, 1909), i.235, ii.346.

[2] *De reg. princ.*, i.5, p. 6: 'Nam fere omne multorum regimen est in tyrannidem terminatum, ut in romana republica manifeste apparet'. The text has *omnium*, which must clearly be emended to *omne*.

[3] Ibid., ii.8, 27. See above, p. 53.

[4] Ibid., ii.9, 28: '... principatus despoticus dicitur, qui est domini ad servum'.

[5] *Politics*, I.iii.1 sqq.; xii.1.

[6] *De reg. princ.*, iv.8, p. 76: 'In partibus . . . quae hodie Lombardia vocatur, nullus principatum habere potest perpetuum, nisi per viam tyrannicam, duce Venetiarum excepto . . .'.

the same time, he saw clearly that, in terms of constitutional theory, the distinctive feature of the *Signoria* was not tyranny, but autocracy.

In substituting the antithesis *regimen politicum-regimen despoticum* for the antithesis *rex-tyrannus*, Ptolemy thus attunes the traditional medieval formula to contemporary political thinking in Italy. Ever since the beginnings of the *Signoria* in the thirteenth century, Italian citizens had reacted strongly against the new régime. 'It should be a lesson to all to shun the rule of such men . . ., to avoid the servile yoke, and with all one's means to defend liberty until death,' writes Rolandino of Padua in about 1260 of Ezzelino of Romano, the earliest of the Italian despots, who died in 1259 after having ruled oppressively over Verona, Padua, and other northern Italian towns;[1] 'now we see clearly what horrible and nefarious deeds tyrants do in the cities over which they rule . . .' Such republican opposition remained strong and became more articulate in the fourteenth century, while at the same time *Signori* did not lack their defenders and eulogists.[2] Hand in hand with acceptance or rejection of the new régime went attempts to explain its origins. One of its primary causes had been the factionalism of the communes, which had often made it possible for prominent men to rise to power as leaders of parties or social groups. Italian observers were not slow to press home this point. Already St Thomas had stated that 'once the *regimen plurium* begins to be torn by strife, it often happens that one man prevails over the rest, and usurps the people's authority'.[3] Giovanni da Cermenate says, around 1315, in his *Historia*, that where the citizens prefer their private interest to that of the community, they provoke the people to set up a despot.[4] Once more, Filippo Ceffi's

---

[1] *Cronica in factis et circa facta Marchiae Trivixanae*, ed. A. Bonardi, in Muratori, *Rer. Ital. Script.*, new ed., viii.1 (Città di Castello, 1905–), 109. On Rolandino's chronicle, see B. Schmeidler, *Italienische Geschichtsschreiber des xii. und xiii. Jahrhunderts* (Leipzig, 1909), 45 sqq. On Ezzelino, see now *Studi Ezzeliniani* (Rome, 1963).

[2] I intend to discuss this subject in a separate article.

[3] *De reg. princ.*, i.5, 6: 'Exorta namque dissensione per regimen plurium, contingit saepe unum super alios superare et sibi soli multitudinis dominium usurpare . . .'

[4] Ed. A. Ferrai (Rome, 1889), 64: '. . . ubi sic vivitur, quod vitio civium commune bonum propriae utilitati postponitur, potentiores . . . tyrannicum imperium in urbe provocent'. This passage was written before 1317: cf. p. xxvi. One of the inscriptions of the fresco of the Bad Government in the Palazzo Pubblico in Siena reads: 'In this town, selfishness has subjected Justice to Tyranny' ('Per volere el ben proprio in questa terra/Sommess' è la Giustizia a Tyrannia'). See Rubinstein, 'Political ideas in Sienese art', 188.

collection of model speeches may serve to illustrate what by the early fourteenth century had become a current theme of Italian political thought. His *Dicerie* contain a speech to be held on the occasion of the election of a *Signore*. 'We are now facing,' it reads,[1] 'the worst calamity that may befall a free city; for ruthless war [another MS. adds: 'and cursed discord'[2]] has reduced us to grant to someone else the liberty and justice which we have possessed for so many years . . .' Later on in the century, the Florentine chronicler Marchionne Stefani put such sentiments into a nutshell:[3] 'it is better to achieve internal peace and not to have discord, than to have first discord, then a tyrant, and then peace'.

The controversy over the relative advantages and defects of the republican and monarchical régimes, which was to become so important in fifteenth-century humanism,[4] already accompanies the expansion and consolidation of the *Signoria* in the late thirteenth and early fourteenth century. While Brunetto ranks monarchy lowest,[5] he still accepts it as one of Aristotle's 'true' constitutions. Yet he wholly rejects, at least for Florence, autocratic government: 'I do not know anyone,' he says in his *Tesoretto*,[6] 'whom I would wish to see as absolute ruler of my city'. His condemnation of despotism was echoed, about half a century later, by Francesco da Barberino: 'Only fools live in towns ruled by tyrants'.[7] Francesco da Barberino had finished the text of his *Documenti d'amore* by 1313; in 1313 or 1314, Mussato composed his tragedy *Ecerinis*.[8] Modelled on Seneca's tragedies, it recounts the misdeeds of Ezzelino. In his person, Mussato attacks Cangrande della Scala, lord of Verona,

---

[1] Op. cit., 61: 'Tra tutti gli altri casi e avvenimenti che possono avvenire alle libere cittadi ora siamo noi al più forte, però che, per asprezza di guerra, siamo condotti a donare la nostra libertade e giustizia, la quale abbiamo posseduti per molti anni'. For the second part of this speech, see below, p. 66.

[2] MS. Vat. Pal. Lat. 1644, ed. L. Biondi, *Le dicerie di ser Filippo Ceffi* (Turin, 1825), 2: 'e per maladetta discordia'.

[3] *Cronaca fiorentina*, ed. N. Rodolico, Muratori, *Rer. Ital. Script.*, new ed., xxx, I (Città di Castello, 1903–55), p. 209: 'è meglio pacificarsi insieme e non avere discordia, che tiranno dopo discordia, e poi pace . . .'

[4] See F. v. Bezold, 'Republik und Monarchie in der italienischen Literatur des 15. Jahrhunderts', *Historische Zeitschrift*, new ser., xlv (1898), 433–68.

[5] Above, p. 51.

[6] 'Ond'io non so nessuno   la mia cittade avere
ch'io volesse vedere   del tutto ala sua guisa'
(op. cit., 8).

[7] 'Nela terra del tiranno/folli son quey che vi stanno' (op. cit.), ii.219. On the date of composition, ibid., IV.xli.

[8] Ed. L. Padrin (Bologna, 1900).

'always the seat of tyrants'.[1] In 1315, Mussato was crowned in Padua with the poet's laurel, and it was decreed that his play was to be publicly read every year in that city.[2] The sentiments it revealed were doubtless shared by many Italian citizens, and not solely in the surviving city-republics, as is shown by the republican risings against the *Signoria* in Modena and Reggio in 1306.[3] In the passage from the *De regimine principum* we have already quoted, Ptolemy of Lucca says that 'some regions are of servile nature, and these must be governed by despots [*principatu despotico*] . . . but those that are of virile spirit and of brave heart, and confident in their intelligence, can only be governed by a republican régime'.[4] In northern Italy, permanent authority, *principatus perpetuus*, could, according to Ptolemy, be achieved only by tyrannical means, with the exception of Venice. The Italian islands, on the other hand, Sicily, Sardinia, and Corsica, always had tyrants.[5]

Domini or *capitani perpetui* was a current title of the Italian *Signori* in the early fourteenth century.[6] In the constitutional development of the *Signoria*, the first step was the election of the new lord as *Podestà* or Captain of the People, with powers and terms of office in excess of those laid down by the statutes; the next step was election for life with full powers; the following one, the transfer of this authority to the *Signore*'s heirs, once more by way of election; the final one, the election of the lord as hereditary ruler. This final step was taken in 1359 when Cansignore and Paolo Alboino della Scala were elected *generales domini* 'for themselves and their heirs and forever'.[7] While elections of the despot's successor remained the rule throughout the fourteenth century, they were not more than a façade of *de facto* hereditary rule; and their constitutional

---

[1] Ibid., 34: 'O semper huius Marchiae clades vetus . . ./Sedes tyranni . . .'.
[2] Ibid., p. xii.
[3] Cf. the statutes and decrees issued in Modena after the expulsion of the Este, in *Respublica Mutinensis 1306-7*, ed. E. P. Vicini (Milan, 1929-32), which contain violent attacks against the *Signoria* of Azzo d'Este (e.g. i. 18 sqq., 71 sqq.; ii. 51).
[4] *De reg. princ.*, iv.8, p. 76. See also above, p. 52.
[5] '. . . semper habuerunt tyrannos' (ibid.).
[6] To give only one instance: in 1264, Obizzo d'Este was elected *perpetuus dominus* of Ferrara; cf. L. Simeoni, 'L'elezione d'Obizo d'Este a Signore di Ferrara', *Archivio Storico Italiano*, XCIII.i (1935), 165-88. See also Salzer, 104 sqq., and Ercole, 53 sqq.
[7] Salzer, 123-4; Ercole, 67: 'pro se et eorum heredibus et in perpetuum'.

significance was further devalued by the frequent grants of the imperial or papal vicariate to the *Signori*, which invested their autocratic powers with a higher sanction.[1]

Accordingly, the problem of how, and whether, government should be elected, assumed a new meaning in Italian political thought and practice. In the communal statutes, electoral methods, as well as regulations concerning eligibility to government offices, had always occupied an important place. Not surprisingly, the rise of the *Signoria* contributed to the tightening of electoral procedures. While in the despotic states, elections had become a façade of absolute rule, the Florentine republic tried to prevent the concentration of power in single families by complex electoral reforms: in 1328, election by lot, first introduced in 1323, became the normal electoral procedure after the end of the short-lived *Signoria* of Charles of Calabria.[2] Ptolemy of Lucca devotes two chapters to the question whether elective government was preferable to hereditary, and comes out strongly in favour of the former.[3] In this, he is in agreement with his master St Thomas. But St Thomas is concerned exclusively with monarchy;[4] Ptolemy, while also dealing with the problem of imperial elections,[5] focuses his attention, in the contemporary world, on city-republics. He praises the ancient Romans for distributing honours equally according to merit, and points out that the freedom-loving populations of northern Italy, while rejecting the *principatus perpetuus*, accept the *principatus ad tempus*, that is government appointed for limited terms of office. 'The governors (*rectores*) should therefore alternate in the city (*politia*), whether they be called consuls or magistrates';[6] such had been the custom in ancient Rome.[7] Ptolemy thus argues in favour of the traditional communal régime, which was characterized by short terms of office for the highest magistracies. He might have

---

[1] On the grants of vicariates to *Signori*, see Ercole, 283–95, and P. J. Jones, 'The Vicariate of the Malatesta of Rimini' (with bibliography), *E.H.R.*, lxvii (1952), 321–51.

[2] See R. Davidsohn, *Geschichte von Florenz*, iii (Berlin, 1912), 698, 862–5.

[3] *De reg. princ.*, iv.7,8, pp. 74–6.

[4] Cf. *Summa theologica*, ia iiae, qu. 105, art. 1.

[5] *De reg. princ.*, iii.19,20, pp. 60–1. He also mentions the German and French cities: cf. *De reg. princ.*, iv.1, p. 67.

[6] iv.8, p. 76: 'Assumendi . . . sunt rectores vicissim in politia, sive consules, sive magistratus vocentur . . .'.

[7] ii.8, p. 27: '. . . quod in ipsa [civilitate] sit continua de civibus sive extraneis alternatio: sicut de romanis scribitur in I Mach. viii, ubi dicitur quod per singulos annos committunt uni homini magistratum suum dominari universae terrae suae'.

stretched his point by including the election of *Signori* for short periods, as had been customary, in the thirteenth century, during the formative period of the *Signoria*.[1] But his acceptance of Aristotle's preference for the 'middle class', the *mediocres*, as well as of his distrust of the too powerful, the *nimis potentes*, who were liable to act tyrannically,[2] marks the point beyond which Ptolemy was not prepared to go.

Just as popular election is designed to limit the powers of the government, so is its subjection to law. Somewhat surprisingly, at first sight, Ptolemy expounds, without any reservations or criticism, the absolutist doctrine that 'the laws are [in the monarch's] breast', and that 'what pleases the prince·has the force of law';[3] he ignores St Thomas' qualifying comments,[4] as well as the discussions by the civilians.[5] The reason for this cavalier procedure is evident: Ptolemy intends to contrast monarchy with civic government; and civic government is, by its nature, 'subject to the laws'.[6] For by his definition, the *principatus politicus* was government of cities or regions according to their statutes; and this, he adds, 'happens in Italy', just as it had in ancient Rome with the senate and the consuls.[7] In his condemnation of absolute government, Ptolemy was in agreement with contemporary republican opinion in Italy, as expressed, a few years later, by Francesco da Barberino: 'arbitrary rule is a hallmark of tyranny, as one may learn from Livy'.[8] Graziolo Bambaglioli put it similarly:

---

[1] See above, p. 63.

[2] *De reg. princ.*, iv.8, p. 76: 'quia de facili tyrannizant'. Cf. *Pol.* IV.xi.4–11.

[3] iv.1, p. 66: '. . . legibus astringuntur rectores politici . . . quod de regibus et aliis monarchis non convenit, quia in ipsorum pectore sunt leges reconditae . . . et pro lege habetur quod principi placet'; see Kantorowicz, p. 28, n. 15, and below, p. 72.

[4] *Summa theologica*, loc. cit.; cf. ia IIae, qu. 96, art. 5.

[5] On the discussions among civilians on the problem of sovereignty and law, see now B. Tierney, ' "The prince is not bound by the laws." Accursius and the origins of the modern State', *Comparative Studies in Society and History*, v (1963), 378–400 (Accursius 'did not associate the words *legibus solutus* with any ideas of arbitrary government' (p. 390)). On the lawyers' difficulties in trying to reconcile the maxim *princeps legibus solutus* with the *lex digna*, according to which the prince was obliged to observe the laws, see Kantorowicz, op. cit., 104–7. On the prince as *lex animata*, ibid., 127 sqq.

[6] See above, n. 3.

[7] *De reg. princ.*, ii.8, p. 27: 'Politicus [principatus] quidem, quando regio, sive provincia, sive civitas, sive castrum, per unum vel plures regitur secundum ipsorum statuta, ut in regionibus contingit Italiae et praecipue Romae, ut per senatores et consules pro maiori parte ab urbe condita'.

[8] Op. cit., ii.218: 'de istis tyrannis potest intelligi lictera titulivii . . . crudelissima ac superbissima gens sua omnia suique arbitrii facit'.

'No one should govern according to his own will'.[1] While republicans condemned the unlimited and permanent authority of the *Signoria*, a more positive approach to the new régime was making headway. Despotism had evidently come to stay, and its eulogists were eager to point out its benefits. Foremost among these alleged benefits figured peace and civic unity. If disunity was seen to lead to factions and social conflicts, and eventually to the overthrow of the republic and the establishment of a despot, it could also be argued that the latter alone was capable of providing a solution for the endemic problems of communal politics.[2] While republicans branded the *Signori* as oppressive 'tyrants', their supporters praised them as just and benevolent rulers who gave the citizens a sorely needed peace. Filippo Ceffi conveniently summarizes their case in a model speech, to be held when citizens want to elect a new lord. 'It is right that we should elect a just *Signore*, who will be joined to us through love and faith . . . who may guide us to perfect justice, which brings victory abroad and concord at home'.[3] Ferreto de' Ferreti eulogizes, in his *Carmen de Scaligerorum origine*,[4] the despotic rule of the Della Scala of Verona. Composed in 1328-9 by an author who was closely connected with the Paduan literary circle,[5] the *Carmen* is one of the earliest examples of humanist panegyrics on despots. In his *Historia*, Ferreto was to give vent to rather different sentiments;[6] and even his panegyric is not unconditional. For in it, Ferreto draws the picture of a benevolent despot who rules, 'with equal laws', justly and mildly, and protects laws and lawcourts. Accordingly, Cangrande's father, who impersonates this picture, was elected *Signore* spontaneously by the 'free people', the *libera plebs*, of Verona.[7]

[1] Op. cit., 18: 'Non regga alcun rector a volontate'. One of Matteo de'Libri's model speeches denies the *Podestà* a demand for arbitrary powers by reminding him of his oath to observe the laws made by the citizens: 'L'uomini di questa terra . . . fanno loro leggie, alla quale quelle persone che sono in quello luogo là ove siete voi, giurano e sono tenute d'osservare . . .' (*Le Dicerie volgari di Ser Matteo de' Libri da Bologna*, ed. L. Chiappelli [Pistoia, 1900], 5). A shorter version of the same speech is in Ceffi, op. cit., p. 46.

[2] See above, pp. 57-9.

[3] Op. cit., 62: 'A noi conviene eleggere segnore giusto . . . la quale [persona] ci addirizzi a tutta giustizia [MS. Vat. Pal. lat. 1644, ed. Biondi, op. cit., p. 3, adds: "e traggaci fuori di sette e di divisioni"], per la quale [MS. Vat.: "sì che per lui"] s'acquisti vittoria di fuori e concordia dentro'.

[4] Ed. C. Cipolla, *Le opere di Ferreto de' Ferreti* (Rome, 1908-20), iii.1-100.

[5] See Weiss, *Dawn of Humanism*, 11-12.

[6] Cf. e.g. Cipolla, op. cit., i.275, ii.178,185.

[7] 'Cura fuit, leges et plebiscita forumque/Pacifico servare statu, remque omnibus

About four years before Ferreto wrote his *Carmen*, Marsilius composed his *Defensor pacis*. Cangrande had been, at one time, Marsilius' employer, and Marsilius must have been familiar with eulogies as well as with condemnations of the Della Scala.[1] If Marsilius' views on popular sovereignty have to be seen in the institutional setting of the Italian communes,[2] they have also to be appraised as belonging to an age of transition.[3] The first discourse of the *Defensor pacis*, though designed to support Marsilius' attack on the doctrine of papal plenitude of power, has its place also in the Italian debate on despotism and the problems of civic government which had helped to bring about the fall of republican régimes. Of these, the foremost was civil strife. The view that factionalism was responsible for much of the contemporary predicament was shared by Marsilius: 'Into this dire predicament, then, the miserable men are dragged because of the discord and strife among them, which, like an animal's disease, is recognized as the bad disposition of the civil régime'.[4] Almost all the usual causes of such strife, he adds, have been described by Aristotle. This reference to the *Politics* is illuminating: what Marsilius, like Aristotle, is, in this context, primarily concerned with are the political and social conflicts in the city-states. In drawing the conclusions, in its final chapter, from the arguments of the first discourse, Marsilius states that he will 'undertake to discuss specifically the unusual cause of the discord or lack of tranquillity of civil régimes (*civilium regiminum*), which in our introductory remarks we said to have long troubled . . . the Italian kingdom'.[5] Later on in the same chapter he points out that this cause, that is the usurpation of secular power by the papacy, had prevented, and still prevents, the Roman emperor from establishing peace in the *Italicum regnum*; the absence of his moderating action causing strife, 'whence there have resulted divisions among citizens and finally the destruction of Italian constitutions (*policie*) or cities'.[6]

---

equam/Dividere . . .' (op. cit., iii.30–1). 'Libera plebs,/Que talem tibi sponte ducem, non ullius astu,/Non impulsa metu, sed res previsa futuras/Fecisti. plausu populi et plaudente senatu/Eligitur pius Albertus . . .' (ibid., 29).

[1] Above, p. 49, n.4.

[2] Above, pp. 46–7.

[3] See Lagarde's observations, op. cit., ii.103.

[4] I.i.3, pp. 4–5.

[5] I.xix.1, p. 125.

[6] I.xix.12, p. 135. For the meaning of *policia* as 'constitution', see I,ii.2; 11: 'non differt regnum a civitate in policie specie, sed magis secundum quantitatem'; 'policie seu regiminis'.

His conclusions, he says at the end of chapter one, will be most useful 'to citizens, both rulers and subjects'.[1] This statement refers both to his discussion of the question of the relationship between Church and State in discourse two, and to his theory of the state in discourse one. The solutions he proposes, in the first discourse, for the problem of *civilis pax*,[2] while being conceived as having general validity, are focused on the Italian city-states, which will achieve peace by creating and preserving the right political order. Historically, Marsilius appears to believe than an order of this kind existed under the Roman republic, with the result that Italy was then at peace, and that the Italians 'brought the whole inhabitable world under their sway'.[3] We are reminded of the picture Mussato draws of Padua in the good old times, when the citizens were enjoying peace, and hence were able to subject their neighbours.[4]

There is no sign that Marsilius, while referring to the *regnum Italicum*, was thinking of it as of a viable political structure along the lines of the city-states of which it was composed, or that he visualized the role of its *principans*, the emperor, as going much beyond that of a supreme 'moderator'.[5] His view on this matter shows some agreement with Dante's concept of imperial authority in the *Monarchia*. Dante's universal monarchy does not mean the abolition of local and national jurisdictions.[6] While the emperor's supreme task is to establish peace, he also re-orders corrupt constitutions in the single states: it is only a world monarch who can make it possible that 'politizant reges, aristocratici, quos optimati vocant, et populi libertatis zelatores'.[7] There can be little doubt that, despite its universalist formulation, he considered his theory of the empire as having its special application to Italy.[8] But while Dante believed that peace in Italy depended on the existence of an effective universal authority, for Marsilius the Italian *regnum* was the framework for the existing political structures with which he was concerned. His attitude to the question to what extent imperial authority

[1] '... civibus tam principantibus quam subiectis' (I.i.8; 9).
[2] III.iii, p. 611.
[3] I.i.2, p. 3.
[4] Above, p. 58.
[5] Cf. I.xix.12, p. 135: 'propter mensurantis absenciam'.
[6] *Monarchia*, i.14, p. 349.
[7] Ibid., i.12, p. 347.
[8] See H. Löwe, 'Dante und das Kaisertum', *Historische Zeitschrift*, cxc (1960), 530–1.

was desirable in Italy, probably came close to that of the ghibelline *Signori* with whom he had been associated, and who had shown, during Henry VII's expedition, their opposition to any attempt to revive the Hohenstaufen policy of Italian government.[1]

In the doctrines expounded in the first discourse of the *Defensor pacis*, monarchy occupies an important place; but it is clear from the start that Marsilius does not, like St Thomas, refer monarchical rule primarily to national states;[2] it can exist, he says, 'in one city as well as in several'.[3] Admittedly, while refusing to commit himself as to which of the temperate constitutions is the best, he shows, at one point, a slight preference for monarchy.[4] However, the statement that monarchy is *fortasse perfectior*, is hedged with significant reservations. These, while derived from the *Politics*, have contemporary implications: true monarchy consists in rule 'over voluntary subjects and according to the law made for their common benefit'. It is in similar terms that Ferreto defines the ideal *Signore*.[5] Marsilius' reluctance to commit himself to an opinion on the best constitution, reflects a political climate in which men like Ferreto could waver between acceptance and condemnation of contemporary despotism.

It has been noted how closely Marsilius' theory of the relations between the *legislator humanus* and the *pars principans* follows the constitutional practice of the Italian communes.[6] Like the *Podestà*, Marsilius' ruler is elected by the citizens, executes the laws of the city both in his government and in his jurisdiction, and is liable to be punished and deposed for transgressing them.[7] The French version of Giles of Rome's *De regimine principum*, and the Italian translation of it of 1288, could still describe it as normal for the Italian cities that the people

---

[1] See W. M. Bowsky, *Henry VII in Italy* (Lincoln, Nebr., 1960), 126, 197 sqq. On Marsilius' associations with ghibelline Signori, see above, p. 49, n.4.

[2] When discussing kingship at the beginning of the *De regimine principum*, St Thomas refers it to *provincia vel civitas* (cf. i.1,2, pp. 2, 3, 4). In doing so, he evidently follows the *Politics*, but significantly reverses Aristotle's order of precedence: *Pol.* III.xiv.1 reads in the Latin translation: 'Considerandum autem, utrum expediat . . . civitati et regioni rege regi, aut non'. Cf. *De reg. princ.*, i.2; 3: '. . . requirere oportet, quid provinciae vel civitati magis expedit: utrum a pluribus regi, vel uno'.

[3] I.ii.2, p. 11.

[4] I.ix.5, p. 43.

[5] Above, p. 66.

[6] See Gewirth, i.23–24.

[7] I.xv.2,4, pp. 85, 87; xviii.3, pp. 122–3.

elects its ruler and punishes him when he acts wrongly, and that therefore, although it accepts him, it possesses a higher authority.[1] This description could fit both the *Podestà* of the communal age, and the *Signori* of the period when the despotic régime was not fully consolidated. By the time Marsilius was writing, these conditions no longer prevailed in large parts of Italy. Thus his account of the well-ordered city assumes the character of a republican idealization, which has much in common with the picture Ptolemy of Lucca draws of the northern Italian communes; but where Ptolemy gives the mere outlines, Marsilius fills in the details. At the same time, while providing the fullest and most coherent defence of Italian republicanism that had yet been made, Marsilius' theory could ideally also support the case for a law-abiding and truly elective form of the *Signoria*.

Marsilius' lengthy discussion of the question 'whether it is more expedient . . . to appoint each monarch individually by a new election, or to elect one monarch alone with all his posterity',[2] is, like the rest of discourse one, designed to have general application and validity: and, as elsewhere in that discourse, his principal authority is Aristotle. However, his views on this question, like those of Ptolemy, which he largely shares,[3] have their bearings upon contemporary conditions in northern Italy, in terms not only of institutional background, but also of political awareness. He begins by refuting Giles of Rome's arguments in favour of hereditary monarchy.[4] Giles of Rome refers his observations to kingdoms and principalities. Already the Italian version of his *De regimine principum* had substituted 'towns' for 'principalities', and had rendered Giles' text as 'Signorie delle terre e de' reami';[5] and some of Marsilius' counter-arguments are, in their turn, far more relevant to the problems of the Italian city-states than to those of the European

---

[1] *Del reggimento de' principi*, III.ii.2, ed. F. Corazzini (Florence, 1858), 237–8: 'donde noi vedemo comunemente nelle città d'Italia, che tutto 'l popolo è a chiamare ed eleggere il signore, ed a punirlo quand'elli fa male, e che tutto chiamin ellino alcuno signore che li governi, niente meno il popolo è più signore di lui, perciò ch'esso lo elegge, ed esso il punisce quand'elli fa male . . .' Cf. Henri de Gauchi, *Li livres du gouvernement des rois* . . . , ed. S. P. Molenaer (New York, 1899), 301.

[2] I.xvi, pp. 94–112.

[3] See Gewirth, ii.68, n. 1.

[4] This does not become quite clear from Gewirth's remark; see preceding note.

[5] *De reg.princ.*, III.ii.5, fol. 272v; *Del reggimento de' principi*, 241. The Latin text reads: 'dominationem regiam et principatum', and the French version (op. cit., p. 306): 'les reaumes et les seignories'.

monarchies. Thus his assertion that by being permanently deprived of the opportunity to be appointed to the rulership, citizens will justly engage in sedition,[1] is meaningless in terms of contemporary European politics, but highly pertinent to conditions in Italian city-states, where it could serve as an argument not only against hereditary rule, but also against the *dominium perpetuum* of the *Signori*.[2] The very form in which Marsilius puts the problem he intends to discuss, i.e. whether it is more expedient to appoint a monarch to rule with all his posterity, has an air of unreality if referred to the western monarchies, while it makes political sense if applied to the election of *Signori*, who by 1324 had secured *de facto*, though not yet *de iure*, hereditary succession.

Much the same is also true of Marsilius' discussion of the limits set to the authority of the ruler. Marsilius' refusal to allow the *pars principans* arbitrary power (*arbitrium*) outside the field of equity, and his constant insistence that the ruler must observe the law on all accounts, has its counterpart in the statutory prohibitions to grant the *Podestà* arbitrary powers of government and jurisdiction.[3] Thus the statutes of Padua contained a law of 1257 by virtue of which the *Podestà* had to swear the following oath: 'I shall not seek to obtain arbitrary powers (*arbitrium*), nor shall I accept such powers, even though they should be granted me by the council or the general assembly of the people'.[4] Prohibitions of this kind aimed at preventing the establishment of despotic government by the current method of granting unlimited authority to the head of the town.[5] In practice, they proved incapable of checking the advance of the *Signoria*, in view of the overriding power of the *Signori* and their factions. From a legal viewpoint, a case could be made for the right of the general assembly of the citizens to suspend existing statutes and delegate its powers to a single ruler. This was the theory underlying the use of plebiscitarian methods by the *Signori*, although the popular assemblies had long lost their

---

[1] I.xvi.21, p. 109.

[2] See above, pp. 64–5..

[3] Previté-Orton, in his edition of the *Defensor pacis*, 41, n. 1, has pointed, in connection with I.xi., to the arbitrary powers granted to magistrates in contemporary Italian cities, but not to the prohibitions of such grants.

[4] *Statuti del Comune di Padova dal secolo xii all'anno 1285*, ed. A. Gloria (Padua, 1873), 42: 'Arbitrium non petam nec recipiam etiam si per consilium vel per concionem mihi concederetur'

[5] See Salzer, op cit., 66 sqq.

original place in the political structure of the communes.[1]

Marsilius' statement that 'no judge or ruler should be granted *arbitrium* to give judgments or commands without law, in those civil matters that could be determined by it',[2] while derived from the *Politics*, has therefore specifically Italian overtones. To rule 'without the laws or contrary to them', is for Marsilius tantamount to ruling despotically.[3] It is perhaps not surprising that Marsilius does not refer, in the first discourse of the *Defensor pacis*, to the *lex regia*, by which the Roman people had granted the emperor 'all his command and power',[4] but that he does so in the *Defensor minor*, in which he expounds his case for the empire.[5] The question, which so much exercised the jurists, whether by virtue of the *lex regia* the Roman people had divested itself permanently of its power, or whether it had conferred its authority on individual emperors only,[6] could be extended to apply *a fortiori* to any contemporary state,[7] and not only to the emperors as successors of the Roman *princeps*. It was implicitly answered by Marsilius' refusal to allow election of the ruler 'with all his posterity'.[8] Similarly, the absolutist interpretation of the *lex regia* as supporting the claim that 'what pleases the prince has the force of law',[9] which was sometimes qualified by the view, based on the *lex digna*, that the emperor acted voluntarily according to the laws,[10] has no place in Marsilius' doctrine of the supremacy of law. His ruler must 'be regulated by the law',[11] that is by the law that had been created by the people, and is not even entitled freely to interpret it.[12] His constitutional position is the exact opposite to that of the *Signori*, who had full legislative authority and were not

---

[1] Ercole, op. cit., pp. 66 sqq.

[2] I.xi.4, p. 57.

[3] I.xiv.8, p. 82.

[4] *Corpus iuris civilis*, Inst. I.ii.6; *Dig.* I.iv.1; *Cod.* I.xvii.1,7.

[5] xii,1, p. 35. Cf. Gewirth, i.248–50.

[6] See O. Gierke, *Political Theories of the Middle Age*, tr. F. W. Maitland (Cambridge, 1922), 39 sqq.; A. J. Carlyle, 'The theory of the source of political authority in the medieval civilians to the time of Accursius', in *Mélanges Fitting* (Montpellier, 1907), i.181–93; Ercole, op. cit., 228, n. 1; Kantorowicz, op. cit., 103.

[7] Ibid., 298.

[8] Above, p. 70.

[9] *Inst.* I.ii.6; *Dig.* I.iv.1; *Cod.* I.xvii.1. Cf. F. Schulz, 'Bracton on kingship', *E.H.R.*, lx (1945), 136–76; Kantorowicz, 103.

[10] *Cod.* I.xiv.4. Kantorowicz, 104–5; Tierney, op. cit., 308 sqq.

[11] I.xv.7, p. 90.

[12] See Gewirth, i.230.

bound by the statutes; having been granted full *arbitrium*, they might indeed be considered 'not bound by the laws'.[1]

At this point, it is well to bear in mind Marsilius' doctrine of the human legislator. His condemnation of arbitrary government, while being the corollary of his theory of popular sovereignty, is supported by his thesis that the common interest is best secured by those whom it concerns most.[2] One of his arguments by which he tries to prove the location of legislative authority in the people is that individual legislators are liable to make laws to suit their private rather than the public interest: 'the authority to make laws belongs, therefore, to the whole body of citizens or to the weightier part thereof... For since no one knowingly harms ... himself, it follows that all or most want a law conducive to the common benefit of the citizens'.[3] Unlike St Thomas and Giles of Rome, he does not consider a monarch best fitted to procure the common good of the people;[4] and to the objection that the wise few 'can discern what should be enacted ... better than the rest of the multitude', he replies with the Aristotelian argument that the latter 'can discern and desire the common justice and benefit to a greater extent than any part of the multitude'.[5] But being best capable of recognizing its 'common utility', the 'whole body of citizens or the weightier part thereof' is also best qualified to make laws and to enforce their observance,[6] quite apart from having, by virtue of the legal principle *quod omnes tangit ab omnibus comprobetur*, to give its consent to legislation concerning its corporate interest.[7]

Contemporary Italian thought assigned, as we have seen, a decisive role in communal politics to the concept of the common good. Yet even Remigio Girolami, like the Thomist school in general, saw its political significance primarily in terms of the relationship between individual and society, between private

---

[1] Cf. e.g. the election decree of 1299 of Guido Bonacolsi of Mantua, in Salzer, op. cit., 302–3. See Ercole, 103–5; one of the powers granted to *Signori* was to interpret the statutes according to their will. For the use of the formula *legibus solutus* to describe *Signori*, ibid., 106.

[2] I.xii.5, pp. 65–6.

[3] I.xii.8, pp. 68–9. See now, on this whole question, E. Lewis, 'The "positivism" of Marsiglio of Padua', *Speculum*, xxviii (1963), 567 sqq. See also Gewirth, I.203 sqq.

[4] See above, p. 54, n. 3.

[5] I.xiii.4,7, pp. 72–3, 75; cf. Aristotle, *Pol.*, III.xi.14, and also 2–4.

[6] I.xii.5,6, pp. 65–7.

[7] I.xii.7, p. 68. See Lewis, p. 569, and, on the maxim *quod omnes tangit*, G. Post, 'A Roman-canonical maxim, "quod omnes tangit", in Bracton', *Traditio*, iv (1946), 197–251.

and public interest.[1] Marsilius, by incorporating this concept into his theory of legislative authority, firmly rooted it in the legal and constitutional structure of the well-ordered *civitas*. While claiming universal validity for his doctrine of the human legislator, he also gave Italian communal thought a new dimension. Conversely, his picture of the well-ordered state in which legislation is determined by the common interest as recognized by the civic corporation, and in which the *pars principans* is bound by the laws created by that legislation, constitutes an implicit condemnation of arbitrary rule as exercised by Italian *Signori*. Marsilius' reminder, in the concluding chapter of the *Defensor pacis*, that his advice not to grant the ruler full powers was one of the principal teachings of his work, thus assumes the significance of a political message to his countrymen:[2] 'The subject multitude will also learn [from this book] the extent to which it is possible to see to it that the ruler . . . does not assume for himself arbitrary powers (*arbitrium*) to pass judgments or to perform any other civil acts contrary to or apart from the laws'. While he was writing the *Defensor pacis*, the Da Carrara were consolidating their ascendancy in Padua, after their initial failure to establish a permanent *Signoria* in 1318.[3] A few years later, Mussato, their relentless enemy, described, in his *History*, the events of 1318.[4] The warning he addresses to posterity, in this connection, recalls Marsilius' concluding words: 'May future generations of our citizens learn from the records of contemporary deeds by what means this city passed from a republican régime to autocratic rule'.[5]

Soon after completing the *Defensor pacis*, probably in 1326, Marsilius fled to Louis the Bavarian and became one of his chief publicists; in 1327, John XXII condemned him as a heretic. In 1328, he probably assisted Louis' coronation by Roman senators, and was appointed spiritual vicar of Rome. The doctrines by which he had hoped to support the secular powers against the papacy were thus enlisted to serve Louis' cause in his conflict with John XXII.[6] That this involved a

[1] See e.g. Lagarde, op. cit., iii.150–3; Davis, 'An early Florentine political theorist', 668–9; and above, p. 54.
[2] III.iii, p. 612.
[3] Above, pp. 48–9.
[4] *De gestis Italicorum*, in [Padrin], op. cit., 79ff.
[5] Ibid., 90.
[6] See O. Bornhak, *Staatskirchliche Anschauungen und Handlungen am Hofe Kaiser Ludwigs des Bayern* (Weimar, 1933), 16–17; cf. also 35–6, 45–6.

shift in Marsilius' views on government is shown by the *Defensor minor*. This shift is already prepared in the second discourse of the *Defensor pacis*.[1] Designed to prove that the papal claim to plenitude of power destroys peace and disrupts the right order, the second discourse is focused on the relations between the papacy and rulers such as the emperor and the kings of France. The theory of the *legislator humanus*, which Marsilius had formulated against the background of the Italian city-states, is maintained throughout that discourse; but the delegation of the people's authority to the prince, who may thus be considered to act as the *legislator*, is taken for granted. At the same time, there is no question of a permanent abdication of popular sovereignty to the prince. The human legislator retains 'the primary authority to make human laws, to establish the government, to elect the ruler [and] to grant him authority'.[2] In the *Defensor minor*, Marsilius still insists that 'the human legislator alone has the authority to correct rulers for acting negligently or wrongly'.[3] Even as an imperialist publicist, Marsilius remained loyal to his fundamental premises. Evidently, this 'son of Antenor' could not entirely forget the political experience and traditions of his native Italy, which had once provided him with the basis for what he believed to be a universally valid theory of Church and State.

[1] See Gewirth's observations, i.248 sqq.
[2] II.xxx.8, p. 600; see Gewirth, i.255.
[3] ii.7, p. 5.

III

PETER PARTNER

FLORENCE AND THE PAPACY[1]
1300–1375

It is hard to know what the guelf party in fourteenth-century Italy was, and to determine whether it stood either for a political programme or for a political ideal. Contemporaries certainly thought that it did both, and its transmutations invite our own interest and curiosity. Among the guelfs not the least interesting are the Florentines, the 'faithful of holy mother church', who seem to have begun by wearing at least the outward show of religious fidelity in the context of a political alliance, and to have arrived in the end at an attitude towards the head of Christendom which even in appearance was calculating and detached. What a gulf lies—or seems to lie—between the arbitrary intervention in Florentine affairs of Pope Boniface VIII, and the spectacle of Pope Martin V in 1419, striding up and down in impotent anger in his room in Florence, while the urchins mocked him in the streets! The most important point in the transformation of the Florentine attitude to the papacy was the 'War of the Eight Saints' in 1375–8; the present essay seeks to examine the relationship in the preceding three-quarters of a century.

A concept as vague as 'guelfism', which was current in Italian politics for at least a century and a half, can have no meaning at all except in the context of a particular political situation. It is true that most Florentines during the fourteenth

[1] For a chronological table of events, see p. 117.

I wish to acknowledge the kindness of the Director and Faculty of the British School at Rome, for a grant which enabled me to examine the archive sources which have been used in this article.

century would have called themselves 'the faithful and devoted people of holy church, lovers of the *popolo* and the commune, and supporters of the liberty of Florence and of the *parte guelfa*'[1] but this description is so vague that it is almost impossible to speak meaningfully of Florentine policy being more or less 'guelf' at any one moment. All that one can do is to trace the changing attitudes of Florentine statesmen towards the other two great partners in the guelf alliance, the papacy and the Angevin kingdom of Naples. And it is often also relevant to remark upon Florentine relations with the minor partners in the guelf alliance in Italy south of the Po, the 'guelf' communes of Emilia, Tuscany and Umbria—relevant also because regarding these 'guelf' communes Florence spoke often in terms of 'liberty'—'people and communes which are free and self-governing, under the popular rule of the catholic guelf party'.[2]

The complexity of the political and social factors in the guelf alliance of the later Middle Ages can be studied in Jordan's *Origines de la domination angevine en Italie*—which as he himself remarked would be better entitled 'Essai sur les origines et la formation des partis italiens'. Almost any generalization we make about such a complex phenomenon is bound to distort it.[3]

Guelfism differed, for a beginning, regionally. Northerners like Guiglelmo della Ventura thought of it as a division of the cities of Lombardy.[4] Bartolus of Sassoferrato the legist, who came from the papal state, thought of 'guelf' and 'ghibelline' as mere factional labels. The Roman noble Napoleon Orsini remarked in the same vein that 'you will never find a true Roman who is either guelf or ghibelline' and added that he did not really understand what a guelf or a ghibelline was.[5] Yet how persistent even in the papal state was the mentality which insisted on 'guelf' and 'ghibelline' as fundamental political divisions may be seen in the report of the papal rector of the March of Ancona in 1341, who although he knew perfectly well that the 'guelf' Malatesta and their like were as much of a threat to his authority as any ghibelline, yet persisted in using the old

[1] Quoted by G. A. Brucker, *Florentine Politics and Society 1343–1378* (Princeton, 1962), 74.
[2] *Miscellanea di Storia Italiana edita per cura della Regia Deputazione di Storia Patria*, xxvi (1887), 419.
[3] See, particularly, in Jordan's book, 163–72, 193–4, 335–56, 542–58, 610–14.
[4] 'Memoriale', in Muratori, *Rerum Italicarum Scriptores* [=RRIISS], xi, col. 153; and cf. Mussato, 'Ludovicus Bavarus', ibid., x, col. 775.
[5] H. Finke, *Acta Aragonensia*, i (Berlin, 1908), 615–17.

77

terminology and spoke of having 're-introduced the guelfs' into the subject towns.[1] Albornoz, more realistic and more authoritarian, forbade the factions of Viterbo even to use the names of guelf and ghibelline.[2]

Perhaps the best modern formulation is that of Jordan: 'In fact people were guelf or ghibelline either out of self-interest or habit. They were not guelf because they wanted to obey the pope, nor ghibelline because they wanted to oppose the Church and its hierarchy'.[3]

Villani the Florentine chronicler subscribes to the historical myth that the struggle between guelf and ghibelline was principally one between the Church and its enemies, but although this may have been sincerely felt one wonders to what extent—like most popularized ideologies—it was not largely a matter of common form. It might be maintained that fourteenth-century Florence was guelf and Catholic just as eighteenth-century England was Protestant and Whig. The historian of Florence, Davidsohn, has compared the witch hunts of ghibelline suspects in Florence to the no-popery riots in England.

A further recurring element in Florentine 'guelf' ideas is, not unnaturally, that the guelf alliance should be used to defend its members from 'ultramontane' dangers—from the emperor and, later in the century, from the German and English Companies. Like all principles of collective security, this concept was treated by the parties concerned on its merits at any one time. Florence argued the idea of permanently excluding German intervention from Italy, at the time when the struggle with Henry VII was approaching its crisis,[4] and in 1340 told Pope Benedict XII that the Church could be defended only by the united forces of the Italian guelfs[5].

Both the papacy and the Angevins had their own game to play. Only with great reluctance did Robert of Anjou accept the German challenge in 1312. The popes did not oppose the imperial descents into Italy of 1310, 1355 and 1368, and in consequence gave the Florentine guelfs no assistance at these

---

[1] A. Theiner, *Codex diplomaticus dominii temporalis sanctae sedis* (Rome, 1861–2), ii, no. 128.
[2] Ibid. ii, no. 328.
[3] 194; cf. C. Cipolla, *Storia delle Signorie Italiane* (Milan, 1881), 121.
[4] W. M. Bowsky, *Henry VII in Italy. The Conflict of Empire and City-State 1310–1313* (Lincoln, 1960), 164–5.
[5] *Archivio Storico Italiano*, Appendice, vii (1849), 356 ff.

times against the emperors. Benedict XII replied to the Florentines in 1340 by a platitudinous remark which was apposite on almost any of the occasions on which some sort of guelf idea was urged as a political motive—that 'Italian politics are extremely changeable, and that Italians want one thing one day and one another'. On the other hand, both the popes and the Angevins naturally urged the guelf tradition upon Florence and others when it suited them, either against Louis of Bavaria, or against the Visconti and the Lombard ghibellines, against tyrants in the papal state, or against the companies.

In fact being something in the nature of a regional defence system, something of an application of the papal theocratic principle, something (from the Florentine point of view especially) like economic imperialism, guelfism was bound to have a different appearance not only from state to state and region to region, but from one group of social and economic interests to another, both within and without a particular state. The financial backing which the Florentine banking companies gave to the Angevins and the Church resulted in an extremely complex alliance of financial interests which has not been analysed in detail by historians, although the material for an analysis exists, and has been largely sifted by Yves Renouard. It is evidently not enough to say that Florentine financial interests as a whole were inseparable from the papacy and the Angevin kingdom, although from 1266 until the 1320s the stake of Florence in the papal system of international taxation and finance, and her privileged position in southern Italy and France, were so valued as usually to outbalance all other Florentine interests. But even under Boniface VIII and Clement V, Florentine policy did on occasion oppose or disregard the papacy—it was easier of course for Florence to cold-shoulder one of the two leaders in the guelf alliance, than both at once. As the fourteenth century advanced and especially after the bank failures of the early 1340s the Florentine stake in both papacy and the Regno fell, and the balance of interest which bound her to the other two partners began to be dubious. Both early and late it could be true for Florence as for the other guelf communes, that 'guelf' policy was often scarcely or not at all concerned with the papacy.[1]

[1] V. Vitale, *Il dominio della parte guelfa in Bologna 1280-1327* (Bologna, 1901), 97, 141-2.

Early and late also, some political and economic groups inside the communes were far more closely bound to the papacy and the Angevins than others; this could end in clashes inside the commune which meant life and death to those involved (as with the White and Black factions at the beginning of the century), or it could show itself (as it more usually did) in conflicts which only occasionally rise above the surface of communal politics.

It also seems worth emphasizing at the outset that no analysis of Florentine-papal relations can hold good, which does not take proper account of the third partner, the Angevin kingdom. On many occasions, and notably in the early years of Clement V's pontificate and in the later years of John XXII, the policy of the Angevins ran directly counter to that of the popes. The Angevins could be and sometimes were a menace to Florentine independence, just as they menaced the independence of Bologna, Genoa, Brescia and the other guelf communes. There was an attempt to establish an Angevin *Signoria* in 1317[1] which anticipated the event, the *Signoria* of Charles of Calabria in Florence in 1326. In the later years of Robert the Wise there was growing estrangement between Naples and Florence, but the *Signoria* of Walter of Brienne in Florence in 1342 can also be regarded as the consequence, even if indirect, of Angevin policy. Robert's death in 1343 is usually held to be a watershed for Italian politics. The period of confusion and disorientation which followed for the Italian guelfs not only promoted the great revival and expansion of Visconti power in the north and centre of the peninsula, but promoted the growth of a more fluid and (if I may be allowed the word) non-aligned policy at Florence. When Albornoz and Niccolò Acciaiuoli launched the next great wave of clerical and Angevin imperialism in the 1350s, the political climate of Florence had been transformed, and the factions most closely associated with the Angevin and papal courts had effectively dissolved.

Finally, although it only appears above the political surface in the 1340s and 50s when Florence was notably out of sympathy with Angevin-papal policy, there is another factor which is important throughout the period. From the thirteenth century and earlier the guelf communes no less than any other secular

[1] G.-M. Monti, 'Da Carlo I a Roberto di Angio', *Archivio Storico per le provincie Napoletane*, xviii (1932), 137–45.

states had an interest in containing the power of the Church in so far as it affected the native clergy and so far as it encroached on the jurisdiction of the courts. The exemption of the clergy from the normal operation of justice, the operation of the inquisition against the laymen, the papal taxation and the conferment of benefices in prejudice of communal interests, all these could and did irritate Florentine relations with the popes. To be guelf was not necessarily to be either privileged or complacent in these matters.

The fourteenth century opens, in fact, when relations between Florence and the papal court were as tense as at any time until 1374–5. Mathew of Acquasparta excommunicated the Florentine priors on behalf of Boniface VIII in March 1300, opening the way to the *coup d'état* carried out by Charles of Valois at the instigation of the pope in 1301—'he comes alone and unarmed, and with the lance with which Judas jousted, and so he directs its point that it slits open the belly of Florence'.[1] The Black faction (which was in effect the faction of the papal bankers) re-entered Florence with Charles, and remained in power for a generation. Had Boniface lived, or had his policies lived after him, the traditional relationship of Florence with the papacy would have been re-established. But his death and the reversal of his policies brought papal power in Tuscany to its nadir. In Bologna a White anti-Angevin régime ruled, dedicated to the overthrow of the Florentine Blacks. At the conclave of Perugia in 1304–5 the design of Matteo Rosso Orsini for a pope who would avenge the outrage of Anagni was outwitted by Napoleon Orsini, who obtained the election of Clement V, the servant of French policy and of the anti-Bonifacian faction among the cardinals.[2] The result was the utter alienation of Florence from the papacy during the early years of Clement V's pontificate. Alienation from the papacy and not from the Angevin, however. Opposed in this to the French court, Charles of Anjou supported the Bonifacians and the Florentine Blacks. In 1305 he sent his son and heir Robert to become captain of the Florentine league against White Pistoia, in direct defiance of papal orders and of the two nuncios whom Clement V despatched to Italy in September 1305. These returned to the

[1] *Purg.*, xx, 73.
[2] Cf. G. Fornaseri, 'Il conclave perugino del 1304–5', *Rivista di Storia della Chiesa in Italia*, x (1956), 321–44.

papal court with a sad story of utter disunity, war and confusion among the Italian guelfs.[1]

Clement V's choice of a legate to Tuscany in 1306, Napoleon Orsini, was utterly unacceptable to the Florentine Black régime, which was now immensely strengthened by the Black *coup d'état* in Bologna in the spring of the same year. Orsini was snubbed by Florence, expelled from Bologna, and in the end laid both cities under interdict, while he seems even to have preached a crusade against them for the benefit of the White army—a striking if futile application of Boniface's methods against Boniface's policy.

Two things healed the split between Clement V and the Black régime in Florence. In 1309 both parties discovered that each needed the other: Clement V because he needed Florentine aid against Venice in order to recover Ferrara, Florence because she feared the approaching descent of the Emperor Henry VII into Italy (which had been encouraged by the pope, mainly because of the failure of his Tuscan policy). A new legate, the papal nephew Arnauld de Pellagrue, was sent to absolve the Florentines and launch an attack on the Venetians. This solution has been variously judged as the triumph of the Florentines over Clement V, or the victory of Angevin policy— the second interpretation seems preferable.[2] But it seems important that this bitter quarrel, healed not through idealism but on grounds of pure political opportunism, preceded what has been termed, perhaps with some exaggeration, the 'rebirth' of Italian guelfism.[3]

It was the accomplishment of Henry VII to unite the Italian guelfs not for but against him, and to make them once more into a more or less permanently linked body which continued to serve the ends of papal policy and Angevin and French imperialism until the ignominious collapse of the political schemes of John XXII, in the summer of 1332. Henry achieved this unwanted result, I would suggest, by two main means.

---

[1] A. Eitel, *Der Kirchenstaat unter Klemens V* (Berlin, 1907), 18–19; R. Davidsohn, *Forschungen zur Geschichte von Florenz* iii, (Berlin, 1896–1908), 287–95; E. Goeller, 'Zur Geschichte der italienischen Legation Durantis', *Römische Quartalschrift*, xix (1905), 16–24.
[2] R. Davidsohn, *Geschichte von Florenz* iii, (Berlin, 1896–1927), 343 and 364 ff.; Eitel, 28 9, 193 4.
[3] Bowsky, 'Florence and Henry of Luxemburg, King of the Romans; 'The Rebirth of Guelfism', *Speculum*, xxxiii (1958), 177–203.

First, he demanded that the guelf communes recall the ghibelline and White exiles. Such a demand was absolutely unacceptable, because it posed insoluble legal problems of property restitution and meant not reconciliation but counter-revolution. Like some apostles of international intervention in our own day, Henry asked too much of human nature. His demand was bound to be rejected, with just the same hastiness as John XXII's demands were rejected, when in 1317 the pope sent his envoys to Lombardy to ask the ghibelline communes to re-admit the guelf exiles.[1] Secondly, Henry stepped on the Sicilian viper. When in 1312 he finally concluded his alliance with Frederick of Trinacria and tore up the fragile treaty of Caltabellotta which had kept the peace of southern Italy since 1302, he finally brought Robert of Anjou (until then hesitating) into the war, and renewed the fighting which intermittently devasted the south of the peninsula until 1372.

As the leader not only of the Tuscan but from 1309 to 1312 of the Roman and indeed of the Italian resistance, Florence was the object of Henry VII's particular dislike. The sentences he passed against the city were still the object of Florentine distress in the 1350s, when they paid Charles IV handsomely to cancel them. And if Florence could be drawn further into the old pattern of guelf and ghibelline hostility, this was achieved by the battle of Montecatini in 1315. The dead on the field cried out for vendetta; when Robert of Anjou made peace with the Tuscan ghibellines a few months later a Florentine poet mocked those who consented to it; if they remembered their dead they would continue the fight to the death: 'Fathers, brothers, cousins, sons. And he who loved his countrymen aright with clenched teeth would grimly fight'.[2]

It would be an error, I think, to suppose that Florence remained for long the centre, still less the leader of guelf policy. If she had revived the guelf organism, she did not control it. Once the Angevin kingdom entered the struggle with Henry VII, and still more when Clement V abandoned his neutrality and pronounced against the emperor in 1313, Florence receded to the position which she was to occupy for twenty

[1] S. Riezler, *Vatikanische Akten* (Innsbruck, 1891), nos. 50, 51, 52. Cf. Bowsky, *Henry VII*, 84–90.
[2] *Poeti del Primo Secolo*, ii (Florence, 1816), 194–5.

years, that of auxiliary in an international struggle in which the
papacy, the French monarchy and the Angevin kingdom
played the decisive roles in shaping and executing policy.[1] It
was a position profitable for the great Florentine companies,
and this period proved the heyday of Florentine commercial
and banking expansion in the Angevin kingdom. But the issues
at stake in the twenty years after 1313 were international rather
than peninsular, still less provincial. John XXII's great military
and diplomatic effort to create a new and stronger extension
of the papal state in northern Italy; Robert of Anjou's attempt
to revive the peninsular hegemony of the Angevins; the policies
of the French monarchy, of the Austrian house, of Louis of
Bavaria, of John of Bohemia—all these, though they affected
local interests in Italy less consistently and effectively than they
were intended to do, nevertheless formed a pattern of international intervention in Italian politics which was too strong
for the Italian states to resist. Florence fought in Tuscany
against Castruccio Castracani and others but she also fought in
Emilia, in Lombardy, in the great struggle for Genoa. When
the Florentine army ran the *palio* under the walls of Milan on
St John's day 1323 it was making a typically regionalist gesture,
but it also, by its presence in the heterogenous Franco-German
guelf besieging army, testified to the renewal of a peninsular
guelf policy firmly inserted into the cadre of Franco-papal
imperialism. It is not surprising that under the strains of this
great war Florentine independence temporarily collapsed, and
that the city submitted in 1325–8 to the *Signoria* of Charles of
Calabria. At this period the Florentine army and that of the
papal legate Bertrand du Poujet were virtually under a single
military command.[2]

Fortunately for Florence, the Angevin monarchy felt the
pressure of the war just as much as its allies, and the Angevin
Signoria was not maintained after Charles' death in 1328. The
time came, moreover, when the whole elaborate and ram-
shackle structure of the guelf alliance collapsed under the

[1] Cf. G. Tabacco, *La casa di Francia nell'azione politica di papa Giovanni XXII*
(Rome, 1953).
[2] Nostra existit intencio, quod Lumbardie et Thuscie exercitus debeant, cum
hoc nececcitas exiget, mutuo se iuuare. *Quellen und Forschungen aus italienischen
Archiven und Bibliotheken*, xxvii (1936–7), 148–9. Cf. Tabacco, doc. 5, 353, and
D. Marzi, *La Cancelleria della Repubblica Fiorentina* (Rocca S. Casciano, 1910),
doc. 6, 629–30.

pressure of internal conflicts which divided its leaders. So also indeed had the ghibelline alliance already done in 1327-9. The effective cause of the split in the guelf leadership was the dealings of the papal Curia and the French court with John of Bohemia. In the summer of 1332 the presence of John of Bohemia in north Italy led to the negotiation of the league of Ferrara. The league which allied Florence with the Este and the Lombard ghibellines against the papal auxiliary John of Bohemia terminates the period in guelf politics which began when John's father Henry VII entered Italy in 1309. It is often reckoned as the point at which the *Signoria* became the determining factor in Italian politics—or if put in a different form, it marks the point at which the French and German interventions in Italian politics, which had held the stage for twenty-five years, now finally broke down and left the political field in Italy comparatively clear for the operation of regional and local forces.

For Robert of Anjou the league of Ferrara meant the beginning of a period of withdrawal and decline in peninsular politics, which lasted until his death. For Florence, it meant the beginning of a period of further expansion in Tuscany which was in the end a crushingly expensive failure. The struggle for the possession of Lucca, which passed into the hands of Mastino della Scala in 1335, led Florence down a ruinous gradient. The papacy at first appeared to encourage this; having accepted Florentine help in 1335 against the Ordelaffi in Romagna, Benedict XII in 1336 congratulated the Florentines and Venetians on their success against the Della Scala, the 'enemies of their liberty'.[1]

But papal no less than Angevin policy was rapidly diverging from that of Florence. Benedict XII was neutral in the wars conducted both by Venice-Florence and by the Visconti against the Scaligeri; and was by no means pleased with the Florentine attitude to Bologna, where Taddeo Pepoli had seized the *Signoria* in despite of the Church in August 1337. Pepoli enjoyed Florentine complaisance if not Florentine support,[2]

[1] J.-M. Vidal and G. Mollat, *Benoît XII (1334-1342). Lettres closes et patentes intéressant les pays autre que la France* (Paris, 1919-50), no. 1094; Raynaldus, ad a., para. 53. For a rather different view to that taken here, see G. Tabacco, 'La tradizione guelfa in Italia durante il pontificato di Benedetto XII', *Studi di Storia medievale e moderna in onore di Ettore Rota* (Rome, 1958), 97-148.

[2] N. Rodolico, *Dal Comune alla Signoria* (Bologna, 1898), 226-7.

and probably some elements at Florence hoped that the city would eventually be *tertium gaudens* in Bologna.

Here is one of the main questions to agitate Florentine-papal relations from the thirteenth century down to the time of Lorenzo the Magnificent. Bologna and the Romagna were legally part of the papal state. The Appenine border which Florence had with this area was one of the most sensitive parts of the Florentine territory. There was not even the sort of relatively satisfactory balance which Siena and Perugia maintained on the other sections of Florence's Appenine frontier; the politics of Bologna were usually unsettled, and the rest of the Romagna was proverbially a prey to the most unruly group of tyrants in Italy, over whom the Church exercised only the appearance of control and sometimes not even that. Florence had little alternative but to intervene pretty largely in the politics of Romagna, to patronize the Bolognese factions and to find herself allies and *raccomandati* among the Romagnol *Signori*. This Florentine diplomatic activity in papal territory was fiercely resented by the popes, and action such as the settlement of the quarrels of Romagnol *Signori* which was arranged through Florentine mediation in October 1339, was ill received at Avignon. Equally, the pope resented the use of rebellious Romagnol subjects as Florentine *condottieri*, such as Malatesta and Galeotto Malatesta, who after their rebellion against the Church in the summer of 1340 continued to be employed by Florence.[1]

Florentine support of Taddeo Pepoli in Bologna, of the Malatesta, the Polenta, the Este was not the only factor to weigh on Florentine relations with Avignon. What above all pressed on Florence were the political and financial results of the failure of the war of Lucca. She had made peace with the Scaligeri (24th January, 1339), but she had contracted a huge debt, and the great Florentine banks were feeling the strain of economic slump and taxation—quite apart from other factors such as the default of Edward III of England. From February 1340 Florence was urging the pope to reconciliation with Pepoli and the Romagnol *Signori*, and was so far successful that Benedict XII in June agreed to accept the Pepoli régime in Bologna. In

---

[1] Vidal-Mollat, nos. 2805, 2834, 2836–7; cf. *Archivio Storico Italiano*, App., vii (1849), 356–7; Theiner, ii, nos. 83, 110.

September the *Signoria* pressed the pope on a significant point, the taxation of the Florentine clergy; they asked for the pope to carry out this taxation for them and to give them the proceeds of two years of the current sexennial tenth. Benedict refused, and in discussion reproached the Florentine envoy with the league which his commune was making with the Este and the Malatesta, 'enemies of the Church', to which the envoy replied that these were not enemies of the Church, 'but rather its old, devoted and trusted friends'. This cavilling may have been based on the so-called 'guelf ideology' but it cut no ice with the pope.

The years 1340–3 were critical for the relations of Florence with the Angevins and the papacy for the rest of the century. They were a time in which Florentine government and society experienced the most serious internal crisis until the time of the Ciompi in 1378. The great bankers were becoming desperate; in November 1340 the Bardi attempted an unsuccessful *coup d'état* which led to their defeat and exile.[1]

In August 1341 Florence bought Lucca from Mastino della Scala, only to find herself immediately attacked by Pisa and the Lombard ghibellines. She had no assistance from either the pope or Robert of Anjou, who were themselves now divided— Benedict XII was now considering following the French lead in coming to terms with Louis of Bavaria, and Robert was organizing a guelf-ghibelline coalition with the object of opposing the descent of Louis into Italy.[2] That she was a party to this coalition got Florence no help from Robert, who still considered that Lucca belonged to him as a result of the negotiations of 1328–9. Thoroughly unhinged by his refusal, Florence made a tentative gesture—of which she rapidly repented—to call on Louis of Bavaria for troops.

Whether because he knew that this approach to the Bavarian had been made, or simply because of the news of the defeat of Florence by Pisa on the Serchio on 2nd October, Benedict XII on 13th October, 1341 signed contracts with the Nicolucci of Siena which virtually ended the banking hegemony of the

[1] A. Sapori, *La crisi delle compagnie mercantile dei Bardi e dei Peruzzi* (Florence, 1926), 117–21.
[2] T. Mommsen, *Italienische Analekten zur Reichsgeschichte des 14. Jahrhunderts* (Stuttgart, 1952), nos. 252–65; Rodolico, docs. 72–3; A. Pepoli, *Documenti storici del sec. xiv estratti dal R. Archivio di Stato fiorentino* (Florence, 1884), doc. 34.

Florentine companies at the papal court.[1] By doing this he signed the death warrant of the great companies, and set in motion forces which made basic changes in the relations between Florence and the papacy. At the same time the Neapolitans began a run on the Florentine banks which broke the Bonaccorsi and some of the smaller firms, though the other big banks still resisted.

What followed is perhaps comparable in some respects to the events of 1301, in that Franco-papal policy cut across Angevin policy in Tuscany. With the consent of the pope and probably that of the king of France, Walter of Brienne, the duke of Athens, was engaged in the service of Florence.[2]

The great bankers sponsored Brienne, who had been vicar in Florence for Charles of Calabria in 1326, for the *Signoria*, and carried out a successful *coup d'état* on his behalf in September 1342. The initial force which caused these events sprang from the internal politics of Florence, but once he was in power, Walter of Brienne was keenly supported by Clement VI and Philip VI. The failure of the Brienne *Signoria* in July 1343 was the work of the magnates, just as his installation had been; the *coup* incurred the displeasure of the pope, the French king, and (King Robert having died at the beginning of 1343) the Neapolitan princes. How the pattern of financial politics was changing under the strains of the Florentine crisis, is shown by the fact that the *coup* against Brienne was led by the bishop of Florence, Angelo Acciaiuoli, in conjunction with the Bardi, Frescobaldi and the great banking families (not least the Acciaiuoli themselves) which until then had been so involved in Angevin and papal finances as to find it very hard to go against Angevin-papal policy.

The removal of the duke of Athens was practically the last effort of the Florentine magnates. For a short time they tried to set up a 'council of fourteen' which would place them firmly in power, but in September this was overthrown by a popular revolution; the great Bardi palace was pillaged by the mob,

[1] Y. Renouard, *Les relations des papes d'Avignon et des compagnies commerciales et bancaires de 1316 à 1378* (Paris, 1941), 198.

[2] C. Paoli, 'Della signoria di Gualtieri Duca d'Atene in Firenze', *Giornale storico degli Archivi Toscani*, vi (1862); idem, in *Archivio Storico Italiano* (1872); cf. Leoni, ibid. (1875); Guerrieri, ibid. (1898); A. Mercati, 'Un tentativo del duca d'Atene di ottenere l'investitura della Romagna', *Rivista storica degli Archivi toscani*, iv (1932).

and the bankruptcy of the Peruzzi and Acciaiuoli followed almost immediately (that of the Bardi was not until 1346). A new period in Florentine government began, in which the new merchant families, the *gente nuova*, were to have a greatly increased share of power. The new circumstances of the Florentine commune were certainly at this point deeply affected by the dislocation of the Angevin government which followed the death of Robert of Anjou. All over the peninsula the guelfs felt the effects of the loss of the man who was, in spite of the lack of idealism in the guelf groups, its leader. For the Florentine bankers the situation was made the more acute, in that Naples was now controlled by a weak and extravagant government, unable and unwilling to support the Florentine banking houses or to repay what it owed them. In fact what is striking about events after 1342 is the ruthless way in which the papacy and the Angevins sought to squeeze the broken banks apparently regardless of the effects which this might have for Florence or for the remaining banks which were solvent.

It is not surprising that the new Florentine régime was not long in running into trouble with the papacy—which was continuing to exhibit its regret for the fall of the Brienne *Signoria*, and suggesting arbitration procedure which might re-establish it.[1] The first mild friction was over a proposal to tax the clergy for the re-construction of the city walls.[2] The major quarrel came in 1344, over a debt due to Pietro Gomez, cardinal-bishop of Sabina, from the Acciaiuoli bank.[3] The proceedings which were to follow, which brought Florence under interdict, were not taken by the new democratic government on behalf of some member of the *gente nuova*, but precisely in favour of a family which though in origin *popolano* was now a great banking house. The Acciaiuoli had had, and were later to re-affirm even more closely, the strongest connections with the Holy See and

[1] Paoli, nos. 372, 373, 376, 380, 381-3; M. Deprez, Clement VI. *Lettres closes, patentes et curiales se rapportant à la France* (Paris, 1898), nos. 330, 574, 1016; *Archivio Storico Italiano* (1898), 303.

[2] Marzi, 650-2; cf. Davidsohn, *Geschichte*, iii, 865.

[3] A. Panella, 'La politica ecclesiastica del comune fiorentino dopo la cacciata del Duca d'Athene', *Archivio Storico Italiano* (1913, pt. 2), 271-370; Brucker, *Florentine Politics*, 131-9; M. V. Becker, 'Some economic implications of the conflict between Church and State in "Trecento" Florence', *Mediaeval Studies*, xxi (1959), 1-16; idem, 'An essay on the "Novi Cives" and Florentine Politics, 1342-1382', ibid. xxiv (1962); 'Florentine politics and the diffusion of heresy in the Trecento: a sociological enquiry', *Speculum*, xxxiv (1959), 60-75; G. Brucker and M. V. Becker, 'The Arti Minori in Florentine politics, 1342-1348', *Mediaeval Studies*, xviii (1956), 93-104.

the Angevin court. They were involved in these events by the subtle and accommodating Angelo Acciaiuoli, bishop of Florence, who played an important part in the overthrow (as formerly in the installation) of the Brienne *Signoria*, and who then rapidly dissociated himself from the magnate faction in favour of the revolution of the lesser guilds.

Disregarding the procedure taken by the Florentine commune to liquidate the Acciaiuoli bank and declare a composition of the assets among its creditors, Cardinal Gomez went instead to the court of the Apostolic Chamber, secured a judgment in his favour for the whole sum, and entrusted the execution of the judgment to the Inquisitor of Florence, Piero d'Aquila. This led to the passing of a harsh law (2nd April, 1345) against ecclesiastical jurisdiction which strengthened the already severe legislation.[1] The commune then impeded the Inquisitor's execution of the papal judgment. The Church promulgated an interdict against the commune (28th March, 1346) to which the commune retorted by the passage of a second stringent law against the ecclesiastical courts (4th–5th April, 1346), and the institution of fourteen 'defenders of liberty' (21st–22nd April, 1346) whose function was to defend the new legislation—a touch of guelf irony was shown in the requirement that the two lawyers among the fourteen defenders were to be 'amatores sancte romane ecclesie'. The interdict lay on the city until 28th February, 1347, when the Pope in return for concessions by the commune which by no means fully satisfied what he asked, lifted it and also took steps to replace the unpopular Inquisitor by Fra Lapo Arnolfi, whom the Florentines had asked for as a new Inquisitor throughout the negotiations. The new laws remained in force: the conflict had ended in a manner distinctly unfavourable to the Church.

No doubt the changed social emphasis of the Florentine régime after 1343 was an element in determining relations with the Church; the less established families and the members of the lesser guilds were more vulnerable to, and consequently more resentful of clerical jurisdiction than the magnates, particularly perhaps in the enforcement of the canon laws against usury. But this anticlericalism was nothing new in Florentine society, nor was it peculiar to the lesser guilds. At least equally important were the changed political conditions of

---

[1] G. Salvemini, *Studi Storici* (Florence, 1901), 69–79.

Italy after Robert of Anjou's death. The Church was immensely weakened by this, and weakened still more by the murder of Andrew of Hungary in September 1345. The Holy See was unable to prevent the complete dislocation of the royal house of Naples, with the worst results for papal policy in the papal state and in central Italy in general. In the Romagna and the March the influence of the Malatesta extended in the mid-'forties virtually untouched by papal government. In 1345 Clement VI was forced to make an important concession to Taddeo Pepoli's régime in Bologna which amounted to a partial recognition of the *Signoria*;[1] it was in this period also that the main concessions were made to the Este of Ferrara, which were decisive for the development of the institution of the 'apostolic vicariate'.

The papal legate, cardinal Bertrand de Déaulx, who was despatched to Italy in the summer of 1346 was destined for a frustrating and ineffective legation. He did not even call at Florence (still under interdict), although he spent a long time at Siena on his way south to Naples. In 1347 his whole policy collapsed, first of all under the impact of the establishment of Cola di Rienzo's revolutionary régime in Rome (with which Florence showed herself fully willing to co-operate) and then with the complete impotence of the legate and the Neapolitan government in face of the invasion of southern Italy by Louis of Hungary in the winter of 1347-8.

It is scarcely to be wondered at that knowing how weak the papal and Angevin position in Italy was, and knowing also of the negotiations for the recognition by the papal court of the Emperor Charles IV, Florence treated the Church with less than enthusiasm; one does not have to look only to the social analysis of the Florentine régime to explain this. The Tuscan league with Perugia, Siena and Arezzo which was formed by Florence in April 1347 was specifically directed against the ultramontane threat of Charles IV, against whom the papacy seemed to offer no protection.[2] Like Robert of Anjou's league of 1341, this one provided for the adhesion of ghibelline powers. These leagues, to which the Pepoli of Bologna were loosely attached, were renewed in 1349; to the Hungarian and the

---

[1] Theiner, ii, no. 145; cf. Rodolico, 141.
[2] G. degli Azzi-Vitelleschi, *Le relazioni fra la repubblica di Firenze e l'Umbria nel secolo xiv*, ii (Perugia, 1904-9), 82-3; Mommsen, *Analekten*, no. 268; Muratori, *RRIISS*, xv, pt. 1, 207-12.

Luxembourg danger was now added a new one, that of the mercenary Company of Duke Werner, which having served Louis of Hungary had now split.[1] From now onwards the danger of the mercenary companies in central Italy was to be an important factor in Florentine policy, and one which inclined her on the whole to extend and emphasize the collective security arrangements which she maintained with the other Tuscan guelfs.

The Church could not contemplate embarking on a policy of revindication of its rights in Italy so long as the civil war in the Neapolitan kingdom was going against its protegés, Queen Joanna and Louis of Taranto. Florence although frequently asked by the Neapolitan government for help had so far refused or evaded it. At last in the summer of 1349 the victory of Louis of Taranto and the truce between the royal family and Louis of Hungary seemed to promise a certain improvement in the situation in south Italy. Florentines were deeply implicated in the Neapolitan revival: the bishop of Florence, Angelo Acciaiuoli, was chancellor of the kingdom and his relative Niccolò Acciaiuoli was becoming the main political personage of Naples. But the clock could not be put back, either in Naples or in Avignon. Although with the turn of Angevin fortunes the Acciaiuoli and a small group of Florentine business men were re-establishing themselves in Naples, and although Clement VI and the Apostolic Chamber were beginning to turn back to the employment of Florentine banks for the purposes of papal finance, the scale on which Florentine business and banking was re-engaged could never be, either in Naples or Avignon, what it had been before the financial crash of the beginning of the decade. Clement VI in the later part of his pontificate was using eight or ten small Florentine companies to carry out credit operations which his predecessors had formerly been able to entrust to one or two. In spite of the Black Death there was a revival of Florentine business activity in the early 'fifties; but the pattern of Florentine trade and banking had now changed, and where formerly it was the magnates who controlled the Florentine government, the Florentines in Naples and Avignon were (with one or two exceptions) now relatively modest

---

[1] *Archivio Storico Italiano*, app. vii (1849), 367–9; cf. K. H. Schäfer, *Deutsche Ritter und Edelknechte in Italien während des 14. Jahrhunderts*, i (Paderborn, 1911), 84ff; Marzi, 654 ff.

financial operators who in Florence amounted not to the ruling clique nor even to a faction competing for power, but to fragments of factions.[1]

In the early 1350s it seems to be impossible to distinguish clearly between the Florentine parties by reference to their attitude to the papacy, or to distinguish between Florentine banking houses which pursued a persistently pro-papal or antipapal policy. The two so-called oligarch and anti-oligarch factions which dominated Florentine politics at this time both included families with important Angevin and papal interests. The Alberti and Acciaiuoli who were 'recognized as allies of the *gente nuova*'[2] were both among the main firms operating at Avignon and Naples. Perhaps it would be fair to mark off the Acciaiuoli, who had had poor treatment (which they doubtless remembered) from the papacy, and who, although the dominant Florentine firm at Naples, never again entered business at Avignon. The Alberti on the other hand became the most important of the Avignon bankers, and also retained substantial business at Naples. This connection was naturally reflected in their politics: they entertained Albornoz in their house, and earlier had in 1350 opposed the party which favoured a Florentine take-over in Bologna. But at the same time some of the leading families of the so-called oligarch party also retained important banking interests in Avignon and Naples—for example, the Baroncelli and Soderini. And it would also be false to think of the papal-Angevin banking connection as something essentially concerning only the magnate houses, to the exclusion of the *gente nuova*. For example the small banking house of Lapo di Ruspo, a rich member of the *gente nuova*, was after 1342 much employed by the papacy; he was also used as a papal moneyer. Some of his sons were accorded knightly status and were shown a favour by the popes which other Florentines must have found rather irritating, particularly when Urban V intervened with the *Signoria* on their behalf to have their tax assessments reduced.[3] Other members of the *gente nuova* who were prominent papal bankers were the Rinuccini and

---

[1] Renouard, 197 ff.; Brucker, *Florentine Politics*, 9ff., 139 ff.
[2] Brucker, 125.
[3] Florence, Archivio di Stato, Capitoli, xvi, fol. 56r. Cf. Brucker, 21n., 196n.; Renouard, 409 et *passim*; H. Hoberg, *Die Einnahmen der apostolischen Kammer unter Innocenz VI*, 314, 391. Lapo di Ruspo was Florentine ambassador at Avignon in 1359: Signori Missive della Prima Cancelleria, vol. 12, fol. 7or.

Davizzi—altogether it would seem exceedingly unsafe to equate the *gente nuova* with antipapalism.

In the spring of 1350 Clement VI's nephew Astorge de Durfort, the papal rector of Romagna, was provoked at last to reply to the seizure of Faenza by the Manfredi by military action, and perhaps tried to begin to reconstitute the papal temporal power. Probably carrying out a predetermined plan, he seized by a ruse the person of his ally Giovanni Pepoli the co-dominus of Bologna, and in alliance with Mastino della Scala commenced a campaign designed to bring the tyrants of Romagna to obedience and to restore Bologna to the direct rule of the Holy See. But it was Mastino della Scala's troops who took Pepoli; they insisted on his being allowed to ransom himself, whereupon the released prisoner promptly went to Archbishop Giovanni Visconti of Milan and 'sold' Bologna to the Visconti—a transaction judged by an intelligent and well-informed contemporary to have been the ruin of Lombardy.[1]

The sale of Bologna to the Visconti in October 1350 began, as Azario implies, a cycle of destructive wars which devastated Lombardy and Emilia for twenty years—indeed, in an extended sense, for the rest of the century. And the entry of the Visconti into the field also profoundly affected Florence. Of the double expansion which was the object of Visconti military and economic policy—into Liguria and into central Italy, the second directly menaced Florence and Tuscany.[2] Formerly Astorge de Durfort's campaign to subdue the Romagnol *Signori* and to recover Bologna had been viewed by Florence with distaste if not hostility. It may be that Florence had actively feared the construction of a strong papal state on her borders, though she knew well how far this was from being politically possible. What was more to the point was that attempts to revindicate papal

[1] Pietro Azario, who was in Bologna in 1351. 'Chronicon', Muratori, *RRIISS*, xvi, cols. 328, 525 and cf. 326. For the ransom, Schäfer, i, 146; cf. A. Sorbelli, *La signoria di Giovanni Visconti a Bologna e le sue relazioni con la Toscana* (Bologna, 1901), 9 ff. It is untrue that Clement VI entirely failed to finance Durfort's mercenaries: G. Mollat, *The Popes at Avignon* (London, 1963), 120. See Renouard, 250–7; Theiner, ii, no. 199; Schäfer, i, 86, 138–9.

[2] Cf. *Archivio Storico Italiano*, app. vii (1849), 382; Marzi, 698. Et come l'arcivescovo di Melano, venendo con sospecto a fare questa impresa, certi di suo consiglio Toscani dissono: Che pensate voi? Avuta Bologna voi avrete Pistoia etc.

sovereignty in the papal state had at once brought the papal agents into conflict with the largely guelf *Signori* (including the *Signori* of Bologna) with whom Florence had for long established a network of patronage relations. The Malatesta, Polenta and some other *Signori* of the March were material for Florentine mercenaries and *raccomandati*. For this reason the Florentines had discouraged Astorge de Durfort in his attacks on the Romagnol *Signori* and particularly on the Pepoli *Signoria* in Bologna, and offered their mediation—indeed offered to take over the rule of Bologna.[1]

But as soon as the Visconti accepted the dominion of Bologna, the attitude of Florence to the Church, which had during the preceding years been distrustful and distant, changed overnight, and fear of Visconti expansion into Tuscany completely overtook annoyance at papal policy in Romagna. Florence was— quite rightly—suspicious still of papal policy, and recalling that earlier in the year Clement VI had threatened 'more or less threateningly' to call Charles IV into Italy; similar 'threats' came from Naples.[2] In truth neither Florence nor Clement VI was really in a position to resist Giovanni Visconti, and both pursued a policy of appeasement. Nor was the Neapolitan kingdom, still traversed by war, in any stronger position; although Niccolò Acciaiuoli wrote from Naples to his Florentine friends to persuade them to send support for the civil war in the south, he could not offer the firm alliance against the Visconti which alone could serve as a base for full co-operation between Naples and Florence. The guelf block could not be satisfactorily reconstituted because its constituents were too weak. When war with the Visconti came in July 1351, Florence had to fight alone, or rather with no more aid than the Tuscan communes could give her. The passionate appeal made by Florence to Clement VI against the Visconti, 'those insatiable dogs, the persecutors of the faithful' fell on deaf ears, as did the references of the Florentines to the 'devoted Italian sons of the Church who bear the venerated name of the *parte guelfa*'. These appellations were common form, as both sides knew. From the autumn of 1351, while Florence negotiated independently

---

[1] Sorbelli, *passim*; *Archivio Storico Italiano*, app. vii (1849), docs. 26–7, pp. 369–72, misdated; Marzi, docs. 102–19, pp. 687–700; F. Baldasseroni, 'La guerra fra Firenze e Giovanni Visconti', *Studi Storici*, xi–xii (1902–3).

[2] E.-G. Léonard, *Histoire de Jeanne Ire, reine de Naples*, ii (Paris, 1932–7), 315; Marzi, 697; *Archivio Storico Italiano*, app. vii (1849), doc. 37, p. 380, misdated.

with Charles IV the papacy negotiated with the Visconti.[1]

In April 1352 the final gesture of papal appeasement was made: the archbishop of Milan was conceded Bologna as a papal vicariate. Florence and the Tuscan guelfs were not included in the peace (though they had asked to be) and all they got out of it was the declaration of a truce, which seems to have been ignored. They had to make their own terms with Milan.

The peace of Sarzana[2] which Florence and the Tuscan and papal state guelfs negotiated with the Visconti in 1353, was for Florence the most important diplomatic settlement of the period; one which was constantly referred to by Florentine statesmen in subsequent years, and which dictated the main lines of Florentine policy towards Milan until 1370, if not until the 1380s. The main effect of this peace was to stabilize political and commercial relations between Milan and the Tuscan communes by guarantees that the Visconti would not intervene in Tuscany, nor the Tuscan guelfs in Emilia or Lombardy. The principles of the peace of Sarzana have to be considered in any assessment of Florentine policy, which while it contained a certain element of 'republicanism' in relation to the ghibelline tyrannies, also perforce had to give even greater emphasis to the commercial interests of the city.[3]

Milan also had overriding commercial interests. The Milanese economy needed the débouche into the markets of central Italy which Bologna offered. But this outlet was useless unless it led into Tuscany, for whose markets the western route through Lucca was insufficient. If Tuscany could not be conquered by the Visconti (and guelf resistance combined with the refusal of Pisa to play her old part of ghibelline base in Tuscany meant that it could not), then peaceful trade relations were essential. It is significant that the treaty dealt with questions of customs duties on Florentine trade with Bologna and of the textile trade between Florence and Milan. Thus the commercial interests of

[1] See the article of Baldasseroni, and Sorbelli's book, cited above, and also Mommsen, nos. 275–9, 358–68.

[2] The best text seems that in Muratori, *RRIISS*, xv, pt. 1, 212–94.

[3] N. Rubinstein, 'Florence and the despots', *Transactions of the Royal Historical Society*, 5th ser., ii (1952), 41–2; Baldasseroni, *Studi Storici* (1903), 41–94. Sorbelli, 73–4 and Mollat, English tr., 124–5, are wrong in maintaining that the treaty was signed through papal intervention; the Church in fact took no part in the negotiations.

both states were involved, and continued to be involved even after Bologna passed out of Milanese control. With the exception of a few months in 1370, the peace of Sarzana regulated relations between Florence and Milan until 1390, when the great war between Florence and Gian Galeazzo Visconti at last broke out.

The main signatories to the treaty with the Visconti were Florence and her 'guelf' allies, Perugia, Siena, Arezzo, Pistoia. The history of this 'guelf' league goes back into the events of 1266—eventually to the Tuscan League of the turn of the twelfth century and earlier still. The fourteenth-century history of the leagues begins (if we disregard the Black guelf policy and the war with Pistoia) with the combinations against Henry VII in 1310, and then rapidly becomes part of the diplomatic history of the wars of Robert of Anjou and the papacy.[1] Although Florence frequently in the course of these leagues referred to the 'liberty' of the Tuscan communes and may have meant it, in practice her policy was little influenced by such ideological considerations. The only thing which tended to make her appear the leader of the 'free' communes, was the degree to which her policy diverged from her monarchic partners in the 'guelf' block, the Angevin kingdom and the papacy. It is well known that Villani maintained that 'the guelf party is the foundation of the liberty of Italy, the enemy of all sorts of tyranny; so that if a guelf becomes a tyrant, by necessity he becomes a ghibelline'. But this is a generalization which the facts have more than once contradicted.[2] The Malatesta did not, because they were tyrants, become ghibellines,[3] nor did Ghiberto da Correggio; nor did the Florentines break off relations with the Pepoli or Giovanni da Oleggio in Bologna, because their rule was tyrannical. Guelfism was not an 'ideology', but a set of regional alliances and factional alignments, which produced a particular state of mind. Of course the

[1] Bowsky, 'Florence and Henry of Luxemburg', *Speculum*, xxxiii, quoted above; idem, *Henry VII*, 37 ff., 80 ff., 141 ff.; Davidsohn, *Geschichte*, iii, 380 ff., 385-6, 418-19, 441-2, 517-18, 589, 605-6, 621, 627n., 663, 726; cf. P. Sambin, 'La lega guelfa in Lombardia nel biennio 1319-20', *Atti del R. Istituto Veneto, Scienze, Lett. ed Arte*, cii (1942-3), 371-85; J. Schwalm, *Mon. Germ. Hist., Const. et Acta Publica*, vi, pt. 1, nos. 539, 552-3, 555, 557 (particularly important), 569-73, 649.
[2] Jordan, *Origines de la domination angevine*, 612. Cf. the extremely careful and accurate analysis of Rubinstein, article cited in *T.R.H.S.*, 5th ser., ii (1952), 38 ff. H. Baron, 'A struggle for liberty in the Renaissance', in *American Historical Review*, lviii (1953), at pp. 270-1, is considerably less careful.
[3] Cf. Theiner, ii, no. 128.

Florentines and the Tuscan communes in general had a strong
bias in favour of the free commune as against the *Signori*; but
how far this bias actually determined policy is extremely hard
to know. What actuated these people was not a set of ideas but
the desires to pursue factional interests, and to seek satisfaction
and vengeance in factional quarrels. One doubts if the ghibellines of Arezzo, when they were 'shamefully and by candlelight'
expelled in 1341 by 'la crudele e guelfa parte', attributed any
feeling for communal liberties to their Florentine masters.[1]
Equally, Florence refused to aid Perugia in her rebellion against
the papacy in 1368, which did not suit Florentine policy, but
fomented and welcomed the rebellion of 1375, which did.[2] Still
less did Florence heed the appeal which the commune of
Bologna made to her in 1361, asking her not to risk the destruction of those areas in Italy which were coveted by the fury
of tyrants.[3]

The treaty of Sarzana is not merely an agreement between
the guelf communes and the Visconti, but a handbook to the
factions of central Italy and principally of the papal state. The
astonishingly long lists of 'sequaces, complices et adherentes'[4]
to the Visconti on one side and the guelfs on the other include
half the important families and communes of the papal state,
going as far away as Fabriano, Matelica, Fermo in the March
of Ancona. The treaty shows how inevitable it was that
Florence should always be deeply implicated in the politics of
the papal state. The factions in Gubbio and Urbino, in Todi
and in the March were all the very stuff of Florentine and
Milanese policy.

In June 1353 Cardinal Gil Albornoz was appointed papal
legate in Italy. His appointment marks a new period in papal-
Florentine relations, which may be conveniently said to last
until his death in 1367. Albornoz set in motion a fresh assault by
papal-Angevin imperialism, the most sustained and important
effort which the two powers had made to achieve hegemony in

[1] 'Cronica di Arezzo di Ser Bartolomeo di Ser Gorello', Muratori, *RRIISS*, xv, pt. 1, 42.
[2] Cf. Brucker, *Florentine Politics*, 269–70; G. Pirchan, *Italien und Kaiser Karl IV. in der Zeit seiner zweiten Romfahrt*, ii (Prague, 1930), 227*–8*. Degli Azzi, *Le relazioni*, i, xvii, comments on Florentine neutrality in 1367–9, 'fa meraviglia che i Fiorentini, così gelosi di lor libertà, tenessero in così poco conto l'altrui.'
[3] O. Vancini, *Bologna della Chiesa* (Bologna, 1906), doc. 27, 197–8.
[4] Cf. G. Soranzo, 'Collegati, raccomandati, aderenti negli stati italiani dei secoli xiv e xv', *Archivio Storico Italiano* (1941), 3–35.

Italy since the period of John XXII and Robert of Anjou. In the course of this attempt the papal legate stirred up central Italy by a series of bloody wars, which began as an attempt to impose internal order in the papal state, and ended as a great struggle with the Visconti *Signoria*. He was not entirely unsuccessful; once during the lifetime of Albornoz and again in 1373 the Visconti power was forced to its knees. But in the end the effort was too much for the decadent Angevin power and for the papacy, already subject to severe international pressure, to support. The papal successes were achieved at the price of great moral and material sacrifice. By setting all the powers of Italy at one another's throats and by spending the treasure of the Catholic Church on a reckless scale, Albornoz and his successors achieved impressive political results. But the moral cost, particularly in the resentment which heavy papal taxation for these purposes aroused, was immense; and the political victory over the Visconti was only temporary, within a very few years to be utterly lost in the chaos of the Schism and the shipwreck of the Angevin monarchy. When Niccolò Spinelli, the pupil of Albornoz and ex-chancellor of the Angevin kingdom, cast up the balance of the attempt to restore papal temporal power when he reflected on it at the end of the century, he pronounced it to have been a disastrous failure.[1]

What was the place of Florence in this new series of aggressions carried out by what purported to be the guelf powers? From start to finish her attitude to the papacy was hesitant and shifting, never that of a convinced and committed ally, seldom that of a determined opponent. In the twenty years that had passed since the end of the last great papal war Florentine interests had become too variant, too contrasting with those of the papacy and the Angevins, to be the basis of a firm alliance. The pressures of the various factions in Florentine politics swung her policy towards the papacy in various directions during this period, but there was also a genuine uncertainty about where her true interests lay. On the one hand she was bound to want to restrain the attempt which the papacy now launched to unify the papal state on the model of the north Italian *Signorie*; this attempt meant papal action against a large number of *Signori*

---

[1] G. Romano, 'N. Spinelli diplomatico del sec. xiv', *Arch. Stor. per le provincie Napoletane*, xxvi (1901), 483–96. The brilliance and fundamental importance of this article has only recently come to be recognized outside Italy.

and communes who were Florentine clients, and it also menaced Florence with the appearance of a new unified territorial block on her borders, which she felt it her duty to oppose just as she opposed the Visconti.[1] She also felt perhaps rather less bound to the papacy after the submission she made to Charles IV in 1355; she continued to fear rather than to love the empire, but the recognition of legal obligation which she had now made towards it continued to influence Florentine policy for over a century[2]. There was also the anticlericalism endemic in Florentine society high and low, which was written into the communal statutes, and which periodically produced conflict with the papacy. This anticlericalism at certain times—particularly in the period immediately preceding the outbreak of the war of the Eight Saints—had a most important effect on foreign policy.

On the other hand, other forces pushed Florence in a different direction, more favourable to papal policy. The financial interests which bound Florence to Avignon and Naples, though much weakened, were far from exhausted. Through the Alberti, certain of the Ricasoli[3] and many smaller banks, the Soderini and Acciaiuoli, Albornoz continued to exert considerable pressure on Florentine politics. As almost his first act when he first visited Florence in October 1353, Albornoz in a high-handed manner ordered the commune to cancel a sentence for murder brought against a papal protégé;[4] and in 1360 he was asked—though he refused—to sponsor a *coup d'état*. The appearance of the great free mercenary companies on the Italian scene also acted to push Florence towards the papacy, because although Albornoz as much as anyone else was responsible for encouraging and employing the companies, the Church was inevitably very important in any collective security system to defend the Tuscan communes against them. But Albornoz's mismanagement of the companies' issue in 1359 alienated Florence from him for some years, and perhaps had permanent effects.

[1] See Romano's comments in an earlier part of the same article, ibid., xxv (1900), 437–441.
[2] N. Rubinstein, 'The place of the Empire in Florentine 15th century Diplomacy', *Bulletin of the Institute of Historical Research*, xxx (1957).
[3] Albertaccio Ricasoli, e.g. often acted as a papal diplomatic agent. Cf. Filippini, *Studi Storici*, v (1896), doc. 8.
[4] F. Baldasseroni, 'Relazioni tra Firenze, la chiesa e Carlo IV 1353–55', *Archivio Storico Italiano* (1906), pp. 323–6.

Finally a certain ideological conservatism; the tendency to moralize and over-simplify political issues through the artificial and misleading terminology of 'guelf' and 'ghibelline' and the maintenance through thick and thin of the historical myth of a Florence which had always been devoted to the cause of the Roman Church and the Angevin monarchy—this also played its part. In these debates the class and factional disputes in Florence, and the financial interests of the *Parte Guelfa* and the papal bankers, were important. But here one tends to lose one-self in plot and counter-plot; a faction or a family which is pro-papal in one year may not be so in another. There were loyalties, but to faction rather than to principle.

The first few years of the papal reconquest by Albornoz showed once again how impossible it now had become to align and identify the interests of the three 'guelf' powers. For Florence from 1353 to 1355 the overwhelming problem was Charles IV, with whom first the papacy and then Florence had flirted, each in despite of the other, and who now marched into Italy in 1355 in despite of the wishes (though with the nominal consent) of both. Neither Innocent VI nor Niccolò Acciaiuoli was able or perhaps willing to assist Florence against the imperial threat. Papal resources were entirely devoted to the re-conquest of the papal state, for which Albornoz and Innocent requested—and received—some Florentine help. The Neapolitan kingdom exhausted itself in the great Sicilian expedition of 1353–4, at the end of which it had no military power left to back up the ambitious revival of the guelf block which Niccolò Acciaiuoli was proposing to the Florentines. In any case the purity of Acciaiuoli's 'guelf' motives was open to suspicion; there was also discussion of a possible league between Naples and Milan, on the suggestion that 'the king (of Naples) is the head of the guelf party and he (Visconti) head of the ghibelline party, so that if they are in alliance the whole of Italy will follow me'.[1]

Florence could not welcome the way in which Albornoz at this delicate moment insisted on stirring up the Italian hornets' nest. She was particularly hurt that he should choose to attack that unimpeachable guelf, Galeotto Malatesta, whom Florence wanted to employ to defend herself against the company of Fra Moriale. Earlier papal officials had been willing to excuse the

[1] Léonard, *Histoire de la reine Jeanne*, iii, 523 (25 September 1354).

Malatesta on the ground that though they tyrannized, it was for the guelf cause.[1] Now at the end of 1353 the Church summoned him to justice—to the displeasure not only of Florence but of the Angevin kingdom, in which he played an important part. Not surprisingly, the settlement which Malatesta agreed with Albornoz in June 1355 was negotiated mainly through Florentine mediation.[2]

The continuing friction was reflected in a renewal of the anti-clerical question. At the beginning of 1355 controversy broke out with the Church on three grounds: on the incorporation of the anticlerical laws of 1345–6 in the revision of the *statuto del capitano*, through the hanging of a priest, and through renewed attempts by the commune to tax the clergy—not remarkable, at the moment when it had to meet the financial demands of Charles IV. The bishop of Florence, Acciaiuoli, placed the city under interdict, and Innocent VI protested energetically and with some effect. The commune disclaimed the action it had taken, without cancelling the legislation. In 1357, when the commune urgently needed papal military support against the companies, the quarrel was revived, this time over the jurisdiction of the court of the Inquisitor. Renewed protest by the pope about the offending statutes this time achieved little more than hitherto, and laws against 'the Catholic faith and ecclesiastical liberty' were suspended only for a short time.[3]

In 1354 the ex-stipendiary of Albornoz, the French mercenary leader 'Fra Moriale' (Montréal du Bar) having been bought off or warned out of the territories of the Church, devastated Tuscany and exacted 25,000 florins from Florence before he

[1] Theiner, ii, no. 128, at 110, 115.
[2] Baldasseroni's article quoted above; F. Filippini, 'La riconquista dello Stato della Chiesa per opera di Egidio Albornoz', *Studi Storici*, vii (1898), 503 ff.; idem, *Il cardinale Egidio Albornoz* (Bologna, 1933), 87; *Archivio Storico Italiano*, app. vii (1849), no. 64, p. 400; Léonard, *Histoire de la reine Jeanne*, iii, 520 ff.; F. Cerasoli, 'Clemente VI e Giovanna I di Napoli', *Arch. Stor. per le prov. Napol.*, xxii (1897), docs. 36, 40, 41; G. Gerola, 'Fra Moriale in Toscana', *Archivio Storico Italiano* (1849), no. 64, p. 400; Léonard, *Histoire de la reine Jeanne*, iii, 520 ff.; F. Cerasoli, (1906), 267–70; Brucker, *Florentine Politics*, 172 ff.; Theiner, ii, nos. 270, 283, 285.
[3] Panella's article cited above, *Archivio Storico Italiano* (1913), 323–7; F. Baldasseroni, 'Una controversia tra Stato e Chiesa in Firenze nel 1355', ibid. (1912), 39–54; Brucker, *Florentine Politics*, 157–9. Cf. the bull of 9th March, 1357, Vatican Archives, Reg. Vat. 244 H, fol. 49r, displicenter audivimus, quod olim antecessores vestri civitatem florentinam regentes, quedam statuta in derogacionem officii inquisitionis pravitatis heretice, inconsultis motis condiderunt . . .

retired again to the papal state to meet his death at the hands of Cola di Rienzo.[1] This was the beginning of an intensification of the question of the companies, which after the departure of Charles IV in 1355 came to be one of the main worries of Florence. The Great Company of Conrad of Landau, the largest and most dangerous of them all, was in the service of the anti-Visconti alliance in the Bolognese *contado* in 1354, and in the kingdom of Naples in 1355. It stayed there until the summer of 1356, when the plague of locusts passed through the papal state (exacting a bribe from Albornoz) and went north to serve the imperial vicar Markward of Augsburg. In mid-June of 1357 it came south to the Romagna. On 26th–27th July it fought an indecisive battle with the army of Albornoz near Forlì, and in August the legate and Florence combined to buy it off for a large sum.[2] In the following year it returned from Lombardy once more to Romagna, and exacted in March a fresh tribute from the new legate, Androin de la Roche, and the *Signori* of Romagna.

For two years at least, when the company threatened to return to Tuscany in 1359, Florence had been closely co-operating with the Church and the guelf communes in organizing collective defence and bribery. In July 1358, while Androin de la Roche still was in command on the papal side, the Florentines saw eye to eye with the Church; they particularly liked the proposal made by the legate that the Visconti of Milan should enter a league with Florence and the Church against the companies.[3] The recall of de la Roche and the return of Albornoz to Italy as legate in the autumn changed the situation. Instead of a legate whose main interest—like that of Florence—was collective security, there was again the man with a policy of aggression and conquest, who was already beginning to see his way to defiance of the Visconti and the recovery of Bologna. When Albornoz visited Florence in November and proposed a new league, the commune looked at the proposal with considerable suspicion in case it should lead them into war with Milan. Everyone, including the 'oligarchic' Simone Peruzzi, agreed

---

[1] Gerola's article quoted above; Filippini, *Studi Storici*, v (1896), doc. 8.
[2] Schäfer, *Deutsche Ritter*, i, 88–91, ii, 49; L. Sighinolfi, *La signoria di Giovanni ad Oleggio in Bologna* (Bologna, 1905), 154 ff., 209 ff.; Villani, vii, 75–6, 85, viii, 18, with mistaken dates; Theiner, ii, nos. 327, 329; Florence, Arch. di Stato, Riformagioni e Atti Pubblici, 10th August, 1357, 29th August, 1357.
[3] Ibid., Signori Missive della Prima Cancelleria, vol. 12, fol. 38r.

that the peace of Sarzana must not be broken.[1] With regard to the legate, Florence's position was the weaker in that Siena and Perugia had quarrelled and could not be brought into the league, and that her own dispute with Pisa still went on. It was strengthened however by the close relations between Florence and Milan. The Visconti had lent troops to both Florence and the legate, and they kept in extremely close touch with the former.

When it became evident that Florence was not going to conclude an alliance for any purpose wider than that of resisting the company, Albornoz's position hardened, and his overbearing temperament led him to commit what may have been an error. By mid-February 1359 it was evident to the Florentine ambassadors at Cesena that Albornoz would probably again buy off the company, and that he was not prepared to fight it. Florence was in a most difficult situation, in that she could not fight the company without Albornoz, and therefore was in effect compelled to abide by his decision, however much she disliked it. Bernabò Visconti was offering to put up 2,000 horse if Florence and the Church would together contribute 2,000; this was a proposal rapturously welcomed by Florence, but abhorrent to the legate.[2] Albornoz claimed that the papal state was in no position to fight—an odd statement for a man who was planning one of the biggest wars of the century—and in March Florence was dragged, loudly protesting, into an agreement (which she did not ratify) to pay a vast tribute to the company.[3]

Dedicated as it was to the freedom of its commerce and to the advancement of its own hegemony in Tuscany, Florentine policy desired the fragmentation of power in Italy. Conditions between the death of Archbishop Giovanni Visconti in 1354 and the seizure of Bologna by Albornoz in 1360 on the whole were

[1] Brucker, 176–81 and further 235, where Peruzzi says the same thing in 1367. Arch. di Stato, Consulte e Pratiche, vol. 2, fol. 10v, die xxvi novembris. Simon' de Perrozis consuluit quod liga fiat cum ecclesia et domino Bononie et aliis ut retulit Philipus Magalottis pro parte ecclesie legati. Salvo semper quod non contrafiat paci cum Mediolano vigenti. Part of this, not very accurately, in Filippini, *Albornoz*, 184.
[2] Arch. di Stato, Signori Missive, vol. 12, fol. 77r.
[3] Ibid. Signori Responsive, filza 5, nos. 1, 2, 14, 17, 33, 37 bis, 38. Missive, vol. 12, fols. 71r–8r, 82r–8r. Especially fol. 85v, ibid., letter of 19th March: vogliamo che gli (Albornoz) diciate che essendo noi disposti atare la santa chiesa della quantita che per Niccolo vi facemmo dire, ci pareva e pare che da esso accordo levar si dovesse, ma stando egli pur fermo non possiamo piu, benche ci paia malpartita.

not unfavourable to Florence; she might experience crises from her inability to deal with Charles IV or the companies, but the other Italian powers were extremely divided and did not threaten her directly. The Visconti had to fight an extensive war in Lombardy to defend their hegemony after the death of the archbishop, and in the course of this, in 1355, Giovanni di Oleggio the Visconti vicar in Bologna proclaimed himself independent.

The reconquest of the papal state by Albornoz in some ways irritated Florence, but did not directly threaten her. The Angevin kingdom was not tied into papal policy as closely as either Acciaiuoli or Albornoz wanted; the factions in Naples and Provence were too powerful, particularly the faction of Robert of Durazzo which was strong in the Sacred College. There was also a powerful group in the Sacred College, which might be termed a peace party, and which wanted a policy of balance and co-existence with the Visconti. This group scored an important success in 1357 with the conclusion of an agreement with the Visconti under which the Holy See promised not to impede the Visconti from recovering Bologna.[1]

As long as papal policy towards the Visconti was uncertain and floating, it was relatively easy for Florence to continue the policy of neutrality which the peace of Sarzana dictated. As soon as the Holy See proceeded to an open break with the Visconti, the Florentine position became extremely difficult. Florence did not want a great war, because whichever side won she would be threatened by the victor. From the time of the return of Albornoz to Italy in the autumn of 1358 the legate was working to make the papal court break the promises made in the agreement of 1357, and to attack the Visconti. Florence knew this, and it was partly the knowledge that this element in Albornoz's policy was the real reason for his refusal to fight the company in 1359, that made the Florentines so angry. Already by March 1359, while the negotiations with the company were going on in Cesena, Albornoz had secretly caused Innocent VI to tolerate Giovanni di Oleggio's *de facto* position in Bologna, and to accept a *census* payment from him in token of papal

---

[1] Filippini, *Albornoz*, 153 ff.; idem, in *Studi Storici*, v (1896), docs. 46–7; G. Biscaro, 'Le relazioni dei Visconti con la Chiesa', *Archivio Storico Lombardo*, n.s., ii (1937), 127 ff., 179–80. Francesco degli Atti the cardinal-archbishop of Florence was among the negotiators of this agreement.

overlordship; the pact of 1357 with the Visconti was thus already violated.[1]

In the summer of 1359 Oleggio's position in Bologna became virtually untenable because of the fall of Pavia to the Visconti. His Lombard allies deserted him, and he had no course left but to turn to Albornoz, who assisted him, as Villani remarks 'just as the kite waits for its prey'. Albornoz may be presumed to have asked the pope for permission to take over Bologna. Innocent and the cardinals hesitated and wobbled up to the very last moment; on 1st February, 1360, the pope had three bulls drawn up: the first stating that the vicariate granted by Clement VI to the Visconti in Bologna remained in force, the second leaving action over Bologna to Albornoz's discretion, and the third instructing him to accept Bologna.[2] The peace party in the Sacred College eventually lost the day: in March Albornoz accepted Bologna from Oleggio and the great war with the Visconti began.

The war between the Visconti and the Church fairly rapidly came to involve the whole plain of Emilia. Florentine policy was, essentially, to preserve the integrity of Tuscany: although with many anxieties and hesitations she stuck for a decade to the position that if the Visconti refrained from intervention in Tuscany, she in her turn would respect the peace of Sarzana. Papal exhortations to Florence to enter the war, particularly fervent after the papal victory of San Ruffilo in 1361, were disregarded.[3] This did not mean hostility to the Church: on the contrary Florence actually congratulated Albornoz (or rather, his nephew) on the fall of Bologna in 1360, and on occasion

---

[1] Sighinolfi, 260, 409–12. Oleggio was not made papal vicar, as he says, though on 22nd January he was told to pay 6,000 florins census for Bologna, Reg. Vat. 241, pt. 1, fols. 16v–17r. On 11th June the Pope refers to a *cedula* presented by the Bolognese on Oleggio's behalf, and asks Albornoz to ascertain Oleggio's intentions. Reg. Vat. 240, pt. 1, fol. 50.

[2] Calendared by Werunsky, *Excerpta ex registris Clementis VI et Innocentii VI* (1885), nos. 511, 512, 513. Biscaro, *Archivio Storico Lombardo*, loc. cit., prints them inaccurately and with the wrong date. The text in Reg. Vat. 241. For drafts contemplating various alternative courses, Professor C. R. Cheney kindly referred me to the article of H. Tillman, 'Ueber päpstliche Schreiben mit bedingten Gültigheit im 12. und 13. Jahrhundert', *Mittheilungen des Instituts für oesterreichische Geschichtsforschung*, xlv (1931), 191–200. Villani is well-informed about these events, ix, 65, 73, hora si, hora nò si dicea, con poco honore della chiesa di Roma.

[3] Arch. di Stato, Capitoli, xvi, fols. 43r, 44r; Martène and Durand, *Thesaurus Novorum Anecdotorum*, ii (Paris, 1717), cols. 1024–5, 1035–6; Capitoli, xvi, fol. 53v, dated 20th May, 1363. Florentine replies to papal exhortations, L. Tanfani, *Nicolò Acciaiuoli* (Florence, 1863), docs. 12–14, 16.

would promise the cardinal to 'follow his advice in everything'.[1] But she remained obstinately neutral; Florentine letters both to papal agents and to Bernabò Visconti, where they touched on the war, were stamped by deliberate obscurity. Nor did Florence even try to mediate; the earlier papal-Visconti negotiations went on without her participation.[2]

The war was an embarrassment to Florence, and it left her without allies outside Tuscany in the event of an attack by the companies. But it was also an opportunity for Florentine imperialism. While the war continued it was unlikely that either the Visconti or the Church would oppose Florentine aggression against the other Tuscan towns. Florence was able to bully Pisa and eventually to go to war with her in 1362-4. Papal diplomacy worked hard to stop the Pisan war, which it viewed as an obstacle to Tuscan participation in the Visconti war, but it is doubtful if this diplomacy had much effect. Only when the expense and frustration of the war had discouraged Florence, and when the conclusion of peace between the Visconti and the Church threatened to leave the former free to intervene in Tuscany, did Florence finally make peace (August 1364).[3]

The Church lost no opportunity to place pressure on Florence. The hoary question of the debts of the Acciaiuoli bank was revived in 1360, and the commune was intermittently under interdict from 1361-2 on account of 5,000 florins said to have been deposited with it by the Church in 1316.[4] The question of ecclesiastical jurisdiction again became acute; in 1364 the commune protested vigorously to Albornoz about the cases brought by Lucio de Callio the Apostolic Collector against

[1] Signori Missive, vol. 12, fol. 138r, to Gomez Albornoz. Ibid., fol. 138v, to Cardinal Albornoz, 18th May, 1360, about reconciliation between Florence and Perugia. A vestris paternis consiliis et suasionibus debitis non intendimus declinare . . .

[2] Signori Missive, vol. 12, fols. 131v-2v (two versions), a letter to Bernabò about Bologna dated 1st April, 1360. Florentine embarrassment is acute. Tanfani's doc. 13, dated 9th July, 1360, makes it clear there was no Florentine mediation at this point.

[3] G. Mollat, 'Deux frères mineurs, Marc de Viterbe et Guillaume de' Guasconi, au service de la papauté (1363-1375)', Archivum franciscanum historicum, xlviii (1955), 52-72. Other documents in Capitoli, xvi, fols. 43v, 46rv, 47rv, 52v, 53v, 54, and cf. Lecacheux-Mollat, Lettres secrètes et curiales du pape Urbain V (1362-1370) se rapportant à la France (Paris, 1902-55), nos. 1070, 1228, 1241; Archivio Storico Italiano (1851), 81-2; Signori Missive, vol. 13, fol. 7r. The peace in Archivio Storico Italiano (1888), 145-65.

[4] Signori Missive, vol. 12, fol. 159; Riformagioni e Atti Pubblici, 13th January, 1362, bull to Andrew Bishop of Rimini; Capitoli, vol. xvi, fol. 45r, 45v; cf. Martène and Durand, ii, cols. 877-8.

Florentines for 'usury and engrossing'. At the same time the commune was having to defend itself at Avignon against accusations that it had passed new laws against ecclesiastical liberty and papal agents. There may have been no new laws against clerks, but the old ones remained on the statute books, and were being suspended only for short periods still in 1368.[1]

Urban V had succeeded to the papacy in 1362. If it is granted that the great objects of his policy were the peace of Italy and the prosecution of the crusade, it must still be added, from a Florentine point of view, that the carrying out of this theocratic policy could hardly avoid extensive papal intervention in Tuscany. Immediately the peace between Pisa and Florence was concluded, the pope pressed hard to include all the Tuscan communes into a league against the companies, which he now —somewhat belatedly—recognized as the great evil of Italy and as a threat to the papal enclave of Avignon. The negotiations for this alliance went on three years, but the original objective became overlaid by two subsequent developments— the gradual breakdown of the peace concluded with the Visconti in 1364, and the emergence and execution of the papal plan to return to Italy. It was in this period that the clashes of opinion between the Florentine factions favouring and opposed to the papacy, became more important. As long as the Visconti were at war with the Church the issues were pretty clear; neither the 'guelf' nor the 'popular' groups wanted to break the peace of Sarzana. But now that the papacy was pursuing a policy ostensibly no longer directed against the Visconti, now that Androin de la Roche the advocate of peace was again in charge of papal headquarters at Bologna, the issues became somewhat blurred.[2]

Not even the question of collaboration with the Church against the companies was a simple one. From the summer of 1364 onwards (when the Pisan war ended and the unemployed Hawkwood had to be compensated) Florence concluded a series of deals to buy off the main companies. The pope continually accused the Florentines of dragging their feet in the

<hr>

[1] Signori Missive, vol. 13, fols. 9v, 16r, 25v, and cf. the reference to the prosecution of Simone dell'Antella, ibid, fol. 44r (May 1365). For 1368, see Pirchan, *Italien und Karl IV.*, i, 232, n.

[2] Cf. Pirchan, *Italien und Karl IV.*, 5–9, 16–35. The documents published by A. Sautier, *Papst Urban V. und die Soldnerkampagnien in Italien in den Jahren 1362–1367* (Zürich, 1911) are particularly important.

negotiations, but in fact as soon as Florence decided on armed action against the companies, all the tribute money they and other communes had paid would go for nothing, and this was something which a city of merchants refused to accept. In the emphatic instructions to the Florentine envoys to the Curia in August 1365, which form a justification of Florentine policy towards the papacy during the preceding decade, the commune represented that the legates no less than the communes had bribed the companies, and that it was madness not to do so.[1] To the constant frustration of the Curia, the Florentines held fast to this argument, and when the 'great' league against the companies was finally concluded in September 1366 it was the reverse of what the pope wanted, in that it envisaged joint action only against future companies, and excluded action against the four major companies actually in existence. The treaty of 1366 was a sore disappointment to the pope; it failed to achieve any of the real aims of papal policy, and it is not surprising that by the end of 1367 it had quietly expired.[2]

It is indeed hard to blame Florentine policy for its reluctance to follow blindly in the wake of the Curia. From the spring of 1365 onwards when Charles IV visited Avignon the Tuscan communes were seriously disturbed at the prospect of a future second Italian expedition by the emperor, and very rightly refused to be reassured by the pope's insistence on Charles' good intentions.[3] The papal league against the companies was not backed up by sufficient military force even by the papal legates.[4] But what was most disturbing of all was the steady deterioration of relations between the papal camp and the Visconti. Florence from an early point represented to the pope (as she had earlier in 1358-9) that the Lombard *Signori* (i.e. the Visconti) should be brought into the league against the companies. In 1365 the Curia was willing at least to contemplate

---

[1] *Archivio Storico Italiano*, App. vii (1849), docs. 83-5.
[2] Arch. di Stato, Riformagioni e Atti pubblici, 28th December, 1367, 2nd January, 1368. Cf. Pirchan, i, 8n.
[3] *Archivio Storico Italiano* (1851), doc. xvii; ibid., App. vii (1849), doc. 87. Cf. Pirchan, i, 22.
[4] Lecacheux-Mollat, nos. 2360 (also in Theiner, ii, no. 415), 2362 (also Theiner, ii, no. 414), 2390, 2391. Last is in Reg. Vat. 244 F. fol. 133r. Quia dubitantur a pluribus dicentibus te non habere gentes armigeras pro colligatione quam in Tuscia tractari facimus ... Cf. nos. 2392-3, 2403, 2423-4 (in Theiner, ii, nos. 422-3; another text in Reg. Vat. 244 F, fol. 150).

this as a possibility; by the autumn of 1366 it was a most remote possibility.[1]

The diplomatic and material support which Florence gave to Urban V in order to facilitate the return of Pope and Curia to Italy in 1367 was fully in accordance with the main lines of Florentine policy in the past. But the commune had made plain even when it sent a 'guelf' embassy to the Curia under the verbose Lapo da Castiglionchio, that this co-operation did not mean the tame abandoning of her position over the companies.[2] The pope immediately on his return to Italy initiated a league with Naples and the *Signori* of the Po valley, which while it sought to conceal its purpose was plainly directed against the Visconti. Florence refused firmly to join—keeping up her insistence that a league formed to keep the peace of Italy must include and not exclude the Visconti. The League of Viterbo (July–August 1367), however, while it excluded Florence did include Siena and Perugia, which was an important step, most disagreeable to Florence, towards splitting the Tuscan communes.

It is not possible here to follow the intricate diplomacy of the years 1367–9, which has been fully expounded by Pirchan in his definitive book.[3] The appearance of Charles IV in Italy in the spring of 1368 upset the existing Italian balance of power—as the appearance of the emperor always did—and placed the Tuscan towns in an extremely uncomfortable position. Having decided at the turn of 1367–8, after a keen internal debate, to continue to reject the papal alliance, Florence now found herself exposed to new external pressures. She found that she could only deal with the emperor, in effect, through the mediation of the Curia. She found it also impossible to avoid accepting for the time being a measure of papal control in Tuscany unequalled since the time of Bertrand du Poujet in the second decade of the century. Having used to place pressure on Florence a means which would one day prove fatal—the temporary denial of corn exports from the papal state—the pope at the beginning of 1369 sent the able and experienced Niccolò Spinelli to Florence to

---

[1] The 1366 league left room for the other Italian powers to adhere to it. Urban V was still extremely anxious to keep the peace with Bernabò when he wrote to Albornoz on 14th March, 1366, Quare cum nostre intencionis existat quod dicta pax prout ad nos et subditos nostros pertinet efficaciter observetur, Reg. Vat. 244 F, fol. 58 (not in Lecacheux-Mollat). But by the autumn he had serious doubts about the Visconti, Pirchan, i, 18 ff.

[2] *Miscellanea di storia italiana*, xxvi (1887), 403–7.

[3] I follow Pirchan in the next paragraphs.

negotiate the Florentine settlement with Charles IV. With Spinelli, the chancellor of the Regno, went Manupello Orsini the logothete—a pretty clear indication of how completely identified Angevin and papal policy were in this period. The price exacted from Charles IV by the Curia was the acceptance of Cardinal Guy of Boulogne as imperial vicar-general in Tuscany. San Miniato, which had rebelled against Florence, was in Guy's custody, and admitted Florentine administrators only under a form of compromise. The height of paradox was now reached in that it was the extremist guelf faction in Florence which for a short time appeared to be the 'imperialist' party.

This unpromising beginning of imperial intervention in Tuscany led however to developments far from unwelcome for Florence. In April 1369 a *coup d'état* in Pisa overthrew the Raspanti régime patronized by the emperor, and had the effect of freeing Lucca from Pisa—an event watched in Florence with incredulous pleasure. Florence was then able to make an extremely profitable commercial treaty with the new régime in Pisa, and to enjoy, from the departure of Charles IV in the summer of 1369, a position in Tuscany which was in many ways improved.

Bernabò Visconti was tempted by these events in Tuscany into making a false move. The continued resistance of San Miniato to Florence, and the prompting of the deposed and exiled Doge of Pisa, his protégé Giovanni dell'Agnello, encouraged Bernabò to try once more the old game of intervention in Tuscany. Milanese support of San Miniato combined with the well-founded report that Bernabò was trying to obtain Pisa and Lucca from the emperor as an imperial vicariate, did for Florentine policy what twenty years of papal blandishment had been unable to do. In November 1369 the first of a series of leagues between Florence and the Church was signed with Urban's brother cardinal Anglic Grimoard at Bologna. The Visconti replied in the following spring by granting Giovanni dell'Agnello a substantial force to try to secure the *Signoria* of Pisa.[1]

[1] F. Landogna, 'La politica dei Visconti in Toscana', *Bollettino della Società storico Pavese di S. P.*, xxviii (1928), 80 ff., and idem in *Archivio storico Lombardo*, 1 (1928), 136–43. For the league between Florence and the papacy see J. Glénisson, 'La politique de Louis de Gonzague seigneur de Mantoue', *Bibliothèque de l'Ecole des Chartes*, cix (1951), esp. at p. 243n. The last of these leagues was on 24th October, 1371 (ibid., and cf. L. Mirot, H. Jassemin and J. Vieilliard, *Grégoire XI. Lettres secrètes et curiales* (Paris, 1936–57), no. 2390).

Thus when Florence actually went to war beside the Church it was to defend Tuscany, and although she was to some extent concerned in the fighting in the Modenese, her main effort (a not too successful one) was against Hawkwood in Tuscany. It was in any case a half-hearted war on either side, and Bernabò, Florence and the Church were all glad to make peace in November 1370.

It is impossible to summarize in a few paragraphs the detailed course of the events which led Florence into war with the papacy in 1375; the aim of the present essay is rather to suggest the historical origins of some of the causes of the conflict. On the papal side a powerful factor was certainly the accession to the papal throne in 1370 of Gregory XI, one of the most energetic and active popes of the period. The concept of a close union of the Italian policies of the papacy and the Neapolitan kingdom, which lay at the root of the policies of both John XXII and Albornoz, was fundamental also to the work of Gregory XI, who in 1372 launched one of the most determined military and political assaults against the Visconti, among the many which the popes sponsored in the course of the century. Niccolò Spinelli, the pupil of Albornoz, held an important and honoured part in this operation, and it may be argued that when Spinelli presided over the reduction of Vercelli in October 1373, he had come as near as any man came in that period to bringing the great Visconti power to its knees.

The political climate in Florence at this time was very ill-suited to appreciating or assisting a great imperialistic enterprise of this kind. The tensions within the Florentine régime, which are better known to us than ever before through Brucker's important book, were now approaching a crisis. In this atmosphere of social and economic malaise, in which the rich merchants who were closest to the papacy daily lost ground to the popular factions, the faculty to conduct a supple and accommodating diplomacy which had always belonged to Florence in the past, began to wear thin if not to disappear. 'Former restraints and controls were less effective; compromise and conciliation were no longer meaningful words in the Florentine political vocabulary'—these words which are applied by Brucker to communal politics of the time have a certain application also to foreign policy.[1] Florentine nerves, in

[1] Brucker, *Florentine Politics*, 264.

fact, were worn to the point where normal diplomacy becomes difficult.

It is hard otherwise to explain that irritants in the relations between Florence and the papacy which had shown themselves on many occasions in the past, should now assume such an overwhelming importance in Florentine minds. It is true that the activities of Cardinal Guy of Boulogne in Lucca and San Miniato had given Florence ground for some suspicion, but in fact he quit Tuscany without giving much trouble in the spring of 1370, and there was no friction between Florence and the papacy in Tuscany proper until the papal-Angevin army operating in Lunigiana on the north-west Florentine border created a minor crisis in the autumn of 1372. There was further suspicion when at the same period Gregory intervened in the dispute between Florence and the bishop of Arezzo over Castiglione Aretino, in the extremely sensitive frontier area which was to be the scene of heavy fighting a century later, at the time of the Magnificent. This was not the first time that the papacy had intervened in the area, but the move came at a time when repeated statements had to be made by the pope and his agents that the Church had no territorial ambitions in Tuscany.[1] On the other side of the Florentine Appenine border, Cardinal Pierre d'Estaing, the cardinal of Bologna, was suspected of raising trouble with the dissident Ubaldini.[2]

It is hard also to see why papal occupation of Perugia in 1371 was quite as bitterly resented as it seems to have been, nor why the admittedly tactless and overbearing papal agent there earned quite as much suspicion as he apparently did among the other Tuscan towns. After all, Perugia had from 1369–70 been an important centre of Visconti influence in Tuscany, and its subjection relieved Florence from worry on this score. But the evident intention of the Curia was to carry out a thorough re-organization of this part of the papal state, to be effected first by Cardinal Philippe de Cabassole, and then after his death in August 1372 by the abbot of Marmoutiers. Not only Florence but Siena, which had entered the papal alliance in 1367 when

[1] Theiner, ii, no. 519, and cf. Mollat, 'Relations politiques de Gregoire XI avec les Siennois et le Florentins', *Mélanges d'Archéologie et d'histoire*, lxvi (1956), 335–76, esp. 360; also Mirot-Jessemin-Vieilliard, no. 2975. For Castiglione Aretino and the dispute with the bishop of Arezzo, see *Archivio Storico Italiano*, App. vii (1849), 423; Arch. di Stato, Capitoli, xvi, fol. 57; Lecacheux-Mollat, no. 2090. This was still an issue in 1375, Theiner, ii, no. 567.

[2] Brucker, 272 ff.

Florence refused, was now subject to fanatical suspicions of papal plots.[1] What touched Florence more nearly was the expedition of the Angevin-papal force under Amedeus of Savoy to Tuscany in 1373–4, made at the request of Lucca to protect her from the companies.[2]

If the Florentines feared the resurgence of papal-Angevin power, they also had some idea of its weaknesses. In the autumn of 1373 the Curia was concerned about the possible alliance of Florence with Louis of Hungary. The papal court had on occasions in the past talked about calling in the Hungarians to Italy once more, but now that the threat of a new Hungarian claim to the throne of Naples was on the horizon, it found the idea most disagreeable.[3]

Inevitably in this period of tension the disputes about ecclesiastical jurisdiction came again to the surface. In 1372 there was a quarrel about the trial by the commune of a sergeant in the employ of the Church in Florence. In the following year the intervention of the commune in an advowson case which had been decided in a papal court, led to the commune's being placed under interdict. In 1374 Andrea Peruzzi the sub-collector of the Apostolic Chamber in Florence was reprimanded for his laxness in admitting the validity of communal legislation about the jurisdiction of the bishop and of the 'dieci di liberta'.[4]

The state of our knowledge does not yet enable us to assess accurately the course of papal-Florentine relations from 1370 to the outbreak of war in 1375; in particular it is unclear what serious diplomatic rupture, if any, had occurred in the course of 1374, that would make the pope already on 25th January, 1375, refer to military precautions taken against Florence in the Romagna and other parts of the papal state.[5] What had happened between March 1374 when it still seemed possible that Florence would aid the Church against the Visconti, and the end of the year? The formation in March of a Tuscan league which excluded the papacy may partially explain such a sharp deterioration of relations, but in itself it is insufficient.

---

[1] Mollat's article in *Mélanges* (1956), quoted above.
[2] Cf. A. Segre, 'I dispacci di Cristoforo da Piacenza', *Archivio Storico Italiano* (1909), at 47, n., Mirot-Jassemin-Vieilliard, nos. 2858–9; L. Mirot, *La politique pontificale et le retour du Saint-Siège à Rome en 1376* (Paris, 1899), 32–3; R. Archivio di Stato in Lucca. Regesti, vol. ii, pt. 2 (Lucca, 1903), 59 ff.
[3] Ibid., no. 3085.
[4] Ibid., nos. 3432, 3555; Mirot, 30–1.
[5] Theiner, ii, no. 566.

Nor was the question of papal grain supplies to Florence sufficiently acute to cause war.[1] In spite of some recent valuable contributions the immediate pre-history of this war has yet to be written.

What does seem plain is that the foreign policy of Florence towards the papacy, which had until 1370 been in its essentials consistent, appeared in the five years which followed to find it impossible to keep a balance between conciliating and respecting the papacy, and preserving against the Curia the essential interests of Florence in Tuscany. It is hard not to blame this inability to keep a political middle course on to the internal disequilibrium of the Florentine régime. It was not that the foreign policy of the 'guelfs' was irreconcilable with the policy of the popular party; as is frequent in constitutional governments the real differences of opinion about foreign policy between these parties were narrower than they appeared to the contestants. In particular there was no serious disagreement about what Florence's policy should be towards Milan, and this was the most fundamental of all the issues.

The argument that a restricted group of prosperous Florentines enjoyed special commercial advantages and special patronage from the papacy and the papal state, and was therefore the object of jealousy from the under-privileged, may be true, but it is one that holds good also for most of the preceding century. It was only the partial breakdown of the internal balance of power in Florence, which made the less favoured groups take an extreme view of these privileges, and disregard the fact that many of the economic benefits of the papal-Angevin connection extended to Florentine society as a whole.

It is difficult to conclude, then, in the present state of the evidence, whether the 1375 war was an aberration in Florentine policy due to the political decadence of the régime, or whether the war was the natural outcome of long-standing irritants and tensions, which no reasonably firm Florentine government could avoid. What may, I think, be asserted, is first that the central point in dispute was Florentine leadership and hegemony in Tuscany, and secondly that an armed conflict between Florence and the papacy had only become feasible or

---

[1] J. Glénisson, 'Une administration mediévale aux prises avec la disette. La question des blés etc.', *Le Moyen Age*, lvii (1951), and cf. L. Mirot, 'La question des blés dans la rupture entre Florence et le Saint-siège', *Mélanges*, xvi (1896).

conceivable at the end of a long period of intermittent tension, which may perhaps be said to have started with the expulsion of the duke of Athens from Florence in 1343.

Certainly the *causa causans* of the war was Florentine fear of the mercenary companies, and annoyance that the papacy instead of co-operating with her in collective defence against them, used the danger which they represented for Florence as a bargaining counter to induce the commune to obey papal wishes. In 1375 as in 1358–60, these wishes were for Tuscan help against the Visconti. It is possible to make a parallel between the negotiations of November 1358–March 1359, in which Albornoz deliberately exposed Florence to the threat of aggression by the great company, and those of June 1375, in which the papal envoys deliberately exposed her to the threat of aggression by Hawkwood. In the first case this led merely to strained relations and bad tempers; in the second it led to war.[1] Even the suspicion in June 1375 of papal implication in the 'plot' against Florence in Prato, has a very close parallel in the invitation to Albornoz to sponsor a Florentine *coup d'état* in 1360.

It is difficult to make any hard-and-fast generalization about the significance of the War of the Eight Saints in Italian politics, save that it immediately precedes a period in which most of the cards, Italian, international and clerical, were to be re-shuffled. The next wave of Visconti imperialism was to be opposed not by the papacy nor by the Angevin kingdom, but by Florence. The papacy after 1378 was made impotent in Italy by the Schism; the Angevin kingdom also was in full political decadence. So the roles were reversed, and the popes practised neutrality while the Florentines fought the Visconti. The identity of papal with Neapolitan interests was shattered for ever by the overthrow of Queen Joanna in 1381 and the decay of the Regno; when the Regno again became a great power under Ladislas of Durazzo it was in opposition to the papacy. The decay of France was a further factor; from the early fifteenth century it was Spanish and not French power which held the initiative in southern Italy. The empire was scarcely a factor in Italian politics, or no more than a tangential one. Thus all the bricks with which the historical myth of 'guelf and ghibelline' was constructed fell finally apart. They had in fact been

[1] Cf. Brucker, *Florentine Politics*, 286–91, and p. 104 above.

gradually falling apart ever since the league of Ferrara and the failure of John XXII's Italian policy in 1332, and the belief of the Florentine 'archguelfs' in the absolute identity of Florentine and papal interest had been growing steadily less credible since then. But although there was no absolute identity of interest, there continued to be a considerable correspondence of interests. By her support of the Council of Pisa in 1409 and of the Council of Florence in 1439 Florence did her best for the welfare of the Church as she understood it. And the fifteenth century also saw the growth of a new common interest—that of the stability and balance of power of Italy.

CHRONOLOGICAL TABLE

1301 November	Charles of Valois enters Florence.
1302 . .	Peace of Caltabellotta between Angevins and Frederick of Aragon (August); *Unam sanctam* published (November).
1303 . .	Boniface VIII taken at Anagni (September). Death of Boniface VIII and election of Benedict XI (October).
1304 July .	Death of Benedict XI.
1305 June .	Election of Clement V.
1305–6 . .	War of Florence against Pistoia.
1306 February	Overturn of White régime in Bologna.
1309 July .	Clement V confirms election of Henry VII.
1310 October .	Henry VII enters Italy.
1311 April .	Clement V cancels acts of Boniface VIII in *Rex gloriae*.
1312 . .	Alliance of Frederick of Sicily with Henry VII. Henry VII's battle for Rome (April–June) against Florentine-Angevin forces. Bull *Romani principes* against Henry VII (March); Henry attacks Florence (September).
1313 . .	Death of Henry VII (August), Matteo Visconti lord of Milan (September).
1314 . .	Uguccione della Faggiuola, lord of Pisa and Lucca. Double election of Frederick of Austria and Louis of Bavaria to empire (October).

1316 August	.	Election of John XXII.
1317 April	.	Bull *Si fratrum* proclaims devolution of imperial rights to papacy during vacancy of empire.
1317–23 .	.	War between Angevin and Visconti for Genoa. Renewal of Este *Signoria* in Ferrara (August '17).
1318	. .	First excommunication of the Lombard tyrants.
1320	. .	Bertrand du Poujet opens campaign against Visconti in Piedmont. War between Florence and Castruccio Castracani lord of Lucca.
1322	. .	Frederick of Austria loses b. of Mühldorf to Louis of Bavaria (September). Temporary displacement of Visconti from rule of Milan.
1323	. .	Siege of Milan by guelf army.
1325 August	.	Florentine defeat at b. of Altopascio.
1326–8 .	.	*Signoria* of Charles of Calabria in Florence.
1327 March	.	Louis of Bavaria enters Italy.
1328	. .	Coronation of Louis in Rome (January). Death of Castruccio Castracani (September).
1330	. .	Louis of Bavaria returns to Germany (January). John of Bohemia enters Italy (December).
1332 September		Guelf-ghibelline league of Ferrara against John of Bohemia.
1333 April	.	Defeat of John of Bohemia and Bertrand du Poujet by forces of league at Ferrara.
1334	. .	Rebellion of Bologna against papal rule and recall of Bertrand du Poujet. Death of John XXII and election of Benedict XII.
1336–9 .	.	War of Florence and Venice against Della Scala for possession of Lucca.
1337 August	.	Taddeo Pepoli, lord of Bologna.
1341–2 .	.	Florentine purchase of Lucca, and unsuccessful war with Pisa and Visconti for its possession. Peace between Church and Visconti.
1342 May	.	Election of Clement VI. *Signoria* of Walter of Brienne Duke of Athens in Florence.
1343	. .	Death of Robert of Anjou (January). Expulsion of Duke of Athens (July).
1345 September		Murder of Andrew of Hungary and crisis of royal house of Naples.

1347 . . Rule of Cola di Rienzo in Rome. First ravages of great company of Werner of Urslingen. Louis of Hungary's first invasion (December).

1350 . . Astorge de Durfort's campaign to re-impose papal rule in Romagna. Louis of Hungary quits Regno (September). Sale of Bologna by Pepoli to Archbishop Giovanni Visconti (October).

1351 . . War of Florence with Visconti.

1352 . . Final reconciliation of Church with Visconti and cession of Bologna by Church to the Archbishop (April). Negotiations of Florence with Charles IV. Election of Innocent VI (December).

1353 . . Peace of Sarzana between Florence, Tuscan communes and Visconti (March). Arrival of Albornoz in Italy as legate in lands of Church (September).

1353–4 . . Re-conquest of Patrimony by Albornoz. Process against Malatesta (July–December '54).

1354 October . Charles IV enters Italy. Death of Archbishop Giovanni Visconti.

1355 . . Charles IV in Tuscany (January); submission of Florence (March); coronation of emperor in Rome (April), Giovanni di Oleggio lord of Bologna. Return of emperor to Germany. Malatesta subdued by Albornoz (June).

1356 . . Revolt of Genoa and Pavia against Visconti rule. Fall of Faenza to the legate Albornoz (September).

1357 . . Conrad of Landau and great company in Lombardy. General league against Visconti and war of Modena (June). Legate and Florence buy off great company (July). Replacement of Albornoz by Androin de la Roche (August).

1358 . . Peace made by league with Visconti (June). Great company moves towards Tuscany and is defeated in Appenines (July). Albornoz in Italy for second legation in place of de la Roche (October).

1359 . . Pact of Albornoz with company (March). Capitulation of Ordelaffi of Forlì to Church (July). Fall of Pavia to Visconti.

1360	. .	Bologna transferred by Oleggio to the Church (March). Outbreak of war between Church and Visconti. Louis of Hungary intervenes for Church (September).
1361 June	.	Papal victory over Visconti at San Ruffilo. Plague in Italy.
1362	. .	League of Lombard and Romagnol *signori* with cardinal against Visconti (April). Florentine war with Pisa (June). Election of Urban V (November).
1363 November		End of second legation of Albornoz.
1364	. .	Peace between Church and Visconti (February). Peace between Florence and Pisa (August).
1365	. .	Charles IV in Avignon (May–June).
1366	. .	Urban V condemns the companies (April). Papal league against future companies (September).
1367	. .	Arrival of Urban V in Italy (May). Leagues of Viterbo against Visconti (July–August). Revolt of San Miniato against Florence (September).
1368	. .	Outbreak of hostilities between Visconti of Milan and the league (April). Arrival of Charles IV in Italy (May). His reception in Rome (October). Rebellion of Perugia against Church (autumn).
1369	. .	Florentine settlement with Charles IV. (February). Overthrow of Raspanti in Pisa (April). Charles IV leaves Italy (August). League of Florence with Church against Visconti (November).
1370	. .	Urban V returns to Avignon (September). Peace between Church, Florence and Visconti (November). Election of Gregory XI (December).
1371 summer	.	Renewal of war between Visconti and allies of Church. Return of Perugia to papal allegiance.
1372 June	.	Visconti victory at b. of Rubiera.
1373 October	.	Fall of Vercelli to papal-Angevin forces.
1375	. .	Peace of Church with Visconti. 'Plot' against Florentine rule in Prato (June). Florentine

	alliance with Visconti (July). Rebellion of Perugia and other cities in papal state (December).
1376 . .	Rebellion of Bologna. Florence under interdict (March). Arrival of Gregory XI in Italy (December).

IV

Anthony Luttrell

THE CRUSADE IN THE FOURTEENTH
CENTURY[1]

The crusade was essentially a Latin movement, and the crusaders' ideal of a holy war remained foreign to other Christians. During the crusading period the Latins, responding to social, economic and demographic forces within the West, invaded the eastern Mediterranean and established colonial bridgeheads in Syria, Greece and elsewhere. This heroic phase of a perennial conflict of East and West which had its roots deep in antiquity was no straightforward confrontation of Christendom and Islam, since the Latins, while reacting in a crude militaristic way against Muslim expansion around the Mediterranean, also attacked Orthodox Greek and other Christians. Oriental Christians, such as the Nestorians and Maronites, were tolerated by their Muslim rulers for, despite Islam's origin as a militant religion, its holy war or *jihad* demanded the enlargement of its domain rather than the forcible conversion of all unbelievers. The Muslims, ignorant of and uninterested in the Latins, saw little difference between the crusaders and their

[1] The standard work is A. Atiya, *The Crusade in the Later Middle Ages* (London, 1938) [cited as Atiya]; but see the extensive criticisms of F. Pall in *Revue historique du Sud-est européen*, xix (1942), 527–83. The pioneer works, J. Delaville le Roulx, *La France en Orient au XIVᵉ siècle*, 2 vols. (Paris, 1886) and N. Iorga, *Philippe de Mézières (1327–1405) et la croisade au XIVᵉ siècle* (Paris, 1896), remain important. S. Runciman, *A History of the Crusades*, iii (Cambridge, 1954), 427–64, covers the period as an 'epilogue'. *A History of the Crusades*, ed. K. Setton, i–ii (Philadelphia, 1955–62), is especially valuable on the Oriental background, necessarily neglected here; vol. iii should eventually constitute the standard work and bibliography for the fourteenth century. Meanwhile, H. Mayer, *Bibliographie zur Geschichte der Kreuzzüge* (Hanover, 1960) and the many recent works cited below provide further references. *The Cambridge Medieval History, iv: The Byzantine Empire*, 2nd. ed. (Cambridge, announced for 1965), appeared too late to be of use here.

other enemies, whether Christian or not.[1] Far more dangerous to Islam were the Mongols, whose defeat by the Egyptian Mamluks in 1260 was a decisive event which perhaps saved both the Muslim and Christian West from the Asiatic barbarians. Subsequently the Mongols were converted to Islam and in 1291 the Mamluks finally completed the reconquest of Syria, where the Latins had long been clinging defensively to a coastal strip originally secured during a period of Muslim disunity. Thereafter Christendom was expanding only in north-east Europe and, marginally, in Spain. In certain ways Latin Europe was entering a period of economic and spiritual stagnation. The crusade was no longer a movement of populations or of colonial conquests but a largely defensive struggle against Islam.

In the fourteenth century the Latins were beginning to identify Christendom with Europe and to distinguish Christians outside Europe as belonging to *la crestienté d'outremer*.[2] Some people, particularly readers of William of Tyre's popular crusading history which opened with Heraclius' seventh-century wars in the holy land, perhaps thought in terms of an East-West duel. Generally, however, the crusade was viewed not as a continuous struggle between civilizations or continents but as a particular event or expedition with a religious character, a *sanctum passagium*, a *negotium crucis* or an *armata christiana*. The crusader was *cruce signatus*, a *peregrinus* who fought as an *athleta Christi* and a *fidelis pugil ecclesie*; men spoke of the *recuperatio terre sancte* and Guillaume Adam wrote a *De modo sarracenos extirpandi*.

The crusading ideal reflected basic impulses to wage holy war against the infidel and to defend or conquer territory; it involved especially the recovery of the holy places in Syria. The mechanism of the crusade survived, and its symbol, the cross, retained a potential vitality. The age of children's and shepherds' crusades, disorganized collective migrations, anti-Jewish riots and other irrational symptoms of social unrest associated with crusading fanaticism was not altogether past. As late as

[1] C. Cahen, 'L'Islam et la Croisade', *Relazioni del X Congresso internazionale di scienze storiche* [cited as *Relazioni*], iii (Florence, 1955); F. Gabrieli, 'The Arabic Historiography of the Crusades', in *Historians of the Middle East*, ed. B. Lewis-P. Holt (London, 1962).
[2] D. Hay, *Europe: the Emergence of an Idea* (Edinburgh, 1957), 50-1, 56-68, 73-6, gives examples.

1344 the Latins' capture of Smyrna aroused considerable popular ferment, with reports of visions and miracles and with enthusiastic bands setting out from Italy for Jerusalem.[1] But the fall in 1291 of Acre, the last major Latin outpost in Syria, seemed a divine judgment upon the Latins. After decades of failure that mystical exultation which infused the earliest crusades with the character of a spontaneous mass movement had largely evaporated, and crusading preachers and tax-collectors met increasingly widespread disinterest and hostility. The emergence of more sophisticated forms of urban society in the West had reduced many of the pressures which had originally stimulated Latin aggression and the development of the crusading mystique. Living standards had improved and men had less reason to leave their lands, businesses and women-folk to embark on increasingly hopeless ventures; in particular, they feared the sea.[2]

The growth of the pilgrimage habit which took people peace-fully to Rome, Santiago, Canterbury and other centres, as well as to the holy places, diluted popular warlike zeal; so did pacifist notions that the conversion of infidels was preferable to their destruction. The importance of studying languages like Greek, Arabic, Hebrew and Mongolian was realized during the thirteenth century. The friars made converts in many parts of India, China, central Asia, eastern Europe, Spain and North Africa, but the results were largely disappointing and the missionary movement gradually lost strength. The last Latin archbishop of Pekin was murdered somewhere in China in 1362, and after the Ming dynasty replaced the Mongol khanate in 1368 foreign cults there were suppressed. The Dominican William of Tripoli in his *De statu sarracenorum* strongly dis-approved of the use of force and genuinely tried to understand Muslim viewpoints. The great Mallorcan philosopher Ramón Llull, who himself preached and disputed in Tunisia, en-couraged the use of the sword—even against the Christian Greeks—for the recovery of Jerusalem, but he also advocated missionary work to convert infidels 'through the way of love'. Though it was accepted that Christianity and Islam had much

[1] P. Alphandéry-A. Dupront, *La Chrétienté et l'Idée de Croisade*, ii (Paris, 1959), 258–70, *et passim*.
[2] P. Throop, *Criticism of the Crusade: a Study of Public Opinion and Crusade Propaganda* (Amsterdam, 1940); S. Runciman, 'The Decline of the Crusading Idea', *Relazioni*, iii (1955).

in common, most missionaries failed to understand Islam and made little attempt to advance arguments likely to impress anyone not already converted; many were concerned chiefly to achieve martyrdom. Thus Llull's treatise on the Trinity was being debated, peaceably but without effect, at Fez in 1344; in the following year a Franciscan provoked his own death by crying out against Islam—in French—during the sultan's Friday prayer in a Cairo mosque. The study and translation of Muslim writings commonly led to the dissemination of crude and nasty-minded anti-Muslim propaganda concentrated on such themes as Mohammed's alleged sexual immoralities and perversions, rather than to a better understanding of the foe. In reality much of this Latin writing was aimed at preventing the Christian minorities under Muslim rule from passing to Islam, while the conversion of schismatic Greek and Armenian Christians was commonly regarded as more important than their defence against the infidels.[1]

The crusading theorists, anxious to exclude a rabble of undisciplined peasantry, made their appeal to the princes who could provide the efficient fighting forces essential to military success. The holy war was part of the chivalric ideal, and it was the feudal class in society which preserved the spirit of aggression and continued to form the backbone of the great crusading expeditions. Knights like Chaucer's pilgrim or magnates such as Henry Bolingbroke still regarded the crusade, whether in Prussia, Spain or the Levant, as a normal opportunity for travel and adventure.[2] Such crusading could cover a variety of activities. For example, when Henry of Grosmont, earl of Derby, and Richard, earl of Arundel, appeared as crusaders at the siege of Algeçiras in 1344 their real purpose was to conduct diplomatic negotiations; and they were accompanied by Derby's sister with whom Arundel was having an affair.[3] Crusading enthusiasm was kept alive through the foundation of chivalric orders, as also by treatises on knighthood, chronicles

[1] In addition to Throop, see N. Daniel, *Islam and the West: the Making of an Image* (Edinburgh, 1960); R. Southern, *Western Views of Islam in the Middle Ages* (Cambridge, Mass., 1962); R. Sugranyes de Franch, 'Els projectes de creuada en la doctrina missional de Ramon Llull', *Estudios lulianos*, iv (1960).

[2] M. Bowden, *A Commentary on the General Prologue to the Canterbury Tales* (New York, 1957), 44–73; lists of crusaders in Atiya, 517–28.

[3] *The Complete Peerage*, i (London, 1910), 243; material kindly made available in K. Fowler, *Henry of Grosmont, First Duke of Lancaster, 1310–1361* (unpublished Ph.D. thesis: University of Leeds, 1961), 153–63, 588–9.

and historical romances of the kind Peter IV of Aragon recommended knights to read at table or when unable to sleep.[1] There was even a propaganda piece at a royal banquet at Paris in 1378 in which the towers of Jerusalem were defended by turbaned Saracens reciting prayers in Arabic and attacked by crusaders in moving boats who fell off scaling-ladders to provide comic relief; apparently the same properties were later used for the Fall of Troy.[2]

The essential manpower, money and enthusiasm came above all, as they always had, from the Frankish heartlands. Levantine rulers, Greek, Armenian and Latin, journeyed to Dijon, Paris and London seeking assistance; the great crusading enthusiasts, like the Gascon Pierre Thomas and his biographer the Picard Philippe de Mézières, were French-speaking, as were many of the Hospitallers who held Rhodes. In northern and western Europe, where exaggerated chivalric sentiments of courage and honour were manifested in duels and tournaments, the holy war was something more than a pious dream and could arouse genuine fervour among men who had no personal stake in the crusade. Like that of the universal church, the crusading ideal was changing and waning, yet it was still a deeply ingrained habit of thought which had real meaning in many spheres of life.[3]

Though the church by itself could achieve little, the direction of the crusading forces traditionally lay with the papacy, especially as the German emperors played little or no part. The popes conceded the indulgences and spiritual rewards, authorized the collection or appropriation of ecclesiastical revenues, appointed the leader and performed other acts canonically and juridically necessary to qualify a war as a crusade.[4] These powers allowed the pope to try to control the direction of the crusade. In 1309, for example, Clement V withheld money and crusading indulgences from a campaign in Granada because he was organizing an expedition to the Levant.[5] The fiscal and administrative machinery, the prestige

---

[1] *Tractats de Cavalleria*, ed. P. Bohigas (Barcelona, 1947), 142, *et passim*.

[2] L. Loomis, 'Secular Dramatics in the Royal Palace, Paris, 1378 . . .', *Speculum*, xxxiii (1958).

[3] J. Huizinga, *The Waning of the Middle Ages* (London, 1924), 74–94.

[4] M. Villey, 'L'idée de la Croisade chez les juristes du moyen-âge', *Relazioni*, iii (1955).

[5] V. Salavert, *Cerdeña y la Expansión mediterránea de la Corona de Aragón*, ii (Madrid, 1956), docs. 323, 332, 340, 345.

and leadership of the papacy were bound up with the holy war, but the persistent preaching of crusades against schismatics, heretics and other Christian enemies of the church, or merely to raise taxation, produced an increasingly bitter literature of criticism, much of it in the vernacular. 'His every enemy was Christian', wrote Dante condemning Boniface VIII, while a fiasco such as Bishop Dispenser's political crusade of 1383 appalled John Wyclif and many others. Following its attempt to control Italy by imposing Angevin rule at Naples, the papacy fell under French influence and from 1309 was established at Avignon. French policy was often determined by men devoid of chivalric ideals such as the chauvinistic lawyers Pierre Dubois and Guillaume de Nogaret, who conceived of the crusade as a political expression of the lay state and hoped to use it as a cover for French dynastic ambitions against the Greeks in *Romania* and as an excuse for royal taxation of the clergy. The French popes did attempt to prevent the many and various wars which attracted and absorbed the chivalric impulses, the desire for plunder and the economic resources essential for an effective crusade, but they expended much of their own wealth and energies on the struggle for control in Italy. The slow emergence of lay states and their mutual rivalries in the West militated against success, as did economic and demographic decline, recurrent plague and social conflict. In the end the crusade seemed possible only in the intervals of the Anglo-French war.

The fall of Acre in 1291 closed a stage but was scarcely a turning point. The holy war preserved the pattern, set long before, of a slow monotonous struggle interrupted by major expeditions, truces and defeats. During the thirteenth century the crusade acquired the character of a steady defensive retreat in which a dwindling band of Latin *colons* and their half-caste mercenaries, aided by the knights of the military orders from the West, sought to hold the great stone strongholds of the desert with thoroughly inadequate resources. As the Frankish nobility of *outremer* retired to Cyprus the wealth of Syria gradually passed to the Italian merchants, whose willingness to bargain with rather than fight against the infidel became an established characteristic of crusading affairs. The Latins relied on their control of the sea for essential reinforcements, but the occasional expeditions which princes or great nobles brought from Europe were often of a pilgrim rather than a crusading nature; they secured only temporary relief for the enfeebled Frankish kingdom. After 1291 the Latins withdrew to Cyprus, placing the sea between themselves and the Mamluks, and only occasionally employed their naval superiority in crusading assaults on Egypt and Syria; the Armenian Christians resisted doggedly in the mountains of Cilicia.

One chance of recovering Syria lay in the Mongols. The appearance of these nomadic hordes early in the thirteenth century enormously enlarged the known world and placed the crusade in a new and larger context, for the Mongol empire stretched from China to the Mediterranean and the Ukraine. Despite the Mongols' gradual conversion to Islam, Latin merchants and missionaries travelled along the caravan routes of central Asia and China throughout the fourteenth century, and both Christians and Mongols proposed grandiose alliances against the Mamluks. In 1307, for example, Mongol envoys at the papal curia offered over 100,000 horse for a joint campaign. The Mongols, however, were unreliable and destructive. They disrupted the course of eastern European history and it was probably fortunate for Christendom that they impinged on the Mediterranean world only for brief periods.[1]

The contemporary Tunisian politician Ibn Khaldun condemned the Bedouins of the desert as landlubbers, while in Egypt the Mamluks, cavalrymen who despised navies, lacked the naval spirit and strength to make much impact at sea. Real changes in the balance of Mediterranean power during the fourteenth century came with the emergence of a new barbarian force, the Turks, who steadily advanced overland against weakening Byzantine resistance and harassed the Latins in the Aegean. The Latins diverted crusading resources to defend the Balkans but their interventions were chiefly maritime in nature; not until 1396 did they assemble a substantial land force to oppose the Ottomans, who crushed it at Nicopolis on the Danube. Elsewhere the Muslims, having lost their predominance at sea centuries earlier, lay behind a frontier running along the Mediterranean roughly from Gibraltar to the Bosphorus.

[1] G. Soranzo, *Il papato, l'Europa cristiana e i tartari* (Milan, 1930), 352, *et passim*; cf. L. Olschki, *Marco Polo's Asia* (Cambridge, 1960).

Though the Moors and the Turks had considerable fleets, the Latins mainly controlled the sea, its islands and its trade. They could launch surprise amphibious attacks on the Muslim coasts but faced the problems of finance and shipping involved in raising and concentrating men and supplies at the end of long lines of communication. Whether directed against the Moors of Spain and the Mahgrib, towards the recovery of the holy places in Syria or to the defence of *Romania*, the crusade was staged primarily within a Mediterranean arena, even if the vital aggressive impulses behind it often stemmed from beyond its peripheries, from the continental hinterlands of the Franks and Turks. The Latins had little choice but to attack across the Mediterranean; yet their assaults on its southern coastline failed and even in the Aegean, where they had colonial and commercial positions to sustain, they had only very limited success. Fundamentally this was the result of growing contradictions between the enthusiasms and aims of the northern crusaders and the interests of the maritime powers on which they depended for transportation and supplies. Because the Mediterranean Latins were reluctant to launch attacks on their Muslim neighbours for ideological reasons alone, and were apt to obstruct the crusade or to abuse it as a cloak for their own commercial or dynastic ambitions, the crusaders could never fully exploit Latin naval superiority. In the resulting stalemate significant gains were only made overland, by the Christians in Spain, by the Muslims in Armenia, Anatolia and the Balkans.

The Mediterranean world, though vast in terms of the weeks needed to traverse it, possessed certain unities. By the fourteenth century the development of the compass and other aids to navigation had made even winter sea-voyages much easier. The Mediterranean joined rather than divided the peoples of its islands and ports, its coastal plains and mountain slopes, who shared the heritage of Rome and whose culture was urban rather than nomadic. The encyclopaedic scholar-statesman Ibn Khaldun, with his subtle geohistorical and sociological insights, understood much of this. He knew regions like Egypt and Spain where there were important religious minorities, and he realized that economic, social and other common factors tended to outweigh religious divergences. Following the great commercial revolution of previous centuries the Mediterranean constituted an economic unit. Its trade was controlled by the

Latins who carried cloth, timber and metals to Muslim ports such as Tunis, Alexandria or Caffa in the Crimea, and returned with precious Oriental stuffs and spices. Grain was shipped enormous distances and an extensive interior commerce in such commodities as wines, fish and honey continued to flourish despite economic fluctuations and major crises like the Black Death. The great merchant powers, Genoa and Venice, the smaller maritime republics like Pisa and Dubrovnik, and such powerful trading towns as Naples, Barcelona and Palermo, customarily opposed breaking the truces with the Muslims from which they profited so highly, though, when their shipping was attacked or their lucrative Black Sea trade endangered, Genoa and Venice prepared reluctantly to fight.[1]

Since most of the Asian and all the African caravan routes towards Europe terminated in Muslim ports, schemes for economic warfare, involving a police-force of galleys, trade with Asia through Christian Cilicia, and the production of commodities such as cotton in Christian lands, were generally accepted as desirable. In practice, however, papal prohibitions against trading with the infidels in iron, wood and other raw materials they badly needed, and in slaves—Tartars, Bulgars, Turks and Greeks who often became Mamluk soldiers—proved largely ineffective and were gradually relaxed. When the Hospitallers attempted to interfere with the Genoese slavers in 1311 the Genoese, who specialized in the Egyptian slave trade, actually bribed the Turks to attack Rhodes.[2] A blockade which could only be enforced by those who stood to lose by it had little chance of success.

The crusaders realized that the key to their fundamental objective in Syria lay in Egypt, which they twice invaded, unsuccessfully, during the thirteenth century. The Mamluks constituted an alien ruling class, a military oligarchy of slave origins which controlled an efficient army and an excellent bureaucracy and could tax the wealth of the corn-producing

---

[1] Ibn Khaldûn, *The Muqaddimah: an Introduction to History*, trans. F. Rosenthal, 3 vols. (London, 1958). Cf. F. Braudel, *La Méditerranée et le monde méditerranéen à l'époque de Philippe II* (Paris, 1949); M. Mollat *et al.*, 'L'économie européenne aux deux derniers siècles du moyen-âge', *Relazioni*, iii (1955); J. Heers, *L'Occident aux XIVᵉ et XVᵉ siècles: aspects économiques et sociaux* (Paris, 1963).

[2] J. Delaville le Roulx, *Les Hospitaliers à Rhodes jusqu'à la mort de Philibert de Naillac, 1310–1421* (Paris, 1913), 10–11.

Nile valley and the luxury trade from India through the Red Sea to the Mediterranean. After inflicting their first great defeat on the Mongols in 1260, the Mamluks made their state the focus of orthodox Muslim religion and culture, for the Mongols had destroyed the religious pre-eminence of Baghdad. The aggressive Sultan Baybars and his successors attacked both the Il-khanid Mongols whose power was centred in Persia, and their Latin and Armenian allies. The Mamluks sought support from Byzantium, the Seljuks of Rum in Anatolia, the Mongols of the Golden Horde on the Volga, and certain Latin rulers such as Manfred of Sicily. They extended their power to the Sudan, expelled the Latins from Syria and ravaged Armenian Cilicia, but an attack on Cyprus in 1271 failed. The Latins' chances of success were slight, and the twenty-five galleys sent from Cyprus to assault Alexandria in 1292 only provoked the Sultan Al-Ashraf Khalil—shouting 'Cyprus, Cyprus, Cyprus'— to order a hundred galleys to be built for a counter-attack. Renewed Mongol attacks in Syria in the following decades impeded those plans but the Latins neglected various opportunities of co-operating with the Mongols, who were reported to be willing to grant them Jerusalem.[1] The Latins still dreamed of reconquering Syria themselves. They had faced the strategic problems involved long before 1291. Considerations as to numbers of men and ships, advice about the climate and the local inhabitants, the arguments for a blockade of Egypt, and the idea of uniting the military orders were all advanced in manuals which were originally commissioned at the Council of Lyons in 1274 from such experts in Eastern affairs as the Dominican William of Tripoli and the Franciscan Fidenzio of Padua. After 1291 the masters of the military orders, the king of Naples, an Armenian prince, the Venetian Marino Sanudo, and others drew up reports.[2] These were essentially variations on the earlier proposals and they provided information to a wide public; the papal library alone contained over twenty manuals of this sort in about 1375.[3]

Despite this theorizing, it fell chiefly to the feeble Latin

---

[1] G. Hill, *A History of Cyprus*, ii (Cambridge, 1948), 167, 204–5, *et passim*.

[2] In addition to Throop and Atiya, see J. Verbruggen, *De Krijgskunst in West-Europa in de Middeleeuwen: IXᵉ tot begin XIVᵉ eeuw* (Brussels, 1954), 465–88 (French summary: 575–7).

[3] G. Golubovich, *Biblioteca bio-bibliografica della Terra Santa e dell' Oriente francescano*, i (Quaracchi, 1906), 410–12.

powers in the East to assist the Armenians in Cilicia, where the Mamluks steadily advanced overland in a protracted war of ambushes, sieges and truces. In Cyprus the Lusignan kings and their nobility retained both their titular claims in the kingdom of Jerusalem and the old weaknesses of the Latins of *outremer*; closely inter-married, given over to feuds and frivolous luxuries, they had become partly Oriental and preferred trade and intrigue to warfare which might bring complete disaster.[1]

In 1291 the military orders retreated to Cyprus with their numbers sadly reduced and their prestige low. In 1309 the Teutonic Knights, who had contracted out of the Mediterranean struggle, established their headquarters at Marienburg, utilizing in crusades against the pagan Lithuanians and in their colonization of Prussia the experience and techniques acquired in Syria.[2] The Templars, after the protracted *affaire* in which the gravest and not altogether unjustified suspicions were cast on their morality and crusading enthusiasm, were suppressed in 1312 and their lands transferred to the more active Hospitallers. Between 1300 and 1304 Guillaume de Villaret, master of the Hospital, twice took aid to the Armenians.[3] But neither Cilicia nor Cyprus offered a satisfactory base and from 1306 to 1310 the Hospitallers were conquering Rhodes from the Greeks, assisted in 1309 by a meagre force assembled by Pope Clement V for a crusade. The Hospitallers fortified Rhodes and organized themselves there as an independent state, while they incorporated the Templars' possessions into the European estates from which they drew their incomes. Clement V tried to involve them in a 'crusade' against the Catalans at Athens. The Hospitallers sought instead to implicate Catalan and Aragonese strength in the Levant by fostering Jaume II of Aragon's marriage to Marie de Lusignan in 1315; the Cypriot princess, however, died childless and the project foundered.[4] Catalunya-Aragon lacked the resources to sustain effective military action in the East, but the Aragonese crown advanced Catalan commercial interests in Syria, Egypt and Tunis by diplomatic means, and sought prestige through special agreements negotiated in Cairo for the release of Christian prisoners,

---

[1] Cf. S. Runciman, *The Families of Outremer* (London, 1960).
[2] F. Carsten, *The Origins of Prussia* (Oxford, 1954), 5–9, 52–72, *et passim*.
[3] H. Finke, *Acta Aragonensia*, iii (Berlin, 1922), 146.
[4] A. Luttrell, 'The Aragonese Crown and the Knights Hospitallers of Rhodes: 1291–1350', *English Historical Review*, lxxvi (1961).

for pilgrims to visit Syria and for Aragonese protection of the holy places.[1]

The dispute among the experts as to whether an overland advance from Cilicia into Syria was preferable to an amphibious assault on Egypt was largely academic, for the essential Western aid, the money, fleets and armies, the unity of purpose, the gifted leadership and careful preparations called for by the theorists were not forthcoming. Edward I's French and Scottish wars, for example, resulted in shipping vital to the crusade being transferred from the Mediterranean to the Channel. In crusading affairs the papacy was traditionally tied to France, and the French crown tried to exploit both the vulnerable situation of the Avignonese popes and the genuine crusading enthusiasm of a small group of French nobles so as to secure the maximum financial advantage for the minimum of crusading activity. Clement V granted huge sums, but the next pope, John XXII, who himself subordinated the holy war to his German and Italian quarrels and ambitions, proved reluctant to concede further tenths. A small Franco-papal fleet was made ready to blockade Egypt, only to be handed over to the king of Naples and destroyed by the Genoese in 1320. In general the pope and cardinals opposed expenditures on small and insufficiently prepared campaigns which, even if initially successful, could never achieve lasting results in Egypt or Syria. They favoured sending military and financial aid to Cilicia, where the Mamluks captured Laiazzo in 1322, but in 1323 the Armenians themselves advised against a minor expedition which would only provoke renewed Mamluk attacks.[2]

In 1331 Philip VI of France promised a crusade for 1334 and John XXII finally granted the tenths. Philip took the cross in 1333 as a diplomatic expedient and four French galleys did join the Christian fleet which defeated the Turks on the Aegean in 1334, but the crusade proper was postponed. By September 1335 John XXII's successor Benedict XII and his cardinals realized that the king's objectives were primarily financial, and when they probed his delegates as to Philip's real intentions the marshal of France lost his temper and replied with *verba*

[1] F. Giunta, *Aragonesi e Catalani nel Mediterraneo*, ii (Palermo, 1959), 7–18, *et passim*; P. Vilar, *La Catalogne dans l'Espagne moderne*, i (Paris, 1962), 366–499, *et passim*.
[2] G. Tabacco, *La casa di Francia nell'azione politica di Papa Giovanni XXII* (Rome, 1953), *passim*.

inordinata et indecencia. Meanwhile Armenian appeals for help in 1335 met no effective response and in January 1336, when the preaching of the crusade in Cyprus was reported to be dangerously provocative, Benedict ordered its suspension until an expedition was ready in the West. Philip had prepared men and ships in Languedoc but they were destined for the English war, and in March 1336 Benedict postponed the crusade indefinitely on the grounds that Anglo-French and other hostilities were imminent and that he feared the consequences of an unsuccessful crusade. Soon after, Philip moved his fleet to the Channel and, though Benedict refused to grant tenths to finance the Anglo-French war, Philip spent on it the crusading monies already raised and tried to get more.[1] Benedict's moves were largely forced upon him, but papal insistence on unity and peace as an essential prerequisite to a crusade tended to become an excuse for permanent, and apparently miserly, inactivity. When Benedict refused in 1336 to help finance an expedition which the Venetians and Hospitallers proposed to organize, crusading activity ceased almost totally.[2] Furthermore, he allowed the Hospitallers' incomes, which should have been devoted to crusading purposes, to be used instead to build up an enormous credit with the pope's own hard-pressed Florentine bankers.[3] Benedict's treasure was expended by his successor Clement VI, who demonstrated what papal enthusiasm could accomplish when the campaign he initiated captured Smyrna from the Turks in 1344.

The Armenian Christians suffered from Mongol and Turkish as well as Mamluk attacks. They were hampered by their strife with the rulers of Cyprus and by endless doctrinal disputes with the Roman church. The Hospitallers and others provided some assistance, and John XXII sent money through the Bardi, his Florentine bankers. Yet, of 30,000 florins he promised in 1324, less than 17,000 florins reached Cyprus; some 2,600 of these

---

[1] G. Daumet, 'Benoît XII et la croisade', in his *Benoît XII (1334–1342): lettres closes, patentes et curiales se rapportant à la France,* introduction (Paris, 1920), xliv–lix; Hill, ii, 299, n. 1. There is much disagreement about these problems; J. Viard, 'Les projets de croisade de Philippe VI de Valois', *Bibliothèque de l'Ecole des Chartres,* xcvii (1936), seems unsatisfactory, cf. E. Lunt, *Financial Relations of the Papacy with England: 1337–1534* (Cambridge, Mass., 1962), 88–94, 525–31.

[2] A. Luttrell, 'Venice and the Knights Hospitallers of Rhodes in the Fourteenth Century', *Papers of the British School at Rome,* xxvi (1958), 203.

[3] A. Luttrell, 'Interessi fiorentini nell'economia e nella politica dei Cavalieri Ospedalieri di Rodi nel Trecento', *Annali della Scuola Normale Superiore di Pisa: lettere, storia e filosofia,* ser. II, xxviii (1959), 317–20.

were expended on arms, provisions and ship-building in Cyprus, and the Armenians actually received less than 11,000 florins.[1] In 1335 the pilgrim Jacopo da Verona, reporting atrocity stories heard from Armenian refugees he met in Cyprus, denounced the rich Cypriots who prospered from their trade in Cilicia and Syria, careless of the fate of the Armenian Christians and the holy places.[2] Soon after, Clement VI, faced with the Anglo-French war, abandoned the papacy's traditional reliance on the French as the major instrument of the crusade. Instead he utilized Italian strength, and Italian interests diverted crusading activity away from Cilicia towards Smyrna and the Aegean. Hospitaller and Cypriot forces brought temporary relief to the Armenians in 1347, but after 1351 they received little help until Pierre I de Lusignan, king of Cyprus, garrisoned the Cilician port of Gorighos in 1359 and captured Adalia from the Turkish emir of Tekke in 1361.

The crusade against the Mamluks had deteriorated into sporadic piracy when Pierre I, convinced of his divine mission to recover his ancestors' kingdom of Jerusalem, organized the only major crusading expedition of the period generated by a Levantine power and dominated by a leader of real prestige. Between 1362 and 1365 Pierre, accompanied by his chancellor Philippe de Mézières and the papal legate Pierre Thomas, made an extensive tour of Europe where their essentially Frankish, chivalric fanaticism succeeded in raising money, ships and men and in turning the Latins' resources away from the defence of the Aegean back towards an old-style crusade. In September 1365 some 165 ships assembled at Rhodes, and the Turkish emirs from the nearby coasts hastened to offer tribute. The objective, a well-kept secret, was the immensely wealthy port of Alexandria which, as expected, was inadequately defended. A landing was effected after some hard fighting and, though some of the barons were reluctant to assault the city, a few crusaders got into the town through a water conduit; others soon scaled the walls, the gates were opened, and there was little further resistance. Colossal pillage and massacre followed. The king, the legate and the chancellor wanted to hold Alexandria, probably hoping to blockade Egypt and thus

[1] Hill, ii, 275-8, et passim; J. Richard, Chypre sous les Lusignans: Documents chypriotes des Archives du Vatican (XIVe et XVe siècles) (Paris, 1962), 36-49.
[2] Liber peregrinationis di Jacopo da Verona, ed. U. Monneret de Villard (Rome, 1950), 17-18.

drastically reduce the sultan's revenues. But the crusaders were dangerously short of men and horses. The majority, including the king's two brothers and the admiral of the Hospital, were half-hearted and anxious to secure their enormous plunder and, as the Egyptian army approached, they forced Pierre to sail away. Hopes of further success were deliberately ruined during 1366 by the Venetians who deterred prospective reinforcements, which included Amedeo of Savoy and Bertrand du Guesclin, by falsely announcing the conclusion of peace; they also negotiated with the Mamluks in order to safeguard their own Egyptian commerce. The crusade lost all impetus. In 1367 Pierre I sacked Tripoli and other places in Syria, but after his assassination in 1369 peace with the Mamluks was concluded in 1370.[1]

In Cilicia the situation remained desperate. Pierre I's death left the Christians without effective leadership; in 1373 the Genoese secured control of Famagusta in Cyprus; and in 1375 the Armenian kingdom collapsed and King Leo VI was incarcerated in Cairo. In Egypt the Mamluks took revenge upon their Christian subjects, taxing them heavily to pay for the crusaders' unrestrained vandalism. The Copts, who were often rich merchants or bureaucrats and had long been accused of aiding the Latins and committing outrages such as destroying mosques with naptha, suffered particularly. The Christians' morale fell, and many went over to Islam.[2]

There was never another grand assault on Egypt or Syria. The truce suited the Mamluks who faced political problems, drought, plague and economic decline in Egypt.[3] They profited greatly from the organized groups of pilgrims who flocked guidebook in hand to Jerusalem and Cairo[4] and from taxation of the Latin merchants who flourished at Beirut and Alexandria. Latin piracy and the more carefully regulated *guerra di corsa*, an economic activity with its own rules,[5] were directed against Christians as well as Muslims, and for long provoked the Mamluks to little more than the frequent seizure of Christian

[1] Atiya, 301–78; Hill, ii, 299–416; J. Gay, *Le pape Clément VI et les affaires d'Orient, 1342–1352* (Paris, 1904), 20, 133–50; J. Smet, *The Life of Saint Peter Thomas by Philippe de Mézières* (Rome, 1954), 96–141.

[2] M. Perlmann, 'Notes on anti-Christian Propaganda in the Mamluk Empire', *Bulletin of the School of Oriental and African Studies*, x (1940–2).

[3] D. Ayalon, *Gunpowder and Firearms in the Mamluk Kingdom* (London, 1956), 103–6, *et passim*.

[4] H. Prescott, *Jerusalem Journey* (London, 1954).

[5] Mollat *et al.*, in *Relazioni*, iii (1955), 760–1.

merchants and their goods. In 1403 the Genoese under the French marshal Boucicault pillaged a number of ports on the Cilician and Syrian coasts, but their scheme to attack Alexandria was betrayed by the Venetians and foiled by adverse winds; the campaign ended in a major sea battle with the Venetians off Modon.[1] Emmanuele Piloti, a Cretan merchant long resident in Egypt, judged that Boucicault could have surprised and captured Alexandria. He also stated that the Mamluks were seriously short of wood for ship-building, and that the Hospitallers stopped their Rhodian subjects carrying Dalmatian and Cilician timber to Egypt;[2] yet in 1366, even before they had completed their conquests in Cilicia with its rich forests, the Egyptians were able to procure enough wood from Syria to build well over 100 ships.[3] By 1426 their fleet was strong enough to reduce Cyprus and its king to tributary status, and Mamluk progress was only halted by the successful defence of Rhodes in 1444.

At the western end of the Mediterranean the *reconquista*, both a colonizing movement and a holy war, traditionally absorbed Spanish crusading vigour and enthusiasm. Ramón Llull, Philippe de Mézières and others considered it part of the crusade: the Christians would advance by way of Granada and Africa to the holy places.[4] After the great conquests of the thirteenth century there was a pause in the *reconquista*. The Moors rallied in their mountain kingdom of Granada. The Christians fought each other and settled the extensive lands already won in Valencia and Andalucia, a process sometimes involving bitter strife with the conquered population, for anti-Muslim attitudes and prejudices could be hard to unlearn.[5] Catalan mercantile interests, especially those of Barcelona, were concentrated on the continuous struggle to control Mallorca, Sardinia and Sicily, and thus to secure the routes to their Levantine and African markets. The Aragonese crown engaged only intermittently in border warfare with the Moors on the Valencian frontier, representing it as a crusade in order to

[1] Delaville, *La France en Orient*, i, 436–46.
[2] *Traité d'Emmanuel Piloti sur le passage en Terre Sainte (1420)*, ed. P.-H. Dopp (Louvain-Paris, 1958), 156–7, 201, *et passim*.
[3] Atiya, 372, 375, n. 1.
[4] Ibid., pp. 80–1, 147.
[5] R. Burns, 'Social Riots on the Christian-Moslem Frontier (Thirteenth-Century Valencia)', *American Historical Review*, lxvi (1961).

persuade reluctant popes to grant ecclesiastical revenues. When Alfonso IV of Aragon genuinely tried to launch a crusade in Granada between 1328 and 1331, the jealous Castilians obstructed him. Castile, the dominant partner, profited from the combined operations in the campaign which ended in Castile acquiring Algeçiras in 1344. The Moorish fleet, mainly supplied by the African states, won a great battle against the Castilians in 1340, and only Genoese assistance later enabled the Castilian, Portuguese and Catalan galleys to cut off reinforcements for Algeçiras by blockading the Straits of Gibraltar.[1] Thereafter the crusading element was seldom dominant in Spanish affairs, and both Castilians and Aragonese allied with the Moors; in 1386 even the duke of Lancaster was accused of plotting to partition Castile with Mohammed V of Granada.[2]

In North Africa Catalan, Genoese and other trading interests dictated a largely peaceful approach, exemplified in a curious and lasting Sicilian-Tunisian feudal condominium over the island of Pantelleria. Piratical Christian attacks, such as the Genoese sacking of Tripoli in 1355, the combined Pisan, Genoese and Sicilian occupation of the island of Gerba in 1388, and the Valencian and Mallorcan expedition of 1399 to Bona, were matched by well-organized Muslim razzias on Malta, Sicily and places farther afield; a truce, an exchange of prisoners and the resumption of commerce normally followed fairly quickly on such incidents.[3] Though the Latins usually defeated them at sea, the Berbers had a considerable navy and in 1377, for example, the pope was alarmed by their attacks around Narbonne and by the presence of a dozen Berber galleys off Gaeta.[4] In 1390 the Genoese, anxious to crush these corsairs, enlisted the crusading enthusiasm of a body of French and some English knights under the duke of Bourbon and

[1] See F. Soldevila, *Història de Catalunya*, i (revised: Barcelona, 1962); J. Robson, 'The Catalan Fleet and Moorish Sea-power, 1337–1344', *English Historical Review*, lxxiv (1959).

[2] P. Russell, *English Intervention in Spain and Portugal in the time of Edward III and Richard II* (Oxford, 1955), 33, n. 1, 36, 444. On the crusade and *reconquista* in Spain see also J. Goñi Gaztambide, *Historia de la bula de la Cruzada en España* (Vitoria, 1958).

[3] R. Brunschvig, *La Berbérie orientale sous les Hafsides: des origines à la fin du XVe siècle*, 2 vols., (Paris, 1940–7) i, 110–225; F. Giunta, 'Sicilia e Tunisi nei secoli XIV e XV', in his *Medioevo mediterraneo: saggi storici* (Palermo, 1954), 151–66.

[4] *Lettres secrètes et curiales du Pape Grégoire XI (1370–1378)*, fasc. iii, ed. L. Mirot et al. (Paris, 1942), no. 2053; cf. Brunschvig, i, 195–7.

transported them to attack the Tunisian port of Mahdiya. But the crusaders were short of horses and when they proved unable to capture the town or to deal with the skirmishing and guerrilla tactics of the armies of Tunis and Bugia, the Genoese merely extorted from the Berbers a truce favourable to themselves and another old-style crusade had failed.[1] Yet Latin Christendom was ready to penetrate with vigour into areas beyond the shores of the familiar Mediterranean world. There were contacts with the Christians of Ethiopia and even suggestions that the Latins should maintain a fleet in the Red Sea or Persian Gulf to cut off Egyptian trade with India. Men knew that caravans crossed the African desert to Timbuctu to bring back gold and slaves from the Niger, and Mansa Musa's empire of Mali appeared on a Mallorcan *mappamundi* as early as 1339.[2] Genuine crusading sentiments, as well as gold and slaves, motivated Portuguese expansion along the African coastline which began with the capture of Ceuta in 1415 and ultimately led to a new Christian confrontation with Islam in the Indian Ocean.

The most important aspect of the fourteenth-century crusade was not the recovery of the holy places but the defence of *Romania*, the Greek empire dismembered by the crusaders in 1204 and restored in an enfeebled form in 1261. The Latin idea of an aggressive holy war was altogether alien to the Greeks,[3] but as Byzantine power declined they became seriously dependent on Latin support, especially from the Genoese. The Mongol invasions and the consequent breakup of the Seljuk empire of Rum produced an unsettled situation in Anatolia, where late in the thirteenth century a number of semi-nomadic Turkish emirates began to emerge. To some extent their success depended on enthusiasm for the holy war, and especially on the *ghazi* warriors. 'A *ghazi*', wrote the Turkish poet Ahmedi towards 1410, 'is the instrument of the religion of Allah, a servant of God who purifies the earth from the filth of polytheism; the *ghazi* is the sword of God, he is the protector and the refuge of the believers. If he becomes a martyr in the ways of God, do not believe that he has died; he lives in beatitude with Allah, he has eternal life.' The Muslims regarded the

[1] Atiya, 398–434.
[2] Ibid., 63, 65, 121, 277; R. Mauny, *Tableau géographique de l'Ouest africain au moyen âge* (Dakar, 1961).
[3] P. Lemerle, 'Byzance et la Croisade', *Relazioni*, iii (1955).

Christian Trinity as polytheistic. However, it was mainly for loot and pay that the Turks, and many Greeks as well, followed the opportunist Anatolian emirs who fought both for and against the Christians, often as mercenaries. The emirs, who needed lands and booty for their followers, finally dominated the whole of western Anatolia including Bithynia, the province facing Constantinople.[1]

Latins and Greeks distrusted one another profoundly. In 1282 Michael VIII Palaeologus and the Sicilian Vespers upset Charles of Anjou's schemes for conquest in Byzantium,[2] but in 1301 Charles de Valois, brother of Philip IV of France, married Catherine de Courtenay, heiress of the titular Latin emperors of Constantinople, and revived the traditional plans for a dynastic crusade in *Romania*, justified by Greek treachery and schism and as a necessary prelude to the recovery of Jerusalem. The Greeks of Asia Minor were so hard pressed by the Turks that in 1308 some were even prepared to submit to Charles de Valois but, even with papal and Venetian support, he could never gather the requisite force. The Angevin rulers of Naples and Taranto had claims and ambitions in Epirus and Albania. Effective power in the Morea was divided between the representatives of the Angevin princes of Taranto and Achaea, who normally resided in Italy, and the intensely chivalric feudal barons in their great castles. In 1311, however, the tough Catalan mercenaries, who in 1303 had fought the Turks in Anatolia with notable success but were later betrayed by their Greek employers, slaughtered large numbers of the Frankish nobility of Achaea at Cephissus near Thebes; they then set up an independent régime around Thebes and Athens and, while the Valois and others schemed to use them as crusaders, the popes complicated attempts to resist the Turks by excommunicating the Catalans and encouraging attacks upon them.[3]

Wars, Turkish raids and the slave trade progressively reduced the population and prosperity of Greece and the Aegean islands,

---

[1] These subjects are controversial: P. Wittek, *The Rise of the Ottoman Empire* (London, 1938); G. Georgiades Arnakis, *The Early Osmanlis ... 1282–1337* (Athens, 1947) [in Greek with English summary]; G. Ostrogorsky, *History of the Byzantine State* (Oxford, 1956); P. Lemerle, *L'émirat d'Aydin, Byzance et l'Occident* (Paris, 1957).

[2] D. Geanakoplos, *Emperor Michael Palaeologus and the West, 1258–1282* (Cambridge, Mass., 1959).

[3] R. Burns, 'The Catalan Company and the European Powers, 1305–1311', *Speculum*, xxix (1954); K. Setton, *Catalan Domination of Athens, 1311–1388* (Cambridge, Mass., 1948).

yet their fertile lands and pleasant climate continued to attract astute traders and landless cadets. As in Syria and Cyprus a mercantile Mediterranean element replaced the Frankish aristocracy. Italians in particular came as Angevin officials, as ecclesiastical benefice-holders and as adventurers hoping to secure estates and rents through purchase, marriage, princely favour or conquest. The Morea, like the rest of *Romania*, was an under-developed area suitable for colonial exploitation; it exported grain, wines, honey and other primary products, and absorbed Western manufactures, chiefly cloth.[1] The Latin colonists were prepared to defend their domains but, hopelessly divided among themselves and often under attack from the Byzantine enclave around Mistra in the south-east Morea, they lacked the strength to combat the Turkish razzias effectively. The Venetians profited from their carefully regulated trade in the Morea and in their own colonial territories throughout *Romania*, but were always reluctant to assume expensive military and administrative responsibilities. They occupied only the strategic ports of call at Coron and Modon in the southern Morea and islands such as Crete and Negroponte (Euboea) which protected the shipping lanes to Trebizond and the Crimea, great markets both for the products and slaves of the Black Sea area and, especially after the fall of Acre in 1291, for luxury silks and spices from India, China and Persia. Venetian rivalry with Genoa for the control of these vital routes was intense. The Genoese had an autonomous colony at Pera on the Golden Horn opposite Constantinople, where they were uneasily allied to the emperor; they had fewer outposts to defend and exercised less control over their citizens' Levantine affairs. The Venetians' crusading policies were usually more clear cut. After 1302 they hoped to oust the Genoese by supporting Valois schemes for conquest at Constantinople; then, realizing that these projects were impracticable, they sought to safeguard their commerce through a rapprochement with Byzantium.[2]

[1] B. Krekić, *Dubrovnik (Raguse) et le Levant au moyen âge* (Paris, 1961), 158, *et passim*; P. Topping, 'Le régime agraire dans le Péloponnèse au XIV siècle', *L'hellénisme contemporain*, ser. II, x (1956).
[2] F. Thiriet, *La Romanie vénitienne au moyen âge: le développement et l'exploitation du domaine colonial vénitien (XIIe–XIVe siècles)* (Paris, 1959), 155–66, *et passim*; P. Argenti, *The Occupation of Chios by the Genoese and their Administration of the Island, 1346–1566*, 3 vols. (Cambridge, 1958); G. Pistarino, 'Nella *Romania* genovese tra i Grechi e i Turchi: l'isola di Chio', *Rivista storica italiana*, lxxiii (1961).

More dangerous to the Latins than the Turks advancing overland in Anatolia were the coastal emirates whose raiders took to the sea, recruiting renegade Greek sailors and plundering the Aegean for slaves and spoil. In 1304 they raided the island of Chios and thereafter the Greeks largely relied on the Genoese under Benedetto Zaccaria to defend Smyrna and Chios. After 1310 the Hospitallers, having conquered Rhodes from the Greeks, gained a series of naval victories against the Turks; the most notable was won with Genoese support off Chios in 1319. Turkish aggression was forced northwards away from the emirate of Mentesche on the coast opposite Rhodes, towards the area around Smyrna and the territories of the emirate of Aydin in central Ionia. In 1327 the Venetians, sensing a new threat, tried to bring Andronicus III Palaeologus, the Genoese Martino Zaccaria of Chios and the Hospitallers into a coalition to defend Smyrna. Instead Andronicus seized Chios and imprisoned Zaccaria in 1329, while the port at Smyrna fell to the great Turkish warrior Umur, who in 1334 became emir of Aydin. For some twenty years, sometimes in alliance with the Greeks or Catalans, more often at their expense, Umur conducted an amazing series of razzias in Thrace, Thessaly, Bulgaria and other parts, and became a major menace to Christian shipping in the Aegean, attacking Monemvasia, Naxos, Negroponte and other places. In 1332 the Venetians succeeded in forming a union against Umur in which they considered including the Turkish Karaman emir at Konya. An insurrection in Crete delayed operations during 1333; then in 1334 galleys sent by Venice, the Hospitallers, the pope and the kings of France and Cyprus assembled. They won a considerable naval victory, but dispersed without inflicting permanent damage on Umur whose raids continued.

Following the inactivity of Benedict XII's pontificate the enthusiastic Clement VI gathered a force from Venice, Genoa, Rhodes and Cyprus. In 1344 it surprised and captured Smyrna, the principal centre of Turkish piracy, and burnt much of Umur's fleet in the most positive and lasting Christian success of the century. Clement also launched a predominantly French crusading expedition but the response was undistinguished and the best available leader, Humbert du Viennois, was inept; he reached Smyrna in 1346, fought an indecisive engagement, opened truce negotiations and sailed away. Smyrna had been captured by those Levantine powers it particularly threatened, but none of them wanted the onerous responsibilities of its defence. In 1346 the Genoese betrayed the alliance and established themselves permanently on Chios which controlled the rich mines of nearby Phocaea, the principal source of the alum essential to Europe's textile industry. The Venetians quarrelled with the Hospitallers, who were left to defend Smyrna with papal assistance. In 1347 the Hospitallers defeated the Turks at sea off Imbros but only Clement's determination prevented their concluding a truce with the Turks at Smyrna. Umur's death in 1348 brought little immediate advantage to the Latins, for they faced a general economic and financial crisis and a catastrophic plague, the Black Death. The Venetians bargained hard for a new league which would protect their interests at the general expense but, after its renewal in 1350, they refused to pay their quarter share of the 12,000 florins needed to maintain 120 mercenaries at Smyrna. Meanwhile the Genoese gained control of access to the Black Sea and threatened Venice's hitherto prosperous commerce in *Romania*. In 1351 Venice went to war with Genoa on this issue, allying with the Turks, disrupting the whole Mediterranean and bringing the crusade to a standstill.[1]

A series of leagues designed to serve Genoese and Venetian interests and dependent on their seapower could not ensure continuous operations against the Turks. Papal intervention was limited by its expense. John XXII's four galleys each cost 600 florins monthly in 1334, and Clement VI's crusading expenditure of over 110,000 florins between 1345 and 1348 was exceptionally heavy. Subsequent popes, spending much more heavily on their Italian wars, regarded even 3,000 florins yearly for Smyrna as a burden.[2] From Avignon the Turks seemed remote. Influential cardinals like the great pope-maker Talleyrand were actively involved in preaching and organizing crusades, but few had experience of the East. Often cautious and reactionary, the cardinals could invoke bureaucratic curial procedures to obstruct or delay action.[3] The popes were

---

[1] Lemerle, *Aydin*, 19–238; Thiriet, 165–9; Luttrell, 'Venice', 203–5.

[2] Y. Renouard, *Les relations des papes d'Avignon et des compagnies commerciales et bancaires de 1316 à 1378* (Paris, 1941), 32 (tableaux A, C), 166–9, 249, 327–30, *et passim*.

[3] B. Guillemain, *La cour pontificale d'Avignon, 1309–1376* (Paris, 1962), 140, 222, 247–50, *et passim*; Atiya, 118, 306.

subject to countless pressures and Innocent VI, in particular, was changeable and easily influenced. He tried to end the Venetian war with Genoa, and he later resuscitated the Aegean league which defeated the Turks off Megara in about 1359.[1] When the ravages of the Catalans, Greeks and Turks threatened to produce a revolt at Corinth, the city and its defence were entrusted in 1358 to the Florentine Niccolò Acciaiuoli. Yet in 1359 Innocent declined Acciaiuoli's offer to arm a crusading fleet on the grounds that policy had already been decided by a committee of cardinals and could not be changed.[2] And by empowering the papal captain of Smyrna, the Florentine Hospitaller Niccolò Benedetti, to trade at Alexandria in order to pay for the garrison and fortifications, Innocent was financing one struggle at the expense of another. A more serious example of confused policy-making was the replacement of the Venetian archbishop of Crete Orso Delfini as papal legate commanding the successful Aegean league by a fanatical Carmelite, Pierre Thomas. The new legate reached Constantinople with a small force in 1359 and destroyed the Ottoman Turks' fort at Lampsacus in the Dardanelles, but his intransigent attitude towards all schismatics, coupled with the inadequacy of Latin military assistance, destroyed the slender possibilities of cementing an ecclesiastical union with the Greeks. Pierre Thomas then went to Cyprus, and the defence of *Romania* was neglected while he diverted papal, Hospitaller and Cypriot forces to Armenia in 1361, and later to Alexandria.[3]

With Smyrna captured and Umur dead the aggressive warrior elements of Anatolia, held in check on the Aegean by the Latins, gravitated away from Ionia towards Thrace. For centuries western Anatolia had been a bulwark of Byzantine power, but after their restoration in 1261 the Palaeologi had caused widespread discontent there through heavy taxation and their brutal persecution of the supporters of the former Lascarid régime at Nicaea. The frontier defences crumbled as Turkish raids and infiltration interrupted communications and aggravated economic decay. The Palaeologi, distracted by their

[1] Luttrell, 'Venice', 205–6. Cf. F. Giunta, 'Sulla politica orientale di Innocenzio VI', *Miscellanea in onore di Roberto Cessi*, i (Rome, 1958).
[2] J. Buchon, *Nouvelles recherches sur la principauté française de Morée*, ii (Paris, 1843), 135–6, 143–60.
[3] Smet, 84–97, 201–12 (on Smyrna, 206) ; Luttrell, 'Venice', 206.

Balkan problems, failed to react with sufficient vigour and in 1301 Osman, the founder of the Ottoman dynasty, won a notable victory near Nicaea. Osman and his son Orhan were petty raiders, chiefs of one of the many tribal units which had reasserted their identity after the Mongol conquests had released them from Seljuk domination. While a number of stronger Turkish emirates emerged in central and south-west Anatolia the Ottomans, a weaker group, were pushed to the fringe of the old Seljuk territories. This situation, however, enabled the Ottomans to canalize warlike enthusiasm against the Greeks and their wealth, first in Bithynia itself and subsequently in the Balkans.

In Bithynia the Ottomans captured Brusa in 1326, Nicaea in 1331 and Nicodemia in 1337. They overran the countryside, starved the cities into surrender and divided the great estates among their semi-nomadic followers who needed the pasturage and rendered cavalry service in return. The Anatolian peasants had to pay tribute but their desperate condition improved under Ottoman protection. The Ottomans' lack of religious or racial fanaticism facilitated the process of assimilation between Greeks and Turks. The Christians were treated with toleration and their collaboration sought; some Greeks learnt Turkish, some became Muslims. The Turks themselves were often unorthodox, and their culture derived from Persia rather than from the Mamluk-dominated Arab world. There was little co-operation between Mamluks and Turks in attacks on the Cilician Christians, though after the Latin sack of Alexandria in 1365 the Egyptians did propose a joint blockade and invasion of Cyprus and Rhodes. None the less Islam constituted an element of cohesion in building up support for the Ottomans and, to a limited extent, it inspired *ghazi* and dervish enthusiasm on the frontier, even if a greater incentive there was the pay and plunder provided by enterprising leaders such as Umur and Orhan, for whom war was an economic rather than a spiritual necessity. The first four Ottoman leaders, capable and determined men who enjoyed long reigns and kept power firmly in the hands of the dynasty, slowly created an Anatolian hegemony. They partially subdued the neighbouring emirates, gradually attracting supporters away from the older tribal groupings and absorbing them into the wider and more profitable sphere of Ottoman allegiance, a process which depended above all on success against the Christians.

The Ottomans profited from John V Palaeologus' struggle
with his father-in-law John Cantacuzenus. Cantacuzenus tried
to use the Latins against the Turks and the Turks against the
Serbs, and he married his daughter to the Ottoman Orhan. So
there had long been Turks serving in the Balkans when, following an earthquake in 1354, the Ottomans occupied Gallipoli
and installed themselves permanently across the Dardanelles.
The Latins were slow to act upon the need to co-operate with
the Palaeologi. In 1353 Innocent VI replied to an appeal from
the Greeks still resisting at Philadelphia in Anatolia that the
price of Latin assistance was complete submission in matters of
faith. Then Stephen Dushan, who had extended Serbian power
into Albania, Epirus and Thessaly and threatened Byzantium
with extinction, proposed an ecclesiastical and political union
with the Latins whose seapower he needed; but his death in
1355 deprived Innocent of the champion he hoped might defend
Romania against the Turks.

In 1355 John V, threatened by Turks and Serbs, revived the
old project for the union of the Greek and Roman churches but,
partly because Innocent could provide no significant military
aid in return, the proposals lapsed. In 1360, when the papal
legate abandoned both the Greeks and the Latins in *Romania*,
the Latin naval league collapsed at once and all the available
crusading forces were subsequently employed against the
Mamluks; by 1361 Demotica and Adrianople in Thrace were
in Ottoman hands. Genoa and Venice gave the Greeks some
support and Amedeo of Savoy sailed to recapture Gallipoli in
1366, but John V, who even visited the pope at Rome in 1369,
sought in vain for substantial Western help. Most Greeks were
reluctant to accept the Roman church; many preferred co-
existence with the Turks. The Balkans in general, hopelessly
divided in race, politics and religion, provided only fragmentary
opposition to the disciplined Ottoman troops. After crushing
Serbian resistance at Cernomen in 1371 the Turks penetrated
the valleys and plains of Macedonia and Albania and reached
the Adriatic, devastating the crops and country. They were
quite unable to settle or administer so much territory at once,
but Ottoman successes made it increasingly easy to secure
service from the Balkan and Anatolian nobles and their followers. There was probably a majority of Christian troops in
many Ottoman armies.

In 1372 Pope Gregory XI, despairing of the West, encouraged the Levantine Latins to act in union and summoned them to an abortive conference at Thebes. Abandoning the insistence on ecclesiastical union, he also planned to send a small expedition of Hospitallers, the most he could hope to raise, to assist the Greeks in the Aegean or in the Dardanelles, where the Latins had conspicuously failed to use their seapower to obstruct Turkish communications. Then in 1373 John V, desperately poor, isolated in the face of a revolt by his son Andronicus and disillusioned with the Latins, became a tributary of the Ottoman Murad. This situation was not novel, but the pattern of affairs in which one or more of the Palaeologi were usually allied with the Ottomans against their own kinsmen, with Venice and Genoa taking opposite sides, now assumed permanent shape. In 1376 Andronicus allied with Murad and the Genoese, and handed back Gallipoli to the Turks; the Venetians occupied the island of Tenedos to counter the threat to the Dardanelles, and war with Genoa followed. In this strife the religious issue counted for little.[1]

Financial difficulties and the papacy's return to Rome in 1377 delayed the Hospitallers' expedition, and it was eventually diverted to protect the Latins in Greece. In 1377 the Hospitallers leased the principality of Achaea for five years from Joanna of Anjou, queen of Naples, and acquired the port of Vonitza in Epirus which was being attacked by the Albanian despot of Arta, Ghin Boua Spata. Early in 1378 a small force of Hospitallers under their master, Juan Fernández de Heredia, reached Vonitza. Then Gregory died and Urban VI, his successor, apparently failed to dispatch reinforcements.[2] Later in 1378 the Albanians, who probably had Turkish support, ambushed and defeated the Hospitallers near Arta. Soon after Latin Greece was thrown into confusion. The Acciaiuoli at Corinth were attacking the Catalans, and Thebes was captured by bands of Navarrese mercenaries who then invaded the Morea and set up a principality there. The Hospitallers eventually evacuated mainland Greece altogether in 1381.[3]

[1] In addition to Wittek and Georgiades Arnakis, see Smet, 64–80, 193–212; G. Dennis, *The Reign of Manuel II Palaeologus in Thessalonika: 1382–1387* (Rome 1960), 26–40, 52–6.
[2] Luttrell, 'Venice', 206–9; 'Interessi', 322–4; on Urban VI, C. du Boulay, *Historia universitatis parisiensis*, iv (Paris, 1668), 521.
[3] R.-J. Loenertz, 'Hospitaliers et Navarrais en Grèce, 1376–1383: régestes et documents', *Orientalia Christiana Periodica*, xxii (1956).

After the schism in 1378 the Avignonese pope, Clement VII, sought prestige by assisting the Hospitallers, most of whom supported him, in the defence of Rhodes and Smyrna. The Roman popes made contacts with the Palaeologi. Both sets of popes authorized crusades, some of them against their rival's supporters, but neither initiated any positive crusading action.[1] The Greeks' fate again depended largely upon Venice. Venetian traffic in *Romania* had been dwindling for several decades and had become less important than that in Egypt and Syria, partly because the breakup of the Mongol empire disrupted the caravan routes across Asia to the Black Sea. However, the Venetians were concerned to preserve their access to the products of the Black Sea area. They tried to slow down the Turks' advances while making trade agreements with them; in 1385 they refused to help the Greeks defend Thessalonika, but on other occasions they provided discreet assistance, as at Constantinople in 1395. Ottoman successes also compelled the Venetians to occupy certain strategic positions: Corfu, the key to their Adriatic lifeline; Argos and Nauplia in the Morea; and, in 1395, Athens.[2]

As the conflict became increasingly continental its Mediterranean aspects grew marginal and only the mountains held up the Turks. The Greeks, mingling defiance with appeasement, lost Serres in 1383 and Thessalonika in 1387. More important, the Serbs were defeated and Balkan resistance broken at Kossovo in 1389; Bulgaria was conquered by 1393; Constantinople besieged in 1394; the Morea ravaged in 1395. Then, with the Greeks in despair and the Latins in schism, the threat to Hungary and the lands across the Danube produced a reaction. Sigismund of Hungary with his vassal princes from Wallachia and Transylvania collected a great army. It included Germans and other northerners, but the union of the Polish and Lithuanian ruling houses in 1386 involved the Poles in struggles to the east and prevented the realization of the much-discussed Polish campaign against the Turks. A lull in the Anglo-French wars allowed the departure under Jean de Nevers, son of the duke of Burgundy, of a large chivalric Franco-Burgundian

---

[1] O. Halecki, 'Rome et Byzance au temps du Grand Schisme d'Occident', *Collectanea Theologica* (Lwow), xviii (1937); Dennis, 132–50.

[2] Thiriet, 353–63; Dennis, 123–7, *et passim*. Cf. F. Thiriet, 'Quelques observations sur le trafic des galées vénitiennes . . .', *Studi in onore di Amintore Fanfani*, iii (Milan, 1962), 502–3, 505–16.

contingent, genuine crusaders some of whom had fought at Mahdiya in 1390. No English participation was organized although both popes gave their blessing. Venetian, Genoese and Hospitaller forces arrived by sea and sailed up the Danube to Nicopolis where a horde of crusaders converged, slaughtering many Bulgarian Christians. Delayed by their lack of siege-engines, they indulged in demoralizing debauchery while Bayezid, the Ottoman leader, hurried up with his army and his Serbian vassals. There were probably some 20,000 men on either side. The French magnates were arrogant and over-confident, and their chivalric jealousies and quarrels led them to ignore Sigismund's more mature judgment. Without any proper plan of battle, they charged wildly at the auxiliary troops in the Turkish van and, when they had to dismount to uproot rows of pointed stakes, Sigismund's vassals fled at the sight of their riderless horses. The Turks' losses were heavy, but the superior disciplined mobility and the effectiveness of their archers allowed the regular Turkish cavalry to cut down the exhausted and largely horseless crusaders. The Christians suffered a colossal defeat.[1]

The news of Nicopolis provoked incredulity and dismay in the West. Many blamed the Hungarians, while Philippe de Mézières diagnosed a profound moral malaise in Christian society and called for a new crusade. The Franco-Burgundian nobility had been crushed and cruelly humiliated; it never again launched a major crusade. The Latins, however, could not altogether ignore the perilous situation of Constantinople. Isolationist Venice negotiated with Bayezid, but reluctantly sent aid to Constantinople to prevent the Turks acquiring control of the Straits and a stranglehold over Venetian grain supplies from the Black Sea. The Morea was ravaged again in 1397; then the Hospitallers occupied Corinth and defended the isthmus for seven years, probably saving the Morea from Turkish occupation. In 1399 the French marshal Boucicault, a veteran of Nicopolis, conducted a minor crusade designed to protect the interests of Genoa, then under French control. With an entourage of experienced warriors and with Venetian and Hospitaller assistance, he evaded twenty-seven Turkish ships

[1] Atiya, 435–62, and A. Atiya, *The Crusade of Nicopolis* (London, 1934); these works require considerable modification as, e.g., in C. Tipton, 'The English at Nicopolis', *Speculum*, xxxvii (1962).

and relieved Constantinople. Boucicault pillaged a number of villages on the Turkish coast and then, leaving a small Latin garrison at Constantinople, he returned to France to seek further help. The Emperor Manuel accompanied him and toured the courts of Europe, but with little result.[1]

While the Ottomans consolidated their territorial gains in the Balkans and Anatolia, Byzantium survived largely because the Turks lacked the naval strength to blockade Constantinople and the artillery to capture it.[2] But the overgrown Ottoman state was vulnerable in Asia. There the Turco-Mongol conqueror Timur, after defeating the Mamluks in Syria in 1400, won a decisive victory over the Ottomans near Ankara in 1402. Then, having captured Smyrna from the Hospitallers, he withdrew from the western fringes of the enormous Asiatic world and died in China in 1405. The Ottoman state was dismembered and almost destroyed. The Turks remained in Europe, but there followed some twenty years of comparative peace in the Levant. Constantinople was safe after seven years of siege, and in 1403 Christian truces with the Mamluks and Turks marked the end of an epoch.[3] The Latins had at last made good use of their seapower. Their support for the Greeks, though scanty, was extremely important in the crucial years between Nicopolis and Ankara.

Too often the Latins lost battles. The Mamluk state was efficiently organized for war by a military oligarchy. Standing armies and better tactics, weapon-drill and discipline, not numerical advantage, ensured Mamluk and Ottoman superiority. The Latins, like the Muslims, produced numerous treatises on the arts of war. They knew, in theory, the importance of bringing the enemy to battle and destroying him, and of tactical points such as sending out scouts and regrouping after a cavalry charge. Yet even when seapower and surprise brought initial successes the crusaders seldom ventured inland, and lack of stamina, of resources and of proper planning usually meant that advantages gained were soon lost. Pierre I of Cyprus raised

---

[1] R.-J. Loenertz, 'Pour l'histoire du Péloponnèse au XIVᵉ siècle, 1382–1404', *Revue des études byzantines*, i (1943), 186–96; Delaville, *La France en Orient*, i, 337–83; Thiriet, 362–7.

[2] Atiya, 466.

[3] P. Wittek, 'De la défaite d'Ankara à la prise de Constantinople', *Revue des études islamiques*, xii (1938), 6–25. 1403 also saw an Aragonese-Sicilian truce with the Berber states (Brunschvig, i, 223–5).

a powerful force and successfully concealed its objective during the lengthy preparations necessary; he captured Alexandria but could not hold it. The Latins had shallow-draught barges which landed cavalry directly on to the beach, but horses were expensive and difficult to transport and, as at Mahdiya in 1390, their shortage could be crippling. In a fortified position the defenders still enjoyed the advantage. The Muslims employed naptha against wooden siege-engines, and although artillery came into use among the Latins, Moors, Berbers and Mamluks —but not the Ottomans—during the fourteenth century, only in the western Mediterranean did it play even a minor and indecisive part in Christian-Muslim conflicts. The Latins in their heavy armour suffered from heat, thirst and exhaustion, while bad wine and disease undermined their morale. The Muslims, lightly armed and extremely mobile, often avoided battle with the heavy Latin ironclad shock-troops, preferring to wear them down with guerrilla and skirmishing tactics. Experience and determination could overcome such manœuvres, as Ferdinand of Castile, victor at Antequera in 1410, showed in Spain where there was permanent contact with the Moors.[1] The Hospitallers provided a small but experienced standing army, available for crusading expeditions and often invaluable in covering a rearguard action. Western princes, however, tended to cut off their supplies, and the Hospitallers could seldom afford a proper navy, but at Rhodes they provided a secure base for crusading operations; they defended the Morea for seven critical years and held Smyrna until 1402. By contrast, the average crusader's excessive desire for personal glory or salvation repeatedly militated against success; at Nicopolis it was disastrous.

In 1365 Philippe de Mézières had to restrain Pierre Thomas from leaping into the water and singlehandedly precipitating a premature attack on Alexandria. Yet this spirit was the essence of the crusade. On the next day Pierre Thomas, as papal legate, stood high on a galley holding aloft a cross and blessed the crusaders: 'Chosen knights of Christ, be comforted in the Lord and His Holy Cross; fight manfully in God's war, fearing not your enemy and hoping for victory from God, for today the

---

[1] Atiya, 18–21, 482, et passim; Verbruggen, 575–7, et passim; Ayalon, 1–44, 141–2, et passim; Brunschvig, ii, 75–98; G. Scanlon, A Muslim Manual of War (Cairo, 1961), 4–21, et passim; I. MacDonald, Don Fernando de Antequera (Oxford, 1948), 33–51, et passim.

gates of Paradise are open.'[1] This concept of holy war could be exploited or perverted by colonialists, merchants, and free-booters, kings, popes and republics only because it retained some meaning in the Latin conscience. Men, though not necessarily less religious, were turning away from the church and its institutions, including the crusade, yet traditional ideals survived alongside growing pacifist and anti-crusade sentiment. For many the failure of the *gesta Dei per Francos* was explicable only in terms of a divine judgment upon their sins; and their sins included greed, jealousy, disunity and a stupid lack of planning. Until the schism the popes tried to encourage the crusade but, like the secular princes, they gave precedence to their problems in the West. The crusade could never become a coherent foreign policy for Christendom, the successful defence of which necessitated something more permanent than an irregular series of chivalric expeditions with varied objectives. Once resistance against the Turks had become the first essential, Tunis, Egypt and even Armenia were false objectives, and Jerusalem a mere distraction. The crusade lost almost all its appeal as a popular movement, and during the fourteenth century came to depend, except where Latin lands or interests were directly threatened, on small groups and individuals: a pope; the duke of Burgundy; the Hospitallers; or bodies of French nobles. The crusade's betrayal by those whose economic position it threatened seemed inevitable. Emmanuele Piloti, the Cretan merchant in Egypt, saw that materialist urban patriciates rather than chivalric princes were predominant in the Mediterranean world and, convinced of the immutable nature of the trade between the Orient and the Mediterranean and of the Christians' dependence upon it, he realized that a blockade was unenforceable. In his crusading treatise he argued that the conflict between crusading and commercial objectives could only be resolved by harnessing the Latins' sea-power and their desire for gain to a crusade in which the great commercial powers would seize control of Egypt and its wealth, and of the holy places as well.

By 1402 the crusade had failed to recover Jerusalem, to succour the Eastern Christians, or to defend the Balkans, though Cyprus, the Aegean islands, parts of Greece, and Constantinople

[1] Smet, 103, 131.

were still in Christian hands. Eastern Europe protected itself more successfully during the fifteenth century than the West had the Balkans in the fourteenth. For many crusaders the holy war came to involve the defence of their homelands, and John Hunyadi in Hungary and Serbia, Skanderbeg in Albania and other great patriots fought to save Europe from the Turks. Western European forces occasionally participated, as in the Varna crusade of 1444; the Hospitallers repulsed Mamluk and Ottoman attacks on Rhodes; the Council of Florence sought theological agreement between Latins and Greeks; and, after the fall of Constantinople in 1453, Pius II and other popes belatedly projected crusading expeditions.[1]

The papacy also encouraged the renewed, oceanic expansion of Christendom, in which financial, nautical and colonial techniques largely developed in the Levant were transferred by Italian merchants and sailors to the Atlantic world. Following the discovery of the first Atlantic islands before 1339 by Lanzarotto Malocello, an Italian galley-captain in Portuguese service, a series of Mallorcan, Catalan, Castilian and Portuguese expeditions, some with genuine missionary aims, set out for the Canaries. The Portugese advance along the African coast, inaugurated in 1415 with the capture of Ceuta from the Moors, soon received official papal patronage as an extension of the *reconquista*. The chivalric Portuguese leaders' crusading sentiments were partly sincere. They really hoped to find a Christian ally, perhaps even a black Prester John, in Africa or Asia; they were not totally cynical in claiming that by securing gold and slaves from West Africa, for centuries a Muslim zone of influence, they were impoverishing Islam and that in enslaving the natives they were making new Christians.[2] The completion of the *reconquista* in Spain by the capture of Granada in 1492 coincided with the opening of a new field for the *conquistadores* in America. In 1513 the Portuguese Albuquerque, having destroyed the Mamluk fleet in the Indian Ocean, considered that it would be easy to land a force in the Red Sea, capture Mohammed's body at Medina,

[1] O. Halecki, 'The Defence of Europe in the Renaissance Period', *Didascaliae: Studies in Honor of Anselm M. Albareda* (New York, 1961).

[2] J. Vincke, 'Die Evangelisation der Kanarischen Inseln im 14. Jahrhundert im Geiste Raimund Lulls', *Estudios lulianos*, iv (1960); G. Pistarino, 'I Portoghesi verso l'*Asia* del Prete Gianni', *Studi medievali* (Spoleto), III ser., ii (1961), 113–37, *et passim*; P. Russell, *Prince Henry the Navigator* [=*Diamante*, xi (1960)]; R. Mauny, *Navigations médiévales sur les côtes sahariennes antérieures à la découverte portugaise (1434)* (Lisbon, 1960, 53–70).

and exchange it for the temple at Jerusalem.[1] Christendom had outflanked Islam on the oceans, while on land the Christians of eastern Europe, who had sheltered the West from the barbarians for so long, gradually halted the Turks. The objectives of the holy war had always changed as circumstances altered and, although enthusiasm for the crusade progressively declined, its ideals survived the disaster at Nicopolis in 1396 just as they had the fall of Acre in 1291.

---

[1] *The Commentaries of the Great Afonso Dalboquerque,* trans. W. Birch, iv (London, 1884), 37.

V

JOHN LE PATOUREL

THE KING AND THE PRINCES IN FOURTEENTH-CENTURY FRANCE

The history of medieval France is often presented as though the process by which power and authority was centralized in the king's hand and ultimately made effective thoughout the king-dom was the only matter of consequence in the political develop-ment of the country. The monarchy is indeed important for, historically, it represents the principle of French unity, and unity triumphed in the end. But there were other possibilities. Monsieur Pocquet du Haut-Jussé has shown how two French dukes, the dukes of Burgundy and Brittany, behaved like independent princes in the fifteenth century,[1] and suggested that they should not be treated necessarily as traitors and rebels when they opposed the king, but as builders of subordinate states, very similar to the kingdom in their organization, some-times in advance of it, more often modelled upon it. France, like Germany and Italy, passed through an 'age of princi-palities';[2] and, though her experience was shorter than theirs, unity under the king was not the only possible outcome. It is in any case a commonplace that the monarchy eventually took over the princely governments as the basis of its provincial organization.

The more sinister side of this phase was brought out in a short paper by Monsieur Perroy,[3] wherein he showed how the

---

[1] B.-A. Pocquet du Haut-Jussé, *Deux Féodaux, Bourgogne et Bretagne* (1935).
[2] B.-A. Pocquet du Haut-Jussé, *Les Papes et les ducs de Bretagne*, 2 vols. (1928), xi–xiii.
[3] E. Perroy, 'Feudalism or Principalities in Fifteenth-century France', *Bulletin of the Institute of Historical Research*, xx (1947), 181–5.

princes and magnates of the fifteenth century, not content with establishing their independence in fact, plundered and pillaged the monarchy, so that the civil wars of the fifteenth century in France, as in England, were struggles for the royal patronage, the royal revenues, ultimately for the monarchy itself. As Perroy observed, however, the process by which these counts and dukes (whom it is convenient to call 'princes') had established their high degree of independence has not been studied as a general phenomenon. It is not that local and regional monographs are lacking; they abound; and many of them represent historical writing on as high a plane, by any standards, as works on a national or wider scale. But they have, in general, treated each duchy, county or seigneurie by itself;[1] whereas the growth of regional autonomies, organized internally as kingdoms in miniature and approaching independence in their relations with the king, with one another and with external powers, seems to be characteristic of late-medieval France as a whole. The object of this paper is to show some of these fifteenth-century principalities in the making, and to suggest that, at the stage they had reached already in the fourteenth century, their progress towards autonomy has to be taken into account in any consideration of the politics of that time.

By the early part of that century the king's authority and his government had advanced a long way from the primitive feudal kingship of the eleventh and twelfth centuries.[2] Partly by good fortune, partly by successful warfare, partly by the growth of a higher ideal of kingship, the king had been able to insist, in the later part of the twelfth and the early part of the thirteenth century, on a much clearer definition of the relationship between the great lords and himself, whether based technically on liege homage or not, as with the duke of Burgundy in 1186, the Plantagenet lands in 1200, with Brittany in 1213, with the reconstituted Aquitaine in 1259; and, largely as a result of King Philip Augustus' successful war with King John, the king of

---

[1] At first sight *Histoires des Institutions françaises au Moyen Age*, ed. F. Lot and R. Fawtier, i, *Institutions seigneuriales* (1957) (hereinafter cited as *Inst. seign.*) seems to be the general work that is required; but it is in fact a collection of unrelated monographs which is not concerned with establishing general tendencies or comparative constitutional development.

[2] Convenient summary, with essential references in R. Fawtier, *L'Europe Occidentale de 1270 à 1328* (Histoire générale: Histoire du Moyen Age, ed. G. Glotz, vi, i, 1940).

France had raised himself in wealth and prestige clear above any of the lords, however independent they might seem to be. In his later life, and certainly in retrospect, King Louis IX had made the monarchy almost sacred. In secular matters, the king had come to claim sovereignty both within his kingdom and in his relations with external powers: *rex in regno suo est imperator*. Not only did he insist on the normal feudal services, service in the field and in his court, the right to *aides*, but he was claiming to legislate for the whole kingdom, to take action, judicial or other, in any part of the kingdom in the interests of peace and justice, claims which were based upon a higher notion of kingship than feudalism offered, upon the idea of descent from the great Charlemagne, the king's consecration, the miraculous power of healing and the tradition of Saint Louis. These claims, it is true, were not all accepted all the time; it was sometimes necessary, particularly in matters of military service and taxation, to accept compromises, though this could be done without surrendering the principle. But whatever compromises might have to be made, the claims were being asserted ever more frequently and confidently.

To translate these claims into practice, the king had already built up a governmental structure of some maturity; but though it was rapidly acquiring a professional, bureaucratic complexion, the king was still effectively in command. The chief central institutions, *conseil, parlement* (high court) and *chambre des comptes* (accounting department), were being formed by groups of professionals within the old *curia regis*, and were only just beginning to have a separate identity as autonomous departments. They were beginning also to work permanently, with their accumulating bulk of records, in the king's palace in Paris, making it necessary for the king to have what amounted to a duplicate organization (*chambre aux deniers, maîtres des requêtes de l'Hotel*, etc.) in his household, to follow him in his itineration. In moments of crisis the king would call great assemblies which, in some sort, represented the people of his kingdom; but it is not at all clear how these were related to the normal conduct of affairs. Local government was in the hands of officers called *baillis* in some parts of the kingdom (mostly in the north) and *sénéchaux* elsewhere. Originally members of the king's court sent out to supervise the older *prévôts, vicomtes* and castellans, they had settled down into more or less stable territorial units with almost every function of local government on their hands. Naturally they soon needed assistants, notaries, who drew up private acts and sealed them with a royal seal of contracts, judges, and receivers who took over their financial duties, both collecting and accounting.

In principle this organization was concerned with the royal domain, now very considerable, and the king's relations with his direct vassals; but already, owing to the development of the idea of kingship, the king's increasing need of money and the enthusiasm of his officers, it was reaching out much further. From the middle of the thirteenth century the king's court (later, specifically, the *parlement*) was developing the doctrine that, if a seignorial court failed to do justice or gave a false judgment, an appeal might be made; and the grounds of appeal were constantly being widened. Potentially this brought everyone in the kingdom, whoever his lord might be, within the purview of the king's court; while the protection which might have to be given to appellants, and the inquiries which might be necessary for the hearing of the appeal, were bringing the king's officers into every great fief. Monasteries and towns might seek the king's protection or the privilege that their litigation should come only before the king's court; landowners might seek to put themselves directly into the king's homage; enclaves of royal domain and ecclesiastical lands might likewise bring the king's officers into the great fiefs on the king's business. In the early fourteenth century the indications were, indeed, in spite of the reaction which these developments produced in 1314–15, that principles already enunciated, and governmental machinery that was being rapidly perfected, would soon make the unity of the kingdom under the king's rule a reality. Yet within a hundred years France was beginning to look more like a loose confederation of principalities under a king whose authority was virtually excluded from them.

Some general reasons for this failure are obvious; military defeat; the inability to mobilize the king's resources in men and money to full effect. But while, if attention is fixed upon the king and his government, it seems that by the beginning of the fourteenth century they must be well on their way to breaking down the autonomy of the great lords, these great lords, for their part, had been building governments of their own within their *seigneuries*; and as the king's officers were concerned to magnify the king's authority and to make it effective throughout the kingdom, so the seignorial officers, who also had careers to make, were concerned to establish their lord's exclusive authority within his lordship, and to make it effective and even sovereign.

The duchy of Aquitaine,[1] as it existed towards the end of the thirteenth century, consisted of most of the ancient duchy of Gascony, the Bordelais, the Agenais, Saintonge south of the River Charente and certain lands in the 'Three Dioceses' of Limoges, Cahors and Périgueux, a large discrete principality with boundaries (legal as well as territorial) which were in constant dispute. It was unlike most of the other principalities of France in that its duke, being also the king of England, was usually an absentee ruler; but the habit which English historical atlases have of colouring the king-duke's lands red, as though they were part of some medieval British Empire, gives a very wrong impression. Edward I, king of England and duke of Aquitaine, owed his duchy to legitimate and continuous inheritance, ultimately from Duke William X and his predecessors; his great-grandfather, Henry II, had been duke of Aquitaine before he was king of England. Aquitaine was as much a part of the kingdom of France as Brittany or Burgundy; Henry III had done liege homage for the duchy in 1259.

In the twelfth century Aquitaine had been an enormous, loosely constructed, feudal principality, formed by the union of the earlier duchies of Aquitaine and Gascony, and centred on Poitiers. Much of it was held by semi-independent barons who might respond to inspiring leadership or pensions, but could hardly be disciplined. When, after 1154, the duke was also duke of Normandy, count of Anjou, king of England and, later, effective overlord of Brittany, Aquitaine could only be governed by frequent visits or by partial delegation (to Queen Eleanor or to Richard, for example); but at all times, it seems, the

---

[1] Y. Renouard in *Inst. seign.*, 157–83 and references there; P. Chaplais, 'Le Duché-pairie de Guyenne', *Annales du Midi*, lxix (1957), 5–38, lxx (1958), 135–60 and 'Gascon Appeals to England (1259–1453)', unpublished London Ph.D. thesis (1951). Only the 'positions' of J.-P. Trabut-Cussac's thesis on 'L'Administration anglaise en Gascogne sous Henri III et Edouard Ier de 1252 à 1307' have been published, though many of his conclusions are embodied in F. M. Powicke, *The Thirteenth Century* (1953), ch. vii. But there is still no general account of the development of government in the duchy during the thirteenth and fourteenth centuries. What follows is based chiefly upon the published rolls of the English chancery.

administration was directed by one or more seneschals holding
'vice-regal' powers, who, though they did not have the institutions
that the justiciars of England and Normandy had at their
command, nevertheless held equivalent status and functions.

The constitutional history of Aquitaine in the thirteenth
century is a function of two developments: the progressive in-
frequence of the king-duke's visits, hitherto an essential element
in the government of the duchy, and the definition and
departmentalization of the seneschal's office. King John was in
Aquitaine at some time during each of the first four years of his
reign, in 1206 and in 1214; Henry III very briefly in 1230, for
longer periods, when serious business could be done, in 1242–3
and 1253–4; Edward I for ten months in 1273–4 and for more
than two years in 1286–9; Edward II and his successors not at
all. It was necessary, therefore, to build up an administration
that would function competently in the king-duke's lengthening
and ultimately permanent absence; though it must have been
some time before it was generally understood that his absence
would be permanent.

For some time the duchy was not treated as an administrative
unit. There were seneschals of Gascony, of Poitou, of La
Marche, of the Three Dioceses (Limoges, Cahors and
Périgueux), or two of these might be combined; it was not until
the transfer of the Agenais in 1279 raised the whole question
that the seneschal of Gascony was made seneschal 'of Aquitaine',
and the seneschals of the Three Dioceses, the Agenais, Saintonge
and Gascony 'outre Landes' subordinated to him. In this way a
coherent administration was at last achieved. But this territorial
extension, added to the economic development of the duchy (of
which the growth of the wine trade and the proliferation of
bastides are the most conspicuous evidence), relations with
neighbouring principalities and judicial innovations which often
required the seneschal's presence in Paris, so increased his
responsibilities, that there was no longer any possibility that
they could be discharged by one man. During King Henry's
visit in 1242–3, a financial officer was appointed to assist the
seneschal, hitherto responsible for collection, expenditure and
accounting; during his visit of 1253–4 the earliest recorded
financial officer with the title 'constable of Bordeaux', was
appointed. During the next thirty years the constable took over
more and more of the financial administration until, in the

ordinances of 1289, he was given full responsibility. Likewise the seneschal could no longer personally attend to all the courts that were coming to be held in the name of the king-duke. More and more of these were being held by men who described themselves as 'lieutenants of the seneschal' and who were, in increasing proportion, professional lawyers. By 1290 a complete governmental structure had been created. The king-duke had just spent some while in the duchy, and it was no doubt expected that he would return from time to time. He had appointed a lieutenant, who represented his authority in a more immediate sense than the seneschal could now do; and with seneschal, an official council, sub-seneschals, constable, receivers and judges, a clear chain of command and a workable distribution of duties, the ducal government seemed competent to deal with anything short of an overwhelming emergency. What is important, however, is that this administration had been built upon native tradition. The law was the law of the country, whether *droit coutumier* or *droit écrit*; the courts were of the kind to be found in southern France; the internal financial administration seems to be similar to that of contemporary Brittany or Burgundy; the seal of the court of Gascony seems, in origin, very like the seal of the court of Burgundy. The king-duke governed the duchy as duke of Aquitaine, not as king of England, and there was certainly no transplantation of English institutions to Aquitaine as there was, for example, from England to Ireland. Aquitaine was the king-duke's inheritance, Ireland his conquest.

From 1202 until 1259, the relation between the duke of Aquitaine and the king of France was one of war or, at best, of truce; but as part of the treaty of 1259 King Henry did liege homage both for what he still held *de facto* and for what was then given him by the treaty, and he accepted a peerage of France as duke of Aquitaine. This meant that as the appeal jurisdiction of the courts of the king of France developed, appeals would be made from the duke's courts in Aquitaine, and the duchy thus laid open to the centralizing activities of the French royal officers. These caused more trouble in Aquitaine than in most of the other great fiefs; partly, no doubt, because the duke was also a king, but much more because there were few clear-cut boundaries. In the Three Dioceses, especially, fiefs owing direct allegiance to the king of France were interspersed with those of the duke of Aquitaine, and conflicts of jurisdiction could hardly be avoided. Appeals were indeed so frequent, and often so important politically, that the king-duke soon found it advisable to be permanently represented in Paris by a body of lawyers, who formed themselves into a 'council', to watch over his interests. Naturally he did what he could to provide a complete judicial service for his Aquitanian subjects. He could hear cases in England or send out commissions of oyer and terminer; he could see to it that a case was not taken to Paris before all the 'grades' of appeal in Aquitaine had been exhausted; he could anticipate royal legislation.[1] But before the war of 1294 he did not affront the system; he might himself initiate litigation in the court of the king of France; it was part of the natural order of things.

Much was changed by the war of 1294 in Aquitaine, as in the almost contemporary war in Flanders. A dispute over jurisdiction led to the seizure of Aquitaine by the king of France and war. It was in the lengthy negotiations that followed the truce of 1297 that the English lawyers began to argue that Gascony (they do not seem to have distinguished between Gascony and Aquitaine in their argument) was an 'allod', had always been an 'allod', and that nothing in the treaty of 1259, as it had been carried out, had altered its status.[2] Whether there was any legal or historical foundation for this argument is a matter for discussion; what is important is that the duke's officers were finding it difficult to secure their lord's rights through protest and the ordinary process of law; they were being driven to attack French sovereignty as it was developing and to assert the independence of the duchy.

By the treaty of 1303 the *status quo ante*, in name at least, was restored; but all the old difficulties remained, and it has long been held that they were among the causes not only of the war of 1324-7, but of the greater war which broke out in 1337, for both started with a confiscation of the duchy for alleged failure, on the part of the king-duke, to act as a loyal vassal. Whatever motives King Edward III may have had for assuming the title

---

[1] P. Chaplais, 'La souveraineté du rois de France et le pouvoir législatif en Guyenne au début du XIVe siècle', *Moyen Age*, Livre Jubilaire, 1963, 449-469.

[2] P. Chaplais, 'English Arguments concerning the feudal status of Aquitaine in the fourteenth century', *Bulletin of the Institute of Historical Research*, xxi (1948), 203-13; 'Le Traité de Paris de 1259 et l'inféodation de la Gascogne allodiale', *Le Moyen Age*, lxi (1955), 121-37.

'king of France' in 1340, that claim, and the state of war or truce which made up Anglo-French relations for the next hundred years and more, meant that Aquitaine was *de facto* independent of the kingdom of France until its final conquest in 1453; and in all the negotiations of those years, whatever military extremity they might be in, the English insisted on nothing less. A principality, independent of the Valois king of France, yet within the kingdom as traditionally understood, had been formed.

In the early years of the fourteenth century, Brittany[1] was a well-found feudal principality.[2] The ruling dynasty had been established when King Philip Augustus married Peter of Dreux, a member of a junior branch of the royal family which had no connection with Brittany, to Alice, daughter of Constance of Brittany by Guy of Thouars. Peter ruled first on behalf of his wife (1213–21), then for his son during his minority (1221–37). John I ruled on his own account from 1237 until 1286, and his son and successor, John II, from 1286 until 1305. As these were able and constructive men, their long lives gave Brittany a period of stability which it badly needed; for the duchy they had taken over was little more than a duchy in name, disunited and weak.

In Carolingian times Brittany had been a kingdom, but it had disintegrated into a number of counties and they into smaller *seigneuries*. The ducal title survived only as a decoration for the counts of Rennes, who were, however, gathering the other counties into their hands. Some measure of unity had been achieved under King Henry II after 1166, and under his son Geoffrey, who was duke from 1181 to 1186, but this unity had not survived the troubled years from 1186 to 1213. Peter of Dreux found a remote and isolated country, in which the ducal

---

[1] Dukes: Peter I, 1213–37; John I, 1237–86; John II, 1286–1305; Arthur II, 1305–12; John III, 1312–41; (Charles of Blois, 1341–64; John of Montfort, 1341–5); John IV, (1345–64) 1364–99.

[2] B.-A. Pocquet du Haut-Jussé, 'Le Grand Fief breton', *Inst. seign.*, 267–88, and references there given; with two important articles by the same writer, 'Les Faux Etats de Bretagne et les premiers états de Bretagne', *Bibliothèque de l'Ecole des Chartes*, lxxxvi (1925), 388–406, and 'La Genèse du législatif dans le duché de Bretagne', *Revue historique de Droit français et étranger*, 4ᵉ series, xl (1962), 350–72. Add (for Peter I), Sidney Painter, *The Scourge of the Clergy, Peter of Dreux, Duke of Brittany* (1937), and (for John IV), J. Calmette and E. Déprez, *La France et l'Angleterre en conflit* (Histoire générale, Histoire du Moyen Age, ed. G. Glotz, vii, i, 1937), 197–230.

domain was small; almost the whole of the north and west was under the lordship of the Penthièvre family and the vicomtes of Léon who scarcely admitted the suzerainty of the duke; the duke had little control over his barons and almost none over his bishops. To set up a firm ducal government was a work of some moment. Peter of Dreux made war inside and outside the duchy; John I was more peaceful and patient; together they enlarged the ducal domain out of all recognition, defeated and largely dispossessed the lords of Penthièvre and the vicomtes of Léon, established the rule that baronial fortifications required a ducal licence, and built several ducal castles at strategic points. They struggled to establish the rights of wardship and relief over their barons, partly for revenue, more perhaps, as a symbol of suzerainty; and they eventually compromised with the *droit de rachat* which preserved the principle and was probably more profitable in practice. With the Church they were less successful; but at least they had proclaimed the principle that the bishops should hold their temporalities of the duke and that he should have some say in their appointment.

In all this the dukes were assisted by two factors peculiar to Brittany, by the traditional connection with the earldom of Richmond in England and by the Breton coast-line. As long as the kings of England were dukes of Aquitaine, they had a direct and practical interest in the country which lay across their communications; and as long as they hoped to recover something of the position in northern France which they had lost in 1204, they looked to the duke of Brittany as a valuable ally. During the twelfth century the great earldom of Richmond had come to be held by the dukes of Brittany; and during the thirteenth, though Peter of Dreux had but the slenderest possible claim to the earldom, he and his successors were allowed to possess it whenever relations between the kings of England and France made it possible or the duke of Brittany was prepared to face the difficulties of a double allegiance. It may well be that the kings of England did not merely permit this connection, but used it as an instrument of policy; to the duke of Brittany, Richmond was at least a very considerable if somewhat uncertain source of revenue.[1] The coast-line of

---

[1] P. Jeulin, 'Un grand "Honneur" anglais: Aperçus sur le comté de Richmond', *Annales de Bretagne*, xlii (1935), 265–302, does not exhaust the subject by any means. There is no satisfactory study of the Brittany-Richmond relationship as a whole. See G. E. C. *Complete Peerage*, s.v. 'Richmond' (779–824) for chronology.

Brittany provided revenue through the right of wreck. In the twelfth century this had been exercised by any seigneur who could lay claim to a stretch of the sea-shore; but during the thirteenth the duke, by various means, made it a ducal prerogative and then (or possibly earlier) converted it into something rather different. Instead of claiming the wrecked ship and all its contents, a barbarous custom which it might not always be easy to exercise effectively in practice, the duke devised a form of sealed document which guaranteed the holder, on any one voyage, from seizure in case of misadventure on the Breton coast. These *sceaux* or *brefs*, as they were called, were sold to masters of ships not only in the Breton ports, but in Bordeaux and La Rochelle as well. Since this was virtually a toll on all shipping passing the coast, it became a regular, increasing and very profitable source of revenue.[1]

In the course of the thirteenth century, therefore, the duke had acquired sufficient wealth and sufficient control of his duchy to stand out as one of the great barons of France. He had married his daughters into French baronial families; he had taken part in crusades and royal expeditions; John II was brother-in-law to King Edward I; moreover, in addition to the connection with Richmond, the two marriages of Arthur II brought the county of Montfort and the *vicomté* of Limoges into the ducal family. For administrative purposes the duchy was divided into eight *bailliages*, each administered by an officer generally called a seneschal. These seneschals held courts, partly of first instance for men of knightly rank, partly for appeals from inferior ducal or seignorial courts; from the seneschals' courts (save that of Nantes), appeals could be made to the court of the seneschal of Rennes, and from Rennes and Nantes to the ducal *curia*. Revenue was collected partly by the seneschals, partly by *ad hoc* farmers of towns, forests and the like; most expenditure was by assignment upon these local collectors, and accounts were presented, probably quite irregularly, at the ducal court. When this court sat for judicial business, it was coming to be called the duke's *parlement*; and though there was as yet little trace of a *chambre des comptes*,

---

[1] H. Touchard, 'Les brefs de Bretagne', *Revue d'Histoire économique et sociale*, xxxiv (1956), 116–40, argues for a thirteenth-century origin; B.-A. Pocquet du Haut-Jussé, 'L'Origine des brefs de sauveté', *Annales de Bretagne*, lxv (1958), 255–62, for a twelfth-century origin.

surviving fragments[1] of accounts and the preparation of *brefs* for distribution to the ports both imply the rudiments of a financial organization within the ducal *curia*.

But the duke was the liege man of the king of France. In 1297, indeed, the king had formally recognized Brittany as a duchy and had created a peerage for the duke, partly as a compliment, more, one must think, to bind him more firmly to the monarchy. The king could, and did, demand military service and levy subsidies in Brittany; litigants could, and did, appeal from the duke's *parlement* to the king's *parlement*; and, as in Aquitaine, royal officers entered Brittanny to protect appellants, those who had obtained royal *sauvegardes* and those who had contrived to put themselves under the king's direct vassalage. Nor were these officers always restrained from attracting litigants to the king's *parlement* or the assizes of the king's *baillis* of Tours and the Cotentin before all the judicial resources of the duchy had been exhausted. The duke, while not contesting the king's sovereignty in principle, protested against these extensions of its exercise; protested so frequently and obtained so many re-iterated promises that the immediate impression must be that protests and promises were ineffective. But since, in fact, very few Breton appeals seem to have reached the French courts,[2] it is more likely that the duke was holding his own by continuous vigilance; and there is evidence that his officers were building up a useful body of precedents for successful resistance.

The great crisis in the development of Brittany as an autonomous principality came in the 'War of Succession' of 1341–64. It began with an unequivocal recognition of royal sovereignty by both claimants, Charles of Blois and John of Montfort, when they submitted their offer of homage to the king, and judgment between them could only be made in the king's *parlement* 'garnished' with peers. But this dispute was quickly swept into the current of war between Edward III and Philip VI. Both kings had tried to pre-judge the issue; Edward III had as strong an interest in Brittany as any of his predecessors, strengthened indeed by his ambitions in France, while the king of France was obviously concerned to prevent the establishment of English forces in the duchy. In the event, Edward

---

[1] B.-A. Pocquet du Haut-Jussé, 'Le plus ancien rôle des comptes du duché. 1262', *Mémoires de la Société d'Histoire et d'Archéologie de Bretagne*, xxvi (1946), 49–68,
[2] B.-A. Pocquet du Haut-Jussé, *Les Papes et les ducs de Bretagne*, i, vii.

succeeded not only in putting down garrisons in Brittany and keeping an army of occupation in part of the duchy, but also in maintaining a body of native support for young John de Montfort (son of the claimant of 1341, who had died in 1345) and the elements of a civil administration in his name; while John was brought up in England. When he came of age, Edward turned all this over to him and gave him the military support which enabled him to defeat and kill Charles of Blois at Auray (1364), and to win his duchy by judgment of battle and in defiance of the king of France and his court.

When peace was made, the relationship of the duke of Brittany to the king of France was subtly changed. King Charles V demanded liege homage, but had to be satisfied with an ambiguous formula which, in the next century, was converted into an explicit denial that homage was liege. John IV, as he is styled, called himself duke of Brittany *Dei gracia*; his successor staged a ceremony in Rennes Cathedral that was closely modelled on the royal coronation. Already, in 1341, both Charles of Blois and John de Montfort, in the case they put to the *parlement*, recalled that Brittany had once been a kingdom 'and still has the dignity of a kingdom', adding significantly, 'and the said royal dignity has been in no way impaired by the peerage of France'.[1] Such phrases were commonplace under John IV. They were made the foundation for his claim to 'regalities such as coinage, rights over churches, wreck and other things included *in his quae sunt Regalia Regni*';[2] the king should be satisfied with his right of ultimate judicial appeal. In 1394 two Breton clerks surprised the papal court by declaring that the duchy of Brittany did not lie within the kingdom of France, nor was the duke subject to any secular prince.[3]

These claims were accompanied by a rapid development in the ducal institutions of government. The duke's *curia* still consisted chiefly of bishops and barons, though the professional element was growing. In its narrowest form, it was the duke's council; in fuller session, for judicial and political matters of importance, it was his *parlement*, with a *président* or *juge universel*,

---

[1] 'Et tient encore les Noblesses de Royaume, . . . et ladite Noblesse de Royaume n'a pas été ostée par la Pairie de France,' Dom Lobineau, *Histoire de Bretagne*, (1707), ii, col. 480.

[2] 'Choses Royalles, comme monnoyes, garde d'Eglises, bris de mer et autres choses continus *in his quae sunt Regalia Regni*'. Ibid., col. 646.

[3] B.-A. Pocquet du Haut-Jussé, *Les Papes et les ducs de Bretagne*, i, 420.

though the duke often presided in person 'assis en sa majesté';
in its fullest form, when it might include representatives of the
towns, it was still officially styled *parlement*, though in the next
century such meetings would be regarded as meetings of 'the
estates'. The duke was beginning to levy his own taxation,
insisting that only he could do so in Brittany, in the form of
fouages and customs on goods entering and leaving the ports.
These taxes required the consent of a reasonably full session of
the *parlement*, as a matter of political prudence rather than of
constitutional necessity, for representatives of those to be taxed
were still not always included. The consequent increase in ducal
revenues necessitated the appointment of a '*trésorier et receveur
général*', responsible both for the older revenues (domain,
justice, *brefs*, etc.) and the new forms of taxation, and also a
much clearer definition of the *chambre des comptes* as a professional
body of auditors under a president. In addition, there was a
chancellor who, besides attending to the normal duties of
chancellor, presided over the council and acted as the duke's
chief adviser, a marshal who directed the duke's still somewhat
undeveloped military resources, and an admiral who organized
the convoying of merchantmen and the impressment of ships
for naval expeditions and coastal defence.

In short, by the end of the fourteenth century, the duke of
Brittany was contesting all but a residual sovereignty in the
king of France and had built up the institutions of government
in the duchy to a point at which they would support his
sovereignty 'in practice'. Whether he desired a higher degree of
independence, it is hard to say; his relations with England at the
time were both an opportunity and an obstacle. Edward III
had not given him his assistance during the 'war of succession'
for nothing. Duke John IV found himself bound to his English
father-in-law by debts, English garrisons and English 'military
experts', not to mention his English upbringing and his two
English wives. When the Anglo-French war broke out again in
1369, loyalty to the king of France and neutrality were probably
equally impossible for him; and when he made his alliance with
Edward in 1372 and Richmond was restored to him, a French
punitive expedition soon drove him into exile. For five years
King Charles V administered the duchy. When, however, the
king decided to annex the duchy to the domain, the Breton
nobility, even Charles of Blois' widow, protested, formed

leagues, and invited Duke John to return. But when he came back and was seen to lean too heavily on English support in order to ward off the French armies, the same Bretons assembled at Rennes and appealed to King Charles for an accommodation. The moral is clear. The Bretons wanted a duke who would maintain the quasi-independence built up during the thirteenth and fourteenth centuries and neutrality in the Anglo-French war; to be tied not so closely to France that commerce with England and elsewhere was difficult, not so closely with England that peaceful relations with France were impossible. For a moment at the end of his life, temporarily improved relations between England and France enabled John IV to enjoy the earldom of Richmond and the duchy of Brittany together once more. His successors in the fifteenth century, though they continued to use the title, never possessed the earldom; but they won the independence in all but name which he never quite achieved.

The county of Flanders[1] was among the most precocious of the feudal principalities of France.[2] Its organization dated, in the main, from the great days of the eleventh and twelfth centuries when Flanders had enjoyed a real independence and its rulers took a not inconspicuous part in the affairs of Europe. The counts' strength in their county was based on the circumstances in which it had come into being. Descended from the Carolingian counts of the original county of Flanders, they had converted their official functions into a lordship and the royal lands to their own use; by warfare and by other means they had added county to county; they had acquired control over church lands and established their right to waste lands including the land that was being recovered from the sea. They were thus wealthy; they could build castles and establish their monopoly of military service within their territory; they co-operated in the enforcement of the Peace of God and converted it into the

---

[1] Counts: (with Hainault)—Baldwin VIII, 1191–5; Baldwin IX, 1195–1205; Jeanne, 1205–44 (married 1, Ferdinand of Portugal; 2, Thomas, Count of Maurienne); Margaret, 1244–78 (married 1, Bouchard of Avesnes; 2, William of Dampierre); (Flanders)—Guy of Dampierre, 1278–1305; Robert of Béthune, 1305–22; Louis of Nevers (II), 1322–46; Louis of Male, 1346–84.

[2] F. L. Ganshof, 'La Flandre', *Inst. seign.*, 343–426 and references there given: in particular, H. Pirenne, *Histoire de Belgique*, i (5th ed. 1929), ii (4th ed. 1947); R. Monier, *Les Institutions centrales du comté de Flandre* (1943), *Les Institutions financières du Comté de Flandre* (1948).

count's peace. They had, in fact, resisted the disintegrating tendencies of feudalism to a quite remarkable extent; the count had made himself *dominus terrae*.

In all this, the counts of Flanders were no doubt assisted by the fact that they had acquired lands in Germany as well as in France, by the situation of their lands at the extremity of either kingdom, and also by the enormous development of the towns in Flanders which they were able to assist, to their very great profit. In the contemporary sense they were vassals of the king of France for their French lands and of the king of Germany for those in Germany, and, when it was convenient, they performed their feudal duties; but neither king had any control over them. They were accustomed to conduct their 'foreign policy' among the principalities that were forming in the ancient Lotharingia, and even further afield. At least from the beginning of the twelfth century they were vassals of the king of England for a pension. From time to time the counts ruled other principalities as well: Philip of Alsace held the county of Vermandois in right of his wife; the count of Flanders was also the count of Hainault through much of the thirteenth century; Guy of Dampierre was also marquis of Namur. Such unions were personal and did not often endure; but they added wealth and prestige.

In the government of Flanders, local institutions, until the thirteenth century, were more remarkable than those at the centre. The basis of local government was the *châtellenie*, a district dependent upon a comital castle, administered by a *châtelain* to whom the count had delegated military, police and judicial functions. The courts he held were public courts, in which the judges were benches of *échevins*. For financial purposes the county was divided into *métiers* (*officia*), in which the count's revenues were collected and at least partly spent by 'notaries'. During the twelfth century *baillis* (very similar to the king's *baillis*) were superimposed. They were the count's agents, appointed, removed and paid by him; they took over the holding of the *échevinages*, both urban and rural, and the local feudal courts. At the centre was the count himself, itinerant with his household and court (so far as they can be distinguished). These were of the usual kind save that the office of chancellor (which was combined with that of general receiver of the revenues) had been given to the provost of Saint-Donatien at Bruges in 1089, to be held by him and his successors for ever. During the thirteenth century, however, with the growth of the revenue, the 'notaries' were replaced by local receivers, the chancellor's financial responsibilities taken over by the 'receiver of Flanders', and the local receivers' accounts were presented to a *Cour des Hauts Renneurs*—a very early example of professional audit.

This powerful, well-organized and idiosyncratic principality had been built up while the king was still remote and weak; during the thirteenth century it was subjected to a determined campaign to bring it under royal control and administration. The campaign was conducted in two phases. During the first, which extends from the beginning of the century to the time of Guy of Dampierre, the king was primarily concerned to secure fidelity. The participation of Ferdinand of Portugal, husband of the Countess Jeanne, in the Anglo-Imperial coalition that was smashed at Bouvines, enabled King Louis VIII to impose a peace by which he annexed the western part of the county (Artois) and imposed sanctions which would guarantee the loyalty of countess, count, their vassals and the towns (Treaty of Melun, 1226). When the Countess Margaret succeeded in 1244, a dispute broke out between the children of her two marriages, and this dispute was referred to King Louis IX. The king ruled that Flanders should go to Guy of Dampierre and Hainault to John of Avesnes. It was a measure of the king's authority that he not only settled the succession to Flanders (which his predecessor had been unable to do in 1127), but to Hainault as well, and Hainault was not within his kingdom. On the ground that he had no right to do this, John of Avesnes repudiated the agreement and, in alliance with other princes of the Low Countries who feared the extension of French influence, attacked Flanders. The Countess Margaret was very glad to accept French assistance, and Guy of Dampierre owed his county very largely to the king. He began his rule in 1278 as a faithful vassal.

Royal intervention in the internal affairs of the county, which marks the second phase, was occasioned by events in the towns. The enormous economic development of Flanders had expressed itself in the growth of a number of manufacturing towns whose size and wealth gave them greater political consequence in the county than either nobility or clergy. Their wealth may be measured by the fact that in 1305, Ypres, Bruges and Ghent alone were assessed at 38 per cent of a sum which had to be raised in the county. Such power had early manifested itself in political action. It was the resistance of the towns which prevented the king from imposing a count on the county in 1127–8. Later in the twelfth century the count found it advisable to consult representatives of the seven largest towns (Arras, Bruges, Douai, Ghent, Lille, Saint-Omer and Ypres—reduced to five after 1226 and to three after 1312 by French annexations) on matters of general concern. But internally, the towns were divided between the rich merchants who dominated the municipal governments and the craftsmen, many of whom were wage-earners in the modern sense.

In order to control the towns which, under weaker or more distant rule might have formed city-states like those of north Italy, Count Guy seemed to support the 'commons' in their often legitimate grievances against the patrician-dominated town governments; and this, when the king's *parlement* was ready to receive them, provoked appeals from the municipalities. The royal officers moved quickly. The *baillis* of Amiens and Vermandois took Flanders into their jurisdiction and royal *sergents* were sent in to protect the appellants. The count's resistance led eventually to a French invasion and the incorporation of the county into the royal domain, with the count and his sons prisoners in Paris (1300). Autonomous Flanders might have come to an end at this point, like Normandy in 1204, but for a revolt in Bruges and the defeat of the French punitive expedition at the astonishing battle of Courtrai (1302). To some extent this was a flash in the pan; the subsequent fighting was not all to the advantage of the Flemings, and the king of France imposed a ferocious peace (Athis-sur-Orge) in 1305, gradually modified in the course of the next fifteen years. As a result of this treaty, the *châtellenies* of Lille and Douai were annexed to the royal domain (1312) but there was no longer any question of annexing the whole of Flanders.

There was another element in the situation. For two centuries at least, the count of Flanders had been in close relation with England, partly because the Flemish towns grew ever more dependent upon England for the wool they made into cloth. Politically this relationship had not always been fortunate. The alliance of 1213–14 led to the disaster at Bouvines and the Treaty of Melun; Count Guy's alliance with Edward I (who as duke of Aquitaine was also faced by the problem of French administrative expansion) in 1297 was equally disastrous, for Edward's help came too late to save him from French invasion. But the economic relationship lost none of its urgency. When Edward III sought to draw Flanders into a coalition of princes in the Low Countries, as war with France was approaching, he met with a blank refusal from Count Louis of Nevers who, owing his county to the king's support at the time of the great revolt of 1323–8, would not be detached from his loyalty for any reason whatever. But when Edward applied the pressure of blockade there was such distress in Flanders that the Three Towns (that is, the three remaining 'good towns' which the count had been accustomed to consult, Ypres, Bruges and Ghent), led by James van Artevelde of Ghent, took matters into their own hands and negotiated treaties first of neutrality then of alliance with Edward. This extraordinary situation persisted for many years. The great towns, and all that part of the county which they controlled, recognized Edward as king of France and gave him more than token military support; while Count Louis remained faithful to King Philip and died fighting on his side at Crécy. From time to time there was a temporary accommodation, for only the count could give lawful authority to public acts in the county; but unless some way could be found to reconcile the economic interests of the towns, their social problems, the authority of the count and the sovereignty of the king, no stability was possible.

This seems to have been understood by Count Louis' successor, Louis of Male. The problem was thrust upon him at once, for as soon as he had done homage to King Philip, the towns put pressure on him to ally himself with King Edward. His solution was the ambiguous Treaty of Dunkirk (1348) which, given obedience to the count, allowed the agreements which the towns had made with Edward to remain in force. Such a settlement could only be made in time of truce; but it was Louis' achievement to maintain good relations with both England and France, rather than a negative neutrality, through most of his rule. By diplomatic skill and good fortune in war he was able to settle his relations with Brabant and the combined counties of Hainault, Holland and Zeeland very much to his advantage; and, secure on that side, he was able to make his own terms when he found the kings of France and England bidding against one another for the marriage of his daughter and heiress, Margaret. In the end, the king of France won. Louis' price was the restoration of the castellanies of Lille and Douai. Margaret was married to Philip the Bold, the king's brother and duke of Burgundy; and the ultimate consequence of this marriage was the fateful union of Flanders and Burgundy in 1384.

During the 1360s and '70s Count Louis had achieved a remarkable degree of independence diplomatically, and this was backed both by economic prosperity and by developments in government. Given reasonable dynastic good fortune, it is likely that Flanders would have been as independent as Brittany in the fifteenth century, even if there had been no union with Burgundy. Its government was being centralized and professionalized. The old comital *curia* had contracted, early in the century, into a more professional council, from which the nobility, as such, almost disappeared. This council could meet in a full session as the *Grand Conseil*, which might include representatives of the towns; it was developing a judicial 'department', the *Audience*, which was encouraging the appeal system within the county and coming to have some of the characteristics of a *parlement*, and a *chambre légale*, a diminishing survival of the old feudal jurisdiction of the *curia*. The men who staffed the council, in its various forms, were appointed, dismissed and salaried by the count; as in Brittany or Aquitaine they were professionals, jurists and doctors of law who had a definite interest in developing the authority of the count's courts. Financially, a transaction known as the 'transport de Flandre', by which the king of France had conveyed part of the indemnity exacted by the Treaty of Athis to the count in return for the definitive cession of Lille and Douai in 1312, had provided him with a regular and profitable source of revenue, for the count continued to raise the 'indemnity' for his own purposes; otherwise, and perhaps for that reason, taxation does not seem to have advanced far beyond individual bargains with the towns before the union with Burgundy. The *receveur de Flandre* was supplemented by a *souverain bailli*, a general supervisor of the administration; the functions, though not the title, of chancellor were taken from the provost of Saint Donatien and given to a *chancelier du comte*; and the auditing of all but the traditional domain revenues was given to an increasingly professional commission of the council soon to be known as the *chambre des comptes*. This centralizing policy, which was seen for what it was by the great towns jealous of their autonomy, was one cause of the revolt of 1379–85; but it was giving Flanders that practical independence which the other principalities in their several ways were achieving. King Charles V had to negotiate with Louis of Male on the marriage question almost as though he were a foreign prince; appeals to the *parlement* of Paris, though technically possible, were so rare that the comital courts were sovereign in practice,[1] and there was no longer any question of French administrative intervention within the county.

It was the dynastic union of the duchy of Burgundy[2] and of the county of Flanders in 1384 that formed the basis of the 'Burgundian state' of the fifteenth century.[3] The two principalities had this much in common that they were both situated on the frontier of the kingdom and both were able to profit by the opportunity to acquire lands in the empire; and after the union it was possible to standardize their administration to some extent. But their historical development had been very different.

The history of Flanders from the ninth to the end of the twelfth centuries had been one of almost continuous expansion from a central nucleus; and the count, preserving much of the Carolingian order and adding to it his enormous wealth as a landowner, was able to build up a compact and well-organized principality. The history of Burgundy, over the same period, was one of disintegration. Its origin lay in the relatively small part of the ancient kingdom of Burgundy that was left to West Francia in the partitions of the ninth century, and it was

[1] R. van Caeneghem, 'Les Appels flamands au parlement de Paris au moyen âge', *Etudes d'histoire du droit privé offertes à Pierre Petot* (1959), 61–8.

[2] Dukes: (Capetian)—Hugh III, 1162–92; Odo III, 1192–1218; Hugh IV, 1218–72; Robert II, 1272–1306; Hugh V, 1306–15; Odo IV, 1315–49; Philip of Rouvres (1349–60), 1360–1. (Valois)—(King John II, 1361–3); Philip the Bold, 1363–1404.

[3] J. Richard, 'Les Institutions ducales dans le duché de Bourgogne', *Inst. seign.*, 209–47 and references there given; in particular—J. Richard, *Les Ducs de Bourgogne et la formation du duché* (1954); H. Jassemin, 'Le contrôle financier en Bourgogne sous les derniers ducs capétiens', *Bibliothèque de l'Ecole des Chartes*, lxxix (1918), 102–41 (but cf. Richard, *Les Ducs de Bourgogne*, 441 ff.); *Registres des Parlements de Beaune et de Saint-Laurent-lès-Chalon*, ed. P. Petot (1927), intro.; and for the later fourteenth century, R. Vaughan, *Philip the Bold* (1962), with excellent bibliography.

organized then as a 'duchy', that is, a group of counties under a royal officer with special military powers. The office of duke was not strictly hereditary, though there was a strong hereditary tendency, until King Henry I established his brother Robert as duke in 1032. Robert founded the Capetian line of dukes which persisted until 1361; but the duchy which he ruled was much smaller than its Carolingian predecessor. The dukes lost control of the counties in which they were not themselves count, and even those they held disintegrated into ecclesiastical immunities and lay *seigneuries*, so that the Carolingian administrative framework had entirely disappeared before the end of the eleventh century. The duchy survived to form the basis of a feudal principality chiefly because the ducal family itself survived, and because the dukes, though there were no great figures among them, managed to retain some control of castle-building as a vestige of their original military authority.[1] They were therefore able to organize a number of *châtellenies* which provided the nucleus about which they were later able to rebuild their authority. But within the duchy of Burgundy, however defined, there were several prelates (the bishop of Langres for example) who held their lands independently of the duke, many royal enclaves, many allods. The duchy was simply a bundle of rights, not yet indivisible, and with very little territorial or political consistence.

When something like a 'war of independence' was being fought in Flanders during the thirteenth and the earlier part of the fourteenth centuries, the dukes of Burgundy were loyal and co-operative vassals of the king. Duke Hugh III, it is true, had acquired lands in the empire by his marriage with Beatrice of Albon, and seems to have thought, at one moment, of playing off emperor against king. But when the lord of Vergy, whom he had occasion to chastise, appealed to King Philip Augustus, the king intervened to great effect; after that there was no question but that the duke of Burgundy was the liege vassal of the king of France, as that was coming to be understood, and often closely connected with him by family ties. Very few obstacles were placed in the way of the development of French royal sovereignty over Burgundy or the entry into the duchy of French royal officials. This, no doubt, was largely because the conception of

[1] This is Richard's thesis.

Burgundy as a territorial entity was itself only just beginning to form. But as the duke gradually built up his domain by purchase and other usual means, and as he gradually defined and standardized his relations with his vassals, he was perpetually brought into contact with other authorities—the king, the greater churchmen, the counts of Champagne—who were doing the same thing and competing with one another for the homage of landowners converting their allods into fiefs. In the process, the dukes and their rivals defined their respective spheres of interest; the notion of a ducal *baronnie* was formed—a bundle of inalienable rights, a stretch of territory in which the duke was *dominus terrae*, an indivisible inheritance. Even at the end of the thirteenth century this was still rather more doctrine than fact, and it was not undisputed; so far as it was law it depended on judgments of the king's court.

In these circumstances it is not to be expected that the political institutions of the duchy would be very precocious. The ducal household and the ducal *curia* were of the usual kind save in one important particular. At the turn of the thirteenth and fourteenth centuries, it became the custom to delegate the hearing of appeals and other judicial work of the *curia* to *auditeurs des causes d'appeaux*. These were ducal councillors, professional lawyers, who formed themselves into a court which did much of the judicial work of the *curia* in the fourteenth century, though the *curia* still held *jours généraux* at Beaune from which the *parlement* of Burgundy grew as a formal institution later in the century. Local government shows the usual progression from the purely domanial agents of the twelfth to the *baillis* of the thirteenth and fourteenth centuries; but the evolution was slow and late. Until the end of the thirteenth century the accounts of local and other officers were still being heard, in principle and often in fact, by the duke himself whenever and wherever it was convenient; a ducal receiver to centralize receipts did not appear until then, and the beginnings of a *chambre des comptes*, in the sense of a small group of councillors detailed to hear accounts, but still unspecialized, cannot be put before the beginning of the fourteenth century.

A quickening of development can be detected under Duke Odo III; and it is significant that this came at a time when, as ruler of the counties of Burgundy and Artois, in right of his wife, he had other things to attend to besides the duchy. But the real organization of ducal government was the work of King John II and the French royal administration. When Odo III died in 1349, his heir Philip of Rouvres, was an infant. Philip's mother, Jeanne, took as her second husband the duke of Normandy who, in 1350, succeeded to the throne of France as King John II. Though he moved carefully, King John was in charge of the duchy, as guardian, by 1353, and this meant that the administration was taken over by French royal officers. Late in 1360, King John reluctantly delivered Burgundy to young Philip, who died of the plague within a year. The king then took possession of the duchy claiming to be the heir; but in 1363 he gave it as an appanage to his son Philip, known to history as Philip the Bold. This did not mean that the activity of French lawyers and administrators came to an end in Burgundy by any means; Philip the Bold was very much a French prince, spending a good deal of his time in Paris. In the great reorganization of his dominions carried out in 1386, after he had taken over the government of Flanders and other territories, French personnel and French administrative experience and practice were still very prominent.

The reconstruction of Burgundian institutions on the model of the French monarchy can be seen in almost every sphere of ducal government in the years between the death of Odo III and the reorganization of 1386. King John had introduced royal officers into the ducal council, making it, since he himself was necessarily absent from the duchy for most of the time of his wardship, a more definite and more professional body than it had hitherto been. Likewise the detailing of two or three of these councillors regularly to audit accounts, the provision of a *clerc des comptes* and of a place in which they could meet regularly, soon made the embryonic *chambre des comptes* at Dijon into a replica of its counterpart in Paris. For judicial purposes, the royal officers worked to make the occasional *jours généraux* of the ducal *curia* into a *parlement* on the Parisian model. They were not whole-hearted in this, perhaps, and they were not wholly successful; for there was already a court of appeal in Burgundy, the court of the *auditeurs des causes d'appeaux*, and though appeals therefrom to the Burgundian *parlement* were coming to be allowed, there was always the *parlement* of Paris ready to accept litigation and to get round any rules of restraint that it might be forced from time to time to make for itself. Besides, there were many seigneurs in Burgundy, chiefly ecclesiastical, from whose courts an appeal could lawfully be made directly to the *parlement* of Paris. By maintaining a number of proctors in Paris and at the courts of the royal *baillis* of Sens and Mâcon (as the duke of Aquitaine had to do at Paris and in the courts of the *baillis* of Toulouse and Périgord), the duke did what he could to preserve his rights as a peer; but he cannot be said to have been more than moderately successful. Like the duke of Aquitaine and the other great lords, he himself used the royal courts when it was convenient to do so. Successful resistance to French judicial sovereignty in Burgundy was not made until the fifteenth century. Finally, the first assembly recognized as the Estates of Burgundy was summoned by King John in 1352. Before then the dukes had occasionally asked for subsidies on a purely local basis, as the king did in France; but it was the desperate needs, first of the king and then of the duke, in the 1350s and 1360s, which established the institution.[1] The substitution of ducal for royal taxation, on a permanent basis, came a little later. Philip the Bold secured a grant of *aides* to be levied in Burgundy on the authority of the estates of the kingdom from King Charles V, and then continued to levy them for himself on the authority of the estates of Burgundy.

In so far, therefore, as Burgundy emerges as an autonomous principality before the union with Flanders, with characteristic institutions of government, these were, if not created, at least greatly hastened in their development by the king himself, his officers and his lawyers—naturally in imitation of royal institutions. It is a far cry from Flanders or Aquitaine.

This same tendency towards the growth of independent principalities in France can be seen in its earlier stages in the counties of Champagne or Toulouse,[2] both annexed to the Crown in the course of the thirteenth century; it can also be seen in small-scale affairs like the county of Forez (where a *chambre des comptes* developed very precociously in the early fourteenth century, in direct imitation, it seems, of the royal institution), the county of Beaujolais,[3] or the minuscule county of Guînes

---

[1] J. Billioud, *Les Etats de Bourgogne aux XIVe et XVe siècles* (1922).
[2] *Inst. seign.*, 71–99; 123–36.
[3] For Forez and Beaujolais, see E. Perroy, 'L'Etat bourbonnais' in *Inst. seign.* 289–317.

with its institutions of the Flemish type.[1] There are many others. At its most spectacular it can be seen in the Pyrenean *vicomté* of Béarn,[2] where the *vicomtes*, having been vassals, in the contemporary sense of the term, of the dukes of Gascony during the eleventh century, transferred their allegiance to the king of Aragon in the middle of the twelfth, and returned to do homage to Henry III of England and Aquitaine in 1242. Amid these changes the *vicomte*'s vassalage cannot often have had much practical import; and Gaston Fébus took what might seem to be the final step when he specifically refused liege homage for Béarn to the Black Prince in 1364. Gaston, in the end, out of dislike for Matthew de Castelbon, his nephew and nearest surviving heir, bequeathed his dominions to the king of France (Treaty of Toulouse, 1390); but after his death the *cour majour* and the *cour des communautés*, hitherto separate institutions, met together spontaneously as the first assembly of the Estates of Béarn and assisted Matthew to negotiate the king's renunciation of the treaty, thus preserving the 'sovereignty' of Béarn to the extent that it had been achieved up to that point. As in Brittany influential men worked for independence when their lord seemed to fail them.

Perhaps the most striking example of the tendency is to be found in what may be described as the 'posthumous' history of the duchy of Normandy.[3] When the duchy was annexed to the royal domain in 1204 its individuality was not destroyed. Though the office of seneschal was abolished, and many offices filled by men taken from the royal administration, the duchy preserved its law and most of its institutions. The exchequer continued as the high court although, as the practice of appeals to the king's court developed in the thirteenth century, it had to allow appeals from its judgments; and it continued to act as the central financial institution of the duchy, though it accounted to the king's officers in Paris. But as the royal *baillis* attacked the judicial privileges of the seigneurs, in Normandy as elsewhere, as the king developed his claims to levy general taxation during the reign of Philip IV, and as appeals from the

---

[1] Le Patourel, 'L'Occupation anglaise de Calais au XIVe siècle', *Revue du Nord*, xxxiii (1951), 236–7 and references there given.

[2] P. Tucoo-Chala, 'Les Institutions de la vicomté de Béarn', *Inst. seign.*, 319–41; also *La Vicomté de Béarn et le problème de sa souveraineté* (1961).

[3] A. Coville, *Les Etats de Normandie* (1894); J. R. Strayer, *The Administration of Normandy under Saint Louis* (1932); R. Besnier, *La Coutume de Normandie: Histoire externe* (1935).

exchequer to the king's court seemed to endanger the autonomy of Norman law, the Normans joined in the movement of 1314 and 1315, and secured the one effective provincial charter that was given at that time, the famous 'charte aux Normands'. This provided that there should be no further appeals from the exchequer to the *parlement* of Paris, that there should be no taxation without consent, save in a defined emergency, and that Norman customs should be respected. The assemblies called from time to time in Normandy to consent to taxation enabled the Normans to make collective protests against anything they considered to be an infringement of their liberties, and to maintain their consciousness as a people distinct from others within the kingdom of France. By the end of the century it could be said in Normandy, as in Brittany, that 'le duché n'est pas du royaume'[1]—and this in a dukeless duchy whose only dukes in the fourteenth century, and those in name only, had been heirs to the throne.[2]

These brief sketches should show that the tendency towards the formation of autonomous principalities was general in the France of the fourteenth century, and that there was more to the political development of France in the thirteenth and fourteenth centuries than the progress of the monarchy. The means by which autonomy was achieved differed from principality to principality, and the whole process would be more comprehensible if a comparative constitutional history of the great French fiefs had been written. That would be a big undertaking; but already the outline is clear.

The great fiefs of the eleventh and twelfth centuries were, in a sense, as independent as those of the fifteenth century. The duke of Normandy or the count of Flanders might recognize the king as his suzerain and might occasionally attend his court; but they might also make war upon him and among themselves and establish independent relations with countries outside the kingdom. But towards the end of the twelfth century and in the thirteenth the king was in various ways able to insist on liege homage; and this carried with it a recognition of his judicial and legislative sovereignty—in practice, the submission of the great

---

[1] E. G. Léonard, *Histoire de la Normandie* (1944), 69.
[2] John, created duke in 1332 (succeeded to the throne in 1350), Charles in 1355 (succeeded in 1364).

lords to the jurisdiction of the king's court, acceptance of the appellate jurisdiction of this court and the administrative intervention of the king's officers in the great fiefs to protect appellants, to collect taxation and so forth. To some extent the development of princely independence can be represented as a reaction to this extension of the royal government, as a resistance leading to the formation of their own hierarchy of courts, their own financial administrations, their own bodies of professional administrators who imitated and rivalled the king's lawyers and administrators. The kingdom and the principalities were growing up together as rival organizations.

But this is not the whole story. Although professional councils, *chambres des comptes, parlements,* and estates were coming into being in all the principalities (sometimes with different nomenclature), and very similar conventions, say, in the use of seals, these institutions did not all originate or develop in the same way. One or two of the principalities (Flanders and Normandy were examples) were in advance of the monarchy in the twelfth century; others were more backward. Each had its own peculiar circumstances. In Flanders it was a position at the extremity of the kingdom, a Germanic population at the centre, the survival of Carolingian institutions, relations with external powers including England, and above all an exceptional economic development; in Burgundy a close relation between the ducal and the royal families; Brittany had her position on the sea routes, her relations with England and her Celtic nucleus; Aquitaine, a relationship first with the Angevin empire and later with England, and all the ramifications of the wine trade. Politics and personalities also played their part. The very fact that the history of each of the principalities has hitherto been studied separately is in itself significant, for they had many of the characteristics of states in miniature.

In the fourteenth century the monarchy was challenged as it had not been challenged since the turn of the eleventh and twelfth centuries. Organized resistance to royal centralization among the seigneurs of the second rank showed itself in the leagues of 1314 and 1315; the professionalization of council, judiciary and finance was appearing in the princely governments as in the royal government; the economic development of the twelfth and thirteenth centuries had begun to produce taxable wealth for princes as well as for the king; and the princes were coming to look upon their lands not as so many units of property but as political entities with interests which might not coincide with those of the kingdom as seen by the king. In many of them a critical point in their development was reached in the fourteenth century: Flanders in the 'war of independence' and the 'neutrality' of Louis of Male; Brittany in the 'war of succession'; Burgundy in the minority and premature death of Philip of Rouvres and the reconstruction of the ducal government by royal officers; Aquitaine (in relation to the Valois kings of France) in Edward III's assumption of the title 'king of France' in 1340; Béarn when Gaston Fébus refused homage in 1364. Edward III's attempts to make capital out of the resistance to royal centralization, and, in Flanders, Normandy, Brittany and elsewhere to identify his cause with local interests,[1] all suggest that the first phase of the Hundred Years War, while fundamentally a war of succession, also showed some of the characteristics of a French civil war in which the princes, led by the duke of Aquitaine who was also the king of England, fought against the efforts of the king of France to make the unity of his kingdom a reality. And they were so far successful that the issue between king and princes was in doubt for a century or so.

[1] Cf. Le Patourel, 'Edward III and the Kingdom of France', *History*, xliii (1958), 173–89.

VI

James Campbell

ENGLAND, SCOTLAND AND THE HUNDRED YEARS WAR IN THE FOURTEENTH CENTURY[1]

Geoffrey le Baker says that in 1333 Edward III, like the apostle, put away childish things.[2] He means that when he intervened to help Edward Balliol displace David Bruce from the Scottish throne Edward broke the treaty of Northampton, concluded in his minority. His motives are not far to seek. Robert Bruce had inflicted on England the worst humiliations

---

[1] W. C. Dickinson, *Scotland from the Earliest Times to 1603* (1961) is the most recent general account of medieval Scotland, with a good bibliography. J. H. Ramsay, *The Genesis of Lancaster*, 2 vols. (Oxford, 1913) and E. W. M. Balfour-Melville, *Edward III and David II* (1954), contain the best accounts of Anglo-Scottish relations; see also E. Miller, *War in the North* (Hull, 1960). The most relevant printed record sources are *Foedera*, ed. T. Rymer, 20 vols. (1704–35), new ed. 4 vols. (Record Commission, 1816–69)—all references below are to the latter edition unless otherwise stated—*Rot[uli] Scot[iae]*, ed. D. Macpherson, J. Caley and W. Illingworth, 2 vols. (Record Commission, 1814–19); *The E[xchequer] R[olls of] S[cotland]*, vols. i–iii, ed. J. Stuart and G. Burnett (Edinburgh, 1878–80); *C[alendar of] D[ocuments] R[elating to Scotland]*, ed. J. Bain, 4 vols. (1881–8); *[The] A[cts of the] P[arliaments of S[cotland]*, vol. i, ed. T. Thomson and C. Innes (Record Commission, 1844); and *[The] Parl[iamentary] Rec[ords of Scotland in the General Register House Edinburgh]*, ed. W. Robertson (Record Commission, 1804)—this work, which contains valuable and otherwise unprinted documents from the manuscript in H.M. General Register House, Edinburgh, known as the Black Book, was withdrawn and few copies exist. The principal Scottish chronicles are those of Fordun, *Chronica Gentis Scotorum*, ed. W. F. Skene, 2 vols. (Edinburgh, 1871–2); Bower, *Joannis de Fordun Scotichronicon cum Supplementis et Continuatione Walteri Boweri*, ed. W. Goodall, 2 vols. (Edinburgh, 1759); and Wynton, *The Original Chronicle*, ed. F. J. Amours, 6 vols. (Scottish Text Society, 1903–14). Froissart gives much information on Scotland; all the references below are to the edition of S. Luce, G. Raynaud, L. Mirot and A. Mirot (in progress, first 13 vols., Paris, 1869–1957), unless that of Kervyn de Lettenhove, 25 vols. (Brussels, 1867–77), is specifically cited.

[2] Ed. E. M. Thompson (Oxford, 1889), 50.

it had suffered since the loss of Normandy. But when he died he left an infant heir and a kingdom that did not seem likely to be able to maintain what he had won. Scotland's resources were inferior to those of England and the Crown's control over them less. It is, at least, symbolic of the power of the Scottish nobility that the Gough map of *c.* 1360 notes in Scotland, not, as it sometimes does in England, the administrative counties, but the *comitatus* of the earls. Bruce's triumph had been not only in a struggle against England but also in a long civil war which had accompanied it. Much land had changed hands and much resentment remained. Scotland was vulnerable, yet rich enough to offer more than the opportunity for revenge. Her wealth derived largely from foreign trade and above all from the export of wool. This averaged at least 5,500 sacks annually between 1327 and 1333 and was nearly all from the eastern and especially the south-eastern ports. Berwick was the most important of these. Its average annual export was over 1,800 sacks in these years and its customs revenue, at an average of about £640 a year, was the largest single regular item in the revenue of the Scottish Crown.[1] The area which England could most easily conquer was also that most worth conquering.

After his victory at Halidon on 19th July, 1333, it seemed that Edward III, at the age of twenty, might dispose of Scotland as best suited him. He imposed a settlement whereby much of the south, including Edinburgh itself, was to be joined to England and the rest ruled by Balliol under strict conditions of vassalage. The next four years were devoted to the consolidation of his success. He moved his central administration to York and led an army into Scotland every year, that of 1335 one of the largest he was ever to raise.[2] But by the time the French war began in 1337 he was far from having defeated the supporters of David Bruce. He held the main fortresses as far north as Stirling and Perth and from them controlled some, but by no means all, of southern Scotland. The Highlands were inaccessible; the violent campaign of 1336 had failed to secure the area between the Dee and the Moray Firth, where David's followers retained the vital port of Aberdeen and kept some kind of administration going; there was considerable resistance elsewhere. Sir

[1] *E.R.S.*, i, nos. III, IV, X, XIV, XVI, XIX, XXII.
[2] A. E. Prince in *The English Government at Work*, i, ed. J. F. Willard and W. A. Morris (Cambridge, Mass., 1940), 332–76; R. Nicholson, 'An Irish Expedition to Scotland in 1335', *Irish Hist. Studies*, xiii (1963), 197–211.

Andrew Moray and the other Scottish leaders controlled wide areas and considerable forces and were able to take the offensive.[1]

The English failure is easy to explain. There was no chance of avoiding resistance. Those whom Edward sought to expropriate were too numerous and too powerful.[2] The geography of Scotland favoured those who chose to resist and the devastation and opportunities of war made it easy for them to find followers. Edward lacked the means to suppress the guerrilla war they waged. He could hold towns and fortresses at a price: by 1337 garrisons in, and repairs at, Edinburgh, Roxburgh, Perth and Stirling were together costing about £10,000 a year while his income from Scotland probably did not exceed £2,000[3]. Large areas and a wide allegiance could be won by the use of big armies, but were lost when they left. As the French had found in Flanders, and Edward was again to find in France, the relation between the income of a king and the pay of a soldier was not such as to permit the permanent occupation of a country in the face of widespread resistance from its inhabitants. Edward's efforts in Scotland created conditions which made pacification harder to achieve. Power on the Scottish side lay with leaders who were often doing well from plunder and ransoms and who did not spare their own countrymen.[4] According to Fordun Sir Andrew Moray did much for the freedom of Scotland, but 'all the country he passed through he reduced to such desolation and distress that more perished afterwards through starvation and want than the sword devoured in time of war'. Like Robert Bruce after 1306 such men built up their power by having booty won within Scotland to offer. It was to be feared that they might turn south of the border as he had done after 1311. If Edward's grip on southern Scotland were to slacken, the conditions he had created there could generate

---

[1] For the scanty records of the administration of David's lieutenants, see *E.R.S.*, i, 435–68; *Handlist of the Acts of David II*, ed. B. Webster (Edinburgh, 1962, duplicated).

[2] David Dalrymple, Lord Hailes, *Annals of Scotland*, ii (Edinburgh, 1797), 159–62; R. C. Reid, 'Edward de Balliol', *Trans. Dumfriesshire and Galloway . . . Antiquarian Soc.*, 3rd ser., xxxv (1956–7), 59–62; *Chronicon de Lanercost*, ed. J. Stevenson (Bannatyn and Maitland Clubs, 1839), 276; *C.D.S.*, iii, 318–47.

[3] These rough figures are based on *C.D.S.*, iii, app. iii–vi and nos. 1240, 1241, and *Rot. Scot.*, i, 489b–490a.

[4] *Fordun*, i, 362–3; *Lanercost*, pp. 278, 288; *Murimuth*, ed. E. M. Thompson (1889), 75; H. S. Lucas, *The Low Countries and the Hundred Years War* (Ann Arbor, 1929), 183.

attacks against England on a much larger scale than those which had been in progress since the war began. In so far as there was a risk that northern England might be devastated as it had been under Edward II, his son's position in 1337 was one, not only of expensive frustration, but of danger.

Thus the war with France began at a time when Edward was heavily, or even inextricably, involved in Scotland. Its immediate cause was quite probably the help which Philip VI gave, or threatened to give to the Scots. The links between France and Scotland were old and numerous.[1] Kings of Scotland had married French wives. Some of the Scottish nobility had special connections with France: Edward Balliol was in private life a French landowner with whom Philip VI had a quarrel of his own.[2] There was a considerable trade between the two countries. Many Scots settled in France: a possible originator of the idea of applying the Salic Law to the French succession was called Jean Lescot. Trade and settlement need have had little political effect. Scottish entrepreneurs are to be found all over Europe in the fourteenth century. They appear selling cloth in Pomerania and perpetrating religious frauds in Italy. There were probably more Englishmen settled in France and more Scots in England than there were Scots in France. The important consideration was the value of an independent Scotland to French policy. This had been clear since the time of Philip the Fair and had most recently been recognized by the treaty of 1326 whereby Robert I and Charles IV bound themselves and their heirs to mutual aid against England in war and peace. Philip VI de Valois was not the most imposing of French kings, but he ruled a state whose power was all and more than all than that of the France of Louis XIV was to be in Europe, and he was well capable of protecting a friend or a client.

Philip began by bringing David to France in May 1334, established him at Château Gaillard and gave him a pension to help maintain his little court, which included some of the Scottish bishops, many of whom had gone into exile.[3] In June

---

[1] Francisque-Michel, *Les Écossais en France: les Français en Écosse*, 2 vols. (1862); the catalogue by B. Mahieu and N. Gand de Vernon of the exhibition at the Archives Nationales, Paris, 'France-Écosse' (Paris, 1956), indicates some of the materials from which this outdated work may be supplemented.

[2] *The Brut*, ed. F. W. D. Brie, i (Early Eng. Text Soc., 1906) 273-4; *Inventaire d'anciens comptes royaux*, ed. Ch.-V. Langlois (Paris, 1899), 45.

[3] *E.R.S.*, i, 448-54, 464-8; P[ublic] R[ecord] O[ffice, London], French Transcripts, 8/138, fols. 12, 14, 15.

Philip broke up an Anglo-French conference which seemed just to have reached an agreement on Gascony by saying there could be no settlement in which Scotland was not included.[1] Thereafter he involved the Scottish issue with the other disputes between France and England, claiming the role of mediator. Philip was in a position where he could bring great pressure to bear. Edward was seeking to improve his position in Gascony, where he was very vulnerable and where, having admitted that he owed liege-homage, he had no substantial *quid pro quo* to offer in return for concessions. There was little to deter Philip from adopting David's cause. There were dangers within France but hostility towards England might help rather than hinder him in dealing with these. Edward's continental alliances did not present a serious threat until 1337. Edward had to take Philip's stand on behalf of David very seriously. At the same time he was not willing and may not have dared to make concessions sufficient to satisfy him. English discontent with the treaty of Northampton had helped Edward to establish his power in and after 1330. It had been one of the causes of Lancaster's rebellion, in which most of the leaders of the Disinherited, Beaumont, Wake, Atholl, and Henry Ferrers were, in different degrees, implicated. After the failure of the revolt Beaumont and Wake had retired to France, returning after the coup at Nottingham in the company of other exiles with Scottish claims, Richard fitzAlan and Fulk fitzWarin. There are indications that Edward was not altogether secure in England in the mid-'thirties and the support of these men may have been important to him.[2] His prestige was in any case heavily committed to the Scottish war. He played for time. A series of conferences in which French, English, Scottish and papal representatives participated were held at intervals up to the end of 1336. Nothing is known to have come of them apart from a certain number of truces between the English and the Scots.

From the beginning the French gave the Scots more than

[1] E. Déprez, *Les préliminaires de la Guerre de Cent Ans* (Paris, 1902), 97. For the diplomatic position, see also H. S. Lucas, op. cit., H. Jenkins, *Papal Efforts for Peace under Benedict XII* (Philadelphia, 1933) and R. Cazelles, *La société politique et la crise de la royauté sous Philippe de Valois* (Paris, 1958).

[2] G. A. Holmes, 'The Rebellion of the Earl of Lancaster 1328-9', *Bull. Inst. Hist. Res.*, xxviii (1955), 84-9 and the works cited there; *Lanercost*, 266-7, 279; cf. R. Nicholson, 'The Last Campaign of Robert Bruce', E[ng.] H[ist.] R[ev.], lxxvii (1962), 234.

diplomatic support. Scotland depended upon imports for most manufactured goods and, to some extent, for food. In this, as in all wars with Scotland in the fourteenth century, the English tried hard to prevent the Scots importing the arms, harness and food upon which their ability to resist must largely have depended.[1] Almost as soon as the Anglo-Scottish war began Philip sent ten ships laden with arms and food. These almost certainly did not arrive, but others which followed probably did.[2] French influence helped to prevent the efforts of English diplomacy to cut the Scots off from Flanders, their chief market and—with the possible exception, even in wartime, of England and Ireland—their main source of supply. France did much to further the naval activities of the Scots. English commerce depended on the safety of the narrow seas; the south coast was open to raids; the garrisons and armies in Scotland depended on sea-borne supplies. The Scots took the opportunity to carry on a *guerre de course* with French and Flemish help. Although the scale of this is uncertain it is clear that, together with the need to blockade Scotland, it forced Edward to maintain a considerable and continuous naval effort.[3]

From the beginning of the war with Scotland it was the possibility that Philip might go so far as to send an army to Scotland or to England which did most to make his intervention formidable. Edward ordered extensive precautions against invasion from the sea by the Scots and their foreign allies during the campaigns of the summer of 1333 and of late 1334. The danger seems to have been thought even greater in the summer of 1335. Orders were issued that all ships over forty tons capacity were to be held ready to intercept the invaders. Beacons were to be prepared on hills to warn of their arrival. The fortresses of Wales and the south-east were put in a state of defence. Arrayers were appointed to levy men all over England should the need arise. These precautions were repeated during the campaign of 1336 when, from July, fears centred on the presence of Philip's erstwhile crusading fleet in the Channel

[1] R. Stanford Reid, 'Trade, Traders and Scottish Independence', *Speculum*, xxix (1954), 210–22; 'The Scots and the Staple Ordinance of 1313', ibid., xxxiv (1959), 598–610; 'Sea-Power in the Anglo-Scottish War 1296–1327', *The Mariner's Mirror*, xlvi (1960), 7–23.

[2] C. de la Roncière, *Histoire de la marine française*, i (Paris, 1899), 388–9; Lucas, op. cit., 142–3; *Rot. Scot.*.

[3] De la Roncière, i, 388–98; *The English Government at Work*, i, op. cit., 376–93.

ports. At the beginning of 1337 orders were issued for the collection of another great fleet to resist invasion.[1] These were the first of the invasion-scares which were to occur in every decade of the French war in the fourteenth century. They were burdensome, especially in so far as they led to the arrest of shipping, and expensive. It is unlikely that there was much to justify Edward's fears in 1333 and 1334 and it is not clear how strong they were. In 1335 and 1336 there was real cause for alarm. On 31st July, 1335, the archbishop of Rouen, preaching before the French court, said that Philip intended to send 6,000 men-at-arms to help the Scots, though this was not, so he is said to have said, to interfere with the crusade.[2] At some time in the same year the Constable of France, the count of Eu, was appointed to command such an expeditionary force. A scheme exists, probably drawn up in 1335 or 1336, for the despatch of 1,200 French men-at-arms and 20,000 serjeants to Scotland.[3] A letter of 19th June, 1336, written by someone close to Edward's court, shows what was thought to be known of French plans in England. It contains detailed and alarming information on the collection of a strong fleet and army to be sent to England or Scotland.[4] Some French troops may have been sent to Scotland at this time.[5] It is not known how far Philip went towards putting his project for large-scale intervention into effect, to what extent it was one among several alternative plans, or how far he was himself frightened by Edward's diplomatic and naval activity. But there is quite enough evidence to show that during the campaigns of 1335 and 1336 Edward was rightly frightened of what Philip might do. He took the risk, played for time in his negotiations with France, and made a great and very expensive effort to crush Scottish resistance. He failed and found himself still involved in a war which he could neither win nor abandon and still faced with the possibility of French invasion. Those chroniclers who thought that his intervention on the Continent

[1] For precautions against invasion see especially *Rot. Scot.*
[2] *Chronique parisienne anonyme*, ed. A. Hellot (Soc. de l'hist. de Paris, xi, 1884), 164–5.
[3] De la Roncière discusses much of the evidence for French invasion plans, i, 347n, 391–3. He may well be right in dating the scheme in Bibliothèque Nationale, MS. Français, 2755, fols. 216–21 to 1336 and it is almost certainly for an expedition to be commanded by the Constable (fol. 221) but it could be rather earlier or later.
[4] Cf. *Lanercost*, 286; *Knighton*, ed. J. R. Lumby, i (1889), 477.
[5] *E.R.S.*, i, 451, 453; R. Cazelles, *La société politique . . .*, op. cit., 148–9 (the de Garencières involved was probably Yon, not Pierre).

was a direct response to Philip's threat of intervention in Scotland may well have been right.[1] Edward's reaction was not only characteristically aggressive, but even, perhaps, prudent. Whatever may be said against his activities in the Low Countries from 1337, they did at least ensure that England was not invaded.

Until the summer of 1338 Edward concentrated his war-effort on Scotland. He had about 4,000 troops there at the beginning of the year and a considerable army besieged Dunbar, in vain, until June.[2] Its departure marked the beginning of a defensive war in the north which dragged on, despite abortive negotiations for peace and ill-kept truces, until Neville's Cross was won in October 1346.[3] The English fortresses in Scotland fell quickly. Edward's preoccupations prevented their being adequately supplied with food or money and neither he, nor his grandfather, had spent enough on their fortification. After the fall of Stirling in April 1342 the English retained nothing in Scotland but Berwick, some lands around it, Lochmaben, and the occasional allegiance of some of the weather-cock gentry of the south-west.[4] England's greatest advantage in war against Scotland lay in her capacity to bring her superior wealth and organization to bear by sending armies into the Lowlands so large that the Scots dare not face them in the open field. This was not done between 1338 and 1347, although northern forces did invade Scotland and Edward himself led a considerable army to the border at the end of 1341 and the beginning of 1342. As the English weakened and proved unable to retaliate in great force so Scottish raiding increased in strength. David's return home in 1341—probably in June—was followed by powerful raids in the autumn and in 1342; at least one of them reached the Tyne. Heavy raiding recommenced in 1345 after something of a lull, culminating in the great expedition which came to grief at Neville's Cross. This was one of the rare Scottish armies to include forces from nearly the whole of the kingdom. As in the later campaigns of Robert I and in those of 1384–9, border

[1] E.g. *Grandes chroniques de France*, ed. J. Viard, ix (Paris, 1937), 158.
[2] A. E. Prince, 'The Strength of English Armies in the Reign of Edward III', *E.H.R.*, xlvi (1931), 358–60.
[3] A truce was concluded for a year in 1338. It is uncertain whether the Scots exercised their right to accede to the truce of Esplechin (1340) as they did to that of Malestroit (1343). It is likely that only shorter truces made on the Marches had much effect, cf. *The Priory of Coldingham*, ed. J. Raine (Surtees Soc., 1841), Appendix, cvii.
[4] B. Webster, 'The English Occupation of Dumfriesshire', *T.G.D.S.*, 3rd ser., xxxv (1956–7), 64–80.

warfare snowballed into something more as the prospect of plunder attracted Scots from beyond the Marches. The damage done in northern England in the years before 1346 was considerable, though not so great as it had been in Edward II's reign or as some applicants for financial relief made out. Cumberland, which suffered most, had its assessment for the tenth and fifteenth reduced by more than half between 1336 and 1339: by 1348 ninety-two 'towns' in the county had to be exempted altogether. Northumberland suffered considerable harm even, in 1346, in the far south.[1] Perhaps the most convincing evidence of the power of the Scots is that by 1344 the bishop of Durham had reverted to the ways of Edward II's reign and was raising a tax to buy them off for a few months.[2] The difficulties caused by raiding were exacerbated by the disorderly state of northern England. English and Scottish brigands co-operated and on both sides there were men who were beyond the control of their rulers. In 1339 an attempt to suppress violence in north-west England had to be abandoned because it gave offence and those offended threatened to join the Scots—as many Englishmen had done under Edward II.[3]

In spite of all, the March was defended, and in the end triumphantly.[4] The triumph was partly that of the northerners themselves, partly of the English administrative system. After 1338 Edward left England north of the Trent to look after itself to a large extent. Very few of its levies or magnates were summoned to serve abroad, apart from the bishop of Durham and a few others in 1346. Conversely, few troops from south of the Trent were sent north, except for the campaigns of 1341–2. The taxation of the north was largely appropriated to its defence and was kept under special officers at York. A lieutenant or *capitaneus* was put in command for particular campaigns or crises but much power lay with commissions of northern magnates. Most conspicuous of these were Henry Percy and

---

[1] J. F. Willard, 'The Scotch Raids and the Fourteenth Century Taxation of Northern England', *Univ. of Colorado Studies*, v (1907–8), 240–2; *Cal. Close Rolls 1346–9*, pp. 30–1, 87–8; *C.D.S.*, iii, no. 1441; *Cal. Inquis. Misc.*, ii, nos. 2037, 2051.

[2] *Registrum Palatinum Dunelmense*, ed. T. D. Hardy, iv (1878), 273–7; cf. *The Anonimalle Chronicle*, ed. V. H. Galbraith (Manchester, 1927), 24, 26; and *Coldingham*, Appendix, xvi.

[3] *C.C.R. 1339–41*, 94.

[4] For the following paragraph see especially *Rot. Scot.*, *Rot. Parl.* ii (1783), and J. E. Morris, 'Mounted Infantry in Medieval Warfare', *Trans. Roy, Hist. Soc.*, 3rd ser., viii (1914), 98–102; cf. M. Powicke, *Military Obligation in Medieval England* (Oxford, 1962), 182–212.

Ralph Neville, particularly in regard to the control of expenditure. An important part seems to have been played by northern assemblies which were held in most years. Commissions were sent to these to announce decisions, usually taken in parliament, on the defence of the north and to make arrangements accordingly. Their most important function was probably the conclusion of indentures with the northern lords. The eight counties north of the Trent had considerable military resources. Something of the order of 8,000 archers and hobelars were available for array; 500 or more men-at-arms and a similar number of archers could be raised in the retinues of the magnates, usually, perhaps always, by indenture. Small raids were left to the levies of the March counties and to the magnate retinues which were probably kept on the March for part of most years. If a more dangerous invasion threatened, more troops were summoned from further south. That an army sufficient to defeat the Scots was collected in time and at the right place in 1346 was the result, not of fortunate improvisation, but of the orderly working of a system of defence much of which was at least as old as the reign of Edward I. It worked, admittedly with much default and delay, because the northerners were used to it, because it was to their interest to make it work, and because Edward ensured the co-operation of the magnates by giving them power and money.

The relatively successful defence of northern England and the victory of Neville's Cross are to some extent to be accounted for by the weakness of the Scots. The limited resources and unfortunate history of the Scottish monarchy rarely permitted the king adequate control over the nobility. Little is known of the internal history of Scotland in the years following David's return, but it is clear that he had to face serious disorder. The incidents of which we know most are connected with William Douglas of Liddesdale—who must be distinguished from the future earl.[1] This man was in high favour after 1341 and received many grants. But his anxiety to extend his lands on the March led him to murder Alexander Ramsay in 1342 and, perhaps, to engage in some kind of treasonable negotiation with the king of England. The internal weakness of Scotland may

---

[1] For the Douglases see W. Fraser, *The Douglas Book*, 4 vols. (Edinburgh, 1885); H. Maxwell, *History of the House of Douglas*, 2 vols. (1902); R. B. Armstrong, *The History of Liddesdale* (Edinburgh, 1883).

help to account for the relative peace on the border in 1343 and 1344. Its effect on the conduct of war is clearly to be seen in the campaign of 1346. Scottish armies were not paid by the king.[1] A large army to attack England could be gathered only by a French subsidy or the hope of plunder; and the gathering took time. The main invasion of 1346 did not take place until October, but the English suspected before the end of August what was afoot.[2] Once gathered such Scottish forces were hard to control. Most of the men of the isles and the west who mustered for this invasion went home before it began. When it did begin, the army spent four days besieging the peel of Liddel in the interests of William Douglas of Liddesdale. He had already quarrelled with the earl of Moray while it was being besieged earlier in the year and so had forced the Scots to retire.[3] This time it fell and he at once suggested that the army should return home. Had less time been spent in besieging this minor fortress, David need not have been intercepted at Durham. In short, while the Scots could easily, almost naturally, keep the borders in turmoil, their effectiveness for war on a grander scale was impaired by the weakness of the Scottish Crown.

Satisfactorily though the war ended Edward had had to pay a heavy price in the north after 1337. He lost his dearly-bought chance of gaining southern Scotland. A major recruiting-ground and a considerable part of his income had to be devoted to the Scottish war. He had to spend or owe £30,000 or more on the fortresses of Edinburgh, Perth, Stirling and Roxburgh between the beginning of the war with France and their loss.[4] The campaign of 1337-8 was very expensive. Expenditure through the wardrobe on the winter campaign of 1341-2 and on the maintenance of troops on the March in the following summer amounted to nearly £11,000.[5] The cost of the defence of the north to the king may have diminished in subsequent years but he by no means bore the whole burden of war, especially within England. Many of the parliamentary grievances of the period related to the means whereby he sought to transfer part of it elsewhere—array, purveyance, excessive pardoning—and

[1] D. Hay, 'Booty in Border Warfare', *T.D.G.S.*, 3rd ser., xxxi (1952-3), 158.
[2] *Rot. Scot.*, i, 673b.
[3] *Murimuth*, p. 202.
[4] This estimate is based on *C.D.S.*, iii, *Rot. Scot.*, i, *C.C.R. 1337-9*, 525 and *Rot. Parl.*, ii, 115a-116b.
[5] P.R.O., E.36/204, fols. 102r-105v.

can be amply illustrated in the north. It is true that complaint and evasion often indicate not so much the oppressiveness of exactions as the opportunities for resistance to them in a society which was for many a very free one. Nevertheless, some of these demands, perhaps array especially, imposed heavy burdens. The counties were supposed to pay their levies to the muster, or even beyond, and sometimes to provide them with arms and uniforms. It is not yet clear how much money was involved or who actually provided it but the cost was certainly considerable. On the other hand some nobles and merchants were enriched by the Scottish war and Neville's Cross brought profit to many.

It is difficult to determine how far Scottish attacks were co-ordinated to suit French strategy. Certainly the main invasions were launched when Edward was involved on the Continent. Conversely, the only occasion on which he seems to have contemplated a big attack upon Scotland was in 1344. Concern for the north may have made him more willing to conclude truces with France. In both 1337 and 1341 the conclusion or extension of such a truce was followed by the despatch to Scotland of troops originally intended for the Continent. The only Scottish attack which we can be fairly sure to have been directly instigated by France was that which ended at Neville's Cross. Philip wrote to ask David for help in June 1346 and, more urgently, in July.[1] Philip did the Scots some service when, in 1342, he released the earl of Salisbury from captivity in exchange for the earl of Moray, who was in English hands. It does not seem that he sent much material help. Ships which the English captured in August 1337 were said to have been taking arms, treaties, and a large sum of money from France to Scotland.[2] If so, this interception was very important since this was just the kind of assistance needed to induce the Scots to launch a major attack. French ships and troops, though probably not many of either, took part in the siege of Perth in 1339.[3] According to le Bel and Froissart a certain number of French

[1] There seems no reason to doubt the authenticity of the letters from Philip to David given in Latin translations in the continuation of Hemingburgh, ed. H. C. Hamilton (1849), ii, 420–423. Their form is the appropriate one of letters missive (cf. R. Cazelles, *Lettres closes . . . de Philippe de Valois* (Paris, 1958), 6–17, esp. 9–10) and there is a near correspondence between the places from which they are dated and Philip's itinerary (J. Viard, 'Itinéraire de Philippe VI de Valois', *Bibl. de l'éc. des Chartes*, lxxiv (1913), 569.

[2] *Cal. Pat. Rolls 1334–8*, 513 and *C.C.R. 1337–9*, 172 nearly resolve doubts on the date of this incident, cf. F. Lennel, *Calais au Moyen Age*, i (Calais, 1909), 79.

[3] *Fordun*, i, 363–4; *Wynton*, vi, 124–7; *E.R.S.*, i, 507.

troops—Froissart says 200—fought with the Scots in *c.* 1340–2.[1] There is no evidence that French aid came to Scotland in 1346, apart from Baker's statement that Philip sent a large force.[2] In general it seems that the French received a great deal of useful help from the Scots at small cost.

Neville's Cross left David and many Scottish noblemen in English hands. Edward now held the initiative. Much of southern Scotland was immediately overrun—roughly the modern counties of Berwick, Roxburgh, Dumfries, Peebles and Selkirk. In May and June 1347 Edward Balliol invaded Scotland and penetrated as far as Glasgow with a powerful army. This expedition may have been a serious attempt to establish him on the Scottish throne. If so, it was the last. Another, lesser, incursion was made into Scotland in October and thereafter Edward III's policy on the March was defensive.[3] Until 1355 the truces were nearly continuous, though ill-kept. Little effort seems to have been made to hold the newly-won lands, a large part of which the Scots had regained by 1356. The English kept Roxburgh and considerable areas in Berwickshire and Roxburghshire. They had never lost Berwick and Lochmaben. Edward Balliol exercised what sway he could in the south-west from Hestan Island and Caerlaverock.

In every year from 1347 negotiations went on for David's release. Great problems and opportunities faced Edward here. He did not recognize David as king of Scotland but if he was to profit from his great prize it was very necessary that the Scots should do so. David was childless. Robert Stewart, his half-sister's son and eight years his senior was heir presumptive and ruled Scotland as guardian in his absence. Robert may not have been over-anxious to redeem his uncle. The English did not cause enough trouble after 1347 to make a settlement imperative. David had been badly wounded at Neville's Cross, still had an arrow-head in his head and needed frequent medical care. Were he to be ransomed Robert would be displaced from power. If he were to die soon after being freed the ransom would be wasted. If he were to live he might outlive his heir, or engender another one.

---

[1] Discussed by J. Viard and E. Déprez, *Chronique de Jean le Bel*, i (Paris, 1904). 274n.
[2] Op. cit., 86: Philip does not seem to have used his strong fleet to aid Scotland, Bibl. Nat. MS. Franç. nouv. acq. 9241, fols. 48r–94v.
[3] P.R.O., Various Accounts (E.101), 25/10 gives details of the campaigns of 1347.

Whether or not such considerations weighed with Robert he had every reason to resist the kind of settlement which Edward at first sought. In a letter of 1350 to the pope, David said that Edward required that he or one of his sons should be recognized as David's heir and that England should have the fullest feudal superiority over Scotland.[1] This would have involved the abandonment of Balliol. Edward was ready for this—as he seems to have been ready to abandon de Montfort in 1353— but Balliol was not. In 1349 Edward was already seeking to bring pressure to bear on him to accept a settlement which seems to have been agreed with David and which was thought to have some support in Scotland.[2] By 1351 Balliol may have been looking towards France; for John II then stated that if Balliol abandoned the English cause, as he heard he proposed to, then his French property would be restored.[3] But Balliol had no support worth the name and David was probably willing to accept Edward's terms *faute de mieux*. Robert and the Scots presented the chief difficulty. Edward's chief agent in Scotland appears to have been William Douglas of Liddesdale, who virtually entered his service after being captured in 1346. He was sent, probably in 1351, to offer the Scots David's return and the restoration of the Scottish lands held by England in return for £40,000 and the recognition of the right of one of Edward's sons to succeed to Scotland.[4] The offer was rejected. David was himself sent home in 1352 to put similar terms. These too were rejected. Yet another vain effort was made at a conference at Newcastle in 1353. There are indications that Edward thought he might have to participate in a Scottish civil war to gain his ends and that the Scots themselves feared they might have their king returned to them by main force. On 1st February, 1352, Edward warned his followers in Scotland to be ready to assist William Douglas to maintain David's cause should any rise up against him when he attempted to get an agreement with Edward confirmed.[5] A letter from John of France, probably of September 1351, envisages David's invading Scotland with

[1] E. W. M. Balfour-Melville, 'David II's Appeal to the Pope', *Scott. Hist. Rev.*, xli (1962), 86.

[2] C. Johnson, 'Negotiations for the Release of David Bruce in 1349', *E.H.R.*, xxxvi (1921), 57-8.

[3] *Froissart*, ed. de Lettenhove, xviii, 336-7, cf. 198, n. 1 below.

[4] E. W. M. Balfour-Melville, 'Papers Relating to the Captivity and Release of David II', *Misc. of the Scott. Hist. Soc.*, ix (1958), 1, 3-4, 37, 44-5.

[5] *Rot. Scot.*, i, 748a.

English support and offers to pay for 500 men-at-arms and 500 archers in that eventuality.[1] Knighton has a story that after the abortive conference at Newcastle in 1353 the Scots threatened not to ransom David but to elect another king unless he pardoned all that had been done in his absence and stood up to Edward. He adds that the English council then ordered Northampton, the northerners, and all who claimed lands in Scotland to accompany David there.[2]

In 1354 an agreement was reached on a different basis. An indenture was concluded on 13th July by which it was agreed that David should be released for £60,000, guaranteed by hostages and payable in nine annual instalments, a truce to last meanwhile. A meeting for the performance of the agreement was to be held on 25th August. It does not seem to have been held. But in early October the English prepared the documents necessary for the ratification, David was sent to the north and it seemed that he was about to be released. He was not. Instead another indenture in almost the same terms as the first was drawn up on 12th November. The chief differences from that of July were, firstly that David, who had not been referred to as king of Scotland in the earlier document, was accorded that title when first mentioned—but not thereafter—in this, and secondly that a clause providing for three captured Scottish knights, who may have played some part in arranging the earlier agreement, was omitted. It was agreed that there should be another meeting on 14th January to confirm the agreement if the king of England approved.[3] This meeting may have taken place, but the agreement was not ratified. The most likely

---

[1] *Parl. Rec.*, 100. I have assumed that the Black Book rightly records all four letters on fols. 15–16 as of the same date, but wrongly gives it as 1361. Alternative texts of the first two printed by de Lettenhove (xviii, 336–8) are dated 1351 which accords better with their contents, and especially with the address of the second.

The text of the letter cited above is at least slightly corrupt. Philip had sent a little help to Scotland—20 suits of armour—in 1348 (*Les journaux du trésor de Philippe VI de Valois*, ed. J. Viard (Paris, 1899), no. 1278). See also, for what it is worth, Francisque-Michel, op. cit., p. 64, n. 2.

[2] Op. cit., ii, 75–6.

[3] The indenture of 13th July is P.R.O., Scottish Documents, Exchequer (E.39), 2/36, printed *Foedera*, III, 281–2—wrongly stated there to be the text from the Scotch Roll. The ratifications of 5th October and the documents indicating the preparations for David's release are printed *Rot. Scot.*, i, 768a–774a. The indenture of 12th November is E.39/2/35, inaccurately described in *Foedera*, III, 291. The alleged ratifications dated 5th December of the indenture of 13th July printed in *Foedera*, III, 293 do not exist. Rymer appears to have misread 'd'Octobre' in the ratifications of 5th October as 'Decembre' and to have printed them twice, under both the right date (III, 285) and the wrong one.

explanation of these events is that the July indenture was a consequence of the proposed treaty of Guînes between England and France, drawn up in the previous April.[1] In this John II granted Edward III good terms and agreed, by implication, to renounce the Franco-Scottish alliance. This would have left the Scots hopelessly exposed and bound to come to terms. But the ratification of the treaty of Guînes was not supposed to take place until a meeting was held at Avignon towards the end of the year. It seems likely that the Scots delayed the ratification of the July agreement with the English until they knew whether or not the Anglo-French treaty was to be ratified. That the delay came from their side and not from the English is suggested both by the fact that the November indenture was marginally more favourable to Scotland than that of July, though this is anything but a conclusive argument, and by the apparent completeness of the English preparations to put the agreement into effect in October. It looks as if by 14th January the Scots either knew that the negotiations at Avignon were vain, or were still awaiting news. The French may have already been urging them towards war and in any case were soon to do so.

On 5th March, 1356, the Sire de Garencières received orders from the king of France to go to Scotland with fifty men-at-arms and, more important, 40,000 *deniers d'or a l'escu* to induce the Scots to attack England.[2] He left Paris on his way to Scotland on the 16th. The English had been uneasy about the March since February, although their keeping David in the north until towards the end of that month suggests that they still hoped for an agreement. By June they were aware that there were French in Scotland and feared their participation in an attack by 'the whole Scottish army'. A considerable army was summoned to Newcastle in July and August to be ready to oppose them. Then, probably about Michaelmas, a truce was concluded. Relying on this, Edward took many of the northern magnates with him to Calais at the end of October, including, of all people, the keeper of Berwick. This proved imprudent. De Garencières had not

[1] F. Bock, 'Some New Documents Illustrating the Early Years of the Hundred Years War', *Bull. John Rylands Library*, xv (1931), 60–99; cf. J. Le Patourel, 'Edward III and the Kingdom of France', *History*, xliii (1958), 177.

[2] The main sources for the events of 1355 are the Scottish chronicles, *Scalacronica*, ed. J. Stevenson (Maitland Club, 1836), *Rot. Scot.* and the French records for which see de la Roncière, i, 505–6 and R. Delachenal, *Histoire de Charles V*, i (Paris, 1909), 108.

brought his money with him, but by 15th September he had reached a sufficiently firm agreement with some at least of the Scots for it to be handed over at Bruges on that day to Walter Wardlaw, acting in the name of 'the lords and barons of Scotland'.[1] The Scottish nobles seem, in fact, to have been divided on whether to attack: it may be that only some of them, in particular William Douglas—the future earl—had agreed to the truce. On 6th November the earl of Angus, supported by the earl of March, took the town—but not the castle—of Berwick by surprise. Edward III learned of this either just before or just after he left Calais for England on about 19th November. He went to the north almost at once, summoning a very large army to him. Berwick was quickly recovered. He went on to Roxburgh, where, on 20th January Edward Balliol ceded to him the kingdom of Scotland. Edward entered his new realm with its banner borne before him and advanced to Edinburgh. Although he did a great deal of damage—the 'Burnt Candlemas' was remembered long after—the failure of his victualling ships to arrive compelled him to leave after an active campaign of little more than a fortnight.

Negotiations recommenced almost at once. Edward's victory at Poitiers in September 1356 strengthened his already strong position. He sought to use it to separate the Scots from the French. His instructions to the Black Prince of 17th December, 1356, for the forthcoming negotiations with France said that the Scots were to be excluded from the negotiations, and if possible from the short truce which was to be made with the French. The French were to be told that the Scots had made truces for themselves and had negotiated for peace in the past without the French being represented and were about to do so again.[2] France was not, in any case, in a position to help the Scots, who, left to themselves, concluded an agreement with England at Berwick in October 1357. David was freed on heavy terms which settled no issue but that of his release. The ransom was fixed at 100,000 marks, to be paid in ten annual instalments, a truce to last meanwhile. David was referred to as king of Scotland in the treaty, but nothing was said specifically about the recognition of his claim and in later documents the English avoided giving him the royal title. On the other hand nothing

[1] Bibl. Nat., MS. Clairambault CIX, no. 141, cf. LX, no. 6.
[2] Bull. John Rylands Library, xv, 99.

was said about the recognition of English territorial claims in Scotland: the nature of some of the references to Berwick suggests that the possibility of its return to Scotland—probably in connection with a settlement of the succession in Edward's favour—was contemplated. The Franco-Scottish alliance was not mentioned. The Scots had made no concessions affecting their dynasty, their territory, or their international position, but Edward had at last coerced them into buying back their king. There are many parallels between the negotiations for David's release and those for that of John of France. In both cases the heir, who was left in power at home, had little reason, sentiment apart, to negotiate a ransom, particularly since either king might soon have died. Both captives were willing to grant more generous terms than their countries could stomach. Each ransom was agreed after Edward had made an intimidating military demonstration before or in the enemy's capital. While it is true that in neither case did Edward obtain his full demands, it is equally true that he might never have obtained a ransom at all from either Scotland or France. From a purely military point of view the 1356 campaign in Scotland and that of 1359–60 in France were doubtfully successful. Their political results place them amongst the most effective Edward ever launched.

David remained at peace with England for nearly twenty years after 1357.[1] In June 1359 he tried to escape from the heavy obligation imposed at Berwick by offering to join in a Franco-Danish attack on England provided that France helped him to pay off the ransom and so to regain the hostages. (The alliance with France was still in force, the 'first treaty of London' of May 1358, which required France to sever it, having come to nothing.)[2] The Dauphin offered him 50,000 marks and an agreement may have been concluded.[3] If so, the English invasion of France in October made it abortive. The Scots continued to pay off the ransom, completing the second instalment in January 1360. Thereafter they paid no more until Candlemas

[1] E. W. M. Balfour-Melville, *Edward III and David II* gives the best account of Anglo-Scottish relations 1357–77. The more important documents are printed in *Foedera*, *A.P.S.*, *Parl. Rec.*, *Rot. Scot.* and by C. Johnson, 'Proposals for an Agreement with Scotland', *E.H.R.*, xxx (1915), 476.
[2] Delachenal, ii, 407. The 'second treaty of London' (March 1359) left the question of the Franco-Scottish alliance for later discussion, E. Cosneau, *Les grands traités de la Guerre de Cent Ans* (Paris, 1889), 26.
[3] Arch. Nat., J.677, 7 and 8; Delachenal, ii, 94–105; *E.R.S.*, ii, 52.

1366. This default left them in a very weak position. Edward held their hostages and the conclusion of a peace between England and France in October 1360 meant that there was small chance of French help, even though the provision requiring the abrogation of the alliance between France and Scotland did not become effective.[1] Edward took his opportunity to press again for the succession to Scotland for his house in negotiations which lasted at least until 1365. David was willing to defer or to appear to defer to him, but the Scottish nobility were not. Robert Stewart must have opposed it. Patriotic sentiment no doubt had some effect. Other considerations are suggested by a tract purporting to describe a discussion of the succession issue in a Scottish council.[2] The opponents of an English succession are represented as maintaining that the English had shown in Wales and Ireland that they were not to be trusted, that an English king would be bound to favour his countrymen and the Disinherited, and that the English lacked the will or the means to attack Scotland. The first two points were sound and the third defensible. How little the Scots accepted it is shown by their readiness to accept almost any terms other than the succession of an English prince and by the new and onerous agreement made in 1365. This raised the amount still to be paid for the ransom from 80,000 marks to £100,000, payable in instalments of £4,000 during a twenty-five-year truce, which Edward could terminate at the end of four years at the cost of reducing the ransom to the old figure. As France became stronger the Scots became less accommodating, and the English started to take fright. But the agreement of 1365 was observed until 1369, when the renewal of the Anglo-French war greatly strengthened the Scottish position. In June of that year, the total of the ransom, paid and payable was reduced to the former figure of 100,000 marks. David returned from concluding the new agreement in London to find Charles V's ambassadors awaiting him in Edinburgh. Their and later French offers were unsuccessful in inducing Scotland to make war on England while Edward

[1] The fate of the hostages is obscure. The last reference to one of the twenty heirs of noblemen remaining a hostage appears to be *Rot. Scot.*, i, 930a (1369); two certainly and probably more died in the plague of 1361–2. It may be that releases were made as the ransom was paid. Of the three magnates Angus and Thomas Moray died in 1361 and do not seem to have been replaced and Sutherland is last mentioned as a hostage in 1367 (*Rot. Scot.*, i, 911a) and died before 19th June 1371.

[2] 'Papers relating to the Release and Captivity of David II', op. cit., 36–56.

III lived. Robert Stewart, who succeeded as Robert II in February 1371, lost no time in concluding an agreement with Charles V. But this provided for mutual aid only when the Anglo-Scottish truces should end, or be broken by the English. Another agreement was prepared at the same time which provided that the pope should be induced to annul the Anglo-Scottish truce and that Charles should give 100,000 nobles to pay off the ransom and should send 1,000 men-at-arms to Scotland for two years together with arms and pay for another 500 knights and 500 serjeants. The first agreement was ratified by Robert in October; the second, so far as is known, was not, and was certainly not acted upon.[1] Robert maintained the ransom payments. The last was made on 24th June, 1377, before the Scots had heard of the death of Edward III two days before. After that they paid no more, while war flared up in the Marches.

The years of peace after 1357 brought a certain prosperity to Scotland. The exchequer rolls show the collection of a surprisingly large revenue.[2] The heavy burden of the ransom was met by doubling, trebling, and finally quadrupling the customs. The mere capacity to raise the sums needed is an indication of the wealth of the country and the power of the state. The flow of money into the exchequer, for whatever purpose it was intended, helped the king. David was able, for instance, to rebuild Edinburgh Castle and, in 1363, to put down a rebellion with the aid of paid troops.[3] The period saw the reform of the Scottish currency and to some extent of the law.[4] A good deal of church-building went on and the first important work of Scottish literature, Barbour's *Bruce*, was completed in 1375. There were repeated rebellions against David, but all were more or less successfully repressed. Rebellion was normal in later medieval

[1] *Foedera*, III, 925–6, Register House, French Treaties 2, Black Book, fols. 64–9, *Parl. Rec.*, 120–4, Arch Nat., J.677, 9–13. The more aggressive agreement is known only from letters of Charles copied into the Black Book (fols. 68–9); it may be that the considerable sum of money which Charles had deposited in the monastery of St Catherine in Paris by May 1378 'pour certaines besoignes qui sont entre nous et le roy d'Escoce' and which he was then drawing upon for other purposes had something to do with this, or a similar agreement, *Mandements [et actes divers de Charles V]*, ed. L. Delisle (Paris, 1874), nos. 1712–14.

[2] The account of Scottish finances and exports below is largely based on *E.R.S.*, ii. Burnett's valuable introduction gives some account of the Mercer family (xlii–iii, n. 4).

[3] *E.R.S.*, ii, 164.

[4] I. H. Stewart, *The Scottish Coinage* (1955), 25–31; T. M. Cooper, *Select Scottish Cases of the Thirteenth Century* (1944), p. lxvii.

Scotland, which in this, as in other respects, resembled Anglo-Norman England. Much remains to be done before knowledge of David's later years reaches its limit. But it is likely that Wynton's judgment, that his rule was effective and he kept good order, is more nearly true than is suggested by the strictures of more modern Scottish historians, to whose high standards of political and personal conduct David notably failed to measure up. That he enjoyed the success he did was due largely to his keeping the peace with England, and his ability to restrain the Marchers and so to keep the peace is an indication of his strength in Scotland.

Burgesses were more prominent in Scottish politics after 1357 than ever before. Their regular summons to parliament begins in the 'sixties.[1] In 1364 David granted a general charter which seems to have given the burghs a new degree of monopoly in trade.[2] John Mercer of Perth, probably the greatest Scottish merchant of his day, acted as the chief financial agent of the Crown in the organization of the ransom payments and in other matters and was prominent in a way that no member of his class is known previously to have been. He appears much like a Scottish equivalent of William de la Pole. These things reflect the importance of foreign trade. The exports of wool recorded between 1359 and 1377 averaged about 5,000 sacks annually and the customs on them constituted a high proportion of the royal revenue. Scotland carried on a considerable trade with England, exporting chiefly fish and hides and importing manufactured goods and food. There was a constant demand for English grain in Scotland in the later fourteenth century. Licences to export it were used as diplomatic presents to Scottish ambassadors; English prisoners sometimes paid their ransoms in it. Between 1357 and 1377 licences were issued for the export to Scotland of just over 20,000 quarters.[3] Their issue sometimes had a diplomatic purport. None of the exceptionally heavy exports of 1365 were issued until the new ransom agreement was drawn up on 20th May, while about half of them were licenced on that day. In some ways the most remarkable English export to Scotland was wool. From 1361–2 the custumars' accounts record the export from Scotland of English wool at a

[1] W. C. Dickinson, *Scotland from the Earliest Times to 1603*, ch. xx.
[2] *Early Records of the Burgh of Aberdeen*, ed. W. C. Dickinson (Scott. Hist. Soc., 1957), xcviii.
[3] Nearly all the licenses which were enrolled are in *Rot. Scot.*

rate of custom lower than that normal in either England or Scotland. The most reasonable explanation of this is that the Scots sought to enhance their revenue by encouraging the smuggling of English wool over the border for export from Scotland. The constant efforts of the English authorities to stop such smuggling are thus explained. Between 1362 and 1377 6,619 sacks of such wool were exported from Scotland, 1,800 of them between February 1373 and February 1374. War was almost certain to harm Scottish trade. It could, indeed, lead to circumstances—such as an embargo on English wool-exports to Flanders—which benefited it. But such advantages were outweighed by the vulnerability of the Scottish route to Flanders, running along the east coast of England. As soon as tension increased in the late 'seventies the English started to seize Scottish cargoes. It is probable that even in time of peace most of the English exports of food to Scotland were illicit. For instance, in 1378 a Louth merchant was pardoned for the unlicenced export of 3,260 quarters of grain to Scotland.[1] The Scots nevertheless considered the opportunity to import food from England as one of the advantages of peace.[2] (Such trade was of some importance to the English also; a parliamentary petition on 1394 maintained that many would be unable to pay their rent if they were not allowed to export grain.)[3] Even the smuggling of wool seems to have been affected by war. Recorded exports of English wool from Scotland drop after 1377 to a total of 1,524 sacks between then and 1399. In short, foreign trade was very important for Scotland and its interests were best served by peace with England.

Good relations with England had other attractions for the Scots. For some they were financial. In 1359 the earl of Mar did liege homage to Edward III against all men but David, in return for a promise of 600 marks a year.[4] In the same year the earl of Angus, one of the hostages, agreed to serve him in France with a retinue, though it is doubtful whether he went.[5] Edward seems to have been at some pains to court his more important Scottish hostages, as he later courted those from France. Many

---

[1] C.P.R. 1377–81, 140; cf. Some Sessions of the Peace in Lincolnshire, ed. R. Sillem (Lincoln Record Soc., 1933), 99, 138–9.
[2] N. H. Nicolas, Proceedings and Ordinances of the Privy Council, i (1834), 32.
[3] Rot. Parl., iii, 320.
[4] Rot. Scot., i, 836ab.
[5] Ibid., i, 840b.

lesser Scots entered his service when the French war began again. In 1369–70 the garrison of Calais contained about 140 Scots, though some of these probably came from English Scotland.[1] Edward seems to have been short of trained troops at this time and glad to get them from anywhere. Many Scots simply liked to be able to come to England. The attractions of Edward's court must partly account for David's three known visits after his release. The Scottish nobility were very isolated in wartime and many may have already spoken no language but English. After 1357 many of them obtained safe-conducts to come on pilgrimage to England. Scotland had no university until 1413. Her aspiring clerks had to look southwards. Between 1357 and 1377 two general and sixty-eight individual safe-conducts were issued to enable Scots to attend the English universities. A Scottish gentleman is found coming to London to consult a doctor and a lesser man to learn the art of a tiler.

These advantages were not enough to prolong the period of peace into Richard II's reign.[2] In the last years of Edward III Scottish pressure on the *terra irrendenta* of English Scotland exacerbated the usual hostility between the English and Scottish Marchers. In particular, Percy and Douglas disputed Jedworth Forest. The wardens of the Marches were hardly able to maintain the truce when the chief among their own number sought to break it. Edward repeatedly sent commissions of conservators, some, and, towards the end, all of them non-Marchers, to hold March-days and to restrain his Marchers. Robert sent his sons, Carrick and Fife, to restrain his.[3] These efforts were in vain. Raiding and counter-raiding by important men and large forces started in 1376 and the Marches were soon reduced to a state such as they had been in during the early 1340s. The central authorities still hoped to maintain the truce and sent embassies to the border every year to attempt to do so.

[1] *Issue Roll of Thomas of Brantingham*, trans. F. Devon (1835), 83–5, 162; cf. 282, 337, 410–11; cf. *Froissart*, vii, 232, 235–7, viii, 138, 148; G. S. C. Swinton, 'John of Swinton', *Scott. Hist. Rev.*, xvi (1918–19), 261–79.

[2] The usual sources for Anglo-Scottish relations are supplemented in Richard II's reign by the important diplomatic material in British Museum, MS. Vespasian F vii. Most of it has been printed, but in many different places. All the major English chronicles pay more attention to Scottish affairs after the outbreak of war. There is no reliable modern account of Robert II's reign apart from Burnett's introductions to *E.R.S.*, ii and iii and E. W. M. Balfour-Melville, *James I, King of Scots* (1936), 1–21.

[3] For attempts to maintain the truce, see *Rot. Scot.*, *Wynton*, and the accounts for March-days in *E.R.S.*, ii and P.R.O., Foreign Accounts (E.364).

The English had every reason to be conciliatory. They did nothing to enforce the payment of the remainder of the ransom. Offers were made for permanent peace: in 1378 and 1379 the marriage of Richard to a Scottish princess was discussed.[1] Efforts were made to force the English Marchers to break the vicious circle of reprisals. At the same time considerable garrisons were kept on the border and large forces sometimes accompanied the conservators to remind the Scots of the power of England. That sent with Gaunt to hold a day in 1380 was intended to consist of 14 bannerets, 162 knights, 1,492 esquires, and 1,670 archers and to cost over £5,000.[2] These efforts resulted in the conclusion of a truce within a truce, a *specialis securitas*, in November 1380 which was extended in June 1381 to last until February 1384, when the truce of 1369 was due to expire.

There were strong forces making for war. Frequent negotiations had not saved the English border from serious damage. The *securitas* was badly broken, especially in 1383. The Marchers were resentful and half-rebellious, above all when efforts were made to make them keep the truce. Those of Gaunt as lieutenant on the March contributed to his great quarrel with Northumberland in 1381. The defence of the March had become a serious burden and there were bitter disputes as to whether the whole of it should fall on the Marchers. Richard must have been tempted to launch a major attack on Scotland on the model of 1356 and so seek to put an end to these troubles. On the Scottish side it seems that while the Marchers, and above all the earl of Douglas were for war, Robert still wanted peace. French influence must have been for war and France may have had powerful friends in Scotland. William Landallis, bishop of St Andrews from 1342 to 1385, had lived in France and John II had at least professed to think that he had been active on the French behalf during David's captivity.[3] Sir Nicolas Erskine was in receipt of a pension of 300 gold francs a year from France.[4] William, earl of Douglas, had been partly brought up

---

[1] P.R.O., Diplomatic Documents, Exchequer, 1527.

[2] Advance payments were made on 7th September, P.R.O., Issue Rolls, 478 mm. 26, 27. The arrangements were subject to some alteration but a very large force certainly went north, *Historia Anglicana*, ed. H. R. Riley (1864), i, 446–7, E.364/15 mm. F and M, 16 m.F.

[3] *Parl. Rec.*, 90.

[4] Arch. Nat., J.621, no. 77; Comptes du Trésor, ed. R. Fawtier (Paris, 1930) no. 1469; H. Moranvillé, 'Extraits de journaux de Trésor', *Bibl. de l'éc. des chartes*, xlix (1888), 384; cf. *Froissart*, vii, cv n. 2.

in France, had fought on the French side at Poitiers and, according to Froissart, had been given a pension of 500 livres a year by John II.[1] In 1377 Charles V spent 500 gold francs on a present of armour for him, his son James and Robert Erskine.[2] At least one Scot was high in the French royal service. A 'Johannes le Mercier, de patria Scotie' was in receipt of an annuity of 400 *livres parisis* as *consiliarius regis* in 1384. He had probably been in the French service since at least 1377 and may well be the John Mercer whom Walsingham describes as a trusted adviser of Charles V on matters concerning England.[3] There is thus little reason to doubt that the French were well-informed on Scottish affairs or that they were in direct communication with those Scottish magnates who wished for war with England. In spite of the pressure upon him, from within Scotland and without, Robert II had held aloof from the Anglo-French conflict, content to make his profit by ceasing after 1377 to pay off the ransom. He may have concluded some agreement with Charles V before May 1378 for aggressive action.[4] If so, if did not come into effect. All that he is known to have done before 1384 to help France is to support Clement VII, the French claimant to the papacy. This seems to have had no effect on Anglo-Scottish relations, although the bombastic Clementist propaganda of Thomas of Rossy, bishop of Galloway, may have caused a certain stir in England.[5] But in 1383, probably through fear of what might happen when the truce expired, Robert made an agreement with France. If Scotland and England were to be at war he was to be sent 1,000 men-at-arms, 1,000 suits of armour and 40,000 gold francs before May 1384.[6]

A somewhat obscure series of events followed. On 26th

[1] *Froissart*, iv, 194.

[2] *Mandements*, no. 1564.

[3] *Comptes du Trésor*, no. 1440; *Mandements*, no. 1414; and *Chronicon Angliae*, ed. E. M. Thompson (1874), 198, where Walsingham probably confuses the John Mercer in the French service with John Mercer of Perth; they can hardly be identical because he of Perth died before 14th March, 1381 (*E.R.S.*, iii, 652); it is, however, conceivable that more than one Scottish John Mercer served the kings of France. A French Jean le Mercier very prominent in the financial administration of the French Crown at this time must also be distinguished.

[4] Above, 203, n. 1.

[5] H. McEwan, '"A Theolog Solempne", Thomas de Rossy, Bishop of Galloway', *Innes Review*, viii (1957), 21–9; E. Perroy, *L'Angleterre et le grand schisme d'Occident* (Paris, 1933), 71–6.

[6] Ratified by Charles in June and by Robert in August, Black Book, fols. 69–70; *Parl. Rec.*, 131–2; *Foedera* (1st edn.), vii, 406–7, cf. 391.

January, 1384, England and France concluded a truce until October, in which the Scots could join if they wished. Scotland was not represented at the conference. This was commonly so, partly because it was often the case that neither side wanted it, partly because she could not afford the expense. Big conferences were in more ways than one the clerical equivalent of campaigns.[1] After the old truce expired on 2nd February open war broke out between England and Scotland. It seems that the Scots attacked and took the most exposed of the English fortresses, Lochmaben, before reports of the new truce could arrive. This probably decided the English, who were hesitating between peace and war, to launch a major attack. They may have taken the opportunity to delay the French ambassadors who were taking word of the new truce to Scotland via England. In April Lancaster led an army on a very short campaign to Edinburgh, which he ransomed. Robert wished, nevertheless, to accept the new truce. He was overborne by the Marchers who retaliated in great force with some French freelances in their company.[2] Thereafter the Scots did accept the truce, and its extension until May 1385, agreed at the Boulogne conference, at which they were represented.[3] Their Marchers did not observe it. James Douglas' state of mind in these years may be judged from a letter to Richard II in which he refers to 'Berwike þat standis in Scotlande þe qwhilke toune yhe call yhouris'.[4]

The Scots blamed the French at Boulogne for not having sent troops in 1384. The reproach would not have been deserved in 1385 when it was through Scotland that for the first and last time in the Hundred Years War a major French army invaded England. At the end of May Jean de Vienne, Admiral of France, set sail for Scotland with at least 1,300 men-at-arms, and 250 crossbowmen, together with armour and 50,000 gold francs for the Scots.[5] He was intended to attack from the north while another French army invaded England from the south. The

---

[1] *E.R.S.*, ii, *passim* for the high proportion of the royal income spent on diplomacy.

[2] *Froissart*, xi, 164–75 is the chief authority for the division between the king and the Marchers. His account is partly borne out by English record evidence.

[3] E. Martène and U. Durand, *Voyage littéraire de deux religieux bénédictins* (Paris, 1724), 332–40.

[4] Vespasian F vii, fol. 17 (probably 1383).

[5] Terrier de Loray, *Jean de Vienne* (Paris, 1877) gives the best account of this expedition and prints many of the abundant documents.

southern force never set sail but in July Vienne and Douglas invaded England on the East March. Richard collected the biggest army of his reign, probably nearly 14,000 men, drove the French and Scots north and advanced to Edinburgh.[1] The enemy, who had been there not long before him, moved south-westwards to harry the West March almost undisturbed. The French went home in November ill-pleased with their experiences. They seem to have found only the Marchers and the earl of Moray well-inclined and the chief object of Robert and his subjects to take as much money as they could from them. Richard's invasion, though it lasted less than three weeks, had its effect. A truce was concluded in September, which was probably extended until June 1388.[2] It was in force during the period when the French armada of 1386, fully as dangerous as the Spanish armada of 1588, was threatening England. In 1388 the Scots, tempted by English weakness during the Appellant coup, refused to renew the truce and attacked with forces gathered from the whole kingdom, probably their largest army since 1346. Fife invaded on the West March, Douglas on the East, where he penetrated beyond the Tyne, defeating Hotspur and meeting his death at Otterburn on the way home. Heavy fighting continued until the next year, when the Scots were given the opportunity to join the three-year truce concluded by France and England in June. The English appear to have been reluctant to agree to the inclusion of the Scots. It was to Scotland's advantage that she should adhere; she had been extremely fortunate in the preceding two years and could hardly hope to stand alone against England. Nevertheless, Robert and Fife, who was ruling for him, seem to have hesitated before they agreed to join, which they did before 27th September. Walsingham plausibly says that while the Scottish nobles wanted peace the *vulgus* did not, because they had impoverished themselves to buy equipment for raiding in England.[3] Some of them may have found employment for it in France, where considerable numbers of Scottish archers are found in 1391.[4] The Scots adhered to the extensions of the truce up to and including that from 1394 to 1398. The war was at an end.

[1] N. B. Lewis, 'The Last Medieval Summons of the English Feudal Levy', *E.H.R.*, lxxiii (1958), 1–26.
[2] *Rot. Scot.*, ii, 75b, 85b–86a, 91b, 93b, E.101/73/35.
[3] *Hist. Ang.*, ii, 182–3.
[4] *Copiale Prioratus Sanctiandree*, ed. J. H. Baxter (Oxford, 1932), 220–2.

The Anglo-French war of 1369–89 covered a wider area and was more dangerous and burdensome to England than any she was to fight until the Anglo-Spanish war of 1585–1604—which it resembles in many ways. Scotland contributed largely to the burden and the danger. In the last year of Edward III's reign the defence of the March cost less than £1,000.[1] In 1384 Northumberland was paid £4,000 for defending it for forty-two days. In 1385 and 1386 the cost of the garrisons on the March ran at a rate of about £16,000 a year in war and £8,000 in truce.[2] At the same time Calais, Cherbourg and Brest together cost not less than £25,000 a year while Richard's annual income was of the order of £125,000.[3] A defensive policy was the royal road to ruin. Besides garrisons it required fortifications. The Scottish threat in the north, like that from France in the south, led to the building or rebuilding of many royal and private castles. Roxburgh, Dunstanburgh, Carlisle, Castle Rushen, Durham and Warkworth are only the most conspicuous examples from Richard's reign and the later part of Edward's.[4] Numerous smaller works were built by lesser men. The value of lands on the March was greatly reduced by the fighting. That of one of the most exposed manors, Burgh-by-Sands, went down, according to the *inquisitiones post mortem*, from £21 15s. 4d. in 1339 to 12s. 2d. in 1384.[5] Otterburn must have ensured that the balance of ransoms went against the English.

But in Richard II's reign the English often did better on sea than on land and the war against Scotland was not an exception. Considerable fleets were maintained on the North Sea, partly for use against the Scots. For instance, between December 1383 and Martinmas 1384 Northumberland, as admiral of the

---

[1] E.101/68/140 and 142, 73/21, E.364/9 m.O, 13 m.E, 25 m.C.; J. L. Kirby, 'The Keeping of Carlisle Castle before 1381', *Trans. Cumberland and Westmoreland Arch. and Ant. Soc.*, new ser., liv (1955), 131–9.
[2] *Rot. Scot.*, ii, 62, E.101/68/239 and 242, 73/29–35, E.364/22 m.E, 23 m.G, 32 m.E, 33 m.C; R. L. Storey, 'The Wardens of the Marches of England towards Scotland', *E.H.R.*, lxxii (1957), 593–603.
[3] E.101/68/244, E.364/20m.A, 23 m.F (Cherbourg); E.101/68/237, E.364/20 m.G. (Brest); E.364/22 m.H (Calais); A. Steel, *The Receipt of the Exchequer* (Cambridge, 1954), 49–57, 446; cf. E. Perroy, *Compte de William Gunthorpe, Trésorier de Calais 1371–2* (Arras, 1959), 5–10.
[4] *The History of the King's Works*, ed. H. M. Colvin and others, ii (Oxford, 1963), 567–9, 599, 818–21; W. Douglas Simpson, 'Further Notes on Dunstanburgh Castle', *Archaeologia Aeliana*, 4th ser., xxvii (1949), 1–28; B. H. St J. O'Neill, 'Castle Rushen, Isle of Man', *Archaeologia*, xciv (1951), 1–26; cf. B. H. St J. O'Neill, *Castles and Cannon* (Oxford, 1960), 1–21.
[5] R. L. Storey, 'The Manor of Burgh-by-Sands', *T.C.W.A.S.*, new ser., liv (1955), 126.

north commanded a force whose wages cost, he maintained, £2,186 16s. and which comprised at its maximum 2 knights, 297 men-at-arms and 544 archers and mariners.[1] Such fleets, the numerous privateers of the east-coast ports and the position of the main Scottish trade-route ensured that many Scottish ships and cargoes fell into English hands when the two countries were at war or when relations between them grew tense. The captures were sometimes very valuable; some ships taken in 1380 or 1381 were said to have been worth £10,000.[2] Robert II had to spend over £500 in 1380 on fitting out ships to defend Scottish trade.[3] It is likely that the gains or losses by sea were on at least the scale of those by land, as may well have generally been the case during the Hundred Years War. It is impossible to know exactly how much the English gained since only a proportion of their captures are recorded in the public records. They certainly suffered some losses to the Scottish privateers who were active in the north and Irish seas. But there is little reason to doubt that, on balance, the advantage was theirs.

War between England and Scotland was not to the advantage of the kings of either country. England could, by an effort, overrun southern Scotland, but lacked the resources to occupy it permanently. The Scots had the power to reduce the March counties of England to misery and three times in the fourteenth century they did so. The Marches were not the only part of England to bear the burden of home defence. The not infrequent threat of invasion required garrisons, fortifications and the gathering of ships and men from the maritime counties too.[4] It was thought that the value of a man's arms might well exceed that of the rest of his property if he lived either on the Marches or on the coast.[5] Nevertheless it was only the north which felt the full weight and savagery of war. Its defence diverted men and money that were needed, or could be used more gainfully, elsewhere. Neville's Cross was very profitable for Edward III— David's ransom alone produced 76,000 marks in one form or another—but it was the great exception. Otherwise the English Crown consistently spent far more in the north than it gained. War with England had attractions for the Scots; raiding

---

[1] P.R.O., Memoranda Roll (K.R.), 165 Communia E.T., mm. 24–5.
[2] *C.P.R. 1381–5*, 83–4.
[3] *E.R.S.*, iii, 55, 651.
[4] E.g., *Records of Norwich*, ed. W. Hudson and J. C. Tingey, i (1906), 272.
[5] *Rot. Parl.*, iii, 82.

England was for them what raiding France was for the English. But Scottish trade was vulnerable and Scotland lacked the military power to prevent the king of England marching straight to Edinburgh when he chose and was able to exert his full strength. Each side had more power to harm the other than to profit itself. In the earlier part of the period neither king recognized this. Edward endeavoured to conquer Scotland. David attacked England when he need not have done. Each learned his lesson. Neither Edward, after 1347, nor Richard made war on Scotland until he was driven to it, although the claim to suzerainty over Scotland was always kept alive. David tried hard to keep the peace in his later years. As Robert Bruce had been willing to pay £20,000 for peace when Scotland was strong and England weak, so did Robert II continue to pay off David's ransom for six years, while England was at war with France and doing badly.

Two forces made for war, French pressure on Scotland and that of the Marchers on either side. It was to the interest of the French to be loyal allies to the Scots and so they proved, though they were nearly driven to abandon them between 1356 and 1360. Philip VI saved Scotland during David's minority. The French observed their obligation to include the Scots in their truces with England, while the Scots did not—could not, in fact—observe the reciprocal obligation on them. It was not from France but from the papacy that there came the suggestion, in 1344, and perhaps again in 1375, that Edward should be given Scotland, abandoning his French lands, where the king of Scotland might be compensated.[1] At the same time the French alliance had disagreeable consequences for the Scots. Accounts of what Scottish ambassadors said in negotiations with France reveal a certain rancour and suggest resentment of a subordinate position. Once England and France were at war the interests of the kings of Scotland and of France diverged. It was to the advantage of the one to maintain at least formal peace with England while extorting what concessions he could—the position of Robert II from 1377 to 1384. The other required that the Scots should go to war, as David did up to 1346. On two later occasions the Scots could be induced to intervene only

[1] E. Déprez, 'La conférence d'Avignon (1344)', *Essays . . . Presented to T. F. Tout*, ed. A. G. Little and F. M. Powicke (Manchester, 1925), p. 312; E. Perroy, 'The Anglo-French Negotiations at Bruges 1374-7', *Camden Misc.*, xix (1952), xvi.

by a subsidy, all of it paid directly to the magnates in 1355 and most of it in 1385. There are indications that on each occasion some Scots were doubtful of the prudence of the venture. They were right to be so, for the king of England was in Edinburgh at the head of an army within three months of each attack. The ability of the king of France—and of the king of England—to patronize Scottish notables weakened the power of the Crown. In 1371 Robert II even feared that the French might intervene in the succession dispute which could follow his death. In short, because Scotland was dependent almost for her existence on its value to France she was subject to pressures which threatened to impair her freedom of action. Portugal was in much the same position in regard to England and presents many parallels. For example, Edmund of Cambridge's expedition to Portugal in 1381–2 met almost exactly the same difficulties and followed very much the same unsatisfactory course as that of Jean de Vienne to Scotland in 1385. It was easy for great powers to gather clients and promises in such relatively poor and feeble states. But the political divisions and institutional weaknesses which made this easy made it equally difficult to induce the small states to give more than passive and ambiguous help. They were capable of effective action on a large scale only under the stimulus of great danger or great opportunity. But however ungrateful an ally Scotland proved it was always in the interest of France to support her against England and her kings were never in a position where they had simply to obey those of France.

It was the Marchers rather than the French who did most to bring about war between the kings of England and Scotland in the later part of the century. March society had had to live through so much war that it had come to live by it. Continued war had much the same effect on the border that it did in parts of France. Bodies very like free companies appeared on the Scottish side as they had, in Edward II's reign, on the English. It was impossible to prevent petty warfare on such a frontier and difficult to prevent its escalation into something worse. Faced with this problem, which was as much one of regulating a society as of defending a frontier, the English authorities had, characteristically, developed an institution to deal with it; the wardenship of the Marches reached under Edward III and Richard II what was to be very nearly its final form. The English wardens—little is known of their Scottish counterparts

—were fairly effective, especially in so far as they were backed by the power of the central government in enforcing the payment of compensation to the other side.[1] They could just about keep the peace provided that the Marcher magnates on either side were not inclined towards war. But the magnates often were so inclined. They disputed lands on the border—which were sometimes surprisingly valuable—with rivals on the other side, feuded with them and were often tempted to raid or retaliate. It was very difficult for kings to check such men. The effect of war between England and Scotland was to increase the power of the Marcher houses, above all of those of Douglas and Percy. Neither was of the first importance at the beginning of the century. By its end they were not far from being dominant within their respective states. At the beginning of Richard's reign his government had the greatest difficulty in controlling the earl of Northumberland, as did Robert II in controlling Douglas. At the end of Richard's reign the Percies played a principal part in toppling him from his throne. They did so for reasons very much connected with the March. The war of 1384–9 had left them more powerful than ever. After about 1397 there was renewed tension on the March. It had the same causes as that in the last years of Edward III's reign and the king tried to deal with it in the same way, by taking the conduct of March affairs out of the hands of the Marchers. Lancaster was again appointed lieutenant. Commissions of conservators, full of Richard's friends and servants, were again sent to the March. The Percies, who had other grievances connected with the tenure of March offices, were again displeased.[2] But this time their displeasure had more serious consequences for the Crown. The forces and circumstances that had helped temporarily to humiliate Gaunt in 1381 did much to put his son on the throne in 1399. War in the north had left the Percies too powerful to be overborne. In this, as in other respects, the Scottish wars of Edward III and Richard II resemble the whole Hundred Years War as it used to be seen.[3] In his attack on Scotland Edward merited Stubbs' strictures; it was an ambitious, unscrupulous and extravagant venture. The ensuing

[1] R. R. Reid, 'The Office of the Warden of the Marches', *E.H.R.*, xxxii (1917), 479–96 is the fullest but not altogether a reliable account.
[2] E.g. *Wynton*, vi, 379–81.
[3] For recent views on the Hundred Years War, see e.g. M. McKisack, 'Edward III and the Historians', *History*, xlv (1960), 1–15.

wars were cruel and destructive and chiefly to the advantage of the northern nobility, whose power was so far enhanced as to become a danger to the state. Much is rightly said of the profits of war in the fourteenth century. These wars remind us of the profits of peace.[1]

[1] I am much indebted to Professor M. McKisack and to Dr P. Chaplais for reading this paper and making helpful suggestions; the responsibility for any errors is mine.

VII

H. S. OFFLER

ASPECTS OF GOVERNMENT IN THE LATE MEDIEVAL EMPIRE[1]

'Every kingdom divided against itself shall be brought to
desolation, for its princes have become the companions of
thieves.' Reciting these opening words of Charles IV's Golden
Bull, the young Goethe caused its learned commentator Johann
Daniel von Olenschlager to muse: 'What times those must
have been, when an emperor at a great imperial diet had such
words thrown in the face of his princes'.[2] The impression persists
that the main themes of the history of the late medieval empire
were disunity, disorder, corruption. Yet even in respect of
government this is not wholly fair. Our grasp of these matters,
let it be said at once, remains imperfect. Half a century ago
Ludwig Quidde stated that the constitutional history of late
medieval Germany was as yet unwritten; this still seemed true

[1] [It may be convenient for the reader to be reminded of the succession of rulers
in Germany during the period discussed here:
   Rudolf (of Habsburg), king of the Romans 1273–91.
   Adolf (of Nassau), king of the Romans 1292–8.
   Albert I (of Habsburg), king of the Romans 1298–1308.
   Henry VII (of Luxemburg), king of the Romans 1308; emperor 1312–13.
   Lewis IV (of Bavaria), king of the Romans 1314; emperor 1328–47.
      (Frederick the Fair of Habsburg, anti-king 1314–22; nominally joint king
      with Lewis 1325–30).
   Charles IV (of Luxemburg), king of the Romans 1346; emperor 1355–78.
      (Günther of Schwarzburg, anti-king 1349.)
   Wenzel (of Luxemburg), king of the Romans 1376–1400 (1419).
   Rupert (of the Palatinate), king of the Romans 1400–10.
   Sigismund (of Luxemburg), king of the Romans 1410 (1411); emperor 1433–7.
   Albert II (of Habsburg), king of the Romans 1438–9.
   Frederick III (of Habsburg), king of the Romans 1440; emperor 1452–93.
   Maximilian (of Habsburg), king of the Romans 1486; emperor 1508–19.]
[2] *Dichtung und Wahrheit*, i, 4. The bull was combining Luke xi, 17 with Isaiah
1, 23.

in 1958 to Quidde's successor in charge of the first series of the *Reichstagsakten*.[1] But much work has been done during the last sixty years or so. Though no new synthesis holds the field, perhaps some indications of the ways in which scholars' ideas and researches have been moving may be useful.

In the fourteenth and fifteenth centuries 'the empire' was a highly equivocal expression. It could be used to denote an area or a community or a mode of government or even the royal insignia, kept from 1424 onwards at Nuremberg.[2] In the background of these meanings was implicit some idea of Germany. By this time the expansive period of medieval German history had ended. The great eastward flow slackened markedly about the middle of the fourteenth century. A strong Slavonic state emerged in Poland-Lithuania, while in Bohemia powerful religious and social emotions nourished Czech particularism. The aggressive ambitions of France and then of Burgundy made themselves felt in the west, where the 'Netherlands' continued to drift outside the political ambit of the Rhineland. But despite these marks of recession the area of Germany remained very large, and men did not commonly have all of it in mind when they talked of the empire. Often they seem to have been thinking of a corridor of territories through which ran the axis Regensburg–Nuremberg–Frankfort–Mainz–Cologne–Aachen, the axis being eccentric until it reached the Rhine and the corridor extending further south and south-west than towards the north. When complaint was heard that this or that king had been absent from the *Reich* for years, it meant that he had not been seen in Franconia, Swabia or the Rhineland. This restricted conception took little notice of parts of Germany immensely important in her national history: the Hanseatic north, for instance, and Prussia. The reason is clear: these areas now had only slight connexion with the government of the empire. A history of the late medieval empire is, then, a good deal less, if also something more, than a history of Germany itself.

Holy since Barbarossa's time, holy and Roman since William of Holland's, after the middle of the fifteenth century the empire

[1] Cf. H. Heimpel, 'Deutsche Reichstagsakten, ältere Reihe', *Die Historische Kommission bei der Bayerischen Akademie der Wissenschaften 1858–1958* (Göttingen, 1958), 92.
[2] 'Insignia, que imperium dicuntur': Mathias von Neuenburg, *Chronica*, ed. A. Hofmeister (M.G.H. *S.S.* n.s. iv), 444.

began to be called 'the Holy Roman Empire of the German Nation'.[1] Possibly national feeling had something to do with the addition, though evidence of a heightened German consciousness can be found much earlier, during the excitements of 1337–9, for instance, or in the writings of Dietrich of Niem and Henry of Langenstein.[2] But the new title should not be misunderstood. It did not claim for the Germans an inalienable right to universal empire: rather it was intended almost as a synonym for Germany itself—for that part of the empire occupied by the German people. This attempt to shake off the incubus of classical and earlier medieval tradition had only limited success. The assumption of the author of the *Reformatio Sigismundi* (1439) that empire and Christendom were still convertible terms was widely shared. The care of Christendom's common interests, whether in restoring unity to a Church rent by schism or in waging war on heretical Hussites and infidel Turks, was thought to lie inescapably on the empire and its ruler. 'Promoted by divine providence to be a head of Christendom' was how Sigismund understood his position.[3] Though the story of his reign did not belie his words, it showed how these continuing universal responsibilities could distract the king from the business of governing Germany. Out-of-date claims which could neither be abandoned nor made good were onerous. The territories listed in Wenzel's grant of the imperial vicariate to Sigismund in March 1396 included Apulia, Calabria and Sicily.[4] It is natural to dismiss this as fantasy. Yet only a few years later the Rhenish electors could use Wenzel's grant of the duchy of Milan to Giangaleazzo Visconti as serious grounds for accusing the king of dilapidating the empire.[5] The reign of Wenzel's supplanter, Rupert of the Palatinate, foundered on the extensive obligations he was forced to undertake before his election: to heal the schism in the Church by the

---

[1] K. Zeumer, *Heiliges römisches Reich deutscher Nation* (Weimar, 1910), 37.

[2] Cf. A. Diehl, 'Heiliges römisches Reich deutscher Nation', *Hist. Zts.*, clvi (1937), 457 ff.; E. E. Stengel, in *Deutsches Archiv f. Gesch. d. Mittelalters*, ii (1938), 300, n. 1; H. Heimpel, *Dietrich von Niem* (Münster, 1932), 220–2.

[3] 'Von gottlicher schickunge ezu einem haubt der Cristenheit gefodert' (25th October, 1433): *Deutsche Reichstagsakten, ältere Reihe, hrsg. durch die Histor. Kommission bei d. Bayerischen Akademie d. Wissenschaften* [=*R.T.A.*] (Munich, 1867 ff.), xi, no. 87.

[4] *R.T.A.*, ii, no. 247; cf. A. Gerlich, *Habsburg–Luxemburg–Wittelsbach im Kampf um die deutsche Königskrone* (Wiesbaden, 1960), 91–3.

[5] *R.T.A.*, iii, no. 9, art. 2a (Christmas 1397); ibid., no. 204, art. 2 (20th August, 1400).

advice of the ecclesiastical electors and to reunite Milan and Brabant with the empire.[1] Only intermittently was it recognized how the empire as area and community had shrunk since Hohenstaufen times: its ruler was still called, and believed himself to be, *semper augustus, zu allen zeiten merer des reiches*.

As a mode of government the empire was in theory a monarchy. Though there was no king of Germany by that name, the principle that the duly elected king of the Romans had forthwith full power to rule the empire could not be effectively impugned in Germany after the electors' declaration at Rhens in July 1338. Complicated transactions with the Curia about papal recognition of the new ruler took place at the beginning of the reigns of Charles IV, Wenzel and Rupert; but their relevance to the situation north of the Alps was probably small. Already crowned in Germany, the king of the Romans became emperor after coronation at Rome by the pope or his delegates. This step was somewhat a matter of chance. Wenzel, Rupert and Albert II never achieved the imperial title; Charles IV became emperor in 1355, eight years after he had begun to reign; Sigismund had to wait twenty-two years and Frederick III twelve. The monarch's authority as king or emperor was supreme; he promulgated laws for the empire *de imperialis potestatis plenitudine, von Romischer kuniclicher macht, kraft und gewalt*. In official usage, at least, the formula 'Emperor and Empire', *Kaiser und Reich*, remained largely tautological throughout the Middle Ages; the institution was identified with the monarch's person.[2] Thus in August 1338 the Alsatian towns could pledge their support 'to our lord the emperor Lewis, who is the empire'.[3]

Reality did not match the theory. Obviously the late medieval empire was not in fact a system of government in the control of a single ruler. A Heidelberg professor—perhaps it was Conrad of Soest—lifted the veil when he wrote in 1408: 'Every nobleman, however modest his standing, is king in his own territory; every city exercises royal power within its own walls'.[4] Half a century later Aeneas Sylvius denied that monarchy existed in Germany.

[1] *R.T.A.*, iii, no. 200; cf. Gerlich, 346.
[2] R. Smend, 'Zur Geschichte der Formel "Kaiser und Reich" in den letzten Jahrhunderten des alten Reiches', *Historische Aufsätze Karl Zeumer . . . dargebracht* (Weimar, 1910), 442, 447.
[3] 'Unsern herren keiser Ludwigen, der daz rich ist': K. Müller, *Der Kampf Ludwigs d. Baiern mit d. römischen Curie*, ii (Tübingen, 1880), 358, doc. no. 5.
[4] *R.T.A.*, vi, no. 268.

The Germans were revelling in a plurality of princes. While they paid lip-service to the emperor as king and master, really he had no power: *nulla eius potentia est*. They obeyed him just as much as they wanted to, and their inclination to obey was minimal. The prelates, the lay princes and the towns were governing their subjects in independence.[1] Aeneas knew what he was talking about, from service in the imperial chancery and close acquaintance with some of the most intelligent Germans of his time. But if not a monarchy, what was the empire?

Corporative ideas did something to help. Admittedly the emperor was head, but there were also members of the empire: the princes, lay and ecclesiastical, led by the electors; the non-princely nobility; the towns, imperial and free; the lesser nobles, often of ministerial origin (the *Ritterschaft*). The attitude of these imperial estates towards the empire was ambivalent. They were proud to belong to it and to stand in direct relation to its head; but all desired for themselves as much freedom as possible within it. While the stronger among them were busily consolidating and extending their territories the small fry sought to escape these voracious pike by insisting that they too were independent members of the imperial body. When in 1426 the Swabian *Ritterschaft* formed their league to protect their common interests and ensure that they should 'continue as members of the empire' they were using language which, though commonplace, was meaningful.[2] With the more powerful estates consciousness of being limbs of the empire led to more positive conclusions. The possibility of distinguishing between the realm itself and the ruler's person had been understood from the early eleventh century, if not before.[3] By the late Middle Ages this distinction had been developed to support the claim that the interests of the empire did not invariably coincide with those of the emperor. Then it might be for the members to take action on behalf of the whole body even against the head. If so, a special responsibility was felt to rest upon the electors as *principaliora membra imperii*. Lupold of Bebenburg's teaching that

---

[1] Aeneas Silvius, *Germania*, ed. A. Schmidt (Cologne, 1962), 57, 68.

[2] 'Auch dass sie als Glieder beym heiligen Reiche bleiben mügen': quoted by C. F. Stälin, *Wirtembergische Geschichte*, iii (Stuttgart, 1856), 448.

[3] On the well-known phrase in Wipo: 'si rex periit, regnum remansit', *Gesta Chuonradi imperatoris*, ed. H. Bresslau, p. 30, cf. H. Beumann, 'Zur Entwicklung transpersonaler Staatsvorstellungen', in *Das Königtum, seine geistigen u. rechtlichen Grundlagen*, ed. Th. Mayer (Lindau and Constance, 1956), 212 ff.

in choosing the king of the Romans they represented the empire could be extended to other activities on their part.[1] In June 1400 the Rhenish electors threatened Wenzel that if he did not appear to meet them at Lahnstein they would feel themselves released from the oaths they had made to his person, though their obligations to the Holy Roman Empire were to remain binding.[2] Wenzel's deposition a couple of months later on the grounds that he was useless to the empire gave sharp point to the distinction.[3] Nothing less than active copartnership in the empire was claimed for the electors by the terms of the league of Marbach, formed under the leadership of Archbishop John II of Mainz against Rupert in 1405.[4] When the citizens of Cologne complained to Sigismund about the behaviour of their archbishop, Dietrich of Mörs, they got but cold comfort in return, according to Eberhard Windecke: 'he could do nothing for them; the electors were themselves the law'.[5] The facts of power make clear that, whatever theory might suggest, the working constitution of the late medieval empire was dualistic.

But it was not nearly so. Among the different estates capacity for effective political action varied enormously. If the electors had the prestige, superiority in physical resources lay increasingly with other territorial princes. Weaker estates, the non-princely nobles, the towns, the *Ritterschaft*, unable to create significant territories for themselves, had good reason to fear those who could. Mutual rivalries and suspicions made it impossible to harness all the estates for common action against the king. The same factors encouraged individual members among them to seek strength by union with selected allies. Late medieval Germany saw a vast activity of the federative principle, *Einung*.[6] The multitude of leagues defies classification. There were leagues between towns, between knights, between peasant communities, but also leagues in which towns, knights, princes and all sorts of nobles were mingled pell-mell. They did not amount to a federal constitution, or even to a

---

[1] Lupold of Bebenburg, *De iure regni et imperii*, ch. 5 (Basle, 1566), 353.
[2] *R.T.A.*, iii, nos. 146–7.
[3] *R.T.A.*, iii, no. 204.
[4] *R.T.A.*, v, no. 489.
[5] 'Do sprach der konig . . . die korfursten weren selber das recht': *Eberhard Windeckes Denkwürdigkeiten*, ed. W. Altmann (Berlin, 1893), 101.
[6] Cf. E. Bock, 'Monarchie, Einung u. Territorium im späteren Mittelalter'. *Hist. Vierteljahrsschrift* [=*H.V.*], xxiv (1929), 568.

system of confederations: 'public life was dominated by a con-fusion of confederations subsisting side by side.'[1] As Samuel von Pufendorf realized, there lurked in the empire some indefinable element which made it irreducible to any of the classical categories of political science.[2]

No simple formula can be found to describe the development of this complex structure; the lines of stratification were con-stantly being fractured. The story of the late medieval empire can no longer be presented in the old terms of the collapse of a formerly strong unitary monarchy, brought to ruin by ambitious and self-seeking territorial princes who had succeeded in usurping the prerogatives of sovereignty. As we recognize more clearly how the intensity with which government can be exercised depends on the relation between what is to be governed and the technical resources available for governing, we are less likely to expect too much of even the ablest medieval rulers. When the level of technical resources was low, the well-governed unit was commonly the small one. The sheer extent of Germany made direct rule by the king impossible once demands on government had become more exacting as the result of population growth and the intensification of settlement. The territorial magnates filled the gap, and it is pointless to abuse them as particularist and disruptive elements for doing what was needed and the king was unable to do.[3] During the last thirty years few books about constitutional developments in late medieval Germany have aroused more discussion than O. Brunner's *Land und Herrschaft*. Perhaps its most valuable lesson is so obvious that it is often overlooked: that medieval con-stitutional problems have the right to be studied in terms of their own times and circumstances, rather than in those suggested by later experience.[4]

A glance at what fifteenth-century Germans thought about the empire reveals much diversity and also a fundamental agreement. Among the town chroniclers Diebold Schilling of Berne has no doubt that 'Heilig rich' and 'Tutsch nacion' are

---

[1] L. Quidde, *Histoire de la paix publique en Allemagne au moyen âge* (Recueil des Cours de l'Académie de Droit International, xxviii, Paris, 1930), 551.

[2] [Severinus de Monzambano], *De statu imperii*, vi, 1 and 9, ed. F. Salomon (Weimar, 1910), 116, 127.

[3] Cf. K. S. Bader, 'Volk, Stamm, Territorium', in *Herrschaft u. Staat im Mittelalter*, ed. H. Kämpf (Darmstadt, 1956), 267–8.

[4] O. Brunner, *Land und Herrschaft*, 4th edn. (Vienna and Wiesbaden, 1959), 111 ff.

one. But while he accepts without discussion the universal mission of the empire, it becomes a concrete institution for him only in so far as it provides for the security of his own imperial city and its allies.[1] This attitude, combining the widest conceptions of the empire with the sentiment that in fact it is embodied in the free and imperial towns, is typical.[2] The Augsburg chronicler Burkard Zink complained that the imperial cities were failing to maintain their union among themselves and were seeking alliances with the lords: 'and thus the empire is wholly rent asunder'.[3] For Zink as for Schilling, the towns were the empire; and the quality of individual kings was measured by the extent to which they cherished urban interests.

Schilling was Swiss, of course; but the history of the Swiss cantons in the late Middle Ages was still part of German history. Their emergence represented a successful protest of the old law and its freedoms in face of the newer aggressive efficiencies of the territorial princedoms. By making good the claim to depend directly from the empire they ensured their independence from Habsburg, into whose territory they seemed fated to be absorbed, and also they legitimatized their own exercise of authority. From 1438 onwards, with Habsburgers as kings, the allegiance of the Swiss to the empire was inevitably strained; the gamekeeper, they feared, might turn poacher. Even so, their reluctance to leave the empire is remarkable. Like other German territories, the Confederation was jealous of its freedom of action, and on these grounds refused to accept the decisions of the reforming diet at Worms in 1495. Nevertheless, it has been claimed with some force, even after 1495 the Swiss did not desire separation; though ultimately it came, its story lies wholly outside the Middle Ages.[4] The Swiss chroniclers of the fifteenth century, just as the articulate elements in the south German towns, no doubt viewed the empire in the light of particular interests. But for all of them it seemed a permanent part of the settled and proper order of things.

The same conclusion was implied by many of the theoreticians.

[1] Diebold Schilling, *Berner Chronik*, ed. G. Tobler, i (Berne, 1897), 131.
[2] Cf. H. Schmidt, *Die deutschen Städtechroniken als Spiegel des bürgerlichen Selbsverständnisses im Spätmittelalter* (Göttingen, 1958), 64 ff.
[3] 'Also ist das reich alles zertrent': Burkard Zink, *Augsburger Chronik*, ed. F. Frensdorff (*Chroniken d. deutschen Städte*, v), 231.
[4] Karl Mommsen, *Eidgenossen, Kaiser und Reich* (Basel, 1958), 292.

To the greatest of them, Nicholas of Cues, writing in 1433, it was obvious that the emperor's power had declined markedly since Otto I's time, when imperial edicts were armed *potentia et vigore*. The situation was critical; unless his recommendations were carried out, Nicholas declared, the empire was doomed; in the ensuing confusion the lower orders (*populares*) would devour the princes, just as these were now gobbling up the empire. But Nicholas himself, one feels, was hardly convinced by this alarmist language. He thought that salvation could be found by return to the old trodden ways: regular annual assemblies of the princes; the establishment of a dozen or more standing imperial tribunals; use of ballot in future imperial elections; a permanent imperial army maintained by contributions from throughout the empire.[1] Not everything in these proposals did in fact represent return to the tried ways of the past; much was sketchy and indefinite; some was naïve. Interest attaches less to the proposals than to the fact that Nicholas believed in them. If they could be adopted, in his view a reformed empire was still possible.

Writing from a very different level of experience and ability the unknown author of the *Reformatio Sigismundi* (1439) contributed less directly to the argument. The perspective of his writing is eschatological; though his sense of actuality never dissolves completely, his passionate concern for the right ordering of Christian society is that of a moralist rather than a political thinker. Perhaps his disposition was more conservative than is often assumed—not that he believed that things should remain as they were, but rather that they should again become what they ought to be. But though no precise view of the empire is offered by the *Reformatio*, it remains for the author a fundamental institution coterminous with Christendom; he does not despair of its future.[2] No more did Peter of Andlau in his *Libellus de caesarea monarchia* (1460). The message of this feeble and derivative piece is that the empire will last until the coming of Antichrist. Admittedly, Frederick III is in a weaker position than the first Caesars. Nevertheless he is their legitimate

---

[1] *De concordantia catholica*, iii, 25–39, ed. G. Kallen, *Opera omnia Nicolai de Cusa*, xiv, 3 (Hamburg, 1959), 420–56.
[2] The manuscript basis of the edition by K. Beer, *Die Reformation Kaiser Sigmunds* (Beiheft to *R.T.A.*, 1933) is incomplete. A new edition by H. Koller for M.G.H. appeared in 1963. What is said above owes much to Lothar Graf zu Dohna, *Reformatio Sigismundi* (Göttingen, 1960), 52 ff.

successor; power lies to his hand, if only he will bestir himself to use it.[1]

Behind all these ideas, with their mingling of present and remote past, of the parochially narrow with the ecumenically wide, lies consciousness that the empire is, and must continue. Some of this consciousness has justly been called negative.[2] The weaker estates were far more likely to show awareness of their imperial status when they felt their independence threatened than when the empire called on them to fulfil their duties. But we may easily underestimate how strongly there persisted a feeling of the potentiality latent in the empire. Just past the middle of the fifteenth century an electoral memorandum emanating from Trier expressed it thus: 'In people, towns, fortresses and all other things which pertain to lordly great affairs our nation is master over all other nations, provided that it is rightly ordered and governed.'[3] It was for the empire to supply this right ordering and governance at the highest level. To maintain peace and justice was its primary concern, as Frederick II had emphasized in 1235.[4] No heavier charge could be found to lay against Wenzel's rule than that war was everywhere and no one knew before whom he should seek justice.[5]

The empire's overriding responsibility for *pax et iustitia* was the business in the first place of its head, but also of its members. At any particular time it was the comparative weights of these elements which swayed the balance in the empire's divided constitution.

A basic fact of kingship in Germany at this period was the way in which its elective nature was stressed and exploited. Only few and obscure voices were raised in the cause of sense against the theory that elective monarchy was superior to other kinds.[6] It is useless to debate whether Albert I, had he escaped being

---

[1] Peter von Andlau, *Libellus de caesarea monarchia*, ii, 18–20, ed. J. Hürbin, *Zts. d. Savigny-Stiftung f. Rechtsgeschichte, Germanist. Abt.* [=*Z.R.G. G.A.*], xiii (1892), 215–17.

[2] Cf. K. S. Bader, *Der deutsche Südwesten in seiner territorialstaatlichen Entwicklung* (Stuttgart, 1950), 58.

[3] Printed by L. von Ranke, *Deutsche Geschichte im Zeitalter der Reformation*, 6th edn., vi (Leipzig, 1882), 13.

[4] In the preamble to the *Landfriede* of Mainz, M.G.H. *Const.*, ii, no. 196, p. 241, the collocation of *pax* and *iustitia* occurs three times in seven lines.

[5] *R.T.A.*, iii, no. 9 (Christmas 1397).

[6] Cf. A. Werminghoff, 'Zur Lehre von der Erbmonarchie im 14. Jahrhundert'. *H.V.*, xx (1922), 150 ff.

murdered in 1308, might have made the Crown hereditary in the Habsburg family. He did not do so, and for the next 130 years no Habsburger was uncontested king in Germany. The important part played by election in making the king had inescapable consequences. Since he could not rely on the Crown remaining in his dynasty after his death (to contrive this for Wenzel taxed the ability of Charles IV, while it seems doubtful whether Maximilian's election was actively promoted by his father at all),[1] the king was bound to do the best he could for his family while he was alive. An elective kingship was necessarily devoted to the pursuit of dynastic power, *Hausmacht*. Before his death Lewis the Bavarian had established members of his family in possession of Tirol, Brandenburg, Hainault, Holland and Zeeland. The acquisition of Brandenburg for the Luxemburgers, completed in 1373, ranks among the most arduous achievements of Charles IV. Only the tireless attention paid by Frederick III to Habsburg family interests, often under discouraging circumstances, made it possible for his heir to play an active part in European politics.

It is futile to accuse these kings of behaving as step-fathers towards the empire. They could make a show of ruling only by deploying their *Hausmacht*. The empire itself had little to offer the king by way of physical or financial support. By this time he had lost control over the imperial churches and their lands; no territory of consequence, except the imperial towns, came to him as king of the Romans; income from such regalian rights as remained was often anticipated for years in advance and these sources were frequently in hazard as the result of being pledged time and again to Crown creditors. Material from which to write a continuous financial history of the late medieval empire does not survive.[2] From year to year revenue from the chief source, the imperial towns, may have varied between about ten and thirty thousand guldens, an excessively narrow basis for the credit operations which had to be undertaken in any emergency and which in the end were commonly

[1] Cf. E. Bock, 'Die Doppelregierung Friedrichs III. u. Maximilians 1486–1493', in *Aus Reichstagen des 15. u. 16. Jahrhunderts. Festgabe dargebracht der Histor. Kommission . . . von den Herausgebern der deutschen Reichstagsakten* [=*A.R.*], (Göttingen, 1958), 283–5. R. Buchner, *Maximilian I* (Göttingen, 1959), 26, puts forward the view that Frederick wished for Maximilian's election though not for its consequences.
[2] E. B. and M. M. Fryde give a useful conspectus in *The Cambridge Economic History of Europe*, iii (1963), 507–18.

backed by the king's dynastic resources. Though the king was still feudal suzerain of Germany, enfeoffing the princes with their territories, this did not put an adequate armed force at his disposal. In face of the Hussite threat in 1422 the summer diet at Nuremberg demanded specified contingents of troops from named members of the empire, together with a fractional tax on incomes or property from those on whom a quota of service was not imposed, as well as a harsh levy from the Jews.[1] These measures were no more effective than the attempt five years later of the papal legate and the estates to finance an imperial army against the Hussites by elaborate tax proposals on persons and property throughout the empire.[2] Feeling against the foreigner might allow Frederick III to bring together an imperial army to relieve Neuss from Charles of Burgundy in 1475, but he met humiliating discomfiture when he tried to enforce by arms an imperial sentence against his vassal Frederick the Victorious of the Palatinate. As was to be expected, at the centre of the wide proposals for reform in 1495 lay a scheme for a general tax, the Common Penny, to be raised for the purposes of 'maintaining peace and justice in the empire and withstanding the enemies of Christ, the Turks and other enemies of the Holy Empire and the German Nation'.[3] Not least amongst the reasons for the failure of the Common Penny was Maximilian's insistence that the proceeds of it from the Habsburg hereditary lands should come under his control, rather than that of the imperial diet. He can hardly be blamed for not accepting a mediatization of his *Hausmacht* which might have undermined his position in the empire. The king's authority and his power as territorial dynast were inseparably connected.

This limited the possible candidates for the office. Four families—Habsburg, Nassau, Wittelsbach and Luxemburg—monopolized the throne from 1272 to 1486; at times there was talk of widening the circle, but nothing came of it.[4] These families did not serve the empire badly. In their differing ways

---

[1] *R.T.A.*, viii, nos. 145, 147, 152–4; cf. H. Herre, 'Das Reichskriegssteuergesetz vom Jahre 1422'; *H.V.*, xix (1920), 13 ff.

[2] *R.T.A.*, ix, no. 76.

[3] K. Zeumer, *Quellensammlung zur Geschichte der deutschen Reichsverfassung* [=Zeumer, *Quellen*], 2nd edn. (Leipzig, 1913), no. 176.

[4] Cf. Gerlich, op. cit., 274 for an agreement reached in September 1399 between the electors and a number of princes to accept a future king only from the houses of Bavaria, Meissen, Hesse, Hohenzollern or Württemberg.

nearly all the German kings from Rudolf of Habsburg to Maximilian were able, Rudolf and Charles IV outstandingly so. Perhaps the only exceptions were Adolf and Wenzel; and even for Wenzel something can be said, at least down to 1389.[1] The Crown's problems were institutional rather than personal, and it would be wrong to underrate the technical standards of such government as these kings did offer. Quite recently more light has been thrown on the considerable achievements of Lewis the Bavarian as a legislator;[2] work on the registers of the imperial chancery under Sigismund and Albert II shows that office as an efficient organ of administration under the king's control, and no longer exclusively a clerical preserve. Only in Frederick III's reign did a change for the worse take place.[3]

Procedure for electing the king was codified in the Golden Bull of 1356.[4] The Bull's great merit was that it provided lasting rules for an orderly succession to the throne. At a first reading it is disappointing to find this fundamental law devoting so many of its articles to the small change of ceremony. But they, like the unrealistic demand that the lay electors should be instructed in the Latin, Italian and Slavonic tongues, and the attempt to apply to those who plotted against an elector's life the sanctions of the Roman law of treason, were of the very stuff of the mid-fourteenth century.[5] The Bull was little concerned with new principles; the electors had long enjoyed the constitutional standing and most of the privileges ratified in 1356. Its purpose was to place beyond the doubts which had worked so mischievously in the past the details of what was at once a great ceremony and a vital political transaction: to settle finally who were entitled to elect and how they were to proceed. It did not prove a perfect rule for the future; Wenzel's election during his father's lifetime, though not forbidden by the Bull, neglected some of its prescriptions; only the timely death of Jost of

[1] H. Weigel, 'König Wenzels persönliche Politik', *Deutsches Archiv f. Gesch. d. Mittelalters*, vii (1944), 133–99.

[2] H. Lieberich, 'Kaiser Ludwig der Baier als Gesetzgeber', *Z.R.G. G.A.*, lxxvi (1959), 176–219, 241–5.

[3] Cf. H. Koller, *Das Reichsregister König Albrechts II* (*Mitteilungen d. Österreich. Staatsarchivs. Erg. Bd. iv*, Vienna, 1955), 1–11.

[4] Cf. K. Zeumer, *Die Goldene Bulle Kaiser Karls IV*, 2 vols. (Weimar, 1908); text, ibid., ii, 5–48 and Zeumer, *Quellen*, no. 148.

[5] On the long controversy between Mainz and Cologne as to which archbishop should take the king's right hand, see H. Foerster, 'Kurköln u. Stadt Köln i.d. Goldenen Bulle Kaiser Karls IV', *Rheinische Vierteljahrsblätter*, xix (1954), 59–63.

Moravia offered a clear way out of the complicated situation in 1410.[1] But the real grounds for criticizing the Bull are that it was too successful. In the long run it petrified what it had sought to make stable and regular.

In general the eastern electorates played a secondary part. As long as the Luxemburgers survived the Bohemian vote was under their control; afterwards, despite George Podiebrad's ambitions to shape imperial policy in the early 'sixties, doubts could be felt whether Bohemia stood on quite the same footing as the other electorates.[2] Little effective intervention could be expected from Brandenburg or Saxony until the Hohenzollerns (1415) and Wettiners (1424) had become established. The lead fell to the Rhinelanders, the archbishops of Mainz, Cologne and Trier, and the count palatine. Mainz, with its great historic claims, its archchancellorship of the empire in Germany, and its initiative in the business of royal elections now secured by the Golden Bull, outranked the other two archbishoprics. The count palatine, the only prince before whom the king could be called to answer legal complaint, had too the duty of governing the empire as vicar in the area of Frankish law when there was no king. Mainz and the Palatinate can hardly be said to have dominated the electoral college, but for more than a century after the Golden Bull they were its most consistently influential members.

The special union for joint action, the *Kurverein*, to which the electors on occasion resorted, was always a weighty demonstration. At Rhens in July 1338, between April and September 1399, at Bingen in January 1424, electoral unions originating on the Rhine decided great matters of imperial politics.[3] They rejected papal interference in the making of the king of the Romans, prepared the deposition of Wenzel and election of Rupert, manifested electoral solidarity for policies to be achieved, if need be, in the king's despite. A peak was reached after Sigismund's death, before Albert II had accepted the kingship: the March *Kurverein* of 1438 declared for German neutrality between the conflicting claims of Pope Eugenius IV

---

[1] R. Lies, 'Die Wahl Wenzels z. Römischen Könige i. ihrem Verhältnis z. Goldenen Bulle', *H.V.*, xxvi (1931), 93–5; J. Leuschner, 'Zur Wahlpolitik im Jahre 1410', *Deutsches Archiv f. Erforschung d. Mittelalters*, xi (1955), 506 ff.

[2] Cf. Zeumer, *Goldene Bulle*, i, 170, 234, 245–55.

[3] Zeumer, *Quellen*, nos. 141a, 141c. *R.T.A.*, iii, nos. 41, 51, 56–8, 204; cf. Gerlich, op. cit., pp. 328, 336. *R.T.A.*, viii, no. 294; cf. H. Angermeier, 'Das Reich u.d. Konziliarismus', *Hist. Zts.*, cxcii (1961), 559–60.

and the Council of Basle.[1] Though the Golden Bull's provision for regular annual meetings between king and electors was disregarded, the electors habitually claimed extensive influence in imperial affairs, even when there was no *Kurverein* for a specific purpose. At times—in 1399–1400, for instance, and from 1405 to the end of Rupert's reign—that influence seemed decisive. Between 1417 and 1430, favoured by Sigismund's long absences, they took over much of the business of government, not always with the king's approval. For much of Sigismund's reign, indeed, they were not just the elective body and highest council of the empire, issuing their individual letters of consent (*Willebriefe*) to royal grants. They arrogated to themselves joint rule with the king, whether he liked it or not.

Such examples should not be pressed too hard; the electors' position was not on the whole as strong as they might suggest. Electoral policy towards pope and council in the *Kurverein* of 1446 did not prevail; Frederick III had other views, and it was he alone who arrived at the concordat of 1448 with Pope Nicholas V.[2] Effective action by the electors depended on unity, and this was not easy to create or maintain. The territories of the four Rhenish electors were not merely contiguous, but confused; the geographical texture of the Palatinate, it has been said, resembled a sponge, in the holes of which lay the most important places, all belonging to Mainz.[3] It was a pattern highly apt to breed controversy. Though as an economic region the middle Rhineland imposed on its rulers some degree of joint action in matters of communications, tolls and currency, from this there grew no steady habit of political co-operation. A particular emergency might bring the Rhenish electors together, to act with impressive effect, but soon local rubs and rivalries would set them at odds again. Within a few years of being made king by the Rhenish bloc Rupert had no more bitter opponent than John II of Mainz; the early 1460s are full of the strife between Frederick the Victorious and Archbishop Adolf II. Above all, the numerical preponderance of the Rhinelanders in the electoral college, the result of old history, perpetuated by the Golden Bull, found no justification in the real balance of forces in late medieval Germany. Even in union

[1] *R.T.A.*, xiii, no. 144; cf. Angermeier, 567.
[2] Angermeier, 575; Zeumer, *Quellen*, no. 168.
[3] The description comes from E. Ziehen, *Mittelrhein u. Reich i. Zeitalter d. Reichsreform*, i (Frankfurt a.M., 1934), 162.

the Rhenish electorates were not big enough nor strong enough nor well enough placed to sustain a dominant role when power had moved elsewhere, to the south and the east.[1] The pretensions of the electors to make decisions for the empire rang hollow when some of the most important political factors in Germany had no electoral voice—the Swiss Confederation, the Wittelsbachers in Bavaria, the Habsburgers in their land of Austria 'which is known to be the shield and heart of the Holy Roman Empire'.

This phrase comes from the *Privilegium maius*, a falsified re-handling in 1358–9 of Barbarossa's privilege for the duchy of Austria.[2] It may well be that in substance the falsification did not go far beyond the genuine privilege of 1156, except in making some high faluting ceremonial claims for the duke and asserting for his territory the judicial immunity of the *privilegium de non evocando*.[3] But it is very likely that Duke Rudolf IV of Habsburg instigated the forgery with the Golden Bull in mind. In 1356, together with the rest of southern Germany, Austria had been excluded from the select circle of electors and so from what Rudolf considered its due influence in the empire; in part the *Maius* was intended to redress the situation. It contained a typical programme of princely 'liberty', reducing to a minimum Austria's obligations to the empire while insisting on the empire's duty to aid the duke. 'In matters favourable to itself it is a member of the empire; not so, when the relation is vexatious.' What Pufendorf said of fourteenth-century Austria had the *Maius* in view.[4] But the comment can be applied further afield. The liberties which Rudolf falsely claimed were granted by Barbarossa he did in fact to a large extent enjoy. So too did many other territorial rulers at this time.

With the princes indeed lay not only the future (as we are often told) but also much of the present. Compared with them the lesser nobility and the towns had little weight in politics. The means chosen by the *Ritterschaft* in its struggle for independence were probably more reputable and intelligent than is

---

[1] Cf. B. Schmeidler, 'Die Bedeutung d. späteren Mittelalters f. d. deutsche u. europäische Geschichte', *H.V.*, xxix (1935), 100.

[2] Text: M.G.H. *Const.*, i, no. 455, pp. 683–5, and A. Lhotsky, *Privilegium maius. Die Geschichte einer Urkunde* (Munich, 1957), 84.

[3] Lhotsky, 24.

[4] [Severinus de Monzambano], *De statu imperii*, ii, 4, ed. Salomon, p. 53: 'Ergo in favorabilibus est membrum Imperii, in odiosis non item.'

sometimes assumed;[1] in their leagues the lesser nobles could be useful allies. But they were hardly an independent force in the empire. No more were the towns in the fifteenth century. By this time the will for positive political action which had characterized the league of Rhenish towns in 1254 seemed dead.[2] Though numerous, the towns were mostly small: among three thousand or so perhaps only a couple of hundred could boast of more than a thousand inhabitants, with a dozen modest giants exceeding ten thousand.[3] Their resources in money, credit and man-power were far from contemptible; the service quotas of 1422 assessed more than a quarter of the imperial army against the free and imperial towns.[4] But with a few exceptions (Nuremberg, Berne, Zürich, for instance) they failed to create for themselves territories of any importance. Individual citizens, as the history of early capitalism shows, abounded in energy and enterprise, yet the corporate psychology of the towns had become defensive, their consciousness of the empire negative. How shrewd Charles IV had been in preferring to support the princes was shown by the towns' nerveless reaction to encouragement from Sigismund. Probably they never fully recovered from the rough handling given them by the nobles and princes in the 1380s.[5] Even the Hanseatic towns, among whom a far stronger and more aggressive political ethos prevailed than in the south, seemed past their peak by 1400.[6]

There was no lack of dynamism among the princes. By the second half of the fifteenth century they were emerging as personalities: Albert Achilles in Franconia and Brandenburg, Frederick the Victorious in the Palatinate, Eberhard the Bearded in Württemberg, Albert the Wise and George the Rich in Bavaria, and a dozen more. Perhaps there is some danger of forgetting how much was still provisional and incomplete in their territorial constructions and how far short

[1] Cf. H. Obenaus, *Recht u. Verfassung d. Gesellschaften mit St. Jörgenschild in Schwaben* (Göttingen, 1961).
[2] Cf. E. Bielfeldt, *Der Rheinische Bund von 1254. Ein erster Versuch einer Reichsreform* (Berlin, 1937), 33.
[3] H. Bechtel, *Wirtschaftsgeschichte Deutschlands von d. Vorzeit bis zum Ende des Mittelalters*, 2nd edn. (Munich, 1951), pp. 255-6.
[4] Herre, 'Reichskriegssteuergesetz', p. 33.
[5] The situation *c.* 1500 has been described by H. Gollwitzer, '*Capitaneus imperatorio nomine*. Reichshauptleute in Städten u. reichsstädtische Schicksale im Zeitalter Maximilians I.', *A.R.*, 273-8.
[6] Cf. F. Rörig, 'Aussenpolitische u. innerpolitische Wandlungen i.d. Hanse nach d. Stralsunder Frieden (1370)', *Wirtschaftskräfte im Mittelalter* (Cologne, 1959), 161-6.

within them they fell of what the modern world would recognize as sovereignty. The rise of the princes to supremacy within their territories was by no means a story of unbroken success.[1] Bad luck or management in a dynasty could lead to paralysing divisions and dissensions. The chaotic internal conditions in Brandenburg under the Wittelsbachers and Luxemburgers are a commentary on that theme.[2] In Bavaria from 1392 to 1448 the duchy was split between four ruling lines, Munich, Ingolstadt, Landshut and Straubing; not until the first decade of the sixteenth century were its rich potentialities brought together in a single hand and its unity made secure. Such circumstances could gravely hinder the princes in their efforts to master the Church, the nobles and the towns in their territories. They could not afford to be nice about the means they used. There are grounds for supposing that the forged *Privilegium maius* was even more serviceable to the Habsburgers as a means of asserting their supremacy within Austria than of emphasizing their quasi-autonomy in the empire.[3] Even so, it has been argued, not till the sixteenth century was the *Landeshoheit* of Habsburg in Austria complete.[4]

The territorial ruler indeed rarely exercised a solid and uniform authority over a neatly defined geographical area. Rather, he is to be pictured struggling with an untidy bundle of rights and superiorities, very diverse in nature and origin. Over some of them his control was still precarious. Feudal ties, paying little heed to emergent territorial boundaries, added their complications. Not everywhere did the lesser nobles submit to the prince; in Württemberg, the Kraichgau and the Rheingau, for instance, they eventually escaped into the status of imperial knights. Sharp definitions were wanting; in a single

---

[1] H. Spangenberg, *Vom Lehenstaat zum Ständestaat* (Munich and Berlin, 1912), 120 ff.
[2] Cf. H. Spangenberg, 'Landesherrliche Verwaltung, Feudalismus u. Ständetum i.d. deutschen Territorien d. 13. bis 15. Jahrhunderts', *Hist. Zts.*, ciii (1909), 512 ff.
[3] Lhotsky, *Privilegium maius*, 30.
[4] Cf. O. H. Stowasser, 'Zwei Studien z. oesterreich. Verfassungsgeschichte', *Z.R.G. G.A.*, xliv (1924), 146; id., *Das Land und der Herzog* (Berlin, 1925), 7 ff.; id., 'Die Entwicklung des Landes Oesterreich', *Vierteljahrschrift f. Sozial- u. Wirtschaftsgeschichte*, xix (1927), 429 ff. Of course there are dangers in generalizing from the experience of a particular area. How little, e.g., O. Brunner's conception of *Land* as a community living and working under a unity of law (*Landrecht*), largely based as it is on evidence from south-east Germany (*Land und Herrschaft*, 180–96, 231–9), fits conditions in the mark of Meissen has been pointed out by K. Bosl, *Hist. Zts.*, cxci (1960), 350, with reference to H. Helbig, *Der Wettinische Ständestaat* (Cologne, 1955).

area the rights and claims of various territorial rulers and lords might lie intermingled and overlapping.[1] Only by unremitting effort in administration could the princes consolidate their territories and their own position. This proved their ladder to success. Attempts to turn the prince's council into an instrument of the noble estate giving mandatory advice failed; the council did not become part of the constitutional machinery of the territory but remained an organ of administration.[2] The prince appointed as advisers and administrators those whose abilities could serve him best; as the fifteenth century wore on more and more was heard of the professional bureaucrats, often now trained in Roman law and moving for advancement from one territory to another.[3] Not infrequent complaints about the *doctores* bear involuntary witness to their efficiency.[4] These complaints continued long, and warn us not to antedate establishment or acceptance of the new techniques. In the electorate of Mainz, which we might expect to have been pretty forward in this field, administration was not brought under the control of central departments until the second half of the fifteenth century.[5]

A territory was something more than the expression of a dynasty's will for power. As in the empire itself, so there was a dualism in territorial constitutions. The prince had to reckon with his estates—the churchmen, the nobles, the towns and in a few instances the peasants.[6] Their composition and the extent to which they worked with or against the ruler varied greatly from territory to territory. In ecclesiastical principalities facts of church organization and the canon law might cause departures from the usual pattern. Thus in Mainz relations between the prince-archbishop and his estates were in a sense distorted by the claims of the cathedral chapter. Towards the archbishop the chapter acted as an estate, but to the other estates of Mainz —the nobles, the *Landschaft* of the Rheingau, the towns of the *Oberstift*—it appeared as part of the ruling lordship, the *Herrschaft*, itself.[7] But however they might be organized, the estates

---

[1] Cf. A. Werminghoff, *Ludwig von Eyb* (Halle, 1919), 58 ff.

[2] Spangenberg, *Vom Lehenstaat zum Ständestaat*, 71–3.

[3] Cf. Henny Grüneisen, 'Herzog Sigmund von Tirol, der Kaiser u. die Ächtung d. Eidgenossen, 1469. Kanzlei u. Räte Herzog Sigmunds', *A.R.*, 157–61, 211–2.

[4] F. L. Carsten, *Princes and Parliaments in Germany* (Oxford, 1959), 11, 355–6.

[5] B. Witte, *Herrschaft und Land im Rheingau* (Meisenheim/Glan, 1959) 141–2.

[6] The nature of the medieval estates is well brought out by Brunner, *Land und Herrschaft*, 394 ff.

[7] Witte, 186.

fulfilled indispensable functions. Without their help it was difficult for the prince to raise taxes; only they were able to protect the community of the territory from the results of dynastic accident or caprice. As guardians of the unity of the territory it was their duty to combat patrimonial conceptions in the ruling house. A chronicler tells us how in 1347, after the death of Count Adolf II, the knights of Mark rejected the demand of his brother Eberhard that the county should forthwith be divided between him and Adolf's son Engelbert. Though it was proper, they conceded, that decent provision should be made for Eberhard, it was essential that the county should be kept as a single unit: and so Engelbert III was brought in as sole ruler.[1] The accent was not always merely on conservation. The action of the estates might also be constructive. Even under the thrusting Dietrich II of Mörs (1414–63), it has been claimed, the development of the territory of Cologne was as much the work of the estates as of the archbishop.[2]

At times the estates met of their own volition. The view that only by converting such meetings into a periodic official occasion, the *Landtag*, did the princes manage to draw the teeth of a threat to their own power, is probably too schematic.[3] The joint meetings of the estates at the summons of the prince, becoming more frequent as the fifteenth century wore on, 'did not come into being as a planned move by one side or the other, but grew up because they fulfilled a useful purpose'.[4] It remains true that they could prove formidable to an unwise or unfortunate ruler, as the dukes in Württemberg experienced; their very existence imposed some limitation on the free play of the princes' ambitions.

There was, then, no single machine of government for the empire. Its politics were shaped by the interplay between head and members, both acting more commonly within the context of this or that league or union than as individuals. Thus authority at a high level in Germany was diffused, at a time

---

[1] Levold von Northof, *Chronica Comitum de Marka*, ed. F. Zschaeck (M.G.H. *S.S.* n.s. vi), 12.
[2] G. Droege, *Verfassung und Wirtschaft in Kurköln unter Dietrich von Moers, 1414–1463* (Bonn, 1957), 205–7.
[3] Spangenberg, *Vom Lehenstaat zum Ständestaat*, 113, 137–51.
[4] Carsten, *Princes and Parliaments*, 428.

when elsewhere it was becoming more concentrated. We ought not to assume too readily that all the results were bad—that therefore the citizen of Bremen or Augsburg or Leipzig had less chance of realizing his human potentialities than his counterpart in Rouen or Bristol or Barcelona. There is a thought-provoking discrepancy in late medieval Germany between vigorous cultural and economic achievement on the one hand and the complications and incoherencies of governmental structure on the other.[1]

But undoubtedly these structural peculiarities in Germany did pose severe problems. Abundant illustration of this can be found in the sphere of justice. Within their territories the princes now controlled the courts. But what if a territorial court judged perversely or denied justice? What if the subjects of one prince were at odds with those of another, or with some lesser member of the empire whose independence might be jeopardized by submission to the jurisdiction of a neighbouring territory? What remedy could be found for the confusions caused by the simultaneous existence of innumerable sources and varieties of law: popular, feudal, ministerial, manorial, urban, in all their differing provincial and territorial forms? The widespread reception of Roman law (as adapted to current needs by the fourteenth-century legists) helped to supply Germany's want of a single common law, even though we cannot assume that this process was rapid or smooth or universal.[2] But as a supreme imperial tribunal the *Reichshofgericht* proved hopelessly inadequate. The *Hofrichter* exercised no jurisdiction over princes; he had neither professional assistants nor means of ensuring the execution of his judgments; commonly a member of the higher nobility, his impartiality might be suspect to other classes; as he worked at no fixed centre but followed the royal court, access to him was difficult. He and his court could contribute little to the maintenance of justice; after 1451 we hear no more of them.[3] Yet baulked as it was by this defective machinery, the desire for imperial, supraterritorial justice remained strong enough to give fresh life to anomalous survivals from the past.

[1] Cf. H. Heimpel, 'Das deutsche Spätmittelalter. Charakter einer Zeit', *Hist. Zts.*, clviii (1938), 233.
[2] Cf. P. Vinogradoff, *Roman Law in Medieval Europe*, 2nd edn. (Oxford, 1929), 119–45.
[3] A. Schulte, 'Der hohe Adel des deutschen Hofrichters', *Festschrift G. von Hertling . . . dargebracht* (Kempten and Munich, 1913), 539 ff.; H. Mitteis, *Der Staat des hohen Mittelalters*, 3rd edn. (Weimar, 1948), 412.

Only thus can we understand the esteem enjoyed in the later Middle Ages by such a court as the 'Hofgericht' at Rottweil in Swabia. By exploiting the facts that it was held on imperial territory and under royal authority it was able to exercise jurisdiction far beyond its original limited competence. The activities of the Westphalian 'free courts', the *Vemgerichte*, were basically similar, for they too claimed to do justice on authority from the king, at a time when the royal *Bannleihe* had long ceased for the courts in the territories. Favoured by Charles IV and Sigismund, and also by the archbishops of Cologne, who saw in them possibilities of promoting their territorial influence in Westphalia,[1] by the early fifteenth century the *Vemgerichte* had achieved an importance not to be disregarded. Their members, the *Freischöffen*, could be found in many places outside Westphalia, participants in a secret alliance, sworn at their initiation to silence about their knowledge of the courts' workings; on them lay the duty of executing the judgments of the *Vemgerichte*. Undoubtedly at times the actions of this secret society were irresponsible and oppressive; the wish to curb them appears clearly in the so-called *Reformatio Friderici* in 1442.[2] But it is certain that in practice the workings of the 'free courts' were not as considerable nor as dreadful nor as abusive as they appeared to the age of Goethe and Kleist.[3] Their significance lay neither in their efficiency nor in their somewhat spurious mystery. Like the Rottweil court they represented a wholly insufficient attempt to supply from local resources the lack of that supreme imperial tribunal which circumstances continued to demand.

Meanwhile recourse to forcible self-help, vendetta, the *Fehde*, was prevalent. It would be a mistake to infer too hastily from this that might alone was right. At least in theory *Fehde* was not the arbitrary exercise of purposeless and unlimited violence, but a process directed to the recovery of right and the re-establishment of peace. Declaration and conduct of *Fehde* were governed by well-understood conventions with an internal logic of their own. That this was a practice ingrained in the legal conscious-

[1] Cf. E. Bock, 'Der Kampf um die Landfriedenshoheit in Westfalen u. die Freigerichte bis zum Ausgang d. 14. Jahrhunderts', *Z.R.G. G.A.*, xlviii (1928), 379 ff.

[2] *R.T.A.*, xvi, no. 209.

[3] T. Lindner, *Die Feme* (Münster, 1888), xxi. For activity of these 'free courts' outside Westphalia, see C. W. Scherer, *Die westfälischen Femgerichte u. die Eidgenossenschaft* (Aarau, 1941), 21 ff., 52 ff.

ness and habits of German noble society, not just a symptom of the failure of medieval government to meet its obligations, has rightly been stressed by Otto Brunner.[1] *Fehde* found its counterpart in the numberless standing arrangements for settling disputes by arbitration which bulk so large among the documents of this period.[2] In the case of such associations as the St George societies of the Swabian knights arbitral procedures between the members seem quite as important as the protection of their political and class interests against outsiders.[3]

But it would be folly to ignore the disastrous effects on wholly innocent third parties of the plundering and wasting which might accompany *Fehde*. Those who have penetrated most deeply into its nature do not deny that it was an evil.[4] The evidence for a slow but persistent pressure to outlaw *Fehde* is therefore a cogent argument against too pessimistic a view of fifteenth-century Germany. Ineffective proposals in 1431 and 1438 to prohibit *Fehde* were followed in 1442 by the attempt to protect the defenceless against its consequences.[5] In 1467 the sanction of the Roman law of treason was invoked for an imperial decree making recourse to *Fehde* illegal during the next five years;[6] after being renewed in 1471, 1474, 1480 and 1486 (for ten years) the prohibition was made perpetual at the great reforming diet at Worms in 1495.[7] Mere legislation could not, of course, immediately abolish a deep-rooted practice. As many of the less powerful estates of the empire well understood, to declare *Fehde* illegal without providing an acceptable substitute by way of process in the courts was beating the air.[8] Nevertheless, between 1400 and 1500 *Fehde* had become increasingly disreputable. Joint action by the emperor and the estates had played some part in bringing this about.

[1] *Land und Herrschaft*, part i (*Friede und Fehde*), 1–110.
[2] Cf. Ingeborg Most, 'Schiedsgericht, rechtlicheres Rechtgebot, ordentliches Gericht, Kammergericht', *A.R.*, 116 ff.
[3] Cf. Obenaus, *Recht u. Verfassung d. Gesellschaften mit St. Jörgenschild*, 39 ff., 93.
[4] Brunner, *Land und Herrschaft*, 80–95, 106.
[5] *R.T.A.*, xvi, no. 209.
[6] Cf. Ingeborg Most, 'Der Reichslandfriede vom 20 August 1467. Zur Geschichte des Crimen laesae maiestatis u. der Reichsreform unter Kaiser Friedrich III', *Syntagma Friburgense. Historische Studien Hermann Aubin dargebracht* (Lindau and Constance, 1956), 191 ff. See too the remarks of H. Conrad in *Z.R.G. G.A.*, lxxv (1958), 394.
[7] Zeumer, *Quellen*, no. 171 (1486), no. 173 (1495); cf. Quidde, *Paix publique*, 547–9; E. Molitor, *Die Reichsreformbestrebungen d. 15. Jahrhunderts bis zum Tod Kaiser Friedrichs III* (Breslau, 1921), pp. 166–7.
[8] Cf. Obenaus, 227.

The theatre for co-operation or controversy between head and members was the diet, the *Reichstag*, in which Ranke recognized the fundamental institution of the late medieval empire.[1] Experience has falsified his estimate that the sources for the history of the diets down to 1519 could all be printed in a couple of quarto volumes after a few years' work.[2] Fourteen volumes of *Reichstagsakten* have been needed to cover the years 1376–1439; another nine will bring the story only as far as 1477.[3] Not until this enterprise is complete will a satisfactory account of the diet as an institution be possible. During the fifteenth century much about the *Reichstag* was still fluid and uncertain; only towards the end of the century were its composition and procedure made more regular and formal by the influence of Berthold of Henneberg, archbishop of Mainz. Clearly by this period the old supreme feudal court of the German ruler, the *Reichshoftag*, had been superseded in idea and practice; the fifteenth-century diet was not a feudal court but an assembly of the estates of the empire.[4] Any conceivable subject might be brought before it. Concern with external affairs bulked large: relations with pope or council, defence against Hussites, Turks or Burgundy. Of internal matters perhaps two were the object of most lively and persistent interest: care for the general public peace in Germany (the *Landfriede*) and reform of the imperial constitution. More must be said of these, at the risk of doing some violence to the facts by separating problems which rarely arose in isolation. For frequently the emperor, calling a *Reichstag* to raise help against the Hussites or the Turks, would be faced by the estates wishing to talk of the *Landfriede* or imperial reform.

The last great act of Hohenstaufen legislation in Germany had been the *Landfriede* promulgated by Frederick II at Mainz in 1235.[5] Many of its principles passed as generally desirable

---

[1] *Deutsche Geschichte im Zeitalter der Reformation*, 6th edn., i (Leipzig, 1881), Vorrede, v.

[2] Cf. Heimpel, 'Deutsche Reichstagsakten, ältere Reihe', 86.

[3] On present editorial problems see W. Kaemmerer, 'Zum gegenwärtigen Standort der Reichstagsakten', *A.R.*, 11 ff.

[4] H. Spangenberg, 'Die Entstehung des Reichskammergerichts u. die Anfänge der Reichsverwaltung', *Z.R.G. G.A.*, xlvi (1926), 245, n. 2.

[5] Text of Latin version: M.G.H. *Const.*, ii, no. 196, 241–7; German version: Zeumer, *Quellen*, no. 58. On the priority of the Latin version see H. Mitteis, 'Zum Mainzer Reichslandfrieden von 1235', *Z.R.G. G.A.*, lxii (1942), 13 ff. [=*Die Rechtsidee in der Geschichte* (Weimar, 1957), 387 ff.]; E. Klingelhöfer. *Die Reichsgesetze von 1220, 1231/2 u. 1235* (Weimar, 1955), 97 ff.

into the legal consciousness of Germany. But the collapse of Hohenstaufen rule frustrated Frederick's intention that responsibility for maintaining the public peace throughout Germany should rest with the emperor and his *Hofrichter*. However usefully the principles of the *pax publica* might serve as the basis for penal legislation against crimes of violence, its effectiveness as an institution was increasingly restricted by the princes' claim to exclusive rights of justice over their own subjects. Moreover the executive machinery tended to slip out of the king's hands. For much of the fourteenth century, so far as the device of the *Landfriede* was maintained at all, it was by the efforts of particular leagues and unions in various parts of Germany. Initiative in forming them might come from the king; more often it was taken by the territorial rulers in ways best suited to serve their ambitions. The *pax publica*, nation-wide in its original conception, seemed fated to become an adjunct of territorial or regional policy.[1]

The last third of the fourteenth century saw a determined attempt by the Crown to recover control over the *Landfriede*. Charles IV showed the way.[2] But it was under Wenzel that appeared an approach towards a new pattern of local organizations which would maintain the public peace under the authority and in the name of the Crown and be strong enough to escape being dominated by the territories. The towns greeted a first scheme to divide Germany into circles with distrust, for it would have involved them in co-operation with the princes and nobles whom they hated and feared.[3] But after their defeats in 1388 Wenzel was able to promulgate a general *Landfriede* on these lines at Eger in May 1389. Within each of five circles—the Rhineland, Franconia, Bavaria, Swabia and Thuringia—care of the *pax publica* was to be entrusted to an executive committee of nine: a captain appointed by the king, four members chosen by the towns and four by the other estates.[4] Little came of the plan. But at least it had indicated how, by a process of devolution which left wide scope for political manœuvre, the king might hope to fulfil effectively, if

---

[1] Cf. Quidde, *Paix publique*, 511–31; E. Bock, 'Kampf um die Landfriedenshoheit in Westfalen', cited above, p. 238, n. 1.
[2] Molitor, 22.
[3] Quidde, 534 ff.
[4] *R.T.A.*, ii, no. 72, arts. 2, 39, 40; 35, 37, 38; 44.

indirectly, his duty of maintaining peace throughout Germany.[1]

The lesson was not wholly lost on Sigismund. Possibly he had it in mind to seek as head of a national *Landfriede* the power which otherwise kingship had ceased to offer.[2] But he was unable to give the problem the consistent attention it deserved and his support of the towns and the *Ritterschaft* could do little to redress a balance now swinging decisively in favour of the princes. In face of the Hussite menace in 1431, it is true, private war was proscribed throughout the empire for the first time since the Diet of Roncaglia in 1158, even though this held good only for the duration of the campaign which ended so disastrously at Tauss. Whether Sigismund exercised any real control over affairs in Germany during the last few years of his reign is disputable. What is certain is that at this time reform of the imperial constitution became a lively issue. How far demand for reform is to be explained as resulting from ill-success in the Hussite wars and the contemporary debate at Basle about reform of the Church, how far by reference to the internal situation in Germany and the newly-found strength of the electors, are matters of opinion.[3] The demand itself continued to echo for the rest of the century.

Perhaps historians have been too ready to blame the fifteenth-century reformers for failing to achieve aims which they did not pursue nor could reasonably have pursued, like the establishment of a strong unitary monarchy.[4] They wanted the government of the empire to be made capable of discharging its duties. In theory imperial prerogatives were already adequate to protect the integrity of Germany from foreign attack, preserve the public peace and make justice readily available. The trouble was that these prerogatives were not being fully exercised. The call, then, was less for revolutionary changes than for such rehabilitation and modification of the constitution as would enable the empire to do what was expected of it. At this point, however, confusion was engendered by conflicting views about what the empire was. The emperor was bound to see the matter in personal terms. Much history

[1] For a less favourable view of the Eger *Landfriede* see H. Angermeier, 'Städtebünde und Landfriede im 14. Jahrhundert', *Hist. Jahrbuch*, lxxvi (1956), 44–6.

[2] Molitor, 26.

[3] Cf. H. Angermeier, 'Das Reich u.d. Konziliarismus', 553–67.

[4] Cf. H. Angermeier, 'Begriff u. Inhalt d. Reichsreform', *Z.R.G. G.A.*, lxxv (1958), 197–205.

suggested that he was the empire; proposals for reform which would enable him to be so more effectively (by providing him with funds or troops, for instance) were welcome; all others were to be rejected as diminishing not only his own dignity but also that of the empire which he incorporated. On the other hand there was the claim of the estates to be considered necessary elements of the empire's authority. By reform they hoped to convert a significant part of the emperor's personal powers into impersonal institutions, capable indeed of working efficiently, but ultimately controlled by themselves and so not likely seriously to impair their independence. Their policy was to bring the respective positions of emperor and estates into line with the current facts of power. They could claim, not wholly paradoxically, to be envisaging reform in a conservative fashion: organs they controlled were to exercise in the name of the empire capacities already to be found there, though detained for the time being by an emperor not strong enough to put them to good use.

The short reign of Albert II marked a first climax in the movement for reform. The electors' proposals for a general *Landfriede* at the Nuremberg diet in July 1438 would have abolished recourse to private war. The whole empire save Austria and Bohemia was to be divided into four circles. Over each a prince was to be appointed captain by the king, to do justice in his name in cases of appeal from the ordinary courts.[1] The danger that this scheme would deliver the circles into the hands of the greater princes was countered by amendments which Albert's counsellors suggested. There should be six circles rather than four; in each the captain should be elected by the estates of the circle and aided by ten counsellors chosen from the lords, lesser nobility and the towns.[2] By this plan a far-reaching delegation of authority would have endowed the circles with a considerable degree of self-government. Perhaps by this date in Germany there was no longer a real possibility of movement in the direction of provincial autonomy under control of the local estates rather than towards territorial consolidation under the supremacy of the princes.[3] But though these interchanges in 1438 produced no practical results, they illustrate what very

[1] *R.T.A.*, xiii, no. 223.
[2] *R.T.A.*, xiii, no. 224.
[3] Cf. Molitor, 97 ff.

different ideas about reform were held by the king and the princes. The former wished to use it to strengthen his own hand in Germany; the circles organized as his counsellors proposed would undoubtedly have offered opportunities for political manipulation by the Crown. To the princes, on the other hand, reform seemed a means of subordinating to themselves the less powerful estates of the empire.

Possibly even at the time of Albert's death in 1439 'there was still hope that the empire could be governed and the constitution be reformed'.[1] As yet the lines along which the constitutional relationship between the king and the particularist powers would develop had not become completely rigid. In this respect, it would seem, the reign of Frederick III was decisive. Perhaps we need to know more about the activities centring on the archbishop of Trier, James of Sierck, in the early 'fifties.[2] But for decades, it seems safe to say, imperial reform ceased to be a serious programme and became a party cry in the rivalries of the territorial princes. Thus the real issue between Wittelsbach and Hohenzollern in their long struggle was lands and power in southern Germany; their talk of *Reichsreform* was camouflage.[3] Despite his extraordinarily high conception of imperial majesty Frederick III made little attempt to rule Germany. Interest in the constitutional problem, still real under Sigismund and Albert, flagged until 1486. Characteristic of the change is the contrast offered to the schemes of 1438 by Frederick's so-called *Reformatio* of 1442. For the most part the *Reformatio* repeated existing and unchallenged law. No reform of the judicial system was envisaged, nor any devolution of responsibility to regional authorities; *Fehde* was tolerated, as long as it was kept within the rules. No provision was made for executing the *Reformatio*, which was indeed sadly destitute of any leading idea, either progressive or conservative.[4] And after 1444 Frederick was seen no more in the empire for twenty-seven years.

Discussion of this period cannot go deep until the *Reichstagsakten* for it have been published. It was not wholly barren for the constitutional problem; slowly some things stirred. From 1467

[1] Heimpel, 'Deutsche Reichstagsakten', 106.
[2] Cf. V. von Kraus, *Deutsche Geschichte im Ausgange des Mittelalters*, i (Stuttgart and Berlin, 1905), 310–20; H. Weigel, 'Kaiser, Kurfürst u. Jurist', *A.R.*, 80–115.
[3] Molitor, 116.
[4] *R.T.A.*, xvi, no. 209; cf. Molitor, 109; Quidde, *Paix publique*, 543.

onwards, as we have seen, the pressure against *Fehde* increased. But if self-help were to be prohibited effectively a supreme imperial court was needed, to do what the now defunct *Reichshofgericht* had never succeeded in doing. In his *Kammergericht* the king already had a partly professional court; shortly after the Grosse Christentag in 1471 Frederick, it seems, gave this court a new establishment and farmed it to Archbishop Adolf II of Mainz, who brought it to a state of some efficiency during the next few years.[1] Though Adolf's death in 1475 checked this development, the interest of the archsee of Mainz had been awakened, and in June 1494 we find Archbishop Berthold of Henneberg taking charge of the *Kammergericht* as of right. For years Berthold and his fellow reformers had been urging the need for a permanent imperial court independent of the emperor. Frederick's tenacity had foiled their attempt at Frankfort in 1486 to impose on him a tribunal divorced from his entourage, passing judgment in its own name as well as his, and with a composition on which his influence would have been markedly less than that of the estates.[2] But the reformers were not permanently to be denied. The setting up of the *Reichskammergericht* as supreme court for the empire at the diet of Worms in August 1495 met many of their wishes; for all its limitations, this proved perhaps the most central and lasting achievement of the whole reform movement.[3]

Berthold's leadership was vastly important for the emergence at this time of a comprehensive policy of reform.[4] Though much of the legislation at Worms bore the marks of compromise, its range was impressive: *Fehde* abolished, at least in principle, for all time by the *Ewige Landfriede*; a supreme court organized by the *Reichskammergerichtsordnung*; proposals for a general system of taxation, the Common Penny, as the basis for an imperial army; the diet itself to become an assembly meeting regularly to

[1] Cf. Spangenberg, 'Entstehung d. Kammergerichts', 286–8; J. Lechner, 'Reichshofgericht u. königliches Kammergericht i. 15. Jahrhundert', *Mitteilungen d. Instituts f. österreich. Geschichtsforschung*, Erg. Bd. vii (1907), 109 ff. While only 2 sessions of the court are known in 1466, 11 in 1467 and 1 in 1468, in 1471 the number had increased to 36 and in the next year to 85.

[2] Molitor, 182,

[3] Zeumer, *Quellen*, no. 174; cf. R. Smend, *Das Reichskammergericht* (Weimar, 1911), 1–23.

[4] Cf. F. Hartung, 'Die Reichsreform von 1485–1495. Ihr Verlauf u. ihr Wesen', *H.V.*, xvi (1913), 24 ff., 181 ff.; K. S. Bader, 'Kaiserliche u. ständische Reformgedanken i.d. Reichsreform d. endenden 15. Jahrhunderts', *Hist. Jahrbuch*, lxxiii (1954), 74–94.

exercise extensive powers in accordance with defined procedures. A campaign which produced results on such a scale as this was clearly not negligible. But the press and complexity of political events during these years, which nearly coincide with the period (1486–93) when Frederick and Maximilian were reigning in double harness,[1] make it difficult to isolate reform and bring it into focus. In 1488, for instance, the Swabian League was born, perhaps the strongest, best articulated and most interesting example of confederative practice in late medieval Germany. Originally it had nothing to do with reform, for it was rooted in the political circumstances of the south-west, where fear of the Wittelsbachers and the Swiss caused the princes, the towns and the lesser nobility to band together for mutual protection. Only gradually, as it gained strength and Maximilian became concerned with the fate of the Habsburg *Vorlande*, did the Swabian League come to be intimately involved in the politics of the empire and the reforming movement.[2]

Then too there is much to puzzle us in the attitudes of the chief actors in this drama. Almost any talk of reform offended Frederick's sense of majesty; he would listen at all only if by so doing he could hope to get help for Habsburg policy. On the other hand Maximilian's approach to this problem, it can be argued, was a good deal more positive. He seemed willing to accept some diminution of the Crown's theoretic rights in return for an increased efficiency in imperial government to be reflected in financial and military support for his own schemes.[3] Seventeenth-century scholars gave all the credit for the reforming legislation of 1495 to Maximilian, none to Berthold of Henneberg.[4] Though we know better, Berthold's personality has remained elusive.[5] There is no doubt, however, that this

[1] E. Bock, 'Die Doppelregierung Friedrichs III u. Maximilians 1486–1493', *A.R.*, 283 ff.

[2] E. Bock, *Der Schwäbische Bund u. seine Verfassungen 1488–1534* (Breslau, 1927), 9; F. Ernst, 'Reichs- und Landespolitik i. Süden Deutschlands am Ende d. Mittelalters', *H.V.*, xxx (1935), 726.

[3] Cf. Bock, 'Doppelregierung', 324–7.

[4] F. H. Schubert, 'Die Reichstage Kaiser Maximilians I. i. Urteil d. 17. Jahrhunderts', *A.R.*, 242.

[5] I have not seen K. S. Bader's essay *Ein Staatsmann vom Mittelrhein: Gestalt u. Werk d. Mainzer Kurfürsten u. Erzbischofs Berthold v. Henneberg* (Mainz, n.d.). That E. Ziehen's learned but disorderly *Mittelrhein u. Reich i. Zeitalter d. Reichsreform*, 2 vols. (Frankfurt a.M., 1934–7) writes Maximilian down excessively in favour of Berthold has been made clear by H. Baron, 'Imperial Reform and the Habsburgs, 1486–1504', *American Hist. Review*, xliv (1939), 293 ff.

great prelate from the heart of Germany, whose house had rendered notable services to the Crown during the fourteenth century, did combine with his passionate loyalty to the empire clear ideas of what needed to be done if it were to play a worthy role in Germany and western Europe.[1] For him the empire was far greater than its monarch, and there was urgent need to strengthen it against the particularist elements in Germany, which were represented just as much by the territorial interests of the king as by the strivings of the princes towards irresponsible independence.[2] Only by turning its administrative institutions into bureaucratic departments of state and so freeing them from the king's personal whims could they be made strong enough to serve their proper purposes. In their technical aspects Berthold's ideas deserved and enjoyed some success. But from the point of view of politics, most would agree, they came too late. Admirable as was his sense of responsibility, Berthold looked too much to the past with its intimations that the electors in union might lead the empire's estates in controlling a system of government directly effective throughout Germany.[3] He failed to get honest support from Maximilian or many of the princes for a permanent collegiate executive for the empire: a *Reichsregiment* in which electoral influence would predominate. After all, Maximilian had good grounds for claiming that it was his business to rule the empire; and the princes had passed the point of being ready to tolerate the amount of imperial government which Berthold's schemes envisaged. The pertinacity with which he fought them through to partial acceptance at Worms in 1495 forbids us to discount him as a mere doctrinaire. Some of his reforms continued to work usefully until the end of the Holy Roman Empire in 1806. But though he has no real competitor for the title of the last statesman of the medieval empire, his understanding of its structural changes had fallen behind the times. By 1500 the shell of that superior authority under shelter of which the territories had grown seemed very thin. How tough it still remained the story of the next three centuries was to show.

[1] Berthold was the seventh son of Count George I of Henneberg-Römhild (in the basin of the upper Werra, south of Meiningen in Thuringia). In Count Berthold VII of Henneberg-Schleusingen the family had produced one of the most important figures in imperial politics between 1310 and 1340; cf. Ziehen, i, 167–9.

[2] Cf. F. Hartung, 'Berthold von Henneberg, Kurfürst von Mainz', *Hist. Zts.*, ciii (1909), 539.

[3] Cf. Bader, 'Reformgedanken', 89.

VIII

DIMITRI OBOLENSKY

BYZANTIUM AND RUSSIA IN THE LATE MIDDLE AGES

'Russia, as I have said earlier, is a highly populated country; the length and breadth of the land occupied by its inhabitants cannot at all easily be measured; the annual produce harvested from its crops is very large and varied; a considerable amount of silver is produced from there, mined in the country; and because that country is gripped by cold owing to its distance from the sun, nature, as you would expect, breeds a large number of thick-fleeced animals which are hunted and whose hides are exported by the local inhabitants to every other land and city, bringing them much gain. And in the neighbouring ocean fishes are caught some of whose bones provide useful enjoyment for satraps and princes and kings and for nearly all those who lead a refined life, and are distinguished men. I forbear to mention how much more abundant wealth the Russians obtain in addition by exporting these objects abroad.'[1] This description, written about 1355 in Constantinople by the Byzantine historian Nicephorus Gregoras, illustrates the interest which the Byzantines retained, after four and a half centuries of trade with Russia, in the economic resources of the country, and particularly in the raw materials exported from the steppes and forests north of the Black Sea. Their trade

---

[1] Nicephorus Gregoras, *Historiae Byzantinae*, lib. xxxvi, cap. 21–2, iii (Bonn, 1855), 512. The exact meaning of the penultimate sentence of this passage is hard to discover, owing to the vagueness of Gregoras' language. V. Parisot believed that he is alluding to the ivory obtained from the tusks of walruses and narwhals in the White Sea and the Arctic Ocean, and to objects of luxury (e.g. musical instruments) manufactured from it: *Livre XXXVII de l'Histoire Romaine de Nicéphore Grégoras* (Paris, 1851), 266–78.

relations with Russia, after a temporary eclipse due to the Mongol invasions and to the Latin conquest of Constantinople, revived in the fourteenth century,[1] though the benefit they brought to Byzantium was reduced by the fact that the Black Sea trade was then controlled by the Genoese and the Venetians. However, food supplies from the northern coast of the Black Sea remained of vital importance to Constantinople, and the expulsion in 1343 of the Genoese and the Venetians by the Tatars from the port of Tana near the estuary of the Don, and the subsequent siege by the same Tatars of the Genoese colony of Kaffa in the Crimea, resulted in an acute shortage of bread and salted fish in the Byzantine capital and other cities of the empire.[2] Russian money was as necessary to Byzantium as Russian raw materials. The authorities of Constantinople, faced with the financial ruin of their state, reduced to pawning the Crown jewels and to using leaden and earthenware goblets at the feast of the emperor's coronation in 1347,[3] were now, for any extraordinary expense, wholly dependent on foreign aid. In 1346 an earthquake seriously damaged the church of St Sophia. The ruler of Muscovy sent a large sum of money for the repair of the building.[4] A further sum was sent in 1398 by the grand prince of Moscow, Basil I, to the aid of Constantinople, blockaded at that time by the Turks; a donation intended, in the words of a contemporary Russian chronicle, as 'alms for those who are in such need and misery'.[5] Each of these gifts was obtained through the good offices of the primate of the Russian Church who, as an appointee of the patriarch of Constantinople and the representative of the emperor, was expected to promote both the ecclesiastical and the secular interests of the empire in Russia. A further contribution from the Russians was sought in 1400: the patriarch of Constantinople wrote to the primate, the Metropolitan Cyprian, urging him, 'as a friend of the Byzantines' (ὡς φιλορρώμαιος ἄνθρωπος) to start another fund-raising campaign; he was to assure his Russian flock that it was more

---

[1] For trade relations between Byzantium and Russia in the late Middle Ages, see M. N. Tikhomirov, *Srednevekovaya Moskva v XIV–XV vekakh* (Moscow, 1957), 121–31; 'Puti iz Rossii v Vizantiyu', *Vizantiiskie Ocherki*, ed. Tikhomirov (Moscow, 1961), 3–33.

[2] Nicephorus Gregoras, *Hist. Byz.*, lib. xiii, cap. 12: ii, 683–6; cf. W. Heyd, *Histoire du Commerce du Levant au Moyen Âge*, ii (Leipzig, 1936), 187–8.

[3] See G. Ostrogorsky, *History of the Byzantine State* (Oxford, 1956), 469–70.

[4] Nicephorus Gregoras, *Hist. Byz.*, lib. xxviii, cap. 34–6: iii, 198–200.

[5] *Polnoe Sobranie Russkikh Letopisey*, xi (St Petersburg, 1897), 168.

meritorious to contribute money for the defence of Constantinople than to build churches, to give alms to the poor, or
to redeem prisoners: 'for this holy City', wrote the patriarch,
'is the pride, the support, the sanctification, and the glory of
Christians in the whole inhabited world'.[1]

It was not for economic reasons alone that the Byzantines
became, in the second half of the fourteenth century, increasingly aware of the advantages to be derived from their relations
with Russia. The military and political situation of Byzantium
justified the gravest anxieties. The Ottoman Turks, established
in Europe since the middle of the century, took no more than
four decades to seize most of what remained of Byzantine
territory, conquer Bulgaria, and crush the resistance of the
Serbian state. By the end of the century, except for its de-
pendency in the Peloponnese and a few islands in the Aegean,
the empire was reduced to Constantinople, and the position of
the capital, blockaded by the Turks, seemed desperate. It was
clear that only foreign military aid on a massive scale could save
the dying empire. The emperors' hopes were mainly focused on
obtaining help from the West: John V's visit to Italy (1369–71)
failed to achieve anything; Manuel II's journey to Italy, Paris
and London (1399–1403) was not more successful; and the
Hungarian attempt to reconquer the Balkans from the Turks
came to ruin at the battle of Nicopolis (1396). In their desperate
search for allies, the Byzantine authorities could not fail to
observe the significant changes that were taking place in the
second half of the fourteenth century on the confines of eastern
Europe. In the Russian lands, which around 1300 had formed a
congeries of petty principalities virtually independent of each
other and subject to the formidable power of the Golden Horde,
two political structures had now emerged, competing for the
allegiance of the eastern Slavs: the grand duchy of Lithuania
and the principality of Moscow. The territories of the former
comprised most of western and south-western Russia, and, since
about 1362, included the ancient Russian capital of Kiev;
Muscovy, still the smaller of the two, was claiming, with growing conviction and success, to embody the political and cultural

---

[1] Τὸ γὰρ καύχημα τῶν ἀπανταχοῦ τῆς οἰκουμένης χριστιανῶν, τὸ
στήριγμα, ὁ ἁγιασμός καὶ ἡ δόξα ἡ πόλις ἐστὶν αὕτη ἡ ἁγία. *Acta Patriarchatus
Constantinopolitani*, ed. F. Miklosich and I. Müller, ii (Vienna, 1862), 361. The
results of this appeal are unknown.

traditions of Kievan Russia, a state with which Byzantium had enjoyed particularly close and mutually beneficial relations in the early Middle Ages. The Muscovite princes, thrifty, persistent and unscrupulous, pursuing at first a policy of abject submissiveness to the Golden Horde, had embarked, with the blessing of the Church and the support of their *boyars*, on the task of 'gathering' the whole of eastern Russia under their sway. By the end of the fourteenth century the power of Muscovy had greatly increased. Among the many causes of its eventual triumph over its rivals we may single out—next to the support consistently given to its rulers by the Russian Church—the belief which was growing in Russia that the prince of Moscow was alone strong enough to stand up to the Tatars and to achieve one day the long-awaited liberation of the country. This faith acquired substance in 1380, when the Russian troops, commanded by Dimitri, prince of Moscow, defeated a large Tatar army at Kulikovo by the River Don. Contemporary Russian sources hail this victory as a great triumph for Muscovy and for the Christian faith; and although from a short-term point of view Kulikovo proved a Pyrrhic victory—two years later Moscow was sacked by a Mongol vassal of Timur—its effect on the prestige of the principality of Moscow, both inside and outside Russia, was lasting and considerable.

The Byzantine government was well aware of these changes which were affecting the balance of power in the lands to the north of the Black Sea, an area which, since the early Middle Ages, the imperial diplomatists had scrutinized with peculiar care.[1] To ensure the friendship and loyalty of the peoples who dwelt in this area had been a cardinal principle of the empire's foreign policy during its heyday in the ninth, tenth and eleventh centuries, when Byzantine influence and prestige throughout eastern Europe were at their height; in the fourteenth and early fifteenth centuries, when Byzantium was a second-rate power, fighting for its life, such a policy had become more essential than ever. It was also far more difficult to implement. The Byzantines, however, still held two trump cards: the fascination exerted by the city of Constantinople on the minds of the men of eastern Europe; and the unifying force of Orthodox Christianity, of which the Byzantines were regarded (at least until 1439) as the

---

[1] See D. Obolensky, 'The Principles and Methods of Byzantine Diplomacy', *Actes du XIIe Congrès International d'Études Byzantines*, i (Belgrade, 1963), 45–61.

most authoritative exponents, and whose administrative centre and spiritual heart were in Constantinople. In the absence of a foreign policy based on power, the Byzantines were reduced in the fourteenth century to playing these cards as best they could. During the period between 1350 and 1453, Byzantine foreign policy in eastern Europe was increasingly driven to rely on the good offices of the Church, whose supreme executive organ, the Oecumenical Patriarchate, in striking contrast to the versatile opportunism of the imperial government, was assuming the role of chief spokesman and instrument of the imperial traditions of East Rome. Hence, in practical terms, the authorities of Byzantium were faced with a double programme of action: they were impelled, on the one hand, to consolidate and extend the spiritual authority of the Oecumenical Patriarchate over the nations of eastern Europe; and, on the other, to ensure the loyalty of these same nations to Byzantium by making diplomatic concessions to their national susceptibilities; and this, particularly in the fourteenth century, meant granting a measure of self-government to those churches outside the empire which owed allegiance to the see of Constantinople. The fact that the empire's foreign policy in eastern Europe was then primarily directed towards these two goals explains the dominant role played by ecclesiastical affairs—and to a large extent by ecclesiastical diplomacy—in the history of Russo-Byzantine relations in the period under review.

The ecclesiastical relations between Byzantium and the Russian lands in the fourteenth century were mostly concerned with the vexed problem of the jurisdiction, place of residence, and method of appointment of the primates of the Russian Church. Until the Mongol invasions of the thirteenth century these dignitaries, who were appointed by the patriarch of Constantinople, resided in Kiev. In 1300, owing to the political fragmentation of the realm, the devastations of Kiev by the Mongols, and the growing political ascendancy of north-east Russia, the metropolitan moved his residence to Vladimir, whence in 1328 it was transferred to Moscow. These successive moves had as yet no significance *de jure*, and the primate of the Russian Church retained until the mid-fifteenth century his traditional title of 'Metropolitan of Kiev and of All Russia'. In practice, however, from the early fourteenth century the metropolitans increasingly identified themselves with the policies and aspirations of the princes of Moscow. It was only natural that Moscow's rivals for the still contested political hegemony over Russia sought to deprive their opponent of the considerable moral and political advantages derived from the presence within the city walls of the chief bishop of the Russian Church. Their best hope lay in persuading the Byzantine authorities to set up separate metropolitanates in their respective territories. Throughout the fourteenth century Constantinople was bombarded with such requests—from the princes of Galicia, from the grand dukes of Lithuania and, in one case, from the king of Poland; these demands, usually backed by promises, threats or financial bribes, were often successful; and with bewildering and unedifying frequency the emperors and the patriarchs of Constantinople[1] set up in the fourteenth century separate metropolitanates for Galicia and for Lithuania, only to abolish them a few decades, or years, later.[2] The rise of these splinter churches signified the retreat of the Byzantine authorities before the political or economic pressure of rulers who controlled portions of west Russian territory; while their successive abolitions represented as many concessions made by the imperial government and Church to the wishes of the Muscovite sovereigns who, for political reasons, were anxious to exercise through their own metropolitans an ecclesiastical authority over the Russian communities outside the boundaries of the Muscovite state. The Byzantine authorities undoubtedly preferred to see a united Russian Church governed by a single primate: tradition, administrative convenience, and a reluctance to submit to foreign secular pressures, caused them to

[1] The prerogative of promoting bishoprics to the rank of metropolitanates was, at least after 1087, generally considered to belong to the emperor. Alexius Comnenus issued a law to this effect: see Migne, *P.G.*, cxxvii, cols. 929-32 (no. 7). Most Byzantine canonists seem to have accepted its propriety: see Balsamon, *In Can. XII Conc. Chalced.*, *P.G.*, cxxxvii, cols. 432-3 (for a contrary view, however, see Zonaras, ibid., cols. 433-6); and in 1335 this imperial prerogative was vindicated once more by Matthew Blastares (Σύνταγμα κατὰ στοιχεῖον, ed. G. Rhalles and M. Potles, Σύνταγμα τῶν θείων καὶ ἱερῶν κανόνων, vi (Athens, 1859), 274-6). Imperial initiative in the creation and abolition of metropolitanates naturally tended, whenever the sees in question were situated outside the empire's confines, to link very closely the decisions taken in Constantinople to organize or reorganize the ecclesiastical administration of these territories with the interests of Byzantine foreign policy.

[2] See E. Golubinsky, *Istoriya russkoy tserkvi*, ii, 1 (Moscow, 1900), 96-7, 101-4, 125-30, 147-8, 153-4, 157-60, 177-87, 190-3, 206-11, 342, 388-9; A. M. Ammann, *Abriss der ostslawischen Kirchengeschichte* (Vienna, 1950), pp. 88-98, 106-10, 120-3; A. V. Kartashev, *Ocherki po istorii russkoy tserkvi*, i (Paris, 1959), 297-9, 303-4, 313-23, 332-3, 338, 346.

favour a centralized solution; and in the second half of the fourteenth century this solution became the more acceptable to them, as it coincided with the wishes of the Muscovite rulers, whose power commanded increasing respect, and whose military and economic resources the empire in its dire predicament so desperately needed.

The problem of the extent of the Russian metropolitans' jurisdiction was bound up with the question of how, and by whom, they were to be appointed. On this question the Byzantines and the Russians held strong, and often conflicting, views. The former, who regarded the metropolitans of Russia as valuable diplomatic agents, capable of using their moral and spiritual authority to ensure the loyalty of their Russian flock to the empire, were naturally anxious to retain control over the appointment and consecration of these dignitaries; and, for equally obvious reasons, the Muscovite sovereigns, while accepting the principle that their metropolitans were to be approved and consecrated by the patriarchs of Constantinople, wished to have as much influence as possible on their selection. These conflicting claims were for a long time resolved by compromise: from 1237 to 1378 Byzantine and Russian candidates were, with striking regularity, appointed in turn by the patriarchs to the metropolitan see of Kiev and All Russia. There are grounds for believing that this regular alternation was the result of a special agreement concluded between the Byzantine and the Russian authorities.[1] The problems involved in the appointment of the metropolitans of Russia became the central issue in the diplomatic relations between Byzantium and Muscovy in the late Middle Ages. Its historical importance far transcends the level of the obscure and often discreditable manœuvres ascribed to both parties in the documents of the time. Behind these dubious operations, affecting their outcome or flowing from their cause, we can discern the diplomatic techniques employed by the Byzantine patriarchate and by the Muscovite experts on foreign affairs; the conflict and alignment of different ecclesiastical programmes within Byzantium and Russia; the changing pattern of power politics in eastern Europe; and—the most significant in the long run of these factors—the slow crystallization in Muscovy of a new attitude

[1] See D. Obolensky, 'Byzantium, Kiev and Moscow. A Study in Ecclesiastical Relations', *Dumbarton Oaks Papers*, xi (1957), 23–78.

towards the Byzantine empire, an attitude closely linked with the development of post-medieval Russian nationalism.

All these factors were already present in some degree in the circumstances that attended the appointment in 1354 of the Russian bishop Alexius as metropolitan of Kiev and All Russia. The decree of the Synod of the Byzantine Church, signed by the Patriarch Philotheus on 30th June of that year, states unequivocally that the Synod's decision to appoint Alexius was influenced by the wishes of 'the great king' of Russia.[1] But it also claims that the appointment of a native to the metropolitanate of Russia is an unusual and dangerous step, which must not be regarded as a precedent. This synodal decree, at times evasive and disingenuous, clothed in the expert phraseology of East Roman diplomacy, is remarkable for its desire to satisfy the demands of the Muscovite authorities, and for its assertion that the appointment of a native Russian 'is by no means customary nor safe for the Church'. The first of these features can be explained by the political and ecclesiastical situation in eastern Europe: in 1354, the very year in which the Ottomans established themselves on European soil at Gallipoli, and in which the Venetian ambassador to Constantinople informed his government that the Byzantines would readily submit to any power that would save them from the Turks and the Genoese,[2] the East Roman government was not unnaturally disposed to lend a favourable ear to the demands of a friendly state from which at least economic assistance could be expected —the principality of Moscow and its 'great king'. The patriarch, too, had his reasons for being conciliatory towards the Muscovite ruler. Philotheus consistently strove to consolidate the authority of the see of Constantinople over the nations of eastern Europe. The Balkan Slavonic churches were in 1354 slipping away from his control; the more reason for making sure of the continued loyalty of the Russians, the most numerous of the foreign proselytes of Byzantium. Yet this concession to the Russian demands must have been costly to the patriarch's conscience: for it involved a betrayal of his conviction that the Church should not submit to any form of secular pressure.

---

[1] The text of the decree is printed in *Acta Patriarchatus Constantinopolitani*, i, 336–40. The Muscovite prince is termed ὁ μέγας ῥήξ, and acknowledgment is made of the pre-eminence of his power (ὑπεροχῆ ῥηγικῆς ἐξουσίας).

[2] See Ostrogorsky, *History of the Byzantine State*, 473, 475.

Philotheus was a leading member of the party of 'zealots' in the Byzantine Church, who, in opposition to the 'politicians' or 'moderates', insisted on the freedom of ecclesiastical appointments.[1] The acceptance of a candidate for a high ecclesiastical post in deference to the wishes of a secular ruler—and a foreign one at that—was a serious derogation of the principle of 'strictness' in the application of canon law and a capitulation to his opponents who, in accordance with the opposite principle of 'economy', believed that the Church in its relations with the secular powers, both at home and abroad, should not intransigently reject all concessions and compromises. This painful dilemma in which Philotheus found himself in 1354 no doubt accounts for his cavalier treatment of historical truth: for the Synod's bland assertion that the appointment of a native Russian to the see of Kiev and All Russia was 'by no means customary' is contradicted by the fact that for the past 117 years there had been—if Alexius himself is included in the list— three Russian and three Byzantine holders of this post.[2]

The Synod's resolve not to tolerate any more Russian metropolitans proved wholly ineffectual, for during the six years that elapsed after Alexius' death in 1378, the patriarchate agreed on three different occasions to the appointment of a native primate.[3] Its inconstancy was further demonstrated by its failure to give adequate support to Alexius himself, who until 1361 had the greatest difficulty in maintaining his rights over Kiev against Olgerd, grand duke of Lithuania, and his nominee, Roman, whom the patriarch had appointed metropolitan of Lithuania in 1354. In 1373 the Patriarch Philotheus sent an envoy to Russia, to investigate the complaints received from the Lithuanian ruler about Alexius' conduct. Two years later this patriarchal envoy, Cyprian, was appointed by the patriarch metropolitan of Kiev and All Russia, with the proviso that the latter half of his title, which implied jurisdiction over the Muscovite Church, would become effective as soon as the accusations against Alexius could be substantiated. However,

---

[1] On the 'zealot' and the 'moderate' parties in the Byzantine Church, see A. Vasiliev, *History of the Byzantine Empire* (Oxford, 1952), 659–70.

[2] On this point, and for an analysis of the Synodal decree of 30th June, 1354, see Obolensky, 'Byzantium, Kiev and Moscow', loc. cit., 37–44.

[3] See Obolensky, op. cit., 43, n. 82. Later, however, the Patriarchate was more successful in enforcing its will: there were no native metropolitans of Russia between 1390 and 1448.

as we learn from a Byzantine source,[1] the patriarch's commission of inquiry found these accusations devoid of substance, and was impressed by Alexius' immense popularity in Muscovy. He was allowed to retain his authority over the Muscovite Church.[2]

These dubious manœuvres were scarcely calculated to enhance the popularity of the emperor and patriarch in Muscovy. The Russians found it hard to forgive the humiliations which the Byzantine authorities had so unjustly imposed on the Metropolitan Alexius, who was not only a highly respected spiritual leader, but something of a national hero. The patriarch's decision to appoint Cyprian as primate of All Russia while the case of Alexius was still *sub judice*—taken in order to please the Lithuanian ruler—was, despite the fact that it was later rescinded, felt to be a bitter humiliation. The Byzantines themselves were impressed by the 'great tumult', the 'uproar', and the 'attitude of revolt' which this affair provoked all over Russia.[3] And in 1378 Cyprian complained that as a result of these events the Muscovites 'were abusing the Patriarch, the Emperor, and the Great Synod: they called the Patriarch a Lithuanian, and the Emperor too, and the most honourable Great Synod'.[4]

But worse was to come. In 1379, a year after Alexius' death, his successor-elect, the Russian cleric Michael Mityai, chosen by the grand prince of Moscow and already accepted by the patriarch, set out from Moscow to Constantinople for his consecration. But as the Russian ships sailed down the Bosphorus, a few miles from his destination, Michael suddenly died. His Russan escort, thoughtfully provided by the prince of Moscow with blank charters adorned with his seal and signature, and with a considerable sum of money, used the former to substitute the name of one of their party, the Archimandrite Pimen, for that of the defunct Michael, and distributed the

---

[1] The decree of the Patriarchal Synod of June 1380: *Acta Patriarchatus Constantinopolitani*, ii, 12–18.

[2] See Golubinsky, op. cit., ii, 1, 182–215; Ammann, op. cit., 95–100; Kartashev, op. cit., i, 317–22.

[3] Θροῦς δ'ἐπιγείρεται μὲν πλεῖστος ἀνὰ πᾶσαν τὴν ῥωσικὴν ἐπαρχίαν καὶ στάσις καὶ ὄχλησις οὐ μικρά: Synodal decree of 1380: *Acta Patriarchatus Constantinopolitani*, ii, 14.

[4] *Russkaya Istoricheskaya Biblioteka*, vi (St Petersburg, 1880), col. 185; the abusive term 'Lithuanian' was clearly intended to suggest that by appointing Cyprian the Byzantine authorities had shown favouritism to the Grand Duke of Lithuania, Muscovy's political rival and enemy.

money as bribes to officials in Constantinople. With the help of these forged documents they persuaded the Patriarch Nilus to consecrate Pimen as 'Metropolitan of Kiev and Great Russia'. This sordid and disreputable deal, for which the Russian envoys and the officials of the Byzantine patriarchate must bear joint responsibility,[1] resulted in a period of extreme confusion in the affairs of the Russian Church, which lasted for twelve years and ended with the acceptance by the Muscovites of Cyprian as metropolitan of Russia (1390).

The Muscovite Prince Dimitri, who on these two occasions (in 1375–6 and in 1379–80) found himself a victim of these machinations of Byzantine diplomacy, could hardly have been expected to entertain feelings of goodwill towards the authorities of Constantinople, and especially towards the emperor, whose influence on the appointment of the metropolitans of Russia was usually only too apparent. It is, however, in the reign of Dimitri's son and successor, Basil I (1389–1425), that occurred the first recorded instance of a revolt by the Russians, not indeed against the authority of the Constantinopolitan Church, but against the claims of the Byzantine emperors to exercise a measure of direct jurisdiction over the whole Orthodox Christian world. Some time between 1394 and 1397[2] Antony IV, patriarch of Constantinople, sent a letter to Basil I of Moscow, rebuking him for having caused his metropolitan to omit the emperor's name from the commemorative diptychs of the Russian Church.[3] The patriarch reprimanded the Muscovite ruler for having expressed contempt for the emperor and having made disparaging remarks about him. He took a particularly grave view of the fact that the Russian sovereign had declared: 'We have the Church, but not the emperor'. To acknowledge

[1] Our principal sources for the history of this affair are the fourteenth-century acts of the Synods of Constantinople and the sixteenth-century Muscovite Chronicle of Nikon. Golubinsky (op. cit., ii, 1, 242 ff.) and Kartashev (op. cit., i, 323–33) suppose, on somewhat inadequate evidence, that this fraudulent deal was initiated by the Byzantine officials. On the other hand, an attempt (likewise unconvincing) to exonerate the Patriarch and to place the entire blame on the shoulders of the Russian envoys, is made by A. A. Takhiaos (Ἐπιδράσεις τοῦ ἡσυχασμοῦ εἰς τὴν ἐκκλησιαστικὴν πολιτικὴν ἐν Ῥωσίᾳ, 1328–1406 (Thessalonica, 1962), pp. 113–15).

[2] For the dating of this letter, see Ostrogorsky, History of the Byzantine State, 492, n. 1.

[3] The text is printed in Acta Patriarchatus Constantinopolitani, ii, 188–92; cf. Russkaya Istoricheskaya Biblioteka, vi, Appendix 40, cols. 265–76: an English translation of about two-thirds of the letter can be found in Social and Political Thought in Byzantium, ed. Ernest Barker (Oxford, 1957), 194–7.

the authority over Russia of the patriarch but not of the emperor is, as Antony points out, a contradiction in terms: for 'it is not possible for Christians to have the Church and not to have the empire. For Church and empire have a great unity and community; nor is it possible for them to be separated from one another'. And, in an attempt to save Basil I from the consequences of his grievous error, and in pursuance of his own duty as 'universal teacher of all Christians', the patriarch solemnly reiterates the fundamental principle of Byzantine political philosophy: 'The holy emperor,' he writes, 'is not as other rulers and governors of other regions are . . . he is annointed with the great myrrh, and is consecrated *basileus* and *autokrator* of the Romans—to wit, of all Christians'. These other rulers exercise a purely local authority; the *basileus* alone is 'the lord and master of the inhabited world', the 'universal emperor', 'the natural king' whose laws and ordinances are accepted in the whole world. His universal sovereignty is made manifest by the liturgical commemoration of his name in the churches of Christendom; and, as the patriarch's letter unequivocally implies, the grand prince of Moscow by discontinuing this practice within his realm had deliberately rejected the very foundations of Christian law and government.[1]

There are few documents which express with such force and clarity the basic theory of the medieval Byzantine state. The Patriarch Antony's letter contains a classic exposition of the doctrine of the universal East Roman empire, ruled by the *basileus*, successor of Constantine and vicegerent of God, the natural and God-appointed master of the *Oikoumene*, supreme law-giver of Christendom, whose authority was held to extend, at least in a spiritual and 'metapolitical' sense, over all Christian rulers and peoples. The fact that this uncompromising profession of faith was made from the capital of a state that was facing political and military collapse, only emphasizes the astonishing strength and continuity of this political vision which pervades the entire history of the Byzantine body politic. 'The doctrine of one oecumenical Emperor,' writes Professor

[1] 'Hear what the prince of the Apostles, Peter, says in the first of his general epistles, "Fear God, honour the King". He did not say "Kings", lest any man should think that he had in mind those who are called kings promiscuously among the nations; he said "the King", showing thereby that the universal King is one.' *Acta Patr. Constant.*, ii, 191; Barker, op. cit., 195.

Ostrogorsky, 'had never been laid down more forcibly or with more fiery eloquence than in this letter which the Patriarch of Constantinople sent to Moscow from a city blockaded by the Turks.'[1]

What significance should we attach to the refusal of the Muscovite sovereign to recognize, in the late fourteenth century, the universalist claims of the Byzantine emperor? This question can best be answered by considering how far, and in what sense, these claims were acknowledged in Russia before and after the reception of the patriarch's admonitory letter by Basil I. Direct evidence on this point is not abundant, and doubtless for good reason: the Russian rulers, however genuine their reverence for the city of Constantinople and its supreme authorities, were always careful to safeguard their own political prerogatives and anxious, within the scope allowed them by their Mongol overlords, to be seen to exercise their national sovereignty. Some indication of their attitude to the emperor of Byzantium has nevertheless been preserved in the documents of the time. In the late thirteenth or early fourteenth century a Russian ruler is said to have borne the Byzantine court title of 'steward of the Emperor's Household'[2]—a sign of his recognition of the traditional right of the emperor to bestow such titles on distinguished subjects or dependent princes; and the same ruler is said to have sent an envoy to Andronicus II, who conveyed to the emperor 'the reverent homage' of his Russian master.[3] The authenticity of this form of address is possibly suspect, and its servility may reflect no more than the wishful thinking of the Byzantine author who records the event. But it is not impossible that the Byzantine title was borne by at least one Russian ruler. The next piece of evidence comes from the mid-fourteenth century. In a letter written in September 1347 to Symeon, the grand prince of Moscow, the Emperor John VI Cantacuzenus stated: 'Yes, the Empire of the Romans, as well as the most holy Great Church of God is—as you yourself have written—the

---

[1] *History of the Byzantine State*, 492.
[2] A rough English equivalent of ὁ ἐπὶ τῆς τραπέζης.
[3] 'Ο βασιλεὺς τῶν 'Ρὼς ὁ ἐπὶ τῆς τραπέζης τῆς ἁγίας βασιλείας σου προσκυνεῖ δουλικῶς τὴν ἁγίαν βασιλείαν σου: H. Haupt, 'Neue Beiträge zu den Fragmenten des Dio Cassius', *Hermes*, xiv (1879), 445; see also Nicephorus Gregoras (*Hist. Byz.*, lib. vii, cap. 5, i, 239); cf. A. Vasiliev, 'Was Old Russia a vassal state of Byzantium?', *Speculum*, vii (1932), 353–4; Obolensky, *Byzantium, Kiev and Moscow*, 30–1, ns. 32, 41.

source of all piety and the teacher of law and sanctification'.[1] This statement clearly implies the existence of an earlier letter —not extant—written by the Russian sovereign to the emperor, in which the former explicitly acknowledged the legislative authority of the *basileus* over Russia.[2] And in 1452, the year before the fall of Constantinople, the grand prince of Moscow, Basil II, wrote to the last emperor of Byzantium, Constantine XI, in these terms: 'You have received your great imperial sceptre, your patrimony, in order to confirm all the Orthodox Christians of your realm and to render great assistance to our Russian dominion and to all our religion'.[3] The idea that the emperor enjoys certain prerogatives in Russia is, though veiled in diplomatic language, clearly apparent in these two texts.[4] His universal authority was further emphasized in the Byzantine collections of canon and imperial law which enjoyed great authority in Russia throughout the Middle Ages.[5] And the teachers and guardians of canonical rectitude in Russia, the primates of the Russian Church, could be expected, especially when they were Byzantine citizens, to instil in their flock an awe-struck reverence for the emperor's supreme position in Christendom. It would be quite misleading to try to interpret the relations between the emperor and the princes of Russia in terms either of medieval suzerainty and vassalage, or of the modern distinction between sovereign and dependent states. The Byzantines themselves sometimes thought of the Christian nations of eastern Europe in terms of Roman administration, and described their relationship to the imperial government with the help of technical terms once used to designate the status of the 'foederati' and 'socii populi Romani', autonomous subject-allies of the Roman empire.[6] However, in the last resort, any attempt

---

[1] Ἡ βασιλεία γοῦν τῶν Ῥωμαίων, ἀλλὰ δὴ καὶ ἡ ἁγιωτάτη τοῦ θεοῦ μεγάλη ἐκκλησία ἔνι, ὡς ἔγραφες καὶ σύ, πηγὴ πάσης εὐσεβείας καὶ διδάσκαλος νομοθεσίας τε καὶ ἁγιασμοῦ. *Acta Patriarchatus Constantinopolitani*, i, 263. The μεγάλη ἐκκλησία is the Patriarchate of Constantinople.

[2] It may be noted that one of the official titles of John Cantacuzenus was ὁ βασιλεὺς τῶν Ῥώσων: Cantacuzenus, *Historiae*, lib. iv, cap. 14 (Bonn), iii, 94. It can be regarded as certain, however, that no Russian ruler would have dreamt of acknowledging that the *basileus* was 'Emperor of the Russians'.

[3] *Russkaya Istoricheskaya Biblioteka*, vi, col. 577.

[4] See M. D'yakonov, *Vlast' Moskovskikh Gosudarey* (St Petersburg, 1889), 13–22; P. Sokolov, *Russky arkhierey iz Vizantii* (Kiev, 1913), 35–9, 305–6; Vasiliev, *Was Old Russia a vassal state of Byzantium?*, loc. cit., 359.

[5] See F. Dvornik, 'Byzantine Political Ideas in Kievan Russia', *Dumbarton Oaks Papers*, ix–x (1956), 73–121.

[6] See Obolensky, *The Principles and Methods of Byzantine Diplomacy*, 56–8.

to define the political relations between Byzantium and medieval Russia in precise legal or constitutional terms will obscure and distort their true picture. It is certain that, in practice, the Russian sovereigns would never have tolerated, except in ecclesiastical matters, any direct intervention of the emperor in the internal affairs of their principalities; and that their relationship to the *basileus* was something different from their very tangible allegiance to the khans of the Golden Horde who, between 1240 and 1480, imposed tribute and conferred investiture upon them.[1] But at the same time it cannot be doubted that from the conversion of Russia to Christianity in the tenth century to the fall of Byzantium in 1453, the Russian authorities—with the sole recorded exception of Basil I of Muscovy—acknowledged, at least tacitly, that the *basileus* was the supreme head of the Christian commonwealth, that as such he possessed by divine right a measure of jurisdiction over Russia, and that, in the words of the Patriarch Antony, 'it is not possible for Christians to have the Church and not to have the empire'. The difficulty of reconciling the national aspirations of the Russian sovereigns of the Middle Ages with their acceptance of the emperor's supremacy will largely disappear if Russo-Byzantine connections are viewed not from the standpoint of modern inter-state relations, nor in terms—unhappily fashionable—of a struggle between Russian 'nationalism' and Byzantine 'imperalism', but in the context of a supra-national community of Christian states—the Byzantine *Oikoumene* of which Constantinople was the centre and the whole of eastern and south-eastern Europe the domain—and which, as most Russians thought until 1453, was destined to foreshadow on earth the Heavenly Kingdom, until the last days and the coming of Antichrist.[2]

We have no direct knowledge of the effect which the patriarch's letter had on Basil I. It seems likely that the emperor's name was restored before long to the diptychs of the Russian Church: for already in 1398 the Muscovite government

[1] It is noteworthy, however, that the title of *tsar* (the equivalent of *basileus*) was, in general, applied by the Russians in this period only to the Byzantine emperor and to the khan of the Golden Horde.

[2] For the idea of the Byzantine *Oikoumene*, see the following studies by G. Ostrogorsky, 'Avtokrator i Samodržac', *Glas Srpske Akademije Nauka*, clxiv (Belgrade, 1935), 95–187; 'Die byzantinische Staatenhierarchie', *Seminarium Kondakovianum: Recueil d'Études*, viii (Prague, 1936), 41–61; 'The Byzantine Emperor and the Hierarchical World Order', *The Slavonic and East European Review*, xxxv (1956–7), 1–14.

sent a large sum of money to the Emperor Manuel II for the defence of Constantinople.[1] And the tone of profound respect with which, as we have seen, Basil I's successor addressed the *basileus* a year before the fall of Constantinople strongly suggests that, so long as this city remained in Christian hands, the Russians never again revolted against the ordered hierarchy of the Byzantine *Oikoumene*.

The preceding survey will have suggested that the attitude of the Russians towards Byzantium in the late Middle Ages was to a marked degree ambiguous: thus their strong resentment of the methods employed by the Byzantine authorities in the second half of the fourteenth century in making appointments to the Russian metropolitan see did not prevent them from contributing generous sums of money for the architectural and military needs of Constantinople; and Basil I's ill-tempered gesture of bravado against the emperor's authority should not obscure the fact that both his predecessors and his successor recognized, at least tacitly, the oecumenical jurisdiction of the *basileus*. This emotional polarity in the Russian response to Byzantium, this complex amalgam of attraction and repulsion, is traceable through the entire history of Russia's relations with the empire. The memories of the wars waged by the Russians against Byzantium in the tenth century, whose more vivid episodes were proudly recorded by Russian chroniclers, contributed to the rise of a national heroic tradition which left its mark on the country's medieval literature; in the struggle for native metropolitans, which began in the eleventh century and reached its climax in the fourteenth, the Russians came to resent the insistence of the patriarchs on selecting their own candidates when they felt strong enough to do so, and to despise the ease with which, whenever the empire was weak, the Byzantine authorities yielded on this issue to Russian secular pressure or to the lure of Muscovite gold. And more generally, the superior skill of the Byzantine diplomatists, whose policy towards Russia was aimed at securing military and economic assistance, and ensuring the loyalty of the Russians to the Church of Constantinople,[2] tended to instil in the victims of this diplomatic game

---

[1] See above, p. 249.
[2] See M. V. Levchenko, *Ocherki po istorii russko-vizantiiskikh otnosheny* (Moscow, 1956), 441 and *passim*.

of chess a distrust of Byzantine motives and a conviction that
'the Greeks'[1] were political intriguers and much too fond of
money. The aphorism 'the Greeks have remained tricksters to
the present day', coined by a Russian chronicler of the eleventh
or early twelfth century,[2] was no doubt frequently and pointedly
quoted in medieval Russia.

Yet this accumulated legacy of pride, bitterness and distrust
paled before the vision, revealed to the Russians of the Middle
Ages, of what Byzantium stood for in the things of the mind and
the spirit. The immensity of the debt which their country owed
to the civilization of the empire was apparent wherever they
might look: religion and law, literature and art, bore witness to
the fact that the Russians, for all the original features in their
cultural life, had been, and still were, the pupils of East Rome.
In the fourteenth and early fifteenth centuries Byzantine
cultural influences, after a period of decline due to the Mongol
invasions, were reviving in Russia; and the work of the Byzantine painter Theophanes, who lived for some thirty years in
Russia and produced his masterpieces in Novgorod and (after
1395) in Moscow, shows how close was the connection between
late medieval Russian painting and the Palaeologan art of
Constantinople.[3] The devotion of the Russians to the mother
Church of Constantinople and to its patriarchs was, despite the
frictions over primatial appointments, genuine and profound;
and not once, at least until 1439, did they seriously entertain the
idea of severing their canonical dependence on the see of
Constantinople which went back to the early days of Russian
Christianity. For this loyalty there was indeed much justification. The Byzantine metropolitans of Russia were for the most
part worthy and zealous men; the emperors and the patriarchs
were often genuinely concerned to see the Christian faith
flourish in Russia; and Russian monasticism, nurtured in the
traditions of Constantinople and Mount Athos, was in the
second half of the fourteenth century powerfully reviving under
the leadership of St Sergius of the Monastery of the Holy Trinity

---

[1] It is noteworthy that in the Middle Ages the Russians, as well as the Balkan
Slavs, invariably referred to the Byzantines as 'Greeks', and not as *Rhomaioi*.

[2] *The Russian Primary Chronicle (Povest' vremennykh let)*, ed. V. P. Adrianova-
Peretts and D. S. Likhachev (Moscow, 1950), i, 50; English translation by S. H.
Cross and O. P. Sherbowitz-Wetzor (Cambridge, Mass., 1953), 88.

[3] See V. N. Lazarev, 'Etyudy o Feofane Greke', *Vizantiisky Vremennik*, vii
(1953), 244–58; viii (1956), 143–65; ix (1956), 193–210; *Feofan Grek i ego shkola*
(Moscow, 1961).

and in close contact with the contemplative schools of Byzantine hesychasm.[1] But the prevailing attitude of the Russians towards Byzantium was not simply that of pupil to master: it was, in a sense, more simple and spontaneous, and is perhaps best epitomized in their reverence for the city of Constantinople, which, in their own language, they called *Tsargrad*, the Imperial City. In the eyes of the Russians—and indeed of all eastern Christendom—Constantinople was a holy city not only because, being the New Rome, it was the seat of the *basileus* and of his spiritual counterpart, the oecumenical patriarch. The city's essential holiness lay in the supernatural forces abundantly present within its walls: the many relics of Christ's passion and of the saints; the numerous churches and monasteries, storehouses of prayer and famed shrines of Christendom; and above all the patronage of the city's heavenly protectors, the Divine Wisdom, whose temple was St Sophia, and the Mother of God, whose robe, preserved in the church of Blachernae, was venerated as the city's Palladium.[2] These visible signs of divine favour surrounded Constantinople in the eyes of all eastern Christians with an aura of sanctity which could only be rivalled by the glory of Jerusalem: indeed, Constantinople was often thought of as the New Jerusalem. The Russian pilgrims and travellers who visited the city in the late Middle Ages and whose writings have come down to us display, before the number of its relics and the holiness of its sanctuaries, the same open-eyed wonder and religious awe which they reveal in their descriptions of the Holy Land;[3] more than one of them dwells on the breath-taking beauty of the church of St Sophia, and on the loveliness of the liturgical chanting therein; and occasionally they seem to catch an echo of that excitement with which the envoys of Prince Vladimir of Russia are said to have described to their sovereign the public worship in St Sophia in the late tenth century: 'We knew not whether we were in heaven or on earth; for on earth there is no such beauty or splendour'.[4] For the Russians of the Middle Ages Constantinople was indeed, as it was for its own citizens, 'the eye of the

---

[1] For the hesychast influences upon the monastic school of St Sergius, see Takhiaos, op. cit., 42–60.
[2] See N. H. Baynes, *Byzantine Studies and Other Essays* (London, 1955), 240–60.
[3] See *Itinéraires russes en Orient*, translated by Mme B. De Khitrowo, i, 1 (Geneva, 1889).
[4] *The Russian Primary Chronicle*, i, 75; English translation, 111.

faith of the Christians' and 'the city of the world's desire'.[1]

The vision of Constantinople as the New Jerusalem was tarnished and partially obscured in Russia as a result of the Council of Florence, which marks a decisive turn in the relations between Muscovy and Byzantium. The proclamation on 6th July, 1439, of the union between the Greek and the Latin churches was an event of major importance for the whole of Christendom: but it was in Russia that its long-term effects were the most far-reaching and significant.[2] A Russian delegation, headed by Isidore, the Greek metropolitan of Kiev and All Russia, attended the sessions of the Council, and its two bishops, Isidore and Avraamy (Abraham) of Suzdal', signed the Decree of Union. In March 1441 Isidore, now a cardinal and an apostolic legate, returned to Moscow. The Latin crucifix which he caused to be carried before him while entering the city, and his liturgical commemoration of Pope Eugenius IV in the cathedral of Moscow, exacerbated the Muscovites' anger and resentment at their metropolitan's behaviour at the Council, which they regarded as a betrayal of the Orthodox faith. By order of the Grand Prince Basil II, Isidore was deposed, arrested and imprisoned in a monastery; six months later he escaped abroad, perhaps with the connivance of the Russian government. Muscovy thus explicitly rejected the Union of Florence.[3]

---

[1] Τῆς Χριστιανῶν ὀφθαλμὸν ὑπάρχουσαν πίστεως: L. Sternbach, 'Analecta Avarica', in the *Rozpzawy* of the Academy of Cracow, XV (1900), 304.—'Η κοσμοπαμπόθητος αὕτη πόλις: Constantine the Rhodian, in *Revue des Études Grecques*, IX (1896), 38.

[2] The effect of the Council of Florence on the Russian attitude to Byzantium will be discussed rather briefly, as detailed treatments of the problem are readily available. See, in particular, F. Delektorsky, 'Kritiko-bibliografichesky obzor drevne-russkikh skazany o Florentiiskoy Unii', *Zhurnal Ministerstva Narodnogo Prosveshcheniya*, ccc (July, 1895), 131–84; P. Pierling, *La Russie et le Saint-Siège*, i (Paris, 1896), 7–104; E. Golubinsky, *Istoriya russkoy tserkvi*, ii, 1 (Moscow, 1900), 424 ff.; I. Ševčenko, 'Intellectual Repercussions of the Council of Florence', *Church History*, xxiv (1955), 291–323; M. Cherniavsky, 'The Reception of the Council of Florence in Moscow', ibid., 347–59; O. Halecki, *From Florence to Brest (1439–1596)* (Rome, 1958), 42–74; G. Alef, 'Muscovy and the Council of Florence', *The American Slavic and East European Review*, xx (1961), 389–401.

[3] Isidore, a trained theologian, had played a leading part in securing Greek agreement to the Decree of Union. His Russian companions at Ferrara and Florence, however, appear to have been poorly equipped for the theological discussions of the Council. See Ševčenko, op. cit., 307–8. However, Father J. Gill's view (*The Council of Florence* (Cambridge, 1961), 361) that 'the reasons for Vasili's [i.e. Basil II's] rejection of Isidore and his mission were probably purely political' is scarcely convincing. The Muscovites may not have had very clear views on the *Filioque*, but their opposition to Latin doctrines and customs and to the Papal claims were genuine and long-standing.

In the course of the next twenty years a number of works dealing with the Council of Florence were produced in Muscovy; they included a brief and artless travelogue by a member of the Russian delegation to the Council; a slightly longer and far more informative report, later included in several sixteenth-century Muscovite chronicles; two successive versions of an account of the Council and of its reception in Muscovy by the monk Symeon, another member of the Russian delegation; and finally, *A Selection from Holy Scripture against the Latins and the Story of the Convocation of the Eighth Latin Council,* a turgid and repetitious pamphlet of uncertain authorship, which appeared in 1461 or 1462.[1]

The historical value of these writings as documents on the Council of Florence is slight. These Muscovite pamphlets are too biased, their special pleading is too crude, their authors' understanding of the discussions at Ferrara and Florence too deficient to make them of much use as independent sources on the Council itself. But their interpretation of this event gave rise to a historical myth which acquired body and consistency in Russia during the decades that followed the Council of Florence, and which, illustrating the changing Russian attitude to Byzantium, is highly germane to the subject of this essay. The premises of this myth were simple in the extreme: the Greeks, by signing the Decree of Florence on terms imposed by the pope, betrayed the Orthodox faith, and the emperor and patriarch fell into heresy; the principal cause of this regrettable lapse was the Greeks' fondness for money, for they had been shamelessly bribed by the pope; by contrast, the Orthodox faith is preserved untainted in Russia, thanks to the Muscovite sovereign Basil II, who exposed the traitor Isidore and confirmed the true religion of his ancestors. The contrast between the tragic inconstancy of the Byzantines and the inspired faithfulness of the Russians is vividly drawn in the two following passages of the *Selection*: addressing the Emperor John VIII, the

---

[1] The text of the first four of these works is printed in V. Malinin, *Starets Eleazarova monastyrya Filofei i ego poslaniya* (Kiev, 1901), Appendices, 76–127; for a German translation of the travelogue, see 'Reisebericht eines unbekannten Russen (1437–1440)', trans. G. Stökl, in *Europa im XV. Jahrhundert von Byzantinern gesehen* [*Byzantinische Geschichtsschreiber*, hersg. von E. v. Ivánka, ii, Graz, 1954], 149–89. The *Selection* is published in A. Popov, *Istoriko-literaturny obzor drevne-russkikh polemicheskikh sochineny protiv Latinyan* (*XI–XV v.*) (Moscow, 1875), 360–95. For a discussion of these documents, see the works cited above (p. 266 n. 2) and also H. Schaeder, *Moskau das dritte Rom,* 2nd edn. (Darmstadt, 1957), 21–38.

author exclaims: 'O great sovereign Emperor! Why did you go to them [i.e. to the Latins]? How could you have entertained a good opinion of such people? What have you done? You have exchanged light for darkness; instead of Divine Religion you have accepted the Latin faith; instead of justice and truth you have embraced falsehood and error. You who formerly were a doer of pious works, how could you now have become a sower of tares of impiety? You who formerly were illumined by the light of the Heavenly Spirit, how could you now have clothed yourself in the darkness of unbelief?' And in the contrasting tones of exultation in which the author addresses 'the divinely enlightened land of Russia', a new and significant note is sounded: 'It is right that you should rejoice in the universe illumined by the sun, together with a nation of the true Orthodox faith, having clothed yourself in the light of true religion, resting under the divine protection of the many-splendoured grace of the Lord . . . under the sovereignty of . . . the pious Grand Prince Vasily Vasilievich, divinely-crowned Orthodox Tsar of all Russia'.[1]

The inversion of the former relationship between Byzantium and Russia is not less striking here for being implied: the emphasis on the universality of the Orthodox faith, the title of tsar applied—still prematurely—to the Muscovite ruler, and even the imagery of light, with its religious and imperial associations, all suggest that for the author Moscow and not Constantinople was now the providential centre of the true Christian religion. It should be remembered, however, that this passage was written eight or nine years after the fall of Constantinople, in the last years of the reign of Basil II, at a time when Muscovy, having weathered an acute political crisis and a civil war that had lasted through most of the second quarter of the fifteenth century, was fast evolving into a centralized, autocratic monarchy, which during the next twenty years was to impose its sovereignty over the greater part of Russia and gain its final freedom from Mongol domination.[2] This new conception of Muscovite Russia, no longer on the periphery of the Byzantine *Oikoumene*, but now the very centre and the heart of Orthodox Christendom, was later to form the starting point

[1] Popov, op. cit., 372, 394–5. Cf. Cherniavsky, op. cit., 352–3.
[2] For the internal history of the principality of Muscovy in the fifteenth century, see L. V. Cherepnin, *Obrazovanie russkogo tsentralizovannogo gosudarstva v XIV–XV vekakh* (Moscow, 1960), 715 ff.

of the theory of Moscow the Third Rome.[1] But the Muscovite ideologues of Basil II were not yet ready to draw the logical conclusions from their view of the Greek sell-out at Florence and from their belief in the historic destiny of their own nation. Hesitantly and ambiguously at first, they groped for new formulae to express the link they felt existed between the Byzantine betrayal of Orthodoxy and Muscovy's mission in the world: and it remains to consider how the Muscovites sought to determine their country's relationship to the empire during the twelve years between Isidore's expulsion from Russia and the fall of Constantinople in 1453.

To the Muscovites, who were consistently opposed to the idea of doctrinal agreement with the Latin Church, the acceptance of the Union of Florence by the supreme authorities of Byzantium came as a severe shock. Four and a half centuries of unwavering loyalty to the Church of Constantinople had left them unprepared for the sudden discovery that—as the primate of the Russian Church expressed it so tersely in 1451—'the Emperor is not the right one, and the Patriarch is not the right one'.[2] Their embarrassment was increased by the urgent need to appoint a successor to Isidore; and so, once again, the question of the appointment of the metropolitan of All Russia became for a while the crucial issue in the relations between Russia and Byzantium.

After Isidore's flight from Moscow in September 1441 three courses of action were open to the Russians: they could break off canonical relations with the Patriarch Metrophanes, on the grounds that by accepting the Union of Florence he had become a heretic, and proceed to elect a new primate; or they could take the latter action without rejecting the patriarch's jurisdiction, in the hope that the Byzantine authorities could eventually be induced to sanction the election; or else they could play for time, pretend to ignore the union between the Greek and Latin churches, and meanwhile seek permission from Constantinople to elect and consecrate their metropolitan in Russia, hoping that the anti-unionist party in Byzantium, known to be on the ascendant, would soon triumph over the

---

[1] An analysis of the theory of Moscow the Third Rome, which acquired final form in the sixteenth century, lies outside the scope of this essay, which is concerned with the relations between Byzantium and Muscovite Russia until the fall of the empire in 1453.

[2] *Russkaya Istoricheskaya Biblioteka*, vi, col. 559.

adherents of the Florentine agreement. The first course of action was far too drastic and revolutionary for the conservative and law-abiding Muscovite churchmen, and there is no evidence to suggest that the Russians in 1441 seriously contemplated a move which would have cast them adrift from their mother Church. In fact they adopted the third, and later the second, course of action. In 1441 Basil II wrote a letter to the patriarch, saluting him as the supreme head of Orthodox Christendom, complaining of Isidore's treacherous behaviour, and mentioning the fact that before the latter's appointment as primate of Russia (1436), the Muscovite authorities had vainly attempted to persuade the emperor and patriarch to appoint as metropolitan the Russian Bishop Iona (Jonas). Courteously and with curious diffidence, the Muscovite sovereign then proceeded to ask the patriarch, and through him the emperor, for a written authorization to have a metropolitan elected in Russia by a national council of bishops, tactfully avoiding any mention of his own candidate, Bishop Iona, and stating the ostensible grounds for his request: the authority of canon law; the difficulties of the long journey between Moscow and Constantinople, made more hazardous still by the Mongol incursions into Russia and 'the disturbances and upheavals in the lands that lie near to ours' (perhaps a semi-ironical allusion to the parlous state of the Byzantine empire); and—rather surprisingly—the fact that discussions of state secrets with the metropolitan must be held, if he is a Greek, in the presence of interpreters whose discretion cannot always be trusted and who thus endanger national security. And Basil II concludes his remarkably shrewd and skilfully argued letter by declaring his intention to maintain the close relations which had always existed between Christian Russia and 'the holy Emperor' and to continue to recognize the spiritual jurisdiction of the patriarch.[1]

The fate of this letter is unknown; there is indeed no certainty that it was even sent. For the next seven years Russia remained

---

[1] *Russkaya Istoricheskaya Biblioteka*, vi, cols. 525–36. The same letter, with appropriate variants, was addressed two years later (1443) to the Byzantine Emperor John VIII. See *Polnoe Sobranie Russkikh Letopisey*, vi (St. Petersburg, 1853), 162–7. The arguments of A. Ziegler (*Die Union des Konzils von Florenz in der russischen Kirche* (Würzburg, 1938), 102–7) who regards the letter as spurious and maintains that it was composed in the 1460s, in order to justify *post factum* Basil II's decision to have Iona consecrated metropolitan in Moscow, seem to the present writer unconvincing. For discussions of this letter, see Golubinsky, op. cit., ii, 1, 470–8; Kartashev, op. cit., i, 357–9.

without a metropolitan. For Basil II these were difficult years: he had a civil war on his hands, and for several months in 1445 he was a prisoner of the Tatars. The next move to end the ecclesiastical impasse was made in December 1448, when a council of Russian bishops, convoked by Basil II, elected Bishop Iona of Ryazan' as metropolitan of All Russia.

The die was cast; Iona's election and consecration were a direct challenge to the patriarch's authority. It seems that the Russians, even at this late hour, were extremely perturbed by the consequences of their own audacity. An influential minority in Muscovy held that Iona's appointment was uncanonical.[1] For more than three years the Russian authorities awaited the Byzantine reaction in anxious silence. Finally, in 1452 Basil II wrote a last letter to Constantinople, addressed to the new emperor, Constantine XI. It was as respectful in tone as his letter of 1441: indeed, he went as far as to acknowledge that the emperor possessed by virtue of his sacred office certain prerogatives in Russia.[2] But, behind the now expert phraseology of Muscovite diplomacy, two new notes are sounded in this letter: self-justification for what, from the Russian as well as from the Byzantine point of view, was an act of ecclesiastical insubordination; and an allusion, veiled yet pointed, to the fact that a considerable section of Byzantine society remained strongly opposed to the government's acceptance of union with Rome:[3] 'We beseech your Sacred Majesty not to think that what we have done we did out of arrogance, nor to blame us for not writing to your Sovereignty beforehand; we did this from dire necessity, not from pride or arrogance. In all things we hold to the ancient Orthodox faith transmitted to us [from Byzantium], and so we shall continue to do . . . until the end of time. And our Russian Church, the holy metropolitanate of Russia, requests and seeks the blessing of the holy, divine, oecumenical, catholic, and apostolic Church of St Sophia, the Wisdom of God, and is obedient to her in all things according to the ancient faith; and

---

[1] See Kartashev, op. cit., i, 360.

[2] See above, p. 261.

[3] The Metropolitan Iona, in a letter written in January 1451, alleged that the only strongholds of the unionist party in Constantinople were St Sophia and the Imperial palace, while the remaining parts of the Byzantine capital (as well as Mount Athos) remained entirely devoted to Orthodoxy: *Russkaya Istoricheskaya Biblioteka*, vi, col. 558. Though something of an exaggeration, this statement shows that the Russians were well informed about the strength of the anti-Unionist group in Constantinople.

our father, the Lord Iona, Metropolitan of Kiev and All Russia, in accordance with the same faith, likewise requests from her all manner of blessing and union, except for the present recently-appeared disagreements'.[1]

This final attempt of the Russians to square the circle by reconciling their traditional loyalty to the Church of Constantinople with their unwillingness to remain dependent on a unionist patriarch, was soon rendered obsolete by rapidly moving events. On 7th April, 1453, Mahomet II laid siege to Constantinople, and on 29th May the city fell. The Union of Florence collapsed with the Byzantine empire, and the Church of Constantinople reverted to Orthodoxy. Basil II's letter remained unsent in the state archives of Muscovy.[2] The theological obstacle to Russian ecclesiastical dependence on Constantinople had disappeared, only to be replaced by a political one, which in the eyes of the power-conscious Muscovite rulers proved the more insuperable of the two: the Church of Constantinople was now in the power of a Moslem state, and the patriarch received his investiture from the Ottoman sultan. And so the Russian Church retained the autonomous status it had acquired *de facto* in 1448, a status which in 1589, by common consent of the other Orthodox churches, was converted to that of an autocephalous patriarchate.

Thus at the end of our story, in the final chapter of the history of Russo-Byzantine relations, there comes to light, in the Russian attitude to Byzantium, the same polarity, the same ambiguous blend of attraction and repulsion, which we discerned in the earlier phases of this relationship. A distrust of Byzantine diplomacy and an abhorrence of its works—yet an open-hearted and probably disinterested desire to come to the aid of the holy city of Constantinople; resentment of the emperor's endeavours to control too closely the affairs of the Russian Church—yet a willingness to acknowledge his

---

[1] *Russkaya Istoricheskaya Biblioteka*, vi, cols. 583–4.

[2] Golubinsky (op. cit., ii, 1, 487–8) and Kartashev (op. cit., i, 362) suggest that the letter was never sent off because the Muscovite authorities, having learnt of the solemn proclamation of the Union by Constantine XI in St Sophia on 12th December, 1452, decided that further negotiations with Constantinople on ecclesiastical matters were useless. This does not seem altogether convincing, as Constantine had for some time past openly displayed his pro-unionist sympathies. Could it be that the Russians were deterred from sending Basil II's letter by news of the growing military isolation of Constantinople, which further increased with the completion, in August 1452, of the Turkish fortress of Rumeli Hisar on the Bosphorus?

oecumenical authority, and so his prerogatives in Russia; a dogged and umbrageous striving for political self-determination —yet a perpetual longing for the fruits of Byzantine civilization; scandalized horror at the readiness of the Byzantine authorities to barter the Orthodox faith for the empire's security at the Council of Florence—yet an equally strong reluctance to sever the canonical dependence of their Church on the patriarchate of Constantinople: the two panels of the diptych that was medieval Russia's image of Byzantium seem to be poised in continuous equilibrium.

Yet this last impression is illusory. For the Russian view of Byzantium was in the fifteenth century no longer part of a fixed and incontrovertible vision of reality; it was being subverted and refashioned by the rapidly developing national conscious-ness of th Meuscovites and by a series of violent shocks ad-ministered from the outside world; two of these shocks had something of a traumatic impact on Russia: they were provoked by the Council of Florence and the fall of Constantinople; their effect was both immediate and delayed, and they produced waves of reaction whose repercussions are traceable well into the sixteenth century. The immediate effect of the Council of Florence was, we have seen, one of alarm and consternation; and only gradually did the idea gain ground in some official circles in Muscovy that the Byzantines, by uniting with the Latins, had forfeited their right to be regarded as the leaders of Christendom. As for the fall of Constantinople, it had on the minds of the Muscovites an impact even more powerful; and the Russian reaction to this event was marked by the old and now familiar ambivalence. The more sententious of the Mus-covite ideologues proclaimed that the fall of Byzantium was God's punishment for the Greek betrayal of Orthodoxy at Florence, a view which was then fairly current in the eastern Christian world, and indeed among the Greeks themselves.[1] The first to expound it in Russia was the Metropolitan Iona, in these words from a letter he wrote in 1458 or 1459: 'As long as its people adhered to Orthodoxy, the Imperial City suffered no ill; but when the city turned away from Orthodoxy, you know your-selves, my sons, how much it endured'.[2] And in another letter,

---

[1] See Ševčenko, *Intellectual Repercussions of the Council of Florence*, 300, and n. 60; Gill, *The Council of Florence*, 391.

[2] *Russkaya Istoricheskaya Biblioteka*, vi, col. 623; cf. Ševčenko, ibid., 309; Schaeder, *Moskau das dritte Rom*, 44.

written in 1460, the metropolitan was more explicit still: referring to 'God's punishment' meted out to Constantinople for its
rejection of Orthodoxy, he quotes the words of St Paul: 'If
any man defile the temple of God, him shall God destroy'
(1 Cor. III, 17).[1]

But the spontaneous Russian response to the fall of Constantinople did not wholly accord with this factitious, meta-
historical theory which seems to have been propagated in
ecclesiastical circles close to the Muscovite court. There is
reason to believe that the feelings first aroused in Russia by the
events of 29th May, 1453, were those of horror and pity. The
destruction of the Christian empire, the end of 1,100 years of
history, the desecration of St Sophia, the sufferings now
endured by the Byzantines—these events, whose magnitude
it was difficult to comprehend, invited comparison with the
greatest calamities of human history and suggested that the end
of the world was near.[2] Soon after the fall of Constantinople, a
Byzantine writer, John Eugenicus, wrote a lament 'on the
capture of the Great City'.[3] Translated into Russian not later
than 1468, it became part of Muscovite literature, and can thus
be held to reflect a common attitude of Greeks and Russians
to the fall of Byzantium.[4] With impassioned rhetoric and
moving despair the author mourns 'the glorious and much
longed-for City, the mainstay of our race, the splendour of the
inhabited world', the church of St Sophia, 'that heaven on
earth, that second paradise', the schools and libraries now
destroyed, and the citizens of Byzantium, 'the holy nation',
'the people of the universe', now driven from their homes and
scattered like leaves in autumn; the Mother of God, age-long
guardian of Constantinople, has now, he says, deserted Her

[1] Ibid., vi, cols. 648–9.
[2] For the belief, current in Russia, that the world would end in 1492, see
Malinin, *Starets Filofei*, 427–43; Schaeder, op. cit., 49–51; A. Vasiliev, 'Medieval
ideas of the end of the world: West and East', *Byzantion*, xvi, 2 (1942–3) 462–502.
[3] One of the manuscripts of this work—Τοῦ νομοφύλακος Ἰωάννου διακόνου
τοῦ Εὐγενικοῦ μονῳδία ἐπὶ τῇ ἁλώσει τῆς μεγαλοπόλεως—was published by
S. P. Lambros in Νέος Ἑλληνομνήμων, v, 2–3 (1908), 219–26. On John Eugenicus,
the brother of Mark (the celebrated Metropolitan of Ephesus) see K. Krumbacher,
Geschichte der byzantinischen Litteratur, 2nd edn. (Munich, 1897), 117, 495–6;
Gill, op. cit., *passim*.
[4] The Russian translation is still unpublished. See N. A. Meshchersky,
' "Rydanie" Ioanna Evgenika i ego drevnerussky perevod', *Vizantiisky Vremennik*,
vii (1953), 72–86; I. Dujčev, 'La conquête turque et la prise de Constantinople
dans la littérature slave contemporaine', *Byzantinoslavica*, xvii (1956), 280–3; idem,
'O drevnerusskom perevode "Rydaniya" Ioanna Evgenika', *Vizantiisky Vremennik*,
xii (1957), 198–202.

city; and stunned by the magnitude of these disasters, the author can find no analogies save in the great catastrophies of mankind: the destruction of Jerusalem, Christ's death on the cross, and the last days of the world.[1]

Side by side, not always or necessarily in conflict, these two reactions to the fall of Byzantium, the nationalistic and the apocalyptic, are traceable through Muscovite literature of the late fifteenth and early sixteenth centuries. The latter left traces in an account of the siege of Constantinople by Nestor-Iskender, a Russian conscript in the Turkish army who took part in the capture of the city; and in an early sixteenth-century historical compendium, the *Chronograph* of 1512. The former, nationalistic, interpretation became one of the elements in the tradition glorifying Moscow as the Third Rome, which was given substance and form in the sixteenth-century writings of Philotheus of Pskov.[2] Gradually, as the spiritual and emotional shock caused by the fall of Constantinople wore off, and the Muscovites became increasingly conscious of their own national heritage, this interpretation carried the day, and in the sixteenth century there were few Russians left who, from the self-contained, self-satisfied, and power-conscious world of Muscovite nationalism, could still look back with nostalgia to the oecumenical traditions and European horizons of Byzantium.

[1] Lambros, loc. cit., 219, 220, 221, 222, 224, 226.
[2] For these works, see Schaeder, op. cit., 38–49, 65–81.

IX

P. S. Lewis

FRANCE IN THE FIFTEENTH CENTURY: SOCIETY AND SOVEREIGNTY

'Tout', thought Michelet, 'influe sur tout'; and this resounding observation is, though still respectable, now only too plainly a truism. The politics of a particular society, for instance, are most clearly and most fully understood as an emanation of it; and it is the purpose of this paper to discuss in these terms the internal politics of fifteenth-century France.

But what does one mean by 'politics' in the France of the later Middle Ages? Naturally they were limited in scope, since the number of questions which had to be discussed and the number of those who were important enough to discuss them, the members of the 'political society', were limited; and government, though ideally it concerned itself with such concepts as justice and the good administration of the whole community, was often more vitally concerned with the management of the political society on questions other than these. And what does one mean by 'society'? Not only were there in it the divisions of the group, the class; there were the divisions of the region, the *pays*, the locality. This localization was a function partly of geography, partly of historical development. The boundaries of these local compartments were as difficult (or as easy) to overleap as those of class. There was nothing to stop (though there were things to hinder) a determined bourgeois or a determined peasant from rising into at least the lower ranks of the nobility; there was nothing to stop a member of one of those local communities, those micro-societies, from entering, through seigneurial or royal service, through the Church, through a simple acceptance of the wider world, the macro-society of the great, of the government, of the cosmopolitan; but there was much to hinder it and much that was regional remained in the thinking of even the most cosmopolitan.

These boundaries, immunities in a loose sense, were reinforced by the often frail formalities of privileges, of charters, of immunities in a strict sense: of liberties for regions, of liberties for social groups, of liberties for individuals. There were people who thought in terms of a unity, as there were people who thought tenderly of classes other than their own. There were people who acted for the common good and there were more who said that they did; but the latter were often found out, as Louis XI and Thomas Basin (on opposite sides) found out the leaguers self-styled of the Public Weal. Between such individualists conflict could naturally be acute. Royal officers attacked noble and clerical immunists; they and the immunists attacked each other. Social conflict in later medieval France was not essentially one of class: it was of every individual immunist, whatever his class, against his immediate enemies, occasionally in alliance with his peers or with his neighbours. Against the kingdom, the unity, the macro-society, was set the micro-society, the *pays*; and against both was set the individual.

The fragile unity had its most potent expression in the idea of the king, in the image of a perfect government, and to some extent in the actual efficacy of the king, the person, in the controller, more or less, of a far from perfect government. The image of sovereignty[1] naturally differed for different people: a *juponnier* in Orléans might deny the king outright and cry 'Kings, kings, kings: we have no king but God!'; an elderly inhabitant of the *Massif central* might have strange superstitions about the Royal Mark. The views of those who were inarticulate on paper, peasant or noble, are hard to discover. Some may have seen the king only in the most general terms, as the most impressive figure in an impressive cortège on the road, a 'royal ceremony', indulged in by Charles V, according to Christine de Pisan, only to impress 'the most worthy status of the high crown

---

[1] The sources of material given without reference in this and the three following paragraphs will be found in 'Jean Juvenal des Ursins and the Common Literary Attitude towards Tyranny in Fifteenth-Century France', *Medium Aevum*, xxxiv (1965).

of France' upon his successors[1]—and also, presumably, upon the bystander. A mere royal presence could be terrifying enough, even to an experienced Italian ambassador.[2] But the image of government of those who were articulate on paper, the men of letters, was more formal than this. It was compounded of notions legal, theological, moral, some indeed from a remote past and some concocted in a less respectable present. Its ingredients could, according to taste or to disingenuousness, be so treated as to produce an image of royal right or of royal duty; its theories so handled as to exhort resistance or to deny resistance utterly. In so far as people thought about politics abstractedly at all in later medieval France, it was in its terms that they made plain their views.

The king was a spiritual and a public being as well as a private one. The Gallican controversy had reinforced his original divinity. A number of popular miracles, now attached to Clovis, illustrated the particular regard with which the Crown of France was held in Heaven: the origin of the *fleurs-de-lys*, the origin of the oriflamme, the miraculous descent of the *Sainte-ampoule* and the power which, it was generally held, its chrism conferred upon the king to touch for the evil found ready pictorial expression in popular abbreviated chronicles.[3] In more extravagant moments it might be held that, in touching for the evil, the king performed miracles in his own lifetime. The king was the head of the body politic and, it could be argued by Jean de Terre-Vermeille about 1420, resistance was thus unnatural as well as sacrilegious. It could be argued, *quia quod principi placuit legis habet vigorem*, that the king was above the law. The very misfortunes of France had reinforced the image of the saviour of France,

> For his loss is our ruin
> And our safety with him lies.

The misfortunes of war had indeed weakened the willingness of the articulate to think of resistance. The English, who killed their kings, were regarded with a fascinated and rather formal

---

[1] *Le Livre des fais et bonnes meurs du sage roy Charles V*, ed. S. Solente, [Société de l'histoire de France], i (Paris, 1936), 51.

[2] *Dépêches des ambassadeurs milanais en France*, ed. B. de Mandrot and C. Samaran, [Société de l'histoire de France], i (Paris, 1916), 238.

[3] 'Two Pieces of Fifteenth-century Political Iconography', *Journal of the Warburg and Courtauld Institutes*, xxvii (1964), 317–19.

horror: a horror, again, expressed in pictorial form.[1] Resistance
had once been preached, as late as the first decade of the
fifteenth century by the doctors of the university of Paris; it was
to be preached again after its end. But in the course of the
century only Thomas Basin, who had been involved in the war
of the Public Weal, justified rebellion; for the rest, the literary,
though they made their distinctions between king and tyrant,
though they preached the moral duty of the anointed of heaven
and the head of the body politic, though they pointed to the
customary awful warnings of scripture, antiquity and even
recent history, though they fulminated against tyranny, for the
rest the literary refused to countenance resistance. The intellectual victors were the king's lawyers in *parlement*. For them it
was temerarious 'to talk of the king's authority, it's sacrilege to
debate it . . .; for the authority of the king . . . is greater than
advocates could express it and it is not subject to the opinions
of doctors'. The latter, with other literary men, adopted an
elegiac attitude and said, with Commynes, 'when all's said and
done, our only hope should be in God'.

The king, then, 'has no other control over him than the fear
of God and his own conscience'. It was to be hoped that these
were efficacious; but too often hope was deferred. If sovereignty
was never challenged, the actions of the sovereign and, more
often, of his servants were accused in diatribe and in action. A
hopeful reluctance to tarnish the image of sovereignty led in the
former to a reluctance to accuse the person of the sovereign; in
the latter there was no such inhibition. Charles VI and Charles
VII had the example of Richard II of England before their
eyes; Louis XI in his later days cowered behind remarkable
systems of physical defences. While the men of letters, a peaceful crew on the whole, regarded the *voye de faicte*, the way of
action, with abhorrence, others less peaceable might not. The
ideas of the articulate, even the notions of the inarticulate, did
not create the political movement of late medieval France:
they were its creation. The motivity of politics and the motivity
of political theory had a more practical source.

Why did people behave as they did? First we must ask how
they did behave. Charles VI was mad, Charles VII at least
politically inexpert until comparatively late in his reign (though
he became very dexterous), Louis XI, though a remarkable

[1] Ibid., pp. 319–20.

man, not necessarily a very efficient one.[1] The English war, and with it the problem of all those who had accepted the sovereignty of the king of England and France, dragged on until the 1450s and the threat of renewed war remained. The revenue from the *domaine*, the royal estates, was far too low for the purposes for which it was intended. And yet Charles VII and Louis XI could at times act with considerable authority. But perhaps we should distinguish between the groups or the individuals to whose detriment such strength was shown. What were the power relationships between the king, the government, and these groups or individuals? What was this interplay of sovereignty and society?

The question of the king's income gives us our first set of problems. A rich king with a taste for power can buy troops to browbeat the unbribable and can bribe the unbeatable. But first he must get the money; and if he lack the strength that comes from wealth to do so his position is, understandably, impossible. Extraordinary revenue came from taxation; and taxation, in principle, was granted by representative assemblies.[2] 'What touches all should be approved by all' had and still did echo from one end of France to another. Specific privileges protected the rights of specific *pays*; some were dearly cherished. But privileges and laws were, like the political theory of later medieval France, *ex post facto* things: a king who needed not to consult the estates for practical reasons needed very rarely (unless the idea had been ingrained even in him by long years of practice) to consult them for theoretical reasons. For what practical reasons did Charles VII· (for it was he alone in the fifteenth century who consulted assemblies with any regularity) feel it necessary to allow his subjects their rights?

He had not (and neither had that paragon Charles V) any special affection or reverence for representative assemblies: he and his entourage seem to have thought, as Charles V and earlier kings had thought, that public opinion needed to be wooed in, preferably, as large an assembly as possible. Now late-medieval Frenchmen had on the whole a profound dislike of general assemblies, of the whole kingdom, say, or of Langue-

[1] R. Doucet, 'Le Gouvernement de Louis XI [X]', *Revue des cours et conférences*, (1923–4), 661–9.
[2] The sources of material given without reference in this and the seven following paragraphs will be found in 'The Failure of the French Medieval Estates', *Past and Present*, xxiii (1962), 3–24.

doil or of a Languedoc larger than the three *sénéchaussées* of Toulouse, Carcassonne and Beaucaire-Nîmes. Though a number of rationalizations of this phobia could be produced (the hazards of the roads in wartime, the cost of travelling vast distances in France, the language barrier between north and south, the difficulties of accommodating a large assembly) its essential cause lay in the long-standing particularism of provincial France. Why should Rouergue be dealt with in the same assembly as the rest of the kingdom, or even in the same assembly as the rest of the Midi? Why should the representatives of the *sénéchaussée* of the Landes (the problem was the same for the duke of Aquitaine) be in the same assembly as those of the Bordelais? It was, in any case, impossible to expect a large assembly like that of the kingdom or that of Languedoil to make a final grant. Charles VII and his entourage, like Charles V and others before them, seem to have wanted large assemblies more for political reasons than anything else: general support was necessary in order to woo the smaller regional assemblies which actually granted the taxes into granting them. Such general support seems to have been necessary primarily in times of defeat, under Charles V as under Charles VII. But large assemblies had a tendency to become tiresome with their grievances; and Charles VII, like Charles V before him, was quite prepared to let general assemblies slip out of existence with the first upsurge of returning victory. They began to slip after the coronation at Reims; they finally vanished after the estates of Orléans in 1439; and they left very few wracks behind.

There remained the regional assemblies, possibly more fervent in defence of local liberty. Some, indeed, remained so. But none presented much obstacle to a determined ruler out for income. 'Charles VII', wrote Commynes, 'never raised more than eighteen hundred thousand francs a year; and King Louis, his son, was raising at the time of his death forty-seven hundred thousand francs, without counting the artillery and other things like that':[1] and, painfully, he was right. The rectitude of using what were in origin taxes for the war for comparatively peaceful purposes was still disputable in the mid-century; but even the reformers of the Cabochian movement in 1413 had

---

[1] P. de Commynes, *Mémoires*, ed. J. Calmette and G. Durville, [Classiques de l'histoire de France], ii (Paris, 1925), 220.

allowed Charles VI half his extraordinary revenue for non-military purposes.[1] It was upon taxation that the wealth of the king depended; and that taxation he got with very little trouble.

The pressing need of war presumably encouraged the tax-payer while the war remained: 'defence of the realm' was a well-established criterion for subvention.[2] The threat of war remained after 1453, though some people at least were not convinced that it was enough to justify permanent taxation.[3] There was indeed local resistance from some of the regional assemblies that survived: from those of the Dauphiné, for instance, or from those of Rouergue. Various forms of pressure could be exerted; but determined and independent estates like those of the Dauphiné could still extract a soft answer from Louis XI in the 1470s and ensure that the taxes of the *pays* rose by two-thirds instead of by one and two-thirds. But the estates of the Dauphiné were rather exceptional. Elsewhere the regional assemblies, where they survived, were less successful. Why was there so little resistance?

Methods of coercion could be successful. In 1462 the Millavois were threatened with a fine of 'a hundred marks of silver and with the seizure and sale of our goods and with the arrest of our persons and on top of that with the penalty of being rebels and disobedient to the king our lord' if they did not accede to a 'particular demand' made by royal commissioners in the face of resistance and wholesale bribery by the estates of Rouergue. The habit of backstairs representations in which a number of towns indulged could hoist them with their own petard. A lack of cohesion amongst the members of the same order in an assembly, that essential individualism, might provide a general ground for the weakness of the regional assemblies. For what interest had they in co-operation? Rodez during the English occupation had run an intelligence service for the count of Armagnac out of urban revenues; Millau in 1369 had carried its doubts about the sovereignty of Charles V to Montpellier, Avignon and Bologna, had held a service for Sir Thomas Wettenhall, English seneschal of Rouergue who died of wounds at Montlaur, and had replaced the arms of England with those of France only on the orders of his French

[1] 'Jean Juvenal des Ursins', op. cit.,
[2] J. R. Strayer, 'Defense of the Realm and Royal Power in France', *Studi in onore di Gino Luzzatto*, (Milan, 1949) i, 289–96.
[3] 'Jean Juvenal des Ursins', op. cit.,

successor.[1] At an individual level the same divergence of interest could be found in members of every order of an Estates. The concept of co-operation, of common action (though it existed) developed very slowly in France. There were so few pressures to foster it.

Why should one engage in united action? As a landowner, ecclesiastical or lay, what interest had one in uniting to oppose taxation? One was on the whole oneself exempt: one attended an assembly in order to consent to the taxation of one's tenants. It could be argued that one had an interest in protecting the source of one's own revenue, that one could be more valiant in defence of this than the bourgeoisie which claimed to represent the *tiers-état*. Some landowners may have been, if only for reasons of prestige, solicitous of their subjects; but the remoteness of the sting of taxation provides at least a *prima facie* case for the apparent lack of resistance of the first two orders to the abolition or coercion of their assemblies. And bourgeois, too, could become exempt from taxation. 'A very large number of the richest people are exempt and don't pay anything', complained the *mairie* of Dijon in 1452, '. . . the merchants and smaller people pay all.'[2] Whole towns could opt out of the taxation system (but with this we will deal later). It can be argued that in the end the taxpayer was left unprotected before the ravening wolf. A Jean Juvenal des Ursins could raise his voice in their protection; but few would raise a hand.

Grievances against the government, infringements of the privileges of the *pays*, these, certainly, might lead the members of an assembly to voice a common complaint. But (however much they might recognize piously their duty of justice) kings did not call assemblies to listen to grievances against themselves and their officers. Since no assembly summoned by the Crown in France acted as a law court or had anything to do with the process of legislation (other than presenting its *cahiers de doléances*) the sole reason for the summoning of an assembly was to raise money. And to his doing this arbitrarily rather too few

---

[1] *Comptes consulaires de . . . Rodez*, ed. H. Bousquet, I, *Cité*, ii, [Archives historiques du Rouergue, xvii], (Rodez, 1943), *passim*; *Documents sur la ville de Millau*, ed. J. Artières, [Archives historiques du Rouergue, vii], (Millau, 1930), 145–95 *passim*: P. Chaplais, 'Some Documents regarding the Fulfilment and Interpretation of the Treaty of Bretigny 1361–1369', *Camden Miscellany*, xix, [Camden Third Series, lxxx], (London, 1952), 51–78.

[2] F. Humbert, *Les Finances municipales de Dijon du milieu du xiv⁰ siècle à 1477*, (Paris 1961), 247.

potential members of an assembly seem to have been prepared to object strongly enough to make it advisable for a king to summon them.

Why did they object strongly enough in the areas in which estates survived? This is the most puzzling question. One is forced to answer it in terms of the general historical development of a particular *pays* which gave its inhabitants some will for an assembly which those of other areas lacked. Any more particular common reasons seem impossible to divine. And properly, of course, one should go below the *pays* and its general social composition to the actual individuals who, at all the moments in the life of an assembly, made its existence. But the biographical method is difficult, if not impossible, to apply to these estates. The reasons for action of a Jean Juvenal des Ursins, archbishop duke of Reims and *premier pair* of France, at the estates general of Tours in 1468 are clear enough from his speech itself and from the voluminous collected works in which it survives;[1] the reasons for action of someone more obscure at an obscure local assembly are silent in the silence of the inarticulate.

But in any case Charles VII and Louis XI got their money. They also, in the same fit of absence of mind, got a standing army. How much this was regarded as the seal of despotism is disputable. Jean Juvenal, who had a ready eye for tyranny, at least overlooked it.[2] We know too little about the composition of the companies of *gens d'ordonnance*, too little about their loyalties, too little about the loyalties of their commanders. The claim made in the same military *ordonnance* of 1439 that only the king could raise a private army clearly was ignored by magnates in times of stress. The military situation remained at least open: the battle of Montlhéry in 1465, for instance, was very nearly a draw with the advantage, if any, on the side of the rebels. But at least Charles VII and Louis XI were rich enough to invest in military power which forced the discontented of the Praguerie and the Public Weal in turn to resort to arms; and, as we shall see, to invest in the tacit bribery which softened the winter of their original discontent.

These kings, then, were comparatively wealthy; the strength which they needed to take their taxes on the whole arbitrarily

---

[1] Bibliothèque nationale, ms. fr. 2701.
[2] 'Jean Juvenal des Ursins', op. cit.

was the strength of victory and of the essential unwillingness to object if those non-taxpayers who were in principle the guardians of the unfortunate contributor. And with the disappearance of assemblies the king was left even more clearly *vis-à-vis* a kingdom composed of individuals or of groups of individuals. These, privileged, immune, with rights in principle irrefrangible, now played essentially a lone game with the government. They made (occasionally successfully) attempts at coalition; but the game was essentially an open one, with a ruler who was quite prepared to print his own aces. He made the law, despite the theory that some laws were fundamental; the courts were his, despite the view that they acted as a check upon arbitrary action. An idea in the air, such as that of the priority of the duty of the subject (who owed obedience) over that of the vassal (who had his rights), investigated by Jean de Terre-Vermeille about 1420, could bear fruit in Louis XI's dealings with François II of Brittany.[1] Religion, Claude de Seyssel's third curb[2] upon monarchy, was, though these men were pious, hardly much of a check upon them. In 1465 Louis XI was alleged to have said 'that he needed to do as the brothers of St Francis did, that is, to play the hypocrite'. This, though Louis could also deny that duplicity was his custom,[3] was hardly encouraging for those who wished to put their trust in princes.

How was the game played? One must remember its complication. No king could act alone: he had his entourage, his counsellors, his 'favourites'; he had his civil servants. In this welter of governance the individual will of the king might be hard to identify: the members of the entourage and the civil servants naturally had their own games to play. The great, too, had their entourages, their counsellors, their civil servants; the interplay of interests quickens. And there could at times be a confusing lack of hostility between major protagonists: politics could be a curious love-hate relationship. To a certain extent the bickerings were the bickerings of the members of a single team who might, on the whole, agree about many things but who disagreed about who was to play where. And though to our hindsight men's interests *vis-à-vis* the government might seem fairly clear, in the immediacy of the royal presence, in the

[1] Ibid.
[2] *La Monarchie de France*, ed. J. Poujol, (Paris, 1961), 115–19.
[3] *Dépêches des ambassadeurs milanais*, op. cit., iv (Paris, 1923), 156, 74.

interplay of interest and personality, strange things could happen: the actions of a moment need not be wholly calculated, nor wholly rational.

The structure of government was on the whole simple enough. The king, like every magnate, had a council to help him rule; he had an administration to deal with his estates and with the collection of extraordinary revenue. The last and the central financial and judicial organizations were naturally more complicated than those of a simple magnate; they and the royal chancery, though its methods and its diplomatic might be copied closely by those of the princes, naturally dealt with a far greater body of business than those of a magnate; but royal and seigneurial administrations were sufficiently alike for their personnel to be interchangeable. These officers naturally had their own fortunes to look to. Their shortcomings, the failure of 'justice', figured largely in the lamentations of reformers; the king's tolerating their malefactions was bitterly attacked.[1] But to what extent were his own servants under his control? Did he indeed encourage them to create his 'tyranny' for him? Or did the civil servants create the king's tyranny for their own ends? Was royal lawyers' eagerness to defend the rights of the Crown, for instance, simply a natural lawyer's eagerness to create long and lucrative lawsuits as, it was argued in 1484, magnates' apparent eagerness for estates stemmed from a desire to collect their expenses as commissioners to them? How could a king[2] control his officers? Stability in office, though eagerly claimed by the officers, was not yet an assured thing; venality of office, though practised, not yet wholly approved of; plurality and non-residence, though common enough to be normal, still formally frowned upon.[3] The Crown still had in principle at least some hold over its servants; but whether the final sanction of dismissal or even of condemnation was exercised may have depended more upon the political position of the officer than upon the degree of his malefaction. Given the nature of government, whose men were the civil servants? Could any man rely upon an attachment to the person of the king alone?

[1] 'Jean Juvenal des Ursins', op. cit.

[2] J. Masselin, *Journal des Etats généraux de France tenus à Tours en 1484*, [Documents inédits sur l'histoire de France], (Paris, 1835), 636.

[3] The latest and in some ways the most searching discussion of these problems and of the position of lawyers in later medieval France in general may be found in B. Guenée, *Tribunaux et gens de justice dans le bailliage de Senlis à la fin du moyen âge (vers 1380–vers 1550)*, (Paris, 1963).

Certainly the need for patronage in acquiring office seems to have been a considerable one. The rivalry of patrons, egged on by their own civil servants to find them royal office, has been seen as prodromic of civil war;[1] and patronage was required not only by those who hoped for office but by those already royal officers who hoped for seigneurial service to increase their income or who hoped for advancement in that of the Crown or who needed protection in keeping the places they had already acquired. Some, admittedly, suffered from the conflict of loyalty thus created. Jean Cadier, royal *élu* in the Bourbonnais, who was also a household servant of Jean II, duke of Bourbon, and then auditor of accounts for him at Moulins, was attacked during the onslaught on the duke in 1480 for infidelity to the Crown which could hardly be thought extensive.[2] But if there was danger in serving too loyally a patron there was also danger in serving too loyally the Crown: the punishment of Jean de Doyat, *bailli* of Montferrand, who had led the local attack on Jean II de Bourbon, was an awful warning to those too zealous in the interests of the Crown of what might happen when, on the accession of a minor king, a magnate's influence might again be formidable.[3] A civil servant had naturally to judge his chances in the same way as minor *seigneurs* caught between greater powers had to judge theirs. In 1457 maître François Hallé, *conseiller du roy*, was appointed judge of the *chambrerie* by the *chambrier* of France, Jean II de Bourbon.[4] Twenty-three years later he was his most implacable opponent as king's advocate in *parlement*.[5] He, certainly, had not made the mistake of Jean Cadier. In the same way as their actions in defending the king's interests might be independent of the will or even of the knowledge of the king, so the civil servants' actions as clients could not be wholly subservient to the interests of their patrons. If extreme conflict arose between their masters, they had to choose; but only when their seigneurial patron was pretty firmly defeated were they likely to lose his protection. And such open conflict was not on the whole normal. Much more

[1] E. Perroy, 'Feudalism or Principalities in Fifteenth-Century France', *Bulletin of the Institute of Historical Research*, xx (1945), 184.
[2] H. de Surirey de St.-Remy, *Jean II de Bourbon, duc de Bourbonnais et d'Auvergne (1426–1488)*, (Paris, 1944), 188–90.
[3] A. Bossuat, *Le Bailliage royal de Montferrand (1425–1556)*, (Paris, 1957), 55–6, 79–80.
[4] Letters of 17th March, 1457, Archives nationales, P.1358² cote 536.
[5] Surirey, op. cit., 184–7, 195.

characteristic possibly was an uneasy neutrality in which it was possible to serve both or, indeed, many masters.

But too much generalization on this subject is probably unwise. The precise interplay of patronage and the civil service is all too little known. A civil servant, especially a courtier civil servant might become himself important; he might so embed himself at court that his patron might almost become his client. Arguably the *épuration* of officers in 1461 could be seen as the product of the accession to power with Louis XI of a party of 'outs'; arguably there was a riposte of the disinherited in 1465 with the war of the Public Weal. Admittedly the mortality in 1461 in the class of courtier civil servants *par excellence*, the *baillis*, was considerable; but it was very much less in 1465. Michel Juvenel des Ursins, who went out as *bailli* of Troyes with his brother the chancellor of France in 1461 and came back with him in 1465 is one of the few clear cases of the return of the old 'ins'; but Guillaume Juvenel des Ursins in 1461–5 was far from completely 'out'. The higher civil servant himself was an integer in the problem: he might still retain some independence of both patron and Crown.

But for these men friends, if no particular friend, were still essential. Guillaume Juvenel des Ursins was advised when he became chancellor by his brother Jean 'not to think you can resist the will of those who will be at court: because that will only have you suppressed and thrown out. It's much better to have patience and dissemble and be the cause of making less trouble, since one can't profit by being too firm and losing one's job: messire Arnault de Corbie used to . . .'.[1] To deplore the nervous strain of being a courtier was an established literary affectation. 'The court', wrote Alain Chartier, 'is an assembly of people who under the pretence of acting for the good of all, come together to diddle each other; for there's scarcely anyone there who isn't engaged in buying and selling and exchanging, sometimes their income, sometimes their old clothes—for we of the court are high-class merchants, we buy the other people— and sometimes for their money we sell *them* our own precious humanity.' The corruption of the court was deplorable. 'The abuses of the court and the habits of courtiers are such that no one lasts there without being corrupted and no one succeeds

[1] 'Jean Juvenal des Ursins', op. cit.

there without being corruptible.'[1] But corrupt, nerve-racking, or not, the court was nevertheless the source *par excellence* of political power. The problem of the control of this nuclear reactor was naturally a considerable one: it depended primarily on the personality of the king and upon the ability of the men to whom, inevitably, he was forced to delegate power. Charles VI's incapacity caused a civil war; the way in which Charles VII in the 1420s and early '30s was captured by 'favourites' has led to recondite speculation upon the state of his mental health. But in the end Charles learned how to manage the court, to choose the best man for a particular job, 'one at the war, another in the financial departments, another in the council, another running the artillery'. 'Eventually', wrote the Burgundian chronicler Chastellain, 'since he had an expert knowledge of the people around him and since he had everything under his eye, misdeeds as well as virtuous actions, it became so dangerous to be in his entourage that no one, however great he was, had the faintest idea where he stood; and so everybody watched their step very carefully, in case, if they put a foot wrong, they should be caught on the hop.'[2] This was the essence of personal rule: it was impossible to avoid the employment of men who would be remarked upon as 'most accepted the most familiar in speaking to the king';[3] it was imperative to keep them under control. Kings, Louis XI once told Commynes, do not naturally love those to whom they are beholden;[4] and certainly Louis XI was not without ingratitude. It was little wonder courtiers' nerves suffered.

But while they kept their nerve (and their place) courtiers could prosper themselves and could prosper the affairs of others. The inter-relation of the court and the powerful outside interests has not been studied for the fifteenth century:[5] but clearly such an inter-relationship existed. Amongst the *alliances* of Gaston IV, count of Foix, are two in which intimate servants of the dauphin promised to maintain him in the good graces of

[1] Alain Chartier, *Le Curial*, ed. F. Heuckenkamp, (Halle, 1899), 22, 23, 6,7.
[2] *Oeuvres de Georges Chastellain*, ed. Kervyn de Lettenhove, ii (Brussels, 1863), 183-4.
[3] Malletta on Josselin du Bois, *Dépêches des ambassadeurs milanais*, op. cit., ii (Paris, 1919), 364-5.
[4] Commynes, op. cit., i (Paris, 1924), 251-2.
[5] For a discussion of it in an earlier period, see R. Cazelles, *La Société politique et la crise de la royauté sous Philippe de Valois* (Paris, 1958).

their master:[1] such services were part of courtly existence. But the powerful outside interests, the great, had themselves a place at court; and in the same way as kingship demanded the management of the entourage, so it demanded the management in personal terms of the great. It was when such management failed, when the great left the court to nourish their grievances and dream of revenge, that the drums of war were heard. But how were these men to be managed?

The most powerful group were the magnates. They, and all nobles, faced a number of problems.[2] Their income from land had probably fallen as a result of the demographic crisis of the Black Death and the subsequent epidemics and as a result of the war; holdings abandoned to the enemy[3] might increase the enemy's spoils of war but they were clearly of little use to oneself. And the very conditions of seigneurial existence brought their own difficulties. A noble must live nobly, he must live magnificently, he must dispend. The dispendiousness of Jean, duke of Berry, 'in his time a worthy prince and honourable', who 'delighted greatly in precious stones, entertained strangers most willingly and gave them his own most liberally'[4] was legendary and the inventory of his goods after his death fabulous; but others, too, had their minor Aladin's caves; and for others, too, the claims of prestige demanded considerable expenditure. Then there were the problems of the family. The dower interests of one's mother, the claims to marriage-portions and inheritances of, especially, one's possible numerous younger sons and daughters, legitimate or illegitimate, warred in the dutiful seigneurial breast with the interest of the principal heir, the maintainer of the line. Then there were the problems of one's soul and those of one's friends and relations. Not only did prestige demand a distinguished funeral: the establishment of chaplainries, masses, perpetual lamps might lead to the nibbling away of the patrimony. Then there were the problems of living in the practice of arms: capture and ransom could be costly and

---

[1] See the article cited below (p. 293, n. 4), p. 172.

[2] For a discussion of those faced by the nobility of the south-west, see R. Boutruche, *La Crise d'une société: seigneurs et paysans du Bordelais pendant la guerre de cent ans* (Paris, 1947), 233–94.

[3] Even if the results of such patriotism could be mitigated: A. Bossuat, 'Le Rétablissement de la paix sociale sous le règne de Charles VII', *Le Moyen Age*, lx (1954), 143–44.

[4] Jean Juvenal des Ursins, *Histoire de Charles VI*, ed. Michaud and Poujoulat, [Nouvelle collection des mémoires. ii], (Paris, 1857), 532b.

even disastrous for oneself and for those loyal friends whom one could persuade to stand surety for one.[1] All of these problems could lead to dispute: with creditors, with one's indignant family and with others with some legal claim to a part of one's property, with one's indignant captors; and in the same way a conflict over one's judicial rights could arise with one's neighbours and with neighbouring royal officers. Dispute and conflict meant lawsuits; and lawsuits were costly and tiresome. The web of his own existence was something every seigneur had to come to terms with.

Not all, of course, failed to do so. The mortality rate of seigneurial families may seem to be high in the fifteenth century; but one has to allow in it for the normal failure of families due to failure to produce a male heir.[2] And there could be compensations within the web of seigneurial existence itself. Prosperous marriages might balance disastrous births and deaths: the trade in marriage-portions was not all one way. The Church was a repository made for unwanted sons and daughters; informed manipulation of customs of seigneurial inheritance might allow one to disinherit the unwanted and to create, as the Albrets created, a family inheritance custom. If the balance in the ransom and booty trade was tilted firmly in favour of the invader and his adherents at least the latter prospered amongst Frenchmen; and some loyal patriots might make a lucky windfall. An intelligent administration of one's estates might still bring in something from this failing source. But one source more might salvage especially the powerful: the patronage of the Crown, those pensions, those gifts, those offices, the struggle for which became only too clearly a large part of the content of the seigneurial attitude towards politics.

In the same way as the king pensioned the civil servants and for the same reasons of weakness as kings in France had always allowed the nobility exemption from taxation, the king pensioned the great. Up to half the revenue of the dukes of Burgundy at the turn of the fourteenth century came from such extraordinary sources; up to half the revenue of the dukes of

[1] A. Bossuat, 'Les Prisonniers de guerre au xve siècle: la rançon de Jean, seigneur de Rodemack', *Annales de l'Est*, 5, ii (1951), 145–62.
[2] E. Perroy, 'Social Mobility among the French *Noblesse* in the Later Middle Ages', *Past and Present*, xxi (1962), 31–2.

Bourbon in the later fifteenth century.[1] But those very acquisitions from an impotent Crown could hinder their recipients' action. At what stage, pressed possibly by the king or by his servants with or without his knowledge or consent, did one adopt the *voye de faicte*? Dunois, the Italian ambassador pointed out with his usual shrewdness in 1465, 'has lost an excellent position and eighteen thousand francs which he had from the king of France between offices and pension'[2] through his participation in the war of the Public Weal; one might easily be led to submit for gains rather less than one had hoped for when one realized that one might lose all. The unreality of politics in the later fifteenth century, the curiously ambiguous attitudes of government and magnates, stemmed from the nature of the things over which there was conflict.

The nature of the pressure the magnates felt from the 'government' naturally varied precisely from person to person. Conflict over the duke of Brittany's royal rights, conflict over the propriety of the count of Foix's ruling by the grace of God, the interminable pressure of the royal officers of the *bailliage* of Montferrand upon those of the duke of Bourbon's *sénéchaussée* of Riom, conflicts essentially of prestige and position and to a certain extent of the income which maintained both, purely human dislike between persons: these were the pressures that might drive a magnate into open resistance. The *douceurs* of favour, the settlement of conflict (temporarily) in one's terms, an increase in one's pension, even the apparent proffer of purely human affection: these were the pressures that might bring one back into the fold. Though their revolt in the 1460s might bear the proud name of the Public Weal, nothing, it could be argued, was further from its participants' minds. Any theoretical approach to politics other than the crudest seems to have passed the magnates by;[3] not because they were unsophisticated, incapable, uncultured, unintelligent, but because their position was very much one of the *status quo*, interpreted in their favour. They were rebels; but they were hardly revolutionary.

How much of a danger were they to a king determined, like Louis XI, say, not to have 'an equal in his kingdom'?[4] In time

[1] M. Mollat, 'Recherches sur les finances des ducs Valois de Bourgogne', *Revue historique*, ccxix (1958), 314; Surirey, op. cit., 92–7.

[2] *Dépêches des ambassadeurs milanais*, op. cit., iii (Paris, 1920), 90–91.

[3] 'Jean Juvenal des Ursins', op. cit.

[4] *Dépêches des ambassadeurs milanais*, op. cit., ii, 204.

of open conflict much depended on their wealth and their ability to raise forces; in 1465 Malletta thought 'all these *seigneurs* are short of cash or have no men except their gentlemen and subjects under their command'.[1] But what was the nature of the political pyramid beneath each prince, which might be useful not only in war but also in the no less complicated games of peace? To a certain extent there still seems to have been in France some reliance upon the purely feudal nexus: the duke of Bourbon still seems to have thought it worth while to call out his vassals and rear-vassals in Forez in April 1465.[2] But there were also more sophisticated means of linking seigneur and seigneur, seigneur and servant. Most spectacular of these, it has been alleged, were the princely orders of chivalry; but though the Burgundian *Toison d'or*, the Breton *Hermine* and the Orléans *Porc-épic* may have had a clearly political purpose, the purely chivalric seems to predominate in such exercises in an eccentric social convention as the *Ecu d'or*, the *Ecu vert à la dame blanche*, the *Fer de prisonnier*, the *Dragon* and the *Croissant*.[3] There were less cumbersome ways of collecting allies.[4] The feudal nexus had, with such things as the money fee for term of life, become etiolated enough; but with the final collapse of the idea of homage as an additional security to mutual interest it was still imagined that stability could be given to the shifting sands of interest by different oaths or by new methods of providing reward. The formal contracts, the *alliances*, which bound together on equal terms the princes of the fifteenth century are notorious; and some magnates at least experimented with the use of *alliances* with inferiors and created a diplomatic parallel to that of the English 'bastard feudalism'. In those who dealt with the administration of his estates a magnate might find a loyal nucleus for his affinity; and some seigneurs at least wooed clients with sinecure household office and pensions on the royal pattern. The acquisition of allies by these methods seems naturally to have been most rapid when magnates were faced, in the time of incompetent kings and of civil war, with the need to defend their interests: the evidence, for instance, for *alliances*

[1] Ibid., iii, 161.
[2] Letters of 27th April, 1465, Archives nationales, P.1402¹ cote 1225.
[3] 'Une Devise de chevalerie inconnue, créé par un comte de Foix? Le *Dragon*', *Annales du Midi*, lxxvi (1964), 77–82.
[4] The sources of material given without reference in this and the following paragraph will be found in 'Decayed and Non-Feudalism in Later Medieval France', *Bulletin of the Institute of Historical Research*, xxxvii (1964), 157–84.

with subordinates seems to get thinner after about 1450, though the princes had no less need to defend their interests against Louis XI than they had had against each other in earlier days. But we know all too little about French 'non-feudalism'; and how the leaguers of the Public Weal really raised their forces is throughly obscure.

How valid had these created loyalties been? Some of the *allié* families of the house of Foix seem to have shown considerable tenacity in fidelity between the 1370s and the 1440s. One should possibly not underestimate the ability of a seigneur paramount in his *pays* to command local loyalty. Of the contracts made with men further removed from the epicentre of his power one may have more doubt; their validity probably grew less as they approached those agreements of temporary convenience, the contracts in which the princes of the civil war confessed their eternal devotion to each other. For the *allié* the problem was much the same as for the client civil servant whom he resembled closely in position: at what stage was it prudent to stop risking all for one's lord? Loyalty was naturally a business much more complicated than simple apparent interest for men whose families had long attachment to those of their patrons: interest ran much deeper than the advantage of a moment. Loyalty to a seigneur in his *pays* might become inherent: in the south-west, in the north-east it might supplant the claim of sovereignty. How was a king to deal with this? The claim to rule by the grace of God was the first thing to be attacked: sovereignty was not mocked. And even loyalties apparently inherent could be sapped. Garsias du Faur, member of a loyal family of comital servants, chancellor of Jean V, count of Armagnac, expert negotiator of difficult matters, found happy employment as a president of the *parlement* of Toulouse after the fall of Lectoure.[1] The career of Philippe Pot, godson of Philippe le Bon, member of the *Toison d'or*, who abandoned the duke's grand-daughter for the novel office of *grand sénéchal* of Burgundy and a pension of 4,000 *livres tournois* from Louis XI and who was quite prepared to preach, in the interests of the Beaujeux, the doctrine of popular sovereignty at the estates general of 1484; or of Philippe de Commynes, who abandoned Charles le Téméraire for Louis in 1472 (but who ended up on the opposite

---

[1] A. Viala, *Le Parlement de Toulouse et l'administration royale laique (1420–1525 environ)*, (Albi, 1953) i, 124–5.

side in 1484) illustrated the way in which at times the most
devoted servant might seem to be in the game for money rather
than for love. The arrogation of superior interest, the creation
of a greater loyalty to the Crown, were clearly necessary acts for
a determined monarch. The great military *ordonnance* of 1439
forbade private armies: how much notice of it was taken by
prospective commanders and prospective troops depended
largely on the weight with which the royal hand was felt in their
locality. Naturally a king could not rule his country without the
co-operation of its magnates; but co-operation had degrees. In
1465 Malletta, who had a healthy respect for the mere force of
suzerainty, thought 'the subjects of these lords [of the Public
Weal] have nevertheless great fear to contradict the king':[1] a
king's rule, too, had degrees.

A king must rule: the greatest trouble comes when he does not,
not when he does. Chastellain clearly thought that in the end
Charles VII could rule; and that Louis XI could do so many
thought during his lifetime: long after his death the testimony
that he was feared above all is formidable. Both he and his
father faced magnate revolt; the fact that this occurred might
be evidence of their failure as kings but their success in suppressing it, or in avoiding its consequences, is at least tribute to
their ability after the event. 'In the kingdom of France,' wrote
Sir John Fortescue with some justice, 'they've never changed
their king, right from the time the country was first inhabited
by the French, except through the rebellion of such mighty
subjects':[2] French magnates, at least, sometimes tried like the
English to kill their kings. Charles VII and Louis XI escaped
assassination, death in civil war, usurpation; the *voye de faicte*
succeeded only in acquiring for those who undertook it the most
temporary of extra advantages. The problem of the overmighty
subject was to haunt many other kings than these; and each
was to fence with the spectre according to his own skill. Charles
VII and Louis XI may be judged on theirs.

If the major struggles of politics were thus personal rather
than 'constitutional', if the government could avoid 'constitutional' assemblies and could, on the whole, deal successfully with
magnates and their political pyramids, how did those inhabitants of the kingdom who had no assembly to protect them and

[1] *Dépêches des ambassadeurs milanais*, op. cit., iii, 161.
[2] *The Governance of England*, ed. C. Plummer (Oxford, 1885), 129.

no wish to adopt the *voye de faicte* fare in their relations with it? Churchmen, in principle, might be pacifists *par excellence*: what was the relationship of their section of society with the Crown? Essentially, in this political context, one thinks of the upper clergy as the political group *par excellence*. Certainly it is their interests which come out most clearly in the 'Church's' dealings with the government. Their relationship was a complicated one, involved in the complexities of ecclesiastical and, later, of Italian politics. Two objects of conflict may be isolated in the three-cornered struggle of pope, king and clergy: benefices and taxation. Essentially the greater clergy were out for the maximum independence they could get; and they fought for it enshrined in the liberties of the Gallican Church, classically expressed in the Pragmatic Sanction of Bourges of 1438 but current long before, occasionally in a more violent form. The attitude of the government varied. Briefly, Charles VII accepted the Gallican Pragmatic and wooed the pope with breaches of it; Louis XI accepted submission to the pope and bullied him with threats of the Pragmatic. On the whole there was more to be got for the Crown from the second process.

But as well as having problems *vis-à-vis* the pope—and the king—*qua* taxpayers and collators, the upper clergy had their problems *vis-à-vis* the king alone *qua* tenants, immunists and mere subjects. In the estates general of 1484 they might dwell long on the Pragmatic and the 'rights and liberties' of the Gallican Church, which 'king Clovis, St Charlemagne, St Louis, Philippe le Bel, king Jean, Charles V, Charles VI and latterly Charles VII', so they imagined, had defended: but they also dwelt on its 'prerogatives, privileges, rights, immunities, liberties and franchises', grievously diminished by the government of Louis XI.[1] A considerable amount of heated information on this problem under Charles VII (to whose reputation distance lent enchantment) is provided by Jean Juvenal des Ursins, successively *évêque-comte* de Beauvais, *évêque-duc* de Laon, *archévêque-duc* de Reims.[2] The two problems of the temporal and of temporal and spiritual jurisdiction were to a certain extent confounded in that they might both be 'grieved' by the actions of the *parlement* of Paris: a court which since the earlier

---

[1] Masselin, op. cit., 663, 665.
[2] Especially in the treatise, Verba mea auribus percipe, Domine, of the 1450's [Bibliothèque nationale, ms. fr. 2701, fols. 107vb–113vb].

fourteenth century had been extending its competence over ecclesiastical affairs and whose actions created one particular aspect of 'gallicanism'.[1] *Parlement* was not necessarily prejudiced against ecclesiastics, any more than Louis XI was prejudiced against nobles; but its actions and possibly more direct ones of the government provided the stuff of ecclesiastical complaint. That the king should provide remedy 'in preserving the name *most Christian*'[2] fell on the whole on the deaf ears of those who were prepared to use sweeping theories of sovereignty to limit the jurisdiction of the Church; however much they were prepared at the same time to uphold its Gallican liberties.

Under such pressure what could an ecclesiastic do? He could complain bitterly of such tyranny; he could threaten the sanctions of moral law; he could excommunicate. But the penalties of excommunication could be avoided[3] and moral sanctions and bitter complaints broke no bones. There remained the personal influence of each churchman; but this of necessity remains obscure. Few became more openly political in defence of their liberties. There were political bishops: Martin Gouge, bishop of Clermont, Guillaume de Champeaux, bishop of Laon, Thomas Basin, bishop of Lisieux, Jean Balue, bishop of Evreux, for example; but these men were politicians, members of a political entourage, rather than ecclesiastics forced into politics by intolerable interference with the rights of the Church. They belonged to the world of the court, not essentially to that of the Church; and although it could be argued that many high ecclesiastics might have passed through the court, it is as courtiers that those who remained politicians *par excellence* should be thought of, not as churchmen oppressed by tyranny. For these there was little remedy; and their moral views provided little danger for the government.

The upper bourgeoisie, were they much danger? Again one must probably exclude the courtiers, the politicians amongst them and think only of those whom their towns thought of as 'notable people and of some rank, who would be bold enough to talk in person'[4] to the king. Jacques Coeur apart, there were

[1] G. Mollat, 'Les Origines du gallicanisme parlementaire aux xive et xve siècles', *Revue d'histoire ecclésiastique*, xliii (1948), 90–147.

[2] Masselin, op. cit., 666.

[3] M. Morel, *L'Excommunication et le Pouvoir civil en France du droit canonique classique au commencement du xve siècle* (Paris, 1926).

[4] *Registres consulaires de la ville de Lyon*, ed. M. C. and G. Guigue, i (Lyon, 1882), 331.

few great bourgeois who lived, as it were, 'bourgeoisly' in the practice of trade. Their interests on the whole were those of their town: it is as bourgeois of Lyon or of Tours or of Rodez that one should think of them in this political context. What were the interests of their towns? Again, one defines them as liberties and immunities: the privileges of the town jealously guarded against infringement, prudently reconfirmed at regular intervals, the immunities of the town in matters of jurisdiction, the liberty of the town from some forms or all forms of taxation. It was these that sent the notable bourgeois on long and perilous journeys through France at the town's expense, to the king's courts and the king's courtiers. It was in defence of these that towns offered shy (or not so shy) presents to influential people, as Millau offered its congratulations to a newly appointed official of the *parlement* of Toulouse because he 'can do a great deal of good to the commons and in particular to the inhabitants of the town' or as Lyon gave ten *livres tournois* to the dauphin's secretary in 1420 'so that he should speak well of the town to monseigneur le dauphin' when the town had failed to send him troops.[1] The backstairs representations of such urban communities were an established thing by the fifteenth century;[2] and so were remissions of taxation for such virtuous causes as urban fortifications. But such representations brought, as we have seen, their own dangers: towns delivered themselves into the hands of the wolf.

A wolf capable, like Louis XI, of ravening ravened. Remissions were still made of taxation; but the private milking of important towns was continuous.[3] And the influence of the government was not confined to this. In so far as the upper bourgeoisie, superior members of the guilds, members of that mystical *maior et sanior pars* which provided the members in turn of the smaller and upper councils of the town, felt any pressure from the inferior artisans, from the lower bourgeois of the larger and lower councils or from those who were not bourgeois at all but simple 'inhabitants', royal support in the form of favourable theoretical regulations and practical support if the *menu peuple* broke into open violence was all too desirable to them. The government had no interest in proletarian revolt; but protection, against such things as combinations, for instance, was

[1] Viala, op. cit., i, 158; Guigue, op. cit., i, 252.
[2] 'The Failure of the French Medieval Estates', op. cit., 14.
[3] R. Gandilhon, *Politique économique de Louis XI* (Rennes, 1940), 286–91.

still desirable.[1] Caught between the inevitable millstones, the upper bourgeoisie had every interest in the end in playing in with the Crown.

And the *menu peuple*, in the towns, in the country, were they much danger? A combination of violent Parisians and left-wing university theorists could force a reforming ordinance out of the government in 1413. But although urban revolt was sporadic throughout the fifteenth century and although Jean Juvenal des Ursins could make dark hints of uprisings, more general insurrection is hard to find;[2] nor, even if it had come about, is it easy to see that it would have been of more danger than the *Jacquerie* or the *Tuchins*. Although it is not very likely that in 1422 the *populaires*' 'purse is like the cistern which has collected and still collects the waters and the drains of all the riches in this kingdom',[3] it still remained true that—allowing for a delay because of the war—in France as elsewhere labourers agrarian and industrial were very much better off than they had been before or, before very long, than they were to be again.[4] The seigneurial reaction of the later years of Louis XI's reign, the bad harvests of the last years: these might have been predisposing causes of revolt; but none seems to have occurred. For those who had suffered so much and who still suffered a little, it may have been that peace was worth it at any price. But peasant and urban revolts were not, in later medieval terms, serious political things.

There were those who thought tenderly of the *menu peuple*; there were forces—and not only theories of general subjection—which tended towards the unity of the orders of society (and it must be remembered that the orders were the upper orders); there were contradictory interests which cut across the stark lines which we have described; there were nobles of perhaps unusual loyalty to the Crown; there were royal officers who were prepared, on the surface at least, to protect those whom they administered from their more rapacious colleagues. On the surface of things the submarine currents are blurred, confused, less visible. And it is hard, perhaps, to justify an analysis which

[1] H. Sée, *Louis XI et les villes* (Paris, 1891), 30–7; Gandilhon, op. cit., 161 ff.
[2] Sée, op. cit., 176–83; 'Jean Juvenal des Ursins', op. cit.
[3] Alain Chartier, *Le Quadrilogue invectif*, ed. E. Droz, [Classiques français du moyen age], 2nd edn. (Paris, 1950), 34.
[4] E. H. Phelps Brown and S. V. Hopkins, 'Wage-rates and Prices: Evidence for Population Pressure in the Sixteenth Century', *Economica*, new series, xxiv (1957), 289–306.

shows an awareness of politics in terms of which very few people in the fifteenth century would have thought. But there are vivid flashes of insight recorded on the surface into motive and behaviour, into attitude and interest: one may perhaps make an approximation to the fifteenth-century way of thinking and the fifteenth-century way of action valid in modern terms. And perhaps as a result a number of problems are clarified.

They concern primarily the development of tyranny in France, the collapse of formal 'opposition', the birth of the *Ancien régime*. Arbitrary taxation and the over-notorious standing army were achieved essentially because of its weakness: the 'opposition' had no interest in opposing. Hostility to the government was aroused primarily by the more direct action of the king or his entourage or his servants upon some fairly powerful political figure or body. One should not underestimate the initiative of the entourage or the servants: to a considerable extent the tyrant was incapable of controlling the instruments of his tyranny. Since there was no peaceful means of expressing this hostility, if one could not remove its cause by counter-influence or counter-action in the courts, one was left with the *voye de faicte*, the way of direct action. For some groups in society this was unthinkable for practical reasons which the articulate, the literary, rationalized into principle. For some, who did not think in terms of political theory, it was thinkable: and with these rebels—or at least with their leaders—the unwieldy tyranny had, on the whole, to deal softly. Popular revolts, on the other hand, were negligible. But no one, except possibly members of the *menu peuple*, objected overmuch to the system. The practice of arbitrary rule in France was too deep-rooted for this. Yet it terrified Sir John Fortescue,[1] who had spent eight long and impoverished years in exile on the Meuse. The English were different, thought Fortescue; but for the causes of the difference between English and French society in the later Middle Ages one must retreat to the dimmest confines of their history, as one must advance into later periods to understand the consequences of the political *conjoncture* of the fifteenth century. Michelet's *vie intégrale* is not only '[ne] véritablement la vie qu'autant qu'elle est complète'; dominated by its past, it dominates its future.

---

[1] *Governance*, op. cit., 113–16; *De Laudibus Legum Anglie*, ed. S. B. Chrimes (Cambridge, 1942), 80–6.

X

D. M. Bueno de Mesquita

THE PLACE OF DESPOTISM IN
ITALIAN POLITICS

In this essay, the later Middle Ages will mean no more than a traditionally accepted chronological period in the history of Europe, approximately between the years 1250 and 1500. In Italy, the period largely coincides with the Renaissance, another traditional term which sets the peninsula somewhat apart from the rest of Europe. This difference of terminology raises complex problems of definition, 'periodization' and reciprocity of influences with which we shall not be concerned here. It also indicates one of the reasons for the peculiar interest which attaches to the Italian experience in these centuries. In politics as well as in art, Italy in the later Middle Ages has been seen as the breeding ground of new ideas and practices, as the fore-runner that gave exemplars to the states of western Europe in early modern times. Here, in the field of international relations, the technical problems of maintaining a 'balance of power' were tackled for the first time,[1] and diplomacy became a con-tinuous science if not yet a fully professional occupation.[2] Here, in the perhaps too famous phrase of Burckhardt, 'the State as a work of art' was born; or, in more modern terms which Burckhardt with his remarkable intuition had already in part anticipated,[3] the absolute power of the prince harnessed the

[1] A convenient summary by E. W. Nelson may be found in *Medievalia et Humanistica*, i (1943), 124–42.
[2] The most recent account is by G. Mattingly, *Renaissance Diplomacy* (1955), 55–118.
[3] See the pages on the Este of Ferrara, in *Civilization of the Renaissance in Italy*.

mechanism of bureaucratic administration to its purposes.[1]
And here some historians have recently discerned, not 'a world
dominated by mere power-politics', but a full awareness of the
momentous issues raised by a conflict between the forces of
freedom and tyranny.

Whichever theme we take, what is commonly called
'despotism' bulks large in it. In 1250 we are still, as far as Italy
north of Rome is concerned, in the age of the communes, the
self-governing cities. By the fifteenth century five regional states,
with their centres at Milan, Venice, Florence, Rome and
Naples, effectively controlled the politics of the peninsula,
though they did not rule the whole of its territory. Only one of
these five states strictly conformed to the pattern of a 'despotism',
the rule of a prince with acknowledged title to absolute power.
Yet when John Addington Symonds wrote in 1875 that 'the
fourteenth and fifteenth centuries may be called the Age of the
Despots in Italian history',[2] he followed a fashion which has
continued largely to prevail;[3] it is written into the titles of the
two most recent large-scale accounts of Italian history in the
later Middle Ages, widely as they differ from one another in
their points of view.[4] This emphasis on the *Signorie* owed something to the brilliant setting of the Renaissance courts. But they
were also the most characteristic autochthonous product of
Italian politics in the later Middle Ages, and they were best
equipped to display those features which seemed to anticipate
early modern political practice.

For Sismondi, whose *History of the Italian Republics* formed a
textbook of liberal thought in the early nineteenth century, they
were an evil product. Italy had lived through the most glorious
age of her post-Roman history between 1150 and 1250, when
the free and industrious citizens of the communes fought to
defend their right to govern themselves, against the would-be
tyranny of the Hohenstaufen emperors from Germany; the
'despots' were tyrants, wicked men who destroyed liberty from
within. Later in the nineteenth century, 'despotism' came to be

---

[1] Briefly discussed by F. Chabod in *Actes du colloque sur la Renaissance 1956* (1958),
65–8.
[2] J. A. Symonds, *Age of the Despots*, 3rd edn. (1926), 77.
[3] H. Baron, *Crisis of the early Italian Renaissance* (henceforth quoted as *Crisis*),
i, 11, emphasizes the oversimplification of this view.
[4] N. Valeri, *Signorie e Principati* (1949) (vol. 5 of *Storia d'Italia Illustrata* published
by Mondadori); L. Simeoni, *le Signorie* (1950) (in *Storia politica d'Italia* published
by Vallardi).

linked with the newly achieved political unity of Italy; it had not in fact united Italy, but it could be studied as a force tending to unification, the natural goal of Italian history, and therefore as a beneficial force. At the same time a fuller knowledge of the apparently chaotic conditions of the self-governing communes in the thirteenth century suggested that the rise of 'despotism' was not a cause of their decay but a consequence of their political bankruptcy; 'in contrast to a freedom which led to anarchy and to disintegration, the *Signoria* represented a higher form'[1]—a higher form of government because it was to some extent able to break through the barriers of communal society and to inaugurate a policy of 'social justice'.[2] In the twentieth century, a closer analysis of the social structure of politics and of the actual workings of government (rather than its formal declarations) has done a good deal to undermine these optimistic assumptions. 'The political practice of the *Signori* displays no other principles save that of the defeat of every attempt at resistance to them.'[3] Finally, tyranny has been seen as the challenge which evoked from the citizens of Florence a heroic response in the defence of their republican liberty. The Florentines, in a lone stand at a supreme crisis, accepted 'a challenge of history to save a chance for liberty in all Italy by securing the survival of the Florentine Republic'.[4]

My purpose in these pages is to consider what the phenomenon known as 'despotism' meant in Italy in the later Middle Ages, and there is no room for a detailed analysis of this fresh and significant interpretation of the Italian political scene.[5] Nevertheless, an understanding of the character of resistance to tyranny, of the motives that inspired it and the meaning of the liberty that it invoked, may serve to clarify some of the causes and intentions of tyranny itself. If liberty and tyranny are antithetical, it will help to know precisely what liberty signified; the more so as the word, already vested with a powerful emotive force, was widely used in different contexts, and recent

---

[1] G. Romano, in *Arch[ivio] St[orico] Lomb[ardo]*, xix (1892), 589.

[2] See below, p. 322.

[3] F. Cognasso, in *Arch. St. Lomb.*, 8, vi (for 1956), 17.

[4] H. Baron, *Crisis*, i, 157, describing the theme of the contemporary Florentine writer Goro Dati.

[5] Of which the chief exponent has been Dr Hans Baron. It will be evident that I do not accept all his conclusions; and also, I hope, that like every student of Italian history in this period, I am deeply in his debt.

historians have not always very carefully distinguished between them.[1]

This may seem of little moment, since the obvious and recognized mainspring of Florentine policy, included in all the contexts of liberty, was the resolute defence of the independence of the city, of its government by the citizens or a part of them, against all threats of external interference or dominion. Basically, this was what 'republican liberty' meant; and its continuity with the traditions and practice of government established by the communes—'that civic freedom which had been characteristic of Italian civilization during the Middle Ages'[2]—is not in dispute. The communes of the Lombard league, defending their 'ancient customs' against Frederick Barbarossa in the twelfth century, did not concern themselves much with political theory, or challenge the supreme *auctoritas* of the emperor; they fought for what they had got, the practice of government by men chosen from among themselves, as a guarantee against alien exploitation. When men called this 'freedom', they still used custom to sanction it; thus the Bolognese declared in 1289 that their acceptance of the pope's sovereignty must not infringe their 'ancient and wonted freedom'.[3] When Gino Capponi said in 1414 that he would prefer the rule of the *ciompi*, the unenfranchised labourers of Florence, to the tyranny of King Ladislaus of Naples,[4] we may wonder how long his opinion would have stood the test of experience, but we cannot doubt that he was expressing, in the strongest terms he could command, the same hostility to the prospect of an alien and arbitrary rule. In the meantime, however, ancient custom, clarified by unhampered exercise and re-defined in more sophisticated classical terms, had become republican liberty, closely attached to Ciceronian political principles; and—no less important in practice—changing political situations, bringing fresh needs and fresh opportunities, had created new methods of defending the liberty of Florence.

The defence of liberty is the theme of the first substantial body of diplomatic correspondence to have survived in Florence, from

[1] N. Rubinstein, in *Transactions of the Royal Historical Society*, 5, ii (1952), 21–45, analyses the meanings of liberty in fourteenth-century Florence.
[2] H. Baron in *South Atlantic Quarterly*, xxxviii (1939), 439; and similarly in *Journal of the History of Ideas*, iv (1943), 25–6.
[3] Quoted by D. Waley, *Papal State in the Thirteenth Century* (1961), 217.
[4] Baron, *Crisis*, i, 322.

the time of the Italian enterprise of Henry VII, king of the Romans and emperor-elect, in 1310–13.[1] Henry came from Germany, with the backing of the pope, to give peace and order to Italy; his programme included the healing of party conflicts and the return of the political exiles to their native cities. The guelf rulers of Florence at the time did not propose to jeopardize their own control of the government by letting their enemies back into the city. They discerned and expressed, with a political acumen rare in Italy at the time, both the scope and the implications of Henry's project; and the government of Florence took on itself for the first time the burdens of political leadership on a peninsular scale. The material centre of opposition to Henry lay in Naples, with the Angevin King Robert; but Florence was the mouthpiece. Wherever men were prepared to defend their freedom against the tyranny of the German king and his ghibelline associates, Florence offered encouragement and support, in terms carefully adapted to the status of the recipients. Thus, to the pope and to King Robert, they wrote in terms of the old guelf cause to which Henry's venture had restored some meaning; the liberty of the Florentines is their right to be 'devoted servants of Holy Mother Church' and of their lord the king of Naples. When they wrote to Giberto da Correggio, lord of Parma, a crucial figure in their plans for an assault on Henry's position in Lombardy, they spoke of liberty but not of the guelf cause or of communal freedom; here liberty is stripped to its essence, the throwing off of the yoke of servitude to German rule. Within the closer circle of their neighbours in the guelf alliance, the communes of Bologna, Lucca, Siena and Perugia, they wrote fraternally of a common defence of 'freedom and state'; this, like the old Lombard league, was a fraternal association for the mutual protection of freely chosen civic governments—provided always that they were guelf. Towards Pisa, the old enemy, equally republican but ghibelline and appealing to Henry for protection against the machinations of Florence, there was no fraternity; the destruction of Pisa had already taken a place in the catalogue of Florentine political ideas.[2]

---

[1] What follows is based on the selection of Florentine letters published by F. Bonaini, *Acta Henrici VII* (1877), part 2. W. M. Bowsky, *Henry VII in Italy* (Lincoln, Nebraska, 1960) gives a full and useful account of the impact of Henry's enterprise upon Italy.

[2] H. Finke, *Acta Aragonensia*, ii (1908), 527, doc. 351 (winter 1308–9): 'ut . . . civitas Pisana et pars predicta pereat et nunquam resurgat'.

'Popular liberty', the fraternal union of republican cities, continued to play a part in the policies of Florence throughout the fourteenth century. It was largely proclaimed, for instance, during the conflict with the papacy in the years 1375–7 which is known as the war of the Eight Saints. Alarmed by the symptoms of the pope's growing determination to create an effective power on the southern borders of Tuscany, the Florentines invoked the cause of freedom for the communes of the neighbouring papal dominions, groaning under the tyranny of the pope and his French officials.[1] At the same time they wooed their Tuscan neighbours in the name of 'Tuscan liberty', the inviolability of the province from external interference that was vital to their own security. 'Tuscany for the Tuscans' might not necessarily have meant 'Tuscany for the Florentines',[2] but other episodes besides that of Pisa had already indicated the possibility.

In 1336, when a rapid expansion of the power of the della Scala, lords of Verona, had brought the Tuscan city of Lucca under their dominion, the Florentines formed an alliance with the republic of Venice against the common enemy. Their joint purpose was declared in the sort of language that the Florentines had used against Henry VII: 'to destroy and wipe out the tyrannical evil of the della Scala, and to give liberty and freedom to the lands and peoples oppressed by them'. The cities freed from this tyranny were to be restored 'to a peaceful and common state'—an ambiguous phrase, but it seems clear that it envisaged the restoration of a guelf communal régime in Lucca. A year later, when the alliance was renewed, it was agreed that Lucca, once it had been wrested from the tyrant, should be subject to Florence.[3] Florentine political rule in Tuscany had been adumbrated as an alternative to Florentine leadership of the free guelf Tuscan communes, to meet the changed situation created by the menace of Italian *Signorie*.

The true character of this alternative can be clearly discerned in the history of the next hundred years. From 1340 to 1447, the real threat to the inviolability of Tuscany came from north of the Apennines, and Florentine external policy was governed by

[1] See now G. A. Brucker, *Florentine Politics and Society* (Princeton, 1962), 265–315, for the causes of this war and the tone of Florentine propaganda.
[2] Compare N. Rubinstein in the article quoted above, 45.
[3] Ibid., 34; and more fully discussed by G. Tabacco in *Studi di Storia in onore di Ettore Rota* (1958), 119–25.

a remarkably consistent, though not entirely unbroken, resistance to the evident ambitions of the Visconti rulers of Milan. The conflict did much to crystallize the attitude of Florence towards their neighbours. In 1384, the Florentines gained possession of Arezzo—not for the first time, but this time for good—and pushed southward against the rights or claims of Siena.[1] In 1406, Florentine diplomacy, money and troops finally overwhelmed the stubborn hostility of the Pisans and brought Pisa under Florentine dominion. Lucca, the Achilles' heel of Florentine statesmanship, precariously survived spasmodic attacks on her independence.

If we apply a 'realistic' political assessment to this conduct, it makes perfectly good sense. In the new Italy forged out of the ruins of Hohenstaufen imperialism in the century after Frederick II's death, the small city living in republican liberty—or indeed under the absolute rule of a 'despot'—was coming to be seen as a potentially dangerous anachronism. It created a political vacuum that attracted more powerful forces. 'Liberty' had become a privilege that the strong could not afford to allow to the weak. If the Florentines did not take dominion over their neighbours, their enemies would do so.[2] Other and less creditable motives—the prospect of economic advantage; old hostilities that had become woven into a habit of mind—were also involved. When they needed friends, they continued to adopt the language of 'popular liberty'. 'It seems necessary to us,' they wrote in 1400, 'that all those in Italy whose purpose is to live in freedom should form an understanding among themselves, and that each one should assume the charge and concern for the preservation of the others.'[3] But a new version of 'liberty' was taking over—the *libertas Italiae* which entitled them to deny to others what they meant to keep for themselves because otherwise, as they professed to believe, the whole of Italy would fall to the tyrant.

[1] D. M. Bueno de Mesquita, *Giangaleazzo Visconti* (1941), ch. 8. The aggression seems clear, though I would modify some of my more sweeping statements about its scope and purpose. Was it a product of the change of régime in Florence in 1382? The facts do not easily fit any neat answer to this question; e.g. the most violent advocate of war against Pisa in the 1360s was a leader of the 'progressive' party: M. B. Becker in *Medieval Studies*, xxiv (1962), 63.

[2] C. C. Bayley, *War and Society in Renaissance Florence* (Toronto, 1961), 97–100, describing the discussions over the attack on Lucca in 1429.

[3] My *Giangaleazzo Visconti*, 365–6, doc. 15; a convenient example among many that could be quoted.

The prospective victims naturally took a different view. It suited the Florentines to identify tyranny with the rule of a despot. The tyranny of Florence was at least as unwelcome, in Pisa or Siena, as the tyrant of Milan. So, too, when they were able to do so early in the sixteenth century, the aristocracy of the mainland cities subject to Venetian dominion denounced 'the three thousand tyrants', the fully enfranchised citizens of Venice.[1] The Florentines were too realistic a people to be subdued by a principle: the principle of communal freedom to which their neighbours, anachronistically perhaps, were no less heirs than themselves. A fanfare of libertarian trumpets greeted the alliances between the republics of Florence, Venice, Genoa and Siena against Filippo Maria Visconti in the 1420s and 1430s; but it has yet to be shown that any political decisions in these decades were influenced by the noble ideal of a union of free republics.[2] And when the Florentines in 1429 prepared another assault upon Lucca, the Sienese, alarmed for their own freedom, quickly turned to the duke of Milan for protection.

Finally, *libertas Italiae* came to mean Italy for the Italians. Foreshadowed in the literature and propaganda of the fourteenth century, this meaning came to the fore after the war of the Milanese Succession between 1447 and 1454 had transformed the character of Italian political relations. The farsighted decision of Cosimo de Medici to support the bid of the *condottiere* Francesco Sforza for the heritage of Filippo Maria Visconti, and so to prolong the tyranny that the Florentines had denounced and defied for a century, could have only one purpose; the disintegration of the duchy of Milan would create a political vacuum that the republic of Venice would be bound to fill, and grow too powerful in the process. The hostility between Venice and Florence did not spring suddenly to life at this point. The decisive events at the beginning of the century, when Venice took over a substantial dominion on the mainland and Florence acquired Pisa and an outlet to the sea, had prepared the way for it. But from 1450, the unlimited greed and ambition of the Venetians became the dominant theme of Florentine propaganda, and ultimately an enduring historical

---

[1] In 1509: A. Bonardi in *Miscellanea di Storia Veneta*, 2, viii (1902), 362–3.
[2] As Dr Baron appears to suggest: e.g. *Crisis*, i, 342–7.

myth.[1] The free or republican character of governments no longer served even as a political counter.

In the second half of the fifteenth century, Italian statesmen appeared to have found an answer to the problem of isolating and confining the aggression of ambitious states. Fear of Venice rather than the superior force of the dukes of Milan now dominated north Italian affairs.[2] But there was also a growing awareness of the dangers that lurked outside Italy. In 1454, Francesco Sforza and Venice wrote the exclusion of interference by foreign powers into the terms of what became a 'universal league' of the Italian states, designed to discourage attempts to alter the political map of Italy.[3] The league as a political force soon foundered, but its static purpose was on the whole achieved until the full force of a foreign power upset the equilibrium. Then it became clear that the resources of Venice, suspect and vilified, were needed to keep Italy for the Italians. But the last slender hope, a revival of the universal league, collapsed between 1495 and 1498; Florence remained outside it, moved by a unanimous determination, in the most democratic phase of her history, to deprive the Pisans of the republican liberty that they had recently regained. When Machiavelli wrote his great plea for *libertas Italiae* in the last chapter of the *Prince*, Italy for the Italians was already a lost cause, and he was probably too close to and involved in events to observe how entangled the uses of liberty had become. He stated candidly that Pisa had for a century 'been held in servitude by the Florentines' (just as his friend Francesco Vettori admitted that the Florentines governed their *contado*, the district immediately subject to the commune, 'by the method of tyranny').[4] But in full accord with Florentine opinion, he dismissed the Pisan appeal for liberty as 'a refuge in rebellion'.[5]

It is possible to do justice to the significant achievement of the

---

[1] The extract from the memorials of Benedetto Dei, published by G. degli Azzi in *Arch[ivio] St[orico] It[aliano]*, cx (1952), 103–13 affords a virulent example, which brings out the importance of commercial rivalry in the East.

[2] F. Catalano in *Nuova Rivista Storica*, xli (1957), 251 refers to the 'pre-eminent position' of Milan, in the course of an interesting assessment of Italian diplomacy in the second half of the fifteenth century.

[3] R. Cessi in *Atti dell'Istituto Veneto*, cii (1942–3), 99–176 is the best account of the purpose and vicissitudes of the league. See also V. Ilardi in *Studies in the Renaissance*, vi (1959), 129–66. In fact, most of the troubles of the period started in Naples or in Rome.

[4] 'Modo tyrannico': C. C. Bayley, op. cit., 277.

[5] *Principe*, cap. 5; ed. L. A. Burd (1891), 204–5.

Florentines in the later Middle Ages without reading more into 'liberty' than a devoted attachment to their own independence. They attained a remarkably coherent vision of the issues of Italian politics seen in the light of their own interests, and an outstanding capacity for the articulate expression of their own point of view. They maintained their independence, and in doing so they launched a new and constructive movement in the study of history and politics.[1] We may wonder, as the 'civic humanists' did in the fifteenth century, from what source Florence drew her power of survival and her intellectual supremacy.

For 150 years after the proclamation of the Ordinances of Justice in 1293, the supreme executive magistrates of Florence were called the Priors of the Gilds, and the gilds stood at the centre of the city's formal constitution. Their organization reflected that broad diversification of industrial activity which, combined with a social mobility allowing the influx of new blood from the countryside, has been seen as the key to the survival of Florentine republicanism.[2] 'Socio-economic' analysis has recently disproved the belief that the lesser gilds maintained a decisive hold over the magistracies and councils of the republic for a whole generation between 1343 and 1378,[3] and has underlined the evidence that 'political agitation and economic disaffection among il popolo minuto were pervasive throughout the Trecento'.[4] Artisans and shopkeepers did not rule Florence. But as long as the rulers found it worthwhile to give them a sense of identification with the régime,[5] their ideas had a chance to survive in the political language and outlook of the city.

The political programme of the gilds, set out in the Ordinances of Justice, can be described quite precisely as liberty, equality and fraternity. Fraternity was the essence of the medieval gild system, and the first clause of the Ordinances

---

[1] See especially H. Baron in *Journal of the History of Ideas*, iv (1943), 21–48; and more briefly in *South Atlantic Quarterly*, xxxviii (1939), 441–8.

[2] H. Baron in *Comparative Studies in Society and History*, ii (1959–60), 445–9.

[3] M. B. Becker and G. A. Brucker in *Medieval Studies*, xviii (1956), 97. The 'new citizens' who led the attack on the *Parte Guelfa* were men of substance: see the interesting paper by M. B. Becker, ibid., xxiv (1962), 35–82.

[4] M. B. Becker in *Comparative Studies in Society and History*, ii (1959–60), 424.

[5] Becker and Brucker in the article just quoted, 102. Professor Becker seems to give more weight to this in the article quoted in the same note: see especially 68, where the governments of 1372–8 are described as 'the most democratic of all Florentine régimes'.

set it as a goal to be achieved not only within each gild but throughout the whole gild society. Liberty may have meant no more than freedom from the molestations of the powerful families of magnates against whom the Ordinances were primarily directed. Equality meant an equal status for all gilds-men, but not for the *ciompi*. Nevertheless, gild members and their families must have made up a very substantial and indeed a formidable backbone of the Florentine people.[1] The chief magistrates of the city were chosen—by however rigged and weighted a system—from among them, and were under obliga-tion to watch over their interests. 'The Priors and Standard-bearer', runs the preamble to an ordinance designed to restore the spirit of fraternity damaged by the illicit practices of par-ticular gilds, 'among the other duties of their office, are obliged to care and ensure that the gilds and gildsmen of the city of Florence are preserved and live in peaceful and quiet and free state . . . and that equality is maintained among them'.[2]

There was little prospect indeed that these aspirations could be achieved. But they continued to form part of the ordinary vocabulary of Florentine politicians in the fourteenth century.[3] They were even more remote from reality when the humanists took them up in the fifteenth century, and found the secret of Florentine strength in the freedom of all her people equally to take part in government.[4] The force of their argument lay in the long familiarity of the Florentines with language of this kind. They were not the people to be deceived by the curious hybrid of a régime devised by the Medici, and quickly recognized the hand of a tyrant in the electoral manipulations by which the family secured its power. The aristocratic families who regretted their lost control of the state may have drawn arguments from the humanists, but the basic terms of liberty and tyranny in which they expressed their resentment were older than

---

[1] A quarter, or a third, of the population? The Ordinances of Justice (the best edition is in G. Salvemini, *Magnati e Popolani in Firenze* (1899)) assumed that the gilds could muster at any moment a force of at least 4,000 men. The population of Florence at the time was in the region of 100,000: the most recent discussion is by E. Fiumi in *Arch. St. It.*, cviii (1950), 78–118.

[2] Florence, Archivio di Stato: Provvisioni, x, 216t (4th April, 1300).

[3] For instance, G. A. Brucker, *Florentine Politics and Society*, 67, n. 45 (equalitas); 192, n. 169 (fraternitas); 372, n. 111 (libertas popularis), but this was a constant theme: see also M. B. Becker in *Medieval Studies*, xxiv (1962), 64–82.

[4] See e.g. Baron, *Crisis*, i, 354 (Poggio Bracciolini); E. Garin in *Rivista Storica Italiana*, lxxi (1959), 200 (Leonardo Bruni) : compare L. Simeoni, *le Signorie* ii, 655–6 on the actual conditions of the time.

humanism in Florentine political parlance.[1] The lesser men could still be moved by the prospect of a 'large state', that is a form of government in which they had a full chance to participate. This prospect divided them from the *optimates* and so helped the Medici to keep control;[2] but when the two wings of opposition, swollen by desertions from the Medici party, came together at last in the aggravated circumstances of November 1494, the Medici could no longer prevail and the 'large state' came into being.

We may see, then, in the broad structure of the gilds, something that helped to strengthen the sentiment of freedom and an attachment to the republican constitution; and, in the party conflicts which gave some weight to the support of the gilds, a chance to keep their aspirations alive.[3] But the search for a positive key to Florentine democracy should not be allowed to distort the true nature of the problem. For if republican liberty was the heritage of the Italian city-state, it is not its survival but its disappearance that marks a breach of tradition and an outrage to sentiment. There is plenty of evidence, from the thirteenth century to the fifteenth, that the liberty enshrined in the 'ancient customs' of the communes was cherished in the valley of the Po as well as in the Tuscan hills. The cities of Tuscany had their *Signori*, but none of them endured a *Signoria* on the Lombard model, a dynasty vested with absolute power, before the sixteenth century. The Bolognese, in their chequered constitutional history, made use of their strategic political situation and the nominal sovereignty of the pope to preserve their independence; and the Bentivoglio, who established a *Signoria* scarcely less informal than that of the Medici in the fifteenth century, found it convenient to propagate the doctrine that their power was the only means to safeguard the liberty of Bologna.[4] Opportunity and resources offer a rational

---

[1] See e.g. A. M. Brown in *Journal of the Warburg and Courtauld Institutes*, xxiv (1961), 207, on Alamanno Rinuccini's *Dialogus de Libertate*; and a fuller account by F. Adorno in *Rivista Critica di Storia di Filosofia*, vii (1952), 19–40.

[2] See especially the debates in late 1465, described by G. Pampaloni in *Arch. St. It.*, cxix (1961), 11–62, 241–81.

[3] Professor Becker, in the articles quoted above, attributes some part in this to tensions between 'personal' and 'impersonal' forces. If I understand his terms aright, these represent policies or methods favoured by the parties.

[4] C. M. Ady, *The Bentivoglio of Bologna* (1937), 154; the devotion of the Bolognese to their 'liberty' is one of the themes of her book. Its use by the Bentivoglio has been further discussed by R. D. H. Gardner, *Politics and Propaganda under Giovanni II Bentivoglio* (B.Litt. thesis in the University of Oxford, 1963).

explanation of the marked divergence between the fate of the communes in Tuscany and in Lombardy; and, indeed, between that of Florence and of the neighbours increasingly over-shadowed by her power. 'Despotism' was a remedy for a disease that was certainly present in Tuscany; but was it present in so acute a form?

There is in the first place the geographical answer, which the traveller can read from such vantage points as the walls of the old city of Bergamo, looking southward on a clear day. For some 200 miles, from Lake Maggiore eastward to the Adriatic coast, there are virtually no natural boundaries between the Alps and the Apennines, save the Po and its lateral tributaries; and the same conditions are renewed to the south-east, in the narrow strip of the Romagna that lies between the Apennines and the sea. The rivers, and above all the Po, were the highways of the Middle Ages, which did not separate men or cities but brought them closer together. In the great triangle whose base lay on the Adriatic and whose sides were the mountains, the old Roman *civitates* clustered thickly on the ground, drawing their life blood from the rivers. This was a more intensely competitive geo-political environment than that of the Tuscan hills, and if the conflicts it engendered were no more bitter or enduring, they were more acute and their consequences more decisive.

In the second place, the large productive circles among the population of the greater Lombard cities were more exposed on the whole than those of Tuscany to the interference of elements powerful enough to affect the political development of the city. The archbishop of Milan, in particular, was a great landowner in the district dependent on the city, and his estates supported many noble families who held them in fief from him, who attended his court in the city and had their houses there and many other interests besides, including the expectation of a major share in the government of the commune. It would be difficult even here to draw any clear-cut line between 'feudal' and 'commercial' or 'bourgeois' interests in the thirteenth century, but men of this kind led the factions whose conflicts ended in the creation of a *Signoria* in Milan. At Padua, for long the eastern bulwark of communal institutions and the guelf cause, the feudal vassals of the bishop who were active in the city in the twelfth century included the da Romano and the da

Carrara,[1] familiar names in the history of despotism. The same contacts certainly existed in Tuscany, but the larger cities, except for Pisa where maritime enterprise gave a special outlet, seem to have been better insulated against this kind of interference. The feudal antecedents of the leading civic families of Florence in the thirteenth century are seriously in doubt.[2] The bishops of these cities had been less richly endowed with political authority, and this probably helped to lessen the impact of the feudal countryside on civic life.

Third, the region between Alps and Apennines had borne the brunt of military resistance to the Hohenstaufen emperors. War became endemic in this region from the time that Frederick issued his challenge to the communes in 1236, and he left behind him a legacy of virtually permanent military conflict. Once again the impact of these circumstances is most apparent at Milan, which led the opposition to the emperor. The habit of military leadership engendered by the long struggle for liberty was re-inforced by the need for a strong hand to exact the heavy taxation still required, from an economy weakened by an exhausting conflict.[3]

Most of the characteristic conditions which paved the way for the *Signorie* are inherent in these three features, whose pressure was at its highest in the great plain formed by the waters of the Po. 'Factions in search of power'[4] were to be found everywhere, but it was not everywhere that individuals were equipped with the force and the opportunity to take advantage of the situation to their own profit. The prototype of the *Signoria* emerged in the chaotic aftermath of Hohenstaufen failure: represented brutally by Ezzelino da Romano in the east of the plain, and with more political insight by Uberto Pallavicino in the west.[5] These men were military dictators whose original force stemmed from the tenants of their estates, whose sanction (in so far as they had any) derived from the imperial cause, and whose initial success carried them into

[1] From the documents published by A. Gloria, *Codice Diplomatico Padovano 1101–83 (Deputazione Veneta di Storia Patria*, 1879–81).

[2] The fullest recent discussion is by E. Fiumi in *Arch. St. It.*, cxv (1957), 385–439.

[3] See especially the comments of E. Franceschini in *Storia di Milano* (Fondazione Treccani degli Alfieri), iv (1954), 277–87.

[4] F. Cognasso in *Arch. St. Lomb.*, 8, vi (for 1956), 10.

[5] Ibid., 20–43, for recent appraisals of the political position of Pallavicino by U. Gualazzini and E. Nasalli Rocca.

projects too ambitious for their resources to sustain or their neighbours to tolerate. The first family to establish an enduring *Signoria*, the d'Este of Ferrara, flourished as military leaders of the guelf party throughout the eastern end of the plain. The *Signori* were the chosen instruments of party dictatorship; but the fate of the party came to depend on the military and political capacity of its instrument, and those who proved capable outlived the need for party support. Such men were less easily to be found in the Tuscan countryside, and less indispensable in the intermittent warfare of the Tuscan communes.[1]

By 1350, the formative age of the *Signorie* was over, and it was clear that the Visconti, now hereditary lords of Milan, had scooped most of the profit. The cities of central and western Lombardy submitted to their rule—a little less hurtful to civic pride than that of another commune—and remained the hard core of their dominion through the vicissitudes of the next hundred years. They had built their power on the superior resources of Milan, now harnessed more effectively under their control,[2] and they had no serious rivals north of the Apennines apart from Venice, normally concerned in the fourteenth century to limit her commitments on the mainland. Their achievement made them in some respects atypical of Italian 'despotism', in domestic as well as in foreign policy. The problems created by the government of a dominion of this size, with a population of nearly a million subjects,[3] differed substantially from those of a small *Signoria* restricted to one *civitas*, such as that of the Gonzaga in Mantua.[4] They imposed a higher degree of formality and a stronger emphasis on impersonal rules. But if the duchy of Milan was not entirely typical of 'despotic' government in Italy, its particular problems and the more highly evolved forms of government that it devised to meet them give it a special significance; and the records that have survived, particularly for the period of the Sforza, enable us

---

[1] Thus Pisa had to call in the Umbrian Count Guido da Montefeltro from his exile in Piedmont in 1289.

[2] For the importance of Milan, see e.g. G. Barni in *Arch. St. Lomb.*, n.s. vi (1941) 16–17.

[3] K. J. Beloch, *Bevölkerungsgeschichte Italiens*, ii (1940), 239–52 (Parma and Piacenza) and iii (1961), 169–242 (the rest of the Duchy). His evidence, roughly adapted for the late fifteenth century, suggests a population of about 900,000.

[4] The administrative methods of the smaller *Signorie* are in need of further study; but see, for the Malatesta, P. J. Jones in *Italian Renaissance Studies*, ed. E. F. Jacob (1960), 221–44.

to see a good deal of the system at work at the peak of its development.[1]

The stages by which the *Signorie* equipped themselves with a juridical title to an authority unlimited by external restraints do not need to be retold.[2] The powers conferred upon them by the communes, and later by the emperors, ultimately placed them above the law. The dukes of Milan were true masters of their state, and could give commands, as Lorenzo de Medici rather enviously observed in 1485.[3] It was accepted political doctrine that they were 'absolved from the laws'; and,[4] in a sense, that their subjects were not free. When Galeazzo Maria Sforza, who had married a Savoyard princess, proposed to grant certain financial concessions in 1474, he emphasized that this should not be done in such a way 'as to put our subjects in freedom, like those of Savoy'.[5]

This comment must not be taken beyond its immediate context, the absence of a right of consent to taxation; this is another meaning of 'liberty', and since it had quite general currency it affords some indication of what men were really concerned about at the time.[6] The duchy of Milan based its government upon authoritarian, absolutist principles, but it does not follow that it was 'despotic' or arbitrary in its normal practice, that it was what was called a tyranny *quoad exercitium*. 'This is our will' was the ultimate sanction inherent in the system, and often used by the government. But *voluntas*, which in the last resort took the place of *lex*, could be used in the interest of the subject. Part of the 'office' of the prince was 'to set aside the statutes'[7] or, to put it more fully, 'to dispense from decrees and ordinances, for the wellbeing of our subjects, in

[1] The general account that follows of government in the Duchy of Milan is based primarily on the administrative records of the last twenty years of the fifteenth century, in the Archivio di Stato of Milan. Where specific references are given to Cart[eggio] Sf[orzesco] or to Miss[ive], they are to documents in this collection. I hope to publish a more detailed and fully substantiated account later.

[2] See especially E. Salzer, *Anfänge der Signorie in Oberitalien* (Ebering's *Historische Studien* 14, 1900); and F. Ercole, *Dal Comune al Principato* (1929), 53–354.

[3] F. Catalano in *Storia di Milano* (Fondazione Treccani degli Alfieri), vii (1956), 371.

[4] See for instance the argument that 'la vostra Signoria que est supra legem, non serà obligata servare un decreto, quale avesse facto ella medesma'; I. Ghinzoni in *Arch. St. Lomb.*, xi (1884), 510–11, doc. 10 (9th April, 1474).

[5] Ibid., 500, doc. 1 (19th March, 1474).

[6] See my paper in *Italian Renaissance Studies*, ed. E. F. Jacob (1960), 213–14 for some examples.

[7] 'Statutis abrogare': Miss. 173, f. 83t–4 (to Melchione Sturiono, 29th January, 1489).

cases where no wrong ensues to anybody from our doing so'.[1] If the subjects did not have 'freedom', they certainly had rights, which the government declared that it meant to respect.

The test of the way in which the system worked must be the acts rather than the words of the government. It is quite easy to find specific cases which demonstrate the hypocrisy of the concern for justice and welfare constantly expressed by the dukes of Milan.[2] It would be no less easy to find evidence to show that their concern was perfectly genuine. Either course is likely to lead to abstract judgments which will not help us to understand either the men or the pressures upon them. The natural concern of any régime is to survive, an exceptionally acute task in the unstable condition of Italian politics in the later Middle Ages. A government does not stress more than it need, in its daily dealings with its subjects, that it intends to go on ruling them whether they like it or not, but it will take such action as it can to achieve that purpose. When it is equipped for the purpose with a formal doctrine of power absolved from the law, it is subject to an immense moral strain. If the ruler chose to satisfy his inclinations and take what he wanted, there was no human law that could call him to account. Irresponsibility in personal conduct, fed by such a doctrine, accounts for much in the more bizarre and bloodstained episodes of the *Signorie*. There were few who would be astonished or particularly shocked if the prince indulged himself in moderation.

Yet the history of the Visconti and the Sforza suggests that there were limits beyond which it was unsafe for a ruler to trespass, and indeed that the limits became narrower as time went by. Of Matteo II, one of the three nephews of Archbishop Giovanni Visconti who succeeded him in the *Signoria* in 1354, we know too little to be sure why his brothers promptly eliminated him, but the narrative sources hint that he was too disgraceful a character to be safe in power. Giovanni Maria Visconti, the child who inherited the duchy in 1402, grew up violent and incompetent, and was violently removed, by whose hand no one save his brother felt bound to care. Galeazzo Maria

---

[1] Miss. 152, f. 3 (to the Podestà of Lodi's Vicar, 2nd September, 1480).
[2] See for Francesco Sforza, whose reputation in this respect stands high, the cautious scepticism of F. Fossati (who has most fully studied the records of his government) in *Arch. St. Lomb.*, 8, vii (for 1957), 370–83. The evidence used for the 'bad government' of Ludovico Sforza by F. Catalano in *Belfagor*, xi (1956), 412–14, 505–17, is also one-sided.

Sforza, not without qualities as a ruler but who went too far in the bestiality of his private conduct, if the stories told of him are true, fell to an assassin's dagger in 1476. There were no doubt contingent circumstances in each case, but a growing interest in tyrannicide reflected its value as an instrument of human judgment upon those whom human law could not touch.

On the whole, however, the Visconti and the Sforza took the task of governing their dominion seriously. Most of them were superstitious, and all of them were outwardly devout—that is, diligent in observance of the rites of the Church. When the humanists began to take a hand in their education, it was generally to emphasize the congruity between Christian virtues and classical standards of conduct. They could not be totally unaware that the *absolutum imperium* of the prince did not absolve them from the law of God or from responsibility for the well-being of their subjects, as indeed even their secular advisers were at times prepared to remind them. A long legal opinion submitted by a privy councillor for the guidance of Ludovico Sforza in 1481 ends with a two-edged statement that no further conclusion need be offered, 'for his Excellency is far-sighted, and knows well what great bounty God is wont to bestow, especially on princes who live under the law and fear of God'. Ludovico took it in good part, and replied 'that he was willing to do anything rather than end up in hell'.[1]

It was in fact in the interest of the ruler to accept these obligations, for valid principles of government could prove a source of strength to a title that was never wholly secure. How does one man, with the technical resources of government at his disposal in the fifteenth century, impose his absolute and arbitrary will upon a million? In the thriving and relatively sophisticated society of the Italian cities, the methods of Ezzelino da Romano—force of arms and ruthless terror unsupported by more constructive measures—had not proved conducive to permanence. The progress from party leaders to princes called both for a more fully integrated method of government, and for a programme of wider appeal than that to

[1] Raymondino Lupo (Marquis) of Soragna to Dr Jacopo Antiquario (secretary for ecclesiastical affairs) in Cart. Sf. 1085, 29th September, 1481 (there is another legal opinion from Lupo of the same date; this one is marked 'super negotio Clarevallis'). In whatever spirit Ludovico's reply was made, Antiquario thought it worthy of record at the foot of the letter: 'XXXo. Sept. 1481. Rettuli ex ordine que supra narrantur Illmo. d. Ludovico: qui respondit omnia se magis uelle facere quam ad domum diaboli ire'.

the now dubious loyalty of the feudal nobility who had rallied to the ghibelline cause under Archbishop Ottone Visconti in the later thirteenth century.

The new mechanism of government evolved gradually, but under Filippo Maria Visconti in the first half of the fifteenth century it had acquired all the institutions and methods that sufficed with few modifications for the needs of the Sforza.[1] The privy council dealt with all 'affairs of state' that the duke chose to delegate to it; the chancellery was becoming the hub of all business, and its chief, the first secretary, was as near to being a prime minister under the Sforza as the personal control of the duke allowed; the *camera*, better described as an exchequer than as a chamber,[2] collected, administered and accounted for the ducal revenues; and a number of smaller departments dealt with specialized branches of administration. In the cities and other administrative districts, the executive bodies and councils inherited from the communes acted in the diminishing sphere of local government, with correspondingly negligible resources;[3] the *podestà* kept order and did justice; captains commanded the castles and fortresses of the dominion, whose garrisons helped to maintain order as well as security; the referendaries watched over the duke's revenues and accounted for them to the *camera*; and the commissioners created by Filippo Maria Visconti formed the main link in the system, in constant touch with chancellery and privy council, and responsible in each city for the broad sphere of government that was regularly described as 'business of state'. The vicars general, legates of the duke with special authority, were a final co-ordinating agency, for they heard local evidence and submitted a full report on the conduct of provincial officials at the expiry of their term of office—or earlier, if local complaints were loud and substantial enough. Every department and official had standing orders, approved by the duke. On paper, at least, Francesco Sforza took over in 1450 an ordered and closely knit structure of government, with a defined establishment of posts, fixed salaries, short-term appointments of provincial officers and a well designed

---

[1] See the account in C. Santoro, *Uffici del Dominio Sforzesco* (1948), Introduction.

[2] If the divorce of the household from government be any test of a modern state, the Duchy of Milan under the Sforza was certainly modern; but this is not so obviously true under the Visconti—even under Filippo Maria.

[3] Though their importance in liaison with the government has perhaps been underestimated.

machinery for inspecting their competence and honesty before renewing, transferring or promoting them.

The growth of this impressive administrative establishment had its own impact on the manner in which government was conducted. It still depended largely on the constant driving force of the ruler—or perhaps of a reliable first secretary.[1] But its purpose was to create an understandable routine that would relieve the burdens upon the duke. Most of the surviving acts of the Visconti are of a general character, enactments in which they laid down the norms of conduct for their subjects, which tell us little of administrative practice. There is a rough and ready air about the government of Bernabò Visconti in the second half of the fourteenth century, but it appears to have been already embryonically inspired by the ideas to which the administrative records of the Sforza bear abundant testimony.[2] Those records leave no doubt that the purpose of ducal government in Lombardy in the fifteenth century was to maintain a speedy and efficient administration, designed certainly to provide the duke with all the material well-being required for his private and his public state, but designed also to do justice to his subjects, to protect their rights and redress their wrongs. Since the whole system emanated from the power and authority of the prince, it could be and certainly was on occasion used to inflict wrong for the satisfaction of his desires. But the many letters of the chancellery to the duke's officers, privately instructing them in the handling of individual cases, time and again proclaim the traditional concepts of medieval government: the common good; *ius alicui*, to each man his right; special concern for widows, orphans and the poor; care for divine worship; equality of burdens. Officials were indeed often in much need of this kind of education in the performance of their duties. We should not discount the fact that the government was prepared to give it to them, and that these principles, repeated often enough, could create the standards by which it appeared to invite men to judge its acts.

There were obvious practical motives for the attempt to enforce valid principles of government. The dukes of Milan never had strong grounds for confidence in the durability of

[1] Cicco Simonetta, first secretary 1450–79, probably played a major part in the creation of the Sforza state.

[2] The articles of F. Cognasso in *Bollettino della Società Pavese di Storia Patria*, xxii and xxiii (1922–3) are the best account of early Visconti government.

their rule. The disintegration of the state after the death of Giangaleazzo Visconti in 1402, and the difficult transition from the Visconti to the Sforza dynasty in 1447–50, interrupted the continuity of the process by which time and custom become legitimating forces. The size and character of their dominion called for an ordered system of government related to established principles because the likely alternative was chaos that would not satisfy their material needs; but it was also a method of appealing for the support of their subjects on the widest possible basis.

'Despotism', then, can be a misleading term, unless we relate it to older ideas that it had in part accepted. The absolute power of the prince, presented as an answer to the practical needs of the time, was a very present force, but it operated àgainst a discreet backcloth of traditional thought. Some humanist writers in the fifteenth century evolved an embryonic utilitarianism that divorced political right from the question of its origins; the power which a man attained by his capacity to mould the course of events was legitimated by the just exercise of it, and a man who ruled, and ruled justly, was *ipso facto* a lawful ruler.[1] The Sforza were prepared to argue, when it suited them, that their truest shield was the love that their subjects bore them.[2] But such opinions were too novel and too tenuous to command much confidence at the top. The lack of tradition behind them contributed most to their instability, and they looked primarily to traditional sources for a remedy. However the *Signori* attained power, they wanted legal buttresses for the foundation of a stable régime, a title *de jure* rather than *de facto*; and the lawyers, despised as they were by the humanists for their hidebound traditionalism, could best provide it.[3] Lawyers and churchmen continued to sit in the councils of princes, and far outnumbered the humanists in their service.

In the routine of government, then, the absolute power of the

---

[1] C. Curcio, *Politica Italiana del '400* (1932), 87–9. This book contains the fullest analysis of the concept of the prince in Italian political thought in the fifteenth century. See also F. Gilbert in *Journal of Modern History*, xi (1939), 449–83.

[2] The argument was used, for example, to debase the value of the feudal investiture of the Duchy that they were seeking from the Emperor Frederick III: despatch of Carlo Visconti from Trier, 9th November, 1473, quoted by C. A. Vianello in *Atti del Primo Congresso Storico Lombardo* (1936), 249–50.

[3] See the discussions of the best grounds on which to base Francesco Sforza's title to the Duchy, analysed by F. Cusin in *Arch. St. Lomb.*, n.s. i (1936) 3–116.

prince did not defy tradition or destroy rights, but supported and strengthened them. There is a measure of truth in the view favoured around the turn of the last century, that the elements of 'social justice' are to be found in the policy of the *Signorie*— that their actions broadened out from the initial tasks of local pacification and defence into the spheres of impartial justice, the preservation of order guaranteed by the new administrative machinery, the breaking of the feudal power and privilege of the nobility and a restoration of the balance between city and countryside by a reversal of the oppressive policy of communal governments.[1] But there is little sign that they progressed very far in these directions, because a programme of this kind called for revolutionary measures which could not be reconciled with the pressures holding them to traditional ideas of government.

Thus, the dukes of Milan certainly set themselves to restrain the power of the nobility.[2] The concept of the absolute prince, indeed, introduced a new kind of equality in which all men were to be faithful and obedient subjects. But the guarantee to every man of his rights inevitably prolonged a hierarchical order of society, and the society over which they ruled tended in fact to become more aristocratic in its outlook, as the splendours of the court grew to enhance the dignity of the prince. Nor could the permeation of the aristocracy by a new element of service affect privilege, of which the new were as tenacious as the old. Ludovico Sforza wrote on one occasion that he would not commit an express wrong against a gentleman who had deserved well of 'this illustrious state', on the complaint of 'a lot of peasants'.[3] This was a personal outburst, and not the normal language of the chancellery. But the case illustrates one of the social consequences of guaranteeing 'to each man his right', for the 'peasants' were a rural community and they were claiming the liability of the 'gentleman' to contribute towards their assessed taxes in spite of ducal letters of exemption. Whatever principles might be expressed, in practice the affairs of the nobility received careful individual treatment, which took up a large part of the time and personal attention of the dukes.

The guarantee of rights in fact formed part of a programme

[1] See e.g. A. Anzilotti in *Studi Storici*, xxii (1914), 82–93.
[2] For this policy and its limits, see especially G. Barni in *Arch. St. Lomb.*, n.s. vi (1941), 17–40; and also my paper in *Italian Renaissance Studies*, cit.
[3] 'Exemplum litterarum Ill. d. Ludovici ad d. Barth. Chalcum' (the first secretary), 21st April, 1488: Miss. 172, f. 190t.; but cf. below, p. 329.

generically described in the routine language of the chancellery as 'pax et quies': a good and peaceful life, a quiet and good governance. This was what the prince offered to those whose ancestors had been citizens of the communes and who were themselves his subjects. In return, he required 'boni subditi', and good subjects were those who did what the government told them, who behaved themselves decently (*costumatamente*), who were prepared to seek union and concord in good and virtuous living, in *vita civile*.

This emphasis on peace and quiet—which again was not new, and which was used by republican governments as well[1]—has also been observed in such records as survive of the external propaganda of the Visconti in the most aggressive phase of their history.[2] In this field it was attached to the idea of unity, which drew substance not so much from the sentimental force of Italian national feeling in the fourteenth century[3] as from a conviction, already expressed early in the century[4] and later adopted by the Visconti in justification of their ambitions, that only unity of rule could bring peace. Thus Giangaleazzo Visconti always declared himself ready to enter into any agreement that would promote 'the peace of Italy',[5] but he also expressed the view that only unity of rule could guarantee that peace.[6] The argument had some force, as we have seen, for those who mistrusted the intentions of Florence. Peace and quiet, the bargain offered in return for acceptance of absolute rule, is not a heroic form of political motivation, but it had a very real relevance to the conditions of the time within as well as outside the dominion. If it failed to win much lasting loyalty, this was probably less because of its inadequacy than because of the limits upon the government's power to impose it.

The fault did not lie in the government's intentions, nor perhaps very largely in the nature of the human resources through which it had to work. From the fifteenth to the eighteenth centuries, the early modern state whose twin pillars were the absolute prince and the bureaucracy operated in western Europe through officials for whom the normal image is

---

[1] E.g. for Florence, the document quoted above, p. 311.
[2] H. Baron, *Crisis*, i, 28–30.
[3] H. Baron in *South Atlantic Quarterly*, xxxviii (1939), 439.
[4] See e.g. G. Barni in *Arch. St. Lomb.*, n.s. vi (1941), 3–10.
[5] See e.g. my *Giangaleazzo Visconti*, 70, 100, 104, 201, 284.
[6] Ibid., 160.

one of venality, extortion and large illegitimate profit. The temptations were great, but so too were the difficulties under which they worked. Two of the standard themes in the correspondence of the Sforza chancellery were, first, that officials must conduct themselves with the responsibility appropriate to those who bear in their function the person of the prince; and second, and in no less need of constant re-iteration, that officials are entitled to the respect and obedience due to the prince whose person they bear. The dukes of Milan, who drew largely upon the old noble families of the communes though there was plenty of room also for new talent in their service, were always inclined to give a severe warning and another chance to delinquent officials; they were prepared to dismiss them in the last resort. Complaints against officials were frequent but not always well founded, and those whom they were sent to govern wrote some eloquent testimonials (how unsolicited we cannot be sure) in praise of their virtues. The dukes used the well conceived methods of inspection and control at their disposal to maintain standards from their officials that were certainly no worse and may well have been higher than those to be found elsewhere in western Europe.

A far more serious defect, and one equally characteristic of the early modern state, was that the forces at their disposal for the ordinary police tasks of protecting their subjects from violence were very thin on the ground. The 'despotism' of the Sforza was not in any normal sense a rule of terror. Their subjects sometimes expressed a wish that it were more so, when they needed protection from their private enemies; and their officials constantly complained that they could not fulfil their obligation of imposing respect for the law unless they had greater material force at their disposal. The government called on them to use *destrezza*, a sort of tactful guile, and when it did authorize the use of threats *per terrore*, it sometimes added a postscript that the threats were on no account to be put into execution.[1] There seem to have been few troops to spare for the fight against crime, and when they were used for the purpose they often came back empty-handed.

[1] E.g. a letter to the Captain of Melegnano, 12th May, 1497: 'Questo siamo contento che si facia per terrore d'epsi tali, non però che intendiamo in effecto che quando passasse dicto termine ch'epsi habiano decadere se non quanto vorrà la justicia'. In this instance, the device was used at the request of a privy councillor, to secure his own rights: Miss. 206 bis., fol. 81r–2.

These are the perennial problems and difficulties of government, but they are relevant to any judgment upon the character and methods of Italian 'despotism' because they reflect the nature of the society with which it had to deal. There is some evidence that the law-abiding subjects of the dukes of Milan— if we may predicate such persons, and I think we may—were more aware of too little government than of too much: save always in the sphere of taxation, and the tax-collector who went out into the countryside seems to have risked limb, if not life, as almost a normal occupational hazard. The problem of enforcing law was certainly more acute in the mountains than in the plain. In the Lunigiana, for instance, the mountainous region where the Marquises Malaspina had held their fiefs and ruled the roost for five centuries, the representatives of the rural communities, brought together by a vicar general in 1480 in an assembly to make 'public peace between the factions', told him that they wanted 'a virile official, who will do right in the name of your Highness (the Duke) and not of the lords Marquises, for otherwise there will never be peace in the land'. The vicar general had been sent with the large escort of a hundred soldiers to bring some criminals to book, but had not been able to lay hands on the wanted men, and he reported that if he were to prosecute all those who infringed the duke's decrees, it would mean depopulating the region.[1] But the need for forceful and indeed ruthless officials was voiced also in the plain. In Piacenza, probably the third largest city of the dominion, 'the municipal council and the citizens who want to live well and peacefully, alike for the well-being and maintenance of your Excellency's state as for their own interests' made great complaint in 1483 that the city was ill governed for lack of a commissioner (who had been appointed but failed to arrive), so that theft, wounding and murder were daily events.[2] And in 1495 the same section of the community declared that the retiring commissioner was 'a good man, but he errs on the side of too much kindness'.[3]

[1] Melchione Sturiono to the Dukes: Cart. Sf. 1084, 20th December, 1479 (but in the folder for December 1480).
[2] Renato Trivulzio and Conte Borella de Secchi to Ludovico Sforza: Cart. Sf. 873, 22nd April, 1483. This was the beginning of the activities of armed gangs who terrorized the city for at least two and a half years before the government, beset by war and plague, was able to get them under control.
[3] 'Bono, ma pechare da troppo bontà'. Ambrogio del Maino to the Duke: Cart. Sf. 876, 21st March, 1495.

The exercise of absolute power was of its nature subject to distortion if dynastic chance placed it in the wrong hands. Most of the Visconti and the Sforza happened to be responsible men who accepted the heavy burdens of government and saw their interest in doing what they could to satisfy the needs of their subjects. A tradition of government, established certainly from the middle of the fifteenth century, helped to mould their outlook and re-inforce their acceptance of obligations. Their absolute power could be brought to bear effectively against individuals, but they were unable to find a remedy for the natural ills of society, those that sprang from the nature of the men who lived in it. Concerned for the durability of dynasty and régime, they stopped short of hazardous innovations and expedients. They took the social materials that they found in their dominions and manipulated them pragmatically to their own best advantage. With the advent of the Sforza, in particular, political conservatism and consolidation set in. By this stage, an aristocracy of court imbued with principles of service and endowed with land and at least financial franchise seemed the most likely foundation for a stable régime. But the nobility (whether new or old) and their retinues remained the element in society most obviously incompatible with the promise of peace and quiet. The middle class of the cities, and especially of Milan, were probably the most loyal supporters of the dukes,[1] but to build on them would have seemed an outrageous gamble at the time.

Above all, the *Signorie* were caught in the financial dilemma that had helped to create them. The need for an effective mobilization of resources, that had contributed to the rise of the *Signorie* and to the development of administrative method, formed a barrier between the prince and his people. The subjects became aware of the positive evils of absolute power, however beneficent its intentions, when it imposed taxation without consent, and we have seen how closely the sense of

[1] Though cries of 'Franza, Franza' were heard in Milan in September 1499, the support given by the city to Ludovico Sforza in February–April 1500, until his capture made further resistance pointless, is referred to by contemporary Lombard writers: G. A. Prato, in *Arch. St. It.*, iii (1842), 246: A. Grumello (ed. G. Müller, 1856), 50: A. da Paullo in *Miscellanea di Storia Italiana*, xiii (1871), 142; and, for the popularity of Cardinal Ascanio Sforza, 154. In other cities, contemporaries still attributed an important part of the old guelf and ghibelline alignments that were also prominent in Milan: da Paullo, 138–9 (for Lodi); and C. Poggiali, *Memorie Storiche di Piacenza*, viii (1760), 151–2.

liberty or the lack of it was associated with this feature of government.

We cannot safely generalize from the dukes of Milan to the other *Signorie*, though their policies and methods undoubtedly had much in common. The one unquestionable achievement of the Visconti and the Sforza was in some respects a source of weakness, not shared by the lords of single cities. They created a Lombard state which reflected the natural radius of Milanese influence and which their foreign conquerors continued after them. The small *Signore* could appeal to the municipal spirit of the city over which he ruled. The dukes of Milan never entirely overcame the resentment felt in the subject cities at what was bound to seem a Milanese government. When Filippo Maria Visconti died in 1447 and the old noble families of Milan proclaimed the Ambrosian republic, the other cities rejected its authority and the state dissolved. Exemption from the need to attend the central courts at Milan figured among the concessions sought from Louis XII of France when he took over the duchy in 1499.[1] Such sentiments may have been as anachronistic as the Ambrosian republic itself, but the choice between the interests of Milan and of the provincial cities created another dilemma which impeded the growth of loyalty to the dynasty.[2] Liberty in the old municipal tradition of the communes may be placed alongside liberty in its financial sense among the causes of the downfall of the Sforza.

So we come back to the communal tradition which, whether it were expressed in terms of custom or of liberty, continued to be one of the most potent forces in Italian political life down to the end of the Middle Ages and beyond. Even the Ciceronian terms in which the humanists of Florence loved to describe the function of the city-state in the first half of the fifteenth century[3] had been anticipated in the first generation of the organized commune, 300 years before. Two great feudal lords had referred their quarrel to the arbitration of the commune of Lucca, and

---

[1] E.g. C. Magenta, *Visconti e Sforza nel Castello di Pavia*, ii (1883), 477–8, docs. 467–8.

[2] The comment of da Paullo, op. cit., 106, on the dissatisfaction of the 'men of worth of noble blood of Milan', though made in a different context, indicates expectations that would be difficult to reconcile with the interests of the other cities.

[3] E.g. Leonardo Bruni's 'multitudo hominum iure sociata', quoted by C. C. Bayley, op. cit., 342 (and 371 for the text).

the comment written by the notary into the record of the award made by the consuls of the city in 1124 stands out the more vividly against this feudal background: 'for a city[1] is a conscious union of people gathered together to live diligently by law'.[2]

If this was the ideal set before the rulers of the communes, they signally failed to achieve it. Nevertheless it remained as an aspiration, and the powerful impact of the *popolo*, the people organized in the gilds, on the political life of the communes in the thirteenth century expressed their judgment upon the old consular class that had betrayed its true function. It became incorporated in the domestic meaning of liberty adopted by the gilds and freely spoken of by the politicians of Florence in the fourteenth century, the liberty to live diligently by law that depended upon adequate protection against the violence of the noble and the powerful.[3] The civic humanists were inclined to relate it to another meaning of liberty, also inherited from the communes, that of freely chosen government in which every citizen had at least a theoretical right to take part; the rulers of Florence, whose spokesmen they were,[4] could not lose by this appeal to the principle of democratic government in support of their resistance to the attacks of foreign tyrants. Freely chosen government and freedom to live by law, the pillars of Florentine political thought, were both part of the communal heritage. It has indeed been suggested that the short-lived *Signorie* of the first half of the fourteenth century in Florence gave better protection and more impartial justice to the ordinary citizen of Florence than he received from the *optimates* who led the fight against the Visconti.[5] 'Despots' could be as anxious as republics to give incentive and opportunity to those who wished to live diligently by law. Let it be clearly understood by all, the Sforza government wrote to one of its officers, 'that in our dominion

[1] Though it is difficult to estimate the force of *civitas* here (state? city-state? city?), the context suggests a contrast between the city (commune) and its feudal surroundings.

[2] 'Omnium civitatum homines, maxime principalium, omnia civiliter atque oneste agere oportet, et decet. Est enim civitas conversatio populi assidua ad iure vivendum collecti'. *Regesto del Codice Pelavicino* (ed. M. Lupo Gentile) in *Atti della Società Ligure di Storia Patria*, xliv (1912), 72–3, doc. 50 (and published several times elsewhere). I have ventured to read *assidue* for *assidua*.

[3] See especially M. B. Becker in *Medieval Studies*, xxiv (1962), 64–82.

[4] For the humanist chancellors of Florence, see E. Garin in *Rivista Storica Italiana*, lxxi (1959), 189–208; and for their place in Florentine society, L. Martines, *Social World of the Florentine Humanists 1390–1460* (1963).

[5] M. B. Becker in *Comparative Studies in Society and History*, ii (1959–60), 421–39; but cf. H. Baron, ibid., 441–8, and Becker in *Speculum*, xxxv (1960), 41–8.

we wish men to live by the standard of right'.[1] And when right was on the side of a poor man, Ludovico Sforza, in spite of his preference for gentlemen, personally instructed his first secretary to see that justice was done on the man's petition against the officials of one of the great lords of Italy.[2]

In this respect at least, the government of the Sforza, measured not purely by its efficiency but by respect for the law and protection of its subjects, compares not unfavourably with that of other forms of rule in the peninsula. By their time political exhaustion, probably associated with difficult economic conditions, had set a premium on stability, and all practicable forms of government in Italy were in some measure open to the charge of tyranny. The mature aristocratic constitution of Venice, which, as some observers in Florence noted, failed to conform to the principles of the 'large state',[3] owed much to the secret and inappellable political verdicts of the Council of Ten. The Aragonese dynasty which had taken over the ruined fabric of a feudal monarchy in Naples by 1442 found that only a 'despotism' in the Italian manner could solve their problems, but their efforts, in a virtually bankrupt kingdom, ended in widespread disaffection.[4] The closing decades of the Middle Ages were not a creative political era in Italy. The desire for 'peace and quiet', expressed in external relations by the universal league of 1455, was reflected domestically in the growing admiration for the Venetian Senate and for the stability which seemed its paramount virtue.[5]

The methods of the Medici suggest that freedom to live by law was a luxury which only well established 'despotisms' could afford to offer. But in Florence, the idea of freely chosen government still lingered. The Florentine interpretation of Italian history in the later Middle Ages has had a long reign. It has prevailed largely because the Florentines of the time wrote it with an exceptional intellectual clarity and an outstanding capacity to grasp the political principles which could be turned to their own credit. It has gone some way towards

---

[1] 'Cum la norma de la rasone': to the Commissioner of Lodi, 9th April, 1481: Miss. 152, f. 267-267t.
[2] Ludovico Sforza to Bartolomeo Calco: Cart. Sf. 1092, 30th March, 1490. The lord was Giovanni II Bentivoglio of Bologna, who held Covo and Antignate (district of Cremona) in fief from the duke.
[3] G. Pampaloni in *Arch. St. It.*, cxix (1961), 45, n. 103.
[4] See R. Colapietra, ibid., 163–99.
[5] On this other 'myth' of Venice, R. Pecchioli in *Studi Storici*, iii (1962), 451–92.

creating a double standard of judgment. Florentine propaganda, even if it used the language of 'noble political ideals', deserves to be examined with the same caution as that of the other side. If we are to accept Florentine aggression as a necessary means of defending liberty, we cannot lightly dismiss that of Venice as sheer greed. Nevertheless there is some justice in the posthumous Florentine victory. For though their propaganda contained as much hypocrisy as most, their case, and their skill in presenting it, derived from the public discussion of political issues, an integral part of the 'eternal vigilance' which is the price of liberty. Freedom of speech in deliberative and judicial assemblies is the essence of liberty: this was the conclusion drawn by Alamanno Rinuccini, a Florentine of noble birth and humanist inclinations, as he observed the growing tyranny imposed by the electoral manipulations of the Medici.[1] The regular discussion of political issues in the councils of the republic, however ineffective it may have been, continued until the 1470s and gave at least some outlet for political aspirations;[2] it was better than no hope at all of a share in government.

By contrast, the subjects of an absolute prince, even if they were not more oppressively governed, felt more vulnerable to oppression, and remained uncommitted to a government in whose decisions they had no hope of taking part.[3] The dukes of Milan must have felt this dilemma more acutely than the small *Signori*, because they could less easily create political loyalty by identifying themselves with the interests of one city. And political loyalty was a crucial problem for the absolute rulers of Italy, beset as they were by the juridical ambiguities of their title, subject to the hazards of dynastic chance, faced by the survivals of the communal tradition, and armed with the dangerous power of taking for their needs what their subjects had not consented to give. The good order which they promised in return would have seemed a more acceptable commodity if they could have come within measurable distance of attaining it, of suppressing the liberty of men to help themselves at the expense of their neighbours. As it was, their subjects were quicker to see the shortcomings of government than the benefits it conferred, and quicker still to resent the burdens it

---

[1] F. Adorno in *Rivista critica di Storia di Filosofia*, vii (1952), 25.
[2] G. Pampaloni in *Arch. St. It.*, cxix (1961), 53.
[3] The point is made by H. Baron in *South Atlantic Quarterly*, xxxviii (1939), 440.

imposed; it was difficult to convince them that they had much to lose by listening to the often specious promises of others. The long career of Giovanni II Bentivoglio, lord of Bologna, which seemed to contemporaries to exemplify the impotence of men in the hands of fate, illustrates most clearly a predicament common enough in the history of despotism. The old weapons of favour and disgrace, used in the search for political loyalty, in the long run narrowed the basis of support for the prince. Awareness of the narrowing basis of support bred fear of treason stimulated from outside the dominion. And fear of treason bred the tyrannical exercise of power. Once a sense of insecurity had taken hold, the prince had little to fall back on —save the guidance of the stars—when his enemies came upon him from without.

XI

A. J. Ryder

THE EVOLUTION OF IMPERIAL GOVERNMENT IN NAPLES UNDER ALFONSO V OF ARAGON

The conquest of the kingdom of Naples by Alfonso V aggravated the problems of government which had grown with the Mediterranean empire of Aragon.[1] At his accession in 1416 that empire already comprised the six kingdoms of Aragon, Valencia, Sicily, Majorca, Sardinia and Corsica, the principality of Catalonia and the counties of Rosellón and Cerdaña. Institutional conservatism combined with geographical separation, cultural divergence and a long, varied process of expansion had favoured the growth of a federative empire within which each state had preserved much of its administrative and political autonomy. The rulers had met the demands of this situation by moving themselves and their court from one kingdom to another whenever some act of state, and in particular the holding of the representative Cortes, demanded their physical presence. The routine functions of government they delegated to governors or governors-general. The great leap forward to Sicily found these solutions quite inadequate, so Pedro III was compelled by the practical necessities of government, as well as by political considerations, to devolve the full royal authority upon his son Jaime whom he appointed *locumtenens generalis* in Sicily. Jaime was empowered to act in all circumstances as the *alter ego* of his father, so that in theory the administration of Sicily could suffer

---

[1] The imperial character of the Crown of Aragon is discussed by P. E. Schramm, 'Der König von Aragon—Seine Stellung im Staatsrecht (1276–1410)', *Historische Jahrbuch*, lxxiv (1955). Catalan personal names have generally been given their Catalan forms.

no handicap from the king's absence. In practice Pedro retained the ultimate power of withholding his assent to the acts of his vicegerent. The separation of Sicily and Aragon on the death of Pedro III lessened the need for such a complete delegation of royal authority, but the kings of Aragon continued to make use of the *locumtenens* or *locumtenens generalis* in a more localized capacity throughout the fourteenth century. At the very end of the century they began also to develop the office of viceroy. The title appears to have been first conferred upon an official sent to Majorca in 1397, and it was afterwards rapidly extended by Martin I to many parts of his continental possessions in an effort to stamp out private wars.[1] Initially the viceroy appears to have been entrusted with a definite mission of a police or military character and restricted to a province or even a single town. Moreover, he was invested with general but limited powers falling far short of those belonging to the office of *locumtenens generalis*. The Trastámara dynasty, enthroned in Aragon by the Compromise of Casp, found new employment for both offices in the solution of its political and administrative problems. To counter strong separatist tendencies in Sicily and Sardinia, and to prepare him as a suitable candidate for the hand of Giovanna II of Naples, Juan, the second son of Ferdinand I, was nominated viceroy in Sicily, Sardinia and Majorca. Alfonso V was to evolve the offices of viceroy and *locumtenens generalis* still further into a systematic structure of imperial government.

If the addition of the kingdom of Naples to an already heterogeneous group of states raised no essentially new problems of administration, it did present the old ones with fresh force in a new context. Contemporaries of Alfonso, especially his Spanish subjects, were acutely aware of the difficulties raised by his long absence from his western kingdoms—in his reign of forty-two years only twelve were spent there—and by the establishment of the court in Naples during the last twenty years. This displacement of the centre of gravity of the Aragonese empire was openly acknowledged to be but a temporary arrangement, for, from the moment the conquest of Naples was secure, it was understood that on the king's death that kingdom would be separated from his hereditary possessions

[1] J. Lalinde Abadia. 'Virreyes y lugartenientes medievales en la Corona de Aragón', *Cuadernos de Historia de España*, xxxi (1960).

and pass to his illegitimate son Ferrante. Nevertheless, for an uninterrupted space of twenty-six years, beginning in 1432, the government of the Aragonese empire, hitherto bound to its Spanish possessions, depended upon a king campaigning up and down the Italian peninsula or resident in Naples. These circumstances alone would have produced severe stresses in the strongly particularist conventions and institutions upon which the empire had in the past relied. The strain was still further increased by more general and fundamental pressures for change. Within the heartlands of the Crown of Aragon, that is in Aragon, Valencia and above all in Catalonia, a profound economic and social crisis was fast undermining the supports of the established order.[1] In the kingdom of Naples half a century of civil war had wrought havoc with the norms of government and society. Such conditions favoured the strengthening of royal authority and made its exercise necessarily repressive in many directions. Financial pressures too were helping to mould Aragonese institutions to a new form. During the first half of the fifteenth century, developments in the tactics and weapons of war substantially increased the cost of the armies with which Alfonso was continually engaging some of the wealthiest states of Europe. At the same time the cult of magnificence inflated expenditure on the royal court. To find the unprecedented sums demanded by his policy and times, Alfonso was accordingly obliged to search for new methods of taxation and financial administration which, however imperfectly, met the changed needs of the state better than did its older practices.

Conditions within and without the Aragonese empire predisposed it to institutional change, but the quality of that change depended very much upon the character of the king. The oligarchic (*Biga*) and popular (*Busca*) factions in Barcelona recognized this when they called upon Alfonso to pronounce upon their rival claims to control the city, the serfs of Catalonia when they appealed to him against their seignorial masters, and all his subjects who lamented that in his absence the ills of the state could receive no cure. The king to whom they looked was

---

[1] The malaise of Catalonia in the fifteenth century has been the subject of several studies by the late Juan Vicens Vives; among them may be mentioned *Juan II de Aragón* (Barcelona, 1953), *Els Trastamares* (Barcelona, 1957), 'La economía de los países de la Corona de Aragón en la Baja Edad Media', *VI Congreso de Historia de la Corona de Aragón* (Madrid, 1959), *Evolución de la economía catalana durante la primera mitad del siglo XV* (Palma de Mallorca, 1955).

of an autocratic and wily temper. Experience in Spain during the early years of his reign had made him impatient and suspicious of constitutional checks upon royal power which he believed to be more perfect when more absolute. Subsequent involvement in Italian affairs sharpened in him the natural political acumen of the Trastámaras who gained their ends over subjects and foreign opponents by the snare rather than the sword. Eager absorption of Italian humanist thought of the mid-century added a conviction of imperial mission to the chivalresque enthusiasm of his earlier enterprises. A Tuscan-centred view of the Renaissance has obscured the extent to which, after the decay of Visconti Milan, humanists looked to the rising Aragonese power as the likeliest protagonist of Italian regeneration. The brilliant group of *literati*, who made the Neapolitan court once more a noted centre of the arts and learning, were not drawn there solely by the hope of immediate profit: many believed that the future lay with a new authoritarian monarchy as the basis of an order and unity that might transcend the limitations of petty tyrannies and republics.[1] Alfonso responded to this environment with vague and apparently boundless ambitions, and with demonstrations of Caesarean splendour in the spirit of the inscription upon his great triumphal arch in Castelnuovo: Alfonsus Rex Hispanicus Siculus Italicus Pius Clemens Invictus. Little attention has yet been paid by either Spanish or Italian historians to the means by which such a ruler controlled an empire.

Alfonso attempted to solve the problem raised by prolonged campaigns and absence from his several states by a systematic devolution of authority upon a hierarchy of *locumtenentes generales* and viceroys. The higher dignity of *locumtenens generalis* he reserved, with few exceptions, for his nearest relatives, partly to stress that it personified the royal power more perfectly than did any other office, and partly to make the substitution more palatable to constitutional susceptibilities. The first person Alfonso appointed to the office was his wife, Queen Maria, who governed all the Spanish territories as *locumtenens generalis* during

[1] The change which took place in the attitude of humanists to the ideas of monarchy and empire are discussed by Hans Baron, *The Crisis of the Early Italian Renaissance* (Princeton, 1955). But he hardly gives due weight to the impact of the Aragonese incursion into southern Italy when he asserts (p. 348) that the powers of western Europe did not invade Italy until the end of the century. In September 1452 an Aragonese army advanced to within eighteen miles of Florence.

the king's first Mediterranean expedition (1420–3). She re-assumed the office when her husband departed finally from Spain in 1432. In 1436, however, Alfonso decided to relieve her of the responsibility in Aragon, Valencia and Majorca where he transferred the powers of *locumtenens generalis* to Juan, king of Navarre, the eldest and ablest of his three brothers. There is some evidence that Maria continued to exercise a theoretically joint control over those three kingdoms with the king of Navarre, as well as retaining effective authority in Catalonia, for in 1445, when the defeat of Olmedo threatened imminent invasion from Castile, Alfonso named his brother sole *locum-tenens generalis* in Aragon and Valencia. At the same time he instructed that the king of Navarre's powers should extend also to Catalonia and Majorca should the conflict affect them.[1] The crisis passed and Maria retained control of Catalonia and the Balearics until October 1453, when she relinquished it in order to undertake a peace-making mission to her brother the king of Castile. In her place Alfonso appointed Galcerán de Requesens who as governor-general of Catalonia since Dec-ember 1442 had won a merited reputation with the king as a shrewd judge of Catalan affairs.[2] Lacking the aura of royalty which had defended his predecessor, Requesens was subjected to constant attack from powerful groups who resented the king's absence and his own reformist sympathies. The king of Navarre too voiced dissatisfaction at this departure from earlier practice. In face of such opposition Alfonso judged it prudent to remove Requesens after barely six months in office and gave the Catalans a royal but unrelenting *locumtenens generalis* in the person of Juan of Navarre.[3] For himself Alfonso reserved only the power of punishing and pardoning treason. Thus all the Spanish territories of the Crown of Aragon were brought under the control of their prospective ruler.

In Sicily and Sardinia Alfonso maintained the viceregal form of government instituted by his father, appointing most of his viceroys from noble families of Spanish origin which had settled

[1] Archivo de la Corona de Aragón (A.C.A.), Barcelona. Registros del Rey, no. 2690, fol. 178v. Letter to the officials of Aragon, Valencia and Catalonia, 14th October, 1445, fol. 183v. Letter to Queen Maria, 22nd October, 1445.
[2] Galcerán and his brother Bernat de Requesens came from a family which had linked its fortunes to the Trastámaras after Casp. Galcerán was charged with the settlement of the crisis in Barcelona. His support of the *busca* and *remensa* causes earned him the bitter enmity of the Catalan oligarchy.
[3] A.C.A. R.2700, fol. 87r, 31st May, 1454.

in those kingdoms. Viceroys also governed the territories he acquired by conquest or treaty. In those where Aragonese possession had to be established or defended against armed attack, the office was more military than administrative in character. For example, when Alfonso decided to assert his titular rights to Corsica by wresting the island from the Genoese, he appointed a viceroy, Jacme de Besora, who was also to command the invading force.[1] In April 1452, following a treaty with the Albanian leader George Kastriota or Skander-beg, he sent Ramon d'Ortaff to Croia as viceroy of Albania, and two years later extended that official's authority over all vassal princes in Greece and Slavonia. The fall of Constantinople led to a notable increase in the number of the king's Balkan clients, so in September 1455 he appointed another viceroy for the Morea with his headquarters in the town of Castrovilari. Both viceroys were soldiers and had the task of defending and expanding a precarious Aragonese footing that hardly reached beyond their fortresses.[2] These were, therefore, prestige appointments rather than the instruments of effective govern-ment. On the Italian mainland, too, Alfonso regularly employed viceroys in a military capacity. For example, in 1449 he nominated Ludovico Gonzaga, marquis of Mantua, as viceroy in Lombardy, even though the marquis was not a subject but a *condottiere* in his service. Moreover Alfonso possessed nothing in Lombardy save some mercenary troops and forlorn claims.

The conquest, pacification and government of Naples raised peculiar problems in answer to which Alfonso likewise resorted to the use of the viceroy and *locumtenens*. As the provinces of the kingdom fell into his hands, he placed a viceroy in each one to control the royal forces, local militia and regular provincial administration. In 1444 these omnicompetent officials, the majority of whom were Spaniards, still held sway in all the provinces except the Terra d'Otranto and Molise, as well as in Terracina and Benevento—papal cities entrusted to Alfonso for the period of his life. Towards the end of that year another two viceroys were appointed in Calabria to crush a revolt raised by

---

[1] A.C.A. R.2697, fol. 106r, 17th August, 1451. In 1434 de Besora had been viceroy of Sardinia.

[2] C. Marinescu. *Alphonse V roi d'Aragon et de Naples, et l'Albanie de Scanderbeg, Mélanges de l'école Roumaine en France*, i (Paris, 1923). F. Cerone, 'La politica orientale di Alfonso d'Aragona', *Archivio Storico per le Provincie Napoletane*, xxvii and xxviii (1902–3).

Antonio Centelles, the former viceroy of that province. But once internal order had been re-established, the traditional governors of the provinces, the justiciars, began to recover control of many parts of the kingdom, and in the last years of the reign viceroys ruled only in the provinces of Calabria, Terra di Lavoro and the Abruzzi which were strategically important for the defence of the kingdom and contained the greater part of the royal desmesne.[1] After taking the city of Naples in June 1442, Alfonso installed his twelve-year-old son Ferrante as *locumtenens generalis* for the whole kingdom. The first parliament of the reign which met in February 1443 recognized this delegation of authority which, though more nominal than real, quietened Neapolitan fears for the future independence of the kingdom and achieved a uniform pattern of government throughout the Aragonese empire.

It would almost certainly be incorrect to assume that any coherent theory of imperial government lay behind Alfonso's development of the offices of viceroy and *locumtenens generalis*. It is difficult to understand, for example, why a state as important as Sicily should have been entrusted to a viceroy and not to the more exalted *locumtenens*. Also a certain confusion over spheres of authority is sometimes apparent. Mention has already been made of a duplication of the office of *locumtenens generalis* in Spain. A still more anomalous situation arose in the kingdom of Naples in November 1443 when Lope Ximénez de Urrea, the viceroy of Sicily, was appointed *locumtenens generalis* and viceroy in Calabria despite the earlier assignment of general powers over the whole kingdom to Ferrante. For practical purposes, however, the powers and function of each official were defined according to need by the king himself, who also insisted that all important matters outside the scope of routine administration be referred to him for consultation or approval. Often the vice-gerents found the king intervening over their heads, rejecting or reversing their decisions.[2] Thus, although the interposition of *locumtenentes* and viceroys theoretically cut off the direct

[1] The only studies of the Neapolitan administration under Alfonso are the old but still valuable work of L. Bianchini, *Della storia delle finanze del Regno di Napoli* (Palermo, 1839), and two surveys by P. Gentile: 'Finanze e parlamenti nel Regno di Napoli dal 1450 al 1467', *Archivio storico per le provincie napoletane* (1913), and 'Lo stato napoletano sotto Alfonso I d'Aragona', ibid. (1937 and 1938).

[2] Alfonso's intervention in the Majorcan crisis of 1447 is a good example of his methods, A. Santamaría Arandez, *El Reino de Mallorca en la primera mitad del siglo XV* (Palma, 1955).

relationship between the king and his vassals, his sovereign power was exercised in such a manner that he retained a large measure of influence over the affairs of his states. The administrative machinery through which Alfonso maintained his control over the Aragonese empire had to be constructed piecemeal as opportunity or necessity arose. Just as the offices of *locumtenens* and viceroy came to hand from the accumulated experience of his predecessors on the Aragonese throne, so most of the procedures and offices which he adapted to the requirements of imperial government existed already within his dominions. His achievement was to turn well-tried institutions to new uses.

In all the states Alfonso ruled, custom and law gave the king's council a central function in the processes of government, though the composition and powers of the council differed substantially from one to another. The problem of reconciling these differences in one council did not arise because the council of each state now attached itself to the appropriate *locumtenens* or viceroy, not to the king. Therefore, while Alfonso remained in the kingdom of Naples, only the seven collateral officials of that state could sit by right of office in the king's council, and even they might have been diverted with some show of legality to attend upon the *locumtenens generalis* had the king so desired. The freedom which he consequently enjoyed in choosing the members of his council at will made that body especially adaptable to new administrative functions of the royal prerogative.

Borso d'Este, brother of the marquis of Ferrara, visited Naples in April 1444 and soon afterwards wrote an account of the kingdom in which he named those then admitted to the council.[1] The president was Alfonso Borja, bishop of Valencia and later Pope Calixtus III, who also held the office of vice-prothonotary in Naples. His pre-eminence seems to have been attuned to both Neapolitan and Aragonese custom, for while in Naples seniority in the council attached to the office of prothonotary,[2] in Aragon it was given to an archbishop or bishop who had also to be a doctor of laws.[3] There was one other clerical member,

---

[1] C. Foucard, 'Descrizione della città di Napoli e statistica del Regno nel 1444', *Archivio storico per le provincie napoletane* (1877).

[2] R. Trifone, *La Legislazione angioina* (Naples, 1921).

[3] These were the qualifications established by Pedro III for the office of chancellor to which belonged the right of directing proceedings in the royal council. Ref. the Ordinances of Pedro the Ceremonious published by P. de Bofarull y Mascaró, *Colección de documentos inéditos del Archivo General de la Corona de Aragón*, v (Barcelona, 1850), 109 ff.

the Neapolitan Jacobo de Montáquila, bishop of Isernia. After the bishop of Valencia, probably the most influential member was Eximen Perez de Corella, count of Cocentayna, governor of the kingdom of Valencia, majordomo to the king and, jointly with the bishop of Valencia, tutor to Ferrante. The count had been the king's companion in all his Italian campaigns, had won his confidence as a soldier, and later enjoyed it as virtual governor of the kingdom of Naples during Alfonso's absence. As a special mark of favour he was permitted to use the royal arms.[1] Hardly less favoured was the Sicilian noble Giovanni di Vintimiglia, marquis of Gerace. He too had commanded in the king's armies throughout the Italian wars and continued an active military career, notably in Acarnania and the March of Ancona, after the conquest of Naples. In 1430 he was appointed viceroy of Sicily, and became admiral of that kingdom in 1438. His attendance in the king's council must have been irregular because he was often absent from the kingdom. The presence of two relatively minor Neapolitan nobles, Perdicasso Barrile, count of Monteodorisio, and Giorgio d'Alemagna, count of Buccino, is less easily explained, especially since the latter had persevered in his allegiance to René of Anjou to the very end. Possibly it was this example of fidelity, almost unparalleled among the Neapolitan nobility, that had commended the count to Alfonso. Besides these ecclesiastics and nobles, the council included, according to Borso d'Este, a group of financial and legal officials. Prominent among them was Guillem de Vich, master of the audit (*magister rationalis*) in the kingdom of Valencia and treasurer to the king's two daughters—a man well versed in financial affairs and in the intricacies of Castilian politics. De Vich and the count of Cocentayna were the only members of the council who were also admitted to the royal entourage, in their capacities as tutor and treasurer to the king's children. Their influence with the king and council was correspondingly enhanced. Of Pons de Santa Creu, the other Spanish member, little is known except that he was a Catalan and a *doctor decretorum*. The Neapolitan administration was represented by Marino Boffa, a president of the *Sommaria* (the audit office of that kingdom), and Giovanni di Sanseverino,

---

[1] In 1456 he quarrelled bitterly with his former companion in office who, as Calixtus III, refused to confirm the bulls investing Alfonso with Naples, Benevento and Terracina. The insults exchanged suggest a long-standing rancour between the two. J. Ametller y Vinyas, *Alfonso V de Aragón en Italia*, ii (Gerona, 1903), 829.

regent of the supreme court of Naples, the *Vicaria*. For twenty years Boffa had played an important and generally pro-Angevin part in the turbulent affairs of Naples, but in 1438, to save the estates acquired through marriage 'to an heiress, he threw in his lot with the Aragonese party and secured a leading position among the Neapolitan officials around the king.[1] He was one of the viceroys appointed to put down the Calabrian revolt of 1444. Giovanni di Sanseverino had acquired favour through services rendered to Alfonso and his brother Pedro. His reward had been the office of regent of the court of the *Vicaria* for life.

Among these permanent members of the council, Borso d'Este included the seven collateral officials of the kingdom of Naples: the constable, admiral, prothonotary, justiciar, chamberlain, chancellor and seneschal. In theory they controlled the armed forces, the administration and the royal household of the kingdom.[2] In fact most of the offices had long since become merely valuable sinecures for powerful nobles whose attachment to the ruler it was politic to reward or secure. While fighting for possession of Naples, Alfonso had bestowed these offices judiciously among the greatest families, and only later did he venture to introduce Spaniards and favourites.[3] Their instructions carefully enumerated functions and duties which had long since lapsed or passed to other officials. For example, in response to a parliamentary petition that the constitutional position of the prothonotary be respected, the count of Fondi was issued with standing instructions that repeated almost word for word those given to that official in 1294. Behind the unchanging façade the Neapolitan collateral official

---

[1] Cf. E. Pontieri, 'Muzio Attendolo e Francesco Sforza nei conflitti dinastico-civili nel Regno di Napoli al tempo di Giovanna II d'Angiò-Durazzo', *Divagazioni storiche e Storiografiche* (Naples, 1960).

[2] Cf. C. Minieri Riccio, *Cenni storici intorno i grandi uffizii del Regno di Sicilia* (Naples, 1872).

[3] Giovanni Antonio del Balzo Orsini, the greatest of the Neapolitan magnates and Alfonso's most reliable adherent, was given the office of constable in 1435. The prince of Salerno, Raimondo Orsini, was confirmed in the office of justiciar in 1436 as part of the price of his adherence to the king. The Roman branch of the Orsini family provided the chancellor, Orso Orsini. The occupants of the other offices in 1444 were: Giovanni Antonio Marzano, duke of Sessa, admiral; Onorato Gaetani, count of Fondi, prothonotary; Francesco d'Aquino, count of Loreto, chamberlain; and Francesco Zurlo, count of Nocera, seneschal. When the count of Loreto died in 1449 Alfonso gave the office of chamberlain to the Castilian noble Iñigo de Avalos. In 1450 Iñigo de Guevara, half-brother of de Avalos, succeeded the count of Nocera as seneschal. When the chancellorship fell vacant in 1455, it was given to Ugo d'Alagno, the brother of the king's favourite Lucrezia.

collected his salary of six ducats a day, ensconced himself in his estates, and left his office and its duties to deputies appointed by the king. Rarely did he frequent the court and still more seldom attend the council. Their nominal inclusion in the council was, therefore, of practical importance only because it made that body constitutionally competent to advise the king upon Neapolitan business.

The description of the council in 1444 ends with the names of seven persons who were not permanent members but were permitted to attend whenever their other duties allowed. Four of them are readily identifiable as Neapolitan doctors of law in the service of the Crown: Michele Riccio, Cicco Antonio Guindazzo, Angelo Tau and Valla's *princeps iurisconsultorum*, Giovanni Antonio Carafa. The one Borso d'Este named simply 'the judge Matteo' may have been either Matteo di Girifalco or Matteo d'Afflitto, and was certainly a legal official. The remaining two were Colella Monopulo and the bishop of Valencia's secretary Pons who also acted as secretary to the council. From other evidence it is clear that this list is incomplete; many other jurists serving in the courts of the *Sommaria* and *Vicaria* were summoned as need arose to attend to council business. At most sessions of the council, therefore, at least half of those present would be lawyers employed in the administrative and judicial offices of government. The number of Spanish jurists attending the council, small in 1444, later increased. But Alfonso continued to depend mainly upon Neapolitan and Sicilian lawyers who, it has been argued, had kept closer to the practical problems of feudal jurisprudence than their north Italian contemporaries.[1]

Borso d'Este mentioned only this one royal council, and it is probable that the same body, or selected members of it, then served for the business of Naples and the other kingdoms alike. While Alfonso remained within the kingdom any further development may have appeared unnecessary, but his two-year absence in Tuscany (1446–8) produced chaos in the Neapolitan administration. Although Ferrante's powers as *locumtenens generalis* were used to summon a parliament in March 1448, he was still too young and inexperienced to fill that role effectively. The bishop of Valencia, who had presided with great authority over the council, had departed for Rome in 1444, upon his

[1] A. Maffei, *Influssi del rinascimento nei giuristi napoletani* (Naples, 1940).

promotion to the cardinalate and had been succeeded by the less capable Gaspare di Diano, archbishop of Naples. Power and responsibility therefore rested in the hands of three governors whom Alfonso had appointed to assist Ferrante: the count of Cocentayna, the treasurer general, Matteu Pujades, and the secretary Joan Olzina. The absent king was usually too occupied with his military and diplomatic problems to do more than present demands for money which threw the government of Naples into still greater confusion. In these circumstances the administration gradually ran down. Officials went unpaid: even the regent of the *Vicaria* had by 1448 received no salary for five years. Arrears of business in the courts and in the *Sommaria* mounted alarmingly. The fate of the council is obscure, for the royal council functioned now in Tuscany. In all probability the council in Naples was reduced to irregular meetings of a handful of officials: at least such is the impression given by the instructions of 3rd October, 1448, in which Alfonso ordered a reform of that body.[1] Defeat before Piombino had so shaken the king's prestige and credit that restoration of order ·in the government of Naples became imperative if creditors were to be satisfied and fresh funds raised. To that end the count of Cocentayna and the Neapolitan banker, Giovanni di Miroballo, were summoned to Tuscany and after consultations returned to Naples with instructions for major reforms of the administrative and judicial system addressed to the *locumtenens generalis*. The first part of these instructions dictated the composition of a council which was to be established in Naples to advise Ferrante in the government of that kingdom. Like the council of 1444, this Neapolitan council had an ecclesiastical president —the archbishop of Naples—and included a large body of legal and financial officials, for it was designed to function principally as a clearing-house for the business of otherwise un-co-ordinated departments. A quasi-representative element was introduced by the nomination of one member for each of the five wards (*seggi*) of Naples,[2] and the seven collateral officials retained the right to attend the council whenever they were present in the capital. In many ways this reform of the

---

[1] A.C.A. R.2699, fol. 141v.

[2] These five were nominated directly by the king, not by the wards. The first to be appointed were: Petriccone Caracciolo, count of Brienza, Carafello Carafa, Buffardo Cicinello, Matteo di Gennaro and Dragonetto di Bonifaccio. All were long-standing supporters of Aragon.

Neapolitan council was a revival of that body as it had existed under the Angevin dynasty, for the procedure laid down by Alfonso followed very closely that prescribed by Charles I in 1294 and revised in 1352 by Giovanna I. The recognition of the prothonotary's customary right of precedence in the council, as demanded by the parliament of March 1450, completed the formal restoration of a Neapolitan council. But though constitutional forms were respected, the government of Naples became in this reign firmly established upon a bureaucratic council dominated by lawyers who made a life career in the service of the state.

The implementation of these reforms cannot have gone very far when in November 1448 Alfonso returned to Naples. Despite many false alarms he was never to leave it again. Whether his return and settlement in the kingdom caused the Neapolitan council to merge once more in a general imperial council is at present uncertain. However, these last ten years of the reign, during which the king turned his immediate attention from the command of armies to the government of his states, produced important developments in many directions and especially in the field of imperial administration.

Information about the royal council in these years is rather meagre and disappointing, though much may remain undiscovered in the Aragonese archives. In the absence of a Borso d'Este, a series of letters written to the city council of Barcelona by its envoys in Naples afford occasional glimpses of the royal council in action.[1] The impression which emerges is that of an indeterminate body with two fairly distinct forms and functions: a large, ceremonial council and a small, inner council. A council of the former variety met on 10th September, 1450, to discuss the king's projected visit to Sicily: barons and knights from several kingdoms attended as well as envoys from Catalonia and Barcelona. A still larger gathering of 'all members of the council and a great part of the barons of this kingdom' met in Pozzuoli on 10th May, 1454, to discuss whether the king should adhere to the Peace of Lodi. Another council, afforced to such a degree that it resembled a parliament, was assembled to decide whether Alfonso should undertake the crusade. For that purpose all the nobles and important

[1] These letters are in the Archivo de la Ciudad de Barcelona, series x, *Cartas Comunas Originales Recibidas*, vols. 13–28.

persons available in Naples were included in the council which met on 26th August, 1455. These were public issues of great moment to which such councils lent added solemnity, but the conclusions at which they arrived had already been determined in a far smaller body. Admittance to the inner council appears to have depended more upon the nature of the business to be discussed than upon the councillor's rank or office, so that many might receive an occasional summons, but very few attended regularly. In December 1451 Alfonso summoned his council to Capua, where he was hunting, to decide a dispute between the Crown and the city of Barcelona. Besides the king those present were Pere de Besalú, conservator-general of the Royal Patrimony, Rodrigo Falco, a chancery judge, the vice-chancellor, Valenti Claver, the advocate of the Royal Patrimony, Nicola Antonio de Monti, and the secretary Arnau Fonolleda. After the vice-chancellor had presented the case for Crown, the king immediately expressed his approval and allowed the other councillors to speak only briefly. Almost certainly the composition of this council was determined by the matter in hand. As for the king's part in it, there is other evidence that he was a dominant, authoritarian figure in his councils, whether large or small, and extremely adept at concealing his thoughts and intentions.[1] He tended, therefore, to emphasize their executive rather than their deliberative functions.

The absolutist spirit that informed the royal council is rather more apparent in the special councils and offices with which Alfonso built up a centralized administration for the Aragonese empire. These councils not only possessed the powers of supreme tribunals superior to those of the individual states, but their composition and authority were determined solely by the king. The best-known of them—the *Sacrum Consilium*—had functioned for at least ten years as an emanation of the king's council before it was constituted a separate body in 1449. It had emerged as an answer to the problems which a multiplicity of legal codes and customs presented to the king as the ultimate court of appeal in the Aragonese empire. Besides adding to the diversity of law, the Neapolitan adventure substantially

---

[1] Vespasiano da Bisticci, who obtained most of his information about Alfonso from Gianozzo Manetti, described the king as having a secretive nature and a dislike of taking advice, *Vite di uomini illustri del secolo XV*, ed. P. D'Ancona and E. Aeschlimann (Milan, 1951).

increased the number of cases brought to the king's council for judgment. Most of these appeals arose from disputes between feudataries over the possession of lands which had changed hands many times during the years of civil war, and for which opposing sides had issued conflicting privileges. Political prudence demanded that these issues be decided carefully but quickly, for Alfonso's strategy of conquest and pacification depended upon convincing the nobility that they could best guarantee their estates by supporting the Aragonese cause. The exercise of the king's appellate jurisdiction was accordingly delegated to the council sitting as a supreme tribunal for all territories owing him allegiance. Various models and precedents have been suggested for this council, including the appeal tribunal of Valencia and the Roman Rota.[1] Account might also be taken of the policy pursued in Castile by the first Trastámara rulers who, in their revival of the royal council, had developed the *Audiencia* for the exercise of its judicial functions. Cassandro[2] is probably correct in maintaining that the *Sacrum Consilium* evolved gradually within the council, and therefore that its origin cannot be traced to any one act or date. However, it can be identified by name from 1439 onwards. The name *Sacrum Consilium* or *Sacrum Regium Consilium* arose from the ceremonial followed in the tribunal to symbolize the sacred character of the power of final judgment vested in the king and through him in the council. Great emphasis was always laid upon the attachment of the *Sacrum Consilium* to the person of the king, and although Alfonso rarely attended its sessions the council followed his court and recorded its judgments with a formula that attributed them solely to him. 'With God before our eyes and His holy gospels placed before us and studied reverently that our judgment might proceed from His countenance and the eyes of our mind be enabled to discern the right . . . this sentence was delivered by the said lord king or in his behalf by the reverend father in Christ and lord Alfonso, by divine providence Bishop of Valencia.'[3]

Until 1449 membership of the royal council and the *Sacrum*

[1] Cf. B. Croce, *La Spagna nella vita italiana* (Bari, 1922), 43. F. Soldevila, *Historia de Catalunya*, ii (Barcelona, 1935), 57. J. Ametller y Vinyas, *Alfonso V . . .*, iii, 138.

[2] G. Cassandro, 'Sulle origini del Sacro Consiglio napoletano', in *Studi in onore di Riccardo Filangieri*, ii (Naples, 1959).

[3] A.C.A. R.2909, fol. 74v, 12th June, 1944.

Consilium was undifferentiated. One president—first the bishop of Valencia, then the archbishop of Naples—served both bodies, and all members of the council, including the collateral officials of Naples, were entitled to participate in the *Sacrum Consilium*. In practice the attendance seldom exceeded seven—the president, a secretary, a knight of rather lowly rank, and four Crown lawyers—and it was constantly changing, for many of the lawyers and secretaries available in Naples took an occasional share in its proceedings. The task of controlling proceedings and allocating work among the council's lawyers fell to the vice-chancellor as principal legal officer of the Crown. The influence of Aragonese practices is very evident in the introduction of this office into the kingdom of Naples, probably in 1443 when the Sicilian Battista Platamone, already a prominent figure in the *Sacrum Consilium*, was appointed vice-chancellor. Platamone at once tried to extend the competence of his office from Naples, Sicily and Sardinia to the Spanish territories, and thus make it co-extensive with the imperial jurisdiction of the *Sacrum Consilium*. But he ran foul of the requirement that a vice-chancellor of the Crown of Aragon had to be born and effectively domiciled there.[1] As a result of this setback, Platamone remained vice-chancellor only in the eastern kingdoms. His death in 1451, coinciding with that of the vice-chancellor of the Crown of Aragon, Juan de Funes, made it possible for Alfonso to appoint one man to both offices. The choice fell upon Valenti Claver, the senior member of the group of Catalan lawyers serving the king in Naples. In the course of a long official career he had acted as regent of the chancery and *locumtenens* to the chamberlain of Naples, and frequently sat in the *Sacrum Consilium*. Thus, for the remainder of the reign the *Sacrum Consilium* was directed by an imperial vice-chancellor.

Present evidence would suggest that the *Sacrum Consilium* ceased to function in the difficult circumstances of the years from 1446 to 1448 when the king was with his army in central Italy. Reference has already been made to the disarray which then arose in the Neapolitan courts, and it may with reason be suspected that the supreme appeal tribunal faced a similar accumulation of business when Alfonso at last returned to

---

[1] Archivo de la Ciudad de Barcelona (A.C.B.), *Lletres closes*. 323 serie vi, 10, fol. 128r and 193v. In addition to his legal duties, Platamone was frequently employed on diplomatic missions to Italian states.

Naples. That supposition is strengthened by the decree of 13th August, 1449,[1] which formally constituted the *Sacrum Consilium* a supreme tribunal with a form and function akin to those it had assumed between 1439 and 1446, but now sharply defined. To a certain degree the tribunal was still regarded as a special form of the council, for a vague formula safeguarded the 'prerogatives and pre-eminence' of the Neapolitan archbishop and prothonotary in relation to the *Sacrum Consilium* whenever they might be present at court. Otherwise all baronial councillors and the remainder of the collateral officials were excluded. In their place Alfonso appointed six permanent members, all of them lawyers. Each received the relatively high salary of 500 ducats a year as well as a proportion of fees: in return they were forbidden to engage in any private legal practice. Three Neapolitans (Cicco Antonio Guindazzo, Geronimo Miroballo, Michele Riccio), two Catalans (Valenti Claver, Nicolau Fillach) and the Sicilian vice-chancellor Battista Platamone were nominated in the decree to be the first members.[2] These 'our principal and privy councillors' represented some of the foremost legal talent among Alfonso's subjects, and all had distinguished themselves in diplomatic missions and administration as well as in the law courts. In the absence of the archbishop of Naples, the *Sacrum Consilium* met under the presidency of the vice-chancellor in the king's fortress-palace of Castelnuovo. But when the king was absent from Naples it met in the vice-chancellor's house. The procedure and competence of the tribunal were little affected by the decree. It continued to be a court of appeal and first instance for all except criminal cases, and for the whole of the Aragonese empire. It also continued to take cognizance of cases from the *Sommaria* involving points of law. A provision that the preliminary examination of feudal cases should be undertaken by at least three, and other cases by at least two counsellors merely standardized former practice.

To the Neapolitan nobility the reconstitution of the *Sacrum Consilium* appeared, with some reason, as an attack upon the constitutions of the kingdom, designed to enhance royal power at their expense. Therefore, in the parliament of March 1450

[1] The document is printed by A. Caruso, 'Circa l'origine del Sacro Regio Consiglio', in *Il Rievocatore* (Naples, 1956).

[2] Giovanni Antonio Carafa was added in December 1449 and Joan de Copons in 1451.

they petitioned that the tribunal should be permanently installed in the capital, that the prothonotary of the kingdom or a Neapolitan substitute should preside over it, and that some Neapolitan magnates should be appointed members. Alfonso could not admit their thesis that the *Sacrum Consilium* was subject to Neapolitan law without destroying much of its value, but in order not to prejudice the financial aid expected from that parliament he glided over the petition with a promise that the prothonotary or his deputy should preside.[1] That undertaking was patently violated in the following year when the king appointed Arnau Roger de Pallars, bishop of Urgell and chancellor of Aragon, to the presidency of both his general council and the *Sacrum Consilium*.[2] By so doing he showed a marked preference for Aragonese custom which accorded precedence in the royal council to the chancellor and relegated the prothonotary to a place below that of the vice-chancellor. The subordination of Naples to an imperial authority had earlier been emphasized by the decrees of 19th April and 10th August, 1450, with which Alfonso answered the baronial demand for representation in the *Sacrum Consilium*. The purpose of these decrees was to appoint six prominent nobles to the council with salaries of 1,000 ducats a year, but not one of the collateral officials appeared among them.[3] Alfonso thereby established the principle that no subject might enter the *Sacrum Consilium* by virtue of his office, but solely at the king's pleasure. In many ways these salaried noble counsellors had less in common with their Neapolitan predecessors than with the two knights whom Pedro IV promised the Aragonese to maintain permanently in his court to give counsel in the affairs of that kingdom, or with the Castilian *alcaldes de corte*. Their duties were to attend the council at the proper times 'to give counsel, to guide, to govern, to assist and to deal with matters brought to our *Sacrum Consilium* from both this kingdom and our

[1] Article VII of the proceedings of the 1450 parliament printed in J. Ametller y Vinyas, iii, 684–92.
[2] In a letter to the bishop of Vich dated 16th March, 1455, Alfonso notified him of his appointment as president of the *Sacrum Consilium*. Since the same letter gave the bishop leave to return to Spain, the purpose of that appointment is not clear (A.C.A. R.2700, fol. 86v).
[3] The six were Giorgio d'Alemagna, count of Buccino, Petriccone Caracciolo, count of Brienza, Nicola Cantelmo, duke of Sora, Americo di Sanseverino, count of Capaccio, Francesco Pandone, count of Venafro and Marino Caracciolo, count of Sant Angelo. Francesco del Balzo Orsini, duke of Andria, was appointed in August 1453 to fill the vacancy caused by the death of the duke of Sora.

other realms'.[1] Not enough is yet known of the working of the *Sacrum Consilium* in its new form to judge whether the Neapolitan nobles shared effectively in its deliberations, or whether Alfonso took the logical step of appointing similar groups of nobles to represent his other states. That the Duke of Andria asked to be excused permanent attendance and was given a reduced salary on condition that he appeared whenever possible, suggests that the office was not allowed to become another handsome sinecure.

Backed by royal authority and able lawyers, the decisions of the *Sacrum Consilium* soon began to command wide respect even among states outside its jurisdiction. The value of the institution itself was also recognized and similar institutions were established, particularly in states ruled by the Trastámaras. After his father's death, Ferrante maintained a Neapolitan version of the *Sacrum Consilium* for that kingdom. Juan II of Aragon referred to his own *Sacrum Consilium* in a *pragmática* issued in March 1459,[2] and in Sicily a *Sacrum Consilium* assumed control of government on the death of the viceroy in October 1462.[3] The *Sacro Supremo Consejo de Aragón* established by Ferdinand the Catholic in 1493 may well be regarded as a further development of an institution which had already proved its worth in an expanding empire.

If the *Sacrum Consilium* provided a reasonably satisfactory solution to the problem of administering justice, the corresponding but greater problems of financial control were never so effectively mastered. Alfonso's methods of warfare and diplomacy depended as much upon gold as upon iron, so that the effective marshalling of the wealth of his Spanish and Italian states became increasingly a prime object of policy. But enormous obstacles stood in the way of an adequate central direction of finance. Even the treasuries of individual states within the empire received only the residue of a multitude of funds tied to distinct offices which independently disbursed the charges upon their revenues. At least two attempts[4] to overcome the handicaps inherent in such a system by channelling

---

[1] A.S.N. *Privilegiorum*, I, fol. 101, 4th August, 1453.
[2] Cf. A. Masiá, 'El Maestre Racional en la Corona de Aragón', *Hispania*, xxxviii.
[3] Cf. J. Vicens Vives, *Fernando el Católico, Príncipe de Aragón, Rey de Sicilia* (Madrid, 1952), 136–7.
[4] In 1446 the bank of Thomas Pujades was appointed for this purpose in the kingdom of Valencia. In 1448 the experiment was repeated in the kingdom of Naples using the bank of Giovanni di Miroballo.

all receipts and payments of the Crown through a private bank failed in advance because the conception of a revenue composed of discrete funds still dominated both official and private thinking. To this accustomed anarchy in the revenues and accounts of his several kingdoms Alfonso added further confusion by the expedients employed to finance his unending Italian ventures. Indiscriminate drawing upon many treasuries and funds, wide variations in the interest charged on bills of exchange, and fluctuating rates of exchange between the half-dozen major currencies used within the Aragonese empire made accurate accounts and effective audit almost impossible.

Until he had Naples firmly in his grasp, Alfonso worried little about accounts and much about the flow of gold that was turning the tide of war in his favour. Hence, his first step towards the creation of a financial superstructure was the appointment in 1439 of a treasurer general with powers over all treasurers throughout the empire. Matteu Pujades, the first of these officials, spent most of his time in Spain stimulating the flow of money and supplies to Italy. After his death in 1447 the office was shared by Perot Mercader in Spain and Pere de Capdevila in Naples, until 1453 when the disgrace of the latter left it re-united in the hands of Mercader who was then summoned to Italy. The royal treasury which was established in Naples after the capture of the city performed an imperial function because it administered funds drawn from each of the king's states, including all the Neapolitan revenues. Also its officials were frequently despatched from Naples to other territories to conduct inquiries touching upon the revenues, and to supervise operations involving large expenditure, such as the provisioning of fleets, the payment of troops or the building of fortifications. On missions of this nature the treasury official was accompanied by another from the office of the clerk of accounts (*scriva de racio*), an Aragonese institution transplanted to Naples as a necessary adjunct to the imperial treasury.[1] In both departments Catalans and Valencians enjoyed a virtual monopoly of offices.

While this central treasury, despite obvious deficiencies, functioned no worse than its territorial counterparts, the difficulties in the way of a corresponding system of audit proved far more intractable. Within the Crown of Aragon the accounts

[1] Cf. P. de Bofarull y Mascaró, *Colección de documentos inéditos*, v, 161–6.

of officials and of the Royal Patrimony were audited by the
master auditor (*maestre racional*), an office introduced by Jaime
II on his return from Sicily. Its occupant was a member of the
king's council. In 1419 Alfonso began a process of decentraliza-
tion by appointing a *maestre racional* solely for the kingdom of
Valencia, and subsequently gave similar autonomy to the audit
offices of Aragon and Catalonia. The *maestre racional* of Catalonia
also controlled the accounts of Majorca and Sardinia. For Sicily
that function had long been performed by a body of auditors
(*maestre razionali*) similar to the *razionali* of the Neapolitan
Sommaria. The relationship between these various auditing
authorities and the treasurer general remained obscure through
most of the reign, partly because it involved virtually insoluble
technical problems, and partly because the king was concerned
not to allow any administrative checks to impede the supply of
money and materials to Italy. The latter consideration governed
a series of instructions issued to the auditors, ranging from the
reasonably cautious order of September 1442 that any letter
signed by the king and sealed with any of the royal seals should
be accepted as sufficient warrant for payment if accompanied
by the appropriate receipt,[1] to the ill-considered letter of 14th
June, 1448, instructing that the sworn word of the treasurer
general should be accepted in resolving any difficulties in his
accounts.[2] Such central control as did exist was achieved by
referring particular items in the accounts back and forth
between Naples and the relevant audit office. Occasionally too
officials from other territories were ordered to present their
accounts in Naples so that queries arising from transactions with
the central treasury might be resolved on the spot at the king's
discretion.[3] The audit of monies spent within the kingdom of
Naples appears to have fallen within the province of the
Sommaria whatever their provenance.

A much stricter attention to the control of accounts begins to
appear in 1449—in many ways a crucial year in Alfonso's reign.
Besides playing a necessary part in the general reshaping of
imperial institutions, the reforms introduced then and later in
the system of auditing probably reflected the disillusionment

[1] A.C.A. R.2901, fol. 84v, 15th September, 1442.
[2] A.C.A. R.2719, fol. 65. Complications arising from varying interest and
exchange rates on bills of exchange were urged to justify this measure.
[3] The royal procurators of Majorca and Logudoro (Sardinia) were summoned
to Naples for that purpose in 1444.

that came when examination of the deceased treasurer general Pujades' accounts revealed very large sums owing to the Crown.[1] Alfonso's declaration, made to justify the measure of June 1448, that he had full confidence in the discretion, diligence and honesty of the treasurer general then began to appear poorly founded. A *pragmática* dated 20th August, 1449, attempted to improve matters by providing that all treasurers and other receivers of royal revenues should account for it to the *maestre racional* of the state in which it was received.[2] In this manner it was hoped to eliminate some of the difficulties raised by peripatetic treasurers, but the reform did nothing to improve the more complicated audit of payments. Another scandal, which brought about the downfall of the Neapolitan treasurer general in 1453,[3] led to more fundamental and effective changes. One of these, introduced by a *pragmática* which came into force on 1st January, 1455, made use of the office of conservator general of the Royal Patrimony which had been established by Alfonso in 1445 in pursuance of his policy of recovering the alienated lands and revenues of the Crown in his Spanish dominions.[4] Since 1448 the holder of the office, Pere de Besalú, had been in the court of Naples where he won great influence and rewards, among them the office of seneschal and extensive lands in Sicily. To this official Alfonso sought to give a supervisory control over all charges on the revenue by directing, in the *pragmática*, that all forms of bond and promissory notes (*albarana, debitoria, cedule maritate*), and all letters emanating from the Curia concerning Crown lands, rights and revenues should be registered word for word in his office. As a further precaution, no letter was to be accepted for registration unless it bore in the king's own hand the words: 'I have read this and it is my pleasure that it be done'.[5] The conservator general was also to keep a register 'in the manner in which merchants

[1] In his capacity as master of the ports (*magister portulanus*) in Sicily alone, Pujades owed 2,400 ducats (A.C.A. R.2946, fol. 160r). The sequestration of his Spanish property ordered in 1452 was countermanded only in 1458 by the king's will.

[2] A.C.A. R.2720, fol. 123v.

[3] The circumstances of Pere Capdevila's disgrace are still obscure. In July 1453 he was deprived of all his offices in Naples, and an order was given for the seizure of his property and offices in Catalonia, Valencia and Aragon as security for large sums found owing to the Crown after an examination of his accounts (A.C.A. R.2661, fol. 26v, 27th July, 1453).

[4] R. Moscati, 'Nella burocrazia centrale di Alfonso d'Aragona: le cariche generali', *Miscellanea in onore di Roberto Cessi*, i (Rome, 1958), 372.

[5] A.C.A. R.2661, fol. 82v, 22nd December, 1454.

conduct their business': that is, showing all ordinary revenues under the offices through which they were received, and against each fund details of the charges upon it. All this work required a considerable staff the majority of whom were Spaniards. But the important office of advocate of the Royal Patrimony was given to a Neapolitan, Nicola Antonio de Monti, who had been a president in the *Sommaria* and *locumtenens* of the chamberlain of Naples. Both he and Pere de Besalú attended the royal council.

This development of the office of conservator general was followed in the same year by the establishment of a supreme financial council, the *Consilium Pecuniae*. Initially this tribunal may have been regarded as a revival of the older *Magna Curia dei Maestri Razionali* which, under the early Angevins, had been responsible for the audit of official accounts and all consequent legal action. Because the members of this court were elected by the wards of Naples, later rulers had relied increasingly upon officials of the *Sommaria* (originally a department of the treasury that carried out a preliminary audit) over whom they had full control, and by the beginning of the fifteenth century the *Magna Curia* had become nothing more than a source of perquisites for the Neapolitan nobility. The idea that such a tribunal, superior to the *Sommaria*, might be a valuable administrative device if properly constituted appears to have come from Antonio Caruso who had served Alfonso as treasurer of Sicily and also in the *Sommaria*. Under his direction the *Consilium Pecuniae* was installed in the building formerly occupied by the *Magna Curia dei Maestri Razionali*. Nominally its senior members were the justiciar and chamberlain of Naples, which further emphasizes its Neapolitan origins. The most active members, however, were Caruso, Jacme de Pilaya, a lawyer who was also employed in the *Sacrum Consilium* and the office of the conservator general, and Goffredo di Gaeta, a president of the *Sommaria*.

In its first year of existence the *Consilium Pecuniae* concentrated its attention on a series of inquests into the titles by which various tolls and offices were held in the kingdom of Naples.[1]

---

[1] These inquests began with a decree dated 13th February, 1456, annulling all titles to tolls and vacant benefices for which no privilege bearing the great seal could be produced. On 13th March, 1456, the inspection was ordered of all royal grants of benefices, public offices and licences to practise professions. An inquest into the titles to forges and mills began on 20th September, 1456.

Such investigations complemented the registration of titles with the conservator general's office, and it may well be that the attempt to enforce the new regulations for that department had quickly revealed the need for machinery to compel registration and punish illegal occupation of lands, offices and revenues. A policy of fiscal terrorism enforced the council's will. Failure to produce its titles within the given period cost the city of Sulmona a fine of 600 ducats. Those found guilty of any offence were mulcted of enormous sums. A fine of 40,000 ducats was imposed upon the city of Trani for a riot, presumably connected with the inquests. Giovanni de Miroballo, a president of the *Sommaria* and formerly the king's banker, was condemned to pay 30,000 ducats. Many cities and individuals, including Manfredonia and a group of Pisan merchants in Palermo, were fined for trading with Florence in violation of the ban imposed in 1451 on the outbreak of war between the king and the republic. No offence uncovered by its commissioners lay outside the competence of the council. Its far-ranging inquisitions and swingeing fines caused dismay throughout the kingdom, especially since its status as a supreme tribunal permitted no appeal against its sentences, except to the king in person. Even that avenue of escape was evidently closed at first, for the parliament of October 1456 had to petition, with success, that execution of judgment be suspended while an appeal was pending.[1] That same parliament attempted, without success, to circumvent the *Consilium Pecuniae* by asking for a general pardon for all crimes committed in the past, excepting high treason against the king's person, for a general confirmation of titles to land and other possessions, and for the cessation of general and special inquests.

Despite its evident unpopularity, Alfonso refused to weaken the powers of the council in any important particular. On the contrary he proceeded to reinforce the system of financial control established in the office of the conservator general and the *Consilium Pecuniae* by creating a new supreme office—the master-general of the audit (*magister rationalis generalis*). The close relationship between this new office and the *Consilium Pecuniae* was emphasized by the appointment of Antonio Caruso

---

[1] Archivio di Stato di Napoli, *Diversi della Regia Camera della Sommaria*, I, 52 (bis), fol. 171–6. A later copy of the proceedings of this parliament, erroneously ascribed to the year 1452, instead of 1456.

as the first *magister rationalis generalis* on 29th October, 1456.[1] Indeed it is very possible that Caruso was the moving spirit behind the new development which was essential to the successful functioning of the *Consilium Pecuniae* as an imperial tribunal. The privilege appointing him argued the necessity of having a general auditor to control those in the king's several states; it empowered him to call for accounts from any receiver of revenue and to question them even when a subordinate auditor had already issued a quittance. Each year the audit offices of Naples, Aragon, Sicily, Valencia and Catalonia were required to submit to him a statement of the balance remaining after payment of all the charges upon the revenues of those states, thus providing the basis for a rudimentary imperial budget.

Armed with these new powers of inquiry and control, Caruso and his colleagues of the *Consilium Pecuniae* turned their attention in 1457 to highly-placed officials and the usurpation of royal rights and revenues in the Spanish states. In April all privileges, exemptions, graces, etc., granted *ad beneplacitum* in Valencia, Catalonia, Aragon and Majorca were revoked because of alleged fraud and losses to the Crown.[2] At the same time, Jacme de Pilaya, specially commissioned as a procurator fiscal, was investigating the activities of several Spanish officials and institutions, among them the *Generalidades* of Catalonia and Valencia. For that purpose he sent his own agents to Spain. But the inquiry into charges brought by the council against Juan de Moncayo, regent in the office of governor of Aragon, was entrusted to Queen Maria and the king of Navarre. In Naples the royal secretary, Francesc Martorell, faced accusations of bribery and other pecuniary crimes,[3] and towards the end of the year de Pilaya demanded the prosecution of the senior secretary, Joan Olzina, on various charges including bribery, malversation of royal funds during a mission to Spain, and mismanagement of the Aragonese barony of Huesca which he had held on lease from the Crown.[4] Alfonso showed some reluctance to proceed against a man who had served him intimately for twenty-five years and, while approving further investigation, stressed that

[1] A.C.A. R.2602, fol. 153; ref. R.2625, fol. 159. Caruso was given a red banner of office bearing the arms of Aragon, Sicily and Naples.

[2] A.C.A. R.2662, fol. 70r, 25th April, 1457.

[3] Perhaps relating to his office of *magister portulanus* in Sicily from which he still owed large sums to the Crown when he died in 1466.

[4] A.C.A. R.2662, fol. 83r, 29th October, 1457. To the king of Navarre ordering an inquiry into the charges.

he wished to deal leniently with Olzina. Accusations of this nature against powerful officials naturally aroused violent antagonisms and counter-denunciations which the king tolerated, and even encouraged, for much was thereby brought to light and his personal power as final arbiter enhanced. Perhaps the energy displayed by the *Consilium Pecuniae* and its allies, the conservator general and auditor general, would soon have spent itself, or proved self-destructive; certainly it came too late in the reign to uncover many glaring abuses, such as those which Trasselli describes in the finances of Sicily[1]. Nevertheless, this elaborate system of financial control bore witness to a remarkable degree of resourcefulness and adaptability in the king and his administration even in the twilight of the reign.

Within the space of twenty years there had emerged an imperial government in embryo, incomplete but coherent, to match the new dimensions of Aragonese imperialism. Above the carefully preserved, and often strengthened, administrative autonomy of his subject states Alfonso had raised a close-knit system of bureaucratic offices and councils staffed overwhelmingly by lawyers of modest origins. Aragonese, Castilian, Sicilian and Neapolitan precedent and experience all contributed to the evolution of these institutions, and men from every part of the empire served them. It might, with some truth, be argued that they became effective too late in the reign to make a lasting impression upon established institutions, and that the division of Alfonso's empire in 1458 entailed dismantling the central administration. But the experience gained in Naples could not be forgotten either in Spain or in Italy, for it had informed the thinking of a whole generation of the most able minds available to the king's service. A large number of them chose to continue their careers with the new ruler of Aragon, and when that monarchy under Ferdinand the Catholic again faced the problems of empire it resumed the courses charted from Naples by Alfonso the Magnanimous.

---

[1] C. Trasselli, 'Sul débito pubblico in Sicilia sotto Alfonso V d'Aragona', *Estudios de Historia Moderna*, vi (1956-9).

XII

J. R. L. Highfield

THE CATHOLIC KINGS AND THE TITLED NOBILITY OF CASTILE

To discuss the relationship between the Catholic kings and the nobility of Castile, but not of Aragon, might at first sight appear an absurdity, especially in a reign which saw Spain a united country. The story of the nobility of the kingdoms of the Crown of Aragon must indeed be told by some future historian,[1] but it involved at least two important and different factors. Wealth and titles did not march together so closely in Aragon, Catalonia, Valencia and Majorca as they did in Castile even if, there too, no tidy 'heads of the honour' were to be found. Secondly the rulers of the Crown of Aragon were able to reward their nobility with Sicilian and (after 1504) with Neapolitan titles. This they preferred to do, both because of their Italian policy and because they did not wish to build up trouble for themselves by granting titles in Aragon, where the nobility was highly privileged. Thus to discuss Aragon is to discuss Italy and that would be to take too large a step in this essay.

Let us first attempt to relate the Castilian titled nobility to the geography of the peninsula and then reopen for consideration some of the more important problems affecting the nobility and the Crown. It is true that much noble wealth consisted of

---

[1] For Catalonia see S. Sobrequés Vidal, *Els Barons de Catalunya* (Barcelona, 1961), for Aragon, A. Giménez Soler, *Revista de Aragón*, i (1900), for Valencia, S. Carreres Zacares, *Notas para la Historia de los Bandos de Valencia* (1932). I am grateful to Mr P. Rycraft for these references. For a quantatitive analysis of the Spanish aristocracy cf. *Historia social y económica de España y América*, ed. J. V. Vives, ii (Barcelona, 1957), 414–17 and J. Lynch, *Spain under the Hapsburgs*, i (Oxford, 1964), 12–20 (Castile only).

parcels of rights, often widely scattered, which could vary greatly from one generation to another. Again in a given group of holdings it can prove difficult to decide where the most important blocks of lands were to be found.[1] But at the end of the fifteenth century at least, the title often (though not invariably) provides a clue; and in a Sargasso sea of difficulties the *mayorazgo* or imbarrable entail seems to offer a clear channel. The details of the *mayorazgos* describe much of the wealth, and more specifically the landed wealth, of the nobility.

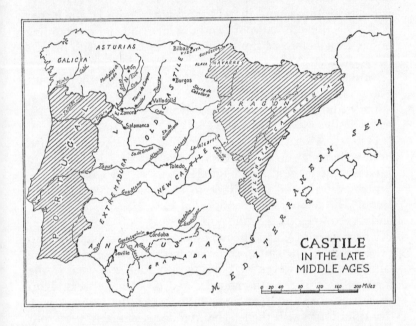

CASTILE
IN THE LATE
MIDDLE AGES

The validity of this essay turns first on whether it is shown worthwhile to pursue this type of evidence as a source for the history of the Castilian nobility. The peerage policy of the Catholic kings will next be considered. Then three other matters touching the nobility (towns, alienations of royal income and the Military Orders) will be reviewed before a return is made to the *mayorazgo*—the centrepiece of noble power. Even after so limited an inquiry it should prove possible to show that the question of the Crown and the titled nobility of Castile at this

---

[1] In lists of lands given in footnotes no claim is made for completeness.

important juncture (1474–1516) must be investigated afresh. For reasons of space no effort will be made to deal with relations between the nobility and the Church.

By 1474 it must have seemed to an outside observer that the Castilian nobility had won in their long struggle with the Crown. True there had been efforts to build up the royal power, especially in the reign of Peter I (1350–69) and John II (1406–54). But though some of the royal institutions had developed in the late Middle Ages, such as the council, the chancery and the audiencia,[1] it had been notable that Peter had lost his throne and that, in the reign of John II, the leader of the royal cause had not been the king, but an outstanding noble, Don Álvaro de Luna, who paid for his zeal with his life. After each successful *coup d'état* an aristocratic clique had been rewarded with a set of 'mercies' and 'donations', that is with grants of rents and lands. The 'mercies' of Henry II (1369–79) —the founder of the Trastámara dynasty—are famous.[2] They were easily excelled by those of John II and Henry IV (1454–74). A veritable aristocratic order of society had seemed to have been set up by the Sentence of Medina del Campo in January 1465;[3] and, although Henry IV had cancelled the Sentence, little had been done to challenge the reality of its terms. The temporary deposition of Henry in the same year had served to emphasize the point.

There were in Castile in 1474 forty-nine noble families with titles of duke, marquis, count or viscount.[4] Some of these families were, however, no more than branches of what in the thirteenth or fourteenth centuries had been single trees. Thus there were five different main branches of the Zúñigas with five titles to go with them. The Mendozas similarly were split into four major families and the Manriques and Velascos into three each. What had originally been four families disposed of

---

[1] L. Suárez Fernández, *Nobleza y Monarquía* (Valladolid, 1959), 34–42.
[2] Ibid., 17–27.
[3] Ibid., 153, *Memorias de Enrique IV: Colección Diplomática* (Madrid, 1913), 486.
[4] A. de Vargas-Zúñiga, *Títulos y Grandezas del Reino* (Madrid, 1956), a convenient but not an infallible repertory. Where not otherwise stated this is the source for the date of promotion to a title. For lands and *mayorazgos* I have chiefly relied on *Registro General del Sello*, ed. Gonzalo Ortiz de Montalván, etc., *Catálogo*, xiii (1935–) in the series *Archivo General de Simancas* and on *Colección de d. Luis de Salazar y Castro*, ed. A. de Vargas-Zúñiga, xxx vols., in progress (1949–). The editor notes whether a document is an original, a copy of an original or a mere copy.

nearly a quarter of the titles of Castile. Convenient though the categories of rank undoubtedly are, it must freely be admitted that some 'lords' were more powerful and wealthy than some of the titled nobility. It was from this group of 'lords' that several of the more important of the promotions under the Catholic kings were to come.

The Reconquest had determined the pattern of noble holdings first between the Douro and the Tagus in southern León and Old Castile, and subsequently in the territory south of the Tagus. The conquest of Andalusia and the acquisition of Murcia in the thirteenth century had led to the most extensive rewards of all for the Castilian nobility. But the impetus of advance had been halted after the battle of Salado (1340) and since then the pattern of holdings had changed, as if it were in a kaleidoscope, partly because of the establishment of the usurping dynasty in 1369, but partly also because five of the *apanages* then set up soon began to disappear.[1]

Galicia in the north-west was the most isolated part of Spain and better supplied with noble families than any other region except Andalusia. The mountainous nature of the country, the need for the Crown to maintain forces on the Portuguese frontier and the opportunity offered to the Galician nobles to play off Castile against Portugal all operated in favour of noble strongholds. On the west and Atlantic coast the powerful family were the Sotomayor, viscounts of Tuy and counts of Carmiña[2]. In south-west Galicia in the province of Orense were the chief holdings of a branch of the Zúñiga. They held the castle of Monterrey and the title of count derived from it.[3] Monterrey controls the upper valley of the Tamega before it flows into Portugal. Between Orense and Lugo were the main properties of the Osorio. Though they claimed descent from Pelayo they had only been counts of Trastámara since 1447 and marquises

---

[1] Suárez, 54–64.
[2] Carmiña is Caminha just across the Miño into Portugal (cf. A. López de Haro, *Nobiliario de Reyes y Títulos*, ii (Madrid, 1622), 61). They were lords of Sotomayor and Pontevedra and of the fortress of Sobroso (1480) (all in Pontevedra) (Salazar, xxviii, 136, *Reg. 1478–80*, pp. 392, 480). After each identified place the name of the appropriate modern province will be found in brackets.
[3] Monterrey had been a viscounty before 1474. For Zúñiga lands at Baides and Galve cf. Salazar, xxviii, 382–3.

of Astorga from 1465.[1] Their lands ran over into León and their headquarters was Villalobos,[2] south-east of the junction of the rivers Cea and Esla (Zamora). Their castle of Astorga (León) dominated the upper Tuerto valley and lay close to the Montañas de León. Another family with lands divided between Galicia and León were the Castro y Osorio counts of Lemos, whose chief fortress was Monforte (Lugo)[3] on the River Cabé. Two Galician families which held titles in 1474, but which died out in the course of the reign, were the Sánchez de Ulloa counts of Altamira[4] and the Villandrando counts of Ribadeo.[5] The latter sprang from Rodrigo de Villandrando, the captain of the Hundred Years War. Ribadeo (Lugo) is a port on the frontier between Galicia and Asturias. The Villandrando lands passed by marriage to the Salinas and Basque branch[6] of the last Galician family in this survey, the Sarmiento, counts of Santa Marta.[7] It was to the Sarmiento that the Catholic kings were increasingly to turn for help in the task of governing a turbulent province.

The old unconquered kingdom of Asturias and the Basque provinces of Castile (Vizcaya, Guipúzcoa and Álava) did not

[1] Cf. grant by Henry IV of the city and marquisate of Astorga to Álvaro Pérez de Osorio on 1st October, 1469 (Salazar, xix, 74). In the *Libro de Asientos* (1447) the first count of Trastámara (d. 1461) had an income from royal sources worth more than 321,000 maravedises p.a. (L. Suárez Fernández, 'Un libro de asientos de Juan II', *Hispania*, xvii (1957), 347). The *Libro* is incomplete. Five of its 341 sheets are missing. Sections labelled *Salvado*, *Juros*, and *Tierra* are most important here since they represent grants thought in 1447 to have been permanently alienated and thus are likely still to have been held in 1474 by the appropriate member of the house concerned. I have worked on a basis of 375 maravedises = 1 ducat = *c.* 9s. 8d. sterling. In 1480 Burón and Navia (both in Lugo) were of the *mayorazgo* of the marquis (*Reg. 1480–4*, p. 91).

[2] *Mayorazgo* of Villalobos founded by 1417 (Salazar, xix, 73).

[3] They also held Sarria (Lugo), Ribera, Cabrera and Coto de Balboa.

[4] The count was *pertiguero mayor* or chief patron of Santiago de Compostela and viscount of Finisterre (1474) (cf. Salazar, xxviii, 136). When the titles died out (1500) that of Altamira was recreated for the grandson of the first marquis of Astorga.

[5] Cf. J. Quicherat, *Rodrigue de Villandrando* (Paris, 1879), p. 4, n. 1, p. 6, n. 1; *Reg. 1478–80*, p. 68. Lands included Navia (Pontevedra), Lobera (Orense), Asperelo and Intremo (both in Galicia) (Salazar, xxviii, 368). In the *Libro* the count of Ribadeo had an income from royal sources of 321,880 m.p.a.

[6] For Diego Gómez Sarmiento, *repostero mayor* or chief butler of John II, *merino* or judge of the sheep-walks of Galicia cf. E. B. Ruano, 'Don Pero Sarmiento, repostero mayor de Juan II de Castilla. Datos, biográfico-documentales', *Hispania*, xvii (1957), 483–504; 'El origen del condado de Salinas', *Hidalguía*, v (1957), 41–8. Salinas de Añana is in Álava. Other properties included La Bastida, Puentelarra, Penacerrada, Marquinez, Astulez (all in Álava), Ocio, Penalva, Lagrán, Lugares de Quintana, Urturi, Retuerto and Sobrón. A *mayorazgo*, licensed on 17th April, 1442, was founded on 29th June, 1463.

[7] Diego Pérez Sarmiento, count of Santa Marta, was *adelantado* or governor of Galicia. In the *Libro* he had income from royal sources worth 212,000 m.p.a.

provide many titled families by 1474. Those which had once held there had for the most part moved the centre of their interests further south as the Reconquest had developed. Thus of the Manrique, who had begun life in the province of Álava, one branch, though they kept their ancient county of Treviño (Burgos/Álava), had advanced their lands south-westwards into Castile. By 1474 they held the title of dukes of Nájera (Logroño).[1] They had a key position on the Navarrese frontier especially in the Sierra de Cebollera and the Upper Ebro valley. Another branch of this family had prospered by marriage with a royal heiress (the grand-daughter of Henry II's brother, Tello) and were through her counts of Castañeda (Santander) and lords of Aguilar de Campóo (Palencia).[2] The Quiñones, counts of Luna, had developed in a different direction. Holding mainly in Castile in the region between Astorga and the port of Llanes (Oviedo),[3] they had acquired important possessions in Aragon and Valencia (Segorbe (Castellón), Alicante and Xecla). The Guevara counts of Oñate (Guipúzcoa) had by contrast remained rooted in the Basque countryside.[4]

The kingdoms of Castile and León still afforded excellent opportunities for noble families to dominate the more important towns and to sit astride the main north-south routes of the wool-trade, both of the 'transhumantes', the sheep passing from seasonal pasture to seasonal pasture (controlled, for example, by the Arévalo Zúñigas at Béjar[5] on the routes known as the *Leonesa* and the *Segoviana*), and of the wool export trade from Burgos to Bilbao, which fell under the influence of the Velasco. They not only had a very strong position in Burgos, but in three different branches of the family had the three titles, Haro, Roa and Siruela respectively, as well as the office of constable of

[1] Diego Gómez Manrique was *repostero mayor* of John II and *adelantado* of Castile (Salazar, xxix, 390). A *mayorazgo* of Amusco (Palencia) was founded on 17th September, 1382 (L. de Salazar y Castro, *Historia Genealógica de la Casa de Lara*, i (Madrid, 1696), 353). Their holdings also included S. Pedro, near Yanguas (Soria) (ibid.). Navarrete and Ocón (both in Logroño) (ibid., xxviii, 132, 260) and Ponferrada (León) (*Reg. 1480-4*, p. 111), cf. Salazar, *Historia de la Casa de Lara*, i, 321-47, ii, 99-180.
[2] Lands also in the Valle del Toranzo (Santander) (*Reg. 1478-80*, p. 143).
[3] *Merinos* of León and Asturias from before 1466 to *c.* 1563-74. For their *mayorazgo* cf. Salazar, xxviii, 339. For their holdings of Onzonilla (León), Villachan and Comes (1480) cf. *Reg. 1480-4*, p. 143.
[4] *Adelantados* of León, 1420-1500, and lords of the valley of Leniz (Guipúzcoa). They also held Villena, Cameno, Hermandades de Barrundia, Gamboa and Eguilar. The father of the first count of Oñate had in the *Libro* royal income of 68,900 m.p.a.
[5] J. Klein, *The Mesta* (Cambridge, Mass., 1920), 19.

Castile (held by the counts of Haro from 1473).[1] The Book of *Asientos* shows that the count of Haro had in 1447 an income from royal sources alone worth more than 1,000,000 m.p.a.[2] In 1469 the first count had become governor of the Basque provinces of Vizcaya and Álava. The neighbours of the Velasco to the west, but hardly their rivals, were the Sandoval y Rojas counts of Castrojeriz (Burgos); as counts of Denia they also held lands near Alicante in the kingdom of Valencia.[3]

At Valladolid on the Pisuerga was the centre of power of the Enríquez, the hereditary admirals of Castile. A semi-royal family in origin, the illegitimate descendants of a half-brother of Henry II, they included both Ferdinand's mother, Juana, and his uncle Alfonso, the third admiral.[4] There were two main families, the admiral's (his eldest son from the second half of the fifteenth century was count of Melgar y Rueda[5]) and that of a cadet line, the counts of Alba de Liste.[6] In the Book of *Asientos* the admiral had an income from royal sources of over 1,000,000 m.p.a., that is more than that of any other non-royal noble family in Castile.[7] A key stronghold of the Enríquez was the castle of Torrelobatón (Valladolid) on the Hornija in the Montes de Torozos.

Close to Valladolid lay Fuensaldaña—the chief fortress of the Vivero viscounts of Altamira.[8] North of it were the lands of the

---

[1] L. Serrano, *Los Reyes Católicos y la Ciudad de Burgos* (Madrid, 1943), 30.

[2] For Haro *mayorazgos* (1448, 1454) cf. Salazar, xxviii, 374. Velasco properties (Haro line) included Haro, Nieva de Cameros and Arnedo (all in Logroño), Briviesca, Medina de Pomar, Salas de los Infantes, S. Domingo de Silos and Frías (all in Burgos), Torrelluecas, Avenzana, Oriñuela and Mabezón (ibid., and Haro, i, 182). The father of the first constable had in the *Libro* royal income worth more than 1,137,200 m.p.a. See also the map (plate ix) in *Inventario del archivo de los Duques de Frías*, ed. de la Peña Marazuela and León Tello, i (Madrid, 1955).

[3] They had been *adelantados mayores* of Castile in 1422 and 1467; their *mayorazgo* had been founded by 1426 (Salazar, xx, 128); their holdings included Valdenebro and Villafrechos (both in Valladolid) and Saldaña (Palencia) (ibid., xxix, 130, 368). In the *Libro* the Rojas family had royal income worth more than 620,000 m.p.a.

[4] License to found a *mayorazgo*, 30th October, 1440 (ibid., xxix, 194); four founded on 10th March, 1473: (1) of Medina de Rio Seco (Valladolid), (2) of Tarifa (Cádiz) and Rueda (Valladolid), (3) of Villada (Palencia), (4) of Vega de Rioponce (Valladolid). Other holdings included Torrelobatón and Valdunquillo (both in Valladolid), Melgar (Burgos), Mansilla (León) and Bolaños (ibid., xxviii, 388-9).

[5] The first count, son of the third admiral, died in 1506.

[6] For their towns of Villada (Palencia) and Villavicencio (Valladolid) cf. ibid., xxviii, 359 and 389.

[7] Suárez, 132.

[8] Cf. *Reg. 1480-4*, p. 266; Salazar, xxvii, 137; *Títulos*, 130 and C. Espejo, 'El contador mayor de Enrique IV, Juan Pérez de Vivero; Notas para su biografía', *Bol. Soc. Cast. Exc.*, iii (1907-8), 346-8, 375-6, 377-9 (Sánchez Alonso, *Fuentes*, no. 1574).

bishop of Palencia. He was in the anomalous position of holding a lay fief, the county of Pernia. This had been granted to Sancho de Rojas, bishop of Palencia, perhaps as a result of his heroic exploits at the conquest of Antequera in 1410. The title was certainly borne by all the bishops after Gutierre de la Cueva (d. 1469).[1] But since the bishops came from different families and did not found dynasties, Pernia was the least threatening noble fief from the royal point of view.

Far more powerful than the viscounts of Altamira or the counts of Pernia were the Manrique de Lara, counts of Paredes de Nava (Palencia), who held very extensive lands north of Palencia in the Tierra de Campos and the valley of the Carrión. Luckily this house had committed themselves to Ferdinand and Isabella as early as 1469, when the latter commanded support elsewhere only among the Enríquez. Rodrigo Manrique, the first count (and the father of the poet, Jorge), enhanced his position on becoming master of Santiago in 1474.[2]

To the west and north-west beyond the Montes de Torozos lay the wheat-growing lands of León, watered by the Esla and other tributaries flowing down into the Douro. Here south of León in the upper Esla valley were the chief lands of the Acuña, dukes of Valencia de Don Juan (also proprietors in Asturias).[3] In that of the Upper Orbigo were those of the Bazán viscounts of Los Palacios de Valduerna;[4] while further down the same valley towards its junction with the Esla were to be found the estates of the immensely strong family of the Pimentel. They were like the Acuñas of Portuguese origin. But they had nearly eighty years before lost their lands in Portugal at Braganza.[5] They took their title of counts of Benavente from the town of that name on the Orbigo. They were powerful also to the north-east between the rivers Cea and Sequillo at Mayorga and Villalón, and at Puebla de Sanabria (close to the frontier of Portugal). It is not surprising to find the Pimentel accused of

---

[1] *Títulos*, 129.
[2] A. Stokvis, *Manuel de Tous les Etats*, ii, 15.
[3] Their title as count went back to 1398 (*Títulos*, 17 and cf. Salazar, xxviii, 120). They had a Portuguese origin. Henry IV gave them Pravia and Gijón (both in Ovideo) and lands in Asturias (ibid., xxviii, 108) and made them dukes (1465).
[4] They held Ceinos (Valladolid) (ibid., 373).
[5] Dias Arnaut, *A Crise Nacional dos Fins do Seculo XIV* (Coimbra, 1960), 247. I owe this reference to Mr P. Rycraft.

treacherous dealings with the Portuguese in the Succession War (1475).[1]

The most crucial centre in southern León was the old Leonese capital, Salamanca, on the Tormes, a southern tributary of the Douro. The great family there were the Álvarez de Toledo, counts (and since 1469 dukes) of Alba.[2] They had advanced rapidly as the allies of Álvaro de Luna and had kept their lands at his downfall. In 1447 the Albas were second only to the Enríquez among the non-royal nobility of Castile. The count himself had income from royal sources worth about 1,000,000 m.p.a.[3] The family also had wide possessions and centres of influence north of the Tagus and the Sierra de Gredos, at Piedrahita (Ávila) and Ávila between Salamanca and Madrid; and also far to the south-west of Salamanca beyond the mountains between the Douro and Tagus at Cáceres and Coria (Cáceres) in Extremadura, where they were the rivals of a branch of the Zúñigas.[4]

In the same mountains and on the southern border of León was the county of Miranda del Castañar, which had been held by another branch of the Zúñiga since 1457. They also had sizable holdings in the Douro valley and in that of its tributary, the Cega.[5]

The lands between the Douro and the Tagus south of the Sierra de Guadarrama had been conquered from the Moors for the most part in the eleventh century. At that time several noble families had come into the upper Tagus valley and into those of its northern tributaries, from the north-east. Among them were the Mendoza, who had previously belonged to Álava in the Basque provinces. By 1366 when Pedro González was *mayordomo mayor* or chief steward to Peter I, they had been given the lordships of Hita and Buitrago (both in Madrid) and had

---

[1] A. Paz y Mélia, *El Cronista A. de Palencia* (Madrid, 1914), p. xxii. In the *libro* the father of the first duke of Benavente had royal income of 451,950 m.p.a.

[2] That is Alba de Tormes (Salamanca).

[3] *Libro*, 338.

[4] Haro, i, 219–28. They were also counts of Salvatierra. Their eldest sons were marquises of Coria (Cáceres) and their eldest sons dukes of Huéscar (Granada). They also had lands at Salvatierra de Tormes (Salamanca) and in the Valdecorneja (Ávila) (ibid.).

[5] At Peñaranda de Duero (Burgos), Iscar (Valladolid) and at Avallaneda, Fuente Alnuxir and Aza (*Títulos*, 68). By marriage they held Candeleda, Alexa and La Puebla (all in Ávila) and Navarrete (Logroño), all to pass (1479) to the count de Treviño (Salazar, xxviii, 131).

reached the rank of *ricoshombres*—nobles.[1] Counts of El Real de Manzanares (Madrid) and marquises of Santillana (Santander) they had royal income in 1447 worth more than 500,000 m.p.a.[2] Since then they had increased their wealth by the marriage in 1460 between the third marquis of Santillana and Maria de Luna which had brought them part of the Luna spoils.[3] Their secular position was enhanced by the political power of the marquis' brother, Cardinal Mendoza. Their support was vital to the establishment of the cause of Ferdinand and Isabella. Though they had possessions in the Carrión valley at Saldaña their chief lands lay between the mountains of the Sierra de Guadarrama and the upper Tagus valley.[4] Their great centre was the town of Guadalajara where they were all-powerful. They also had lands in the province of Ciudad Real (Manzanares). There were two titled subordinate lines of this family. The Suárez de Mendoza, counts of La Coruña, held lands in the valley of a tributary of the Henares.[5] Descended directly from the marquis of Santillana were the counts of Tendilla (Guadalajara). The second count was one of the most interesting members of the Castilian nobility of his day, as befitted a grandson of the first marquis of Santillana. He became one of Ferdinand's key supporters. His correspondence, to which attention has recently been drawn, constitutes one of the most important sources for the history of the reign.[6] Neighbours of the dukes of Infantado in the upper Henares valley were the De la Cerda counts of Medinaceli and marquises of Cogolludo (Guadalajara). They were descended from an illegitimate branch of the Pyrenean family of Béarn. Bernard de Foix,

[1] L. Serrano, *Historia de Guadalajara y sus Mendozas*, 4 vols. (Madrid, 1942), Haro, i, 240–57.
[2] *Libro*, 332–3.
[3] Salazar, xxix, 408.
[4] The eldest son had the title of count of Saldaña from 1462 (*Títulos*, 75). Íñigo López de Mendoza, count of Saldaña, was granted the towns of Barajas and El Alameda confiscated from J. Zapata, cf. A. Huarte, 'Cosas que pasaron en Madrid. La Rebelión de Juan Zapata', *Rev. Bibl. Arch. Mus. Ayuntamiento de Madrid*, xx (1951), 237–58, quoted in *Índice Histórico*, ii (1955–6), no. 7307, p. 48.
[5] At La Coruña del Conde (Burgos), They were also viscounts of Torija (Guadalajara) and had rents in Guadalajara itself (*Reg. 1478–80*, p. 448).
[6] J. C. Adán, 'Andalucía en 1508, un aspecto de la correspondencia del virrey Tendilla', *Hispania*, xxii (1962), 38–80; G. Ibañez de Segovia, 'Historia de la casa de Mondéjar', B.N. MS. 3. 315. License to found a *mayorazgo*, 3rd June, 1478 (*Reg. 1478–80*, p. 89). The counts held Loranca (Guadalajara) and Meco (Madrid) in 1480 (*Reg. 1480–4*, p. 35), La Guardia (Navarre), Aranda del Duero (Burgos) and Mondéjar (Guadalajara) by 1483 (cf. ibid., 169; Salazar, xxviii, 96, 102).

'Bastard' of Béarn, had married the heiress of the La Cerda family of Alfonso X and had become naturalized in Castile in the fourteenth century.[1]

Between the Henares and the Tagus were the main estates of the Silva, counts of Cifuentes. The founder of their line had been *adelantado* or governor of Cazorla (Jaén). He had set up a *mayorazgo* in 1430. He held the post of *alférez mayor* or standard bearer to John II and this became hereditary in his family which by 1504 held no less than four *mayorazgos*.[2]

South of the Tagus lies the dry upland plateau of Cuenca, known as La Alcarria. Here were the lands of the Acuña (counts of Buendía from 1467). They were also lords of Dueñas on the Pisuerga.[3] A younger line of this family, the Vázquez de Acuña, counts of Viana, were made dukes of Huete (Cuenca) in 1474.[4] Huete lies in the *Altos de Cabrejas* fifty-five kilometres west of Cuenca between it and the Tagus valley. To the east of the present Tagus reservoirs in the Sierra de Cuenca the important family was that of the Mendoza counts of Priego.[5] But the more powerful families in the Tagus valley were to be found on its middle reaches further to the west.

In this part of the modern province of Toledo some very wealthy houses were to be found. The most dangerous opponent of the new monarchs was the marquis of Villena of the Pacheco. They were, like the Pimentel, of Portuguese origin. Their most strategic castle was probably that of Escalona (Toledo) on the Alberche, a tributary of the Tagus.[6] But the marquisate of Villena itself was an extensive fief contiguous with the frontier of the Aragonese kingdom of Valencia between Cuenca and Murcia. Juan Pacheco, when he became master of Santiago in 1467, added the strength of the most important of the Military Orders to that of his family possessions. Near Toledo were the lands of another family which tapped the resources of a military

[1] Haro, i, 78–87. They held Medinaceli (Soria) and Arcos (on the Aragonese frontier) (*Reg. 1478–80*, pp. 217, 255).

[2] Salazar, xix, 75. They had lands at Palos (Huelva) and Hormazas (Burgos) (ibid, xxviii, 149 and cf. 150). Cifuentes is in Guadalajara.

[3] Haro, ii, 8 corrected in *Títulos*, 101, cf. Salazar, i, 465, xxix, 123.

[4] *Títulos*, 124.

[5] Haro, i, 376–83. They were *reposteros mayores* to Henry III; their lands included Morón (Soria) and Hueto (Álava) (Salazar, xxviii, 158–9).

[6] For their Portuguese origins cf. Dias Arnaut, 159, 223–4, 245, 250 and cf. F. Pulgar, *Crónica de los Reyes Católicos*, ed. J. de M. Carriazo, i (Madrid, 1943), 57 (grants of Alcaraz (Albacete), Trujillo (Cáceres), Requena (Valencia) and Escalona (Toledo)). They had lands also at Garcimuñoz and Alcalá del Río (*Reg. 1478–80*, pp. 372, 383).

order in addition to its own. These were the Sotomayor, counts of Belalcázar, two of whom were successively masters of Alcántara (1416–46).[1] Also in the middle Tagus group were the Ayala counts of Fuensalida.[2]

Extremadura, like León and Galicia a frontier province which marched with Portugal, was naturally a centre of aristocratic power. It had also been of great strategic value as a base from which to overrun the Guadalquivir valley in the thirteenth century. In the north along the Tagus were the estates of the Manrique, counts of Osorno, who had married into the Enríquez.[3] There too lay an important group of lands belonging to the most dangerous and powerful of the Zúñiga clans, the dukes of Arévalo (Ávila), who also had property at Ávila, Burgos and Salamanca. They were the closest supporters of the first marquis of Villena.[4] Another branch of the same family held the county of Nieva in the mountains to the northwest of Béjar.[5]

In southern Extremadura Badajoz commands the Guadiana valley and the entry into Portugal in much the same way as Zamora does that of the Douro in the north. There were three great families of the Guadiana. The Figueroa had their chief centre at the town of Zafra (Badajoz) in the Tierra de Barros.[6] Like the Pacheco and the Sotomayor they owed much to a military order. Lorenzo Suárez de Figueroa had been master of Santiago (1387–1409). The foundation of a *mayorazgo* in 1404 was followed by the grant of their title of count of Feria in

---

[1] Haro, i, 410–19, cf. Salazar, xxix, 242 and M. Muñoz de S. Pedro, *Don Gutierre de Sotomayor, Maestre de Alcántara, 1400–53* (Cáceres, 1949).

[2] The first and second counts were *alcaldes mayores* or mayors (with judicial authority) in Toledo. They had lands at Cuerva, Guadamur (both in Toledo) and Huecas (cf. E. B. Ruano, *Toledo en el siglo XV* (Madrid, 1961), 108–9).

[3] Cf. Salazar, xxix, 142–3. *Historia de la Casa de Lara*, i, 599–613. Their lands included Osorno (Palencia). They claimed Vega de Ruiponce (Valladolid).

[4] Cf. V. Paredes, 'Los Zúñigas, señores de Plasencia', *Revista de Extremadura*, v–vi (1903–4). They had been governors of the fortress at Burgos for nearly a century (Serrano, *Burgos*, 29). They had castles at Toral and Aviados (Salazar, xxix, 315). One Zúñiga *mayorazgo* was based on lands at Arcos, Santa Cruz de Juarros, Revilla del Campo, Cuzcurrita (all in Burgos), Villatoto (Ávila) and Ciadoncha (Serrano, *Burgos*, 29). To these can be added Guzmán (Burgos), Bañares and Grañón (Logroño), Arévalo (Ávila), Béjar (Salamanca), Curiel, Pesquera, Villaconancio and Encinas (ibid., 193).

[5] The county of Nieva (Cáceres) included Valverde (cf. *Reg. 1480–4*, p. 50). The counts held Huércanos Tobía and rights at Matute (all in Logroño) (*Reg. 1480–4*, pp. 85, 163, 317), at Quintanilla de Nuño Pedro (Soria) (ibid., *1485–6*, p. 12) and the fortress of Los Gallegos y Miramontes (ibid., *1480–4*, p. 69).

[6] Cf. Salazar, xxix, 66–7, 27, 60, 13. They held Salvaleón, Villanueva de Barcarrota and Feria (all in Badajoz), Perales and Solana (ibid., 15, 35).

1460. Henry IV entrusted the government of Extremadura to the second count of Feria, who was a strong supporter of Villena.[1] When in 1474 Villena died, the count of Feria became a key figure in the election of the new master of Santiago (Alonso de Cárdenas).[2] A second Guadiana family were the Portocarrero, counts of Medellín (from 1452). This town lay well up stream from Badajoz and commanded the upper stretches of the valley. The Portocarrero were hereditary *regidores* or rectors of the town of Toro (Zamora).[3] The third family were the De la Cueva, dukes of Alburquerque. After enjoying the mastership of Santiago for a year Beltrán de la Cueva had been persuaded to renounce it so that it could be given to Isabella's brother Alfonso. He gained a duchy in exchange.[4] Alburquerque lies close to the Portuguese frontier, and although it is true that the De la Cueva had great centres of influence at Salamanca in León and at Cuéllar in Castile, the strength of their position close to Portugal tempted them towards a policy of friendship with the Portuguese.

Andalusia was the greatest centre of aristocratic power in Castile. This was particularly because of the rewards which had been handed out there after its conquest from the Moors in the thirteenth century. It was not only the base for any campaign against the kingdom of Granada, but included the great part of the frontier of that kingdom. Thus *La Frontera* was a source of military forces in time of peace.

The wealthiest and most outstanding family were undoubtedly the Guzmán, dukes of Medina Sidonia. They had been settled in Seville since the thirteenth century. By the fourteenth they are found as *ricoshombres* and lords of the port of Sanlúcar de Barrameda (Sevilla) at the mouth of the estuary of the Guadalquivir.[5] They advanced their position both by taking a successful part in the Moorish wars of Alfonso XI and in 1369

---

[1] Salazar, xxv, 408.
[2] Ibid., xxv, 410, 412; xxix, 114–15, 117.
[3] Salazar xxix, 146, 196. They had rights in Écija and Fuentes (both in Seville) (*Reg.* 1478–80, p. 520.)
[4] For a *mayorazgo* of 1472 cf. Salazar, xxix, 416. They had lands at Roa, Aranda (both in Burgos), Molina de Aragón, Atienza (both in Guadalajara), Cuéllar (Segovia), Ledesma (Salamanca), Jimena (?Jaén), Vezmar and Alcarquilla (cf. Pulgar, i, 55; *Reg. 1480–4*, p. 108; Haro, i, 345).
[5] Salazar, xxviii, 141. They had lands at Escamilla (Guadalajara), Niebla, Almonte (both in Huelva) (ibid., xxix, 74), at Lucena (Córdoba), Véjer and Chiclana (both in Cádiz), cf. also P. de Medina, 'Crónica de los duques de Medina Sidonia', in *CODOIN*, xxxix (1861), 5–395.

by backing the winning Trastámaras. As a result they found themselves (1371) counts of Niebla (Huelva) and owned lands covering much of the modern province of Huelva and parts of those of Seville and Cádiz. These were welded into a homogeneous whole by the first count of Niebla.[1] Three times during the fifteenth century a Guzmán controlled the lands of the Order of Alcántara, while both the second and the fourth counts continued to take part in Moorish campaigns in the tradition established by Alfonso Pérez de Guzmán, 'The Good', at the capture of Tarifa (1294). By 1460 they had become dukes of Medina Sidonia, a town forty kilometres east of Cádiz in the modern province of the same name.

The Guzmán were the deadly enemies of two other noble Andalusian familes—a line of the Enríquez and the Ponce de León. Since the Guzmán disputed lands near Niebla with the Enríquez it is not surprising to find that they were at first chary of supporting the cause of a prince who was half an Enríquez himself. By 1474, however, they had come to terms with the winning side, partly through the advocacy of the cause of Ferdinand and Isabella by the chronicler Palencia.[2]

In 1506 on the death of Philip I when there was a real chance of civil strife a league was made of the 'five great ones of Andalusia'. Leaving out the archbishop of Seville and the duke of Medina Sidonia there were the leading representatives of two branches of the Córdoba family and the Téllez Girón, counts of Ureña.[3] The Córdoba like the Guzmán had been *ricoshombres*. They had come south from Galicia to take part in the conquest of Córdoba by Ferdinand III (1236). One family took its title of count from the town of Cabra (Córdoba). They held land also at Iznájar, on the Genil, as well as the town of Baena (Córdoba) near Cabra.[4] In a list of the chief lords of the kingdom of Córdoba made in 1464 the count of Cabra heads the rest. The first count was an expert at making good marriages for his kin among the local Andalusian nobility. A junior branch of the family sprang from Alfonso, brother of the first count of Cabra. The post of *Alcaide de los Donceles* or master of the

[1] Cf. Haro, i, 57–9, Salazar, xxix, 74.
[2] Paz y Mélia, p. xi and Salazar, i, 465, cf. A. Barrantes Maldonado, *Memorial Histórico Español* (RAH), x (Madrid, 1857), 249–71.
[3] Salazar, xxv, 418.
[4] They were viscounts of Iznájar and lords of Baena (both in Córdoba) (*Títulos*, 55).

pages was held by these Córdobas for six generations. The fifth Alcaide was one of the outstanding personalities of the reign.[1] The Aguilar Córdoba founded their *mayorazgo* before 1327. Their two chief towns of Aguilar (granted 1369) and Montilla (both in Córdoba) lay directly between the lands of the count of Cabra and Córdoba itself.[2] This family exercised great influence over the town of Andújar (Jaén), on the Guadalquivir, and over local Andalusian houses holding lands between the Guadajoz and the Guadalquivir. The Great Captain, Gonzalo de Córdoba, was born at Montilla, the younger son of a Córdoba lord of Aguilar.

The fifth family named as that of one of the Grandees in 1464 was that of Téllez Girón (counts of Ureña from 1466).[3] They were especially strong in the present province of Seville round the town of Osuna in the valley of the Corbones. Their power was partly derived from the Order of Calatrava, since the first count had been the illegitimate son of Pedro Girón, master of the order from 1455–66, while another member of the family held the same mastership from 1466–82. The aspirations of this house may be measured by the fact that Pedro had seriously sought the hand of Isabella herself before he died in 1466.[4] Henry IV granted them the right to found a *mayorazgo* made up of lands at Osuna, Cazalla (both in Seville) and Archidona (Málaga).[5]

There is an obvious omission from the list of Grandees of Andalusia already quoted, which must mean that it was drawn up by an enemy of the Ponce de León. Bernáldez likened the Guzmán and the Ponce de León to two columns supported by the city of Seville and the whole of Andalusia.[6] The latter

[1] Salazar y Mendoza, *Origen de las Dignidades* (Toledo, 1618), pp. 104a and b. He became marquis of Comares (see p. 375).

[2] Salazar, xxv, 315, 412–3, 417 and (for Andújar) p. 407. They had lands at Aguilar, Cañete de las Torres, Montilla, Monturque, Hornachuelos, Bujalance (all in Córdoba), Almagro (Ciudad Real), Pedroche, La Rambla and Castillo Anzur (ibid., xxix, 95; J. C. Adán, *En torno al concepto del estado en los Reyes Católicos* (Madrid, 1956), 165, L. M. de Lojendio *Gonzalo de Córdoba* (Madrid, 1942) 60).

[3] They were *notarios mayores* of Castile (Salazar, i, 192). The county of Ureña is in Valladolid province.

[4] Suárez, 156; J. F. O'Callaghan, 'Don Pedro Girón, Master of the Order of Calatrava, 1445–66', *Hispania*, xxi (1961), 385–6.

[5] Ibid., 387, n. 215 (details of lands).

[6] Cf. 'Historia de los hechos de d. Rodrigo Ponce de León, m. de Cádiz, 1443–88', in *CODOIN*, cvi (1893), 143–317. They were granted Medellín in 1429 (Salazar, xxviii, 327) and were lords of Marchena and Mairena (both in Seville), and of Rota and Chipiona (both in Cádiz) (Adán, *En torno al concepto del estado*, 151).

family cannot be denied the description of Grandee in 1474. They had been *ricoshombres*, lords of Marchena (Seville), counts of Arcos (Cádiz) (since 1440), marquises of Cádiz (from 1468).[1]

A less obvious omission from the 1464 list than the Ponce de León is that of the counts of Santisteban del Puerto of the Galician family of Benavides. They were a little removed from the main struggles of Andalusian politics, for their lands lay right up at the head of the Guadalquivir basin in the high ground known as the Loma de Chiclana, between the rivers Guadalimar and Guadalén towards the frontier of the modern province of Ciudad Real. For two generations they held the important office of *caudillo mayor* of the bishopric of Jaén.[2]

That the titled aristocracy of Castile increased in number during the reign of the Catholic Kings has long been recognised. But neither the extent nor the significance of that increase have been assessed. If the six houses, which died out by natural incidence or the marriage of an heiress, are omitted (Vázquez de Acuña (dukes of Huete), Velasco (dukes of Roa), Villandrando (counts of Ribadeo), Sánchez de Ulloa (counts of Altamira), Zúñiga (counts of Pedrosa) and Tovar (counts of Berlanga)), the increase was still about a fifth. Thus it can be readily seen that the Catholic kings made no discernible attempt to restrict the numbers of their new appointments. In granting the title of duke they turned first to their supporters. The Manrique de Lara became dukes of Nájera (1482). The Mendoza who had havered but come across at a crucial juncture, came off with the red hat of a cardinal and the duchy of Infantado, granted to the marquis of Santillana in 1475.[3] The De la Cerda counts of Medinaceli, who had also joined the winning side, gained their ducal title of Medinaceli in 1479.[4] But the Velasco who had for long adhered to the coalitions of the marquis of Villena had to wait until 1492, when the counts of Haro became dukes of Frías. The war against Granada offered an obvious path by which a family which had been on the wrong side could win its way back to favour. The most notable example is provided by the Ponce de León, who, although they were the bitter opponents of the Guzmán, were

---

[1] Haro, i, 198–208.
[2] *Reg. 1478–80*, p. 79, also count of Santa Maria del Puerto (Cádiz).
[3] *Títulos*, 35.
[4] Ibid., 156.

advanced first to be marquises of Cádiz on the capture of Boabdil in 1483 and finally to be dukes of Arcos after the fall of Granada.

A family, which had consistently helped the marquis of Villena, provides a special case. This was the family of Álvaro de Zúñiga, duke of Arévalo and count of Plasencia. Their title of Arévalo was exchanged for that of Plasencia in 1476,[1] but subsequently when the Crown felt stronger in 1485 it once more exchanged the title of this branch of the Zúñiga for that of duke of Béjar. This exchange was made in order to incorporate Plasencia in the royal domain. The arrangement was not agreed to with good grace and the dukes of Béjar were still trying to regain Plasencia in the seventeenth century.[2]

If grants of the ducal title were sparing this was not true of that of marquis. One such grant has already been noticed. There were no less than eleven others. Boabdil was made marquis of Guadix for diplomatic reasons in 1486. But this title naturally had no significance after the Moorish king left Spain in 1493.[3] Two other promotions (those of Rodrigo Díaz de Vivar de Mendoza, to be marquis of Cenete and count of El Cid, and that of Diego Hurtado de Mendoza, to be marquis of Cañete), can be grouped with the rewards which had already fallen to the Mendozas. Rodrigo was the illegitimate son of the cardinal. Diego Hurtado was lord of Cañete (Cuenca). Again the appointment of Garci Fernández Manrique, third count of Castañeda, to be marquis of Aguilar de Campóo (Palencia) in 1484 offered a reward to this branch of the Manrique which was complementary to that already given to the count of Treviño. Of the other three marquises made in Isabella's lifetime that of Andrés de Cabrera to be marquis of Moya (1480) is not difficult to explain. Formerly *mayordomo mayor* or chief steward of Henry IV, he had not only handed over Segovia to Ferdinand and Isabella at a vital moment in 1473 but had married the queen's lady-in-waiting, Beatriz de Bobadilla.[4] Also promoted before 1504 were the Sandoval counts of Denia (made marquises of Denia in 1484) and Luis Pimentel y Pacheco, a cadet of the Pimentel, who became marquis of Villafranca del Bierzo

[1] *Títulos*, 113.
[2] Ibid., 142.
[3] Ibid., 200.
[4] Salazar, i, 213–4, xxvii, 138. Moya is in Cuenca province. For Isabella's second thoughts cf. *Testamento de Isabel la Católica* (Valladolid, 1944), 15–17.

(León) in 1486.[1] Of the old marquises of Henry IV only one was permanently left in the cold—Pedro Álvarez Osorio, marquis of Astorga.

To complete a survey of the new marquises it is necessary to look not only beyond the death of Isabella but also beyond that of her son-in-law, Philip I, in 1506. Between that date and his own death in 1516 Ferdinand tied his promotions of marquises to four Andalusian families, the Córdoba, the Portocarrero and the Mendoza, and that of the governor of Andalusia.

The Córdoba were the most difficult to win over and to trust. One led an open revolt against the royal authorities and was ruined. Another, the Great Captain, so much aroused the king's suspicious nature that he would only grant him an Italian title (that of duke of Sessa).[2] But this did not prevent Ferdinand from advancing the chief representatives of two branches of the family to be marquises of Priego (1507) and of Comares (1516) respectively. Juan Portocarrero was also a powerful Andalusian lord. The Catholic Kings had granted his father license to alter his *mayorazgo* in 1478. A kinsman of the Cárdenas, he was lord of Moguer (Huelva), a town on the estuary of the River Tinto, when he was promoted to be marquis of Villanueva del Fresno (1512–16).[3]

The captain general of Granada, Íñigo López de Mendoza, second count of Tendilla, built up the Andalusian Mendoza. His captaincy covered the difficult years 1507–8. His reward, the title of marquis of Mondéjar (Guadalajara), granted in 1512, was earned many times over.[4] Another Andalusian family, the Ribera, had for several generations held the office of *adelantado* or governor of Andalusia. Marrying into the Mendoza, they advanced to become marquises of Tarifa (1514).

In Murcia the uncrowned kings through most of the reign of Henry IV had been the Fajardo. But their title of counts of Cartagena had died out in 1482, when the main line ran into an heiress. The family had for long controlled the office of governor of Murcia and had founded its *mayorazgo* as long ago as 1438. It had also taken a major part in the conquest of the marquisate of Villena and in the defence of the Murcian frontier

---

[1] *Títulos*, 185.
[2] Lojendio, 318.
[3] *Títulos*, 225. Villanueva del Fresno is in Extremadura.
[4] Cf. Adán in *Hispania*, xxii (1962), 38–80 and see below, p. 367 n. 6.

against Granada until 1492.[1] The appointment of Pedro Fajardo, grandson of the last count of Cartagena, to be marquis of Los Velez, therefore, was no more than the granting of a title in a new and more impressive form to a family whose importance had for long been outstanding.

It would be tedious to comment on all of the fourteen promotions to the rank of count between 1474 and 1516,[2] to which may be added for convenience the two promotions made by Juana and Philip I between 1504 and 1506.[3] But some general points may be made. Six (perhaps seven) of them can be allotted to the period of the Succession War and its after-math (1474–8).[4] Of those appointments three went directly to Mendozas (Pedro González de Mendoza, lord of Almazán (Soria), made count of Monteagudo (Soria), Ruy Díaz de Mendoza, lord of Morón, made count of Castrogeriz and Mariá de Mendoza, lady of Los Molares, who became countess of the same title) and one more went to Alonso Ramírez de Arellano, who though certainly powerful enough in his own right to deserve his promotion to be count of Aguilar de Inestrillas (Logroño), had also married a daughter of the first duke of Infantado.

The remaining twelve appointments reflect the predominance of the nobilities of Galicia and Andalusia and the recognition of this fact by Ferdinand and Isabella. Galicia provided no less than four new counts directly, including its governor, Ber-nardino Sarmiento, made count of Ribadavia, as against one

[1] J. Torres Fontes, *Pedro Fajardo, adelantado mayor del reino de Murcia* (Madrid, 1953), also 'La Conquista del Marquesado de Villena en el reinado de los Reyes Católicos', *Hispania*, xiii (1953), 37–151.

[2] Pedro González de Mendoza, count of Monteagudo (1475), Pedro Dávila, count of Risco (1475), Fernán Álvarez de Toledo, count of Oropesa (1475), Alonso Ramírez de Arellano, count of Aguilar de Inestrillas (1476), Ruy Díaz de Mendoza, count of Castrojeriz (1476), María de Mendoza, countess of Los Molares (?c. 1476), Bernardino Sarmiento, count of Ribadavia (1478), Alvaro de Zúñiga y Guzmán, count of Bañares (also duke of Béjar) (1485), Diego de Andrade, count of Villalba (1486), Pedro de Ayala y Herrera, count of Salvatierra de Álava (1491), Rodrigo de Moscoso Osorio, count of Altamira (re-creation soon after 1500), Pedro de Zúñiga, count of Pedrosa (before 1503), Luis de Tovar, count of Berlanga (before 1504), and Francisco de Guzmán y Zúñiga, count of Ayamonte before 1504.

[3] Alonso de Cárdenas, count of La Puebla del Maestre (Badajoz) (1506) and Luis de Portocarrero, count of Palma del Río (Córdoba) (1506) (Salazar, xxviii, 322) : in addition to Palma, he held Almenara (Castellón).

[4] See the first seven named in n. 2. Despite the assertions of López de Haro it is uncertain whether the grant of the title of countess of Los Molares should be attributed to 1476 (cf. *Títulos*, 147–8).

from Andalusia.[1] Two more appointments, one of a Zúñiga y Guzmán and another of a Guzmán y Zúñiga, were made to families which were a nice amalgam of the nobilities of both provinces.

The question of the relationship between the Crown, the titled nobility and the royal towns is complex and needs re-opening. The position of the seignorial towns is a separate issue. But, as Ruano has shown in his recent study of Toledo, many of the rights and offices in royal towns had been sold to the nobility during the fifteenth century.[2] This had been done by granting away municipal taxes and offices and the command of the royal fortresses which dominated the towns. The constitutions and offices of the towns need systematic investigation. It is remarkable that the *alguacilazgo* or office of high constable of Toledo could be sold by the first duke of Alba to the count of Fuensalida, who bought it for his son for 2,100,000 maravedis.[3] The positions of the Enríquez at Valladolid, of the Velasco at Burgos, of the Mendoza at Toro and Guadalajara need further examination.[4] The commander of the fortress could pull in quite a different direction from the city, as the Zúñiga, duke of Arévalo and Burgos did during its siege in 1475–6.[5] They could act together. The fact that there was no capital and that the Crown continued to migrate encouraged aristocratic domination of towns. There was no temptation to drift to town houses in a capital like London or Paris which the government could control. The example of Toledo shows that once a town had fallen into the hands of aristocratic factions (i.e. Cifuentes and Fuensalida), it may not be assumed that town and Crown could act together. The Infant Alfonso in 1467 had been backed in his rebellion against Henry IV not only by a league of nobles but also by a series of royal towns controlled by the nobility (Burgos, Ávila, Valladolid, Palencia, Zamora, Seville, Córdoba and Cádiz).[6] Military developments were to affect the power of noble garrison commanders in royal towns

[1] Galicia provided the counts of Ribadavia, Villalba, Altamira and Pedrosa, Andalusia that of Palma del Río.

[2] Ruano, *Toledo*, 149–50.

[3] Ibid., 116.

[4] The work has been begun by P. L. Serrano (Burgos), see above, p. 364, n. 1, and F. L. Serrano (Guadalajara), see p. 367, n. 1.

[5] Serrano, *Burgos*, 142–66.

[6] Ruano, *Toledo*, 89–92.

(just as they did that of the Military Orders). Urban citadels, like that of Utrera in 1477, became vulnerable to the latest artillery.[1] But the menace of the noble garrison commander had not yet passed.

The independent voice of the towns had, of course, never been stilled, if it had not been listened to very attentively.

The Cortes of 1422 had asked that powerful men, *omes poderosos*, should not hold high municipal office.[2] The Catholic Kings continued to recognize that this was a desirable aim. Again and again instructions were issued that *regidores* of this or that town (especially in Andalusia) should not live in the houses of gentlemen (*caballeros*). But the reiteration of the instructions suggests that they were not obeyed.[3] Hereditary succession of the office of mayor (*alcalde*) was often banned but frequently still to be found.[4] The greatest positive achievements were those of the *Hermandades*[5] (brotherhoods) and they were made in the face of the most determined aristocratic opposition from, for instance, the duke of Medina Sidonia.[6] How far these were the successes of gentlemen remains to be discussed.

There were certainly positive gains to be recorded in the winning of towns for the royal domain. The policy had already begun even in Henry IV's reign. Thus Badajoz had been brought back in 1470. In 1473 Tordesillas (Valladolid) made clear its anxiety to come under the Crown and succeeded in doing so.[7] Ferdinand and Isabella followed this up with such reacquisitions as Huete from its duke in 1476,[8] Plasencia from its duke in 1485[9] and Cartagena from the marquis of Los Velez.[10] At Orduña (Álava) the town was regained for the

---

[1] The duke of Alba had his own lombards which he lent to the army besieging Zamora. What mattered was whether aristocratic commanders could bring their castles up to date (cf. Adán, *Concepto del Estado*, 149; Diego de Valera, *Crónica de los Reyes Católicos*, ed. J. de M. Carriazo (Madrid, 1927), 51.

[2] *Cortes de los Antiguos Reinos de Castilla y Leon*, iii, 38.

[3] Cf. position at Jaén (1479) (*Reg. 1478-80*, p. 265), at Murcia (1480) (ibid., *1480-4*, p. 42). Similar instructions had been issued by John II.

[4] Cf. the plea brought against the perpetual succession of the posts of *regidor* and *fiel* by the *caballeros* and others of Ciudad Real (1480) (ibid., *1478-80*, p. 353). A post as *regidor* in Valladolid passed in 1480 from his brother to the count of Ribadeo (ibid., 481).

[5] J. Puyol y Alonso, *Las Hermandades de Castilla y León* (Madrid, 1913); Serrano, *Burgos*, 167-90; L. Suárez Fernández in *Cuadernos de List. de España* (1951), 5-78.

[6] Paz y Mélia, *A. de Palencia*, p. xxiii.

[7] Pulgar, i, 45-6 (a case of a town freeing itself from a tyrannical *alcalde*).

[8] *Títulos*, 124.

[9] Ibid., 142.

[10] Ibid., 101.

royal domain but the fortress stayed in the hands of the Ayala.[1]

But in the early years of the reign especially, noble pressures on the Crown were still such that the movement was by no means all one way. Moreover the monarchs positively wished to reward those members of the aristocracy who had supported them. Sometimes, as in and after the Portuguese treaty of 1479, they showed themselves remarkably lenient to their fiercest opponents. At Burgos Isabella insisted that one Ribera should follow another as *alcalde* of the castle.[2] The town submitted most unwillingly to this noble hereditary succession. Again after 1479 the hated Antonio Sarmiento was reinstated despite all protest and his own rebellion against the Crown.[3] The inquest of 1478 shows that the royal authorities seriously wished to build up the royal position again by directing the equivalent of a 'quo warranto' inquisition against holders of alienated revenues. But they were equally prepared to make important new alienations, for example both at Burgos and Segovia, which were very irritating to the municipal authorities.

At Toledo much was achieved by the introduction of the *corregidor*, Gómez Manrique, between 1477 and 1490. But the year of strain (1506–7) saw renewed clashes between the old bands of the counts of Cifuentes and Silva, and this rivalry was still to trouble the city in the seventeenth century.[4] The noble outbreaks of the fifteenth century at Toledo set a pattern for the rise of the *Comuneros* in the sixteenth. As has been pointed out by Ruano these rose at least as much in defence of privilege as of municipal liberties.[5]

In Andalusia the fate of Seville, in some ways, resembled that of Burgos. John II of Aragon had advised his son to seize Seville at an early stage in the Succession War, for 'the master of that city has always controlled the direction of affairs, and as the old saying goes "when they give you the heifer etc".'[6] But once Seville had been won the position there of the marquis of Cádiz was strengthened despite the efforts of the city.[7] At Córdoba, it is true, the exchanges were freed from the control of the

---

[1] *Reg. 1478–80*, 357, 360.
[2] Serrano, *Burgos*, 192–3.
[3] *Reg. 1478–80*, p. 477; Serrano, *Burgos*, 194–5.
[4] Ruano, *Toledo*, 133.
[5] Ibid., 160–2.
[6] Paz y Mélia, *Palencia*, p. xix.
[7] *Reg. 1478–80*, pp. 43, 54, 192.

Aguilar Córdobas, as were those of Écija from the Porto-carrero (later counts of Palma del Río).[1] But after the capture of Loja in the war against Granada that town was handed over to the Great Captain, despite its evident desire to become part of the royal domain, and the Córdoba seignorial administration, though it raised an instant storm, was reinforced by royal officers.[2]

Victory over Portugal and Granada gave the Catholic Kings two great opportunities to strengthen the position of the Crown, and, after Isabella's death, Ferdinand's conquests in Italy and Navarre provided two more. In addition the discovery of the New World offered Castile a chance to multiply new titles and to extend the royal domain. Here we need only consider the first two of these distributions. In the years 1474–9 it seems that once the treaty of 1479 had been settled the Crown used its victory as a chance both to reward its own aristocratic sup-porters[3] and to try to buy the loyalty of its opponents. By 1492 the Crown was, of course, much stronger. But again the loyal aristocratic supporters were rewarded. It must be admitted, however, that a wholesale study of the division of the kingdom of Granada, such as has been carried out for Seville after its conquest in the thirteenth century, is very much needed. In her will indeed Isabella shows how keenly she understood the interests of the royal domain. She specifically made plans for the return of Moya from the marquis of Moya, of rents in Ávila from the duke of Alba, and of Gibraltar from the duke of Medina Sidonia. Moreover she tried to ensure the inalienability of the marquisate of Villena. But she had to admit that she had not been able to build up the domain in her lifetime as she would have wished, and she directed that the aristocrats con-cerned in the specific resumptions named should be compen-sated from the resources of the kingdom of Granada.[4] Like Charles V of France she had to leave instructions in her will for carrying out a policy which she had only been able to fulfil in part.

The Crown certainly gained as a result of its treatment of the

[1] Ibid., 182.
[2] Adán, *Hispania*, xxii, 60.
[3] Cf the grant of 406,000 m.p.a. to the count of Medinaceli (1478) (Adán *Concepto del Estado*, 154).
[4] *Testamento*, 14, 17.

Military Orders. But though the story has been chronicled, the question has not been sufficiently studied to allow an accurate estimate to be made of the effects on the relationship between the Crown and the nobility when this great source of patronage and military power passed to the monarchy.[1] At the end of the fourteenth century it was possible for a master of Alcántara to pursue a foreign policy diametrically opposed to that of the king.[2] Ferdinand I had thought to secure the orders for his sons. But that answer had proved disastrous for the Castilian Trastámaras.[3] The suggestion that the orders should be incorporated in the Crown, made in 1456,[4] was made again by Isabella in 1476 as the best way of calming down the furious quarrel between the rival aristocratic contestants for the mastership of Santiago.[5] The wisdom of such a scheme must have been underlined by the revolt of 1480 on the lands of the Order of Alcántara which had to be forcibly suppressed.[6] Señorita Javierre Mur has recently described the stages of incorporation. It was a lengthy process, drawn out by the necessity to consult the pope at every step. But no systematic study of the orders in terms of their financial and military value has been attempted. It is assumed that they were very wealthy. Their lands were certainly extensive and the anxiety of the nobility to secure appointments in them was very great. There was an important social factor here. In the Spanish orders (as in the Portuguese Order of Avis) from c. 1512–17 marriage was allowed. This probably more than anything else saved the Military Orders from the fate of the Templars or the English monasteries. The Crown and the nobility could jointly exploit them. But the process by which the commanders became merely ornamental has yet to be explored. It had hardly begun in 1516.

The whole question of royal office at this time also needs investigation in order to test how far the royal administration

---

[1] A. L. Javierre Mur in *Fernando el Católico, Vida y Obra*, V Congreso de Historia de la Corona de Aragón (1955), i. 287–300. For a map of the Santiago properties see B. de Chaves, *Apuntamiento sobre el dominio solar que por expressas reales donaciones, pertenece a la Orden de Santiago* (Madrid, 1740). For Calatrava see F. Gutton, *L'Ordre de Calatrava* (Paris, 1955). I owe these last two references to Dr D. Lomax.
[2] Pedro López de Ayala, *Crónicas de los Reyes de Castilla*, ed. E. de Llaguno Amirola, ii (1780), 513–18.
[3] I. Macdonald, *Ferdinand of Antequera* (Oxford, 1948), 74, 94, 102.
[4] Cf. Suárez, 25.
[5] Paz y Mélia, p. xviii.
[6] Cf. *Reg. 1478–80*, pp. 386, 438 (1480).

escaped the control of the Crown. Throughout the fifteenth century almost all the positions in the royal household and the army were filled by the nobility. Each post conveyed revenue to its holder. To be *contador mayor* or receiver general in 1447 was to have an office worth 32,000 m.p.a.[1] At the same date the count of Trastámara was *alférez mayor* or chief standard bearer both for the division of the Cord of St Francis and of the house of the Cord, military appointments worth 36,480 m.p.a.[2] Similarly the offices, such as that of *alcalde mayor* or chief magistrate in any of the provinces, had been alienated to the nobility. Moreover great blocks of royal taxes had been granted away. The Book of *Asientos* shows that in 1447 the office of scribe and the taxes known as *alcabalas* and *tercias* had been most affected. The section in the book known as *salvado*, consisting of revenues worth 2,577,681 m.p.a., was chiefly made up from these taxes and was noted as being permanently alienated. But most of the other royal taxes had also been affected.

Another way in which the Crown had alienated its substance had occurred as a result of the Cortes of Guadalajara. By the Ordinance of Lances then passed royal lands had been allotted to the nobility in return for the promise of a *servitium debitum* on a basis of 1,500 m.p.a. of income (from the lands in question) for every lance.[3] At a cost in alienated rents of more than 3,363,500 m.p.a. the Crown had a force of over 2,300 lances which was in fact controlled by the aristocracy. It would be difficult to have devised a more effective method of maintaining noble power. How battleworthy the lances were in 1474 is hard to tell. But the rents had been lost.

Another kind of alienation revealed by the Book of *Asientos* consisted of hereditary *juros* or annuities. These were sold in large numbers and not only to the nobility. The *juro* for life was damaging to the royal revenue, the hereditary *juro* much more so. This was one of the dangers with which the Cortes of Toledo began to deal (1480).[4] The extent of the achievement has, however, only begun to be seriously examined.[5]

[1] *Libro*, 350–1.
[2] Ibid., 347.
[3] *Cortes de Castilla*, ii, 461–3.
[4] On 5th April, 1480, the scribe of the royal register writes of a general embargo on *juros* as a result of the 'new situation which had arisen since the time of King Henry' (*Reg. 1478–80*, p. 454).
[5] See especially the excellent work of A. Matilla y Tascón, *Declaratorias de los Reyes Católicos sobre reducción de juros y otras mercedes* (Madrid, 1952).

By an Act of Resumption of the same date the Crown tried to recover all rents alienated since 1464. Unalienated rents in 1474 have been estimated at 11,000,000 m.p.a. and some rents (other than *juros*) had been recovered after 1480,[1] but, as has been recently pointed out, vast amounts of rents had been alienated to the aristocracy long before 1464 and remained untouched by the act.[2] A careful quantitative survey of the changing fortunes of royal and aristocratic revenues has not been made.

Finally the problem of Castilian aristocratic power needs also to be approached from the evidence of its central institution. The *mayorazgo* or *maioratus* is, fortunately, a revealing kind of source since it was necessary to put down in the document by which the *mayorazgo* was set up detailed statements of rights and possessions.

As has been seen the *mayorazgo* (which had many forms) was in essence an imbarrable entail.[3] Thirteenth-century *mayorazgos* occur quite frequently, but their number shows a remarkable increase from the middle of the fourteenth century onwards.[4] Originally it seems that a *mayorazgo* could be set up with or without royal permission. But the Crown in the fifteenth century regarded the licence to found a *mayorazgo* as a privilege, which once granted required royal permission again if it needed to be altered.[5] Moreover the Crown insisted that a proportion of the founder's wealth, often a third, be set down in detail before the licence could be granted. It is this practice which makes it a source worth pursuing. Ambitious families might wish to found as many as four *mayorazgos* for different members of a single family. In the sixteenth century the *mayorazgo* spread to non-noble families and in the form of the *mayorazgo corto* became immensely popular.[6] Its economic effect

---

[1] D. D. Clemencín, *Elogio de la Reina Católica Doña Isabel* (Madrid, 1821), pp. 151, 153, cf. *Declaratorias*, 17.

[2] J. H. Elliott, *Imperial Spain, 1469–1716* (London, 1963), 100.

[3] It returned to the Crown only in default of direct male heirs (Sempere y Guarinos, *Historia de los Vínculos y Mayorazgos* (Madrid, 1805), sections, 19 and 30).

[4] Cf. Sempere y Guarinos, s. 19; A. González Palencia, *Mayorazgos Españoles* (Biblioteca Histórica Genealógica), i (1929) (although this is a repertory for the years 1690–1892 it contains copies of earlier *mayorazgos*, some of which are also to be found at Simancas).

[5] For faculty to increase the *mayorazgo* of Alba de Liste cf. *Reg. 1478–80*, p. 320; to remove an agnation clause cf. Salazar, xxviii, 389; to sell part cf. *Reg. 1478–80*, p. 372.

[6] Cf. R. Carr in *European Nobility in the Eighteenth Century*, ed. A. Goodwin (London, 1953), 48–9.

could be very deleterious, since it gave its owner an interest in the income to be derived from the lands and rights, but no corresponding concern for the capital. Nevertheless, since it created great blocks of inalienable land, as a factor stabilizing the wealth of the titled nobility its influence was no doubt very great. Fifteenth- and sixteenth-century *mayorazgos* were still operating at the end of the eighteenth century.[1] Into its full complexities it is not our purpose to enter now. It is sufficient to note that it needs to be the subject of research and that the Catholic Kings accepted it without hesitation as part of the Castilian landscape. An attempt was made to regulate the institution at the Cortes of Toro,[2] but in no hostile manner. The freedom with which licences to found fresh *mayorazgos* were given shows clearly that the Crown had no desire to weaken one of the central institutions of aristocratic power. The lawyers of Philip II were still wrestling with the problem of regularizing *mayorazgos* at the end of the century.[3]

The fact was the Catholic Kings took a great section of the nobility with them in the Succession War and thereafter did much to associate the nobles with the régime. There was point in this. Once the Mendoza had been won over the count of Saldaña could be set to watch over Archbishop Carrillo.[4] With unerring eye the Sarmiento count of Ribadavia was chosen to be governor of Galicia.[5] The most outstandingly successful noble appointment was undoubtedly that of the count of Tendilla to be governor of Granada. With full powers but little material backing he was left to handle a very ugly situation. One of the most interesting achievements of the régime was to have persuaded the count to act as loyally as he did towards the Crown which supported him so inadequately. Some of this may be due to the care with which Isabella always corresponded with the Grandees especially during the war against Granada. Certainly the winning over of the marquis of Cádiz

---

[1] Cf. Arch. Hist. Nac. Consejos. Ejecutoria, 6, 281, leg. 37822 (a *mayorazgo* of Francisco Ramírez, secretary of the Catholic Kings, dated 13th October, 1499 and quoted in full in a plea of 1778).

[2] Sempere y Guarinos, s. 20; Laws of Toro, 27, 40–5 in *Cortes de Castilla*, iv, 205, 209–10.

[3] Cf. Melchior Paláez a Meris, *Tractatus illustrium . . . iurisconsultorum* (Venice, 1584), x, pt. 1, 337.

[4] Paz y Mélia, 299.

[5] By June 1483 (cf. *Reg. 1480–4*, p. 168).

to the régime seems to have been a personal success of the queen.[1] On other occasions she was careful to insist that the Grandees should be consulted as for instance when their approval was sought for the treaty with Louis XI[1] before its publication. The second count of Feria and the third count of Cabra were particularly trusted and were, for example, given the government of Castile and León in 1499 when the Catholic Kings were in Andalusia.[2] The titled nobility also had their part to play on the council, in the army and in diplomacy. But to weigh that up would require an overall survey of each of these branches of royal service.

Twice the success of the royal policy was put to an extreme test. The first occasion came between the death of Isabella in 1504 and that of Philip I in 1506, when the governments of Castile and Aragon once again separated. The dissident members of the Córdoba family, and the dukes of Medina Sidonia and Nájera at once grouped themselves round the weak Hapsburg and began to undo the work of the Catholic Kings. When Philip died they formed themselves up into ominous coalitions and they were to do so again on the death of Ferdinand in 1516. In each instance the royal position was held, but only just, thanks to Ferdinand and Cardinal Cisneros respectively. But historians' relief that the fifteenth-century wars did not again break out has led them too eagerly to suppose that the political and economic power of the aristocracy had vanished away. It is hoped that it has been shown that it had not and that the extent of that power is a subject ripe for exploration.[3]

---

[1] Pulgar, i, 320, cf. ii, 162.
[2] Salazar, xxix, 121.
[3] Since this was written two important new works have appeared, vol. xv of R. Menéndez Pidal, *Historia de España* (Madrid, 1964), with its invaluable opening chapter on Castile by L. Suárez Fernández, and Tarsicio de Azcona, *Isabel la Católica, Estudio crítico de su vida y su reinado* (Madrid, 1964) (see especially 69–74).

XIII

C. A. J. Armstrong

THE LANGUAGE QUESTION IN THE LOW COUNTRIES: THE USE OF FRENCH AND DUTCH BY THE DUKES OF BURGUNDY AND THEIR ADMINISTRATION

The Low Countries in the later Middle Ages provide an example of the interplay of political forces and linguistic conditions.

Netherlandish is the least ambiguous collective name for the Germanic vernacular [other than Friesian] of the Low Countries. Netherlandish came slowly into use from about 1500, predominantly in the southern Low Countries, to distinguish the regional speech from that of High Germans.[1] In some respects 'Dutch' is preferable as a collective name, for it is the English for 'duitsch' or 'dietsch', which was what Netherlanders in the later Middle Ages called their native speech. However, in England 'Dutch' since the seventeenth century has come to be exclusively associated with the northern Netherlands.[2] From an early period 'Flanders' and 'Flemish' were used by foreigners to designate by synecdoche the collective Netherlands and their Germanic vernacular.[3] This is misleading; and in the following pages Flemish will be kept for the

[1] F. Prims, 'De naam onzer taal in de jaren 1480–1540 inzonderheid te Antwerpen', *Verslagen en mededeelingen der koninklijke vlaamsche Academie voor Taal-en-letterkunde* (1939), 274–82 (bibliography).

[2] O.E.D. under 'Dutch'.

[3] Prims, op. cit., 281. L. Van der Essen, 'Notre nom national: quelques textes peu remarqués des xvi et xvii siècles', *Revue belge de philologie et d'histoire*, iv (1925), 121–31.

speech of the county of Flanders. During the Burgundian period, French speakers called the Germanic tongue in the Netherlands *thiois*, and those, who spoke as their mother tongue any of the numerous Germanic dialects of the Netherlands, recognized it as *dietsch* in differentiation from the *waalsch* of their romance neighbours.

Until the recent adoption of a standardized form, the 'Algemeen Beschaafd', in the kingdoms of the Netherlands and Belgium,[1] Netherlandish was not the name of a particular language but the family name for several related dialects corresponding with the principal territories of the Low

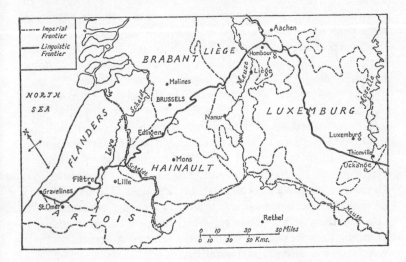

Countries. First Flanders, then in the later fourteenth century Brabant and finally in the seventeenth century Holland assumed the literary leadership of the Netherlandish family.[2]

The literary form was not always fully intelligible to readers in a neighbouring territory. The great Jan Ruusbroec of Groenendael (ob. 1381) wrote his devotional treatise *Chierheit*

---

[1] Despite local difficulties: E. Blancquaert, 'Ter bevordering van het Algemeen Beschaafd in Vlaanderen', *Verslagen . . . vlaamsche Academie voor Taal-en-letterkunde* (1938), 561–9. H. J. E. Endepols, 'Algemeen Beschaafd en Maastricht . . .' *Tijdschrift voor nederlandse Taal-en-letterkunde*, lxv (1947), 101–17. P. C. Paardekooper, *Erzijn geen Belgen* (Antwerp, 1962), 5–6, 15–16, 27–8.

[2] For a literary history of our period, see J. van Mierlo, *De middelnederlandsche Letterkunde van omstreeks 1300 tot de Renaissance* (1940), being vol. ii of *Geschiedenis van der letterkunde der Nederlanden*, ed. F. Baur and others.

der gheesteliker Brulocht in the idiom of Brabant; but at the request of the brethren in Flanders, who could not perfectly understand his vernacular, he had it translated into Latin.[1]

About 1425 English merchants were granted by the town of Middelburg in Zeeland safe conducts expressed in the local vernacular; and a notary of Bruges was engaged to translate into Latin these safe conducts so that they might be universally understood.[2] The Flemish notary, uneasy about his translation, submitted it to a London mercer, who knew Latin and the vernacular of Zeeland. When they failed to reach agreement, another Londoner, who also knew Latin and the language of Middelburg was called in to establish an agreed Latin text. A notary at Bruges must often have had to turn Flemish documents into Latin; but when he had to translate the Netherlandish of Middelburg, a town geographically and commercially close to Bruges, he was not so sure of himself.[3]

Fifteenth-century evidence scarcely supports the theory that the Germanic areas of the Low Countries were moved to joint action by awareness of their common Netherlandish racial and linguistic ties.[4] In 1477 the Duchess Mary at Ghent granted in Netherlandish a general constitution for the Burgundian Netherlands, the so-called Grand Privilège.[5] The three principal Germanic territories, Brabant, Flanders and Holland, insisted on individual charters. They preferred separate charters to the Grand Privilège for many reasons; but by procuring regional charters, they were able, among other things, to formulate their requirements in their own dialects.

French, of a sort, was the speech native to much of the southern Low Countries. Like Netherlandish this indigenous

---

[1] *Ioannis Rusberi de Ornatu spiritualium Nuptiarum* (Paris, H. Stephanus, 1512 fol.), a 1r; J. van Mierlo, op. cit., 126–35. *Biographie nationale publiée par l'Académie royale de Belgique*, xx (1909), 507–99.

[2] In 1465 the privileges of Middelburg were translated into French that they might be better known. J. H. de Stoppelaar, *Inventaris van het oud-archief der stad Middelburg* (Middelburg, 1873), ix.

[3] N. J. M. Kerling, *Commercial relations of Holland and Zeeland with England from the thirteenth century to the close of the Middle Ages* (Leiden, 1954), 168 from P.R.O. C.47, bundle 30/9, no. 13.

[4] But see the works of P. C. A. Geyl particularly *Geschiedenis van de Nederlandsche Stam*, 3 vols. (Amsterdam, 1930–7).

[5] P. van Ussel, *Deregeering van Maria van Bourgondie* (Louvain, 1943), 49–65. F. W. N. Hugenholtz, 'The 1477 crisis in the Burgundian Duke's dominions', *Britain and the Netherlands*, ed. J. S. Bromley and E. H. Kossman (*Historische Studies vanwege het instituut voor geschiedenis der Rijksuniversiteit te Utrecht*, xx, 1964), 37 sqq.

French was divided into local dialects, Picard and Rouchy in the west, Walloon in the east. These dialects, however, were backed by the French of France, which was a more unified language than the Low German to which Netherlandish belonged. The Burgundian government disregarded these local forms of French. Its administrative language, like its institutions, was borrowed straight from the practice of the French Crown. Only thus could the Burgundian power introduce a standard language, which neither the Netherlandish- nor the French-speaking inhabitants of the Low Countries could provide from their own resources.

The frontier between French and Netherlandish dialects roughly followed an east–west line, from Hombourg at the eastern extreme, within ten miles of Aachen, to Gravelines on the North Sea coast. The division between French and German dialects ran in a less direct line from Hombourg in the north to Uckange in the south on the River Moselle inside the old boundaries of Luxemburg.[1]

The internal boundaries of the Low Countries, ecclesiastical and lay, ignored the language frontier; but under medieval conditions juridical and linguistic divisions seldom coincided. The 1056 frontier between the empire and France[2] traversed the southern Netherlands; but neither there nor on any other sector of its course from North Sea to Mediterranean did it divide Germanic- from romance-speaking peoples. The language frontier did not bisect any of the territories, which it crossed in the southern Netherlands, for each one of them was preponderantly Germanic or romance with a minority in area and population belonging to the other culture. The counties of Artois and Hainault together with the episcopal territory of Liège were mainly romance. The county of Flanders and the duchy of Brabant were for the most part Netherlandish, while

---

[1] The map at p. 387 is based on G. Kurth, *La frontière linguistique en Belgique et dans le Nord de la France*, 2 vols. (Mémoires couronnés de l'Académie royale de Belgique, série 8°, 1895). Kurth's conclusions have been criticized, but his work not superseded. Of particular interest for its maps of the area where French, Netherlandish and German converge, J. P. D. Banning, *Gebiedsovergang . . . getoetst aan de praktijk van de inlijving van Eupen-Malmedy door België* (Utrecht, 1949). For the influence of settlement on language, F. Petri, *Zum Stand der Diskussion über die fränkische Landnahme und die Enstehung der germanisch-romanischen Sprachgrenze* (Darmstadt, 1954) and C. Verlinden, 'Frankish colonization: a new approach', *Transactions Royal Historical Society*, 5, iv (1954), 1–18.

[2] L. Mirot, *Manuel de géographie historique de la France*, 2 vols. (Paris, 1948–50), i, 104–16, for fuller references.

the majority of the duchy of Luxemburg fell within the area of Franconian German speech.

The language frontier was no obstacle to various forces within the Low Countries working towards unity. It hindered neither the dynastic union of Hainault and Holland in 1299 nor their joint merger into the Burgundian dominions by 1433. Above all it was no impediment to artistic and economic exchange; and the drama and literature of townspeople furnishes the most convincing evidence.

At the beginning of the Burgundian period *chambres de rhétorique* or *rederijkers*[1] were establishing themselves as convivial and literary confraternities covering a wide social range from burgess to artisan. At the competitions in which the societies from several towns vied with each other in public performances it soon became usual to award prizes for the best production in either language. At the Ghent meeting of 1440 the *chambre* of Tournai won the prize for a composition in French and the *rederijkers* of Oudenaarde for a piece in Flemish. At Tournai, 1455, the French prize went to Lille and the Netherlandish to Ypres.[2]

Until the creation, in 1830, of Brussels as a national capital the language frontier remained remarkably stable. During our period two local fluctuations occurred quite close to each other, the one favourable to French the other to Netherlandish. The west Flemish dialect, extending formerly almost to Boulogne,[3] receded in Artois. Under Burgundian rule Saint-Omer was still a bilingual town, but the progress of French continued.[4] One of the earliest and most scholarly champions of Flemish, Jacob de Meyere (1491–1552),[5] was born close by, just inside Flanders;[6] and his remarks about the retreat of Netherlandish from and around Saint-Omer show a sense for the cultural significance of the linguistic boundary rarely found prior to the nineteenth century.[7]

On the other hand French, established at Ypres since the thirteenth century, was displaced during the fifteenth by a

---

[1] For the importance of *rederijkers* in the development of Netherlandish see J. van Mierlo, op. cit., 214–25.
[2] H. Liebrecht, *Les chambres de rhétorique* (Brussels, 1948), 54–5.
[3] G. Kurth, op. cit., ii, 72.
[4] See references and texts quoted ibid., ii, 75–9.
[5] See *infra*, p. 407, n. 4.
[6] Flêtre (Vletteren) dép: Nord. arr: Dunkerque. Canton Bailleul-sud-ouest.
[7] *Flandricarum rerum tomi*, x (Bruges, Hubertus Crokus, 1531, 8v), fol. 42v.

revival of Flemish.[1] In either case the Burgundian power seems to have been indifferent to the alteration in the language frontier taking place under its administration. Conditions along the language frontier were regulated by the regional constitutions inherited from the pre-Burgundian feudal lords; and in its local government Burgundian rule was on principle a respecter of native customs.

In so far as the Burgundian princes encouraged, and were dependent upon, the local estates of the territories which they ruled, they were indirectly responsible for influencing the linguistic distribution. The assemblies of these estates, by becoming increasingly frequent and important, encouraged the predominant language, e.g. French in Artois and Flemish in Flanders, to assert itself within each territory.[2]

The language frontier owed its prolonged stability to its dependence on local conditions. On the other hand, political, religious and intellectual factors operating on a European scale determined whether French or Netherlandish was at any given period between the thirteenth and the nineteenth century more generally used through the Low Countries as a whole for administrative, literary and social purposes.

As a cosmopolitan vernacular, northern French spread through much of Europe and the Levant from the twelfth century onwards; but during the fourteenth the tide turned, and French receded unevenly. The Low Countries from Luxemburg[3] to Holland early became familiar with French; but by the fourteenth century Netherlandish was growing in importance as the language of the guildsmen, the social class which had gained control of the towns. Between 1305 and 1369 Flanders was reduced to Flemish-speaking Flanders (Vlaanderen binnen der Leye) while French-speaking Flanders (Flandre gallicante) was forcibly annexed to the French Crown. Louis de Male (count of Flanders 1346-84) adopted Flemish

---

[1] G. Kurth, op. cit., ii, 42. G. des Marez, 'Le droit privé à Ypres au xiii siècle', *Bulletin de la commission royale des anciennes lois et ordonnances de Belgique*, xii (1926), 210 ff. E. I. Strubbe, 'Gedingvoerding voor het leenhof te Ieper in de vijftiende eeuw', ibid., xix (1956), 100–72.

[2] C. Hirschauer, *Les états d'Artois*, 2 vols. (Paris, 1923), i, xx ff. W. Prevenier, *De leden en de staten van Vlaanderen, 1384-1405*, (Verhandelingen van de koninklikje vlaambe Academie voor wetenschapen, letteren en schone kunsten van België, klasse der letteren, xliii, 1961), 219–20.

[3] For the special conditions in Luxemburg, see A. Houdremont, *Histoire de la langue française comme langue administrative du pays de Luxembourg* (Luxemburg, 1897).

for many types of document issuing from his chancery,[1] and particularly for correspondence with towns. After twenty years of Burgundian rule the Flemings remembered him as the count with whom they had dealt in their own tongue.[2]

In 1369 Philip 'le Hardi' laid the foundation of the Burgundian power by his marriage to Margaret, heiress of Flanders; but in 1379 the revolt of Ghent threatened to subject not Flanders alone but much of the Low Countries as well to the rule of the artisan class. To Philip, who launched the armies of the French Crown upon Flanders rather than lose his wife's magnificent inheritance in the county, it can only have been an accidental coincidence that his foes were Netherlandish speakers. Nevertheless, the subsequent fortunes of the French language in the Low Countries owed much to his military success. Had he failed in the face of the challenge from Ghent to implant his dynasty in Flanders, French as a denizen language might have disappeared north of the language frontier outside mercantile centres like Bruges.

In the light of their traditions Ghent and her allies could not fail to identify Netherlandish with the defence of their political and social interests. Their sentiments are revealed in the anecdote of Froissart purporting to be the harangue delivered by their leader Philip van Artevelde before the battle of Westrozbeke (27th November, 1382). He bade them do no harm to the boy king of France, whom Duke Philip had brought in the army against them, but they should capture the young Charles VI and carry him back to Ghent to teach him Flemish.[3]

There is no need to suppose that the duke disliked Flemish, even if the story of Jacob de Meyere be true that those Flemings, who were loyal to the comital authority, were forbidden to speak Flemish when following the French army with which Philip 'le Hardi' defeated the forces of Ghent at Westrozebeke.[4] Some such measure may well have been necessary in order to distinguish between friend and foe in the generally hostile countryside of west Flanders. In the fifteenth century the

---

[1] See the large number in *Cartulaire de Louis de Male, 1348–1358,* ed. T. Limburg-Stirum, i (Bruges, 1898).

[2] *Verzameling van xxiv origineele charters . . . van de provincie van Vlaenderen,* Ghent [1787–8, 5–6 ff.]

[3] Froissart, *Chroniques,* ed. Kervyn de Lettenhove, 26 vols. (Brussels, 1867–77), x, 155.

[4] *Annales rerum flandricarum,* ed. S. Feyerabend in *Annales . . . rerum belgicarum a diversis auctoribus* (Frankfurt, 1580 fol.), 217.

Burgundian power tolerated at court and in the army a diversity of tongues so that awkward incidents were not uncommon.[1]

Duke Philip, however, realized that the question of language was involved in the conflict, since, when he decided on negotiating a peace with Ghent, it was in Netherlandish that he had letters close issued in the name of Charles VI[2] offering a truce and safe conducts for negotiators. The use of Netherlandish in a document under the royal seal was a departure from the protocol of the French chancery. The final treaty, dated from Tournai, 18th December, 1385, in which Ghent swore obedience to Philip and his wife as count of Flanders, was also issued in two originals, French and Netherlandish.[3]

According to custom, treaties drawn in the vernacular followed the language of the victorious party; and when Philip 'le Bon' in 1453 vanquished Ghent more effectively than his grandfather in 1382, the peace treaty between the duke of Burgundy and the town was sealed in an exclusively French form.[4]

The bilingual pacification of 1385 indicates the lack of coercive power over which the first duke commanded during his early years in Flanders; but as he consolidated his authority he gallicized the comital administration. The introduction of French was vital to his plan for the standardization of methods and personnel over his northern dominions. His treatment of Antwerp, which was a part of Brabant attached since 1357 to Flanders,[5] is an extreme example of his determination to unify his administration on the basis of French as an official language. At Antwerp, as elsewhere in Brabant, French was previously unknown as an administrative language, whereas in Flanders, a fief of the French Crown, it had been an alternative. However, under Philip's influence French at Antwerp was employed

---

[1] Chastellain, *Chroniques*, ed. Kervyn de Lettenhove, 8 vols. (Brussels, 1863–6) iii, 104. O. de la Marche, *Mémoires*, ed. H. Beaune and J. d'Arbaumont, (4 vols. Société de l'histoire de France, 1884–8), ii, 18.

[2] From Troyes, 6th November, 1385. L. Mirot, 'L'emploi du flamand dans la chancellerie de Charles VI', *Bibliothèque de l'Ecole des Chartes*, lvii (1896), 55–63.

[3] O. Cartellieri, *Philip der Kühne* (Leipzig, 1910), 122, no. 19.

[4] *Collection de documents inédits concernant l'histoire de Belgique*, ed. L. P. Gachard, (Brussels, 1834) i, 142–59. Flemish translations were made for use at Ghent, *Kronijk van Vlaenderen, 580–1467* (Maatschappij der vlaamsche Bibliophilen, Ghent, 1839–40), ii, 198–211.

[5] H. Laurent and F. Quicke, 'La guerre de succession du Brabant 1356–57', *Revue du Nord*, xiii (1927), 82–121.

in all matters in which he or his government were directly concerned.[1]

The first Valois duke founded the tradition that Burgundian central government was conducted in French alone. After his death in 1404, his councillors around his widow—herself a born countess of Flanders—could not deal with a petition in Netherlandish submitted by Bruges and towns in Brabant.[2] The petitioners wasted a week at court while the translation was being made. Even at the time this was considered a notable example of the inconvenience suffered by Netherlandish speakers through the absence of bilingualism at the top of the administration; and later, in 1409, the Flemings were informed in an official *ordonnance* that the chancellor of Burgundy did not know their language.[3]

The two high courts, one for justice the other for finance, but both using French, founded by the first duke, were sited at Lille in French Flanders, not just to be outside Flemish Flanders but because Lille was central for administering Flanders, Artois and Rethel.[4] Philip successfully avoided any direct clash over language, because as a politician he conceded what his administration refused. John his eldest son, heir of Flanders, was given a Fleming as a tutor,[5] and Duke Philip's second son, Anthony, heir of Brabant, received instruction from a tutor[6] chosen by the estates of Brabant.

Of the two branches of the Burgundian dynasty, the senior in Flanders under Duke John (1405–19) and the junior under Duke Anthony (1406–15) in Brabant, the latter was quicker to acclimatize itself linguistically. Unlike his two sons (John IV, 1415–27 and Philip, 1427–30) Anthony was strong intellectually

---

[1] F. Prims, 'Het eerste officieel Fransch te Antwerpen 1380–1406', *Verslagen . . . vlaamsche Academie voor Taal-en-letterkunde* (1933), 763–75. A. Cosemans, 'Taalgebruik in Vlaanderen en Brabant tijdens de middeleeuwen', ibid. (1934), 491–3.

[2] *Handelingen van de leden en van de staten van Vlaanderen, 1384–1405*, ed. W. Prevenier (Commission royale d'histoire, série 4°, Brussels, 1959), 320. W. Prevenier, *De leden en de staten van Vlaanderen, 1384–1405*, p. 220.

[3] *Placcaert boeck . . . van Vlaenderen*, 10 vols. (Ghent, 1639–1766), i, 238, 243. See *infra*, p. 297, n. 1.

[4] R. Vaughan, *Philip the Bold* (1962), 206 ff.

[5] O. Cartellieri, op. cit., 112. Informing his father of the difficulty of raising taxation from the Flemings, John declared in 1394: 'et je meismes leur diz en flamenc au mieulx que je sceuz et peuz'. W. Prevenier, *De leden en de staten van Vlaanderen*, 288, n.

[6] *Geschiedenis van Vlaanderen*, ed. R. van Roosbroeck, F. Quicke and others, 6 vols. (Antwerp, 1936–49), iii, 58.

and physically. Within Brabant, he showed something of a preference for Netherlandish, which he restored to its previous status in Antwerp;[1] and he is thought to have sent at least one Netherlandish letter to a French-speaking community on the language frontier.[2] A son of his, who died in infancy, was buried under an epitaph in Netherlandish,[3] apparently the only member of the Valois dynasty distinguished by a monumental inscription in that language. His career exposes the fallacy of identifying linguistic usage and political loyalty, for Duke Anthony remained devoted to the royal house of France in whose cause he fell at Agincourt.

In Brabant the status of the two languages had received since 1356 some constitutional definition[4]; and the French and Netherlandish parts of the territory had never been severed from one another as in Flanders between 1305 and 1369. An incident during the absence from Brabant of John IV (1415-27) shows how the balance of the two languages was preserved in practice. Thomas, Lord of Diest, and Pierre de Luxembourg had been appointed captains general for the duchy during John's absence, but when Thomas was incapacitated by an accident, the duke had hastily to appoint two other lords who knew Netherlandish of which Pierre de Luxembourg was ignorant.[5]

With the extinction in 1430 of the junior branch ruling in Brabant, the senior branch of the Burgundian dynasty represented by Philip 'le Bon' succeeded to the duchy. His accession oath, 'Blijde Inkomst',[6] provided that the chancellor of

---

[1] F. Prims, 'Het eerst officieel Fransch te Antwerpen 1380-1406', p. 771.

[2] G. Kurth, op. cit., ii, 53.

[3] At the Whitefriars, Brussels (A. Henne and A. Wauters, *Histoire de la ville de Bruxelles* (Brussels, 1845), iii, 157). This church was destroyed by the French bombardment of 1695. The epitaph of William, son of Anthony, had been copied by an antiquary and has been published by C. G. Dallemagne, 'Le manuscrit de l'Ecuyer Charles van Riedwijck. Source commune des travaux sigillographiques et archéologiques de Christophe Butkens et de Mgr P. F. X. de Ram', *Annales de la Société royale d'archéologie de Bruxelles*, xlvi (1942-3), 27 ff. I am indebted for this information to Mlle M. Martens, archivist of the city of Brussels.

[4] Articles, 4, 33, of the 1356 charter guaranteed native councillors also a native bailiff for the *waalse land*. R. van Bragt, *De Blijde Inkomst van de hertogen Johanna en Wenceslas* (Standen en Landen, Louvain, xiii, 1956), 97, 105. Cf. the oath of Duke Anthony, 18th December, 1406, *Placcaerten, ordonnantien . . . van Brabandt*, etc., ed. A. Anselmo and others, 10 vols. (Antwerp-Brussels, 1648-1774), i, 140-4.

[5] A. Uyttebrouck, 'Liste chronologique provisoire des ordonnances du Brabant et du Limbourg, règne de Jean IV', *Bulletin de la commission royale des anciennes lois et ordonnances de Belgique*, xx (1959-60), 257, nos. 172, 177.

[6] The name Joyous Entry, which has had such a success with historians, was first used officially by Philip 'le Bon', R. van Bragt, op. cit., 122.

Brabant[1] was to know Latin, French and Netherlandish, in that order. In the absence of the duke, Brabant was to be governed by four native councillors, to whom Philip might add two councillors from his personal council, who presumably would be French speakers, on condition that they understood Netherlandish.[2]

The *Blijde Inkomst* of 1430, with additions, provided the oath for successive sovereigns of Brabant up to the Emperor Charles V.[3] It contained such important principles that its influence on the trend of Burgundian linguistic policy cannot have been negligible, notwithstanding that the component parts of the Burgundian dominions were each so distinct that the constitution of one territory could seldom seriously affect that of its neighbour.

A linguistic settlement in Flanders was retarded by reaction against the methods of Philip 'le Hardi', on whose death in 1404 the Flemings of Flemish Flanders (Vlaanderen binnen der Leye) tried to dismantle Lille as a central administrative citadel. Already in 1401 the estates complained that the castellan of Lille was a native of Artois and not, as he ought to have been under the 1369 marriage treaty of Philip and the heiress of Flanders, a Fleming of Flemish speech.[4]

The demands confronting Duke John, when he took possession of Flanders in 1405, anticipated those extorted in 1477 from the Duchess Mary. In each case the centralizing and gallicizing procedure of the preceding reign aroused the particularism of Flanders to protect itself by imposing the native speech upon the comital administration. In 1405 Duke John had to agree that communications addressed to him, as count of Flanders, should be in Flemish.[5] Although the finance court (*chambre des comptes*) remained at Lille, the Flemings had their way about the judicial court, council of Flanders, which was uprooted from Lille and transplanted inside Flemish Flanders.[6]

[1] Not the same as the duke's supreme chancellor of Burgundy.
[2] *Placcaerten, ordonnantien . . . van Brabandt*, i, 153 (article 5).
[3] Ibid., i, 168–78, 179–89, iv, 405–17.
[4] *Handelingen van de leden en van de staten van Vlaanderen, 1384–1405*, ed. W. Prevenier, pp. 208–9. J. J. Vernier, 'Philippe le Hardi . . . son mariage avec Marguerite de Flandre en 1369', *Bulletin de la commission historique du département du Nord*, xxii (1900), 94–6.
[5] *Verzameling van xxiv origineele charters . . . van de provincie van Vlaanderen*, 5–6, 39–40. P. Blommaert, 'Inhuldiging van Jan zonder Vrees te Gent 1405', *Belgisch Museum*, i (1837), 83–98.
[6] J. Buntinx, *De raad van Vlaanderen en zijn archief 1386–1795* (Standen en Landen, Louvain, i, 1950).

By 1409 Duke John's government was stronger. An *ordonnance*[1] was issued restoring French as the language for the deliberations of the council of Flanders and for its dealings with the duke and his chancellor. In open sessions the council might follow the language of the parties concerned. This solution was typically Burgundian since it admitted Flemish at the regional level, but preserved French for the serious transaction of the council as an organ of central government.

Evidence does not warrant the allegation that Netherlandish was despised by the Burgundian princes,[2] of whom one at least, Duke John, assumed a Netherlandish motto.[3] The suggestion[4] that they tolerated Netherlandish only because they were conscious that their power reposed on the Flemish rather than the Walloon population derives from the misapplication of a well-known text in Molinet.[5]

The two dukes, Philip 'le Bon' and his son Charles the Bold spoke Netherlandish unaffectedly when they pleased. Philip preferred French when he had to make a precise statement on policy,[6] but was at home in carrying on a social conversation in Netherlandish or Low German (convertible terms).[7] Charles was familiar with Netherlandish from his boyhood at Bruges to the point that when he found himself caught up in a popular riot at Ghent he upbraided in Flemish a

---

[1] Douai, 16th August, 1409, *Placcaert boeck . . . van Vlaanderen*, i, 238–44.

[2] P. Fredericq, 'Een Blik op de geschiedenis der vlaamsche gewesten tot Waterloo', *Vlaamsch België sedert 1830*, (Ghent) i (1905), 74.

[3] *Ik houd*, Monstrelet: *Chronique*, ed. L. Douet d'Arcq (Société de l'histoire de France, 6 vols., 1857–62), i, 123. His first emblem was the hop, a plant of Flemish rather than French cultivation, J. Calmette, *Les grand-ducs de Bourgogne* (Paris, 1949), 113.

[4] P. Fredericq, *Essai sur le rôle politique et social des ducs de Bourgogne dans les Pays-Bas* (Ghent, 1875), 74, repeated curiously enough by H. Pirenne, *Histoire de Belgique*, 3rd edn., (Brussels, 1922) ii, 458 although his general thesis runs contrary to such an idea.

[5] In 'La resource du petit peuple' written between May 1481 and March 1482 (*Les faictz et dictz de Jean Molinet*, ed. N. Dupire [Société des anciens textes français, 1936], i, 136–61) to encourage the resistance of the Walloon districts to their French invaders. The actual text is: 'Puissance sieut la cour du prinche et se tient en Flandres, en Brebant, à Bruges, à Gand, en Hollande et Zelande et en Namur et est trop plus flamengue que walonne', ibid., i, 156. *Puissance* = military forces, which in 1481 had to come from the Netherlandish areas seeing that the southern or Walloon districts were either occupied or raided by the troops of Louis XI. For this reason the court was in the north from which region Molinet foretold Maximilian would lead *Puissance* to the rescue of Wallonie.

[6] 'Table chronologique des chartes et diplômes de Luxembourg 1439–1443', ed. F. X. Würth-Paquet, *Publications de la section historique de l'institut grand-ducal de Luxembourg*, xxviii (1874), 153–4.

[7] O. de la Marche, *Mémoires*, i, 272.

member of the crowd whom he thought was a ringleader.[1]

There was never a doubt that the prince's personal language was French and since the government was based on his personal power French was necessarily the political language. In his autobiographical romance, composed in old age, Maximilian recalled how when he married Mary of Burgundy, in 1477, she and he had to teach each other their own language. Thus, declared Maximilian, he learnt the Burgundian language to govern his wife's dominions.[2] The Burgundian language was nothing other than French,[3] which was (and this is the significance of the passage in *Weisskunig*) indispensable for conducting the government. Maximilian also professed that a prince ought to know the languages of his subjects, and, for this reason, he claimed to have mastered 'Flemish', an attainment which had rendered him—as he supposed—extremely popular.[4] From his own account there is little doubt that he was taught 'Flemish' by the dowager duchess, Margaret of York, widow of Charles the Bold.[5]

The Burgundian power was operated by clerks and knights, who were domestic servants of the dynasty rather than civil servants; and the ducal household was of incalculable influence in propagating French in the Low Countries, since both French- and Netherlandish-speaking subjects of the dynasty coveted a post in it.[6] French was the primary language of the

---

[1] *Collection de documents inédits concernant l'histoire de Belgique*, ed. L. P. Gachard, i, 211–12.

[2] 'Nun erfordert die gross notturft das der jung weyss kunig seiner sprach nemlichen die burgundishe sprach pald iernet damit er seiner gemahl land desterpass regiren mocht'. *König Maximilians Weisskunig*, ed. H. T. Musper, R. Buchner, E. Petermann (Stuttgart, 1956), i, 245.

[3] In the seventeenth century French was occasionally known as Burgundian, e.g. the students' manual, De Pratel, *Manuductio ad linguam Burgundicam* (Louvain, 1689) (C. Moeller, *Eléonore D'Autriche*, Paris, 1895, 72). See also De Reiffenberg, *Histoire de l'ordre de la Toison d'Or* (Brussels, 1830), xxxii. This is not the place to explore the question of divergence from the French of France by the Burgundian court and administration, but verbal differences had started by 1500, see P. Gorissen, 'De historiographie van het Gulden Vlies', *Bijdragen voor de geschiedenis der Nederlanden*, vi (1952), 222.

[4] *Weisskunig*, i. 246.

[5] According to Maximilian he was taught by *ain alte fuerstin* (ibid.) and in a letter written in December 1477 he referred to the dowager of Burgundy as *die alt fraw* (*Maximilians I vertraulicher Briefwechsel mit Sigmund Prüschenk*, ed. V. von Kraus, Innsbruck, 1875, 28). Both expressions are renderings of *Madame la Grande* the form which Burgundian court protocol reserved for dowagers of the ruling house. This form was regularly applied to Margaret after 1477.

[6] Except for the influence of Maximilian there were few foreigners, cf. the Venetian ambassador's report of 1505 on the household of Philip 'le Beau', 'la maggior parte . . . fiaminghi, e pochi di altra nazione', *Relazioni degli ambasciatori veneti al senato*, ed. E. Alberi (Florence, 1839), I, i, 7.

household, because it was the prince's; but the household *ordonnance* composed by Olivier de la Marche for Charles the Bold was translated into Netherlandish.[1] When Philip 'le Bon' was in The Hague he naturally issued letters patent in Netherlandish to grant a chamberlainship to the lord of Montfoort.[2]

Members of the higher bureaucracy, after they had already begun to crystallize into an official class, still clung to French as a status symbol showing their close connexion with the prince. Charles V instructed in 1515 the *Grand Conseil* at Malines to use nothing but Netherlandish in dealing with the affairs of Holland. The councillors agreed to Netherlandish for their written judicial instruments, but refused to give up French for their deliberations and pronouncements, since it was the language which the prince spoke to his household.[3]

With the expansion of the Burgundian dominions under Philip 'le Bon' the officers of the central courts increasingly dealt with papers in Netherlandish on which they sometimes left marginal notes in French;[4] but the practice of translating into French the majority of important documents, normal under the first two dukes,[5] was no longer possible. For this reason the government of Charles the Bold preferred for the office of *maître de la chambre* [des comptes] at Lille the candidate who among other recommendations could show that he possessed a knowledge of Flemish.[6] The coinage, although the central accountancy at the Hôtel des Monnaies in Lille and the accounts of most territorial mintmasters were kept in French, was itself known under bilingual equivalents. After the currency *ordonnance* of 1433 gold and silver of like value and

---

[1] A. Matthaeus, *Veteris aevi analecta* (Leyden, 1698), 10 vols., i, 357–454; O. de la Marche, *Mémoires*, iv, cxix.

[2] 9th November, 1432. But the secretary responsible for preparing the letters wrote his own name in the French form *de la Mandre*, J. F. Niermeyer, *Honderd noord -nederlandse oorkonden en akten* (Groningen, 1939), 98.

[3] P. Wielant, *Recueil des antiquités de Flandre*, in *Corpus Chronicorum Flandriae*, ed. J. J. de Smet (Commission royale d'histoire, série 4°, 1865), iv, 149–50, cf. *supra*, p. 394, n. 4.

[4] T. S. Jansma, *Raad en rekenkamer in Holland tijdens hertog Philips van Bourgondië* (Bijdragen van het instituut voor middeleeuwsche geschiedenis der Rijksuniversiteit te Utrecht, xviii), 75 ff., 163.

[5] Cartellieri, op. cit., 134, the *ordonnance* of 1409 made detailed provision for translation, see *supra*, p. 397, n. 1.

[6] H. Pirenne, *Histoire de Belgique*, 3rd edn., (Brussels, 1922) ii, 457 more fully J. Bartier, *Légistes et gens de finance* (Académie royale de Belgique, classe des lettres, mémoires, collection 8°, vol. L, 1955), i, 421. Already in 1402 Daniel Alarts was appointed a councillor at Lille, because, as his commission stated he, unlike most of the other councillors, knew Flemish. R. Vaughan, *Philip the Bold*, 212n.

pattern were struck throughout the Burgundian Netherlands. The actual coins, however, were referred to by convertible French and Netherlandish names[1] in accordance with the local linguistic usage.

In local affairs the Burgundian administration imitated the ecclesiastical authority, for in 1375 Pope Gregory XI had laid down the principle that parsons ought to know the vernacular of their parishioners. This rule, reaffirmed frequently prior to the council of Trent, actually exercised some practical effect on the filling of benefices in Flanders.[2] When in 1464 the ecclesiastical authority and the secular power were closely co-operating for the promotion of the Crusade, Guillaume Fillastre, bishop of Tournai and councillor of Philip 'le Bon', took steps to have the bull enjoining the Crusade published both in French and Netherlandish in every parish[3] of the diocese.

Correspondence between the ruling house and its *stadhouders* in Holland was conducted in French, because in the fifteenth and sixteenth centuries the provincial governors were the personal representatives of the prince not of the territories in which they held office.[4] Within the county of Holland the native tongue was the administrative language from the start of Burgundian rule.[5] Later it became the practice for *ordonnances* of general application in the Burgundian Netherlands to be issued in French by the council around the duke, sent to the council in Holland (*Raad van Holland*) and translated.[6]

---

[1] From their appearance, e.g. *cavalier* and *ridder* for the 1433 gold issue with equestrian figure of the duke, *briquet* and *vuurijzer* for the 1474 silver issue with the Toison d'Or badge of the flint and steel. For the Burgundian coins, see H. Enno van Gelder and M. Hoc, *Les monnaies des Pays Bas bourguignons et espagnols 1434-1713* (Amsterdam, 1960) and the forthcoming work of P. Spufford on the coinage and monetary policy from Philip 'le Bon' to Philip 'le Beau'.

[2] H. Nelis, 'L'application en Belgique de la règle de chancellerie apostolique, *De idïomate beneficiatorum*', *Bulletin de l'institut historique belge de Rome*, ii (1922), 129-41.

[3] L. P. Gachard, *Rapport . . . sur les documents concernant l'histoire de Belgique qui existent dans les dépôts littéraires de Dijon et Paris* (Brussels, 1843) (première partie, Dijon) 158.

[4] E. Poullet, 'Les gouverneurs des anciens Pays-Bas', *Bulletin de l'Académie royale des sciences, lettres et beaux arts de Belgique*, 2, xxxv (1873), 362-437, 875-921. P. Rosenfeld, *The Provincial Governors from the minority of Charles V to the Revolt* (Standen en Landen, xvii, Louvain, 1959).

[5] This view is corroborated by the large number of different sorts of documents recorded before 1440 by Jan Rosa, secretary of the council of Holland, A. S. de Blécourt and E. M. Meijers, *Memorialen van het hof van Holland . . . van den secretaris Jan Rosa* (Rechtshistorisch instituut, Leiden, serie 1, 1929).

[6] T. S. Jansma, op. cit., 163, n. 3.

The civil, if not the military, officers of the Valois dukes probably believed in the principle that each region should be administered in its own vernacular. In 1471 a legal and a fiscal official from the county of Burgundy visited the Sundgau of Alsace and advised Charles the Bold what form the local administration should take under his rule. They recommended a provincial council modelled on those functioning in other parts of the Burgundian dominions; but they emphasized that the councillors must understand and speak German to be acceptable to the duke's new subjects in Alsace.[1] Actually during the brief Burgundian domination of Upper Alsace (1469–74) French was the official language, because the duke concentrated power in the hands of his local bailiff,[2] a soldier, who maintained a military government.[3]

The government of Philip 'le Bon' was perfectly prepared to state its own case in bilingual form in front of territorial estates when it was a question of securing their submission to Burgundian rule. In 1426 when the pretensions of the duke to rule in Holland were presented to delegates of Dutch towns and knights gathered at Malines, the chancellor of Burgundy, Nicolas Rolin, explained in French the title of the duke as count of Holland, followed by Roland van Uutkerke, one of Philip's Flemish councillors, who spoke in Netherlandish.[4] This procedure was repeated twenty-five years later in Luxemburg. In 1451, Nicolas Rolin, still chancellor, declared before the estates of Luxemburg the rights of his master Duke Philip over the duchy,[5] and Johann de Willer made an identical speech (*teutonice*) in German.

The States-General of the Burgundian Netherlands had,

[1] L. Stouff, 'Les possessions bourguignonnes dans la vallée du Rhin sous Charles le Téméraire', *Annales de l'Est*, xvii (1904), 66.

[2] Peter von Hagenbach, a member of the local nobility, many of whom had for long known *alemant et bourguignon*. H. Brauer-Gramm, *Peter von Hagenbach* (Göttingen, 1957), 13.

[3] Guy de Brimeu, another of Charles's military commanders, who presided at a regional council at Maastricht, also used French although the court's jurisdiction was mainly over Netherlandish speaking populations. P. Gorissen, *De Raadkamer van de hertog van Bourgondie te Maastricht 1473–1477* (Louvain, 1959), 41, 76.

[4] T. van Riemsdijk, 'De opdracht van het ruwaardschap van Holland . . . aan Philips van Bourgondie', *Verhandelingen van de koninklijke Akademie van wetenschappen, afdeeling letterkunde*, [new series] viii, (Amsterdam, 1906), bijlage iii.

[5] 'Table chronologique des chartes et diplômes de l'ancien pays de Luxembourg . . . 1451–1457', ed. F. X. Würth-Paquet, *Publications de la section historique de l'institut grand-ducal de Luxembourg*, xxx (1875), 14.

prior to 1477, no policy of bilingualism. Until 1465 their assemblies were not institutionally established;[1] and Charles the Bold, who made much use of them, imposed French on their public sessions.[2] After Charles' death, in 1477, the States-General were instrumental in dismantling his system of absolutism and in placing the central government under the influence of individual territories, in the first place that of Flanders and Brabant. From 1477 onward, therefore, evidence of bilingualism in the discourses and transactions at the States-General is plentiful.[3]

On both sides of the language frontier there existed jealousy of the Picards and Burgundians proper (*duchois et comtois*), who occupied such a number of lucrative posts in the Low Countries. In 1481 an *ordonnance* was drafted at Ghent for the removal of Burgundians from the household of the Duchess Mary and for the keeping in Flemish of the daily household accounts.[4] In 1483 it was the turn of the estates of Hainault who urged Maximilian to keep no more than sixteen Burgundians and Germans in his service.[5]

Quite understandably French itself was associated in Netherlandish-speaking areas with foreign and autocratic rule. In 1405 the Flemings asked Duke John whether his subjects in the duchy of Burgundy would like him to govern them in Flemish rather than in their own French tongue.[6] The same idea is implicit in the restrictions placed upon the official use of French in Flanders by the charter extorted from the Duchess Mary.[7] The French language provided the formulae, which

---

[1] This view does not coincide with the thesis of the editors of *Actes des Etats généraux des anciens Pays-Bas 1427–1477*, ed. J. Cuvelier, J. Dhondt and R. Doehard (Commission royale d'histoire), série 4⁰ (1948), but see P. A. Meilink, 'Dagvaarten van de Staten-Generaal 1427–1477', *Bijdragen voor de geschiedenis der Nederlanden*, v (1951), 198–212.

[2] *Actes des Etats généraux . . . 1427–1477*, 139 ff.

[3] Ibid., 339. The evidence for bilingualism will be much fuller when the *Actes des Etats généraux* from 1477 to 1506 are published; but for a speech in Netherlandish and French at the meeting of April 1482 see *Bulletin de la commission royale d'histoire*, 3, i (1860), 314, and for frequent evidence of bilingualism at the meeting February–March 1492, ibid., 3, iv (1863), 342, 344.

[4] *Corpus Chronicorum Flandriae*, ed. J. J. de Smet (Commission royale d'histoire, série in 4⁰, 1856), iii, 396–7.

[5] L. Devillers, 'Le Hainaut après la mort de Marie de Bourgogne, 1482–1483', *Bulletin de la commission royale d'histoire*, 4 ,viii (1880), 300.

[6] *Verzameling van xxiv origineele charters . . .*, 5.

[7] Ghent 11th February, 1477. 'Extrait du registre des chartes', ed. O. Dela-pierre, *Annales de la société d'émulation pour l'étude de l'histoire et des antiquités de la Flandre occidentale*, i (Bruges, 1839), 47–8.

unequivocally expressed the prince's prerogative.[1] These formulae were not native to Netherlandish. They were translated into it by officials of the dukes of Burgundy.

There is evidence from all three orders of society to suggest that Netherlandish speakers deliberately used their mother tongue when they wished to advertise their opposition to the Burgundian power. One late example is particularly striking. In 1527 the prelates of Brabant were involved in controversy with the regent, Margaret of Austria, over the fiscal demands of her government. During the discussion before the estates of Brabant, the abbot of Villers, spokesman for the prelates, suddenly stopped addressing Margaret in French and continued in Netherlandish. Margaret took this as a defiance of her government and immediately sequestrated the goods belonging to abbeys of Brabant represented at the estates.[2]

In 1455 the duke of Burgundy and the noble house of Brederode were at variance over the succession in the bishopric of Utrecht, so that Reinoude van Brederode was accused before a chapter of the Toison d'Or held in May 1456 of having broken the statutes of the order by opposing the duke's policy for Utrecht. The lord of Brederode demanded—and received—a copy of the order's statutes in Netherlandish;[3] and twice he spoke in his own defence in Netherlandish before his brother knights. The prosecution followed a bilingual procedure, the chancellor put the duke's case in French and Pieter Bladelin, a Fleming, repeated it in Netherlandish. Although the chapter of the order admitted Netherlandish as an official language, the employment by Reinoude van Brederode of his native language was intended to emphasize that a feudal family of Holland was challenging the Burgundian

---

[1] E.g. 'très redoubté seigneur'='harde geduchte heere'. 'Car ainsi nous plaist-il et le voulons estre fait'='wanttet ons belieft ende aldus gedaen willen hebben', see T. S. Jansma, op. cit., 123, n. 2 and 173.

At the same time a number of words relating to various aspects of political society were borrowed by Netherlandish from the French: Salverda de Grave, 'De franse woorden in het Nederlandsch', *Verhandelingen der koninklijke Akademie van Wetenschappen afdeeling Letterkunde*, (new series), vii (Amsterdam, 1906), 51 ff.

[2] P. Gorissen, 'Le séquestre des biens des abbayes brabançonnes en 1527', *Analecta premonstratensia*, [Tongerloo] xxxi (1955), 65.

[3] To show the social parity of esteem in which Netherlandish was held, it is worth noting that the earliest form of the statutes, prior to November 1440, is extant in a manuscript written in Brabant. G. I. Lieftinck, 'Een uniek handschrift met de middel-nederlandse versie van de statuten van het Gulden-Vlies', *Tijdschrift voor nederlandse Taal-en-letterkunde*, lxvii (1950), 209–14.

dynastic interest. The judicial outcome was a compromise.[1]

At Ghent, where resistance in the fourteenth century was coupled with the official use of Flemish, the approach of the armed conflict with Philip 'le Bon' evoked the same combination. On 15th December, 1451, the captains of Ghent publicly proclaimed that the town's external correspondence would henceforth be conducted exclusively in Netherlandish;[2] and so it remained until the defeat of Ghent in 1453. During their frequent squabbles with the central government towns also invoked their language usage in support of their claims. An episode in the economic rivalry between Bruges and the Scheldt ports assumed the form of a language dispute. In 1500, Bruges had obtained the renewal of its staple rights by letters patent from the chancery of Philip 'le Beau'. These letters were naturally in French; but on their reception at Antwerp and Bergen-op-zoom the magistrates there refused to publish them on the pretext that no Netherlandish translation had been forwarded and that French was not understood at Antwerp![3]

Burgundian rule was indirectly responsible for promoting bilingualism within the ruling class. Fathers anxious that their sons should grow up to hold office had them taught both languages. Jean de Lannoy, a councillor of Philip 'le Bon', when drawing up a programme for the education of his son, admitted that in his own public career a knowledge of 'l'alemant' (Netherlandish) had proved useful. As a language, it was 'très convegnable et très séant'; and he directed that if his son was to study at Paris rather than at Louvain the boy must be accompanied by a priest 'de la langue thioise', because Netherlandish was easy to forget 'et qui ne l'apprent josne jamais ne le parlera droit'.[4] On the other side, Jan van Dadizeele was sent from Flemish Flanders at the age of twelve to Lille and Arras in order that he might learn French.[5] Towns which had

[1] Vienna, Archiv des Ordens vom Goldenen Vliesse, Regest, I, fol. 37v. Baron de Reiffenberg, *Histoire de l'ordre de la Toison d'Or* (Brussels, 1830), 36.

[2] *Dagboek van Gent 1447–1470*, ed. V. Fris (Maatschappij der vlaamsche bibliophilen, 4, xii, 1901–4), ii, 245.

[3] C. J. F. Slootmans, *Jan-metten-lippen* (Rotterdam, 1946), 119.

[4] Quoted, Chastellain, *Chronique*, ed. Kervyn de Lettenhoven, v, 110, and B. de Lannoy and G. Dansaert, *Jean de Lannoy le batisseur 1410–1493* (Brussels, 1937), App. Later Jacob de Meyere claimed that the French disliked Flemish because they found it hard to learn, *Annales rerum Flandricarum*, ed. S. Feyerabend, 217.

[5] *Mémoires de Jean de Dadizeele, 1413–1481*, ed. Kervyn de Lettenhoven (Société d'émulation pour l'étude . . . des antiquités de la Flandre occidentale, Bruges, 1850), 1.

frequent dealings with the court submitted themselves to bilingualism. In May 1434 the pensioner [secretary] of Brussels reserved the right to refuse business at court which had to be done in French;[1] but by 1485 Brussels resigned itself to maintaining two pensioners, the one French the other Netherlandish.[2]

The Burgundian régime provided a geographical framework within which Netherlandish could develop; and the subsequent division of north and south between the United Provinces and Spain probably intensified the fragmentation of the language into dialects within the southern Low Countries. But, Netherlandish could not emerge as a sovereign language so long as the Burgundian régime and that of the Burgundian Habsburgs lasted. However, the first attempt in print to standardize the vocabulary by means of a Netherlandish-Latin dictionary owed something to the Burgundian influence, as it was produced in the chancery of Cleves, a satellite of the Burgundian chancery in the same way as the dukes of Cleves were themselves clients of the Burgundian dynasty. Gert van der Schuren,[3] chancellor of Cleves, who was responsible for this dictionary entitled *Theutonista* or 'Duytschlender',[4] was influenced by the terminology of the Burgundian administration.[5]

For the re-invigoration of literary French in the Low Countries during the fifteenth century no other factor equalled in importance the patronage of the Valois dukes.[6] They respected letters, which for them meant French literature or translations into French. Their preference directly influenced the nobility, and even indirectly acted to the disadvantage of Netherlandish for works which might otherwise have been translated into that language were instead turned into French. About 1453 one of the more important chronicles of Holland

---

[1] J. Paquet, 'La contribution du clergé à l'administration des villes de Bruxelles et d'Anvers aux xiv et xv siècles', *Moyen Age*, lvi (1950), 368.

[2] Their names were Jean Suquet and Gheert van den Hecke, Brussels, 'compte communal', 1485–6, Archives générales du royaume, 30942, fols. 89, 91, 92.

Already in 1404 the town of Nieuport in Flanders had a 'waalsche advocaat', *Handelingen van de leden en van de staten van Vlaanderen*, ed. W. Prevenier, 320.

[3] *Allgemeine deutsche Biographie*, xxxiii (1891), 80–2.

[4] Hain, no. 14513. The Netherlandish-Latin finished March 1476 and the entire work including the Latin-Netherlandish printed at Cologne May 1477.

[5] See *Theutonista* under *fiscus* and *confiscare*, sig. g, 4r.

[6] For an initial bibliography see the works of G. Doutrepont, *La littérature française à la cour des ducs de Bourgogne* (Paris, 1909) and *Les mises en prose des épopées et des romans chevaleresques du xiv au xvi siècle* (Académie royale de Belgique, classe des lettres, mémoires, collection 8°, xl, 1939).

and Utrecht was translated into French. Wolfert van Borselen[1] picked out the Latin text among his manuscripts at the castle of Veere, and hoping that it would interest the duke had a servant of his translate it for presentation to Philip 'le Bon'.[2]

Albert Krantz,[3] a champion of Low German against other idioms, both Germanic and romance, thought that subjects in general copied the speech of their rulers. He instanced the imitation in Mark Brandenburg of the German which the ruling house of Hohenzollern had imported from Franconia and the imitation among the Saxons of Meissen of the speech used by the Wettin dynasty.[4] In this same passage Krantz criticized the *Flamingi* for adopting French; and he obviously had in mind the attraction exercised by the prestige of the Burgundian court.

In the later sixteenth century the poet Ronsard maintained that neo-feudal powers like Burgundy had constituted a threat to the linguistic as well as to the political unity of France.[5] Ever since the reign of Charles VII the apologists of the French monarchy had claimed that territories, including those ruled by the duke of Burgundy, bordering the eastern frontier of the kingdom, were properly part of France, because, among other reasons, their inhabitants spoke French.[6] Nevertheless, any association between language and political loyalty remained in an incipient stage. Governments and scholars were alike more concerned to identify their lands with the former provinces of the Roman empire.

Under Charles the Bold the official view regarded the Burgundian Netherlands as the juridical successor of *Gallia*

---

[1] On him see *The Complete Peerage* . . . *by G.E.C.*, ii (1912), 378.

[2] W. Noomen, *La traduction française de la Chronographia de Johannis de Beka* (The Hague, 1954), 1 ff. Of interest is the editor's study of the political background to the duke's historical reading, lxiii ff.

[3] References in K. Schottenloher, *Bibliographie zur deutschen Geschichte im Zeitalter der Glaubenspaltung* (Leipzig, 1933–40), i, 418; vi, 144.

[4] *Saxonia*, (Cologne, 1520), fol. lib. i, cap. i, a^{iv}. a^v. Written in 1500 after Krantz visited Antwerp in 1491 and 1497.

[5] 'Et ne fay point de doute que s'il y avoit encores en France des ducs de Bourgogne, Picardie, Normandie, Bretaigne, Champaigne, Gascongne, qu'ils ne desirassent pour un estresme honneur que leurs subjets escrivissent en la langue de leurs pays naturels; car les princes ne doibvent estre moins curieux d'agrandir les bornes de leurs seigneuries, que d'étendre à l'imitation des Romains, le langage de leurs pays,' P. de Ronsard, *L'abbrégé de l'art poétique français* [1565] in *Oeuvres complètes*, ed. P. Laumonier (Société des textes français modernes), xiv (1949), 11–12.

[6] The Herald Berry writing in the 1450s. Gilles le Bouvier, *La description des pays*, ed. E. T. Hamy (Recueil de voyages et de documents pour servir à l'histoire de la géographie avant le xvii siècle, xxii, 1908), 52, 108, 112.

belgica[1]; and in the sixteenth century when the language question became a subject of learned controversy there was no mistaking the divergence between the gallicizing tendency of the students of classical antiquities and the attachment of Germanists to Netherlandish.

'Le propre langaige belgien est le gaulois'[2] stated categorically the Fleming, Philip Wielant, when he came to write between 1510 and 1520 the 'Antiquities of Flanders'. He was versatile and knew the common law of Flanders and Holland excellently; but he started his career as an official of the Parlement de Malines under Charles the Bold and remained a man of the central government. He visualized the historical and linguistic development of the Low Countries as springing from *Gallia belgica*. The existence of Germanic speech on the North Sea coast of the Netherlands he explained by the incursions of early teutonic raiders and in the east of the Netherlands by reason of intercourse with neighbouring Germans towards the Rhine. Erasmus of Rotterdam thought of his native Holland as lying on the map between France and Germany, but pertaining more to the former.[3] His recollections of the northern frontier of the Roman empire probably decided his choice for France (Gaul).

Jacob de Meyere,[4] who knew the *Saxonia* of Krantz,[5] whom he admired as a fellow Germanist, possessed both the inclination and the historical knowledge to prove that *Gallia belgica* had been replaced at the end of Antiquity by teutonic settlements between the Rhine and the English Channel. He thought that he could detect a historical process whereby French was gradually regaining the territory and pushing the Germanic language back to the Rhine.[6] His Flemish patriotism led de Meyere into a linguistic jingoism altogether uncommon at the time; and his considerable classical learning gave him another excuse for despising French as a debased form of Latin.[7] Although his inspection of archives was facilitated by official

[1] *Actes des Etats généraux ... 1427–77*, 179–80.
[2] *Corpus Chronicorum Flandriae*, iv, 10.
[3] *Opus epistolarium*, iv, 353–4.
[4] *Biographie nationale publiée par l'Académie royale de Belgique*, v (1875), 534–50.
[5] *Flandricarum rerum tomi x* (1531), fol. 42v. The reference is to the passage of Krantz quoted *supra*, p. 406, n. 4.
[6] *Flandricarum rerum*, fols. 4v, 42–3.
[7] 'Tamen spuma sit linguae latinae', *Annales rerum Flandricarum*, ed. S. Feyerabend, 217.

patronage, the government viewed with displeasure his publication of the 'liberties' of Flanders. The imperial privilege, which de Meyere secured from the Brussels government (19th February, 1537 n.s.) for the printing of his *Compendium chronicorum Flandriae* was granted only on condition that the printed text took account of the corrections insisted on by the council of Flanders and omitted the urban charters.[1] His devotion to the 'liberties' and language of Flanders ranged de Meyere ideologically at least among the opponents of the central government.

With good reason the Burgundian princes and their ministers might have protested that under their régime no language question existed in the Netherlands. In so far as it did exist the question was a technical one. For example, it was not always easy to find officers in the higher grades who were also good linguists. Thus in 1394 the Duchess Margaret protested against the suggested transfer of Jean de Poucques from her household since he was her only *maître d'hôtel* who knew Flemish.[2] If from time to time, differences of language rendered the administration rather more complex than it might otherwise have been, the resulting difficulties were negligible compared with the enormous problems arising from the conflicting economic, legal and social conditions between town and countryside and between one territory and another of the Low Countries.

The reaction of the Burgundian government after 1405 and again after 1477 shows it determined to retain French for its own use.[3] Demands for the adoption of Netherlandish in courts created by the central government were treated as part of a programme to enthrone particularism at the expense of the prince's authority.

On the other hand the Burgundian state never committed itself to a policy of linguistic restriction, let alone of linguistic unification, to enforce which it possessed neither the wish nor the power. Despite its much superior material and moral forces,

[1] 'Les correxions et changemens faitz audit livre par lesditz de nostre conseil en Flandres. Et qu'il obmetra l'insertion des privileges d'aucunes villes . . .', *Compendium chronicorum Flandriae* (Nuremberg, Ioannes Petreius, 1538, 8°), aa, 2, recto.

A. Voisin, 'Examen critique des censures qu'ont subies les *Annales de Flandre* de Jacques Meyer', *Bulletin de l'Académie royale des sciences et belles lettres de Bruxelles*, vii (1840), 236–47 seems to confuse, 241 the *Compendium* with the *Annales*, the former first printed at Nuremberg (1538) the latter at Antwerp (1561).

[2] R. Vaughan, *Philip the Bold*, 212.

[3] See *supra*, 396, 402.

the Crown of France did not proceed to curtail seriously the use of Latin and Provençal in favour of French until the *ordonnance* of Villers-Cotterets in August 1539. As for the Burgundian government: it required from its subjects observance of the Christian religion free of heretical taint, docility in paying taxes and willingness to support the military and economic consequences of an ambitious foreign policy. But, more tolerant than later European governments, it never interfered to teach its subjects what language they should speak or write.[1]

---

[1] Cf. also P. Bonenfant, 'Du *Belgium* de César à la Belgique de 1830. Essai sur une évolution sémantique,' *Annales de la soc. royale d'archéologie de Bruxelles* (1958–61) 31–58.

XIV

J. M. FLETCHER

WEALTH AND POVERTY IN THE MEDIEVAL GERMAN UNIVERSITIES WITH PARTICULAR REFERENCE TO THE UNIVERSITY OF FREIBURG

Most medieval universities had to make special provision for rich and poor masters and scholars, but in Germany this problem was particularly serious. I propose in this essay to examine the reaction of the university authorities to three different groups within the academic society: the wealthy noblemen, the poor scholars and the rich, salaried lecturers. The proliferation of universities during the later medieval period produced in Germany a number of small academic centres very dependent on the nobility for their future expansion. Rich scholars from this class expected preferential treatment in return for their financial support of an essentially local university. On the other hand, the German universities, unlike the provincial universities of France, concentrated on the teaching of the arts. They attracted, therefore, large numbers of poorer, younger students who could not afford the expensive journey to Paris. The surviving statutes of the German universities show that they were conscious of the need to legislate for the special interests of rich and poor students.[1] Moreover, a characteristic of the smaller universities was their employment of a salaried teaching staff distinct from 'ordinary' lecturers. This encouraged the

[1] For a general discussion of the social status of medieval students, see H. Rashdall, *The Universities of Europe in the Middle Ages*, ed. F. M. Powicke and A. B. Emden, (Oxford, 1936) iii, 404–14.

development of a wealthy élite of teachers with interests diver-
gent from those of the remaining masters. Within this privileged
group, the ending of the traditional poverty and insecurity of
the regent master's life brought opportunity for the furtherance
of individual ambitions. This, in turn, was to involve the
universities in further difficulties.

Throughout the medieval period the number of students of
noble birth entering the German universities remained small.[1]
The fame of the celebrated law schools of northern Italy and the
increasing popularity of the 'New Learning' drew many
ambitious nobles south. Nevertheless, German universities
attempted to attract influential students by allowing special
privileges to the nobility. Their motives were not at all altruistic.
A rich nobleman not only brought fame to the university, but
while studying could be compelled to spend money lavishly to
maintain his privileged position, and in his future career would
be expected to support the university in any legal or political
difficulty. To ingratiate itself with Frederick I, the university of
Heidelberg was even prepared in 1474 to allow his son to hear
lectures for the B.A. degree in the electoral castle.[2] The future
prosperity of the university was so closely associated with its
support of the electoral house that requests for privileges such
as this could hardly be rejected.

The young nobleman learned very soon after his entry to the
university that his enjoyment of a special status was closely
associated with his ability to support the university financially.
At matriculation many German universities demanded higher
enrolment fees from noblemen. The statutes of Tübingen, for
example, provide for special charges for nobles, prelates, and
those wishing to be placed 'on the front rows'.[3] References to
this special, reserved seating for rich scholars attending lectures
and important ceremonies appear frequently in university
documents. At Basel privileges were given to those 'with a
particular place on the benches'[4] and at Freiburg to those 'who

---

[1] For a further discussion of the statistics, see F. Eulenburg, *Die Frequenz der
Deutschen Universitäten* (Leipzig, 1904), 66.

[2] E. Winkelmann, *Urkundenbuch der Universität Heidelberg*, (Heidelberg, 1886) ii,
51.

[3] R. Roth, *Urkunden zur Geschichte der Universität Tübingen* (Tübingen, 1877), 59.

[4] C. C. Bernouilli, *Die Statuten der Philosophischen Fakultät der Universität Basel*
(Basel, 1907), 24.

are allocated the highest benches'.[1] Special seating in churches used by the university was also provided for noblemen.[2] Respect for wealth could affect academic standards. A decision at Freiburg to compel all masters of arts to attend daily lectures in the higher faculties was not imposed on noblemen 'because of their distinction and the high level of their scholarship'.[3] More striking was the preference given to the nobility at degree examinations. Successful candidates for the B.A. degree at Tübingen were to be placed in the same order as they had in the Matricula, but noblemen were to be preferred to all others. The examiners for the M.A. degree, on the contrary, were to place the successful applicants in order of mérit. Here again nobility and the prospect of an important career were influential. In deciding the place to be occupied in the list by a successful candidate, the examiners were to consider not just his knowledge, manner of life and his ability to express himself, but his chance of future promotion and his noble birth.[4]

The rich nobleman could not be expected to live under the same restrictions as the ordinary students. He usually had with him a retinue of servants whose entry to one of the burses, the halls of residence for the students, would have dislocated the communal life practised there. He would also have found the simple food served there inadequate to his tastes. Many rich young men were able to employ their own private tutors and, therefore, had less need of the special instruction provided in the burses. Accordingly, university statutes expressly exempt noblemen from the requirement of residence in a burse. It was usually sufficient for them to obtain permission from the university for their lodging in a private house, although at Vienna the statutes also insisted on the appointment of someone to live with such students and be responsible to the authorities for their good behaviour.[5] In recognition of the nobleman's rank, the universities also allowed him to wear distinctive clothing. At Freiburg, he was exempted from the punishment decreed for students 'who go about in tunics that have no

[1] Freiburg, University Archives, Protocollum Senatus, i, fol. 128v. The university archives are at present being reorganized and no permanent shelf numbers have yet been allocated to the MSS. I am preparing an edition of the first volume of the Protocollum Senatus.
[2] Ibid., i, fol. 21.
[3] Ibid., i, fol. 184.
[4] R. Roth, op. cit., 358.
[5] R. Kink, *Geschichte der Kaiserlichen Universität zu Wien*, (Vienna, 1854) ii, 236.

girdle'[1] and allowed to wear the *birretum*, a privilege usually confined to bachelors of the higher faculties.[2] Should a student, able to spend annually more than thirty florins, obtain the master's degree at Leipzig, he was expected to maintain the dignity of the university by purchasing within six months the proper academic dress.[3] The relative liberty allowed to a nobleman concerning his dress could be abused. In July 1470 the rector at Freiburg was instructed to call before him certain nobles guilty of wearing improper dress. They were to be 'piously warned' but also informed that any minor breaches of the statute regulating the dress of students would be tolerated.[4]

During the ceremonies that accompanied the award of a degree the university regents took this final opportunity to extort as much as possible from the successful candidate. Gifts of money, offerings of clothing, and invitations to expensive banquets were required. The rich man at this time was especially vulnerable; as an act of charity he frequently paid for the *prandium Aristotelis*, the degree feast, on behalf of poorer scholars. At Cologne the university officially appointed a rich man to undertake the duty of providing this banquet, and in return endowed him with the honorary title of *primus universitatis*.[5] In such ways, the German universities attempted to impose obligations on their wealthy students to benefit both the university itself and its poorer scholars.

The noblemen attending the universities were too few to affect fundamentally their development in the medieval period. They were a small group with interesting but exceptional privileges. Of more importance were the rich, salaried lecturers within the teaching body of the university itself, who formed a permanent pressure group with their own special interests. Although the earlier German universities attempted to reproduce the regency system of Paris, whereby all official teaching was done by those who had qualified for a degree and had been accepted into the corporation of masters, the smaller universities found that they could not attract lecturers of

---

[1] Freiburg, City Archives, O 38 (The Earliest Latin Statutes of the University), fol. 18v. *The Medieval Statutes of the Faculty of Arts of the University of Freiburg in Breisgau*, ed. H. Ott and J. M. Fletcher (Notre Dame, Indiana, University Press, 1964), 60.
[2] Freiburg, University Archives, Protocollum Senatus, i, fol. 128v.
[3] F. Zarncke, *Die Statutenbücher der Universität Leipzig* (Leipzig, 1861), 315.
[4] Freiburg, University Archives, Protocollum Senatus, i, fol. 22v.
[5] H. Keussen, *Die Alte Universität Köln* (Cologne, 1934), 301–2.

sufficient standing by this method. Universities such as Freiburg or Rostock never had sufficient students to provide an adequate salary from lecture fees alone for an ambitious master. The higher faculties in particular could never be certain of attracting sufficient students to reward adequately a highly qualified lecturing doctor. Nor did the prestige of a regent's position compensate for loss of income as it did, to a certain extent, in the larger and more celebrated universities. To solve this problem many German universities created a number of lectureships in all faculties which were financed directly or indirectly by the university itself and which were allocated annually a fixed sum. The money for these lectures was usually donated by local noble patrons of the university or by town councils. In either case an opportunity was created for continual interference in the university's affairs by the external authorities providing the salaries. The number of lectureships and the salaries paid varied from place to place and from year to year according to the prosperity of the university. At Freiburg in 1489 the university owed money to four doctors, one licenciate, four masters of arts and one 'poet' for official lectures.[1] The duke of Bavaria's foundation charter for the university of Ingolstadt established salaried lectureships in all faculties. There were to be one doctor in theology, two in canon law, one in civil law and one in medicine. For the Faculty of Arts six lectureships were endowed.[2] The salaried lecturers also received free rooms in the university *collegium* or an allowance towards the rent of private rooms. In some universities the lecturers were also paid by the students in the usual manner; in others their lectures were given without charge.

The prestige and financial security enjoyed by the salaried lecturers was quickly reflected in their importance in university administration. By the close of the fifteenth century, the majority of the smaller German universities were controlled by this privileged élite which co-operated closely with the local secular power. At Heidelberg, for example, where the university had been constituted 'on the Paris model',[3] a statute of June 1393 removed effective control from the masters of arts and placed it in the hands of the doctors of the higher faculties.[4]

---

[1] Freiburg, University Archives, Protocollum Senatus, i, fol. 148.
[2] C. Prantl. *Geschichte der Ludwig-Maximilians-Universität* (Munich, 1872), ii, 23–4.
[3] E. Winkelmann, op. cit., i, 3.
[4] Ibid., i, 53–5.

Amongst these, the salaried lecturers were preponderant. The reforming ordinance of Frederick I in May 1452 restricted the representation of the Faculty of Arts on the university council to five members, the dean and four masters chosen from the twelve senior faculty members. The rector and all doctors of the higher faculties had the right to attend the council.[1] The different versions of the foundation letter for the university of Ingolstadt also show this tendency to reduce the importance of the younger masters of arts in the university council and give control to the established doctors.[2] Such a policy prevented the numerical superiority of the Faculty of Arts from being reflected, as at Paris or Oxford, in its preponderance within the administration of the university. In the individual higher faculties the power of the salaried lecturers was unchallenged. Here they must often have been the only regents lecturing. Even on the rare occasions when other doctors were available, the salaried lecturer was allowed a privileged position. At Ingolstadt any matriculated doctor could hold lectures, but he could not do so at any time when the salaried doctors were lecturing.[3] Every dean of the Faculty of Theology at Freiburg between 1460 and 1520 appears also in the list of salaried lecturers for that faculty.[4] Only in the Faculty of Arts was their control incomplete. Even here the strong tendency to restrict positions of responsibility to the senior members of the faculty gave greater opportunity to the secure, salaried lecturers than to the younger, unestablished masters. The virtual monopoly of authority which they enjoyed in the university and in most of the faculties was of great financial importance to the salaried lecturers. They were able to divert into their own pockets many of the additional per-quisites of office originally intended to help the poor regents. At promotions, for example, the gifts and payments made by successful candidates helped to swell their incomes. The donations of food and wine made by students during examina-tions and when receiving degrees also came to a great extent to the salaried lecturers. These incidental gifts added to their normal salary gave them a position which their less privileged colleagues might envy.

It would be expected that the division between salaried and

[1] Ibid., i, 163.
[2] C. Prantl, op. cit., i, 25–6.
[3] Ibid., ii, 26.
[4] J. J. Bauer, *Zur Frühgeschichte der Theologischen Fakultät der Universität Freiburg i. Br.* (Freiburg, 1957), 178–83.

unsalaried lecturers would produce tension amongst the regents. In fact, there is little sign of this in the published documents. Perhaps the influence of the salaried lecturers in the smaller universities and the support they received from the local secular authorities were too strong to be opposed. It is notable that the best documented conflict between the two groups occurred at a large university, Leipzig, and in the Faculty of Arts, where the non-salaried masters still retained some importance within the teaching structure of the faculty. The details of the dispute well illustrate the manner in which control of the Faculty of Arts was passing into the hands of a small privileged group, and how this group then used its authority for its own financial gain.

The foundation document of the university of Leipzig established in 1409 for the Faculty of Arts a *collegium maius*, with twelve salaried masters, and a *collegium minus*, with eight salaried masters.[1] Of these twenty masters, one was to be a theologian and later two other places were reserved for lecturers in the Faculty of Medicine.[2] The foundation of the Collegium Beate Marie Virginis added another four salaried lecturers in the Faculty of Arts.[3] The statutes made for the faculty in the first year of the university's existence granted to all masters the right to attend the faculty council, but in future restricted this privilege to those who had reached their third year as masters.[4] After 1436–7 the right was further restricted to those who had reached the fourth year of their mastership.[5] This restriction of membership of the council to the senior masters inevitably increased the influence of the established salaried lecturers. They were more likely to remain for many years lecturing in the Faculty of Arts because they were assured of their annual income. The statute of 1443, which reserved to members of the council two-thirds of all money collected at promotion ceremonies, was designed to strengthen their financial position.[6] During the following year further statutes consolidated the council's control over the gifts made by candidates receiving degrees.[7] This erosion of the privileges of the masters who were

[1] F. Zarncke, op. cit., 4.
[2] Ibid., 7.
[3] Ibid., 265.
[4] Ibid., 306.
[5] Ibid., 324.
[6] Ibid., 358.
[7] Ibid., 361–6.

not members of the council was not allowed to pass unchallenged. In 1445 an appeal to the chancellor on behalf of these masters produced action to restore the traditional position. A committee was set up to investigate promotion payments, the election of the deans and the choice of examiners.[1] In this case determined opposition had drawn attention to the customary rights of the non-salaried masters, but this opposition seems exceptional and restricted to the artists of the larger universities. In a university such as Leipzig the number and importance of the non-salaried masters of arts was still sufficient to exercise some pressure on the faculty authorities. In a smaller university there were fewer regent masters and consequently the salaried minority was able to exercise control more easily.

An interesting comment on the difficulties created by the establishment of a group of salaried lecturers within the regent body of the Faculty of Arts is recorded in the *Acta* of the rector at Freiburg. In 1490 the dean of the Faculty of Arts appeared before the university to present certain grievances. He stated that in the faculty were many masters 'and they cannot obtain an income or sufficient exercises to pay for their own food and drink'. The reason for this, he claimed, was that after the salaried lecturers of the faculty had given their statutory lectures and exercises, few subjects remained for the other masters to cover. The solution proposed by the dean was to reduce the number of subjects allotted to the salaried lecturers so that there would be sufficient remaining to be shared amongst the other masters. He also proposed that the lecturers should then all be hired by the university and the faculty so that the students need not make any payments to them. The university refused to accept this proposal, declaring that it was bound to carry out the royal ordinance which had established the salaried lectureships.[2] The university, apparently, was not prepared to recognize that the co-existence of the traditional regency system and the practice of hiring lecturers was unfair to the non-salaried masters. This reluctance to break with the system that had been customary since the foundation of the older northern universities is perhaps understandable. Nevertheless, it is apparent from complaints such as these, that in Germany the abandonment of the traditional right of every regent master to

[1] Ibid., 371–4.
[2] Freiburg, University Archives, Protocollum Senatus, i, fol. 154.

lecture in return for fees paid by his students was being seriously considered by the Faculty of Arts.

The financial security enjoyed by the salaried lecturers set them apart from the poor masters so frequently mentioned in the records of the earlier northern universities. With the abandonment of the regent's traditional poverty, many earlier academic restrictions also disappeared. Lecturers grew ambitious for the comforts of a normal, respectable life. In some universities the habit of communal life amongst the salaried lecturers of the Faculty of Arts was abandoned or modified. Instead, the university made payments towards the renting of private houses for its lecturers. In contravention of the faculty statutes official exercises were frequently held in these private houses. Occasionally, usually after some disturbance, the authorities took steps to halt this development and to bring students under closer control. At Freiburg, for example, in 1498 after a quarrel between two students during a town fair, all masters teaching scholars outside the burses were ordered to carry out their future 'resumptions'—revision lectures—and exercises only in the burses. This ruling was to apply in particular to the married lecturers.[1] But despite these occasional attempts to reverse the development, there was a general movement away from the traditional academic practices evolved at a time when both masters and students lived communal lives.

The higher standard of living and the relative security brought by their position encouraged many salaried lecturers to venture on family life. One of the most interesting features of fifteenth-century university life in Germany is the general acceptance of the need to make provision for married lecturers. There were, of course, always traditionalists who wished to revert to earlier days and who poured scorn on their married colleagues. Such a person must have scribbled the often quoted words 'becoming mad, he took a wife' in the matriculation rolls of the university of Vienna.[2] Such phrases, however, give a wrong impression of the universities' general attitude to marriage and such exceptional outbursts of indignation should not be taken as typical of academic thinking on this subject. For those lecturers wishing for a future career in the Church or in

[1] Ibid., i, fol. 186v.
[2] See G. Kaufmann, *Die Geschichte der Deutschen Universitäten*, ii (Stuttgart, 1896), 86n.

the Faculty of Theology, marriage would be out of the question, but for lawyers, medical lecturers and artists married life proved very attractive now that financial security had been attained. For many of these lecturers, marriage with a wealthy widow or a well-endowed daughter brought additional income and an introduction to the middle-class society of the university towns. Unfortunately, these matrimonial adventures were in turn to involve the universities in disputes requiring constant attention. The married men are conspicuous by the frequency in which they appear in descriptions of the universities' legal difficulties and quarrels with the civic administration.

The traditional privileges sought by medieval universities were those thought necessary to protect students and lecturers from the judicial power of the local authorities and to prevent their exploitation by unscrupulous tradesmen.[1] They were granted on the assumption that the university would be able to discipline its own members and prevent their illegitimate use of these privileges. In effect the university became independent of the judicial authority of the city and its members exempt from the taxes and such duties as watch service normally imposed on the burgesses. Purchases of basic necessities such as food and drink could also be made by members of the university without payment of the tolls levied by the city on the transactions made at its market. As we have noted above, in the fifteenth century amongst the salaried lecturers there was a movement away from university communal life towards a more normal manner of living, often involving marriage to a member of some local family. The wife of such a lecturer, her property and her children then fell under the jurisdiction and protection of the university. In such circumstances privileges possessed by a member of the university could be exploited to the benefit of his family and to the harm of the local municipality. It would clearly be impossible for a strong civic council to tolerate the abuse by rich lecturers of privileges originally granted to protect poor masters. On the other hand, the universities would be reluctant to withdraw protection from some of their most influential members. The stage was set, therefore, for a struggle in which both sides could appeal to strongly held prejudices and principles.

---

[1] These privileges are discussed, with particular reference to the universities of Bologna, Padua, Paris and Oxford, in P. Kibre, *Scholarly Privileges in the Middle Ages* (London, 1961).

At Freiburg it is possible to trace in the university records the way in which the tension between the civic and academic authorities continually embittered relations between town and gown. In 1470 the citizens approached the university in an effort to obtain the adoption of a statute prohibiting all salaried lecturers from marrying 'with the exception of medical teachers and lawyers'. Nothing came of this proposal.[1] In the following year the university was involved in a dispute with the town concerning the property of the married men. The question of whether such property could be exempt from civic jurisdiction and taxation was one that could not easily be resolved. The university preferred to remit the case to the royal council for a decision.[2] In this dispute the university must have felt that its position was not very strong, for in the same year it refused to hire a master to lecture except on condition that he did not marry.[3] The dispute dragged on with the town attempting to deprive the married members of the university of certain of their privileges and the rector insisting that the foundation charter must be maintained in its entirety. In April 1473 the quarrel flared up again. On this occasion the central figure was the important lecturer in the Faculty of Arts, John Knapp of Rutlingen. The citizens complained that Knapp had married a wealthy widow, had so deprived himself of the chance of future ecclesiastical promotion and should, therefore, now come under the jurisdiction of the Freiburg burghermaster. When Knapp sought refuge under the protection of the university's privileges, he was arrested. The town's claim was the not unreasonable one that the removal of individuals and property from its jurisdiction could not be tolerated. The loss of income and services previously rendered to the municipality was a severe blow to a relatively small town. Perhaps of more importance was the loss of prestige by the town council at every extension of the university's privileges. During the course of the inquiry an interesting addition to the charge against Knapp was made. He was accused of using his position to engage in trade, such trade, of course, being exempt from the normal duties paid to the town. It was even suggested that his journeys to Rome had been for commercial purposes. Whatever the truth of all these

---

[1] Freiburg, University Archives, Protocollum Senatus, i, fol. 21v.
[2] Ibid., i, fols. 25v–6.
[3] Ibid., i, fol. 29v.

charges, the general situation is clear; a financially secure lecturer was taking advantage of the university's privileges to better his income and social position. As was usual, the case was remitted to the royal council for a decision.[1]

Similar disputes appear frequently in the university records. In September 1480, however, the town council appears to have decided on stronger action to enforce its claims. Three doctors and one master were officially notified that they would be required to assist either in person or by proxy the town's attempt to re-establish a road damaged by flood water. This demand was made only to those 'who possess their wives' property in Freiburg'.[2] The university's protestations were angrily rejected and a further claim was made that such doctors and masters were liable also to service with the watch. The university also stood firm, stating that its members 'should not be instructed to undertake such menial tasks and duties as labouring, keeping watch or guard or any other undignified burdens'.[3] Appeal was once again made to the royal council for a settlement. On other occasions the citizens attempted to force the married men to take an oath to their burghermaster[4] or to prohibit them from making purchases for their students in any place except the common market.[5] These matters were settled amicably. Although in such cases the married men in general are attacked, it is apparent from the names of those involved in these disputes that the citizens were worried about the richer doctors and masters rather than the student body as a whole. It was the group of salaried lecturers who were seeking to expand their income and establish their social position by judicious marriages who aroused the citizens' anxieties. It is also a measure of the importance of this group that it was able to induce the university to defend the privileges of the married men with such vehemence.

The acceptance and defence of the married lecturers also involved the universities in their family affairs. There are frequent references in the Freiburg records to actions taken to protect the dependents of deceased lecturers. In 1478 the town council was warned against attempts to molest the widow and

[1] Ibid., i, fol. 48v.
[2] Ibid., i, fol. 96.
[3] Ibid., i, fol. 97.
[4] Ibid., i, fol. 118v.
[5] Ibid., i, fol. 179v.

son of Matheus Hummel, the first rector of the university. The threat of an appeal to the royal authority 'to safeguard our privileges' was intimated to the burgesses.[1] Again, in June 1490, the university made payments to the widow of Dr Menynger in settlement of the debt it owed to her dead husband.[2] For Dr Northofer's children the university provided guardians who were to ensure that they received possession of their father's goods and were allocated a suitable tutor.[3] In its care for the children of its regents, the university appears to have been especially solicitous. All legitimate sons of regent masters and doctors by a statute of 1480 were allowed to be enrolled in the university Matricula without payment;[4] one son succeeded in following his father as a salaried lecturer.[5] It is clear that the university accepted its obligations to the married lecturer with family responsibilities. It was the town council, which saw itself indirectly being deprived of taxes, dues and services, that strongly opposed this extension of university authority to the property and families of the rich lecturers.

The Freiburg material also illustrates in an interesting manner the close co-operation between the salaried lecturers and the local secular overlord, in this case the house of Austria. In times of conflict with the town, an appeal from the university usually produced a favourable response from the royal council. In turn, the salaried lecturers, particularly in the legal and medical faculties, co-operated closely with the Austrian monarchy and gave professional advice when it was required. In fact, the salaried lecturers' concern for the affairs of the Austrian house was often over zealous. On many occasions the university found it necessary gently to rebuke the royal council for its too frequent employment of the lecturers, who were then distracted from their teaching programme. It is difficult to avoid the conclusion that with this increasing concern for social status and a secure income, the salaried lecturers were sacrificing that independence from secular control that had been the first demand of the masters at an earlier date. By the sixteenth century, most German universities were controlled by the local ruling houses through this dependable group of senior

[1] Ibid., i, fol. 71v.
[2] Ibid., i, fol. 152v.
[3] Ibid., i, fol. 239v.
[4] Ibid., i, fol. 78v.
[5] Ibid., i, fol. 116.

lecturers. It is interesting to note a similar development later in England. The Elizabethan Statutes which set up the Caput at Cambridge and the Laudian Statutes which established the Hebdomadal Council at Oxford[1] gave the English monarchy systematic control of the universities by putting administrative power into the hands of a small group of compliant senior members. By these constitutional changes which are first seen in Germany at the close of the medieval period, the traditional democracy of the north European university system was destroyed. The universities, afterwards, became readily susceptible to governmental pressure.

In sharp contrast to the standard of living enjoyed by the nobility and the salaried lecturers was that of the poor students. The begging letters written by such students in which they describe their wretched condition, have already attracted the attention of historians.[2] Some students suffered from cold; others had to beg from door to door through muddy streets; all complain of the expense of living in a university town and of the poor food that their poverty compels them to eat. Some pardonable exaggeration must be expected in such letters, but they do indicate that for some students life was always uncomfortable and occasionally unpleasant. It was Rashdall's opinion, however, that the poor students formed only a small minority amongst those attending the medieval universities.[3] He speaks of the 'vast majority of scholars' as being from an intermediate social group between the highest and the lowest classes. Nevertheless, the poor scholars were of sufficient importance to attract the attention of the German university authorities and to induce the Faculty of Arts in particular to make generous provision for them.

The first obstacle facing the poor scholar on his entry to the university was the necessity to pay the fee for enrolment in the Matricula. From this fee, a scholar who could satisfy the authorities as to his poverty was usually exempted. For example, at Wittenberg the normal matriculation fee was a quarter florin. Members of the mendicant orders were admitted at a

---

[1] M. H. Curtis, *Oxford and Cambridge in Transition 1558–1642* (Oxford, 1959), 42–5.
[2] For example, C. H. Haskins, in his *Studies in Medieval Culture* (Oxford, 1929).
[3] H. Rashdall, *The Universities of Europe in the Middle Ages*, ed. F. M. Powicke and A. B. Emden, (Oxford, 1936) iii, 408. Other evidence for the number of poor scholars in the German universities is discussed below.

reduced rate, and poor students paid what they could afford 'or are to be enrolled without charge to show God's love'.[1] This *privilegium paupertatis* could be abused, and at Cologne the deceptions practised grew so notorious that the privilege was withdrawn in 1503.[2] On the basis of these matriculation statistics at Cologne, Eulenburg was able to estimate that about 16 per cent of the students were classed as 'poor', and from the records at Leipzig that 9 per cent of the students were so classified.[3] These figures must be considered with scepticism in view of the unreliability of the matriculation tables as an adequate record of all students entering the university, but at least they do suggest a substantial minority of genuinely poor students at Cologne and Leipzig.

Within the university, the poor student was entitled to enjoy various privileges. He was generally exempted from the strict requirements concerning academic dress. The earliest Heidelberg statutes of the Faculty of Arts required from all candidates seeking permission to 'determine'—that is, to complete their B.A. course—an oath that for the ceremony only new gowns should be worn. But the dean of the faculty was also given permission to dispense those students unable to afford a new gown from this requirement. Scholars seeking such a dispensation had first to swear that they were in fact poor, and were then allowed to determine in the gown they already possessed.[4]

From such regulations it is clear that the university authorities had to have some criterion for judging whether or not a student should be classified as 'poor'. At Prague the criterion was simply financial. All students with an income of less than twelve florins per year were classed as 'poor' provided that they could take an oath to this effect to their master or to the rector.[5] At Tübingen the regulations were a little stricter. The statutes of 1488, revising early regulations for the Faculty of Arts, defined a poor student as someone not being able to raise sixteen florins from his own resources and those of his friends. An addition to this statute, however, prohibited the granting of relief to students who might overspend on food and drink either before or after

[1] W. Friedensburg, *Urkundenbuch der Universität Wittenberg;* i (Magdeburg, 1926), 28.
[2] H. Keussen, op. cit., 151.
[3] F. Eulenburg, op. cit., 71.
[4] E. Winkelmann, op. cit., i, 36-7.
[5] *Monumenta Historica Universitatis Carolo-Ferdinandeae Pragensis, Liber Decanorum Facultatis Philosophicae,* i (Prague, 1830), 17.

they applied to the university for this privileged status.[1] At Ingolstadt, enjoyment of the status of a poor student was conditional on the production of adequate testimonial letters sealed in the student's own native town certifying to his poverty. Even then, the student's manner of life at the university was to be noted, so that his privileges might be withdrawn if he showed himself to be undeserving of them.[2]

One of the most important privileges granted to the poor scholars was that of living outside the communal life of the burses. This they shared with the noblemen, but for a very different reason. Poor students were not expected to be able to pay the low fees charged for food and lodging in the officially recognized burses. University statutes assume that rich doctors and masters would employ such poor scholars in their own households. The Freiburg definition of those scholars recognized by the university as *bona fide* students, for example, includes servants 'who live with the said doctors and masters at their expense'.[3] At Basel the statutes of the Faculty of Arts forbid the regent masters to employ anyone except a poor scholar as a servant.[4] So general was this employment of poor students as servants that the disciplinary ordinances of 1507 at Ingolstadt refused to recognize any scholar as 'poor' unless he was employed as a servant living at someone's expense.[5] Apart from serving rich masters and doctors, poor students also supported themselves by working in the burses. References to such scholars appear frequently in the university records. The revised Freiburg statutes of 1495,[6] which exempt only the servants working in the burses from a new procedure for examining students claiming classification as 'poor', would seem to indicate that these servants were regarded as the poorest of all students. There can, indeed, have been little financial reward obtained from work in a burse where the majority of students were themselves not from wealthy parents.

Certain universities also attempted to bring poor scholars under control by providing burses where the standard of living was not so high and the charges more suitable for the less

---

[1] R. Roth, op. cit., 349.
[2] C. Prantl, op. cit., ii, 114.
[3] Freiburg, University Archives, Protocollum Senatus, i, fol. 20.
[4] C. C. Bernouilli, op. cit., 19.
[5] C. Prantl, op. cit., ii, 138.
[6] Discussed below.

well-endowed students. In the first years of its existence, the university of Freiburg took steps to establish three types of burses: 'burses with different charges'. One of these was to be a 'house for poor scholars' charging a fee less than the two others.[1] At Erfurt the *Bursa Pauperum* attempted to provide some security for poorer students reading for arts degrees.[2] But the most interesting attempt to solve in this manner the problem presented by poor students was at Vienna.[3] There, poor scholars were housed in special burses known as *codriae* where lower charges were made and fewer restrictions were imposed. This second characteristic of the *codriae* seems to have attracted the more unruly but not necessarily poorer members of the university. The Faculty of Arts attempted to control these undisciplined students by enacting in 1413 a series of statutes regulating behaviour, and by then adding a codicil that scholars living in the *codriae* who were found guilty of breaking the new rules would be more severely punished than other members of the university.[4] This statute seems to have been only partially successful. At the beginning of the sixteenth century the faculty attempted to clear out of the *codriae* all those living there under false pretences. No student with an income above a certain yearly amount was to be allowed to live in the *codriae*. Those at present living there were to prove that their income was below this figure. At the same time the faculty took steps to regulate the distribution of money obtained by the members of the *codriae* from their legitimate begging activities. The dean of the faculty was also to ensure that specific masters were held responsible for the behaviour of specific scholars.[5] It is apparent from these regulations that if the poverty of these students' lives was not pleasant, at least to some the absence of restrictions on their behaviour was a compensatory factor of some value.

Students who were hardly able to afford their accommodation, food and drink, could not be expected to pay the fees charged by the masters for their lectures and exercises, or offer to the university the statutory gifts required at graduation. Various forms of exemption from these payments were

[1] Freiburg, University Archives, Protocollum Senatus, i, fol. 20.
[2] See G. Oergel's article in *Mittheilungen des Vereins für die Geschichte und Alterthumskunde von Erfurt* (1896).
[3] See K. Schrauf, *Studien zur Geschichte der Wiener Universität im Mittelalter* (Vienna, 1904), for a discussion of the burses established by the university.
[4] R. Kink, op. cit., ii, 255.
[5] Ibid., ii, 314.

incorporated in the statutes of the German universities. The problem of the poor student was essentially one for the Faculty of Arts. In the higher faculties, although a student might have only a small regular income, at least he had the opportunity to earn money by lecturing in the Faculty of Arts where he had usually studied earlier. It is, therefore, the statutes of the faculties of arts which are the richest source of information concerning the dispensations from payment allowed to poor students.[1]

Exemption from payment for official lectures and exercises usually followed automatically after a scholar had been examined by the faculty and classed as 'poor'. At Tübingen, for example, the statutes required the dean to announce once in every six months that any scholar unable to pay for his exercises should appear before a special panel for examination. The panel was composed of the dean, the *conventores* in charge of the burses who would be expected to give evidence of the candidate's manner of life, and representatives of the two philosophical sections, or *viae*, into which the faculty was divided. This committee would then impose on the candidate what proportion, if any, of the fees that it believed he could afford.[2] With minor variations this procedure was in general use throughout Germany. It provided the means whereby a poor student could obtain the minimum amount of instruction necessary for his degree, and also included safeguards for the regents who might otherwise be deprived of their legitimate income.

To allow the poor scholar to participate in a master's private exercises and resumptions was more difficult. Masters undertook such work for the financial reward involved, and over these activities the university had not quite the same close control as it had over the official lectures and exercises. Clearly, if a master was forbidden to take fees from pupils attending his private exercises, he might well decide not to hold these at all. He could do this without loss of status, for such private exercises were not usually required from him by statute. It was here that the poor student was at a disadvantage. At Prague in 1400 the university was compelled to take action against masters who were attempting to evade the statutes regulating lectures and exercises. By teaching subjects outside those approved by the statutes and at

[1] These are discussed in G. Kaufmann, op. cit., ii, 401–6.
[2] R. Roth, op. cit., 349.

different times, the masters were creating a new class of exercises which they termed *declarationes*. Since these were not covered by the faculty statutes, the privilege of free admittance for poor scholars did not apply and such students were excluded. The faculty resolved the problem by insisting that any *declaratio* where more than four students attended was to be covered by the existing statutory regulations governing exercises and lectures.[1]

In most cases a compromise was reached between the masters and the faculty. The masters were not compelled to take poor scholars into their classes, but on the other hand the number of paying students they might receive was restricted. The detailed regulations of 1504[2] for the resumptions held at Vienna in the Faculty of Arts provided for regular exercises on the Grammar of Alexander. Each master was allowed to take only twelve paying pupils, but might take others classified as 'poor'. These pupils were to pay half the statutory fee if they were able. There were special regulations for those masters resuming in the *codriae*; these were allowed to take twenty-four scholars who were to pay half the normal fee if their means allowed. The dean was instructed to examine those students claiming exemption from payment to determine whether they were really poor.[3] At Leipzig poor students were admitted without charge to those resumptions which the salaried lecturers had to hold when they were not lecturing.[4] The addition to the statutes of the Faculty of Arts at Tübingen in 1505 regulated resumptions for the M.A. degree and allowed poor students to attend on payment of half the fee, or a smaller proportion in the case of extreme poverty; such students had to be 'humble, discreet, thrifty and studious'.[5] An interesting situation arose at Freiburg in 1471 when a master having eleven scholars living with him appeared before the university. He was allowed to keep this number, but on condition that in the future he would teach only eight. Any beyond this number were to be poor scholars 'with whom he should and must resume without charge as a service to God'.[6] The intention

---

[1] *Monumenta Historica Universitatis Carolo-Ferdinandeae Pragensis, Liber Decanorum Facultatis Philosophicae*, i (Prague, 1830), 112–13.

[2] The date 1509 in Kink is incorrect. See G. Bauch, *Die Rezeption des Humanismus in Wien* (Breslau, 1903), 105.

[3] R. Kink, op. cit., ii, 317.

[4] F. Zarncke, op. cit., 19.

[5] R. Roth, op. cit., 334.

[6] Freiburg, University Archives, Protocollum Senatus, i, fol. 24v.

behind this legislation seems to have been to share out the available work and income it brought amongst all regent masters, and at the same time to protect the interests of the poor scholars. This was all the more necessary as at the close of the fifteenth century the private resumptions seem to have been increasing in importance. There was a real danger that poor scholars would be excluded from them. Even though this was avoided, the terms on which they gained admittance were not quite as favourable as those they enjoyed in connexion with the official university lectures and exercises.

It would be of little value to allow a student special privileges enabling him to study if his poverty made him incapable of obtaining a degree. Accordingly, the general practice in the German universities was to allow a recognized poor student exemption from the charges imposed at graduation. The 1443 additions to the statutes of the Faculty of Arts at Leipzig, for example, exempted all poor students from the payments required for the B.A. and M.A. degrees. Those claiming this privilege had to produce two witnesses to testify to their poverty.[1] Certain universities modified this liberal policy to require from all students granted exemption a promise to repay the amount they had been excused if at some future date their income permitted them to do so. The records of the Faculty of Arts at Frankfurt for 1515 have references to four scholars classified as 'poor' who have promised to pay the usual fee required for the B.A. degree when their resources allow it. Another student promised to pay after two years.[2] This exemption was clearly a valuable privilege which enabled some scholars to obtain a qualification that they otherwise would have been unable to afford.

For information relating to the privileged position of the poor scholars, we have been very largely dependent on the statutory legislation of the various German faculties of arts. There is little published evidence to indicate the extent to which this legislation was enforced or to show the practical problems encountered in its application. Fortunately, the survival in manuscript at Freiburg of the *Liber Taxatorum*,[3] in which details of the examination of poor students were recorded, allows us an insight

[1] F. Zarncke, op. cit., 358.
[2] G. Bauch, *Das Älteste Decanatsbuch der Philosophischen Fakultät an der Universität zu Frankfurt a. O.* (Breslau, 1897), 52–3.
[3] Freiburg, University Archives, Liber Taxatorum Facultatis Artium.

into the actual working of the system. The city and university archives at Freiburg also contain four different versions of the statutes for the Faculty of Arts: a short German copy written by the first rector of the university, Matheus Hummel, and longer Latin editions dating from *c.* 1463, 1490 and 1504–5.[1] It is, therefore, possible to trace the development of the faculty's legislation for poor students and at the same time study the problems encountered in its treatment of them.

In the German version of the faculty statutes there is no mention of poor students. This is not surprising as the version seems to be little more than a preliminary draft intended to provide the faculty with only essential outline legislation. Nor do the statutes of *c.* 1463 make detailed provision for such students; they are merely mentioned incidentally. The statutes make it compulsory for every scholar, whether studying for the B.A. or M.A. degree, to make his payment to his lecturers during their fourth lecture or exercise. Only scholars who can produce a reasonable reason for exemption are to be excused this payment. Such scholars are to be examined by the dean and his councillors who are to decide how much the scholar is able to pay and then instruct the lecturers to request only this amount.[2] The revised procedure of 1490 makes only minor changes. Like the majority of the 1490 statutes, the section dealing with poor scholars is derived from the Tübingen statutes. Once during every six months the dean is to summon all students wishing to be classified as 'poor' before himself, the *conventores* and representatives of the two *viae*. This committee is then to decide what proportion, if any, of the statutory fee the applicants are able to pay.[3]

The legislation of 1490 was soon modified. On 20th December, 1495, the Faculty of Arts accepted 'certain statutes concerning the examiners and the examinations of poor scholars, which are entered in the *matricula taxatorum*—the lists of those scholars examined'.[4] The *matricula taxatorum* here referred to is the register today entitled *Liber Taxatorum*. The statutes promulgated in 1495 are no longer preserved in this register; it is possible that they were lost before the leaves were

[1] The German edition and the Latin editions of *c.* 1463 and 1490 are preserved in the City Archives. The Latin version of 1504–5 is in the University Archives.
[2] Freiburg, City Archives, O 39, fol. 4.
[3] Freiburg, City Archives, O 39, fol. 5v.
[4] Freiburg, University Archives, Protocollum Facultatis Artium, i, fol. 140.

bound together in their present form. Happily, they are recorded in the 1504–5 Latin edition of the faculty statutes. They are much more detailed than the earlier provisions. The relevant section is headed: *De Taxa*, and begins by repeating the 1490 instructions for the summoning of those claiming to be unable to pay for their lectures and their examination by the dean and his advisers. Now, however, those officially excused payment are instructed to appear regularly before the committee whenever it meets. The faculty will then be able to consider whether the applicant's manner of life is consistent with his continued classification as a poor scholar. Those excused payment are also to take an oath that if they obtain a certain income in the future, they will reappear before the faculty and compensate those masters whose lectures they have heard free of charge. To ensure that this is done, the faculty is to institute a register in which the names of all excused payments are to be recorded. The students, in turn, are instructed to present at graduation a list of all the masters whose lectures they have heard without payment. The faculty, therefore, will have a complete record of all students classified as 'poor' and of those masters to whom money was owed. If a master entitled to such compensation should die, his share of any money received by the faculty would be devoted to 'pious uses', towards the celebration of masses, for example, or towards the support of deserving poor scholars. From these statutes only those acting as servants in the burses were to be exempt.[1]

The *Liber Taxatorum*, in its present form, contains the list of those students examined by the dean and his advisers between 1496 and 1521, with some omissions. But there are also surviving in the register similar lists from 1493–5.[2] This would suggest that the procedure established by the statute of December 1495 was in use at an earlier date. Alternatively, records kept informally before the promulgation of the statute could have been officially recorded in the register later. A similar confusion exists concerning other entries in the *Liber Taxatorum*. There are preserved there several copies of submissions made by poor students on obtaining their degrees. According to the procedure established by the 1495 statute, these list the masters from whom

[1] Freiburg, University Archives, Das Statutenbuch der Philosophischen Fakultät, fols. 23–23v.
[2] Freiburg, University Archives, Liber Taxatorum Facultatis Artium, fols. 9v–10.

lectures have been heard without payment. Yet the submission made by Gregorius Rusch,[1] later to gain a reputation as the author of the Margareta Philosophica, was made in or before 1489 when he was received as a master into the Faculty of Arts.[2] Other submissions recorded in the Liber Taxatorum also date from before 1495. A third type of entry records briefly poor students' promises to recompense at a later date masters deprived of their legitimate salaries, if this is ever possible.[3] These date from before the statute of 1495. Finally, two entries[4] from students excused the usual payments for the degree feast and for Determination promised repayment at a later date, when 'better fortune smiles'. Both these entries antedate by at least five years the 1495 statute.

The survival of this pre-1495 material from a time when the faculty statutes made only elementary provision for the examination and regulation of poor students seems to indicate that the authorities kept informal and temporary records of their proceedings long before the statutes compelled them to do so. It is not difficult to understand the disappearance of such records if they were made only on sheets of paper or unbound gatherings. The preservation of this pre-1495 material at Freiburg seems to have occurred by the chance binding of these sheets and gatherings with the more formal register instituted in 1495. It may be that the German universities had a much more thorough and elaborate procedure for the examination of their poor students than the surviving statutes would suggest. Certainly, at Freiburg the simple processes established by the statutes of c. 1463 and 1490 give little indication of the elaborate precautions taken by the faculty to record the names and obligations of those students to whom it had granted exemption. As in so many cases, the statutes seem here to do little justice to the administrative efficiency of the faculty authorities. The statute of 1495 probably made formal a procedure that had been evolved to meet problems already encountered in the application of existing legislation.

The survival of the Liber Taxatorum enables us to examine in

[1] The submission appears twice in the Liber Taxatorum. Fol. 1 is probably the original document written by Gregorius Rusch himself, and on fol. 7 is a transcript.
[2] Freiburg, University Archives, Matricula Facultatis Artium, i, 32.
[3] Freiburg, University Archives, Liber Taxatorum Facultatis Artium, fols. 6v, 8v–9.
[4] Ibid., fol. 8.

detail the position of the poor students in one small German university at the close of the medieval period. There do not appear to be any foreign students who were granted exemption at Freiburg. One member of a religious order, a Frater Beinhardus Gur, came before the examining committee.[1] The majority of the names in the register are those of students preparing for the B.A. degree; this is to be expected. But there are also a few references to bachelors appearing before the examiners. In 1512, for example, two of the sixteen applicants before Dean Matheus Zeell were bachelors,[2] and in 1517 three out of the twelve applicants before Dean Melchior Vatlin.[3] The regular lists also allow us to estimate the numbers of poor students at Freiburg and enable us to calculate the approximate proportion of the university population which they comprised. During the seven years 1508–14, 792 enrolments were made in the university Matricula.[4] For this period the lists of poor students examined by the Faculty of Arts are complete. One hundred and thirty-four different students appeared before the faculty committee in these years;[5] none was rejected although some were instructed to contribute a proportion of the statutory fees. During these seven years, therefore, about 17 per cent of the official university membership was classified as 'poor'. Such figures must, of course, be accepted with some reservations; matriculation lists are notoriously inaccurate. Nevertheless, the figure of 17 per cent is an interesting one, especially as the figure calculated from the matriculation rolls at Cologne is 16 per cent.[6] It would seem that here we have a reasonable estimate of the proportion of poor students in the German universities at the close of the Middle Ages.

It would hardly be expected that the masters of the Faculty of Arts would administer laxly a privilege which deprived them of part of their income from lecture fees. There must inevitably have been mistakes made in assessing the poverty of students, but perhaps too much attention has been given to the withdrawal of the *privilegium paupertatis* at Cologne in 1503 owing to

---

[1] Ibid., fol. 11v.
[2] Ibid., fol. 17.
[3] Ibid., fol. 21.
[4] The figures are taken from H. Mayer, *Die Matrikel der Universität Freiburg i. Br.*, i (Freiburg, 1907).
[5] In deference to the 1495 statute some students appeared more than once in the lists. Such students have, however, only been counted once.
[6] See above.

its misuse.[1] Certainly, at Freiburg the examiners seem to have taken care to grant exemption from payment only to deserving cases. The *Liber Taxatorum* contains many instances of applicants being instructed either to pay the full lecture fees or to make a partial payment. In March 1498 nine students appeared before the examiners. Only one was excused the entire statutory fees. Five were ordered to pay half and the remaining three were allowed no relief at all.[2] Under Dean Nicolaus Schedlin, who was elected on 31st October, 1509, twenty-nine applicants sought exemption from payments for lectures and exercises, seventeen of them applying for the first time. All were accepted as 'poor' by the examiners, but five were instructed to pay a quarter of the fees and three to pay half.[3] It is also clear that examiners used their powers to adjust the payments required from a candidate if his income increased. Udalricus Rieger appeared for the first time in the taxation lists in 1508, when he was exempted from payment unconditionally.[4] He appears regularly in the lists until 1509. By this date his circumstances must have been improved, for he was then instructed to pay half the statutory fees.[5] It would seem that the examiners at Freiburg carefully performed their duties and endeavoured to ensure that the masters would recover at least part of their fees from those students able to make payment.

The revised statutes of 1495, like those of many German universities, required an oath from poor students that they would pay to the faculty an amount corresponding to the fees they had been excused if their future resources allowed this. Few seem to have done so. The *Liber Taxatorum*, however, does contain occasional indications of this repayment being made. John Kung, who appears in the taxation list for April 1505, later enjoyed a successful academic career at Tübingen as a salaried lecturer in the Faculty of Canon Law. In 1534 he was able to recompense the masters of the Freiburg Faculty of Arts for their earlier generosity.[6] Cristannus Feden did not have to wait quite so long before making repayment. He was granted total exemption from lecture fees in 1507 and was able to repay

---

[1] See above.
[2] Freiburg, University Archives, Liber Taxatorum Facultatis Artium, fol. 5v.
[3] Ibid., fol. 14v.
[4] Ibid., fol. 12v. The date is here given wrongly as 1507.
[5] Ibid., fol. 13v.
[6] Ibid., fol. 11v.

all the masters in 1512.[1] A successful career in the Church gave Melchior Vatlin the means to repay the faculty. He was granted exemption in 1508 and was able to make a satisfactory settlement with the faculty in 1521.[2] But apart from these exceptional cases, there are no records of repayments being made. It is interesting to notice, however, that the three examples quoted above do indicate that the statute requiring future repayment did not remain entirely a dead letter.

The efforts made by the Faculty of Arts to encourage poor students to remain at the university do not seem to have been successful. Most of those classified as 'poor' did not complete their courses. In 1499, twelve scholars appeared before the examining committee;[3] two later obtained the B.A. degree and one the degrees of M.A. and D.Cn.L. While John Keyser was dean of the Faculty of Arts in 1501, fourteen students were granted total or partial exemption from payment of the statutory fees.[4] Only three of these were later awarded any degree, and in all cases it was the B.A. degree, the lowest academic qualification, that was obtained. Of the nineteen students listed as exempt from payment from November 1508 until April 1509,[5] five later obtained the B.A. degree, two the master's degree and one the doctorate in theology. It is difficult to avoid the conclusion that despite the help given to them by the faculty, far fewer than half the poor students of Freiburg were able to proceed to even the lowest degree. The impersonal records of the *Liber Taxatorum* must conceal many individual tragedies and disappointments.

The cleavage between rich and poor in the German universities at the close of the Middle Ages was probably widening. While the group of secure, well-paid salaried lecturers was demanding and obtaining a better standard of living, with comforts previously known only to the middle classes of the towns, poorer students were generally unable to benefit fully even from those privileges granted to them. At an earlier date, university masters and students had been united by their

---

[1] Ibid., fol. 12.
[2] Ibid., fol. 12v.
[3] Ibid., fol. 10v. Biographical details from H. Mayer, *Die Matrikel der Universität Freiburg i. Br.*, i (Freiburg, 1907).
[4] Freiburg, University Archives, Liber Taxatorum Facultatis Artium, fol. 10.
[5] Ibid., fol. 13.

relative poverty; the few noble students were exceptional by reason of their wealth. In the fifteenth century the division between rich and poor appears within the university itself, dividing masters from students and even salaried lecturers from those without salaries. The effect was to restrict that ability for corporate action which had been characteristic of the earlier universities, and to replace it by a mass of conflicting interests within the academic structure. The wretched student, working as a servant in a burse, could have felt little in common with the salaried lecturer, married, living in his private house and often enjoying the confidences of members of the local nobility. The resulting weakness of the German universities and their inability to oppose external pressures was already apparent in the fifteenth century.

XV

E. F. JACOB

CHRISTIAN HUMANISM

The later Middle Ages is a period as rich in intellectual movement as it is abounding in economic and political change. There
could be no greater error than to imagine that Europe was in
some undefined way static until the Reformation and that it
needed Luther and Calvin to confront both the courts and the
studia with serious problems of religion and politics. The French
wars had posed, in an early form, the question of national
sovereignty and national expansion; the Schism and the
General Councils had seen the attempt to apply secular
political theory to the organization of the Church, and the
various heretical movements called in question the very basis of
religious beliefs and practice. And there had been William of
Ockham and his legacy, the experimentalists. Above all, the
layman was being educated and was vindicating for himself a
position alike in the Church and in society, bringing a critical
and often a constructive mind to bear upon contemporary
people and institutions.[1] If in the towns a thinking bourgeoisie
had long been in evidence, the upper middle ranks of rural
society were getting professional training, organizing communities for religious and social purposes, building nobly and
creating schools for grammar and good letters. There was an

---

[1] So too the schoolmaster of the late fourteenth and early fifteenth century. An
admirable English example is given by V. H. Galbraith, 'John Seward and his
Circle', *Medieval and Renaissance Studies*, I, i, 85, based on Merton College MS. 299,
a compendium of epigrams and prose. 'Each tract in the volume is dedicated to
someone, distinguished either in scholarship or in public life, often with a rhetorical
epistola commending his virtues'. Here is a circle not unlike those of northern Italy
of the late thirteenth century described by R. Weiss, *Il primo secolo del umanesimo*
(Rome, 1949); where lawyers and physicians, people on the borders of clerkdom,
met and exchanged opinions on the Latin classics.

increase in personal correspondence, a growth of interest in other people for themselves and of consciousness of the part played by the individual as such.

In this process humanism played a vital role. Humanism is not tantamount to the Renaissance, though it was the main-spring of that movement. It is the study and use of the history, literature and art of Greece and Rome and (this is often too little emphasized) of the tradition handed on to the Middle Ages by the Christian Fathers; but more, it is the habit of mind, exact, sensitive and tasteful, moulded by that discipline and encouraged by learned intercourse and by abundant self-examination. Thus it is more than the accumulation of classical *exempla*: it is their employment for inter-communication and critical judgment. There is, it need hardly be said, a wider and vaguer usage of the term, as P. O. Kristeller has remarked:

'In present discourse, almost any kind of concern with human values is called "humanistic" and consequently a great variety of thinkers, religious and antireligious, scientific or antiscientific, lay claim to what has become a rather classic label of praise. We might ignore this twentieth-century confusion, but for the direct impact it has had upon historical studies. For many historians, knowing that the term 'humanism' has been tradi-tionally associated with the Renaissance, and seeing that some features of the modern notion of humanism seem to have their counterpart in the thought of that period, have cheerfully applied the term 'humanism' in its vague modern meaning to the Renaissance and to other periods of the past, speaking of Renaissance humanism, medieval humanism or Christian humanism in a fashion which defies any definition and seems to have little or nothing left of the basic classicist meaning of Renaissance humanism.'[1]

It is well to be reminded of this danger: but this should not imply that terms like 'medieval humanism' when applied, for instance, to the school of Chartres or to a production like John of Salisbury's *Policraticus*,[2] or 'Christian humanism' when describing treatises by the Victorines or Gerson or a brilliant

[1] *The Classics and Renaissance Thought* (Harvard Univ. Press, 1955), 8.
[2] See Dr Clement Webb's list of sources used by John of Salisbury, *Johannis Sarisberiensis Episcopi Carnotensis Politicratici . . .*, ii (Oxford, 1909), and Hans Liebe-schütz, *Medieval Humanism in the Life and Writings of John of Salisbury* (London, 1950), esp. chapter V, 'Medieval Experience and Ancient Ideas: Political Con-ceptions'.

classicist like Nicholas of Clamanges, are out of place. It would be absurd to deny the title of humanist to a thirteenth-century Franciscan like John of Wales for his *Compendiloquium* and the *Breviloquium de virtutibus*,[1] though John has many characteristic medieval attributes. At the back of this reluctance to concede the title to scholars and theologians in the fourteenth and fifteenth century may lurk the suspicion that they are dominated by a moral and religious purpose rather than by the interest in character as such, and that they are searching for beliefs rather than for the expression of personality. With such is humanism ruled out?

Each generation has made its own selection from antiquity and some have seemed nearer to its essential spirit than others; but from one who joined contemporary Aristotelian cosmology with deduction from ancient history and classical poetry to form the concept of a world order under a single dominant will, the attribute of humanism should not be withheld.

This was Dante's achievement in the *Convivio* and the *Monarchia*. The *Convivio* is an essay on songs which he had written; it only reaches to the fullest degree its ancient sources with the discussion of nobility in Book IV when it is a question of what constitutes the noble nature and how such virtue is best expressed in a political order. Behind the fourth book lie Aristotle's *Politics*, the *Nichomachean Ethics* and the *Metaphysics*, viewed now less along the lines of St Thomas than on those of Averroes and the Arabian commentators. The last book of the unfinished *Convivio* was the first sketch, so to speak, for the most important of his prose works, the *Monarchia*, which lays down, as the principle directing his whole inquiry into that office, the thesis that there is *universalis civilitas humani generis*, a civilized human society which like other things produced by nature has its own objective, one realized by the collective simultaneous efforts (*totum simul*) of individuals to achieve their own natural end of happiness. Dante speaks of the 'human race taken as a whole' as this totality, whose aim is to bring into action the whole power of the possible intellect. Man is distinguished from the brutes, just as he is from the heavenly intelligences, by this potentiality of the intellect, and his highest, because his natural and essential activity is its realization. But for this realization to

[1] See W. A. Pantin, 'John of Wales and Medieval Humanism', *Medieval Studies presented to Aubrey Gwynn S.J.* (Dublin, 1962), 296 ff.

be complete, there must be universal peace; the peace or *concordia* which historically marked the coming of the Redeemer into the world: 'whence it was that to the shepherds there sounded from on high not riches nor pleasure nor honours nor length of life, nor health nor strength, but peace.' That peace the monarch alone ensures.

Here then is the *principium directivum*, that believes in a sum total of human mental activity that can be made to function only under the conditions Dante demands. This activity is not complete—and here there is an echo of the *Politics*, Book I— in the home, the village, the city and even, the *regnum* but in one single universal society, the thinking *humanum genus* considered both as entity and totality, when guided by its imperial charioteer. The next stage in the arguments is to prove that the emperor is the Roman emperor, presiding over an empire which is the working of Providence and was foretold by Virgil, the poet of imperial Rome. Most crucial in Dante's own development were the years 1304–6 during which, if we are to believe Boccaccio and Villani, he was living part of the time in Bologna. Besides law, Bologna specialized in the Latin classics: the *Aeneid*, the *Metamorphoses*, the *Pharsalia* and the *Thebais*, were books read in the poetical course, and Renucci makes the point that in citing their authors Dante seldom goes outside these classical epics.[1]

Above all it was the Virgil of the *Aeneid* that captured him. Virgil, to Dante's younger mind the master of style, now later dawned on him as the historian and prophet of the Roman empire; and with the Latins, from whom of course Livy must not be excepted, went the study of the Bible, particularly Isaiah, the *Visio Pauli*, and the Apocalypse. With Virgil the contact seems to deepen after 1306, the year when the *Convivio* ended with Tractate IV, and the sound is fullest in the letters and the Cacciaguida cantos of the *Comedy*.

In the second book of the *Monarchia* Dante comments on his own misunderstanding of Roman history which produced a *derisiva despectio* for the progress of Rome. But his eyes were opened and the book describes his experience; it is a study of the working of Providence in history. The Trojan legend is combined with the central theme of the *Aeneid*, the foundation of a kingdom in Latium by the noble Trojan Aeneas through the

[1] Paul Renucci, *Dante, Disciple et Juge du Monde Gréco-Latin* (1954), pp. 70–1.

subjugation of Turnus and marriage with Lavinia. The progress of Roman arms and justice leads up to the supreme justification of the Roman empire, the birth of Christ and the Redemption, at a time when the world, through the *pax Romana*, was best disposed to these events. The climax—not a subsidiary argument—is expressed in the major premise of a syllogism. If the Roman empire was not justified by right, the sin of Adam was not punished in Christ. This appeared very paradoxical to some contemporaries: but it is only another way of saying that the redemption of the world from sin is linked with the world domination of Rome. Two points have always seemed to me of particular interest: Dante's treatment of the heroic figures of antiquity and the concept of the justice of Rome as manifested by a *duellum*.

To Dante mythology is history. The gods and heroes take their place in the scheme of Providence both in the *Monarchia* and the *Comedy*, whether in Limbo or in the *Inferno* or above, as Ripheus in the eye of the eagle. Their nobility may not save them in the final count, but when active on earth they played their part in the evolution of the divine justice and· some foretold the destiny of Rome. Following the famous forecast of Anchises in *Aeneid* VI, Jupiter's speech to Mercury concerning Aeneas is used in the *Monarchia* as evidence of this destiny:

> *Non illum nobis genetrix pulcherrima talem*
> *Promissit graiumque ideo bis vindicat armis;*
> *Sed fore qui gravidam imperiis, belloque frementem*
> *Italiam regeret.*

The heroic figure *par excellence* of Aeneas introduces the procession of ancients in the *Monarchia* who were there because of their nobility:

> *Romanus populus fuit nobilissimus, ergo convenit*
> *et aliis omnibus praeferri.*

They have the *premium prelationis*; most of all, the father of the *Romanus populus*, Aeneas, who has two attributes:

> *Rex erat Aeneas nobis quo justior alter*
> *Nec pietate fuit nec bello maior et armis.*

His descent was noble, from Dardanus, son of Zeus, whose mother was Electra, daughter of Atlas from Africa; his wives were noble, Creusa, daughter of King Priam, Dido (for she was openly his wife in spite of Aeneas' repudiation of her claim in the *Aeneid*) and Lavinia, given to him by the dying Turnus, and from that triple concourse—Troy, Italy, Africa—the divine predestination is clear. That predestination is borne out by the miracles attending early Roman history. It could be seen, for example, in the character of and the vision shown by the institutions of Rome, by the collegia, especially the Senate which Cicero called 'the harbour and refuge of kingdoms, peoples and nations', and in the quality of individual Romans, Cincinnatus, Fabricius down to the Marcus Portius Cato (that figure of tedious nobility) who made the unspeakable sacrifice of his life and is lifted above Limbo to be guardian and destined to a place in paradise. All these aimed at the *bonum reipublicae* and by so doing aimed at the objective of law, *finem juris*. What of those who aimed at it but were in conflict among themselves? The *Monarchia* is discreetly silent about Pompey, Marius or Curio who occurs later among the sowers of discord in the *Inferno*, the ninth Bolgia of Circle VIII. Ultimate success because it implied aiming at the common good, is the criterion for inclusion here. Yet it is notable that Julius Caesar, with the hawk eye, whose exploits are magnificently told in *Paradiso* VI, is only here by implication as the first Caesar. It is Justinian who has to do him justice.

The third book of the *Monarchia* contends that the secular emperor who guides the world *per philosophica documenta* to its goal of happiness is in no way dependent upon the ecclesiastical power, whose claims it is Dante's aim to define. The pope leads men to their eternal blessedness through grace and the sacraments, and the resulting society is an empire which is not specifically directed by the Church but complementary and in the closest alliance with it. To the modern reader it is not the less Christian because it is not directed by the papal power.[1] *Monarchia* I is a magnificent vindication of the human reason in politics based on the Aristotelian concept of nature, a lead followed later with significant but questionable results by the Paduan physician Marsilius. The element, however, in Dante which perhaps brings him most securely into the humanist

---

[1] 'Dante's system of thought is cosmic and not specifically Christian': Walter Ullmann, *Principles of Government and Politics in the Middle Ages* (London, 1961), 259: a contrary view.

category is his treatment of the gods and heroes, and his employment of myth in the service of his political argument and of the *Comedy* itself.

For the later Middle Ages mythology seems to have grown in fascination. This was not only because it was hard to draw a firm line between legend and sober history, but because of the allegorical interpretations placed upon early heroic figures, particularly the participants in the siege of Troy or the attack of the seven against Thebes. From a purely historical point of view, it seemed highly desirable to claim a share in the heritage of antiquity, and in the twelfth and thirteenth century the emerging nations appropriated what was especially to their taste. Thus Christian de Troyes can affirm that France has secured the patrimony of ancient culture and virtue.

> *Grece ot de chevalerie*
> *Le premier los et de clergie*
> *Puis vint chevalerie a Rome*
> *Et de la clergie la some*
> *Lui ore est en France venue.*[1]

The Franks, it was claimed, were descendants of the Trojan Francus, just as the origin of the Britannic kingdom was put down to Brutus, after escaping from the siege of Troy; and to the London imagination Brutus was the first duke of London which was christened New Troy. The apocryphal journals of the siege of Troy by the so-called Cretan Dictys and the 'Phrygian' Dares made the ancient worthies even more convincingly historical than Charlemagne, Roland or Oliver. Trojan Aeneas as Dante called him, *de' Romani il gentil seme*, seemed to guarantee the providential destiny of his Italian descendants. Sacred and profane history run parallel. Not only in books like the *Divine Comedy* (particularly *Purgatorio* XII) but as late as the Renaissance, artists are alternating events from the Old Testament and from mythology, such as the punishment of Adam and the Labours of Hercules on the façade of the Colleoni Chapel in Bergamo, or the medallions at the base of the façade of the Certosa at Pavia showing prophets side by side with emperors

---

[1] 'For knighthood and chivalry, Greece had the first honour; then knighthood passed to Rome, and of clergy the sum total has now come to France'; *Cligès* (ed. M. Forrester), 32 f. cited by J. Seznec, *The Survival of the Pagan Gods*, Eng. edn. (London, 1940), 18–19.

and gods.[1] Morally, the gods with their peccadilloes and their pettiness had become figures of spiritual significance. To make the Olympians respectable had been the attempt of writers as early as Sallust, who in his *De deis et mundo* in defending mythology showed that some of the grossest fables, e.g. that of Attis and Cybele, had a moral purpose, illustrating the trials of the soul in its search after God. Legends which Cicero called *superstitiones paene seniles* are given a pious and philosophical explanation.[2] Ultimately the moralizing interpretation derived from the Christian Fathers themselves; at the beginning of the sixth century two great works of allegorical interpretation appeared: the *Moralia* of Gregory the Great, dealing with the Bible, and the *Mythologiae* of Fulgentius Planciades, explaining the significance of the gods and the legends about them. Thus, as Professor Seznec has remarked, in time 'mythology tends to become a *philosophia moralis*' and grew to astonishing proportions,[3] especially where Ovid's *Metamorphoses* were concerned.

Most interesting, perhaps, is the later medieval treatment of mythical figures encountered by Aeneas (*Aeneid* VI) and by Dante himself in the underworld depicted in the *Inferno*.[4] The Giants, the Titans and the personnel of Pluto's entourage including the monsters (like Cerberus) have become part of the administrative structure of the City of Dis, to which Minos allots each soul according to its record. This is included in the later works of mythography, 'companions' to the study of the gods, which took their origin in Martianus Capella and the commentary, on the marraige of Mercury and Philology, of Remigius of Auxerre upon Martianus. The best examples are the treatise called by Mai and Bode 'Mythographus III' (late twelfth–early thirteenth century), but by contemporaries *Scintillarium poeseos* and attributed to 'Albricus' or Alexander Nequam;[5] and a remarkable work, the *Fulgentius Metaphoralis* by the English Franciscan, John Ridewall (1320–30).[6] The

[1] Seznec, op. cit., 30.
[2] Ibid., 85.
[3] Ibid., 90.
[4] I have given an account of these, in relation to Dante's treatment of *Inferno* XXXI, in 'The Giants (Inf. XXXI)', *Essays presented to Eugene Vinaver* (Manchester, 1965).
[5] Miss E. Rathbone, 'Master Alberic of London, *Mythographus Tertius Vaticanus*', *Medieval and Renaissance Studies*, i (1941), 35–8, thinks that this is not Nequam, but one Alberic, canon of St Paul's.
[6] Ed., under this title, by Hans Liebeschütz (Studien der Bibl. Warburg, Berlin, 1926).

Fulgentius Metaphoralis is, just like *Mythographus III*, an illustrated discussion of the iconography of the gods generally in vogue during the fourteenth century. Each god represents, in the way he or she is currently depicted, a virtue or an attribute of some kind, e.g. Neptune, Intelligence: Juno, Memory, considered under the various aspects suggested by the accompanying drawing. Jupiter stands *poetice* for *virtus amoris et benivolencie*. It means warmth of life: for love is fire, moreover ordered love is life.

'I know, says Hugh (of St Victor) addressing his soul in his book on the Soul's Deposit, that your life is an act of loving.[1] Moreover that love is a fire is taught by sacred and profane philosophers, as is clear from Dionysius in his book *On the Angelic Hierarchy*.[2] It is also plain from iconography, where love is wont to be depicted with a quiver containing fiery darts.' The treatise had a wide circulation: some forty manuscripts of it have survived. Other moralized mythologies, like those of Petrus Berchorius (Pierre Bersuire) and the *De Deorum imaginibus libellus*, which Liebeschütz prints, set the later medieval fashion for combining art and allegory in the description of Olympus. It was *Mythographus III* which gave Petrarch the model for his poets of Africa though here the moral and didactic elements are left out. In Book III of the *Punic War* Petrarch describes the figures of the gods and the *formae heroum* in the hall of the Numidian king Syphax with iconographical detail, but without the pious deductions emphasized in the *Mythographus* or the *Fulgentius Metaphoralis*.[3] The denizens of the underworld as Petrarch describes them show the influence of the chapter on 'Pluto, Providencia' (VI) in the latter treatise.

The absence of the moral and the didactic from Petrarch's poem should not lead to the supposition that the great early Renaissance humanist set himself to exclude allegory from his writings. The art of the *quattrocento* suggests a very different conclusion.[4] As to Petrarch himself, the writer of the revealing

[1] 'Scio, dicit Hugo alloquens animam suam in suo libro de arra anime quod vita tua dileccio est. Etiam quod amor sit ignis docent sancti et mundi philosophi, sicud patet ex Dionisio in suo libro de angelica hierarchia. Patet etiam ex poetica pictura, qua solet amor depingi cum pharetra continente ignita iacula,' Migne, *Patr. Lat.*, 176, 951 C. I owe this and the next reference to Dr Liebeschütz.

[2] *De Celesti hierarchia*, XV, 2.

[3] *Fulgentius Metaphoralis*, 79.

[4] Here one may refer to the 'Index of sources' in Professor E. Wind's *Pagan Mysteries in the Renaissance* (London, 1958), 193. The purpose of this outstanding book is to trace the interpretation in works of art, along Platonist lines, of classical mythology and the early mysteries.

Letters, the single-minded follower of *bonae literae*, reveals in at least two of his prose works and in certain of his *Canzoniere* a marked Augustinianism. In the *De sui ipsius ignorantia* he turns away from Aristotelian thought and particularly from the Averroists who were its main upholders; and though he does not fail to emphasize his own literary record and cannot be charged with any exaggerated humility, he understood perhaps as fully as any man of his time the spirit of the *Confessions*, and in the *Secretum* castigated his own failures, and had to acknowledge, in the words of the companion in this dialogue:

'To despise myself is safest of all, to despise others most dangerous and fatuous.'[1]

The element of pride in his own nature he had to control by freely recognizing his own dislike of hearing the truth about himself:

'To hear true testimony about yourself you have termed wounding accusation. For the Satirist's maxim is true. *He will be the accuser who speaks the truth.* No less the saying of the writer of comedy: *Fawning begets friends, truth begets hatred.*'[2]

This self-discipline, not least in morality, he could have learned, his companion in the dialogue said, from Plato, whom he had earnestly studied: this could have overcome the *luxuriae flammae*:

'*Augustine.* You have something here which may, even to the utmost, absolve you from thinking about divine matters. For what else does the heavenly doctrine of Plato teach save that we must guard the mind from the lusts of the body and eradicate evil fantasies, so that it may arise pure and ready to behold mysteries of divinity to which the thought of our mortality is closely adjoined? You know what I am saying, and these things are familiar to you from the Platonic books which you are said to have studied with such avidity.'[3]

As Professor Whitfield has justly remarked: Petrarch's rejection of the primacy of Aristotle rests largely on this conception of Plato as closer to the Christian tradition.[4] This refers to St

---

[1] Secretum sive De Contemptu Mundi, Book II, in *Opera*, (Basel, 1542), i, 342.
[2] Ibid., 343.
[3] '*Augustinus.* Habes igitur quod te vel maxime ab omni divinorum cogitatione dimoveat. Quid enim aliud caelestis doctrina Platonis admonet, nisi animum a libidinibus corporis arcendum et eradenda phantasmata, ut ad providenda divinitatis arcana, cui propriae mortalitatis annexa cogitatio est, purus expeditusque consurgat. 'Scis quod loquor et haec ex Platonis libris tibi familiariter nota sunt, quibus avidissime nuper incubuisse diceris.' Ibid., 346.
[4] J. H. Whitfield, *Petrarch and the Renaissance* (Oxford, 1943), 38.

Augustine's debt to Cicero and Plato: 'the saint had candidly confessed his familiarity with both, as well as his finding in Plato a great part of our faith, while in the Hortensius of Cicero he had found a turning-point by which he was converted to the study of truth alone'.[1] But it might equally apply to the Platonic morality, the *caelestis doctrina* referred to above. This he could not study, as he laments, in the original Greek, but only through the Latin classics, Cicero especially, who, because he was a rhetorician, could particularly touch Petrarch's heart. But here Petrarch remembered, in the preface to his *De remediis*, that he must be on his guard against the pleasure afforded him by an author with an engaging style. Aristotle had said in the *Ethics*:

'It is more difficult to sustain hardships than to abstain from delights. Following whom, Seneca writing to Lucilius says "It is a greater thing to go through with difficulties than to steer a happy course".'[2]

Characteristically, throughout the *De remediis*, it is the other side to the worldly good fortune that is emphasized. All the delights have their penalties and drawbacks, and Petrarch's vast classical and mythological knowledge is utilized in the attempt to expose the materialistic and ephemeral values of the affluent and comfortable life. This *contemptus sui* may not be thought unusual in a humanist so confident in his craft: but the same humanist had the same medieval attachment to European unity as Dante.

It is the Roman character of the papacy which Petrarch emphasizes. In his *Rime* a number are concerned with the return from Babylon (Avignon) and with Philip VI's projects for a crusade. 'The central idea is always the return from exile to the eternal city': 'Tirelessly to each pope Petrarch makes the same appeal'. When, he asks, did one see more peace and justice save when the world had one single head, and that head was Rome? This, he replies, was when God chose to be born of a virgin and to visit his earth. Naturally Virgil was wrong when he spoke of an eternal empire, for all kingdoms perish: but as

---

[1] Ibid. Cf. especially *De Re. Fam. Epistolarum Liber II*, 9, *Opera*, 601, where Petrarch, speaking of 'Augustinus meus' rejects the charge that he had cultivated that father 'with a sort of fictitious regard' and extols him for having found 'a great part of our faith in the Platonic books'. The whole letter (to James Colonna) is of the utmost significance for Christian humanism in the fourteenth century.
[2] *De remediis utriusque fortunae*, Praefatio.

long as the creatures endure, the Vicar of Christ is here below to make a *pax romana* a *pax Christiana*.[1]

The humanist of the fourteenth century is therefore no exclusive devotee of literary composition. Self-awareness, a critical attitude towards self more than others, is his true mark. The receptivity of a scholar like Petrarch, his interest in human character which emerges in the *De remediis* and his readiness to face solitude owes as much to the self-examination of St Augustine as to the moral exhortations of Cicero, Horace and Seneca. The Fathers are asserting their place in Christian theology. This can be seen in the increased acquisition by medieval libraries of Augustine, Jerome, Ambrose and Chrysostom. Augustine is, of course, normally found in libraries of all dates: but in Petrarch's own day a Fellow of Merton, John Staveley,[2] possessed and bequeathed to the college as many as twelve volumes of the saint, and among his books were Bradwardine's *De causa Dei contra Pelagios*,[3] the work largely founded upon St Augustine's doctrine of grace, and written against the followers of Ockham. If we take the Merton College Library alone, some interesting entries will be apparent among gifts recorded in the fourteenth–fifteenth century. William Rede, bishop of Chichester (d. 1385), passed on to the college a number of works given him by the Kent clerk, Nicholas of Sandwich (d. 1370), and left in all to various Oxford colleges as many as 1,250 books.[4] He gave three volumes containing Augustine to Merton, to add to a fine existing stock of *Augustiniana*, one of which contained *tabulae* of the City of God, and also *tabulae* of Chrysostom on Matthew.[5] John Renham, chancellor of Oxford, 1361–2, besides giving Augustine, *De Trinitate*, presented Hugh of St Victor on the *Celestis hierarchia* of the Pseudo-Denys. It was the fifteenth century which, at

---

[1] Cf. the passages cited by M. Gandillac in Forest, Van Steenberghen and Gandillac, 'Le mouvement doctrinal du XIe au XIVe siècle', *Histoire de l'Eglise depuis les origines jusqu'à nos jours*, 13 (Paris, 1956), 429–30.

[2] F. M. Powicke, *The Medieval Books of Merton College* (Oxford, 1931), 120; cf. 23.

[3] The future archbishop was a humanist as well as a theologian. 'He was one of a little group of Merton Fellows including the mathematician John Mauduit, the philosopher Richard of Kilmington (d. 1361), Walter Burley, and Walter Segrave, who were the clerks and companions of that illustrious prelate Richard of Bury, bishop of Durham, the patron of scholars and collector of books.' Powicke, op. cit., 24–5.

[4] 'He had a library of some 370 books. It must have been one of the largest private libraries in England.' Powicke, 31.

[5] Powicke, no. 342, p. 28; for texts, nos. 501 and 573.

Merton, saw bequests of St Jerome.[1] Henry Sever, warden of Merton, 1455–71, in his gift of twenty-one books to the Library, included a commentary on the *De Civitate Dei* along with various writings of Lactantius; a volume of Jerome and a commentary upon Jerome's prologue to St John; and a collected various works of Ambrose and Jerome. The main Jeromes came at the end of the century, at the gift of the warden, the commentaries on Isaiah, Jeremiah, the Twelve Minor Prophets, and on Matthew, Mark, the Apocalypse, the Pauline epistles, etc. Parts of this manuscript[2] are thought to have been copied from the Italian manuscript of Jerome on the epistles given by William Grey of Ely to Balliol College (no. 157, fols. 136–218v).[3] Two other Jeromes, both probably written in monasteries, twelfth–thirteenth centuries, were acquired by Grey for this college;[4] and the Balliol Chrysostom, finished in August 1447, (no. 134), was sent to Grey by the Florentine humanist scribe Antonio Mario himself.[5]

The intake of patrology into the fourteenth and fifteenth century could be illustrated from other libraries. This should not surprise. Quite apart from the Fathers being a repository of Platonic and neo-Platonic speculation and the philosophy of the Hellenistic world, it served as an antidote to the prevalent form of scholastic thought and strengthened the resistance offered to philosophic scepticism; it also constituted a storehouse of style and personal experience (how much so with Jerome's letters!), and plain good sense (nowhere more than in Chrysostom).

Early humanism gladly accepted this patristic inheritance. Of the circle of classically minded academics and officials of the French court in the last twenty years of the fourteenth century, containing men like Gontier and Pierre Col, Jean of Montreuil, Jean Muret, Jacques de Nouvion, the most strongly marked humanist was undoubtedly Nicholas of Clamanges, long resident at the college of Navarre and later secretary to Benedict

---

[1] Nos. 945, 953.
[2] Powicke, no. 1182.
[3] R. A. B. Mynors, *Catalogue of the Manuscripts of Balliol College, Oxford* (Oxford, 1963), 141–2.
[4] Nos. 147, Mynors, 127; 229, ibid., 237–40. The Oxford stationers had for sale books of the twelfth and thirteenth century from monastic scriptoria, which through channels authorized and unauthorized had come on to the market (Mynors, xxvi).
[5] Mynors, xxxi.

XIII. When his friend Jacques de Nouvion died, Nicholas wrote an epitaph in which he described this 'humaniste à la fois et théologien'.[1]

> *Te mores Socratem faciebant, alta Platonem,*
> *In Physicis fueras magnus Aristoteles,*
> *Augustinus eras, divina archana videndo. . . .*
> *Tu preceptor eras summus. . . .*
> *Quid loquar eloquium clarum, dulce atque disertum. . . .*
> *Quid referam moresque graves, moresque modestos?*[2]

I sent you, he wrote to Gontier Col, a few small gifts, but your liberal mind sought to repay me shortly with great interest, for the little quire of my writings, in the shape of a great and noble volume of the holy fathers Jerome and Augustine. Since the place where I write does not abound in such books I am specially delighted, sated as I am with reading the Gentiles which excite tedium more than produce pleasure, and do not refresh the mind anxious to gather fruit, either by comely leaves of elegant words or by vernal flowers of sweet-sounding eloquence. The books of the Fathers are most helpful, abundantly adorned by accomplished prose and producing mature fruit ripened by the sun of justice. In youth we perambulate the gardens of the orators, but spring soon changes to summer, summer to autumn, the youth becomes a mature man and the flowers turn to fruit. In other words, serious work succeeds to the merely charming and attractive: 'For unless the flower fades away, the fruit is never formed'. Ripeness is all. This description of classical antiquity as flowers that in time give place to fruit, *mores graves* and *mores modesti*, cannot be attributed to humanism generally, but the gifts of moderation and *gravitas* are an inheritance from Cicero and Horace and are above all exemplified in Augustine and Ambrose.

We must dwell with these Fathers for a while since they were in great part the vehicle by which the Platonic tradition was passed to the medieval humanist and will reveal the continuity

---

[1] A. Coville, *Gontier et Pierre Col et l'humanisme en France au temps de Charles VI* (Paris, 1934), 96.

[2] 'Thy morals made thee Socrates, the depths of thy mind Plato; in physics thou wast the great Aristotle; Augustine thou wast, beholding divine mysteries. Thou wast the teacher supreme. Why should I speak of thy clear speech, sweet and eloquent, thy character alike grave and modest?' *Opera*, ed. Lydius, Epistolae, no. LXIX, 199, cited by Coville.

of the classical legacy. 'The Christian Church is not the beginning of the Middle Ages: it is the last creative achievement of classical antiquity.'[1] For the first three words substitute 'Christian humanism' and there is much to be said for the apothegm; for it was Plotinus and the neo-Platonists who gave Augustine the idea of a Christian philosophy, and their impact upon his own personal life transformed the Manichean materialist into one who had discovered that God was spirit.[2] In the *De Civitate Dei*, Books VIII and X show Plato and the Platonists as the philosophers who approached nearest to Christianity; it is *Confessions*, Books IV and VII which display the working of the Platonic leaven in Augustine's own life and had a great attraction for the humanist; especially for Petrarch who took with him in his pocket when he made the ascent of Mount Ventoux, a little manuscript of the saint.[3] After his appointment as professor of rhetoric at Milan, Augustine began, he says, seriously to study *quosdam Platonicorum libros*, in which he found the doctrine of the Word who was God and by whom all things were made, and learned what a spiritual substance was.

How did he make the discovery of Christian neo-Platonism? M. Courcelle has suggested convincingly that it was Mallius Theodorus who, at Milan, gave him the Latin translation, by the great Christian neo-Platonist, Victorinus, of Plotinus' *Enneades* as well, perhaps, as the *De regressu animae* of Porphyry. Behind this introduction to Platonic thought stands the figure of Ambrose, whom Augustine calls his 'father'.[4] M. Courcelle shows that Ambrose, preacher rather than philosopher, had within his hands a number of treatises by Plotinus and 'doubtless also of Porphyry', and he has pointed to the striking and often verbal resemblance of some of Ambrose's sermons, to which Augustine listened in 386–8,[5] to *Enneades* 6–7 and to

---

[1] W. R. Inge, 'Plotinus', *Proc. British Acad.*, xv (1929), 20.

[2] In *Confessions*, xvi, 4, Augustine explains how, without aid, he could understand Aristotle's ten categories, at the very mention of which his professor puffed out his cheeks with pleasure and pride; whereas they only confused his conception of God, 'mirabiliter simplicem atque incommutabilem', as if God could be subject to his greatness or beauty . . . 'since thou art thyself thy magnitude and thy beauty'.

[3] Pierre Courcelle, *Les Confessions de Saint Augustin sous la tradition littéraire* (Paris, 1963), 329–51.

[4] *Conf.*, v, 25–25.

[5] Notably to the sermon sequences *De Isaac vel anima* and the *De bono mortis*: Pierre Courcelle, *Recherches sur les Confessions de St. Augustin* (Paris, 1950), 106 ff. For other passages where Augustine has drawn upon Ambrose's reading of Plotinus, cf. 126–33. 'Ainsi plusieurs sermons d'Ambrose ont incité Augustin á certains aspects essentiels de la doctrine Plotinienne.'

Plotinus' treatise *On the beautiful*. As a preacher, Ambrose's work was penetrated by neo-Platonism.[1] Not only in his sermons are there neo-Platonic allusions, but in them are 'whole pages which are paralleled by several treatises of the *Enneades* sometimes cited word for word under the author's name, sometimes paraphrased in a Christian sense'.[2] There were many other reasons why the Middle Ages read Augustine and Ambrose, but the neo-Platonist flavour of the much-traversed *Confessions* and *De Civitate Dei* is a strong explanation.

Apart from Augustine himself, Platonist tradition received in the post-Patristic age a vital contribution from the corpus of Dionysian writings translated into Latin during the ninth century. The works of the Pseudo-Denys are based chiefly on Proclus: 'but the roots of their doctrine of mystical theology is to be sought in the Platonic *Parmenides* or rather in the tendency ascribed to this dialogue in the interpretations of Plotinus, Syrianus and Proclus'.[3] Here one should note the great importance of the commentary of Proclus on the *Parmenides*: as Dr Klibansky has put it: 'Plato's dialectical approach to the One is now transferred to the theologian's approach to the Deity'.[4] Naturally so subtle and varied a system of philosophy cannot even be outlined in a few pages: but to understand something of the spiritual and intellectual problems of the fourteenth and fifteenth century something must be said of the two great and related spheres of thought with which the Platonic inheritance was concerned. These touched both metaphysics and practical conduct. Just as in the later Hellenistic period Proclus was set the task of meeting the supreme religious need of the time by somehow bridging the gulf between God and the soul, so throughout the movement known as Northern Renaissance, and its powerful generator, the *Devotio Moderna*, men set themselves to formulate a philosophy of life that required a special and unique relationship between God and the individual. It was as if the old Hellenistic problem of finding a single philosophy and creating a scheme of salvation against that of the mystery sects had been revived in a peculiarly personal way against the

[1] Courcelle, *Recherches*, 29.
[2] On the exact balance of the influences of Plotinus and Porphyry in his works, see Courcelle, *Les Confessions de St. Augustine dans la tradition littéraire* (Paris, 1963), chapter III.
[3] R. Klibansky, *The Continuity of the Platonic Tradition* (Warburg Lib., 1950), 25.
[4] Ibid.,

heretical societies and within the structure of the Church. The second sphere was that of exegesis. Theologians in their comments and lectures, particularly on the Pauline epistles, had to take account of the new translations of the Platonic dialogues from the Greek and decide how far the apostle could be interpreted from the standpoint of Plato; and that takes the reader to Marsilius, Ficino and John Colet.

Basically, the problem inherited by the later Middle Ages was formulated by Scotus Erigena in the ninth century. It concerned the relation between God and the world and the significance of the act of creation. It was expressed in the premises of Erigena's *De Divisione Naturae*. God creates all, i.e. He is in all and is the essence of all; for He alone really exists and all that really is in the whole of existence is God. In other words nothing of all that exists, exists of itself. The creation is co-essential and co-eternal with God. But in one sense God precedes the world, that is in the order of reason, since, as Erigena observes, He is the cause of all and is Himself uncaused, and all exists causatively in Him from all eternity. All was created from nothing, but by nothing one must not understand the privation of essence, substance and mere accidents, *nihil de nihilo*, but the excellence of the divine superessentiality.[1] To say that God created all things out of nothing is equivalent to saying that God created all things out of Himself. Now, to quote Dr Henry Bett's paraphrase of Erigena:[2]

'The nothing of which the world is created is not mere privation of being. How could privation of relation exist before any relation existed, or negation of existence before existence? But if *nihil* be taken to signify not merely the privation of habitude, or the absence of existence, but the total negation of habitude, existence, substance, accidents and most of all that can be said or thought, then it necessarily means God who is the negation of all that is, being utterly beyond all that is . . . so God makes all, of nothing, that is, he produces of his super-existence, existence; of his super-life, life; of his super-intellect, intellect, and of the negation of all that is and is not, the affirmation of all that is and is not.'

Now while neo-Platonic thinkers lay emphasis upon the goodness of God as the essential source of creative activity and

---

[1] *De Divisione Naturae*, III (Migne, *P.L.* 122) 634 B.
[2] *Johannes Scotus Erigena* (Cambridge, 1925), 34.

therefore of the existence of all that is, their doctrine of the super-existence of God leads to the conclusion which many have found startling, though it occurs in many mystics: that the divine nature, while it is understood to be unintelligible by its very excellence, is not undeservedly described as nothing:

'Per excellenciam nihil non immerito vocitatur.'

As Erigena put it:

'God is above all essence and intelligence, nor are reason or intelligence applicable to Him, nor can He be spoken of or understood, nor has He a name, nor is there a word for Him.'[1] We name Him, yet we cannot name Him, since He is above name.

But as well as goodness, God is knowledge. What knowledge can He have of the *singularia*, the individuals, striving pitifully if they are human beings, to reach Him?

Neo-Platonism conceived of God as essential, eternal unity free from all distinction and variation: how then could it make the transition to the multiplicity, change and variety of the world of phenomena? Historically this had been the reason for the intermediate processes, the emanations, the aeons or intermediate existences characteristic of some of its manifestations. The immense differentiations of the external world have somehow to be explained either as overflowings from the fullness of God or as multiplicity and limitation which are the characteristics of the finite, as unity is the very character of the infinite. This cleavage was perhaps the most difficult problem for neo-Platonism. It was the one that troubled the northern mystics who, to solve it, had recourse to doctrines of special revelation or of ecstatic approach to the deity. The god who cannot be named and cannot be grasped by the finite intellect can be partially known by inference from his works or by analogy with other causes; he may be unknown and unknowable in his positive character but definable by negations; he may be unknown and unknowable, but accessible in a mystical union which is not properly speaking knowledge, being supralogical.[2] It was with such problems that the preacher and the metaphysician alike were faced and the answers given vary from

---

[1] ['Deus est] supra omnem essentiam et intelligentiam cujus neque ratio est neque intelligentia, neque dicitur, neque intelligitur, neque nomen ejus est neque verbum': *De Divisione Naturae*, I (Migne, *P.L.* 122), 510 D.

[2] Proclus, *The Elements of Theology*, ed. E. R. Dodds (Oxford, 1963), App. I, 312.

a pantheism suspected as heretical to the profoundest philosophy of the age.

The emphasis laid upon the cleavage between Creator and created seemed to fit the altering pattern of thought during the fourteenth century. Ockham (d. 1349) and his successors, Bradwardine (d. 1349), Holcot (d. 1349), Buckingham (d. 1331) and Adam of Woodham (d. 1357) had done much to emphasize their incompatibility. It was an emphasis on the limits rather than the scope of reason. A historian of thought has given his opinion that the fourteenth century was nearer to the fourth than to the thirteenth. Where the thinkers of the pre-Scotist era had 'sought to incorporate knowledge into a framework of revelation', Ockham, Bradwardine and Gregory of Rimini had emphasized their incompatibility.[1] Where the Augustinians as well as the Christian Aristotelian 'had striven to find some common ground from which to view both the divine and the created, fourteenth-century thinkers affirmed the absoluteness of their separation'.[2] Such an attitude, when it did not make for philosophic scepticism, led to the longing for direct contact with the divine, for the wholly personal revelation and the inspired recognition which had characterized the Plotinian moments of ecstasy, when the seeker became aware intuitively of the reality he had pursued by negation and in an atmosphere of darkness. The very autonomy and self-sufficiency of the experimental sciences, the great advances in experimental philosophy made by the successors of Ockham both at Oxford and Paris, alarmed the Christian humanist anxious to bridge the gulf, and brought him not to a recrudescence or revision of Thomism, but to the practice of meditation, practical piety and imitation of Christ. The creature had to grow like the Creator.

Thus in the Low Countries in the Charterhouses, cloisters and the smaller towns there started among the working laity a movement which was profoundly to influence northern Europe and to make a notable contribution to Christian humanism both by the teachers it encouraged and by the production of manuscripts and, later, of printed books. The leaders of the *Devotio Moderna* were first and foremost revivalists whose aim was to live in common a life of piety and devotion. They started from a

[1] G. Leff, 'The Changing Pattern of Thought in the earlier Fourteenth Century', *Bull. John Rylands Lib.*, 43, no. 2 (March 1961), 354.
[2] G. Leff, *Gregory of Rimini* (Manchester, 1963), 18.

Divine Unity'.[1] The believer is, so to speak, absorbed in the Trinity:

'Now it is according to its essential existence that the spirit receives the coming of Christ, in the purely natural order, without intermediary or interruption. For the ideal being, and the life that we are in God, in our eternal image, and the being that we possess in ourselves, according to essential existence, know no intermediary nor separation.'[2]

These were counsels for the inner life, and the second passage was one of those which gave Gerson, the chancellor of Paris, good reasons for attacking Ruysbroeck when he maintained that the soul loses its own essence in becoming transformed and absorbed into the divine essence. To Gerson neither sense nor reason could understand the divine essence: only 'pure intelligence' (*intelligentia simplex*) which receives immediately from God the first principles, for it is a light which derives from the infinite light of the primordial intelligence which is God, and of which St John writes: *That was the true light that lighteth every man coming into the world.*[3]

The first half of the fifteenth century was one of enormous advance in humanistic studies, in which Italians were in the lead, particularly in the search for manuscripts. Poggio's example was catching; and the discoveries opened the way to a fuller Plato, and a new emphasis upon composition, pure and simple. Pier Candido Decembrio translated the *Republic* for Duke Humphrey of Gloucester, and at Florence Leonardo Bruni, before 1421, rendered into Latin the *Phaedo*, the *Platonic letters*, the *Gorgias*, the *Apology* and the *Phaedrus*. While Filelfo taught at Florence, Siena, Bologna and Milan, Gasparino di Bergamo was instructing at Pavia, Venice and Padua, Guarino at Ferrara and Vittorino da Feltre at Mantua. A great movement for finer expression based on the classical orators and poets had begun and a critical view of texts long dormant was prevailing.

---

[1] *Oeuvres*, 3, 84 (chapter I, on the text, 'Voyez, l'époux vient: sorte à sa rencontre').

[2] 'Or c'est selon son existence essentielle que l'esprit reçoit la venue du Christ, dans l'ordre simplement naturel, sans intermédiaire et sans interruption. Car l'être idéal et la vie que nous sommes en Dieu, dans notre image éternel, et l'être que nous possédons en nous-mêmes, selon l'existence essentielle, ne connaissent point intermédiaire ni de séparation', ibid., 162 (chapter lviii).

[3] *Gersonii opera*, ed. Dupin, iii, 370–1: Lux quaedam intellectualis naturae, derivata ab infinita luce intelligentiae primae quae Deus est, de quo Johannes: Erat lux vera quae illuminat omnem hominem venientem in hunc mundum.

The pontificate of Martin V saw the influence spreading to the curia (which indeed had under the Avignonese pontiffs been a considerable literary centre), and the presence of cardinals like Giordano Orsini and Giuliano Cesarini, Domenico Capranica, later of Thomas Parentucelli and Aeneas Sylvius, made the Vatican a home of Renaissance culture. But the most distinguished centre of studies in the first part of the fifteenth century was unquestionably Padua, where in the early 'twenties, there was a galaxy of humanists and scientists: the medicals Ugo Benzi of Siena and Paolo Nicolletti of Udine, the mathematicians Prosdocimo di' Beldomandi and Paolo del Pozzo Toscanelli, Vittorino da Feltre and the canonist and theologian just mentioned, Giuliano Cesarini, professor of law. These are some of the people whom a young Heidelberg student, Nicholas Krebs of Cues, found in the university of Padua, where he matriculated in 1417, or in Venice close by. Ugo Benzi, Gemisthes Plethon and Pietro Calabro were notable Hellenists; the combinations of Greek and mathematics made its mark on the young 'Treviran', as he was called: to Toscanelli he was to dedicate his *De transmutationibus geometricis*, to receive from him the translation, by Ambrogio of Camaldoli, of the *Theologia Mystica* by the Pseudo-Denys, and to put him into his dialogue, *De quadratura circuli*. This was the beginning of the cardinal's career which saw his attachment to Orsini's household and his exploits, soon to be famous, in the discovery of classical texts.

But the real significance of his Italian sojourn was that he was laying the foundations of the system of philosophy which was to give vitality and completion to the Christian neo-Platonism of early thinkers. Among the books annotated in his own hand which he left to the hospital of St Nicholas at Cues, are the major works of Proclus, the six books on the *Theology* of Plato,[1] the Commentary on the *Parmenides* (*Exposicio in Parmenidem Platonis*)[2] and the *Elementatio Theologica*;[3] and three codices of the *Pseudo-Denys*.[4] Here also, annotated by the cardinal, is a

[1] J. Marx, *Verzeichis der Hendschriften-sammlung des Hospitals zu Cers* (Trier, 1905), no. 185.

[2] Marx, no. 186.

[3] Marx, 194, wrongly stated by him not to have been by Proclus. The last edition (in the Greek) is by E. R. Dodds (Oxford, 1963).

[4] Containing the De coelesti hierarchia, De ecclesiastica hierarchia, De divinis nominibus, De mystica theologia, Marx, no. 43; printed Paris, 1498.

copy of Eckhart's *Opus tripartitum* which contains the seventeen articles which fell under ecclesiastical condemnation.[1] He also had the *Horologium divine sapientie* of Henry Suso.[2] The Harleian manuscripts in the British Museum contain a number of his classical texts as well as other works annotated by himself.[3] Cusanus accumulated a remarkable collection not only of reforming treatises and sermons, but of theology and philosophy, for in additon to the mystic neo-Platonic line just illustrated, there are the orthodox realist philosophers and a number of scientific and astronomical works. And there is Ramon Lull, that master of the devotional life. A note to one of his manuscripts shows that in 1444, when he was the representative of Eugenius at the diet of Nuremberg, Cusanus bought 'a great solid sphere, an astrolabe and other works, for 38 Rhenish florins'.[4] His interest in medicine is attested to by a substantial number of volumes, some containing collections of treatises. His was a universal spirit.

In the philosophical writing the Proclus-Dionysius element is uppermost. This can best be seen from the first and seminal essay, the *De docta ignorantia* itself, with its emphasis on the two themes—'to know is to be ignorant' (*scire est ignorare*) and the coincidence of opposites. The first is set out (I. Ch. XXVI) in the thesis derived from the Pseudo-Denys and from Scotus Erigena. God, being absolutely greatest is absolutely one. There is no opposite to Him: His unity is not the unity normally opposed by us to plurality: in His oneness, which includes all things, there is no distinction, and so, strictly speaking we cannot give Him any name or names.

'Holy ignorance teaches us that God is ineffable, and this because He is infinitely greater than all that can be named: and because this is verily so, we speak more truly of Him by removal and negation, as great Dionysius did, who would not have Him as truth, nor as understanding, nor as light, nor as any of the terms usually ascribed; whom Rabbi Solomon and all wise men follow: when He is neither Father, nor Son nor Holy Spirit,

---

[1] Printed *Archiv für Litteratur und Kirchengeschichte des Mittelalters*, ii, 616 (fols. 83–228).

[2] Marx, no. 45.

[3] Twenty-eight British Museum manuscripts are listed by Paul Lehmann, *Sitzungsber. Bayer. Akad. Wissenschaften*, Phil-Hist. Abt. (1930), 2, 20 f. Five more are given by B. L. Ullman, *Speculum*, xiii (1938), 194–7.

[4] Marx, no. 24, note (fol. 1) in his own hand. Ibid.

according to this negative theology, according to which He is infinite only.'[1]

The Cusanus idea of the absolute unity and infinity of God implied a doctrine of the relations of the finite to the infinite which demands from the creative intellect 'an effort of abnegation', in order that through this act the creature seeking may come within the *visio* or glance of God, and through instruction perceive what the discursive reason cannot tell him.[2] The second thesis, *coincidentia oppositorum*, was the basis of his great work of political theory, the *De Concordantia Catholica*,[3] written for the Council of Basel in an attempt to reconcile the papal and the conciliar sides: a moderate and flexible statement of the theory of representation and of the occasions when supremacy of the General Council in the Church must apply.

But the great problem remains. How can the eternal undifferentiated Being have any contact with the world and its individuals? How does one pass from that unity to the world of sense perception?[4] Cusanus rejects the neo-Platonist plan of emanations or intermediate evidences between God and the world. In the same manner as he makes the absolute maximum and the absolute minimum coincide in God (which is the foundation of the doctrine of *coincidentia oppositorum*), so he brings together under the single concept of reality God and the visible world, and regards reality as having two aspects, one being God, the invisible and ultimate reality, the other the world, the visible and desired reality. *Quid est mundus nisi invisibilis Dei apparitio? Quid Deus, nisi visibilium invisibilitas?* The two are separate, yet correlated. Reality is not a bare concept:[5] through and by the Trinity it is active and communicating. For Nicholas, the Trinity is the plan of the universe. Scotus and Eckhart had identified Father, Son and Holy Spirit with *essentia, virtus, operatio*. Nicholas adopted these terms occasionally, but more normally identifies them with unity, equality and connexion. Within the Godhead there is this vital three-part principle at work, communicating itself through the Word, with the Spirit unifying whatever is divided. The Word

---

[1] Ed. Hoffmann and Klibansky, 54–5.
[2] Jacob, *Essays in the Conciliar Epoch*, 163, based on *De Visione Dei*, chs. 4, 5, 8.
[3] On which see especially Morimichi Watanabe, *The Political Ideas of Nicholas of Cusa with special reference to the De Concordantia Catholica* (Geneva, 1963), 30.
[4] Jacob, ibid., 164.
[5] *De Docta Ignorantia*, I, c. 25.

was made flesh and acted and acts as the equalizing bond that draws man to man because man is drawn to Him. It is His humanity that supplies the deficiencies:

'The humanity therefore that is in Christ Jesus has supplied all the defects in all men. For since it is the greatest possible, it embraces the whole power of the species in order that such equality of being should belong to every man, that he may be joined to each much more fully than a brother or very special friend. For so acts that extreme fulness of human nature that in each man that adheres to Him by established faith Christ is that same man in most perfect union, saving the number [the individuality] of each.'[1]

In the remarkable tract, the *De Pace Fidei*, written after the fall of Constantinople, the Word acts first as the advocate of the various nations and sects who are being brought by argument to the unity of a single orthodox faith; then, just like St Peter and St Paul, He acts as the party that convinces Greeks, Arabs, Indians and Scythians of the validity in their cases, of the Christian faith. The Word, says the king of heaven, He sent in human form to the various deluded peoples to bear witness that man was capable of free will and so of eternal life which was the ultimate desire of the inner man:

'to wit, the truth which alone is sought and since it is eternal, eternally feeds the intellect. Which truth feeding the intellect is nothing but the Word itself in which all things are enfolded and by which all things are expressed; which also put on human nature, that every man according to the choice of free will in his human nature is assured that he can, through that man who is also the Word, attain the immortal nourishment of truth.'[2]

[1] 'Humanitas igitur in Christo Jesus omnes omnium hominum defectus implevit. Nam ipsa cum sit maxima, totam speciei potentiam amplectitur, ut sit cuiuslibet hominis talis essendi aequalitas, quod multo amplius quam frater et amicus specialissimus cuilibet coniunctus sit. Nam hoc agit maximitas humanae naturae, ut in quolibet homine sibi per formatam fidem adhaerente Christus sit ipse idem homo unione perfectissima, cuiuslibet numero salvo,' *De Docta Ignorantia*, III, 6.

[2] 'Scilicet veritas quae solum appetitur et, uti aeterna est, aeternaliter pascit intellectum. Quae quidem veritas intellectum pascens non est nisi Verbum ipsum, in quo complicantur omnia et per quod omnia explicantur, et quod humanam induit naturam, ut quilibet homo secundum electionem liberi arbitrii in sua humana natura, in homine illo qui et Verbum, immortale veritatis pabulum se assequi posse non dubitaret,' *De Pace Fidei*, ed. Klibansky and Bascour (Medieval and Renaissance Studies. Supplement III. London, 1956), 9. On this use of the terms *complicatio*, *explicatio*, redolent of the Chartres school, see Eduard Zellinger, *Cusanus-Konkordanz* (Munich, 1960), nos. 170, 279. For the *Coincidentia oppositorum* in God, ibid., no. 43.

Two years before the death of Cusanus (1464) Ficino's academy was founded in Florence. Its model was, of course, the academy of Plato himself: but lay religious associations also provided a model, and the appeal of the new society to the educated Florentine was due, as Kristeller has pointed out,[1] not simply to the founder's metaphysical speculation, 'but rather to the moralizing and edifying tone of his letters and discourses in which Christian and Platonist elements were blended and which must have impressed persons who had received both a religious and a classical education'.[2] Ficino, it may be recalled, was a priest; he delivered, in public, sermons as well as lectures on Plato, Plotinus and St Paul, mainly in the church of Santa Maria degli Angeli and to general audiences, not only to his own circle. But these *declamationes* were sometimes turned into letters sent to his own special friends. Particularly characteristic in the collection of Ficino's letters are the 'love letters', the *epistolae amatoriae*, when love is understood in the spiritual sense: as he said to Politian: if a love element is sometimes found in them, this was 'Platonicum illud quidem et honestum non Aristippicum et lascivum'.[3] His major work, the Platonic *Theology*, was 'intended to prove the immortality of the soul and many other teachings of Christianity, and it appears from many of his statements that he believed in the essential harmony of Platonic philosophy and Christian theology and considered it his major task to confirm the teachings of this faith through the rational arguments of his philosophy'.[4]

It is therefore extremely interesting to mark the contact of this thorough-going Platonist with the leading English student of Plato, the Christian humanist John Colet (1466–1529), the founder of St Paul's School and dean of St Paul's. We are fortunate enough to possess, in the All Souls copy of Ficino's *Epistolae*, a volume annotated throughout by Colet which shows that he read the letters in the preparation of a course of free public lectures at Oxford on St Paul's epistles, delivered by him in 1498 and 1499. It has been shown that in the first part of Colet's lectures on the Romans very little interest was shown in Platonism: but in the lecture notes covering Romans VI–XI, the method specially associated with Colet appears: that of

---

[1] P. O. Kristeller, *Studies in Renaissance Thought and Letters* (Rome, 1956), 113.
[2] Ibid., 111.
[3] Ibid., 119.
[4] Ibid., 109.

'examining the historical and grammatical meaning of the text as a whole, relating it to the historical circumstances in which it was written and explaining Paul's meaning in terms of analogous doctrines from the theology of Platonism'.[1] In the (148) marginals and notes the impact of the *Theologica Platonica* (1482) can be seen, but even more so is this the case in the lectures where he seems to be 'systematically de-secularizing' Ficino.[2] In one passage (among many) Colet substitutes St Paul for Socrates: none the less, it is more difficult to show that Colet's reading of the *Epistolae* actually influenced his interpretations of St Paul; on the larger issue whether Colet in his biblical commentary accepted the Platonism of the School of Careggi, there is only evidence on a certain number of limited topics. Colet was, it is true, out for all he could glean from a brilliant master, borrowing what he could: but on certain major issues, such as the conception of the soul and the problem of the superiority of the intellect over the will, he differs from his Italian master, even to the extent of placing, in St Paul's triad of faith, hope and charity, hope first.[3] Thus while Ficino in his first letters to Colet penned in the All Souls volume addresses his new admirer in affectionate terms, as indeed was merited by Colet's description of him as a sun (*me solem saepe vocas*), his graceful declining of the metaphor makes one suspect that he may have foreseen incompatibility with one already known as an English reforming theologian—or was it literary modesty?

'I may seem a sun to you and to others who love me as much

---

[1] Sears Jayne, *John Colet and Marsilio Ficino* (Oxford, 1963), 27. The All Souls volume is the 1495 text printed at Venice. Colet may have brought it back with him when he returned from the Continent in 1495. Jayne shows conclusively that while in Italy, 1493–5, Colet did not meet Ficino.

[2] Jayne's phrase, *Colet and Ficino*, 50.

[3] Hope for Colet corresponds to the first level because one is sustained through the trials of purgation of fleshly sin only by the hope of knowing God; one proceeds to a knowledge of God only by grace which comes from faith; and one's final knowledge of God is not really knowledge at all, but only love or charity', ibid., 63. On the differences between Colet and Ficino, cf. Leland Miles, *John Colet and the Platonic Tradition* (Illinois, 1961), chapter III, 'Colet's concept of Man', especially the summary, 86; 'Colet's psychology is thus seen to be an amalgamation of Pauline, Platonic and other influences. His concept of the soul as the origin of biological life, and his preference for the terms "soul" and "body" rather than the more characteristically Pauline "spirit" and "flesh" are undoubtedly the result of Platonic pressure. The presence of Plato, reinforced by Plotinus, is also evident in Colet's intermittent emphasis on the God-created body as evil—a heresy into which he might have been led by his usually infallible guide, Augustine. However Colet does manage to reject Ficino's Platonic heresy of the soul as the "real Man", and insists instead with Paul that the body is part of personality.'

as you do, but to every one else I am a moon; it is fortunate for me that you have this opinion of me, dear Colet, since it is obviously reflecting to you a much more beautiful Marsilio than the one whose image it is receiving.'[1]

Colet was a lecturer rather than a writer:

'For though elegant both by nature and training, and though he had at his command a singularly copious flow of words while speaking, yet when writing Colet would now and then trip in such points as critics are given to mark, and it was on that account, if I mistake not, that he refrained from writing books.'[2]

Erasmus comes to remind the reader that philosophy and homiletics are only a part of Christian humanism; and that even if the sage and severe inheritance of Plato and the Pseudo-Denys provides the thread of continuity, the *Moriae Encomium* and the laughing satire are equally characteristic. 'Without me', says Folly, 'the world cannot exist for a moment. For is not all that is done among mortals full of folly? Is it not performed by fools and for fools? No society, no cohabitation can be pleasant or lasting without folly; so much so that a people could not stand its prince, nor the master his man, nor the maid her mistress, nor the tutor his pupil, nor the friend his friend, nor the wife her husband for a moment longer, if they did not now and then come together, now flatter each other; now sensibly conniving at things, now smearing themselves with some honey of folly.'[3] And Folly's sister is self-love: and in that there is the vigour and courage of life, ambition and creativeness. These gifts have led lovers of Greece and Rome to make the great effort, as Erasmus did, of combining classicism with Christianity. The union of antiquity with the Christian spirit has not proved an impossible ideal.

---

[1] Jayne, 81.
[2] *Opus Epistolarum D. Erasmi*, ed. P. S. Allen, IV, 523.
[3] Passages cited by J. Huizinga, *Erasmus of Rotterdam* (London, 1952), 70.

XVI

J. R. HALE

THE EARLY DEVELOPMENT OF THE BASTION: AN ITALIAN CHRONOLOGY
C. 1450–C. 1534

The most significant of all architectural forms evolved during the Renaissance was the angle bastion. By resisting the new artillery and providing platforms for heavy guns it revolutionized the defensive-offensive pattern of warfare, and its speedy adoption by state after state during the sixteenth century dramatically affected the appearance of cities throughout Europe—and further afield: the application of the angle bastion to forts and town walls led to a homogeneity of style wherever Europeans settled overseas; from Havana and San Juan in the Caribbean to Mombasa and Mozambique in East Africa and on to Diu and Goa across the Indian Ocean, visitors saw the outlines that characterized townscapes from the Baltic to the north African coast. The international style *par excellence* of the Renaissance was that of military architecture, and its module was the angle bastion. It did not only extend in space, it endured in time. The next period of intensive development in the art of fortification, associated with the career of Vauban (1633–1707), elaborated and re-deployed the basic Renaissance forms, and on sites where attack from the heaviest forms of siege guns was not anticipated, fortifications continued to be built in the manner of the mid-sixteenth century. Neither the star forts built to guard the mouth of the Mississippi in the war of 1812 nor the walls of Fort McHenry as they appeared to the author of *The Star-Spangled Banner* would have appeared strange to

466

Antonio da San Gallo the younger, the Florentine architect who died in 1546.

Not surprisingly, there has been strong competition among architectural and military historians to establish what nation, or what individual, invented the most radically effective architectural element since the arch. This controversy, which was waged most strongly at the turn of the last century, has not yet provided a solution. It has been dogged by chauvinism and obscured by the unfamiliarity of its protagonists with monuments outside their own countries.[1] It has been diverted from methodical fieldwork by the romantic notion that a great breakthrough must be the work of a great man. It has been confirmed by vague terminology and a misunderstanding of the technical terms used by contemporary writers.[2] This essay does not offer a solution: that can only follow from a detailed comparative chronology of military architecture in France, Germany, Italy and the Iberian peninsula from the middle of the fifteenth to the middle of the sixteenth centuries.[3] There can be no doubt, however, that in the first generation of the sixteenth century it was the Italians who experimented most freely, and that it was they who, in the second generation, became the acknowledged leaders, and the most prolific exporters of the new bastioned fortification. A survey which charts the way in which they reached this position is, therefore, of special interest even if it cannot settle, absolutely, the question of precedence.

A glance at the historiography of the subject in Italy will show how necessary it is to take an extensive look at the

[1] Even the opposition of Viollet-le-Duc to the Italians' claims as innovators in the new fortification was not based on a knowledge of the relevant buildings. See his *Dictionnaire raisoné de l'architecture français du XIe au XVIe siècle* (1854–68), under *bastion* and *boulevard*. The same ignorance of fortifications south of the Alps led Cosseron de Villenoisy to claim in his *Essai historique sur la fortification* (Paris, 1869) that the systematized bastioned front was a development of the north, and of the second half of the sixteenth century. A. von Cohausen's assertion that 'der Ausgangspunkt der neueren Befestigungsweise Deutschland war' (*Die Befestigungsweisen der Vorzeit und des Mittelalters*, Wiesbaden, 1898, 331) led him to exaggerate the importance of certain sites (Menzberg, Neckarbischofsheim) in an attempt to combat Italian claims to priority.

[2] The word 'bastion' (*bastione*) first appears in Italian documents of the late fourteenth century and has been the source of much confusion. See P. Pieri in *Archivio Storico per le Provincie Napoletane* (1933), 154.

[3] The suggestion of Turkish precedence, raised from time to time since A. de Zastrow's *Histoire de la fortification permanente* (Paris, 1866, trans. E. de la Barre Duparcq) has been effectively rebutted by L. A. Maggiorotti, 'Le origini della fortificazione bastionata e la guerra d'Otranto', *Rivista d'Artiglieria e Genio* (1931), 93–110, and by Kevin Andrews, *Castles of the Morea* (Princeton, 1953), especially 231–2.

monuments themselves. Contemporary writers are not helpful. Machiavelli's scorn for Italian military prowess led him to ascribe innovations in the art of fortification to the example of the French invaders—though he does not mention bastions in this connexion—in a passage in the *Art of War* (1522) which was echoed almost verbatim in 1562 by the military engineer Girolamo Maggi.[1] The same contempt for his own countrymen led Guicciardini, in his *History of Italy* (written 1536–40) to make the easy conquests of the French the motive for changes in every aspect of warfare, including fortification, though he suggested that a glimpse of new methods was offered by the Turks when they dug themselves in after the Otranto raid of 1480. By the middle of the century writers were prepared to name the inventor of the angle bastion. To Gian Giacamo Leonardi (d. 1562) it was Alfonso I of Ferrara (1505–34),[2] to Vasari it was Michele Sanmicheli (d. 1558); 'before his time they were made of a circular form, by which the difficulty of defending them was much increased'.[3] All these statements can be proved wrong by buildings known to their authors.

Vasari's assertion was repeated in Scipione Maffei's influential *Verona Illustrata* (vol. 3, 1732) and was not seriously challenged until the publication in 1841 of an edition of Francesco di Giorgio's treatise on civil and military architecture.[4] In a series of appendices Carlo Promis made the first critical investigation into the origin of the new fortification. He dismissed the claims of the Turks to be innovators, he destroyed the legend that bastions had been invented in the Hussite wars and subsequently introduced into north Italy by Bohemian engineers; by pointing to works at Florence, Urbino, Bari, Pisa and the island of Rhodes he showed that Sanmicheli could not have been the inventor of the angle bastion, and he began the tradition which gave this distinction to Francesco di Giorgio, who died in 1502. This thesis was taken up and discussed in a brisk but inconclusive manner in technical military journals in France, Germany and Italy, but it was not until 1880 that there

[1] Machiavelli, *Arte della Guerra*, ed. Sergio Bertelli (Milan, 1961), 498–9; Maggi, *De gli ingegni militare*, MS. Biblioteca Nazionale Fiorentina (subsequently referred to as B.N.F.), Palat. 464, 326.
[2] *Trattato delle fortification di nostri tempi*, MS. in Oliveriana Library, Pesaro, no. 220, quoted by L. Serra, 'Architettura militare del Rinascimento nelle Marche', *Rassegna Marchigiana* (1933), 455.
[3] *Vite*, ed. G. Milanesi, 9 vols., (Florence, 1878–85) vi, 353.
[4] *Trattato di architettura civile e militare*, ed. Cesare Saluzzo (Turin, 1841).

was a serious attempt to tackle the subject afresh. In that year, the Dominican father Alberto Guglielmotti produced a history of late fifteenth and sixteenth-century fortification in the present province of Lazio.[1] The first attempt to apply scientific archaeological standards to military works of the Renaissance, his studies of the structure and building history of such forts as the *rocca* at Ostia Antica, Castel S Angelo, and the forts at Civitacastellana, Nettuno and Civitavecchia are still of value, but in a preliminary discussion he made Tàccola (Mariano di Jacopo, d.1458) the inventor of the angle bastion, and used a medal of Pope Calixtus III (1455–8) to show that it was already thought of as an element in a symmetrical-bastioned front. These early dates were greeted with incredulity: the medal was pronounced a forgery, and it was shown that what he had taken to be bastions in the Marciana (Venice) MS. were the attempts of Tàccola to represent juts in the sea-coast on which he drew his quite conventional forts.[2] Since then the claims of other artists and architectural theorists to be the crucial innovators have been put forward, among them Brunelleschi,[3] Filarete, Leonardo da Vinci, Fra Giocondo and Michelangelo. None is convincing, because none has been discussed against the background of the fortifications already in existence when each claimant expressed his ideas.[4] The art historian has not been tempted to do fieldwork, and the architectural historian has not helped him by attempting a study which would perforce include many buildings which cannot be attributed to a great name.[5] These claims are looked at in the chronological study which forms the centre of this essay.

It would be disingenuous not to point out the limitations on the accuracy of such a survey, quite apart from my own errors

[1] *Storia delle fortificazioni nella Spiaggia Romana* (Rome, 1880).

[2] General Schröder, 'Martini e la fronte bastionata', *Archiv für die Artillerie-und-Ingenieur-Offiziere des deutschen Reichsheeres* (August and September, 1891) and E. Rocchi, *Le origini della fortificazione moderna* (Rome, 1894), 3–4, 17–45.

[3] For literature, see below. I do not discuss the claims of Brunelleschi, the latest contender, as the case urged by Pierco Sanpaolesi [*Brunelleschi* (Milan, 1962), 100] is based on one section of the wall of Pisa, the building history of which is not entirely clear.

[4] Ignazio Calvi makes such an attempt in the introductory chapter to his *L'architettura militare di Leonardo da Vinci* (Milan, 1943) but it is neither full nor accurate enough to be convincing.

[5] The last attempt to write a general account of gunpowder fortifications was E. Rocchi, *Le fonti storiche dell'architettura militare* (Rome, 1908). In spite of confused arrangement, and a grave shortage of references, it remains the best introduction to the subject.

of judgment and knowledge. Many forts and town walls of the transition period (*c.* 1450–*c.* 1530) have been destroyed or altered beyond recognition. Fortifications were often built over a period of years and though the ground plan may still reflect the ideas of their planners, important details, especially gunports, parapets and platforms may represent an important divergence from them; such details are, besides, vulnerable to decay and later modification. Details of many forts, especially the angle where the flank of a bastion joins the curtain, are choked with vegetation and cannot be properly seen. Gun chambers and internal passages are frequently blocked by internal collapse, refuse or rebuilding. Among vanished monuments are field fortifications of earth, a medium in which experiment could be especially free. Documentary evidence for the fifteenth century is extremely sparse. Drawings become more copious as the sixteenth century advances, partly because of an increased emphasis on the accurate relationship of the various components of a fort or town wall, partly because of the growing prestige of military architects and the interest in their plans as works of art. Even by the middle of the sixteenth century, however, it is seldom easy to say (where the monument does not exist) whether a plan represents the building itself or a project for it. Very few plans are dated. Models were constantly used, but in contrast with the many models of secular buildings which remain from this period, I know of none of a fort. This may be due to the hazards of travelling to and fro between the architect, the agency responsible for the commission and the masons on the site, it may be due to a lack of interest in military architecture among later collectors, or it may be the result of a desire for secrecy, a reason, possibly, for the destruction of plans as well. Written descriptions are rare. Usually a government record will say 'as in the plan', or 'according to the model' or 'as the architect himself will explain'. This possibly reflects the lack among officials of a technical vocabulary adequate to describe increasingly complex works.

Non-technical drawings, paintings and engravings are all suspect. Artists thought of forts in terms of symbols—like a city in the hand of a patron saint, or the generalized town view in a chronicle chapter heading—and there was a considerable time-lag before a new style of building was generalized into a new type of symbol. Medals were struck to commemorate the building of an important work, but, as with plans, they can be used only with great caution. They may be accurate but represent a plan subsequently changed. They may be symbolic rather than descriptive.[1] These hazards, and the shortage of detailed monographs on individual buildings must blur our vision. Such lacunae led an early student of the subject to give up the search for the origin of the bastion in despair.[2]

Radical changes in fortification only take place when there is a radical change in offensive weapons. It was long thought that the amazement expressed by such writers as Guicciardini and the explosives expert and gun-founder Vanuccio Biringuccio[3] at the superior weapons of the French meant that changes in military architecture must be looked for, first and foremost, in France. It has been shown, however, that, granted the general superiority of French artillery, especially field artillery, Italian siege guns developed steadily from their first recorded employment in the thirteenth century, and that with the increasing use of iron balls in the fifteenth their power was amply sufficient to stimulate innovations in defence. In Italy, moreover, conditions were especially favourable to experiment. The peninsula was divided into many independent and mutually hostile territories. There were many frontiers to defend; recent conquests needed the manacle of a fort, insecure princes needed citadels in which they would be safe from a revolt of their own people. Enterprise was not fettered by a uniform system of licences for castle building. Even after the Peace of Lodi in 1454 there were enough pin-prick wars, especially in central Italy, in the Romagna, the Marche and the heartlands of the papal states, to necessitate a constant vigilance; overseas, and not far overseas, was the growing menace of the Turks. Nowhere else in Europe, moreover, was

[1] On the custom of placing special medals under the foundation stones of fortresses in this period, see R. Weiss, Un umanista veneziano, Papa Paolo II (Venice, 1958), chap. 4. Good examples of misleading medals are the two struck to celebrate the connection of Sixtus IV and of Giuliano della Rovere (later Pope Julius II) with the fortress of Ostia. In both instances the fort is made to look more traditional than it was. P. Verdier, 'La Rocca d'Ostia dans l'architecture militaire du Quattrocento'. Mélanges d'archéologie et d'histoire (1939), 303. They are reproduced in R. Weiss, The Medals of Sixtus IV (Rome, 1961), figs. 37–9.

[2] Luigi Marini, Saggio istorico ed algebraico su i bastioni (Rome, 1801). He comes to the same conclusion in the second dissertation in his valuable edition of the Della architettura militare of Francesco de Marchi, 2 vols., (Rome, 1810) i, 7.

[3] De la pirotechnia (Venice, 1540). This exaggeration of French superiority was challenged by Rocchi (Origini . . ., 83 ff.) and by P. Pieri, Il Rinascimento e la crisi militare italiana (Milan, 1952), sections ii and iii of part two.

the prestige of the architect so high or so articulate, and the military engineer was not yet isolated from the kudos attached to the liberal arts. Alberti pointed out in the middle of the fifteenth century that 'if you were to examine into the expeditions that have been undertaken, you would go near to find that most of the victories were gained more by the art and the skill of the architects than by the conduct or fortune of the generals; and that the enemy was oftener overcome and conquered by the architect's wit without the captain's arms, than by the captain's arms without the architect's wit'.[1] Castiglione commended drawing to the courtier not only as a thing excellent in itself but of the greatest use in planning military operations and designing fortifications.[2] According to Francesco de Hollanda, Michelangelo celebrated the artist's role in war 'especially in designing the form and proportions of citadel and defensive work, and of bastions, ditches, mines, counter-mines, trenches, gun-ports, blockhouses', etc.[3] The close connexion between the arts and fortification hardly needs emphasizing. To restrict ourselves to Florentines: according to Vasari, Arnolfo was not only the designer of the Florentine cathedral and of S Maria Novella but of the city walls; he said that some held the impregnable fortress of the Giusta at S Frediano at Lucca to be the work of Giotto; Brunelleschi designed fortifications at Pisa, Pesaro and elsewhere; Leonardo inspected forts for Cesare Borgia; Michelangelo was put in charge of the fortifications of Florence during the great imperialist siege of 1529–30, and when Cosimo I wished to strengthen the city's fortifications still further he distributed the works among a number of artists, including Benvenuto Cellini.[4] Michelangelo's fame in the liberal arts was mentioned in his appointment as one of the reasons for putting him in charge of the fortifications, but it is from an unfavourable comment on his defences that we have the first hint of an opinion that fortification was, in part at least, a job for soldiers.[5]

---

[1] Preface, *Ten Books on Architecture*, trans. J. Leoni (London, 1955), x.

[2] *Il libro del Cortegiano*, ed. V. Cian (Florence, 1947), 123.

[3] *Da pintura antiga*, ed. E. Radius (Milan, n.d.), 97.

[4] In his *Autobiography* Cellini says that *c.* 1544 he was also asked by Francis I to advise him how to fortify Paris.

[5] The terms of his appointment are quoted in Paola Barocchi's edition of Vasari's life of Michelangelo, 5 vols., (Milan, 1962) iii, 915. On 918 she quotes from the *Breve istorietta dell'assedio di Firenza*: 'E 'perchè l'uffizio del buono architettore è di levar ben la pianta e formare il modelo de' ripari secondo la natura del

During the transition period not only was there no distinction between 'art' and military engineering, but the mathematical interests of art theorists were particularly suited to the development of a type of fortification based on geometrical principles. The cult of harmony, proportion and symmetry among artists fitted the need for precisely angled fire and regular, coherent planning, and if the age produced plans which show more concern for ideal geometrical forms than military practicability, this interest, which was shared by humanist princes, helped the integration of the angle bastion within an ordered system of defence.[1] Such an interest in the new fortification—which, from its dependence on aesthetic theory, its connexion with town planning and its interest in the writings of the ancients, can be called 'humanist' with as much justification as the ecclesiastical architecture of the period—was not restricted to such princes as Sigismondo Malatesta, Lorenzo de' Medici, Federigo di Montefeltro or Francesco Maria della Rovere, it was common to the educated classes, not excluding the clergy: Roberto Valturio was a papal abbreviator, the fortifications of Padua and Treviso were re-cast by the Dominican Fra Giovanni Giocondo. And if the political state of Italy led to an amount of building and remodelling that cannot be matched elsewhere, the movement of innovating military architects up and down the peninsula meant that, with varying degrees of success, their ideas were presented to more conservative administrations and that they learned from one another's work. In 1487 Giuliano and Antonio da San Gallo the elder, who had recently been in the papal states tried, vainly, to persuade the Florentine government not to proceed with the traditional fortress they were building at Sarzana.[2] Francesco di Giorgio, Giuliano da Maiana, Giuliano da San Gallo, Fra Giocondo, Benedetto da Maiano and Antonio Marchesi da Settignano were all in Naples at some period between 1485 and 1495. Francesco di Giorgio met Leonardo in

---

luogo; questo, come di tutti li altri valentissimo, mirabilmente fece. Mail cognoscer da che banda possin esser i ripari offesi, o come difesi, e che effetto fachino in quelli i fianchi e le cannoniere, non uffizio è d'architettore, ma di pratico, valente e buon soldato, che delle fortezza sia stato non solamente speculatore, ma difensore'.

[1] The relationship between geometry and fortifications is discussed in J. R. Hale, 'Some military title pages of the Renaissance', *The Newberry Library Bulletin* (1964), 91–102.

[2] Rocchi, *Fonti* . . ., 136–7.

Milan and Pavia, a fact which complicates attempts to determine the priority of their ideas. Francesco also knew Fra
Giocondo and Baccio Pontelli, who designed fortifications
across central Italy from Ostia to Recanati and Loreto.
Architects who had worked for different states met in conference, as at Civitavecchia in 1515 or were sent on tours of
inspection, as when Antonio da San Gallo the younger,
Michele Sanmicheli and Pierfrancesco Fiorenzuoli da Viterbo
went round the Romagna in 1526 for Clement VII.[1]

Before looking at individual buildings it might be helpful to
state the principle ways in which guns affected the art of
fortification. The thickness of medieval walls was determined
by their height and the need to provide a walk from which
marksmen could shoot, protected by crenellations. The main
danger the defenders faced was at the moment of assault, and
towers, taller than the walls, and unscaleable, were built at
intervals so that attacking parties armed with rams or ladders
could be shot at from the flanks. Walls were machicolated so
that such parties could also be subjected to a curtain of missiles
dropped vertically on their heads. The slung fire of siege
engines was not so accurate that they could land repeated blows
on the same place: their main role, like the mortars which
succeeded them (some of the earliest guns which have survived
are of this form) was to harass the inhabitants, particularly by
hurling incendiary materials over the wall. Neither the ram nor
the mine affected the thickness or height of the wall: this was
determined by the need to prevent scaling and maintain an
effective vertical defence from the machicolation. The gun
provided for the first time a hard-hitting long-range horizontal
blow and by the fifteenth century a reasonably accurate one.
To counter this, walls were made thicker (not necessarily lower,
where time and money allowed) and were scarped, sometimes
very emphatically, on the outside for some two-thirds of their
heights; in this way it was hoped to deflect some of the impact
of the cannon balls. Scarping was accepted the more readily

[1] Their report was printed by L. Beltrami, *Relazione sullo stato delle rocche di
Romagna* . . . (Nozze Emanuele Greppi, Bice Belgioioso, n.p., 1902). It deals with
Imola, Faenza, Forlì, Cesena, Rimini, Cervia and Ravenna. Except for Cesena,
where a more thorough modernization is recommended—lowering of walls,
addition of bastions of some sort (neither text nor drawing is very clear on this
point)—the report is mainly concerned with strengthening the existing works
and clearing ditches. Interesting as it is, this rare work throws no light on contemporary ideas.

because it weakened siege ladders by increasing the angle at which they were set to the wall.[1] Strong scarping was a first reaction, and is rarely found after the fifteenth century, but it had the effect of so seriously reducing the effectiveness of vertical fire that there was little point in having machicolation: in compensation, greater attention was paid to flanking fire.

The importance of flanking fire from towers had always been recognized, and at first the reaction to gunpowder was to build gun towers on the model of the old round or pentagonal towers but thicker, and provided with key-hole or letter-box-shaped loops for hand guns or small cannon instead of arrow slits; for the gun, from the point of view of defence, was first seen as a weapon to be used against assault parties rather than as a long-range deterrent. Gradually, however, it was realized that guns could be used to break up the besiegers' concentrations and dismount their artillery. Heavy guns were no use inside towers: they made too much smoke and their arc of fire was too restricted by loops in immensely thick masonry, so they were placed on platforms on top of the towers. From this moment we are in sight of the bastion, which is not a gun tower but a solid platform thrust forward to obtain as wide a field of fire as possible while retaining the tower's role of providing flank cover to the adjacent parts of a fortification.[2] The tower was basically a defensive, the bastion an aggressive form. When the tower became a platform it had to be still more massive, and for reasons of cost, as well as the convenience of running guns from one platform to another along the wall walks, was dropped to the level of the wall. An object of fortification became to present as few projections to be knocked off as possible: crenellations were replaced by pierced parapets, bastions and walls were designed to present an even silhouette. A scraped platform which had to bear the weight of heavy guns at its edge had no place for machicolation: this absence of vertical defence meant that methodically devised flanking fire now became the only protection against assault. This problem, and the masking of flank batteries (*traditori*—traitors, the Italians called them) from fire from the field became a major point of discussion among early sixteenth-century engineers.

[1] A point made by Alberti and Francesco di Giorgio.
[2] Reluctance to make this distinction has led many a searcher for the origin of the bastion on a wild goose chase back into the fourteenth century.

The bastion developed from the tower,[1] and existing towers suggested two favourable shapes: round or pointed-pentagonal. Medieval Italy provided examples of both in plenty, and the first bastions were built in both forms. The round was probably easier to build (it needed less squared masonry), it provided some deflection to a ball at every point, and it had no vulnerable sharp points; on the other hand it left dead ground at its head which could not be covered by flanking fire, and with the absence of vertical protection from machicolation together with the use of gunpowder in mining, the danger of dead ground became so great that the angle bastion gradually became the norm.[2] Like the exaggeratedly scarped wall, the round bastion taught a useful lesson before it lost favour. Where a scarped round bastion met such a wall a withdrawn flank was created. This evidently suggested the location of the concealed battery. A high proportion of angle bastions were built in the sixteenth century with round protective shoulders, though the future lay with batteries cut back in a straight flank at its meeting with the wall.

A traditional feature which lingered on in transitional fortresses was the *mastio* or keep. Too high to be an effective gun platform it was retained on grounds of prestige, to provide suitably splendid apartments for the prince or castellan, and as a place of refuge. Political instability within a state led to an emphasis on points of retreat within the walls, a preoccupation which reached an extreme in the labyrinthine fantasies of Filarete and Leonardo.[3] Mature gunpowder fortifications laid

[1] The most direct link between the two were the massive corner towers of fortresses which, though at the same level as the walls, were taller than normal bastions in order to retain the prestige and beauty which was considered due to a lofty princely residence. I use the term tower bastion for this short-lived type. As an example see plate 9.

[2] This involved a breach with the advice of the ancients. One school of thought tried to believe, by an optimistic reading of ancient siege tactics, that the Greeks and Romans had known about gunpowder, an attitude sardonically rebutted by Francesco di Giorgio: why don't we find traces of gun loops in these walls, he asks; why did they go on using catapults? (*Trattato* ed. cit., 249). Defending the angle bastion, an anonymous writer of the mid-sixteenth century comments: 'Si come adunque sappiamo, che gli antichi hanno fuggiti gli angoli, ancor che in molte altre cose errassero: cosi noi non potrendo fuggirli per nō lasciar alcuno spatio del recinto indifeso . . .', *Discorsi delle fortificationi*, MS. B.N.F., XIX, 2, fol. 7.

[3] Machiavelli, in the *Art of War* (ed. cit., 496), points out the bad effect on morale of having a place to which to retreat. Sanmicheli made the same point when the Venetians were contemplating building a citadel in Padua in 1544 and asked his advice: 'a mio giuditio è una mala cosa quando quelli che stanno a guardia di una città habbiano speranza de potersi ritirar in uno castello'. C. Semenzato in *Michele Sanmicheli 1484-1559. Studi raccolti dall'accademia di agricoltura scienze e lettere di Verona* (Verona, 1960), 87.

all their emphasis on the *enceinte*, treating it as a continuous gun platform. This function was recognized by the Spanish military engineer Pedro Navarro, when he inspected the walls of Florence with Machiavelli in 1526. 'A city can expect to have more guns than an army can carry with it; whenever you can present more guns to the enemy than he can range against you, it is impossible for him to defeat you.'[1] This is the concept that underlay the changes planned for these walls in the following years by Michelangelo. It was the concept that changed a fort from an inert defensive object to an attacking agent reaching far out against an enemy by means of mutually supporting outworks, the half-moons, crown-works, horn-works and the rest so beloved of Sterne's Uncle Toby.

The theory and practice of gunpowder fortification in the middle of the sixteenth century can be explained by a group of buildings in the Romagna and Marche, and the writings of Leon Battista Alberti and Filarete. In his *De re aedificatoria* (written between 1440 and 1450), Alberti makes no reference to the special nature of guns, as opposed to earlier siege engines, but he emphasizes the superiority of flanking fire to vertical defence, he recommends strong scarping and that 'those parts which are exposed to battery should be made semi-circular, or rather with a sharp angle like the head of a ship'. He also mentions the advantage of having triangular projections from the wall and adds that 'some think no wall is so safe against battery as those which are built in uneven lines, like the teeth of a saw'. He is entirely concerned with defensive strength. There is no suggestion that large guns can be used by the defenders to attack. He is primarily interested in fortifications as giving protection to a city, and, within the city, to the prince: they are necessary to preserve the urban scene, the physical environment of civic life which fascinates him, and he was not moved to rethink them in a way which would take serious account of the new weapon. The same is true of Filarete's *Trattato di architettura* (written *c.* 1460). Like Alberti he is more preoccupied by the ideas of classical writers than by the developments in fire power and their consequences in his own day, and though he provides for gun-loops in the towers and walls of his ideal city—the towers were to be considerably higher than the walls—and

---

[1] Quoted by Machiavelli in his 'Relazione di una visita fatta per fortificare Firenze', printed in Bartelli, ed. cit., 297.

points out that walls now have to be thicker than formerly, his concern with fortifications is to contrive a dignified and solid cladding to the urban environment and the labyrinth-guarded citadel which are the main subject of his treatise. He has been regarded as an innovator because Sforzinda was planned in the form of an eight-point star (Alberti had suggested that a star might be a good shape for a fortress) and because the city's main gate was to be defended by a triangular ravelin, but there is no suggestion that either of these ideas was connected with artillery, offensive or defensive.[1]

In contrast to this basic indifference to the new problems of defence, we have a document[2] which shows the town of Foligno's plans for rebuilding its walls in 1441, after they had been severely damaged by the artillery fire of Cardinal Vitelleschi's siege train in 1439. Among the measures proposed were: scarping of curtain walls; angled scarping on the outer face of round towers; the building of new tower bastions (*torrono*) of angle (*a spigolo*) form, presumably pentagonal, projecting well forward from the walls; pointed ravelins; a *glacis* sloping away from the town 'so that it can all be commanded by anyone standing on the battlements (*merli*)'; on either side of one angle ravelin, gun-loops were to be cut in the curtain wall to cover (*che rade*) its faces.

Drastic rebuilding in Foligno has left no trace of these works, if they were ever carried out. But some of them can be illustrated from analogous works which still survive. The tower bastions must have looked like those at Corinaldo (plate 1) and Morro d'Alba (plate 2). Similar towers and strongly scarped walls can be seen at Ostra and S Arcangelo di Roma (*c.* 1447). The ravelins were probably similar to the one at Corinaldo (plate 3), which is mentioned in an inventory of *c.* 1455.[3] The word *rivellino* or *revellino* does not necessarily refer (as it came to in the sixteenth century) to a small outwork standing at some distance from the wall; it was used to describe works which could be round (like the other ravelin at Corinaldo) or square

[1] Parts of Filarete's treatise have been printed (from the B.N.F. MS., Palat. 372, by W. von Oettingen, *Antonio Averlino Filaretes Tractat ueber die Baukunst* (Vienna) 1890), but the reader should be warned that the editor's interpretive drawings sometimes read progressive points into the text which are not there.

[2] Printed by A. Angelucci in 'Spigolature militare dell'archivio communale di Foligno', *Archivio Storico per le Marche e per l'Umbria* (1886), pp. 477–9.

[3] Printed in the same journal in the same year, 126, by D. Gaspari, 'Fortezze marchigiane e umbre del secolo XV'.

(as at Castel d'Emilio or Certaldo) or, as in this case, presenting an angled face to the field.[1] The importance of the ravelin in the development of the bastion is that it was never conceived as a tower, and its position beside a gate, where the main rush of an assault might be expected, helped its builders to see it in terms of breaking up the attack at a distance as well as harassing it with flanking fire at the gate itself. By the 1360s the tower bastion is in some instances beginning to look like the mature angle bastion. Matteo Nuti's polygonal work in the town wall (1464–9) at Fano, though it has no flanks to speak of, serves the function of a platform (plate 4), and when he placed a tower bastion beside the gate at Cesena[2] (plate 5) in *c.* 1466 it took on an added purposefulness from its ravelin-like position.[3]

The progress towards the angle bastion made between the 1440s and 1460s was restricted in area and carried out, for the most part, in obscure hill towns. It was halted for a while by the adoption of round forms in a series of splendid and conspicuous palace-fortresses: in Naples (Castel Nuovo, 1443–58), near Rome (Tivoli, 1458–64 and Bracciano, 1470–85), in Tuscany (Volterra, from 1472), and in the Romagna itself in a succession of square strongholds with round tower bastions at the corners: Forlimpopoli (1471–80), Imola (1472–3), Pesaro (1474–1505), Senigallia (*c.* 1480) and Forlì (1481–3). In general these buildings are conservative, relying on mass, and accepting large areas of dead ground at the faces of their tower bastions. Gunports are few and small, providing inadequate flanking fire; considerable importance still attaches to vertical defence. Tower bastions and walls are level, and the tops of all the tower bastions provide solid platforms, but their parapet

[1] Though no documents have been produced to date the fortifications of Morro d'Alba, Ostra, and Castel d'Emilio, are so similar in style and detail (especially the round brick gun-loops) that they must belong to the mid-century programme of Corinaldo. The ravelin at Certaldo is probably rather later. It, too, is undocumented.

[2] On Cesena, see F. Mancini and W. Vichi, *Castelli, rocche e torri di Romagna* (Bologna, 1959), 221.

[3] It is tempting to follow the dating of L. Serra which puts the three square corner bastions of the *rocca* at Fano at 1452, and as Nuti's work. All are level with the curtain walls and the faces of the south-eastern one are considerably longer than the flanks, but the evidence for their date is too slight to establish the *rocca* as a remarkable anticipation of the form the mature angle bastion was to take. Detailed work on this fortress, which is at present used, as are so many of its kind as a prison, is of prime importance in charting the development of fortification in this area. 'Architettura militare del Rinascimento nelle Marche', *Rassegna Marchigiana* (1934), 1–2 and *L'Arte nelle Marche. Il periodo del Rinascimento*, (Rome, 1934), 116–17 and (town wall), 107.

embrasures remain too small for the use of heavy guns. They were the last great fortified residences, paying lip-service to the existence of guns, but relying in the main on their magnificent burliness.[1] It is in the Romagna, once again, that progress is most noticeable, with the girth of the tower bastion swelling at the expense of its height, from its slim form at Forlimpopoli (plate 6) to the thicker form at Imola (plate 7) and to the most magnificent round tower bastions of all, at Senigallia (plate 8).[2] Scarcely less important in emphasizing the role of the bastion as a routine element in gunpowder fortification, were the new walls surrounding the town of Colle Val d'Elsa (1479), the abbey of Grottaferrata (1484), the castle at Nepi (c. 1484) and the town wall of Bracciano, which, though undocumented, is closely analogous to the wall at Nepi.[3] The moderate height of the town wall at Colle enabled the tower bastions flanking the Volterra gate[4] to be low in relation to their girth, so that the tower element almost disappears. When Baccio Pontelli (possibly the architect of Senigallia) surrounded the abbey of Grottaferrata with a low wall and round corner bastions at the same level, only their bracketed and vulnerable battlements suggest that he was thinking in terms of a shrunken tower, rather than of a straightforward gun platform. The bastions in

[1] When building operations were recommenced on the Castel Nuovo after the earthquake of 1456, a low terrace, a sort of shrunken outer ward, was built out from its base which could serve as a continuous platform for artillery, but the state of the parapet today makes it impossible to judge whether it was in fact used for anything other than small arms fire. See R. Filangieri, *Castel Nuovo Reggia Angoina ed Aragonese di Napoli* (Naples, 1934), 51–72. Similar action was taken at Gaeta. The tower bastions of the fortified residence were too high to permit of accurate fire from their platforms and the establishment of a gun terrace was a logical compensation for this. A terraced outer ward with round bastions at the same level extends in front of the Orsini castle of Bracciano as well.

[2] On these *rocche*, see Serra, opera cit. and Mancini, op. cit. The *rocca* at Pesaro was the work of Luciano Laurana, architect of the ducal palace of Urbino. Its form is similar to the others, but its state of preservation (including much restoration) worse. The corner tower bastions at Forlì are more tower-like and are above the level of the curtain.

[3] This *enceinte* was designed by Antonio da San Gallo the elder, according to G. Giovannoni, *Antonio da Sangallo il Giovane*, 2 vols., (Rome, 1959) i, 343. It surrounds an ordinary high-towered mid-fifteenth century castle, and was in turn protected by a massive angle-bastioned front designed in 1540 by Antonio da San Gallo the younger. These three layers of fortification give Nepi a special interest which has not yet been properly investigated. Cf. G. Silvestrelli, *Città castelli e terre della regione romana*, 2 vols., (Rome, 1940) ii, 559. The town wall at Bracciano likewise lacks a historian, but see L. Borsari, *Il castello di Bracciano* (Roma, 1895).

[4] All that remains, apart from a circular detached blockhouse with two tiers of letter-box gun slits outside the wall on the earth. Giuliano da San Gallo was concerned with the works at Colle, along with Francione and others. G. Marchini, *Giuliano da Sangallo* (Florence, 1942), 83.

1 Corinaldo, tower in town wall

2 Morro d'Alba, tower in town wall

3 Corinaldo, gate in town wall

4 Fano, Nuti's bastion in town wall

5 Cesena, tower bastion in *enceinte* of the
Rocca Malatestiana

6 Forlimpopoli, Rocca

7 Imola, Rocca

8 Senigallia, Rocca

9 Nepi, *enceinte* of Rocca

10 Sarzana, Rocca

11 Ostia Antica, Castello

12 Ostia Antica, Castello

13 Offida, town wall

14 Brolio

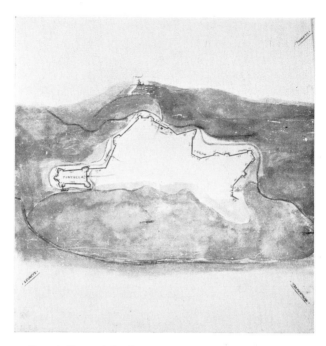

15 Poggio Imperiale, from Francesco de Marchi, *Trattato d'architettura militare*, Florence, Biblioteca Nazionale, 11.1.280, f. 19ʳ

16 Poggio Imperiale, Rocca

17 Poggio Imperiale, Rocca

18 Poggio Imperiale, town wall

19 Rome, Castel S. Angelo

20 Civita Castellana, Rocca

21 Sarzanello

22 Sarzanello

23 San Leo, Rocca

24 Sassocorvaro, Rocca

25 Sassocorvaro, Rocca

26 Cagli, Francesco di Giorgio's tower

27 Mondavio, Rocca

28 Mondavio, Rocca

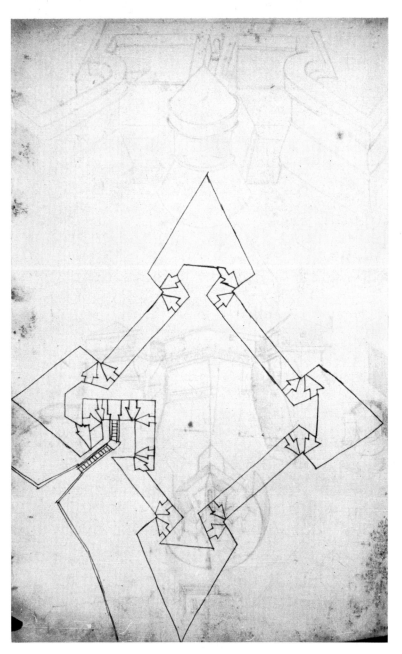

29 Francesco di Giorgio, fortress plan, ms. cit. f. 240^v

30 San Sepolcro, Rocca

31 Nettuno, Rocca

32 Arezzo, Fortezza Medicea

33 Civitavecchia, Rocca

34 Civitavecchia, Rocca

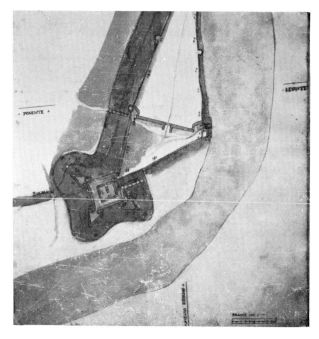

35 Pisa, Francesco de Marchi, ms. cit. f. 8ʳ

36 Livorno, Fortezza Vecchia

37 L'Aquila, Castello

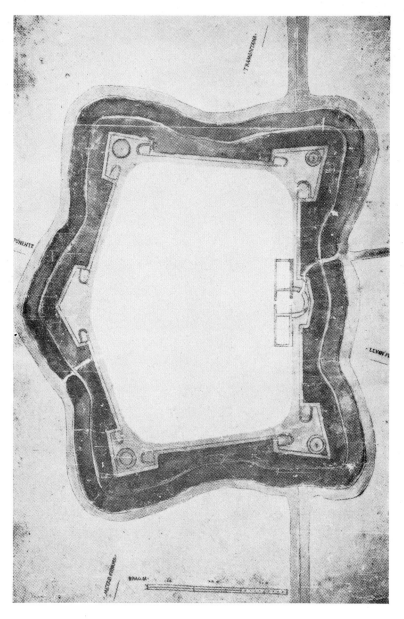

38 Florence, Fortezza da Basso, Francesco de Marchi,
ms. cit. f. 3ʳ

39 Urbino, town wall

40 Loreto, town wall

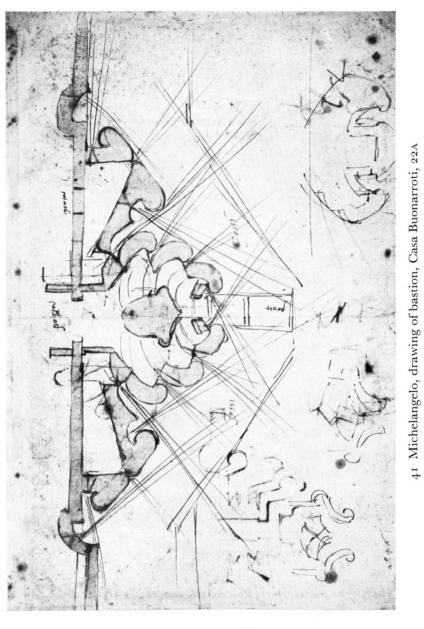

41 Michelangelo, drawing of bastion, Casa Buonarroti, 22A

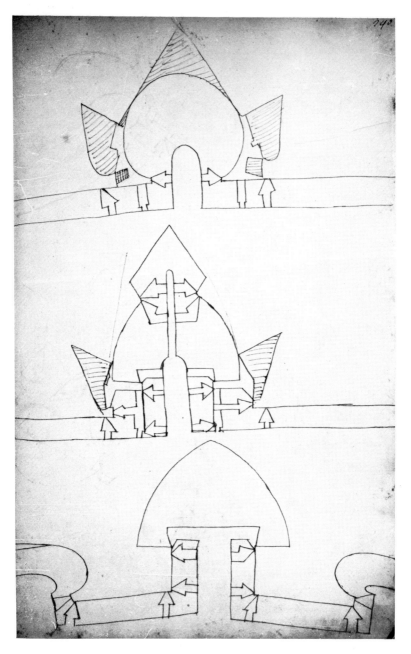

42 Francesco di Giorgio, drawings of bastions, ms. cit.
f. 140^r

the castle *enceinte* at Nepi (plate 9) look more businesslike and though their state of preservation makes it impossible to be sure of this, they were probably thought of as platforms for guns of some weight, as were those of Bracciano, where bastions of a similar shape and size have two tiers of letter-box slits in the flanks, giving a wider traverse than was possible for the round loops at Nepi.

In the evolution of the bastion, the most crucial period was the decade preceding the French invasion of September 1494. In this period a few fortifications mark time: the massive fort of Sarzana,[1] begun by the Florentines in 1487, though its loop-holes provide four tiers of flanking fire, still relies on vertical defence from machicolations: the stone cannon balls embedded in its walls as a decoration come from guns larger than any it could fire itself (plate 10); the similar but slighter Orsini castle at Avezzano (1490) has tower bastions that rise well above the curtain walls. But by the time the French arrive the decision of military architects has been made to reduce the 'tower' aspect of the tower bastion still further, to augment its fire-power, to rationalize the support given by one bastion to another, and to make increasing use of the angled shape.

The *rocca* at Ostia Antica was built between 1482–6. Triangular in form, it has two great drum bastions and a pentagonal one, all level with the curtains (plates 11 and 12). In some ways this fortress, too, marks time, with its keyhole loops, its bracketed machicolation, its tall central watch-tower and its fragile battlements (the massive parapet on the pen-tagonal bastion is due to restoration), but for the first time the flanking fire is well rationalized so that no surface, apart from the heads of the round bastions, is left uncovered; there are embrasures for large guns near the bottom of the outer faces of the pentagonal bastion; the lower gun chambers are connected by a passage running in the thickness of the wall, the lengths of which can be enfiladed from screens pierced with gun-loops in case an enemy should break in. The work of Baccio Pontelli, Ostia is the only transition fort to have received detailed modern attention, and for its beauty as well as its science, it well deserves it.[2] In his works of the late 'eighties, at Osimo and Offida

---

[1] E. Rocchi, 'La citadella di Sarzana ed il forte di Sarzanello', *Rivista d'Arti-glieria e Genio*, (1904) ii, 137–54. Reliable only for Sarzana. Idem., *Fonti* . . ., 136–7.

[2] Verdier, op. cit.

(plate 13) Pontelli gave up round forms and reverted to more tower-like, lightly defended bastions.

If Ostia was the most advanced fortress of its time, the most advanced *enceinte* was certainly that of Brolio,[1] the castle which controlled the approaches to Tuscany from Siena. Ruined in the war with Naples and the papacy in 1478–9, the castle's *enceinte* was completely rebuilt by the Florentines from 1484. At each of the five corners is a square bastion (plate 14). Not all are symmetrical. The four tiers of small keyholes below the cordon in the flanks of most of them are suitable only for small-arms, and the restricted fields of fire are not arranged to provide an accurate coverage of the adjacent curtains or bastion faces, but here is a bastioned front that would be recognizable as such to the engineers of Peschiera, perhaps the most superbly accomplished *enceinte* of the mid-sixteenth century.

Even more instantly recognizable would have been the defences of Poggio Imperiale, commanding another of the valley approaches into Tuscany from Siena. It was the first site in Italy—and no contender has been advanced from elsewhere —to combine a bastioned fortress with a bastioned town wall; planned in 1487, it never attracted settlement from nearby Poggibonsi and remains incomplete, as can be seen from Francesco de Marchi's mid-sixteenth century plan (plate 15). Little is known about its building history;[2] in spite of its unique importance it has been ignored by students of fortification. The works there are mentioned in a document of 1488 with Giuliano da San Gallo as the architect in charge. Another shows them going forward in 1490, a third names Antonio da San Gallo the elder as their superintendent in 1495. Further work is mentioned in 1511, and it is likely that some reconstruction was carried out by Cosimo I during the Sienese war of 1552–7. There seems little reason to doubt that what can be seen today represents the plan devised by Giuliano for Lorenzo the Magnificent, who is known to have supported his criticism of the Sarzana fortifications. There are no inscriptions, but the sculptured emblems of

[1] A. Casabianca, *Le mura di Brolio in Chianti* (Siena, 1900), with plan. The plan in B. Ebhardt, *Die Burgen Italiens*, 6 vols. (Berlin, 1910–27), fig. 434, is misleadingly symmetrical. It is a failing, indeed, of several of his plans. Other relevant plans in Ebhardt are: S Leo (fig. 18), Cesena (fig. 60), Sarzanello (fig. 108), Senigallia (figs. 411–13), Bracciano (figs. 445–50).

[2] E. Repetti, *Dizionario geografico fisico storico della Toscana*, 6 vols. (Florence, 1834–46) *sub*. Poggio Imperiale. It is mentioned briefly in Marchini, op. cit., p. 88 and G. Clausses, *Les San Gallo*, 3 vols., (Paris, 1900) i, 105–6.

the people and commune of Florence, the cross and lily, which are set above the inner gate of the entrance on the south-west, suggest a date before 1512. If any construction, rather than restoration, was carried out under Cosimo I, it was probably the tufa cladding of part of the south-east front of the citadel, though it is difficult to believe that the elegant but vulnerable sally port in the middle bastion (plate 16) can be as late. The bastions of the citadel (plate 17) are solid; the embrasures above the cordon and, where they occur, low down in the flanks or face, are for guns of large calibre. The flanking fire accurately covers the adjacent curtains and faces. The bastions of the town wall are evenly scarped from top to bottom, with no trace of cordon. They vary in size and are provided with keyhole loops in flank and face (plate 18); internal passages connect the chambers in a bastion with others in the length of the wall.[1] Owing to the small aperture of the loops, the flanking fire is not accurate at all points, and the distance between some of the bastions makes it unlikely that small-arms fire would have reached across with any accuracy. There is much tantalizing uncertainty about Poggio Imperiale, but it is reasonably certain that it entitles Giuliano to be considered as the first architect to explore the possibilities of the angle bastion in a large scale and diversified defensive system.

Two further works, one a reconstruction, one a new building, completes the story of Italian gunpowder fortification on the eve of the French wars. In 1492 Alexander VI employed Antonio da San Gallo the elder to modernize the round towers which Nicholas V had erected at the corners of Castel S Angelo[2] in Rome, and Antonio surrounded them with seven-sided bastions. Further additions under Pius IV have obscured much of this work, but the S Matteo bastion, in spite of a conjectural reconstruction of the upper works, shows the nature of Antonio's approach to the bastion (plate 19). Antonio was also the principal architect of Cesare Borgia's palace fort at Civita-castellana,[3] begun in 1494. Pentagonal in shape, the fort retains the conventional central *mastio*; its keyhole and letter-box slits are small and do not provide a perfectly systematized flanking

---

[1] This system of internal works has not been properly unblocked and restored. The second main entrance to the *enceinte* is also blocked: this may well contain an inscription or emblem that would help date it.

[2] M. Borgatti, *Castel Sant'Angelo in Roma* (Rome, 1931), 234–6.

[3] Guglielmotti, op. cit., 139 ff.

fire, but it does away not only with machicolation but with the conventional bracketing that lingered on, as, for instance, at Sarzanello, and of its five bastions, only one is round (plate 20). Sarzanello,[1] a hill-top fort, was designed in 1493 as an equilateral triangle with round corner bastions, conventional in shape and in the provision of keyhole loops for fire towards the field, but possessing flanking embrasures for large guns above the cordon and unusually massive parapets—if these are, indeed, part of the original structure (plate 21). In 1497 the Genoese, into whose hands the fort had come, began the remarkable triangular detached ravelin which juts hugely out towards the edge of the plateau most vulnerable to fire from a nearby hill (plate 22). Without forbears or progeny similar in size, this immense platform completes one of the most strikingly situated and well preserved of transition forts.[2]

We are now in a position to judge the claims made on behalf of Francesco di Giorgio, whose treatise dates from c. 1495.[3] From Saluzzo's edition of 1841 he has persistently been seen as the pioneer of the transition from medieval to modern fortification. In the words of one recent authority: 'Fully comprehending the novel challenge offered to defensive works by artillery, he laid down new principles of construction . . . his work represents the transition from Renaissance fortification, which adapted medieval principles to new needs, to the modern bastioned front'.[4] And in those of another: 'Francesco di Giorgio worked out the new style in fortification . . . he asserted, before anyone else, with the marvellous foresight with which all competent students now credit him, the theory and practice of the bastion, the origin of modern fortification'.[5]

That Francesco was highly conscious of the effect of guns and believed that new methods, relying not on mass but intelligently disposed units, were needed to counter them, there is no doubt.

---

[1] A. Neri, 'Il forte di Sarzanello', *Archivio Storico Italiano* (1885), 345–53.

[2] It is surrounded by a covered way, complete with *places d'armes*. The fort itself shows no trace of later reconstruction and this may mean that the covered way itself is of the early sixteenth century. If this is true it is the earliest of covered ways to have survived. But this would make it an astonishingly sophisticated achievement.

[3] There is no internal evidence, but it is generally accepted as dating from the last years of his life.

[4] L. Serra, 'Le rocche di Mondavio e di Cagli e le altre fortezze di Francesco di Giorgio Martini nella Marca', *Miscellenea di storia d'arte in onore di Igino Benvenuto Supino* (Florence, 1933), 435.

[5] R. Papini, *Francesco di Giorgio Architetto*, 3 vols. (Florence, 1946), 168.

There is also no doubt that he looked upon himself as a pioneer: 'he who can discover the answer to this manner of attack deserves to be called divinely, rather than humanly gifted'.[1] But before turning to his theoretical writings, it would be as well to look at the fortifications he actually built. Only few remain, and one of these, S Leo (plate 23) is attributed to him with some uncertainty. The others are Sassocorvaro (plates 24 and 25), built some time in the 1480s, Cagli (plate 26), built c. 1484 and of which only one detached tower from the wall leading up to the hill fort remains, and Mondavio (plates 27 and 28) of 1490–2. These works are fascinatingly idiosyncratic, but when they are compared with the works we have been discussing they appear quite irrelevant to the answers already proposed to the problem of fortifying against artillery. Towering and under-armed, they represent the massive doodling of a genius who is not prepared to sacrifice fantasy to logic, and it is not surprising that the least eccentric design, that of S Leo, is least certainly his.

The treatise lays down basic principles with firmness: the need to present glancing surfaces by means of scarping and of angled walls; the importance of flanking fire and the enfilading of ditches; the usefulness of outworks: ravelin and blockhouse (*capannato*) to break the force of an assault; the need to sink defences as much as possible from the attacker's fire. The drawings show many forms of bastion, but several of these are not solid and provide walks for small-arms rather than plat-forms for guns. The drawings, moreover, show a marked divergence from the principles of the text. They abound in impractical geometrical fantasies in which he rings elaborate changes on Alberti's suggestions of star and zigzag shapes: his designs abound in superfluous elements which could easily be knocked off, which get in the way of each other's fire, or are so placed as to be too high (as in some examples of *capannati* on towers, or too sunken to be of much use. He is still primarily concerned with the moment of assault rather than with long-range bombardment; he litters his ditches with booby-traps and harassing spurs, *tenailles* and blockhouses. Also, like Filarete, he is concerned with the political security of the prince or castellan within the city and devises complicated routes to the *mastio*. Though aware of the danger of mining, a strong liking for round or very obtuse forms, unprotected by flanking

[1] *Trattato*, ed. Saluzzo, 251.

fire, produces large areas of dead ground. His gun-ports are designed for small-arms, and even those that look suited to heavy cannon in plan reveal his preoccupation with short-range arms when he re-draws them in elevation.[1] One of the only two plans[2] that appears to be abreast of progressive contemporary buildings (plate 29), is matched on the facing page by a bird's-eye view that makes a very similar ground plan look remarkably old-fashioned: the angle bastions are scarped to two-thirds of their height, and continue up to a roofed storey projecting on bracket-corbels until their height is considerably greater than the ground area they cover. In short: while a case can be made from his text that he was abreast of current practice, he was not ahead of it, and his drawings and actual buildings show that he was diverted from dealing with simple, mutually dependent low-lying forms by a scholar's exuberant interest in ideal geometrical patterns, and by the relish for vertical mass he derived from church and palace, the staple of his architectural work.

Claims similar to those made for Francesco di Giorgio have been advanced on Leonardo da Vinci's behalf since J. B. Venturi declared in 1797 that he was 'fort supérieur aux ingénieurs de son temps',[3] but they have usually been made more guardedly because no trace of a bastion (as opposed to ravelin-like approximations to it) appears among his drawings. Leonardo designed no forts himself. The only finished drawing of a fort[4] is of an elaborate Francesco di Giorgio-like structure probably based on buildings he saw when working for Cesare Borgia as inspector of fortifications[5] in 1502. His own ideas are often difficult to interpret: the drawings are frequently so small that details are indistinguishable; lines of fire can be confused with measuring or composition lines; it is not easy to discern levels of building in plans that are not accompanied by elevations or bird's-eye views. But some conclusions can be

[1] Most of his drawings of guns (except for the page of drawings of existing types on fol. 48r) are concerned with short-range 'shrapnel' of various sorts: mortars, shooting baskets or frames full of stones, etc. He suggests, too, giant machines for scorching attackers off the walls by means of catherine wheels (MS. B.N.F. II, i, 141 ff., 198r,v, 215v).

[2] The other (MS. cit., fol. 82r) is for a triangular bastioned fort. There are irregularities in the drawing that suggest that his imagination was more concerned for the triangle shape than for the lines of fire from the bastions.

[3] *Essai sur les ouvrages physico-mathématiques de Léonard da Vinci*, reprinted in G. B. de Toni, *Giambattista Venturi e la sua opera Vinciana* (Rome, 1924), 189.

[4] Reproduced in Calvi, op. cit., fig. 88.

[5] His title was 'architecto et ingegnero generale'.

drawn from the numerous sketches made from the 1480s into the early years of the next century and preserved, for the most part, in MS.B., the Leicester MS. and the Codex Atlanticus.

In the earlier drawings he clings to round towers, strongly scarped at the base, and provided with small and secretive gun-loops right up against the curtain for flanking fire. Pointed shapes he reserves for ravelins. These are often very large, covering an entire curtain, and set in a wide wet ditch. They are open on the inner face, so that they can be covered by fire from the curtain and its towers; the only plan of such a system that has a clearly marked fire pattern[1] emphasizes the mutual defensibility of curtain and ravelin rather than the co-operation of the fire of both out to the field. He does not favour a *glacis*, seeing it as a lodgement in which an enemy can establish himself rather than as an advanced firing position—the true function of *glacis* and covered way. Like earlier theoretical writers, he is mainly concerned with what happens at the moment of assault and when the enemy actually breaks in. He provides round tower bastions with parapet embrasures in the flanks which have double openings: one to sweep the outer face of the curtain and another to enfilade its wall-walk. His project for strengthening the Sforza castle of Milan includes an outer *enceinte*—square, with round tower bastions at the corners—which has a firing gallery on its inner side, so that if the enemy gets through he will come under fire from the defence he has just penetrated. In the later drawings he becomes more concerned than ever with intricate systems of retreat—the medieval principal of outer ward, inner ward and keep from which contemporary practice was escaping—with *capannati*, concentric walls and underwater and underground passages: he is preoccupied with the anatomy, rather than the striking power of a fortress, pays little heed to providing the outer *enceinte* of his labyrinths with flanking fire and increasingly favours a curved surface for parapet, curtain and ravelin. He experiments with various forms of embrasure, but from the point of view of protection, not from that of mounting an effective firepower. Taking his drawings together with those in other contemporary treatises,[2] the conclusion seems inescapable: the revolution in

---

[1] Calvi, fig. 25.
[2] B.N.F. MS. Palat. 767 (Anon); Buonaccorso Ghiberti, B.N.F. MS. Magl. N. XVII. D.2. Both *c.* 1500. Neither has a title.

gunpowder fortification was carried through, not by theorists, even theorists of genius, but by working architects and masons.

This does not exclude the importance of architects of genius in exploiting more fully the measures of lesser men—Baccio Pontelli was possibly, Giuliano da San Gallo certainly, an architect of genius, but men whose genius was as much, or more, speculative than practical were lured from essentials by other considerations: politics, geometry, town planning; the tough outer shell which the new fortification required left a central void which their imaginations longed to fill. While Leonardo was working for Cesare Borgia, and sketching ideal fortress towns, Giuliano was designing or building three actual structures which established the angle bastion—in these instances with round shoulders protecting flank batteries—as the principal and normal element of a fortress: at Borgo San Sepolcro (plate 30), planned in 1500 and built between 1502 and c. 1505; at Nettuno (plate 31), built 1501-3; and at Arezzo (plate 32), planned in 1502, built from 1503.[1]

The story of the bastion in the next thirty years can be quickly told, first in terms of the fort, then of the town wall. Only in the next fort to be built, Bramante's *rocca* at Civitavecchia,[2] begun in 1508, was the round form of bastion still used. The fort is rectangular with four corner bastions, one of which (plate 33) is entirely solid, the others have gun-ports low in the flank, opening from chambers common to both flanks. The great hexagonal tower (plate 34) in the middle of the curtain on the harbour side serves both as bastion and *mastio*; it was completed, after Bramante's death, by Michelangelo. In the following year, 1509, Giuliano da San Gallo designed a fort to hold down Pisa after its capture by the Florentines. In poor condition, and too overgrown to allow details of the bastions to be seen clearly in photographs, its plan (modified in the course of construction[3]) can be grasped from de Marchi's drawing[4]

---

[1] See Marchini, op. cit., for dates. The project for incorporating the *rocca* at Borgo San Sepolcro with a new overall defence for the town (fols. 28r-28(a)r in Ferrante Vitelli's untitled MS. in the library of the Museo del Genio in Rome) was not carried out. One bastion was, instead, greatly extended, c. 1540, on the model of a similar addition made to the *rocca* at Arezzo, ordered by Cosimo I (see de Marchi's plan, B.N.F. II, i, 280, fol. 13r). Unknown to the literature of fortification, the *rocca* at San Sepolcro cries for detailed investigation.

[2] Rocchi, *Fonti* . . ., 145-6. Guglielmotti, op. cit., 189-240.

[3] Cf. Giuliano's original plan in his Sienese sketchbook, ed. Falb (Siena, 1902).

[4] MS. cit., fol. 8r.

(plate 38). The date, (probably 1518 for the design) and the author (probably one of the San Gallo) of the *rocca* which guards the harbour of Livorno (plate 36) are both in doubt.[1] This powerful fortress, unusual for the height of its bastions and the strength of the armament in its concealed flanks, shares with so many of its contemporaries the distinction of being ignored by architectural historians and by a government otherwise so zealous in the protection of the great monuments of the Renaissance. Similar obscurity surrounds the angle-bastioned *rocca* at Bari (probably *c.* 1520);[2] neither it nor the similar *rocca* at Barletta (1532–7) are as advanced as the Tuscan fortresses and cannot compare in strength, firepower or the rational combination of parts with the Fortezza da Basso at Florence,[3] designed in 1533 by Antonio da San Gallo the younger and illustrated here from de Marchi's plan[4] (plate 38). Begun in 1534 and brought rapidly to completion as it can be seen today (except for later masonry in the flank batteries) this fortress, hailed by Vasari as 'untakeable' and by Francesco de Hollanda as 'the finest fort in Europe' is a symbol both of the new Medici domination of Florence and Italian domination of the new fortification.

The use of the angle bastion in town walls was more hesitant than in fortresses. Biagio Rossetti used round bastions in the stretches of the Ferrara wall he built for Ercole I between *c.* 1500 and *c.* 1506.[5] The first walls to be re-built on a large scale were those of Padua and Treviso in face of the threat presented to them by the League of Cambrai, whose armies invaded the Veneto in 1509. On the strength of an assertion by Marin Sanudo that their engineer, Fra Giocondo, 'wanted to make angles in the walls' it has been claimed that Fra Giocondo was the inventor of the angle bastion.[6] It is by no means clear, however, that Sanudo was referring to bastions, and all the indications

---

[1] See Clausses and Giovannoni, opera cit., and G. Nudi, *Storia urbanistica di Livorno* (Venezia, 1959), 82.

[2] G. Bacile di Castiglione, *Castelli Pugliesi* (Rome, 1927), 48–64 (with plan).

[3] MS., cit., fol. 3r.

[4] L. Dami, 'La fortezza da Basso', *Arte e Storia* (1915), 162–4. Also M. Borgatti, 'Le mura e le torri di Firenze', *Rivista d'Artiglieria e Genio*, (1900) iv, 273–322. Originally called the fort of S Giovanni, it was called 'da basso' after the erection of the fort of S Giorgio (the Belvedere) on the heights above the Boboli gardens.

[5] U. Malagù, *Le mura di Ferrara* (Ferrara, 1960), 10.

[6] G. Fiocco in his edition of Vasari's *Vita di Fra Giocondo*, 2 vols., (Florence, 1915) i, 45. The claim is repeated in R. Brenzoni, *Fra Giovanni Giocondo Veronese* (Florence, 1960), 69.

are that Padua (like Treviso) was strengthened with round bastions, first built in a hurry of earth and timber. None of Fra Giocondo's works remains in its original form, but when the fortifications of Padua were consolidated from 1513 under the direction of Bartolomeo d'Alviano, he continued to use round bastions, facing Fra Giocondo's with stone and constructing others. The first angle bastions at Padua date from 1526–30.[1] There are no angle bastions at Treviso. Three angle bastions were added to the wall of Ferrara by Alfonso I between 1512 and 1518,[2] and the town wall of Civitavecchia, planned in 1515 but now destroyed (if indeed it was built according to this plan[3]) was for a regular angle-bastioned front. This design was determined on after those of Antonio da San Gallo the younger had been approved by a group of practising soldiers, including Pedro Navarro and Giovan Paolo Baglioni, and their endorsement of the angle shape led Antonio Fiorentino, who had been present at the conference, to change from the round to the angle shape for the bastions he was constructing for the new *enceinte* of the Castel Nuovo.[4] The town walls of Urbino (plate 39), Pesaro and Senigallia, which were probably begun *c.* 1515[5] used angle bastions, but when Loreto was refortified after the Turkish raid on the nearby Porto Recanati in 1518, the main works consisted of two great round bastions (plate 40), finished in 1521.[6] And when Verona was strengthened from 1520 after its walls had fallen into grave disrepair during the sieges of 1509 and 1516, the new bastions were round, with one exception: Michele dei Leoni's bastion dalla Maddalena of 1527. It was subsequently altered by Michele Sanmicheli, whose own works, employing angle bastions, did not begin there until *c.* 1530.[7]

It is not altogether surprising, then, that among the bastions suggested by Machiavelli and Navarro in 1526 for the walls of

---

[1] G. Rusconi, *Le mura di Padova*, 2nd edn. (Bassano, 1921), 58 ff.

[2] Malagù, op. cit., 21 and A. Frizzi, *Memorie per la storia di Ferrara*, 2nd edn., (Ferrara, 1848) iv, 266, 283.

[3] On the dating controversy (which has not been resolved), see L. Celli, 'Le fortificazioni militari di Urbino, Pesaro e Senigallia del secolo XVI', *Nuova Rivista Misena* (1895), 74 ff.

[4] R. Filangieri, op. cit., 282.

[5] Serra and Celli, opera cit.

[6] Serra, *L'arte nella Marche*, 109–12. I have not been able to find a copy of P. del Monte, *Il santuario di Loreto e le sue difese militari* (Loreto, 1929).

[7] E. Langenskiöld, *Michele Sanmicheli the architect of Verona* (Uppsala, 1938), *passim*.

Florence, the only two whose shape is specifically mentioned were to be round,[1] or that their plans were altered when Michelangelo was put in charge of the fortifications in 1529.[2] None of his work survives as he designed it; what we see is due to Antonio da San Gallo the younger who consolidated the defences after 1534; as only angle bastions can be seen today, it is most likely that Michelangelo's bastions were in that form. In August 1529, moreover, he had been sent to look at the fortifications of Ferrara, where the latest bastions were angled, and in none of his many drawings of the time of the siege is there anything but various forms of angle bastion. These drawings have been studied by Charles de Tolnay, who concluded that 'from the point of view of military effectiveness, the projects of Michelangelo seem to be the most perfect fortification plans of the sixteenth century. In fact, the possibility of a successful enemy attack was reduced to a minimum and at the same time a maximum of active defence was assured'.[3] This is to go too far. In the series of crustacea-like bastions (plate 41) which recall some of the designs of Francesco di Giorgio (plate 42) Michelangelo shows a far greater concern than any previous theorist with the dynamic, attacking role of the bastion, but by clinging to elaborately protected embrasures of small traverse he produced bastions which would be difficult to build, full of vulnerable projections and requiring a numerous armament. The future lay not with these opulent fantasies, but with platforms of simple plan, and wide embrasures or a low parapet over which guns could fire in any direction. That Michelangelo did actually build bastions at Florence is clear from contemporary criticisms[4] that they had too many flanks and too many embrasures, but it is probable that drawings like the one illustrated here are indeed fantasies: doodlings prompted by the actual needs of Florence but following a

---

[1] 'Baluardo tondo'. It may be that the shape is specified on these occasions because the pentagonal shape is taken for granted elsewhere.

[2] 'Governatore e procuratore generale delle fortificazioni della città'. This was on 6th April. From 10th January he had been a member of the *nove della milizia*. Barocchi, op. cit., i, 128.

[3] 'Michelangelo studies', *Art Bulletin* (1940), 136.

[4] De Tolnay, ibid., p. 136, footnote. The fact that these works were hastily made of temporary materials—earth and straw faced with unbaked bricks—rather than San Gallo's disapproval of them may account for their disappearance before Vasari painted the city's southern walls in his fresco in the Palazzo della Signoria.

purely aesthetic impulse towards a more open architectural style.[1]

It was in 1534, the year in which the Fortezza da Basso was begun in Florence, that the angle bastion may be said to have become the norm in town defences. In August of that year Turkish raids on the Lazio coast and at the mouth of the Tiber caused Clement VII to fear for the safety of the capital itself, and after a conference of soldiers and architects, Antonio da San Gallo's plan for an angle-bastioned *enceinte* for the Borgo (the present Vatican city) was approved and begun. These fortifications, and those that were begun soon after on the south of the city[2] between Porta S Paolo and Porta S Sebastiano, became the subject of intense publicity, and not only because they were seen by every visitor to Rome: their progress was attended by much, and often acrimonious debate among the architects, including Michelangelo, who were consulted as each new section was planned. These debates, however, were concerned with the siting of the defences and the length of curtain between bastions: there was never any doubt that the angle bastion was the only form to be used.

The life of the round bastion still flickered on here and there. Paul III himself—he had succeeded Clement VIII just before the Borgo defences were begun—had a round bastion built to defend the entrance to the *rocca maggiore* at Assisi in 1535–8;[3] far in the south, round tower bastions were constructed at Lecce and Cotrone in the 'forties. But these were remote and unimportant exceptions. Controversy remained lively, but it was restricted to various forms of the angle bastion, particularly as to how batteries at various levels were to be so housed in its flanks that their field of fire could be as wide as possible—in order that, in Galileo's terminology,[4] the flanking *tiro che*

[1] With reference to the treatment of space in the Laurentian library and the Capitoline Hill, etc., J. S. Ackerman comments in *The Architecture of Michelangelo*, 2 vols., (London, 1961) i, 53: 'The necessity to find an architectural solution for projectiles in constant radial motion along infinitely varied paths must have helped to remove from his mind the last vestiges of the static figures and proportions of the Quattrocento'.

[2] M. Borgatti, 'Le mura di Roma', *Rivista d'Artiglieria e Genio*, (1890) ii, 325–403, with plans, and 'Il bastione ardeatino a Roma', ibid., (1916) ii, 207–23, with plans.

[3] A. Brizi, *Della rocca di Assisi* (Assisi, 1898), 439–40. Plans.

[4] For Galileo's perfect bastion, which had a large gun chamber (protected by a round shoulder) housing four guns firing (a) out to the adjacent covered way and some distance into the field, (b) along the opposite bastion face, (c) into the opposite bastion face, to dislodge mining parties, etc., (d) into the adjacent curtain and along it, see the diagram in the Florence, 1932 edition of his *Trattato di Fortificazione*, p. 123.

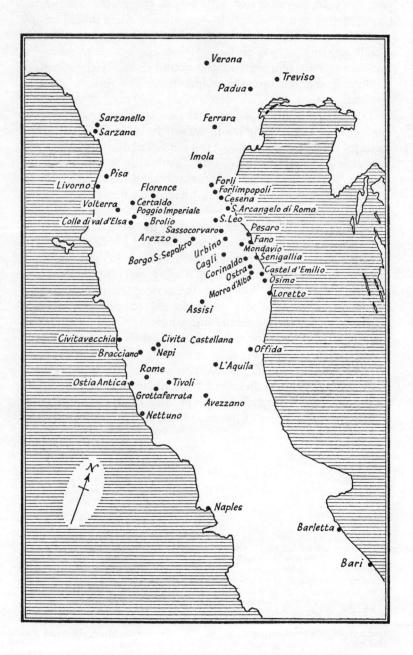

Verona

Treviso

Padua

Ferrara

Imola

Pisa

Livorno

Florence

Volterra   Certaldo
Poggio Imperiale
Colle di val d'Elsa   Brolio
Sassocorvaro
Arezzo

Borgo S. Sepolcro

Sarzanello
Sarzana

Forlì
Forlimpopoli
Cesena
S. Arcangelo di Roma
S. Leo
Pesaro
Fano

Urbino   Mondavio
Cagli   Senigallia
Corinaldo   Castel d'Emilio
Ostra   Osimo
Morro d'Alba
Loretto

Assisi

Civitavecchia   Civita Castellana
Bracciano   Nepi   Offida
Rome   L'Aquila
Ostia Antica   Tivoli
Grottaferrata   Avezzano
Nettuno

N

Naples

Barletta

Bari

striscia could be combined with *tiro che ficca* directed along the covered way and into the field—or whether there should be any batteries at all below the platform. The experiment at L'Aquila (plate 37) in 1535 was an isolated one. Elsewhere, practice did no more than refine upon the round-shouldered models of Giuliano, and the square-shouldered ones of Antonio da San Gallo.

Looking back, then, we see that the core of the development we have been describing lay in central Italy. In the parts of the country most open to northern influence, fortifications remained conservative; nothing new from Lombardy or the Trentino; Venice herself remained reactionary until she employed an architect, Sanmicheli, who had formed his ideas south of the Veneto. From the Spanish-influenced kingdom of Naples we have only the abortive experiment of the gun terrace. Other countries had to adapt fortification to the challenge of gunpowder: the *enceinte* of Mont S Michel (1426–45) is a practical, Dürer's *Etliche underricht, zu befestigung der Stett, Schloss, und Flecken* (Nüremberg, 1527) a theoretical example. Certain specially vulnerable sites were forced to produce defence methods which were possibly independent of Italian example, such as the barbican-bastion in late fifteenth-century Rhodes.[1] The purpose of this essay is no more ambitious than to suggest that the bastioned front, in the treatment of which the Italians were universally acknowledged to be the leaders by the middle of the sixteenth century,[2] was the product of an indigenous and consistent development from the middle of the *quattrocento*.

---

[1] But this does not justify B. M. St J. O'Neil's 'If, therefore, one asks the question, "Who invented the bastion?" The present writer suggests that the answer should be "Pierre d'Aubusson at Rhodes in 1496" '—with reference to the Boulevard d'Auvergne, in *The Antiquaries Journal* (1954), 52. This fine article suffers by ignoring contemporary Italian work and the writings of Italian scholars, especially those of G. Gerola, e.g. 'Il contributo dell'Italia alle opere d'arte militare rodiesi', *Atti del R. Istituto Veneto di scienze, lettere ed arte* (1930), especially 1019 and 1027.

[2] The most thorough survey is provided by L. A. Maggiorotti, *L'opera del genio italiano all'estero*, 3 vols. (Rome, 1936–9). It is, however, a work of propaganda, is inadequately documented, and, in Europe, only covers Spain, Portugal and Hungary.

A SELECT INDEX